THE COMPLETE
GOLFER'S
ALMANAC
1995

A COMPENDIUM OF USEFUL GOLFING FACTS AND INFORMATION

by
James M. Lane

A Perigee Book

A Perigee Book
Published by The Berkley Publishing Group
200 Madison Avenue
New York, NY 10016

Book design by James M. Lane

Cover illustration by Walt Spitzmiller

First.edition: April 1995

Printed simultaneously in Canada.

Library of Congress Cataloguing-in-Publication Data

Lane, James M. (James Max)
    The complete golfer's almanac 1995/James M. Lane. —1st ed.
        p. cm.
    "A Perigee Book."
    ISBN 0-399-52151-8
    1. Golf—Miscellanea. 2. Almanacs, American. I. Title.
  GV965.L25 1995
796.352 02—dc20   94-37049
                                                                 CIP

Printed in the United States of America

10 9 8 7 6 5 4 3 2 1

Quick Index

1995
MAJOR CHAMPIONSHIP PREVIEWS

The Masters

Augusta National Golf Club, Augusta, Georgia

Course designed by—*Alister Mackenzie with Robert T. Jones (1932)*
Course architects—*Perry Maxwell, Robert Trent Jones,*
George Cobb, Jack Nicklaus, Tom Fazio
Defending Champion—*Jose Maria Olazabal*
Golfer's Almanac Favorite—*Greg Norman*
Also watch—*Jose Maria Olazabal, Nick Faldo,*
Davis Love III, Tiger Woods
Key holes—*12, 13, 15, 18*
Television—*USA /CBS*

Notes: Tiger Woods will make his first major championship appearance here. Greg Norman continues to seek his first green jacket on a course seemingly built for his power-and-touch game. Foreign-born players have won six of the last seven titles. Defender Olazabal was also runner-up in 1991.

The U.S. Open

Shinnecock Hills Golf Links, Shinnecock Hills, New York

Course designed by—*William Flynn and Dick Wilson (1931)*
Defending Champion—*Ernie Els*
Last champion at Shinnecock—*Ray Floyd (1986)*
Golfer's Almanac Favorite—*Corey Pavin*
Also watch—*Colin Montgomerie, David Frost,*
Phil Mickelson, Rick Fehr
Key holes—*9, 11, 14*
Television: *ESPN/ABC*

Notes: Shinnecock Hills is regarded as America's most "links-like" course. Accurate long irons and woods, combined with pressure putting, will be the key to victory. Shinnecock features a rare par-three finishing hole on the front nine. Colin Montgomerie finished third in 1992 and runner-up in last year's Open. Both the par-three 11th and the par-four fourteenth are rated among America's 100 greatest golf holes.

British Open
The Old Course, St. Andrews, Scotland

Course designed by—*Unknown*
Subsequent course architects—*Allen Robertson, Tom Morris*
Defending Champion—*Nick Price*
Last champion at St. Andrews—*Nick Faldo (1990)*
Golfer's Almanac Favorite—*Nick Faldo*
Also—*Mark McNulty, Nick Price, Tom Kite, John Daly,*
Bernhard Langer, Anders Forsbrand, Vijay Singh, Joakim Haegmann
Key holes—*11, 14, 16, 17*
Television—*ESPN/ABC*

Notes: The Old Course requires study perhaps more than any other course in the world; hence, golfers who play well here tend to do so consistently. Jack Nicklaus won twice here (1970, 1978) and was runner-up a third time (1964). Given the huge putting surfaces and dry turf, approaches and long lag putts are the key to victory. John Daly has had particular success on this course in the Alfred Dunhill Cup. A win by Faldo would make him the second golfer to win twice at Muirfield and St. Andrews (the first was James Braid).

PGA Championship
Riviera Country Club, Los Angeles, California

Course designed by—*George Thomas, Jr. (1925)*
Defending champion—*Nick Price*
Last champion at Riviera—*Corey Pavin (1994 L.A. Open)*
Golfer's Almanac Favorite—*Fred Couples*
Also watch—*Corey Pavin, Paul Azinger, Jeff Maggert,*
Ernie Els, David Edwards, Hal Sutton
Key holes—*10, 17, 18*
Television—*USA/CBS*

Notes: Horses for courses—Fred Couples has won the Nissan L.A. Open three times here (in 1990, 1992 and 1993) and is popular with the galleries here. Straight driving is the key. Ben Hogan was very successful here in his career and the course became known as "Hogan's Alley." Long drives can pay off on the back nine with the short par-four 10th hole and the long, uphill finishing 17th and 18th holes. Hal Sutton, who made a comeback from total obscurity in 1994, won the PGA here in 1983.

1995 CALENDAR

OVERVIEW: *Includes listing of all major PGA, LPGA, and Senior Tour events. For tournaments, the lead television network is indicated in bold. Television coverage is typically 4:00pm-6:00pm on Saturdays; 3:30pm-6:00pm Sundays, Eastern time. Major championships are typically telecast in their entirety, with the exception of the Masters which follows a standard network schedule. Secondary networks typically carry the telecast in off-air hours and on Thursday and Friday of the tournament. These networks are indicated by an asterisk and italics.*

PGA TOUR

DATES	NETWORK	TOURNAMENT, LOCATION
January 5-8	ABC	**Mercedes Championships** *La Costa Resort—Carlsbad, CA*
January 12-15	TBS	**United Airlines Hawaiian Open** *Waialae Country Club—Honolulu, HI*
January 19-22	ESPN	**Northern Telecom Open** *Tucson Nat'l Golf Resort/Star Pass* *Golf Club—Tucson, AZ*
January 26-29	ESPN	**Phoenix Open** *TPC of Scottsdale—Scottsdale, AZ*
February 2-5	CBS	**AT&T Pebble Beach National Pro-Am** *Pebble Beach, Spyglass Hill,* *Poppy Hills—Pebble Beach, CA*
February 9-12	NBC	**Buick Invitational of California** *Torrey Pines—La Jolla, CA*
February 16-19	NBC	**Bob Hope Chrysler Classic** *Indian Wells, Indian Ridge, Bermuda Dunes,* *LaQuinta—Indian Wells, CA*
February 23-26	CBS	**Nissan Los Angeles Open** *Riviera Country Club—Pacific Palisades, CA*
March 2-5	CBS	**Doral-Ryder Open** *Doral Resort & Country Club—Miami, FL*
March 9-12	NBC	**Honda Classic** *Weston Hills Country Club—Ft. Lauderdale, FL*
March 16-19	NBC	**The Nestle Invitational** *Bay Hill Club and & Lodge—Orlando, FL*
March 23-26	NBC	**The PLAYERS Championship** *TPC at Sawgrass—Ponte Vedra Beach, FL*
March 30- April 2	NBC	**Freeport-McMoRan Classic** *English Tum Golf & Country Club—New Orleans, LA*
April 6-9	CBS *USA*	**The Masters** *Augusta National Golf Club—Augusta, GA*

DATES	NETWORK	TOURNAMENT, LOCATION
April 13-16	CBS	**MCI Heritage Classic** *Harbour Town Golf Links—Hilton Head Island, SC*
April 20-23	CBS	**Kmart Greater Greensboro Open** *Forest Oaks Country Club—Greensboro, NC*
April 27-30	ABC	**Shell Houston Open** *TTC at The Woodlands—The Woodlands, TX*
May 4-7	CBS	**Bell South Classic** *Atlanta Country Club—Marietta, GA*
May 11-14	ABC	**Byron Nelson Classic** *TPC at Las Colinas—Irving, TX*
May 18-21	CBS	**Buick Classic** *Westchester Country Club—Rye, NY*
May 25-28	CBS	**Colonial National Invitational** *Colonial Country Club—Ft.Worth, TX*
June 1-4	ABC	**Memorial Tournament** *Muirfield Village Golf Club—Dublin, OH*
June 8-11	CBS	**Kemper Open** *TPC at Avenel—Potomac, MD*
June 15-18	NBC USA	**US Open** *Shinnecock Hills—Southampton, NY*
June 22-25	CBS	**Canon Greater Hartford Open** *TPC at River Highlands—Cromwell, CT*
June 29-July 2	CBS	**Federal Express St. Jude Classic** *TPC at Southwind—Memphis, TN*
July 6-9	CBS	**Motorola Western Open** *Cog Hill Golf & Country Club—Lemont, IL*
July 13-16	ESPN	**Anheuser-Busch Golf Classic** *Kingsmill Golf Club—Williamsburg, VA*
July 20-23	ABC ESPN	**British Open** *The Old Course—St. Andrews, Scotland*
	TGC	**Deposit Guaranty Golf Classic** *Annandale Golf Club—Madison, MS*
July 27-30	TGC	**The New England Classic** *Pleasant Valley Country Club—Sutton, MA*
August 3-6	CBS	**Buick Open** *Warwick Hills Golf & Country Club—Grand Blanc, MI*
August 10-13	CBS USA	**PGA Championship** *Riviera Country Club—Los Angeles, CA*
August 17-20	CBS	**The International** *Castle Pines Golf Club–Castle Rock, CO*
August 24-27	CBS	**NEC World Series of Golf** *Firestone Country Club–Akron, OH*

DATES	NETWORK	TOURNAMENT, LOCATION
August 31- September 3	ABC	**Greater Milwaukee Open** *Brown Deer Park Golf Course–Milwaukee, WI*
September 7-10	ESPN	**Bell Canadian Open** *Glen Abbey Golf Club–Oakville, Ontario*
September 14-17	TGC	**B.C. Open** *En-Joi Golf Club–Endicott, NY*
September 21-24	TGC	**Quad Cities Open** *Oakwood Country Club–Coal Valley, IL*
	NBC	**The Ryder Cup** *Oak Hill Country Club–Rochester, NY*
September 28- October 1	ESPN	**Buick Southern Open** *Callaway Gardens Resort—Pine Mountain, GA*
October 5-8	TGC	**Walt Disney World/Oldsmobile Classic** *Lake Buena Vista Golf Club–Orlando, FL*
October 12-15	ESPN	**Las Vegas Invitational** *TTC at Summerlin, Las Vegas CC,* *Desert Inn CC–Las Vegas, NV*
October 19-22	TGC	**Texas Open** *Oak Hills Country Club—San Antonio, TX*
October 26-29	ABC	**THE TOUR Championship** *Southern Hills Country Club—Tulsa, OK*
November 2-5	ABC	**Lincoln-Mercury Kapalua Int'l** *Kapalua Resort –Lahaina, Maui, HI*
November 9-12	NBC	**The World Cup of Golf** *Hyatt Dorado Beach–Dorado, Puerto Rico*
November 16-19	CBS	**Franklin Funds Shark Shootout** *Sherwood Country Club–Thousand Oaks, CA*
November 23-26	ABC	**Skins Game** *PGA West, Jack Nicklaus Resort Course–La Quinta, CA*
November 30- December 3	ABC	**JC Penney Classic** *Innisbrook Hilton Resort—Palm Harbor, FL*
December 7-10	ABC	**Diners Club Matches** *TBA*
December 30-31	ABC	**Anderson Consulting World Championship of Golf**

Senior PGA TOUR

DATES	NETWORK	TOURNAMENT, LOCATION
January 9-15	ESPN	**Senior Tournament of Champions** *Hyatt Dorado Beach—Dorado Beach, Puerto Rico*
January 23-29 January 30-	ABC	**Senior Skins Game** *Mauni Lani Resort—Kohala Coast, HI*
February 5	ESPN	**Royal Caribbean Classic** *Links at Key Biscayne—Key Biscayne, FL*
February 6-12	ESPN	**The IntelliNet Challenge** *The Vineyards—Naples, FL*
February 13-19	ESPN	**GTE Suncoast Classic** *TPC at Tampa Bay—Tampa, FL*
February 20-26	ABC	**Chrysler Cup** *Acapulco, Mexico*
February 27- March 5	ESPN	**FHP Health Care Classic** *Ojai Valley Inn & Country Club—Ojai, CA*
March 6-7	TBS	**Senior Slam of Golf** *Cabo del Sol Golf Course—Cabo San Lucas, Mexico*
March 6-12		**The Dominion** *Tle Dominion Country Club—San Antonio, TX*
March 13-19	ESPN	**Toshiba Senior Classic** *TBA*
March 20-26		**American Express Grandslam** *Oak Hills Country Club—Chiba, Japan*
March 27-April 2	ESPN	**The Tradition** *Desert Mountain—Scottsdale, AZ*
April 10-16	NBC	**PGA Seniors Championship** *PGA National Golf Club—Palm Beach Gardens, FL*
April 17-23	ABC	**Liberty Mutual Legends of Golf** *Stadium Course at PGA West—La Quinta, CA*
April 24-30	ESPN	**Las Vegas Senior Classic** *TPC at Summerlin—Las Vegas, NV*
May 1-7	ESPN	**PaineWebber Invitational** *TPC at Piper Glen—Charlotte, NC*
May 8-14	ESPN	**Cadillac NFG Golf Classic** *Upper Montclair Country Club—Clifton, NJ*
May 15-21	ESPN	**Bell Atlantic Classic** *Chester Valley Golf Club—Malvern, PA*
May 22-28		**Quicksilver Classic** *Quicksilver Country Club—Pittsburgh, PA*
May 29-June 4		**Bruno's Memorial Classic** *Greystone Golf Club—Birmingham, AL*
June 5-11	NBC	**BellSouth Senior Classic at Opryland** *Opryland Golf Club— Nashville, TN*
June 12-18		**Dallas Reunion Pro-Am** *Oak Cliff—Dallas, TX*

DATES	NETWORK	TOURNAMENT, LOCATION
June 19-25	ESPN	**Nationwide Championship** *Golf Club of Georgia—Atlanta, GA*
June 26-July 2	CBS	**US Senior Open** *Congressional Country Club—Bethesda, MD*
July 3-9	ESPN	**Kroger Senior Classic** *The Golf Center at Kings Island—Mason, OH*
July 10-16	ABC	**FORD SENIOR PLAYERS Championship** *TPC of Michigan—Dearborn, MI*
July 17-23		**First of America Classic** *Egypt Valley Golf Club—Ada, MI*
July 24-30	CBS	**Ameritech Senior Open** *Stonebridge Country Club—Chicago, IL*
August 1-6	ESPN	**VFW Senior Championship** *Loch Lloyd Country Club—Belton, MO*
August 7-13		**Burnet Senior Classic** *Bunker Hills Golf Club—Coon Rapids, MN*
August 14-20	ESPN	**Northville Long Island Classic** *Meadow Brook Country Club—Jericho, NY*
August 21-27	ESPN	**Bank of Boston Senior Golf Classic** *Nashawtuc Country Club—Boston, MA*
August 28-September 3		**Franklin Quest Championship** *Park Meadows—Park City, UT*
September 4-10		**GTE Northwest Classic** *Inglewood Country Club—Seattle, WA*
September 11-17		**Brickyard Crossing Championship** *Brickyard Crossing—Indianapolis, IN*
September 18-24		**Bank One Classic** *Kearney Golf Links—Lexington, KY*
September 25-October 1	ESPN	**Vantage Championship** *Tanglewood Park—Clemmons, NC*
October 2-8	ESPN	**The Transamerica** *Silverado Country Club—Napa, CA*
October 9-15		**Raley's Senior Gold Rush** *Rancho Murieta Country Club—Sacramento, CA*
October 16-22		**Ralph's Senior Classic** *Rancho Park Golf Club—Los Angeles, CA*
October 23-29	ESPN	**Hyatt Regency Maui Kaanapali Classic** *Royal Kaanapali Golf Club—Maui, HI*
October 30-November 5		**Emerald Coast Classic** *The Moors—Pensacola, FL*
November 6-12	ESPN	**GOLF MAGAZINE SENIOR TOUR Championship** *The Dunes Golf & Beach Club—Myrtle Beach, SC*
December 4-10	ABC	**Diners Club Matches** *PGA West—La Quinta, CA*

LPGA TOUR

DATES	NETWORK	TOURNAMENT, LOCATION
January 12-15		**Chrysler-Plymouth Tournament of Champions** *Orlando, Florida*
January 20-22		**HEALTHSOUTH Inaugural** *Orlando, Florida*
February 16-18		**Cup Noodles Hawaiian Ladies Open** *Ewa Beach, Oahu, Hawaii*
March 9-12		**PING/Welch's Championship** *Tucson, Arizona*
March 16-19	ESPN	**Standard Register PING** *Phoenix, Arizona*
March 23-26	ABC ESPN	**Nabisco Dinah Shore** *Rancho Mirage, California*
March 31 -Apr 2		**Las Vegas Classic** *Las Vegas, Nevada*
April 14-16		**Pinewild Women's Championship** *Pinehurst, North Carolina*
April 27-30	CBS	**Sprint Championship** *Daytona Beach, Florida*
May 5-7		**Sara Lee Classic** *Old Hickory, Tennessee*
May 11-14	CBS	**McDonald's LPGA Championship** *Wilmington, Delaware*
May 19-21		**Children's Medical Center LPGA Classic** *Dayton, Ohio*
May 25-28		**LPGA Corning Classic** *Corning, New York*
May 27-28	ABC	**JCPenney/LPGA Skins Game** *Frisco, Texas*
June 1-4		**Oldsmobile Classic** *East Lansing, Michigan*

DATES	NETWORK	TOURNAMENT, LOCATION
June 9-11		**First Bank Presents the Edina Realty LPGA Classic** *Brooklyn Park, Minnesota*
Jun 15-18		**Rochester International** *Pittsford, New York*
June 23-25		**ShopRite LPGA Classic** *Somers Point, New Jersey*
June 30-July 2		**Youngstown-Warren LPGA Classic** *Warren, Ohio*
July 7-9		**Jamie Farr Toledo Classic** *Sylvania, Ohio*
July 13-16	ABC ESPN	**U. S. Women's Open** *Colorado Springs, Colorado*
July 20-23	NBC	**JAL Big Apple Classic** *New Rochelle, New York*
August 3-6		**McCall's LPGA Classic at Stratton Mountain** *Stratton Mountain, Vermont*
August 10-13		**PING/Welch's Championship** *Canton, Massachusetts*
August 17-20		**Chicago Challenge** *Naperville, Illinois*
August 24-27	PRIME	**du Maurier Ltd. Classic** *Montreal, Quebec, Canada*
September 2-4		**State Farm Rail Classic** *Springfield, Illinois*
September 8-10		**PING-Cellular One LPGA Golf Championship** *Portland, Oregon*
September 14-17		**SAFECO Classic** *Kent, Washington*
September 28-October 1		**GHP Heartland Classic** *St. Louis, Missouri*
October 5-8		**Carolina LPGA Classic** *Charlotte, North Carolina*

DATES	NETWORK	TOURNAMENT, LOCATION
October 12-15		**World Championship of Women's Golf** *TBA*
October 27-29		**Nichirei International** *Ibaragi, Japan*
November 3-5		**Toray Japan Queens Cup** *Japan*
November 30-December 3		**JCPenney Classic** *Tarpon Springs, Florida*
December 8-10	ABC	**Diner's Club Matches** *La Quinta, California*

EUROPEAN TOUR

DATES	NETWORK	TOURNAMENT, LOCATION
January 6-13		**Apollo Week** *San Roque, Spain*
January 19-22		**Dubai Desert Classic** *Emirates G.C., Dubai, United Arab Emirates*
January 26-29		**Johnnie Walker Classic** *Orchard Golf & Country Club, Manila, Philippines*
February 2-5		**Madiera Island Open** *Madeira Santo da Serra, Madeira Island*
February 9-12		**Turespana Open de Canaries** *Campo de Golf da Maspolomas, Canary Islands*
February 16-19		**Lexington S.A. PGA** *Wanderers Club, Johannesburg, South Africa*
February 23-26		**Turespana Open Mediterriania** *TBA, Spain*
March 2-5		**Turespana Masters Open** *Islantilla G.C., Spain*
March 9-12		**Moroccan Open** *Golf Royal de Agadir, Agadir, Morocco*
March 16-19		**Portuguese Open** *Penha Longa G.C., Sintra, Portugal*

DATES	NETWORK	TOURNAMENT, LOCATION
March 30 -Apr 2		**Open de Extremadura** *Golf del Guadiana, Badajoz, Spain*
April 13-16		**Open Catalonia** *TBA*
April 20-23		**Air France Cannes Open** *Cannes Mougains G.C., Cannes, France*
April 27-30		**Tournoi Perrier de Paris** *Golf de Saint-Cloud, Paris, France*
May 4-7		**Italian Open** *TBA*
May 11-14		**Benson and Hedges International Open** *St. Mellion G. & C.C., Plymouth, England*
May 18-21		**Peugeot Open de Espana** *Club de Campo, Madrid, Spain*
May 26-29		**Volvo PGA** *Wentworth Club (West), Surrey, England*
June 1-4		**Murphy's English Open** *Forest of Arden G.C., Warwickshire, England*
June 8-11		**Deutsche Bank Open** *Gut Kaden, Hamburg, Germany*
June 15-18		**Jersey Open** *La Moye (Nicklaus), St. Brelade, England*
June 22-25		**Peugeot Open de France** *Le Golf National, Versailles, France*
June 29-July 2		**BMW International Open** *St. Eurach Land-und, Munich, Germany*
July 6-9	PRIME	**Murphy's Irish Open** *Mount Juliet C.C., County Kilkenny, Ireland*
July 12-15	PRIME	**Bell's Scottish Open** *Carnoustie, Angus, Scotland*
July 20-23	ABC *ESPN*	**British Open** *Old Course, St. Andrews, Scotland*

DATES	NETWORK	TOURNAMENT, LOCATION
July 27-30	PRIME	**Heinecken Dutch Open** *Hilversumsche G.C., Hilversum, Netherlands*
August 3-6	PRIME	**Scandanavian Masters** *Barsebacks, Sweden*
August 10-13		**Hohe Bruke Open** *G.C. Waldviertal, Litschau, Austria*
August 17-20		**Chemapol Trophy Czech Open** *Marianska Lazbe G.C., Czech Republic*
August 24-27		**Volvo German Open** *Nippenburg G.C., Stuttgart, Germany*
August 31- September 3		**Canon European Masters** *Crans-sur-Sierre, Switzerland*
September 7-10		**Trophee Lancome** *St. Nom-la-Breteche, Versailles, France*
September 14-17		**Dunhill British Masters** *Woburn G. & C.C. (Duke's), England*
September 28-October 1		**Smurfit European Open** *Kildare C.C., Dublin, Ireland*
October 5-8		**Mercedes German Masters** *Motzner See G. & C.C., Motzen, Germany*
October 12-15		**Toyota World Match Play Championship** *Wentworth Club, Surrey, England*
October 19-22		**Alfred Dunhill Cup** *Old Course, St. Andrews, Scotland*
October 26-29		**Volvo Masters** *Valderrama, Sotogrande, Spain*

1994: THE YEAR IN GOLF

OVERVIEW: *Includes items of interest concerning the business and organizations, and personalities of golf—significant news regarding golf courses, tournaments, companies, rules, equipment, and the arrival and passing of prominent personalities in the game.*

NOVEMBER 1993

People

In a rules mix-up, **Greg Norman** did not complete the necessary minimum of 60 rounds, and lost the PGA of America's Vardon Trophy to **Nick Price. John Daly** received a three-month suspension from **PGA TOUR** commissioner **Deane Beman** after walking off the course in the middle of the second round of the Kapalua International. **Reg Murphy** was nominated to succeed **Stuart F. Bloch** as president of the United States Golf Association. **Heather Farr** died of complications from breast cancer November 20, age 28.

Places

Vahalla Golf Club, of Louisville, Ky, scheduled site of the 1996 PGA Championship, received a bid from the PGA of America to purchase the club. **Pumpkin Ridge** Golf Club of North Plains, Oregon, was announced as the host of the 1997 U.S. Women's Open. The two-year old course will also host the 1996 U.S. Amateur. **Sharon** Golf Club (Sharon Center, Ohio) was dropped from the list of U.S. Open qualifying sites in 1994 because of its all-male membership policies. The **East Lake** Country Club, where **Bobby Jones** played his early golf, was purchased by **Tom Cousins** for $4.5 million. Cousins announced his intent to restore the club and course as a tribute to Jones.

Business

The **PGA of America** abandoned plans to require a four-year college degree to enter the PGA apprentice program. **Karsten Manufacturing** announced that it would enter the metal woods market. A **Michael Jordan Company** was announced November 19, with a goal of making the game more accessible and affordable. 390 delegates gathered in **Pebble Beach**, California, for a three-day **Women in**

Golf Summit 1993. **Spalding** announced it was ending its sponsorship of the **Golden State** and **Space Coast** mini-tours. **Hooters**, a restaurant chain, announced it would sponsor the **T.C. Jordan Tour** in 1994. **ClubCorp of America** acquired the **Mission Hills** Country Club, host site of the LPGA's Nabisco **Dinah Shore**.

DECEMBER 1993

People

Lanny Wadkins was selected as Captain of the 1995 U.S. Ryder Cup team. **Steve Mona** was named Executive Director of the **Golf Superintendents' Association of America**. **Paul Azinger** was diagnosed with cancer in his shoulder, and left the PGA TOUR indefinitely for treatment. **Peter Jacobsen** announced December 8 that he would leave the ABC golf broadcasting team in order to concentrate more on his playing career.

Places

The **Pebble Beach Co.** sued December 7 to prevent a Houston developer from duplicating Pebble Beach's famed 14th hole. **Golf Digest**'s annual golf course rankings were released, with perennial favorite **Pine Valley** leading the list, and the brand-new **Shadow Creek** vaulting to eighth place in its first appearance in the closely-watched rankings.

Business

The **Western Open** announced that **Motorola** would be its new sponsor, changing the name of the **PGA TOUR's** oldest tourney to the Motorola Open. **NBC** and the PGA TOUR agreed to a three-year contract extension through 1998. The **European PGA Tour** announced a reduction of the captain's wild-card selections from three to two for the **1995 Ryder Cup** matches.

JANUARY 1994

People

The **1994 Curtis Cup team** was announced by the **USGA**, Jan. 23, led by **Carol Semple Thompson** who received her eighth selection to the team, and **Sarah Ingram**, the 1993 Amateur of the Year. **Jack Nicklaus** returned to the winners circle with a victory in the senior division of the **Mercedes Championships**. **Pat Summerall** was dropped from the CBS golf broadcast team Jan. 24 after signing with the Fox network as an NFL announcer.**Charles Price**, long-time golf writer, died Jan. 29, age 68.

Places

KSL, an affiliate of **Kohlberg Kravis Roberts & Co.** announced the acquisition of the **Doral Resort** & Country Club.**Indian Wells** Country Club and **Royal Kenfield** Country Club (Las Vegas, Nev.) were turned over to the auctioneer in a **U.S. Customs** seizure.

Business

Record crowds showed for the annual **PGA Merchandise Show** in Orlando Fla. Over 35,000 professionals, industry executives, and members of the public crowded the Orlando Convention Center for the four-day event. **Callaway** Golf introduced the Big Bertha Irons. **Hogan** introduced Apex irons; **PING** debuted the Ping Zing 2 Irons; **Nicklaus** golf introduced the mid-size N1 metalwoods; **GolfGear International** debuted its two-piece PT518 Airmatch ball.

FEBRUARY 1994

People

Johnny Miller stunned the golf world by winning the **AT&T National Pro-Am** at Pebble Beach Feb. 6, after years of absence from full-time play on the PGA TOUR. **Greg Norman** regained the No. 1 Sony Ranking, displacing **Nick Faldo** after 81 weeks at the top.**James R. Watson**, a turfgrass specialist, was awarded the Donald Ross Award by the American Society of Golf Course Architects. **John Daly**'s three-month suspension from the PGA TOUR was lifted three weeks early by TOUR Commissioner **Deane Beman**. **Lee Trevino** became the third player to amass $4 million in earnings on the Senior PGA TOUR. **Dinah Shore**died Feb. 24, after a brief illness, age 76.

Places

Blackwolf Run, in Kohler, Wisc., was awarded the 1998 U.S. Women's Open. The International TPC of Mission Hills, in Guangdong Province, China, was awarded the 1995 World Cup.Chateau Elan (Atlanta, GA) was announced as the site of the inaugural $1.9 million Sarazen World Open Championship, sponsored by Wilson.

Business

Bullet Golf sued the USGA for banning the Hollow Point driver and the Magnificent 7-wood. The Celebrity Golf Association announced a 6-tournament schedule with purses totaling $1.4 million in 1994. Larry Nelson purchased an undisclosed percentage of Merit Golf. Shell's Wonderful World of Golf was officially revived Feb. 28 with a three-match schedule—the show was a mainstay of televised golf in the early 1960s.

MARCH 1994

People

Deane Beman announced his retirement as PGA TOUR Commissioner Mar. 1. The resignation is effective at the end of 1995. **Phil Mickelson** suffered a broken leg in a skiing accident in Arizona, Mar. 3. CBS golf analyst **Ben Wright** was retained to design the Valley course at the Cliffs at Glassy. **Richard Hill** of Batavia, Ill. became the 400,000 member of the USGA.

Places

Dorado Beach East was announced as the site of the Senior TOUR's Tournament of Champions. The tournament will replace the senior division of The Mercedes Championships played at **La Costa**. **Runaway Bay** Golf Club, in Jamaica, and **Mission Hills** Golf Club, Thailand, were announced as the qualifying sites for the 1994 World Cup at **Hyatt Dorado Beach**, Puerto Rico. The Jack Nicklaus Course at **PGA West** was announced as the site of the new Diners Club matches.

Business

The Golf Channel moved closer to launch with the completion of a $65 million capitalization drive. **Computer Golf** president Paul Spreadbury disappeared after suddenly cancelling his five-tournament series. The **Pro**

Athletes Golf League announced a four-tournament schedule for 1994.

APRIL 1994

People

51 Senior TOUR players, including **Dave Stockton**, **Bob Charles**, **Larry Laoretti**, **Bruce Crampton**, **Jim Colbert** and **Mike Hill** were fined more than $100,000 by the Senior PGA TOUR for purse-splitting in the Merrill Lynch Shoot-Out Championships and the United Van Lines Aces Championships. It was the first instance of proven purse-splitting in many years. Oklahoma State women's coach **Ann Pitts** was awarded $36,000 in damages in a suit charging the university with pay discrimination against women. **Mac O'Grady** claimed that up to seven of the world's top-30 golfers are taking performance-enhancing "beta blockers."

Places

Poipu Bay G.C. was announced as the site of the 1994 Grand Slam of Golf by the PGA of America. **Pebble Beach Co**. president, Thomas A. Oliver, was found guilty of bank fraud.The **Robert Trent Jones Club**, in Manassas, Va., was selected as the host site of the inaugural President's Cup. A four-month delay was announced in the completion of the **World Golf Village**. The new completion date was given as April 1996.

Business

Cheval Country Club was ordered by the Florida Attorney-General to allow women Saturday morning tee-times, following a complaint lodged by a female member at Cheval. **Levi's** announced their entry into the crowded golf fashion market with a line of golf apparel. **Maruman** Golf Japan closed a chapter in their assualt on the U.S. golf equipment market by purchasing Maruman USA for an undisclosed sum. The **Sporting Goods Manufacturers Association** reported that in 1993 exports of golf equipment rose 12.9% over 1992 exports. The value of all exports reached $1.54 billion in 1993. A 12.9 percent growth in golf equipment exports for 1993 was also announced. **Seabury Management** Co. lost in its lawsuit against the PGA of America, in an appeals court decision handed down April 28. Seabury alleged that the PGA breached an agreement with Seabury regarding the East Coast Merchandise Show.

MAY 1994

People

Hale Irwin and **David Graham** were named captains of the United States and World teams, respectively, for the inaugural President's Cup matches. **Seve Ballesteros** resigned from the 1997 Ryder Cup committee, stating that he should not have accepted the appointment when he had previously declared his support for Novo Sancti Petri's application to be the host course.

Places

The **Royal Kenfield** Country Club was purchased for $16.2 million in a U.S. Customs auction. **Indian Wells** was sold in a similar auction May 19 to a subsidiary of ClubCorp of America for $16.5 million. The **Augusta National** Golf Club announced May 2 that, beginning in 1995, a limitation would be placed on the sale of practice-round tickets, after more than 80,000 people attended on the Tuesday of Masters week 1994.

Business

The parent company of **Titleist** and **Foot-Joy** Worldwide, American Brands, announced a major restructuring including the sale of the tobacco division and several major personnel changes at Titleist.**Cleveland Golf** received a $5 million capital infusion from its parent, **Rossignol**, to finance Cleveland's expansion.

JUNE 1994

People

John Daly signed a 10-year, multi-million dollar contract with Wilson. **O.J. Simpson** was dropped June 20 as a director of the Pro Athletes Golf League, after his arrest on double-homicide charges. Golf Digest magazine announced that it will renew its search for the World's Worst Avid Golfer, a title granted to **Angelo Spagnolo** in 1985. **Arnold Palmer** announced that his appearance in the 1994 U.S. Open at Oakmont Country Club would be his final Open appearance. **Tim Finchem** officially succeeded Deane Beman as PGA TOUR commissioner, effective June 1.

Places

South Africa was announced as the inaugural site of the Southern Hemisphere Challenge, pitting golfers from Australasia against Southern Africa. The initial matches were scheduled for February 23-26, 1995. **Pebble Beach** was announced as the site of the inaugural Shivas Irons Games of the Links, loosely based on the book *Golf in the Kingdom* by Michael Murphy. A course redesigned by Donald Ross, the **Oakwood Club** of Cleveland, Ohio, was sold to a real estate development concern for a shopping-center and multi-family housing development.

Business

Club designer **Terry McCabe** won a $5.7 million award from his former employer, **Founders Club**, for breach of contracts relating to McCabe's compensation for design work. The judgement was appealed but subsequently settled for an undisclosed sum. More than 160 new companies applied for booth space at the **PGA International Golf Show** in Anaheim, Calif., to be held August 28-30.

JULY 1994

People

Kim Williams, an LPGA touring pro, was struck by a stray bullet July 4 while shopping in Niles, Ohio. **Anders Forsbrand** was disqualified in the French Open when he ran out of golf balls (after putting two into the water on the 18th hole).**John Daly** suggested in the London *Sun* that a number of PGA TOUR professionals were substance abusers.

Places

The **La Quinta Hotel** was announced as the new site of the Liberty Mutual Legends of Golf, the original Senior TOUR tournament. The Legends had been played in Austin, Texas since its inception in 1978. **Pinehurst Resort** and Country Club announced construction was about to begin onan eighth course, Centennial, from a design by Tom Fazio.

Business

Wilson Golf announced a restructuring of senior management of the company to implementproduct line organization. The **New York Times Co.** sold its three British golf magazines—**Golf World, Golf Illustrated Weekly** and **Golf Industry News**—to Reed Elsevier PLC for an undisclosed sum. Strong second quarter earnings announced for **Callaway, Cobra,** and **Coastcast** gave a fresh

indication of the strength of the golf economy in 1994. Each reported an earnings increase of at least 50% over the second quarter of 1993.

AUGUST 1994

People

The embattled Pro Athletes Golf League—which had recently dropped board member **O.J. Simpson**—suspended operations after dismal ratings for its first event, televised on ESPN. **Lee Janzen** left the TOUR temporarily following hernia surgery July 20. **Nick Price** secured the number-one slot in the Sony Rankings, edging out **Greg Norman** who had spent 20 weeks at the top. The estate of **Heather Farr** sued Karsten Manufacturing, claiming non-payment of medical benefits for the LPGA player who died November 20, 1993. **Paul Azinger** made a return to competitive golf at the Buick Open, following a nine-month period of treatment for bone cancer. Azinger subsequently played in the PGA Championship. Azinger was also appointed President's Cup co-captain by **Hale Irwin. Mark Wiebe** also returned to the TOUR after a long layoff following a skiing accident, by playing in the Sprint International. **Bert Yancey** died of a heart attack August 26, minutes before his scheduled tee-time in the Franklin Quest Championship. **John Daly** was attacked by a spectator at the NEC World Series of Golf after a dispute arose concerning Daly hitting into the groups in front of him on the golf course.

Places

The legal fight to force clubs to make weekend tee-times available to women spread to Connecticut, where three women brought suit against the **Clinton** Country Club for discriminatory tee-time policies. Tom Fazio was retained to design **The Forest Course at Pebble Beach** for the Pebble Beach Co, to bring their collection of courses up to four. **Desert Mountain (Arizona)** began construction of a fourth Jack Nicklaus course—the first private community ever to build four golf courses in one community by a single architect. The LPGA announced a new tournament in 1995, the Pinewild Women's Championship (Pinehurst, N.C.) to replace the struggling Atlanta Women's Championship.

Business

American Golf Corporation announced an

alliance with the **Western States Golf Association** to provide golf instruction, equipment, and scholarships to Los Angeles-area minority youths. **Wilson** announced a 500-dimple golf ball, claiming that the new ball represented the first significant change in golf ball design in some time. The **Space Coast Golf Tour** officially changed its name to the **Gary Player Golf Tour** following the signing of the **Gary Player** Golf Equipment Co. as a title sponsor. The **PGA International Golf Show** in Anaheim, Calif. attracted over 10,000 industry executives and golf professionals.

SEPTEMBER 1994

People

Mac O'Grady conducted the first of his three-day master professional instruction seminars at Rancho Santa Fe, Calif. **Gary McCord** was dropped from the CBS golf telecast team for The Masters, following remarks at the 1994 tournament which were deemed offensive by Augusta National. **Ernie Els** and **Tom Kite** were among leading players who declined to compete in the inaugural President's Cup matches. **Mickey Walker** announced the final selections for the European Solheim Cup team September 4: **Laura Davies, Annika Sorenstam, Liselotte Neumann, Helen Alfredsson, Lora Fairclough, Trish Johnson, Alison Nicholas, Dale Reid, Pamela Wright,** and **Catrina Nilsmark. John Daly** was dropped by Reebok as a sponsor, as controversy continued to swirl around the young Tour star. **Wilson** followed suit October 4.

Places

Tres Vidas (Acapulco, Mexico), a Robert Hagge-designed course along the Pacific Ocean, was announced as the new site of the Chrysler Cup in 1995

Business

A four-event professional golf tour in China was announced, including the $400,000 **Volvo China Open**. The **Veterans of Foreign Wars** announced September 6 their sponsorship of a PGA Senior Tour event, the VFW Senior Championship. The **PGA TOUR** announced September 6 a new eight-man team match-play

event for 1995, featuring teams from the PGA TOUR, the PGA European Tour, the Japanese tour and a combined team from the Australian and South African tours.

OCTOBER 1994

People

Nick Faldo announced that he would rejoin the PGA TOUR in 1995. USGA Golf Journal editor **David Earl** died Oct. 2, in Versailles, France, age 48. **Dick Enberg** was announced as a replacement for **Jim Lampley** as the regular host of NBC golf telecasts in 1995.

Places

Charlotte, N.C. was announced as the home for a new LPGA event, the Carolina LPGA Classic, to finish off the U.S. LPGA calendar beginning in 1995. The PGA TOUR announced that the NIKE TOUR championship would move in 1995 to **Atlanta**. Bizarre floods and heavy rains closed numerous courses in Texas, Georgia, and South Carolina during record flooding. The rain led to the cancellation of the scheduled taping of the Wendy's Three Tour Challenge at **Colleton River** Plantation in Hilton Head, S.C.

Business

The **PGA of America** announced that they would re-examine ticket policies for the Ryder Cup after the 25,000 tickets available for the 1995 event were sold out within 48 hours. Nestle announced that they would withdraw from sponsorship of the Bay Hill Classic after 1995. The **Solheim Cup** announced that teams would increase from 10 to 12 players beginning with the 1996 matches. **Callaway** and **Cobra** reported strong third quarter earnings, both up over 80% over 1993, as evidence continued to mount that 1994 was an excellent year for the golf equipment industry. **Ram Golf** sued **Bobby Grace** for patent infringement September 23, over alleged copying of the Ram Zebra putter. **The PGA of America** announced October 9 that, beginning in 1995, only 25 club professionals would receive exemptions into the PGA Championship. The total was previously 40.

1994 MAJOR CHAMPIONSHIP RESULTS

OVERVIEW: *Complete scores, and prize money for the four major championships on the PGA TOUR, Senior PGA TOUR, and the LPGA Tour.*

PGA TOUR

THE MASTERS
Augusta National G.C.,
Augusta, Georgia,
Apr. 7-10, 1994

JOSE MARIA OLAZABAL	1	**74-67-69-69**	**279**	**$360,000**
TOM LEHMAN	2	70-70-69-72	281	$216,000
LARRY MIZE	3	68-71-72-71	282	$136,000
TOM KITE	4	69-72-71-71	283	$96,000
JAY HAAS	T5	72-72-72-69	285	$73,000
JIM MCGOVERN	T5	72-70-71-72	285	$73,000
LOREN ROBERTS	T5	75-68-72-70	285	$73,000
ERNIE ELS	T8	74-67-74-71	286	$60,000
COREY PAVIN	T8	71-72-73-70	286	$60,000
IAN BAKER FINCH	T10	71-71-71-74	287	$50,000
RAY FLOYD	T10	70-74-71-72	287	$50,000
JOHN HUSTON	T10	72-72-74-69	287	$50,000
TOM WATSON	13	70-71-73-74	288	$42,000
DAN FORSMAN	14	74-69-76-73	283	$38,000
CHIP BECK	T15	71-71-75-74	291	$34,000
BRAD FAXON	T15	71-73-73-74	291	$34,000
MARK O'MEARA	T15	75-70-76-70	291	$34,000
SEVE BALLESTEROS	T18	70-76-75-71	292	$24,343
BEN CRENSHAW	T18	74-73-73-72	292	$24,343
DAVID EDWARDS	T18	73-72-73-74	292	$24,343
BILL GLASSON	T18	72-73-75-72	292	$24,343
HALE IRWIN	T18	73-68-79-72	292	$24,343
GREG NORMAN	T18	70-70-75-77	292	$24,343
LANNY WADKINS	T18	73-74-73-72	292	$24,343
BERNHARD LANGER	T25	74-74-72-73	293	$16,800
JEFF SLUMAN	T25	74-75-71-73	293	$16,800
SCOTT SIMPSON	T27	74-74-73-73	294	$14,800
VIJAY SINGH	T27	70-75-74-75	294	$14,800
CURTIS STRANGE	T27	74-70-75-75	294	$14,800
LEE JANZEN	T30	75-71-76-73	295	$13,300
CRAIG PARRY	T30	75-74-73-73	295	$13,300
NICK FALDO	32	76-73-73-74	296	$12,400
RUSS COCHRAN	T33	71-74-74-78	297	$11,550
SAM TORRANCE	T33	76-73-74-74	297	$11,550
DAVID FROST	T35	74-71-75-78	298	$10,300
NICK PRICE	T35	74-73-74-77	298	$10,300
FUZZY ZOELLER	T35	74-72-74-78	298	$10,300
FULTON ALLEM	T38	69-77-76-77	299	$9,000
FRED FUNK	T38	79-70-75-75	299	$9,000
SANDY LYLE	T38	75-73-78-73	299	$9,000
WAYNE GRADY	T41	74-73-73-80	300	$7,400
ANDREW MAGEE	T41	74-74-76-76	300	$7,400
HAJIME MESHIAI	T41	71-71-80-78	300	$7,400
CONSTANTINO ROCCA	T41	79-70-78-73	300	$7,400
MIKE STANDLY	T41	71-69-79-75	300	$7,400
JOHN COOK	T46	77-72-77-75	301	$6,000
IAN WOOSNAM	T46	76-73-77-75	301	$6,000
JOHN DALY	T48	76-73-77-78	304	$5,250
HOWARD TWITTY	T48	73-76-74-81	304	$5,250
JOHN HARRIS	T50	72-76-80-77	305	Amateur
JEFF MAGGERT	T50	75-73-82-75	305	$5,000

THE UNITED STATES OPEN
Oakmont C.C.,
Oakmont, Pennsylvania
June 16-19, 1994

ERNIE ELS	1	**69-71-66-73**	**279**	**$320,000**
COLIN MONTGOMERIE	T2	71-65-73-70	279	$141,827
LOREN ROBERTS	T2	76-69-64-70	279	$141,827
CURTIS STRANGE	4	70-70-70-70	280	$75,728
JOHN COOK	5	73-65-73-71	282	$61,318
CLARK DENNIS	T6	71-71-70-71	283	$49,485
GREG NORMAN	T6	71-71-69-72	283	$49,485

TOM WATSON	T6	68-73-68-74	283	$49,485
DUFFY WALDORF	T9	74-68-73-69	284	$37,179
JEFF MAGGERT	T9	71-68-75-70	284	$37,179
JEFF SLUMAN	T9	72-69-72-71	284	$37,179
FRANK NOBILO	T9	69-71-68-76	284	$37,179
JIM McGOVERN	T13	73-69-74-69	285	$29,767
SCOTT HOCH	T13	72-72-70-71	285	$29,767
DAVID EDWARDS	T13	73-65-75-72	285	$29,767
FRED COUPLES	T16	72-71-69-74	286	$25,899
STEVE LOWERY	T16	71-71-68-76	286	$25,899
SCOTT VERPLANK	T18	70-72-75-70	287	$22,477
SEVE BALLESTEROS	T18	72-72-70-73	287	$22,477
HALE IRWIN	T18	69-69-71-78	287	$22,477
SAM TORRANCE	T21	72-71-76-69	288	$19,464
STEVE PATE	T21	74-66-71-77	288	$19,464
BERNHARD LANGER	T23	72-72-73-72	289	$17,223
KIRK TRIPLETT	T23	70-71-71-77	289	$17,223
MIKE SPRINGER	T25	74-72-73-71	290	$14,705
CRAIG PARRY	T25	78-68-71-73	290	$14,705
CHIP BECK	T25	73-73-70-74	290	$14,705
DAVIS LOVE III	T28	74-72-74-72	292	$11,514
JIM FURYK	T28	74-69-74-75	292	$11,514
LENNIE CLEMENTS	T28	73-71-73-75	292	$11,514
JACK NICKLAUS	T28	69-70-77-76	292	$11,514
JUMBO OZAKI	T28	70-73-69-80	292	$11,514
MARK CARNEVALE	T33	75-72-76-70	293	$9,578
TOM LEHMAN	T33	77-68-73-75	293	$9,578
FULTON ALLEM	T33	73-70-74-76	293	$9,578
TOM KITE	T33	73-71-72-77	293	$9,578
BEN CRENSHAW	T33	71-74-70-78	293	$9,578
BRAD FAXON	T33	73-69-71-80	293	$9,578
BRADLEY HUGHES	T39	71-72-77-74	294	$8,005
PETER BAKER	T39	73-73-73-75	294	$8,005
GORDON BRAND	T39	73-71-73-77	294	$8,005
BRANDT JOBE	T39	72-74-68-80	294	$8,005
FRAN QUINN JR.	43	75-72-73-75	295	$7,222
PAUL GOYDOS	T44	74-72-79-71	296	$6,595
FRED FUNK	T44	74-71-74-77	296	$6,595
DON WALSWORTH	T44	71-75-73-77	296	$6,595
TIM DUNLAVEY	T47	76-70-78-73	297	$5,105
OLIN BROWNE	T47	74-73-77-73	297	$5,105
BARRY LANE	T47	77-70-76-74	297	$5,105
MICHAEL EMERY	T47	74-73-75-75	297	$5,105
DAVID BERGANIO	T47	73-72-76-76	297	$5,105
JIM GALLAGHER, JR.	T47	74-68-77-78	297	$5,105
WAYNE LEVI	T47	76-70-73-78	297	$5,105
PHIL MICKELSON	T47	75-70-73-79	297	$5,105
TOMMY ARMOUR III	T55	73-73-79-73	298	$4,324
HUGH ROYER III	T55	72-71-77-78	298	$4,324
SCOTT SIMPSON	T55	74-73-73-78	298	$4,324
STEVEN RICHARDSON	T58	74-73-76-76	299	$4,105
FUZZY ZOELLER	T58	76-70-76-77	299	$4,105
DAVE RUMMELLS	T60	71-74-82-74	301	$3,967
DOUG MARTIN	T60	76-70-74-81	301	$3,967
ED HUMENIK	T62	74-72-81-75	302	$3,800
MICHAEL SMITH	T62	74-73-78-77	302	$3,800
EMLYN AUBREY	T62	72-69-81-80	302	$3,800

THE BRITISH OPEN

Turnberry G.C. (Ailsa),
Turnberry, Scotland
July 14-17, 1994

NICK PRICE	1	69-66-67-66	268	£110,000
JESPER PARNEVIK	2	68-66-68-67	269	£88,000
FUZZY ZOELLER	3	71-66-64-70	271	£74,000
ANDERS FORSBRAND	T4	72-71-66-64	273	£50,666
MARK JAMES	T4	72-67-66-68	273	£50,666
DAVID FEHERTY	T4	70-69-66-70	273	£50,666
BRAD FAXON	7	69-65-67-73	274	£36,000
COLIN MONTGOMERIE	T8	72-69-65-69	275	£30,000
TOM KITE	T8	71-69-66-69	275	£30,000
NICK FALDO	T8	75-66-70-64	275	£30,000
TOM WATSON	T11	68-65-69-74	276	£19,333
FRANK NOBILO	T11	69-67-72-69	276	£19,333
RONAN RAFFERTY	T11	71-66-65-74	276	£19,333
JONATHAN LOMAS	T11	66-70-72-68	276	£19,333
RUSSELL CLAYDON	T11	72-71-68-65	276	£19,333
LARRY MIZE	T11	73-69-64-70	276	£19,333
GREG NORMAN	T11	71-67-69-69	276	£19,333
MARK CALCAVECCHIA	T11	71-70-67-68	276	£19,333
MARK MCNULTY	T11	71-70-68-67	276	£19,333
PETER SENIOR	T20	68-71-67-71	277	£12,500
MARK BROOKS	T20	74-64-71-68	277	£12,500
VIJAY SINGH	T20	70-68-69-70	277	£12,500
GREG TURNER	T20	65-71-70-71	277	£12,500
LOREN ROBERTS	T24	68-69-69-72	278	£7,972
TOM LEHMAN	T24	70-69-70-69	278	£7,972
PETER JACOBSEN	T24	69-70-67-72	278	£7,972
ANDREW COLTART	T24	71-69-66-72	278	£7,972
PAUL LAWRIE	T24	71-69-70-68	278	£7,972
BOB ESTES	T24	72-68-72-66	278	£7,972

MIKE SPRINGER	T24	72-67-68-71 278	£7,972
CRAIG STADLER	T24	71-69-66-72 278	£7,972
ERNIE ELS	T24	69-69-69-71 278	£7,972
JEFF MAGGERT	T24	69-74-67-68 278	£7,972
TERRY PRICE	T24	74-65-71-68 278	£7,972
LEE JANZEN	T35	74-69-69-67 279	£6,700
GARY EVANS	T35	69-69-73-66 279	£6,700
MARK DAVIS	T35	75-68-69-67 279	£6,700
JOSE-MARIA OLAZABAL	T38	72-71-69-68 280	£6,100
JEAN VAN DE VELDE	T38	68-70-71-71 280	£6,100
DARREN CLARKE	T38	73-68-69-70 280	£6,100
MASASHI OZAKI	T38	69-71-66-74 280	£6,100
DAVID GILFORD	T38	72-68-72-6B 280	£6,100
DAVIS LOVE III	T38	71-67-68-74 280	£6,100
SEVE BALLESTEROS	T38	70-70-71-69 280	£6,100
DOMINGO HOSPITAL	T38	72-69-71-68 280	£6,100
BRIAN MARCHBANK	T38	71-70-70-69 280	£6,100
JIM GALLAGHER, JR.	T47	73-68-69-71 281	£5,450
HOWARD TWITTY	T47	71-72-66-72 281	£5,450
DAVID EDWARDS	T47	68-68-73-72 281	£5,450
GREG KRAFT	T47	69-74-66-72 281	£5,450
DAVID FROST	T51	70-71-71-70 282	£4,925
TSUKASA WATANREIE	T51	72-71-68-71 282	£4,925
MATS LANNER	T51	69-74-69-70 282	£4,925
KATSUYOSHI TOMORI	T51	69-69-73-71 282	£4,925
TOMMY NAKAJIMA	T55	73-68-69-73 283	£4,700
JOHN COOK	T55	73-67-70-73 283	£4,700
PETER BAKER	T55	71-72-70-70 283	£4,700
BRIAN WATTS	T55	68-70-71-74 283	£4,700
ROSE MCFARLANS	T55	68-74-67-74 283	£4,700
ROBERT ALLENBY	T60	72-69-68-75 284	£4,350
GORDON BRAND, JR.	T60	72-71-73-68 284	£4,350
BERNHARD LANGER	T60	72-70-70-72 284	£4,350
PER JOHANSSON	T60	73-69-69-73 284	£4,350
HAJIM MESHIAI	T60	72-71-71-70 284	£4,350
WAYNE GRADY	T60	73-74-67-75 284	£4,350
CHRISTY O'CONNOR	T60	71-69-71-73 284	£4,350
LENNIE CLEMENTS	T67	72-71-72-70 285	£4,050
CARL MASON	T67	69-71-73-72 285	£4,050
STEVE ELKINGTON	T67	71-72-73-69 285	£4,050
MARK ROE	T67	74-68-73-70 285	£4,050
RUBEN ALVAREZ	T67	70-72-71-72 285	£4,050
WAYNE RILEY	T72	77-66-70-73 286	£3,900
WARREN BENNETT	T72	72-67-74-73 286	Amateur
SANDY LYLE	74	71-72-72-72 287	£3,850
COLIN GILLIES	T75	71-70-72-75 288	£3,775
CRAIG RONALD	T75	71-72-72-73 288	£3,775

JOAKIM HAEGGMAN	T77	71-72-69-77 289	£3,650
BEN CRENSHAW	T77	70-73-73-73 289	£3,650
CRAIG PARRY	T77	72-68-73-76 289	£3,650
NIC HENNING	80	70-73-70-78 291	£3,550
JOHN DALY	81	68-72-72-80 292	£3,500

THE PGA CHAMPIONSHIP
Southern Hills C.C.,
Tulsa, Oklahoma
August 11-14, 1994

NICK PRICE	**1**	**67-65-70-67 269**	**$310,000**
COREY PAVIN	2	70-67-69-69 275	$160,000
PHIL MICKELSON	3	68-71-67-70 276	$110,000
NICK FALDO	T4	73-67-71-66 277	$76,666
GREG NORMAN	T4	71-69-67-70 277	$76,666
JOHN COOK	T4	71-67-69-70 277	$76,666
STEVE ELKINGTON	T7	73-70-66-69 278	$57,500
JOSE MARIA OLAZABAL	T7	72-66-70-70 278	$57,500
BEN CRENSHAW	T9	70-67-70-72 279	$41,000
TOM KITE	T9	72-68-69-70 279	$41,000
LOREN ROBERTS	T9	69-72-67-71 279	$41,000
TOM WATSON	T9	69-72-67-71 279	$41,000
IAN WOOSNAM	T9	68-72-73-66 279	$41,000
JAY HAAS	14	71-66-68-75 280	$32,000
GLEN DAY	T15	70-69-70-72 281	$27,000
MARK MCNULTY	T15	72-68-70-71 281	$27,000
LARRY MIZE	T15	72-72-67-70 281	$27,000
KIRK TRIPLETT	T15	71-69-71-70 281	$27,000
BILL GLASSON	T19	71-73-68-70 282	$18,666
MARK MCCUMBER	T19	73-70-71-68 282	$18,666
CRAIG STADLER	T19	70-70-74-68 282	$18,666
CURTIS STRANGE	T19	73-71-68-70 282	$18,666
CRAIG PARRY	T19	70-69-70-73 282	$18,666
FUZZY ZOELLER	T19	69-71-72-70 282	$18,666
ERNIE ELS	T25	68-71-69-75 283	$13,000
DAVID FROST	T25	70-71-69-73 283	$13,000
BARRY LANE	T25	70-73-68-72 283	$13,000
BERNHARD LANGER	T25	73-71-67-72 283	$13,000
JEFF SLUMAN	T25	70-72-66-75 283	$13,000
BRAD FAXON	T30	72-73-73-66 284	$8,458
RICHARD ZOKOL	T30	77-67-67-73 284	$8,458
BOB BOYD	T30	72-71-70-71 284	$8,458
LENNIE CLEMENTS	T30	74-70-69-71 284	$8,458

WAYNE GRADY	T30	75-68-71-70	284	$8,458
SAM TORRANCE	T30	69-75-69-71	284	$8,458
CHIP BECK	T36	72-70-72-71	285	$7,000
BLAINE MCCALLISTER	T36	74-64-75-72	285	$7,000
COLIN MONTGOMERIE	T36	67-76-70-72	285	$7,000
FRED COUPLES	T39	68-74-75-69	286	$6,030
HALE IRWIN	T39	75-69-68-74	286	$6,030
TOM LEHMAN	T39	73-71-68-74	286	$6,030
BILLY MAYFAIR	T39	73-72-71-70	286	$6,030
GIL MORGAN	T39	71-68-73-74	286	$6,030
DAVID EDWARDS	T44	72-70-74-71	287	$5,200
DAVID GILFORD	T44	69-73-73-72	287	$5,200
NEAL LANCASTER	T44	73-72-72-70	287	$5,200
FULTON ALLEM	T47	74-67-74-73	288	$4,112
BILLY ANDRADE	T47	71-71-78-68	288	$4,112
BOB ESTES	T47	72-71-72-73	288	$4,112
GREG KRAFT	T47	74-69-70-75	288	$4,112
ANDREW MAGEE	T47	70-74-71-73	288	$4,112
FRANK NOBILO	T47	72-67-74-75	288	$4,112
JUMBO OZAKI	T47	71-69-72-76	288	$4,112
D.A. WEIBRING	T47	69-73-70-76	288	$4,112
KENNY PERRY	T55	78-67-70-74	289	$3,158
MIKE SPRINGER	T55	77-66-69-77	289	$3,158
TOM DOLBY	T55	73-68-75-73	289	$3,158
FRED FUNK	T55	76-69-72-72	289	$3,158
DUDLEY HART	T55	72-71-75-71	289	$3,158
HAL SUTTON	T55	76-69-72-72	289	$3,158
BRUCE FLEISHER	T61	75-68-72-75	290	$2,800
RAY FLOYD	T61	69-76-73-72	290	$2,800
RON MCDOUGAL	T61	76-69-72-73	290	$2,800
TOMMY NAKAJIMA	T61	73-71-74-72	290	$2,800
LANNY WADKINS	T61	69-73-73-75	290	$2,800
JAYDON BLAKE	T66	72-71-74-74	291	$2,600
JOHN INMAN	T66	70-72-73-76	291	$2,600
LEE JANZEN	T66	73-71-73-74	291	$2,600
TODD SMITH	T66	74-69-71-77	291	$2,600
PAYNE STEWART	T66	72-73-72-74	291	$2,600
DONNIE HAMMOND	T71	74-69-76-73	292	$2,512
PETER SENIOR	T71	74-71-70-77	292	$2,512
SANDY LYLE	T73	75-70-76-76	297	$2,462
DICKY PRIDE	T73	75-69-73-80	297	$2,462
BRIAN HENNINGER	T75	77-65-78-78	298	$2,412
HAJIME MESHIAI	T75	74-71-74-79	298	$2,412

LPGA TOUR

NABISCO DINAH SHORE

Mission Hills C.C.,
Rancho Mirage, California
March 24-27, 1994

DONNA ANDREWS	**1**	**70-69-67-70**	**276**	**$105,000**
LAURA DAVIES	2	70-68-69-70	277	$65,165
TAMMIE GREEN	3	70-72-69-68	279	$47,553
JAN STEPHENSON	4	70-69-70-71	280	$36,985
MICHELLE MCGANN	5	70-68-70-73	281	$29,940
GAIL GRAHAM	T6	73-71-71-68	283	$21,251
KELLY ROBBINS	T6	73-70-69-71	283	$21,251
BRANDIE BURTON	T6	73-73-65-72	283	$21,251
HOLLIS STACY	T9	72-72-70-70	284	$15,674
NANCY LOPEZ	T9	68-72-73-71	284	$15,674
MEG MALLON	T11	72-75-69-69	285	$12,064
LISELOTTE NEUMANN	T11	76-71-68-70	285	$12,064
DANA DORMANN	T11	73-71-70-71	285	$12,064
DALE EGGELING	T11	71-71-71-72	285	$12,064
KRIS MONAGHAN	T15	70-76-70-70	286	$9,862
VICKI FERGON	T15	69-74-72-71	286	$9,862
LAURI MERTEN	T17	74-74-71-68	287	$8,982
NANCY SCRANTON	T17	75-70-69-73	287	$8,982
BETH DANIEL	T19	76-72-70-70	288	$7,204
JANE GEDDES	T19	70-77-71-70	288	$7,204
PAT BRADLEY	T19	71-75-71-71	288	$7,204
CAROLINE KEGGI	T19	72-73-72-71	288	$7,204
CHRIS JOHNSON	T19	74-73-69-72	288	$7,204
PATTY SHEEHAN	T19	73-71-72-72	288	$7,204
DOTTIE MOCHRIE	T19	74-73-68-73	288	$7,204
AYAKO OKAMOTO	T19	69-74-72-73	288	$7,204
MISSIE MCGEORGE	T19	72-71-70-75	288	$7,204
TINA TOMBS	T28	73-74-72-70	289	$5,670
SHERRI TURNER	T28	72-74-71-72	289	$5,670
VAL SKINNER	T28	72-72-72-73	289	$5,670
MISSIE BERTEOTTI	T28	71-73-72-73	289	$5,670
TERRY-JO MYERS	T32	76-73-71-70	290	$4,913
HIROMI KOBAYASHI	T32	72-77-71-70	290	$4,913
KRIS TSCHETTER	T32	73-69-76-72	290	$4,913
SHERRI-STEINHAUER	T32	76-68-72-74	290	$4,913
JULIE LARSEN	T36	76-70-75-70	291	$3,949
KRISTI ALBERS	T36	77-73-70-71	291	$3,949
CINDY RARICK	T36	72-74-74-71	291	$3,949
DAWN COE-JONES	T36	74-70-75-72	291	$3,949

TOSHIMI KIMURA	T36	71-74-73-73	291	$3,949	DANA DORMANN	T14	71-76-71-70	288	$16,051
MARTHA NAUSE	T36	74-71-72-74	291	$3,949	CHRIS JOHNSON	T14	70-74-73-71	288	$16,051
ALICE MILLER	T36	68-71-77-75	291	$3,949	BARB MUCHA	T17	73-74-75-67	289	$12,257
MUFFIN SPENCER-DEVLIN	T43	74-75-72-71	292	$3,029	NANCI BOWEN	T17	73-75-73-68	289	$12,257
ELAINE CROSBY	T43	74-71-75-72	292	$3,029	TAMMIE GREEN	T17	71-76-74-68	289	$12,257
DANIELLE AMMACCAPANE	T43	71-74-75-72	292	$3,029	DONNA ANDREWS	T17	73-76-69-71	289	$12,257
DEB RICHARD	T43	72-74-73-73	292	$3,029	BETSY KING	T17	74-73-71-71	289	$12,257
TRISH JOHNSON	T43	77-70-71-74	292	$3,029	MISSIE MCGEORGE	T17	75-71-70-73	289	$12,257
JANE CRAFTER	T48	75-75-72-71	293	$2,070	KRIS MONAGHAN	T17	72-72-72-73	289	$12,257
JOANNE CARNER	T48	73-75-72-73	293	$2,070	MARDI LUNN	T17	70-75-70-74	289	$12,257
KAREN NOBLE	T48	72-75-73-73	293	$2,070	ROBIN WALTON	T17	70-70-75-74	289	$12,257
SUZANNE STRUDWICK	T48	76-72-71-74	293	$2,070	JOANNE CARNER	T26	73-75-74-68	290	$9,907
HELEN ALFREDSSON	T48	76-72-71-74	293	$2,070	MICHELLE MCGANN	T26	70-76-75-69	290	$9,907
CINDY SCHREYER	T48	72-74-72-75	293	$2,070	JENNY LIDBACK	T28	73-73-74-71	291	$8,460
JUDY DICKINSON	T48	75-72-70-76	293	$2,070	MISSIE BERTEOTTI	T28	75-70-75-71	291	$8,460
LAUREL KEAN	T48	73-71-73-76	293	$2,070	GAIL GRAHAM	T28	73-71-76-71	291	$8,460
BETSY KING,	T48	70-72-75-76	293	$2,070	BRANDIE BURTON	T28	76-70-73-72	291	$8,460
LISA WALTERS	T48	68-74-75-76	293	$2,070	AYAKO OKAMOTO	T28	74-72-73-72	291	$8,460
CINDY FIGG-CURRIER	T58	75-72-74-73	294	$1,426	JENNIFER WYATT	T28	72-74-73-72	291	$8,460
AMY ALCOTT	T58	74-72-74-74	294	$1,426	TINA BARRETT	T28	73-77-68-73	291	$8,460
SUSIE REDMAN	T60	72-74-77-72	295	$1,197	DALE EGGELING	T35	76-74-71-71	292	$6,891
MELISSA MCNAMARA	T60	74-75-72-74	295	$1,197	PAGE DUNLAP	T35	71-74-75-72	292	$6,891
TRACY KERDYK	T60	74-76-70-75	295	$1,197	AMAIA ARRUTI	T35	75-73-71-73	292	$6,891
LORI GARBACZ	T60	75-74-71-75	295	$1,197	HELEN ALFREDSSON	T35	73-74-71-74	292	$6,891
					JUDY DICKINSON	T39	74-71-79-69	293	$5,562
					CINDY SCHREYER	T39	76-75-71-71	293	$5,562
					MUFFIN SPENCER-DEVLIN	T39	76-72-74-71	293	$5,562
					LISA KIGGENS	T39	75-71-76-71	293	$5,562
					KATHY GUADAGNINO	T39	72-79-69-73	293	$5,562
					LORI WEST	T39	75-73-70-75	293	$5,562
					HOLLIS STACY	45	73-76-72-73	294	$4,760
					BARB BUNKOWSKY	T46	72-76-75-72	295	$4,317
					LAURI MERTEN	T46	74-77-71-73	295	$4,317

MCDONALD'S LPGA CHAMPIONSHIP

DuPont C.C.,
Wilmington, Delaware,
May 12-15, 1994

LAURA DAVIES	1	**70-72-69-68**	**279**	**$165,000**	MARY BETH ZIMMERMAN	T46	74-77-71-73	295	$4,317
ALICE RITZMAN	2	68-73-71-70	282	$102,402	MARIANNE MORRIS	T49	75-76-76-69	296	$3,497
ELAINE CROSBY	T3	76-71-69-67	283	$54,660	NOELLE DAGHE	T49	69-79-78-70	296	$3,497
PAT BRADLEY	T3	73-73-70-67	283	$54,660	NANCY SCRANTON	T49	78-72-74-72	296	$3,497
HIROMI KOBAYASHI	T3	72-73-71-67	283	$54,660	NINA FOUST	T49	76-75-70-75	296	$3,497
LISELOTTE NEUMANN	T3	74-73-67-69	283	$54,660	KRIS TSCHETTER	T49	75-72-74-75	296	$3,497
SHERRI STEINHAUER	T7	75-70-72-68	285	$27,676	ALLISON FINNEY	T54	75-76-75-71	297	$2,822
AMY ALCOTT	T7	71-75-70-69	285	$27,676	LISA WALTERS	T54	74-77-74-72	297	$2,822
BETH DANIEL	T7	72-74-68-71	285	$27,676	CINDY FIGG-CURRIER	T54	75-75-74-73	297	$2,822
PATTY SHEEHAN	T7	72-68-72-73	285	$27,676	PEARL SINN	T57	75-76-75-72	298	$2,130
DOTTIE MOCHRIE	T11	68-78-70-70	286	$20,203	KAREN NOBLE	T57	75-75-76-72	298	$2,130
MEG MALLON	T11	71-71-69-75	286	$20,203	PAMELA ALLEN	T57	75-72-79-72	298	$2,130
VAL SKINNER	13	74-69-72-72	287	$18,266	MICHELLE ESTILL	T57	78-73-71-76	298	$2,130
JULI INKSTER	T14	69-76-74-69	288	$16,051	MARTA FIGUERAS-DOTTI	T57	76-75-70-77	298	$2,130

JODY ANSCHUTZ	T57	76-73-72-77	298	$2,130
JAN STEPHENSON	T63	75-76-74-74	299	$1,660
AMY BENZ	T63	75-74-75-75	299	$1,660
CINDY RARICK	T63	72-74-73-80	299	$1,660
JULIE LARSEN	T66	71-77-80-72	300	$1,384
NANCY RAMSBOTTOM	T66	77-74-75-74	300	$1,384
CATHY JOHNSTON-FORBES	T66	74-75-77-74	300	$1,384
KIM SAIKI	T66	75-75-74-76	300	$1,384
ALICE MILLER	T66	73-77-73-77	300	$1,384
CAROLINE KEGGI	T66	74-75-72-79	300	$1,384
MITZI EDGE	T66	73-74-74-79	300	$1,384

U.S. WOMEN'S OPEN

Indianwood G.C.,
Lake Orion, Michigan
July 21-24, 1994

PATTY SHEEHAN	**1**	**66-71-69-71**	**277**	**$155,000**
TAMMIE GREEN	2	66-72-69-71	278	$85,000
LISELOTTE NEUMANN	3	69-72-71-69	281	$47,752
TANIA ABITBOL	T4	72-68-73-70	283	$31,132
ALICIA DIBOS	T4	69-68-73-73	283	$31,132
AMY ALCOTT	T6	71-67-77-69	284	$21,486
MEG MALLON	T6	70-72-73-69	284	$21,486
BETSY KING	T6	69-71-72-72	284	$21,486
KELLY ROBBINS	T9	71-72-70-72	285	$16,445
DONNA ANDREWS	T9	67-72-70-76	285	$16,445
HELEN ALFREDSSON	T9	63-69-76-77	285	$16,445
LAURI MERTEN	T12	74-68-75-69	286	$12,805
DOTTIE MOCHRIE	T12	72-72-71-71	286	$12,805
LISA GRIMES	T12	72-73-69-72	286	$12,805
MICHELLE ESTILL	T12	69-68-75-74	286	$12,805
JUDY DICKINSON	T12	66-73-73-74	286	$12,805
LAURA DAVIES	T12	68-68-75-75	286	$12,805
MICHELLE MCGANN	T18	71-70-77-69	287	$10,202
JULI INKSTER	T18	75-72-69-71	287	$10,202
BETH DANIEL	T18	69-74-71-73	287	$10,202
JOAN PITCOCK	T18	74-72-67-74	287	$10,202
STEPHANIE MAYNOR	T22	73-70-76-69	288	$9,011
LISA WALTERS	T22	72-73-72-71	288	$9,011
SHERRI STEINHAUER	T22	68-72-74-74	288	$9,011
KRISTEN TSCHETTER	T25	71-73-72-73	289	$8,089
DEB RICHARD	T25	68-74-72-75	289	$8,089
PATRICIA BRADLEY	T25	72-69-70-78	289	$8,089
PAMELA WRIGHT	T25	74-65-71-79	289	$8,089
KAREN LUNN	T29	72-72-77-69	290	$7,371
VICKI GOETZE	T29	71-73-73-73	290	$7,371
DALE EGGELING	T31	67-73-79-72	291	$6,929
JO ANNE CARNER	T31	69-74-75-73	291	$6,929
CAROL THOMPSON	T31	66-75-76-74	291	$6,929
AMY READ	T31	68-72-76-75	291	$6,929
COLLEEN WALKER	T35	73-73-75-71	292	$6,048
HOLLY VAUGHN	T35	74-70-76-72	292	$6,048
JANE GEDDES	T35	73-72-73-74	292	$6,048
KIMBERLY WILLIAMS	T35	72-74-72-74	292	$6,048
MISSIE MCGEORGE	T35	69-73-75-75	292	$6,048
NANCY LOPEZ	T35	73-71-73-75	292	$6,048
DAWN COE-JONES	T35	73-73-71-75	292	$6,048
KRIS MONAGHAN	T35	75-69-72-76	292	$6,048
MICHELE BERTEOTTI	T43	71-73-77-72	293	$4,934
VICKI FERGON	T43	72-72-77-72	293	$4,934
MAYUMI HIRASE	T43	74-72-73-74	293	$4,934
ELAINE CROSBY	T43	74-72-73-74	293	$4,934
SALLY LITTLE	T43	67-76-74-76	293	$4,934
BRANDIE BURTON	T43	70-73-74-76	293	$4,934
NANCI BOWEN	T49	73-74-72-75	294	$4,299
AYAKO OKAMOTO	T49	71-72-72-79	294	$4,299
SHERRI TURNER	T51	72-74-75-74	295	$3,981
DANA DORMANN	T51	73-73-73-76	295	$3,981
EMILEE KLEIN	T51	71-73-69-82	295	$3,981
JAN STEPHENSON	T54	70-77-74-75	296	$3,619
HIROMI KOBAYASHI	T54	71-76-73-76	296	$3,619
NANCY RAMSBOTTOM	T54	71-74-72-79	296	$3,619
CAROLINE PIERCE	T57	74-73-76-74	297	$3,408
SARAH INGRAM	T57	74-71-77-75	297	$3,408
TARA FLEMING	T57	70-75-77-75	297	$3,408
ALICE RITZMAN	T57	73-74-74-76	297	$3,408
MITZI EDGE	T57	72-72-76-77	297	$3,408
TOSHIMI KIMURA	T62	73-72-75-78	298	$3,288
LISA KIGGENS	T62	71-74-73-80	298	$3,288
PAGE DUNLAP	T64	73-71-78-78	300	$3,272
PEARL SINN	T64	74-73-75-78	300	$3,272
JUDY SAMS	66	74-73-76-80	303	$3,272
SARAH MCGUIRE	67	76-71-77-80	304	$3,272

Du MAURIER LTD. CLASSIC

Ottawa Hunt and G.C.,
Ottawa, Ontario
August 25-28, 1994

MARTHA NAUSE	**1**	**65-71-72-71**	**279**	**$120,000**
MICHELLE MCGANN	2	66-71-71-72	280	$74,474
LISELOTTE NEUMANN	3	70-67-71-73	281	$54,346
JANE GEDDES	T4	74-67-70-72	283	$34,888
MEG MALLON	T4	70-72-68-73	283	$34,888
BETSY KING	T4	67-69-74-73	283	$34,888
DAWN COE-JONES	T7	72-70-71-71	284	$20,128
MARIANNE MORRIS	T7	69-72-70-73	284	$20,128
JUDY DICKINSON	T7	72-68-70-74	284	$20,128
KELLY ROBBINS	T7	66-70-73-75	284	$20,128
VICKI FERGON	T11	72-68-75-70	285	$14,223
SHERRI STEINHAUER	T11	68-72-73-72	285	$14,223
PATTY SHEEHAN	T11	71-71-68-75	285	$14,223
AMY ALCOTT	T14	73-70-72-71	286	$12,076
DOTTIE MOCHRIE	T14	67-74-72-73	286	$12,076
JANE CRAFTER	T16	71-74-75-67	287	$9,862
PAGE DUNLAP	T16	72-69-75-71	287	$9,862
ALICE RITZMAN	T16	76-70-68-73	287	$9,862
ROSIE JONES	T16	73-70-70-74	287	$9,862
JENNY LIDBACK	T16	70-72-71-74	287	$9,862
ALICIA DIBOS	T16	71-71-70-75	287	$9,862
SALLY LITTLE	T22	74-72-73-69	288	$7,348
MISSIE BERTEOTTI	T22	70-72-73-73	288	$7,348
BRANDIE BURTON	T22	71-74-69-74	288	$7,348
BARB BUNKOWSKY	T22	74-69-71-74	288	$7,348
KIM WILLIAMS	T22	67-74-73-74	288	$7,348
KAREN LUNN	T22	70-73-70-75	288	$7,348
ANNIKA SORENSTAM	T22	72-67-73-76	288	$7,348
NANCY LOPEZ	T22	67-70-75-76	288	$7,348
LEIGH ANN MILLS	T22	66-72-70-80	288	$7,348
TINA BARRETT	T31	71-75-72-71	289	$5,514
LISA WALTERS	T31	73-72-73-71	289	$5,514
ALICE MILLER	T31	72-71-74-72	289	$5,514
MICHELE REDMAN	T31	72-72-72-73	289	$5,514
HELEN ALFREDSSON	T31	71-73-71-74	289	$5,514
ROBIN WALTON	T31	73-67-72-77	289	$5,514
JENNIFER WYATT	T31	69-72-69-79	289	$5,514
JUDY SAMS	T38	71-72-76-71	290	$4,315
GAIL GRAHAM	T38	72-72-74-72	290	$4,315
LORI WEST	T38	75-71-71-73	290	$4,315
MICHELLE ESTILL	T38	71-72-74-73	290	$4,315
LAURA DAVIES	T38	75-69-72-74	290	$4,315
MITZI EDGE	T43	75-71-75-70	291	$3,542
LORI GARBACZ	T43	74-72-74-71	291	$3,542
STEPHANIE MAYNOR	T43	72-72-76-71	291	$3,542
MISSIE MCGEORGE	T43	74-71-70-76	291	$3,542
DEB RICHARD	T47	68-76-78-70	292	$2,825
CHRIS JOHNSON	T47	70-74-76-72	292	$2,825
CAROLYN HILL	T47	72-71-76-73	292	$2,825
CAROLINE PIERCE	T47	70-72-74-76	292	$2,825
DALE EGGELING	T47	71-70-74-77	292	$2,825
MAGGIE WILL	T52	75-71-75-72	293	$2,173
BARB MUCHA	T52	72-74-75-72	293	$2,173
PAT BRADLEY	T52	73-72-76-72	293	$2,173
AMY BENZ	T52	72-72-73-76	293	$2,173
MARTA FIGUERAS-DOTTI	T52	73-69-75-76	293	$2,173
LISA KIGGENS	T57	73-73-77-71	294	$1,593
JOAN PETCOCK	T57	73-72-74-75	294	$1,593
FLORENCE DESCAMPE	T57	71-74-73-76	294	$1,593
COLLEEN WALKER	T57	73-70-75-76	294	$1,593
SHERRI TURNER	T57	72-71-74-77	294	$1,593
HIROMI KOBAYASHI	T62	72-72-76-75	295	$1,288
MARDI LUNN	T62	71-73-73-78	295	$1,288
VICKI GOETZE	T64	76-70-76-74	296	$1,106
KATIE PETERSON-PARKER	T64	74-72-74-76	296	$1,106
LAURI MERTEN	T64	70-76-74-76	296	$1,106
JAN STEPHENSON	T64	74-71-75-76	296	$1,106
HEATHER DREW	T64	71-74-75-76	296	$1,106
NANCY SCRANTON	T64	75-70-72-79	296	$1,106
KRISTI ALBERS	T70	74-71-78-74	297	$945
PAMELA WRIGHT	T70	73-70-78-76	297	$945
CATHY JOHNSTON-FORBES	72	70-74-76-78	298	$875

Senior PGA TOUR

THE TRADITION

G.C. at Desert Mountain,
Scottsdale, Arizona
March 31-April 3, 1994

RAY FLOYD	**1**	**65-70-68-68**	**271**	**$127,500**
DALE DOUGLASS	2	68-68-69-66	271	$74,800
JIM COLBERT	3	70-66-68-70	274	$61,200

JACK NICKLAUS	T4	70-71-69-68	278	$41,933
JIMMY POWELL	T4	67-69-72-70	278	$41,933
TOM WEISKOPF	T4	68-70-70-70	278	$41,933
GIBBY GILBERT	T7	66-69-73-71	279	$28,900
MIKE HILL	T7	70-70-68-71	279	$28,900
ISAO AOKI	T9	67-69-71-73	280	$22,100
DAVE STOCKTON	T9	68-70-72-70	280	$22,100
TOM WARGO	T9	68-75-65-72	280	$22,100
GEORGE ARCHER	T12	70-70-70-71	281	$17,283
CHARLES COODY	T12	68-67-71-75	281	$17,283
SIMON HOBDAY	T12	68-71-71-71	281	$17,283
JIM ALBUS	T15	73-70-67-72	282	$14,875
BOB CHARLES	T15	71-75-66-70	282	$14,875
JIM DENT	T17	71-69-72-71	283	$12,388
DON JANUARY	T17	67-77-73-66	283	$12,388
CALVIN PEETE	T17	73-66-75-69	283	$12,388
J.C. SNEAD	T17	70-70-68-75	283	$12,388
DICK HENDRICKSON	T21	68-72-71-73	284	$10,200
LEE TREVINO	T21	68-71-72-73	284	$10,200
LARRY LAORETTI	T23	69-74-69-73	285	$9,137
TOM SHAW	T23	67-78-70-70	285	$9,137
BUTCH BAIRD	T25	74-73-70-69	286	$8,287
DEWITT WEAVER	T25	68-71-75-72	286	$8,287
LARRY GILBERT	T27	75-70-73-69	287	$7,225
BOB MURPHY	T27	73-69-74-71	287	$7,225
GARY PLAYER	T27	70-71-72-74	287	$7,225
KERMIT ZARLEY	T27	71-73-70-73	287	$7,225
JACK KIEFER	T31	69-72-78-69	288	$6,247
RICHARD RHYAN	T31	71-75-71-71	288	$6,247
BRUCE CRAMPTON	T33	73-75-73-68	289	$5,482
GENE LITTLER	T33	74-69-73-73	289	$5,482
GRAHAM MARSH	T33	69-68-78-74	289	$5,482
WALTER ZEMBRISKI	T33	73-71-73-72	289	$5,482
TOMMY AYCOCK	T37	71-74-75-70	290	$4,590
DICK GOETZ	T37	74-71-74-71	290	$4,590
LARRY MOWRY	T37	72-70-75-73	290	$4,590
CHI CHI RODRIGUEZ	T37	70-73-72-75	290	$4,590
TOMMY AARON	T41	73-77-74-68	292	$4,080
BOB DICKSON	T41	73-74-72-73	292	$4,080
BOBBY NICHOLS	T43	73-73-77-70	293	$3,740
HARRY TOSCANO	T43	72-73-77-71	293	$3,740
TERRY DILL	T45	73-72-78-71	294	$3,400
BEN SMITH	T45	78-76-70-70	294	$3,400
BRUCE DEVLIN	T47	71-74-76-74	295	$3,060
BERT YANCEY	T47	71-78-72-74	295	$3,060
MILLER BARBER	T49	75-72-75-74	296	$2,635
MIKE HILL	T49	76-76-73-71	296	$2,635
RANDY PETRI	T49	73-74-75-74	296	$2,635
DON BIES	52	70-80-76-71	297	$2,011

PGA SENIORS CHAMPIONSHIP

PGA National Golf Club,
Palm Beach Gardens, Florida
April 14-17, 1994

LEE TREVINO	**1**	**70-69-70-70**	**279**	**$115,700**
JIM COLBERT	2	68-71-74-67	280	$85,000
RAY FLOYD	T3	69-69-69-75	282	$57,500
DAVE STOCKTON	T3	70-69-71-72	282	$57,500
ISAO AOKI	T5	71-71-75-66	283	$32,500
DALE DOUGLASS	T5	70-71-70-72	283	$32,500
CHI CHI RODRIGUEZ	T5	73-72-69-69	283	$32,500
DEWITT WEAVER	T5	72-73-70-68	283	$32,500
JACK NICKLAUS	9	71-71-72-72	286	$20,500
BOB CHARLES	T10	69-74-71-73	287	$16,500
BOB MURPHY	T10	69-75-73-70	287	$16,500
TOM WARGO	T10	72-80-70-65	287	$16,500
JAY SIGEL	13	72-71-74-71	288	$15,000
WALTER ZEMBRISKI	14	70-74-73-72	289	$14,500
TOMMY AARON	T15	71-70-75-74	290	$13,250
GENE BOREK	T15	72-76-71-71	290	$13,250
MIKE HILL	T15	78-72-70-70	290	$13,250
J.C. SNEAD	T15	74-70-75-71	290	$13,250
CHARLES COODY	T19	74-70-74-74	292	$11,000
DICK HENDRICKSON	T19	73-74-74-71	292	$11,000
GARY PLAYER	T19	74-75-73-70	292	$11,000
ART PROCTOR	T19	72-74-74-72	292	$11,000
ROCKY THOMPSON	T19	74-72-70-76	292	$11,000
KIKUO ARAI	T24	72-71-74-76	293	$8,500
LARRY GILBERT	T24	76-73-74-70	293	$8,500
BILL HALL	T24	72-77-74-70	293	$8,500
GRAHAM MARSH	T24	75-73-71-74	293	$8,500
LARRY ZIEGLER	T24	68-77-74-74	293	$8,500
JIM DENT	T29	66-76-79-73	294	$6,250
GIBBY GILBERT	T29	72-78-68-76	294	$6,250
SIMON HOBDAY	T29	76-75-70-73	294	$6,250
JACK KIEFER	T29	73-74-69-78	294	$6,250
GAY BREWER	33	73-73-75-74	295	$5,000
LARRY LAORETTI	T34	73-73-76-74	296	$3,812
RIVES MCBEE	T34	75-75-74-72	296	$3,812

LARRY MOWRY	T34	70-68-85-73	296	$3,812
TOM WEISKOPF	T34	75-73-77-71	296	$3,812
JIM ALBUS	T38	73-74-73-77	297	$2,900
MASARU AMANO	T38	75-76-75-71	297	$2,900
HISASHI SUZUMURA	T38	75-75-74-73	297	$2,900
BRUCE CRAMPTON	T41	77-76-71-74	298	$2,500
JACK FLECK	T41	77-70-73-78	298	$2,500
DICK LOTZ	T41	75-72-81-70	298	$2,500
PAT O'BRIEN	T41	71-71-76-80	298	$2,500
HARRY TOSCANO	T41	75-75-77-71	298	$2,500
TOMMY AYCOCK	T46	73-75-73-78	299	$2,033

U.S. SENIOR OPEN
Pinehurst C.C. (No. 2),
Pinehurst, North Carolina
Apr. 7-10, 1994

SIMON HOBDAY	1	**66-67-66-75**	**274**	**$145,000**
GRAHAM MARSH	T2	68-68-69-70	275	$63,418
JIM ALBUS,	T2	66-69-66-74	275	$63,418
TOM WEISKOPF	T4	72-66-72-67	277	$30,608
DAVE STOCKTON	T4	74-67-68-68	277	$30,608
TOM WARGO	T4	69-70-68-70	277	$30,608
BOB MURPHY	T7	71-70-71-67	279	$21,651
JAY SIGEL	T7	73-66-70-70	279	$21,651
JACK NICKLAUS	T7	69-68-70-72	279	$21,651
ISAO AOKI	10	69-71-73-67	280	$18,313
LEE TREVINO	11	69-71-72-69	281	$17,169
RAYMOND FLOYD	12	69-68-74-71	282	$16,044
DAVE EICHELBERGER	T13	74-72-69-69	284	$14,280
ROCKY THOMPSON	T13	70-74-69-71	284	$14,280
GARY PLAYER	T13	72-67-73-72	284	$14,280
MIKE HILL	16	72-68-70-75	285	$12,760
DEWITT WEAVER	T17	74-73-70-69	286	$11,429
JIM FERREE	T17	71-75-69-71	286	$11,429
KERMIT ZARLEY	T17	74-68-71-73	286	$11,429
BOB DICKSON	T20	76-73-69-69	287	$9,070
MIKE JOYCE	T20	74-73-69-71	287	$9,070
CALVIN PEETE	T20	73-70-72-72	287	$9,070
JIM COLBERT	T20	72-74-69-72	287	$9,070
GIBBY GILBERT	T20	73-73-68-73	287	$9,070
JIMMY POWELL	T25	70-76-73-69	288	$7,287
DALE DOUGLASS	T25	72-68-74-74	288	$7,287
JACK KIEFER	27	69-75-71-74	289	$6,589
LARRY ZIEGLER	T28	71-76-75-68	290	$5,738
JOHNNY STEVENS	T28	75-71-74-70	290	$5,738
TOMMY AYCOCK	T28	74-70-73-73	290	$5,738
LARRY MOWRY	T28	72-73-72-73	290	$5,738
CHI CHI RODRIGUEZ	T32	70-76-76-69	291	$5,050
BILL HALL	T32	70-76-73-72	291	$5,050
TERRY DILL	T32	70-74-72-75	291	$5,050
BEN SMITH	T32	71-73-72-75	291	$5,050
LARRY LAORETTI	T36	75-73-76-68	292	$4,292
BOBBY NICHOLS	T36	76-73-75-68	292	$4,292
BOB IRVING	T36	76-72-74-70	292	$4,292
CHARLES COODY	T36	74-73-73-72	292	$4,292
MARION HECK	T36	76-70-73-73	292	$4,292
BILL MCDONOUGH	T36	76-72-71-73	292	$4,292
BOB E. SMITH	T42	75-73-74-71	293	$3,690
JIM DENT	T42	75-74-70-74	293	$3,690
VINNY GILES	T42	71-70-75-77	293	$3,690
TOMMY AARON	T45	72-76-72-74	294	$3,163
BRUCE LEHNHARD	T45	75-72-72-75	294	$3,163
STEVE BULL	T45	70-72-76-76	294	$3,163
JIM STEFANICH	T45	76-72-69-77	294	$3,163
TOM SHAW	T45	69-72-74-79	294	$3,163
RAY VANYO	T50	72-77-74-72	295	$2,562
J. C. SNEAD	T50	71-75-75-74	295	$2,562
BILL KRICKHAN	T50	74-75-72-74	295	$2,562
BILLY TLE	T53	72-69-80-75	296	$2,318
JACK RULE	T53	71-73-77-75	296	$2,318
JIM COLLART	T55	76-71-79-71	297	$2,230
BOB HOUSEN	T55	76-72-74-75	297	$2,230
MILLER BARBER	T57	74-75-76-73	298	$2,138
DICK HOWELL	T57	73-76-75-74	298	$2,138
ARNOLD PALMER	T57	74-74-73-77	298	$2,138
DEAN SHEETZ	T60	73-74-76-76	299	$2,050
WAYNE CAREY	T60	68-73-78-80	299	$2,050
MIKE MCGINNIS	T62	75-73-78-74	300	$2,022
JOHN REICHERT	T62	74-74-78-74	300	$2,022
GARY WIREN	64	75-72-76-79	302	$2,000
BOB PFISTER	65	76-72-79-78	305	$1,978
LABRON HARRIS	T66	72-77-82-75	306	$1,945
BUDDY OVERHOLSER	T66	76-73-79-78	306	$1,945

FORD SENIOR PLAYERS CHAMPIONSHIP
TPC of Michigan,
Dearborn, Michigan
June 23-26, 1994

DAVE STOCKTON	1	**66-66-71-68 271**	**$210,000**	RIVES MCBEE	T39	73-70-76-74 293	$7,140
JIM ALBUS	2	67-69-72-69 277	$123,200	CHARLES COODY	T42	68-75-80-71 294	$5,880
ISAO AOKI	T3	67-70-73-68 278	$84,000	TERRY DILL	T42	74-71-76-73 294	$5,880
RAY FLOYD	T3	72-68-71-67 278	$84,000	BABE HISKEY	T42	75-75-75-69 294	$5,880
LEE TREVINO	T3	66-69-74-69 278	$84,000	ROGER KENNEDY	T42	69-77-73-75 294	$5,880
JIM DENT	T6	72-67-70-71 280	$50,400	GARY PLAYER	T42	71-72-75-76 294	$5,880
HAROLD HENNING	T6	69-67-74-70 280	$50,400	RICHARD RHYAN	T42	68-72-80-74 294	$5,880
JACK NICKLAUS	T6	68-72-73-67 280	$50,400	TOMMY AYCOCK	T48	73-72-80-70 295	$4,620
JAY SIGEL	9	67-71-73-70 281	$39,200	BERT YANCEY	T48	74-72-78-71 295	$4,620
JERRY MCGEE	T10	69-69-74-70 282	$30,200	LARRY ZIEGLER	T48	76-73-74-72 295	$4,620
BOB MURPHY	T10	69-68-73-72 282	$30,200	DICK HENDRICKSON	T51	74-69-83-70 296	$3,675
TOM WARGO	T10	70-73-71-68 282	$30,200	DON JANUARY	T51	69-74-76-77 296	$3,675
TOM WEISKOPF	T10	65-71-74-72 282	$30,200	DICK LOTZ	T51	70-73-78-75 296	$3,675
JIM COLBERT	T14	69-72-71-71 283	$25,900	BEN SMITH	T51	70-75-82-69 296	$3,675
GRAHAM MARSH	T14	67-71-75-70 283	$25,900	JOE JIMENEZ	T55	74-71-77-75 297	$3,150
LARRY GILBERT	T16	72-67-74-72 285	$21,735	KEN STILL	T55	69-70-79-79 297	$3,150
TOM SHAW	T16	67-78-71-69 285	$21,735	BOB BRUE	T57	70-76-76-76 298	$2,800
J.C. SNEAD	T16	71-68-76-70 285	$21,735	BOB DICKSON	T57	70-70-80-78 298	$2,800
ROCKY THOMPSON	T16	74-68-76-67 285	$21,735	DEWITT WEAVER	T57	77-73-76-72 298	$2,800
DALE DOUGLASS	T20	72-73-72-69 286	$17,920	DON BIES	T60	74-71-75-79 299	$2,380
WALTER ZEMBRISKI	T20	68-71-75-72 286	$17,920	BILL HALL	T60	72-74-79-74 299	$2,380
GEORGE ARCHER	T22	68-73-76-70 287	$15,446	BOB REITH	T60	73-78-79-69 299	$2,380
DAVE EICHELBERGER	T22	76-68-74-69 287	$15,446	JIM FERREE	T63	73-75-80-72 300	$2,030
DICK GOETZ	T22	72-67-76-72 287	$15,446	ORVILLE MOODY	T63	70-78-79-73 300	$2,030
GIBBY GILBERT	T25	71-71-76-70 288	$13,346	RICHARD BASSETT	T65	70-75-85-71 301	$1,680
KERMIT ZARLEY	T25	68-75-76-69 288	$13,346	GAY BREWER	T65	75-73-81-72 301	$1,680
MIKE HILL	T25	66-76-73-73 288	$13,346	ARNOLD PALMER	T65	73-76-79-73 301	$1,680
SIMON HOBDAY	T28	71-71-78-69 289	$11,340	JOHN PAUL CAIN	68	69-70-87-76 302	$1,400
MIKE JOYCE	T28	71-70-75-73 289	$11,340	HOMERO BLANCAS	T69	76-69-80-78 303	$1,232
JACK KIEFER	T28	72-70-73-74 289	$11,340	BILLY CASPER	T69	72-75-81-75 303	$1,232
CALVIN PEETE	T28	71-71-72-75 289	$11,340	WALTER MORGAN	T69	73-79-76-75 303	$1,232
TOMMY AARON	T32	71-71-77-72 291	$9,660	GENE LITLER	72	76-75-82-71 304	$1,064
BOB CHARLES	T32	68-76-75-72 291	$9,660	AL KELLEY	73	75-70-81-79 305	$980
CHI CHI RODRIGUEZ	T32	71-71-76-73 291	$9,660	MILLER BARBER	74	74-74-86-73 307	$924
BUTCH BAIRD	T35	75-71-75-71 292	$8,225	LEE ELDER	T75	78-73-78-79 308	$840
DAVE HILL	T35	70-70-82-70 292	$8,225	CHARLES SIFFORD	T75	77-73-87-71 308	$840
LARRY MOWRY	T35	68-73-76-75 292	$8,225	LARRY LAORETTI	77	81-75-84-70 310	$756
HARRY TOSCANO	T35	68-74-73-77 292	$8,225				
DOUG DALZIEL	T39	75-70-75-73 293	$7,140				
BRUCE LEHNHARD	T39	69-73-78-73 293	$7,140				

1994 TOUR RESULTS

OVERVIEW: *Top finishers, scores, and prize money for all tournaments (through October 30), on the PGA TOUR, LPGA Tour, Senior PGA TOUR, Nike TOUR, European Tour, Women's European Tour, Asian Tour, Australian Tour, Japanese Tour and Senior Japanese Tour. Asterisks not otherwise noted denote playoff victories.*

PGA TOUR

MERCEDES CHAMPIONSHIP
La Costa C.C.
Carlsbad, California
January 6-9, 1994

PHIL MICKELSON	1	70-68-70-68	276	$180,000
FRED COUPLES	2	69-70-69-68	276	$120,000
TOM KITE	3	73-68-69-68	278	$80,000
JAY HAAS	T4	71-71-69-69	280	$46,625
DAVIS LOVE III	T4	71-69-72-68	280	$46,625
JEFF MAGGERT	T4	72-74-65-69	280	$46,625
SCOTT SIMPSON	T4	70-72-70-68	280	$46,625
DAVID EDWARDS	T8	75-68-66-72	281	$34,000
HOWARD TWITTY	T8	72-73-67-69	281	$34,000
GREG NORMAN	10	70-73-69-70	282	$31,000

UNITED AIRLINES HAWAIIAN OPEN
Waialae C.C.,
Honolulu, Hawaii
January 13-16, 1994

BRETT OGLE	1	66-66-69-68	269	$216,000
DAVIS LOVE III	2	68-60-71-71	270	$129,60
JOHN HUSTON	3	70-68-67-67	272	$81,600
COREY PAVIN	4	68-70-70-65	273	$57,600
JESPER PARNEVIK	5	71-66-74-63	274	$48,000
CRAIG PARRY	T6	66-70-72-67	275	$41,700
TED TRYBA	T6	69-71-68-67	275	$41,700
LENNIE CLEMENTS	T8	69-66-70-71	276	$31,200
PAUL GOYDOS	T8	67-73-69-67	276	$31,200
DAVID ISHII	T8	70-67-69-70	276	$31,200
JEFF MAGGERT	T8	69-67-68-72	276	$31,200
DAVID OGRIN	T8	72-69-68-67	276	$31,200
SEIKI OKUDA	T8	71-69-72-64	276	$31,200

NORTHERN TELECOM OPEN
TPC at Starpass and Tucson National,
Tucson, Arizona
January 13-16, 1994

ANDREW MAGEE	1	69-67-67-67	270	$198,000
JAY DON BLAKE	T2	68-69-67-68	272	$72,600
LOREN ROBERTS	T2	68-68-72-64	272	$72,600
VIJAY SINGH	T2	67-68-72-65	272	$72,600
STEVE STRICKER	T2	68-69-68-67	272	$72,600
OLIN BROWNE	6	70-70-66-67	273	$39,600
JIM FURYK	T7	68-68-67-71	274	$35,475
ROBERT GAMEZ	T7	66-71-71-66	274	$35,475
BOB BURNS	T9	70-72-69-65	276	$22,400
DAVID FEHERTY	T9	70-69-67-70	276	$22,400
RICK FEHR	T9	73-68-69-66	276	$22,400
JOHN HUSTON	T9	68-71-70-67	276	$22,400
BILLY MAYFAIR	T9	69-71-68-68	276	$22,400
ROCCO MEDIATE	T9	70-70-71-65	276	$22,400
PHIL MICKELSON	T9	69-70-70-67	276	$22,400
DILLARD PRUITT	T9	64-71-68-73	276	$22,400
MIKE SPRINGER	T9	70-65-73-68	276	$22,400
JIM THORPE	T9	69-70-70-67	276	$22,400

PHOENIX OPEN
TPC of Scottsdale,
Scottsdale, Arizona
January 27-30, 1994

BILL GLASSON	1	68-68-68-64	268	$216,000
BOB ESTES	2	66-68-69-68	271	$129,600
JEFF MAGGERT	T3	70-68-69-65	272	$62,400
BLAINE MCCALLISTER	T3	67-69-69-67	272	$62,400
MIKE SPRINGER	T3	68-68-71-65	272	$62,400
RICK FEHR	T6	66-67-69-71	273	$41,700
TOM LEHMAN	T6	67-68-73-65	273	$41,700
FRED FUNK	T8	69-69-70-66	274	$32,400

Phoenix Open, continued

SCOTT HOCH	T8	72-66-67-69	274	$32,400
PHIL MICKELSON	T8	67-70-71-66	274	$32,400
STEVE PATE	T8	68-69-69-68	274	$32,400

AT&T NATIONAL PRO-AM
Pebble Beach G.L., Spyglass Hill G.C.,
and Poppy Hills G.C.,
Monterey, California
February 3-6, 1994

JOHNNY MILLER	1	68-72-67-74	281	$225,000
JEFF MAGGERT	T2	68-72-72-70	282	$82,500
COREY PAVIN	T2	69-71-71-71	282	$82,500
KIRK TRIPLETT	T2	69-74-67-72	282	$82,500
TOM WATSON	T2	69-67-72-74	282	$82,500
TOM LEHMAN	6	69-68-73-73	283	$45,000
KEITH CLEARWATER	T7	70-70-71-73	284	$36,375
JAY DELSING	T7	66-75-70-73	284	$36,375
DUDLEY HART	T7	65-71-70-78	284	$36,375
BLAINE MCCALLISTER	T7	68-71-72-73	284	$36,375

NISSAN LOS ANGELES OPEN
Riviera C.C.,
Pacific Palisades, California
February 10-13, 1994

COREY PAVIN	1	67-64-72-68	271	$180,000
FRED COUPLES	2	67-67-68-71	273	$108,000
CHIP BECK	3	66-71-72-68	277	$68,000
BRAD FAXON	4	70-71-68-69	278	$48,000
DAVID FROST	5	67-74-71-67	279	$40,000
PETER JACOBSEN	T6	69-71-68-72	280	$34,750
TOM WATSON	T6	69-71-71-69	280	$34,750
LENNIE CLEMENTS	T8	68-74-68-71	281	$28,000
JAY DELSING	T8	67-72-69-73	281	$28,000
CRAIG STADLER	T8	68-69-71-73	281	$28,000
KIRK TRIPLETT	T8	68-76-69-68	281	$28,000

BOB HOPE CHRYSLER CLASSIC
PGA West (Palmer), Bermuda Dunes
C.C., Indian Wells C.C., Tamarisk C.C.,
Palm Desert, California
January 13-16, 1994

SCOTT HOCH	1	66-62-70-66-70	334	$198,000
FUZZY ZOELLER	T2	70-67-66-68-66	337	$82,133
LENNIE CLEMENTS	T2	67-69-61-72-68	337	$82,133
JIM GALLAGHER, JR.	T2	66-67-74-62-68	337	$82,133
PAYNE STEWART	5	67-69-71-68-63	338	$44,000
GUY BOROS	T6	66-67-68-69-69	339	$36,850
KEITH CLEARWATER	T6	67-64-70-68-70	339	$36,850
PAUL STANKOWSKI	T6	67-66-69-68-69	339	$36,850
BOB ESTES	T9	66-69-70-67-68	340	$30,800
JOHN HUSTON	T9	66-68-66-68-72	340	$30,800

BUICK INVITATIONAL OF CALIFORNIA
Torrey Pines G.C., San Diego, California
February 24-27, 1994

CRAIG STADLER	1	67-67-68-66	268	$198,000
STEVE LOWERY	2	67-68-66-68	269	$118,800
PHIL MICKELSON	3	68-69-69-64	270	$74,800
HAL SUTTON	4	68-68-67-69	272	$52,800
MARK CARNEVALE	5	67-69-70-67	273	$44,000
BOB ESTES	T6	70-67-67-70	274	$36,850
ROBIN FREEMAN	T6	68-67-71-68	274	$36,850
KIRK TRIPLETT	T6	71-63-68-72	274	$36,850
MARK CALCAVECCHIA	T9	69-72-69-65	275	$28,600
LENNIE CLEMENTS	T9	66-69-68-72	275	$28,600
PAUL GOYDOS	T9	68-70-70-67	275	$28,600

DORAL RYDER OPEN
Doral C.C. (Blue Course), Miami, Florida
March 3-6, 1994

JOHN HUSTON	1	70-68-70-66	274	$252,000
BILLY ANDRADE	T2	70-68-66-73	277	$123,200
BRAD BRYANT	T2	70-69-69-69	277	$123,200
JIM THORPE	T4	68-72-68-71	279	$57,866
D.A. WEIBRING	T4	74-69-65-71	279	$57,866
LENNIE CLEMENTS	T4	72-70-66-71	279	$57,866
BRUCE LIETZKE	T7	74-69-71-67	281	$43,633
GREG NORMAN	T7	71-74-69-67	281	$43,633
LOREN ROBERTS	T7	73-70-69-69	281	$43,633
MIKE HULBERT	T10	72-74-70-66	282	$35,000
MARK MCCUMBER	T10	76-69-68-69	282	$35,000
LARRY NELSON	T10	73-64-69-76	282	$35,000

HONDA CLASSIC
Weston Hills C.C.,
Fort Lauderdale, Florida
March 10-13, 1994

NICK PRICE	1	70-67-73-66	279	$198,000
CRAIG PARRY	2	68-73-69-67	277	$118,800
BRANDEL CHAMBLEE	3	67-68-72-71	278	$74,800
JOHN DALY	T4	69-70-73-68	280	$43,312
BERNHARD LANGER	T4	67-72-73-68	280	$43,312
DAVIS LOVE III	T4	68-71-70-71	280	$43,312
CURTIS STRANGE	T4	71-67-72-70	280	$43,312
DAVID EDWARDS	8	70-72-69-71	282	$34,100
BRUCE FLEISHER	T9	68-73-70-72	283	$27,500
JIM GALLAGHER, JR.	T9	68-71-74-70	283	$27,500
TOM KITE	T9	71-72-71-69	283	$27,500
SANDY LYLE	T9	71-74-72-66	283	$27,500

NESTLE INVITATIONAL
Bay Hill Club,
Orlando, Florida
March 17-20, 1994

LOREN ROBERTS	1	70-70-68-67	275	$216,000
NICK PRICE	T2	66-72-68-70	276	$89,600
VIJAY SINGH	T2	68-69-68-71	276	$89,600
FUZZY ZOELLER	T2	72-68-67-69	276	$89,600
LARRY MIZE	5	68-69-71-69	277	$48,000
TOM LEHMAN	T6	72-67-68-71	278	$41,700
GREG NORMAN	T6	68-72-71-67	278	$41,700
TOM WATSON	8	69-70-67-73	279	$37,200
ANDREW MAGEE	9	70-67-69-74	280	$34,800
GLEN DAY	T10	70-68-72-71	281	$30,000
BILL GLASSON	T10	70-72-71-68	281	$30,000
D.A. WEIBRING	T10	71-73-70-67	281	$30,000

THE PLAYERS CHAMPIONSHIP
TPC at Sawgrass (Stadium Course),
Ponte Vedra, Florida
March 24-27, 1994

GREG NORMAN	1	63-67-67-67	264	$450,000
FUZZY ZOELLER	2	66-67-68-67	268	$270,000

JEFF MAGGERT	3	65-69-69-68	271	$170,000
HALE IRWIN	4	67-70-70-69	276	$120,000
NICK FALDO	5	67-69-68-73	277	$100,000
BRAD FAXON	T6	68-68-70-72	278	$83,750
DAVIS LOVE III	T6	68-66-70-74	278	$83,750
STEVE LOWERY	T6	68-74-69-67	278	$83,750
GARY HALLBERG	T9	68-69-69-73	279	$65,000
NOLAN HENKE	T9	73-69-69-68	279	$65,000
TOM KITE	T9	65-71-70-73	279	$65,000
COLIN MONTGOMERIE	T9	65-73-71-70	279	$65,000

FREEPORT-MCMORAN CLASSIC
English Turn G. & C.C.,
New Orleans, Louisiana
March 31-April 3, 1994

BEN CRENSHAW	1	69-68-68-68	273	$216,000
JOSE MARIA OLAZABAL	2	63-74-70-69	276	$129,600
SAM TORRANCE	3	67-71-67-73	278	$81,600
DENNIS PAULSON	T4	74-62-75-68	279	$49,600
MIKE SPRINGER	T4	73-69-69-68	279	$49,600
STEVE BRODIE	T7	71-67-72-71	281	$36,150
BOBBY CLAMPETT	T7	70-68-72-71	281	$36,150
CHRIS DIMARCO	T7	76-70-66-69	281	$36,150
DICK MAST	T7	71-69-74-67	281	$36,150

THE MASTERS
Augusta National G.C.,
Augusta, Georgia
April 7-10, 1994

JOSE MARIA OLAZABAL	1	74-67-69-69	279	$360,000
TOM LEHMAN	2	70-70-69-72	281	$216,000
LARRY MIZE	3	68-71-72-71	282	$136,000
TOM KITE	4	69-72-71-71	283	$96,000
JAY HAAS	T5	72-72-72-69	285	$73,000
JIM MCGOVERN	T5	72-70-71-72	285	$73,000
LOREN ROBERTS	T5	75-68-72-70	285	$73,000
ERNIE ELS	T8	74-67-74-71	286	$60,000
COREY PAVIN	T8	71-72-73-70	286	$60,000
IAN BAKER-FINCH	T10	71-71-71-74	287	$50,000
RAY FLOYD	T10	70-74-71-72	287	$50,000

*For a complete summary of all players making the cut at
The Masters, please refer to "1994 Major Championships"*

MCI HERITAGE CLASSIC
Harbour Town G.L.,
Hilton Head Island, South Carolina
April 14-17, 1994

HALE IRWIN	**1**	**68-65-65-68**	**266**	**$225,000**
GREG NORMAN	2	67-66-67-68	268	$135,000
LOREN ROBERTS	3	69-70-68-62	269	$85,000
DAVID EDWARDS	T4	70-71-65-64	270	$51,666
DAVID FROST	T4	70-61-72-67	270	$51,666
NOLAN HENKE	T4	69- 69-66-66	270	$51,666
RUSS COCHRAN	T7	67-67-66-71	271	$40,312
BOB ESTES	T7	65-70-68-68	271	$40,312
LARRY MIZE	T9	67-65-75-65	272	$35,000
JESPER PARNEVIK	T9	68-68-69-67	272	$35,000

KMART GREATER GREENSBORO OPEN
Forest Oaks C.C.,
Greensboro, North Carolina
April 21-24, 1994

MIKE SPRINGER	**1**	**64-69-70-72**	**275**	**$270,000**
BRAD BRYANT	T2	68-71-68-71	278	$112,000
ED HUMENIK	T2	72-65-73-68	278	$112,000
HALE IRWIN	T2	65-73-71-69	278	$112,000
BOB LOHR	5	69-71-69-70	279	$60,000
DONNIE HAMMOND	T6	70-71-69-70	280	$52,125
JOHN MORSE	T6	72-68-67-73	280	$52,125
DAVID EDWARDS	T8	71-74-68-68	281	$42,000
JOEL EDWARDS	T8	69-69-73-70	281	$42,000
DUDLEY HART	T8	75-69-67-70	281	$42,000
MIKE SMITH	T8	69-73-69-70	281	$42,000

SHELL HOUSTON OPEN
TPC at the Woodlands,
The Woodlands, Texas
April 28-May 1, 1994

MIKE HEINEN	**1**	**67-68-69-68**	**272**	**$234,000**
JEFF MAGGERT	T2	70-66-68-71	275	$97,066
HAL SUTTON	T2	68-70-68-69	275	$97,066
TOM KITE	T2	68-65-71-71	275	$97,066

BOB GILDER	T5	66-76-69-67	278	$49,400
VIJAY SINGH	T5	72-67-69-70	278	$49,400
JOHN DALY	T7	68-74-70-67	279	$40,516
GIL MORGAN	T7	70-71-72-66	279	$40,516
PETER JACOBSEN	T7	68-73-69-69	279	$40,516
DAVE BARR	T10	66-72-71-71	280	$32,500
FRED FUNK	T10	71-67-71-71	280	$32,500
CURTIS STRANGE	T10	71-72-66-71	280	$32,500

BELLSOUTH CLASSIC
Atlanta C.C.,
Marietta, Georgia
May 5-8, 1994

JOHN DALY	**1**	**69-64-69-72**	**274**	**$216,000**
NOLAN HENKE	T2	70-67-69-69	275	$105,600
BRIAN ENNINGER	T2	68-67-69-71	275	$105,600
BOB ESTES	T4	71-69-68-68	276	$52,800
DAVID PEOPLES	T4	73-65-68-70	276	$52,800
LENNIE CLEMENTS	T6	68-69-72-68	277	$38,850
RUSS COCHRAN	T6	69-69-69-70	277	$38,850
TOM KITE	T6	66-72-68-71	277	$38,850
BLAINE MCCALLISTER	T6	69-68-69-71	277	$38,850
CLARK DENNIS	10	71-66-72-69	278	$32,400

GTE BYRON NELSON CLASSIC
TPC at Los Colinas,
Los Colinas, Texas
May 12-15, 1994

NEAL LANCASTER	**1**	**67-65**	**132**	**$216,000**
TOM BYRUM	T2	68-64	132	$72,000
MARK CARNEVALE	T2	65-67	132	$72,000
DAVID EDWARDS	T2	67-65	132	$72,000
YOSHINORI MIZUMAKI	T2	66-66	132	$72,000
DAVID OGRIN	T2	64-68	132	$72,000
BRAD BRYANT	7	66-67	133	$40,200
RONNIE BLACK	T8	70-64	134	$31,200
MARK BROOKS	T8	67-67	134	$31,200
BEN CRENSHAW	T8	66-68	134	$31,200
BOB GILDER	T8	67-67	134	$31,200
GREG NORMAN	T8	66-68	134	$31,200
JEFF WOODLAND	T8	69-65	134	$31,200

MEMORIAL TOURNAMENT
Muirfield Village G.C.,
Dublin, Ohio
May 19-22, 1994

TOM LEHMAN	1	67-67-67-67	268	$270,000
GREG NORMAN	2	70-69-70-64	273	$162,000
JOHN COOK	3	67-69-69-71	276	$102,000
DONNIE HAMMOND	4	69-69-70-69	277	$72,000
DAVID EDWARDS	5	69-67-72-70	278	$60,000
ROBERT GAMEZ	6	77-69-66-67	279	$54,000
MARK BROOKS	T7	64-75-70-71	280	$48,375
BEN CRENSHAW	T7	72-66-74-68	280	$48,375
BRAD FAXON	T9	72-68-72-69	281	$42,000
JEFF MAGGERT	T9	71-74-66-70	281	$42,000

SOUTHWESTERN BELL COLONIAL
Colonial C.C.,
Fort Worth, Texas
May 26-29, 1994

NICK PRICE	1	65-70-67-64	266	$252,000
SCOTT SIMPSON	2	66-65-64-71	266	$151,200
HALE IRWIN	3	64-70-68-65	267	$95,200
PETER JORDAN	4	68-70-66-66	270	$67,200
BRAD FAXON	T5	70-66-67-68	271	$51,100
GARY HALLBERG	T5	67-67-65-72	271	$51,100
TOM LEHMAN	T5	66-66-69-70	271	$51,100
PHIL MICKELSON	8	68-68-71-65	272	$43,400
JOHN COOK	T9	66-71-67-70	274	$37,800
MARK MCCUMBER	T9	68-69-67-70	274	$37,800

KEMPER OPEN
TPC at Avenel,
Potomac, Maryland
June 2-5, 1994

MARK BROOKS	1	65-68-69-69	271	$234,000
BOBBY WADKINS	T2	68-67-65-74	274	$114,400
D.A. WEIBRING	T2	70-68-68-68	274	$114,400
LEE JANZEN	T4	70-71-68-66	275	$57,200
PHIL MICKELSON	T4	70-69-67-69	275	$57,200
JOEL EDWARDS	6	71-70-68-69	278	$46,800
CRAIG PARRY	T7	69-71-69-70	279	$40,516

KENNY PERRY	T7	72-72-68-67	279	$40,516
MARK LYE	T7	70-70-69-70	279	$40,516
MICHAEL BRADLEY	T10	70-71-67-73	281	$26,975
ROBERT GAMEZ	T10	72-66-69-74	281	$26,975
KELLY GIBSON	T10	75-64-71-71	281	$26,975
SCOTT HOCH	T10	69-72-67-73	281	$26,975
BRIAN KAMM	T10	69-71-68-73	281	$26,975
WAYNE LEVI	T10	68-70-72-71	281	$26,975
TIM SIMPSON	T10	71-72-70-68	281	$26,975
KIRK TRIPLETT	T10	72-73-67-69	281	$26,975

BUICK CLASSIC
Westchester C.C.,
Rye, New York
June 9-12

LEE JANZEN	1	69-69-64-66	268	$216,000
ERNIE ELS	1	68-66-69-68	271	$129,600
BRAD FAXON	T3	70-68-70-66	274	$69,600
JAY HAAS	T3	68-70-69-67	274	$69,600
BILLY ANDRADE	T5	70-71-66-69	276	$43,800
BOB BURNS	T5	71-67-70-68	276	$43,800
STEVE PATE	T5	66-72-69-69	276	$43,800
MARK BROOKS	T8	71-76-66-70	277	$32,400
ROBIN FREEMAN	T8	69-69-69-70	277	$32,400
HALE IRWIN	T8	70-72-65-70	277	$32,400
JEFF MAGGERT	T8	72-72-64-69	277	$32,400
JOE OZAKI	T8	69-67-69-72	277	$32,400

UNITED STATES OPEN CHAMPIONSHIP
Oakmont C.C.,
Oakmont, Pennsylvania
June 16-19, 1994

ERNIE ELS	1	69-71-66-73	279	$320,000
COLIN MONTGOMERIE	T2	71-65-73-70	279	$141,827
LOREN ROBERTS	T2	76-69-64-70	279	$141,827
CURTIS STRANGE	4	70-70-70-70	280	$75,728
JOHN COOK	5	73-65-73-71	282	$61,318
CLARK DENNIS	T6	71-71-70-71	283	$49,485
GREG NORMAN	T6	71-71-69-72	283	$49,485
TOM WATSON	T6	68-73-68-74	283	$49,485
DUFFY WALDORF	T9	74-68-73-69	284	$37,179

U.S. Open, continued

JEFF MAGGERT	T9	71-68-75-70	284	$37,179
JEFF SLUMAN	T9	72-69-72-71	284	$37,179
FRANK NOBILO	T9	69-71-68-76	284	$37,179

For a complete summary of all players making the cut at the U.S. Opens, please refer to "1994 Major Championships"

CANON GREATER HARTFORD OPEN

TPC at River Highlands,
Cromwell, Connecticut
June 23-26, 1994

DAVID FROST	1	65-68-66-69	268	$216,000
GREG NORMAN	2	69-65-66-69	269	$129,600
COREY PAVIN	T3	65-73-66-67	271	$57,600
DAVE STOCKTON, JR.	T3	66-66-67-72	271	$57,600
STEVE STRICKER	T3	70-67-67-67	271	$57,600
DAVE BARR	T3	68-70-68-65	271	$57,600
KIRK TRIPLETT	T7	71-67-69-67	273	$38,700
WAYNE LEVI	T7	68-66-71-68	273	$38,700
MIKE REID	T9	66-68-69-72	275	$28,800
JOHN COOK	T9	71-67-64-73	275	$28,800
GLEN DAY	T9	72-65-70-68	275	$28,800
CLARK DENNIS	T9	65-72-66-72	275	$28,800
KEN GREEN	T9	69-70-68-68	275	$28,800
PETER JACOBSEN	T9	68-68-70-69	275	$28,800

MOTOROLA OPEN

Gog Hill G.C. (No. 4), Lemont, Illinois
June 30-July 3, 1994

NICK PRICE	1	67-67-72-71	277	$216,000
GREG KRAFT	2	67-70-68-73	278	$129,600
MARK CALCAVECCHIA	T3	67-70-72-70	279	$62,400
BILL GLASSON	T3	66-70-72-71	279	$62,400
SCOTT HOCH	T3	67-69-73-70	279	$62,400
KELLY GIBSON	T6	69-72-72-67	280	$41,700
JEFF SLUMAN	T6	68-69-69-74	280	$41,700
DAVID DUVAL	T8	73-70-70-68	281	$28,000
DAVID FROST	T8	71-68-74-68	281	$28,000
JIM GALLAGHER, JR.	T8	72-68-68-73	281	$28,000
ANDREW MAGEE	T8	70-71-69-71	281	$28,000
TOM PURTZER	T8	68-72-73-68	281	$28,000
LARRY SILVEIRA	T8	73-71-68-69	281	$28,000
DOUG TEWELL	T8	69-72-71-69	281	$28,000

| JIM THORPE | T8 | 71-72-71-67 | 281 | $28,000 |
| MARK WURTZ | T8 | 70-70-70-71 | 281 | $28,000 |

ANHEUSER-BUSCH OPEN

Kingsmill G.C.,
Williamsburg, Virginia
July 7-10, 1994

MARK MCCUMBER	1	67-69-65-66	267	$198,000
GLEN DAY	2	64-68-72-66	270	$118,800
JUSTIN LEONARD	3	67-69-67-69	272	$74,800
MICHAEL BRADLEY	T4	68-69-69-67	273	$45,466
JOHN WILSON	T4	64-70-72-67	273	$45,466
SCOTT VERPLANK	T4	71-69-66-67	273	$45,466
JAY HAAS	T7	69-73-65-67	274	$34,283
TOMMY ARMOUR III	T7	69-71-67-67	274	$34,283
BOB LOHR	T7	61-68-73-72	274	$34,283
JIM FURYK	10	70-70-66-69	275	$28,600

THE BRITISH OPEN CHAMPIONSHIP

Turnberry G.C. (Ailsa Course),
Turnberry, Scotland
July 14-17, 1994

NICK PRICE	1	69-66-67-66	268	£110,000
JESPER PARNEVIK	2	68-66-68-67	269	£88,000
FUZZY ZOELLER	3	71-66-64-70	271	£74,000
ANDERS FORSBRAND	T4	72-71-66-64	273	£50,666
MARK JAMES	T4	72-67-66-68	273	£50,666
DAVID FEHERTY	T4	70-69-66-70	273	£50,666
BRAD FAXON	7	69-65-67-73	274	£36,000
COLIN MONTGOMERIE	T8	72-69-65-69	275	£30,000
TOM KITE	T8	71-69-66-69	215	£30,000
NICK FALDO	T8	75-66-70-64	275	£30,000

For a complete summary of all players making the cut at the British Open, please refer to "1994 Major Championships"

DEPOSIT GUARANTY CLASSIC

Annandale G.C.,
Madison, Mississippi
July 14-17, 1994

| BRIAN HENNINGER | 1 | 67-68 | 135 | $126,000 |

Deposit Guaranty Classic, continued

MIKE SULLIVAN	2	66-69	135	$75,600
TOMMY ARMOUR III	T3	71-65	136	$31,570
GUY BOROS	T3	69-67	136	$31,570
CHRIS DIMARCO	T3	70-66	136	$31,570
SCOTT HOCH	T3	69-67	136	$31,570
DAVE STOCKTON, JR	T3	69-67	136	$31,570
BOBBY CLAMPETT	T8	68-69	137	$20,300
DICKY PRIDE	T8	73-64	137	$20,300
STAN UTLEY	T8	67-70	137	$20,300

NEW ENGLAND CLASSIC
Pleasant Valley G.C.,
Sutton, Massachusetts
July 21-24, 1994

KENNY PERRY	**1**	**67-66-70-65**	**268**	**$180,000**
DAVID FEHERTY	2	65-69-68-67	269	$108,000
ED FIORI	3	66-66-70-70	272	$68,000
CHRIS DIMARCO	4	67-68-70-68	273	$48,000
STEVE GOTSCHE	5	68-70-69-67	274	$40,000
BILLY DOWNES	T6	71-68-69-67	275	$33,500
FRED FUNK	T6	68-66-75-66	275	$33,500
JUSTIN LEONARD	T6	69-68-70-68	275	$33,500
BILL GLASSON	T9	68-68-71-69	276	$23,142
KEN GREEN	T9	68-72-68-68	276	$23,142
JEFF MAGGERT	T9	68-69-71-68	276	$23,142
BLAINE MCCALLISTER	T9	68-73-69-66	276	$23,142
FRANCIS QUINN	T9	67-72-66-71	276	$23,142
GUY BOROS	T9	65-69-70-72	276	$23,142

FEDERAL EXPRESS ST. JUDE CLASSIC
TPC at Avenel,
Potomac, Maryland
July 28-31, 1994

DICKY PRIDE	**1**	**66-67-67-67**	**267**	**$225,000**
GENE SAUERS	T2	67-66-68-66	267	$110,000
HAL SUTTON	T2	67-68-68-64	267	$110,000
NICK PRICE	4	72-66-66-64	268	$60,000
DAVE BARR	T5	66-69-67-67	269	$45,625
RUSS COCHRAN	T5	67-68-65-69	269	$45,625
WAYNE GRADY	T5	70-66-67-66	269	$45,625

PAUL STANKOWSKI	T8	68-67-69-66	270	$37,500
FUZZY ZOELLER	T8	66-65-70-69	270	$37,500
BRIAN CLAAR	T10	69-67-68-67	271	$28,750
JOHN COOK	T10	67-70-65-69	271	$28,750
JIM GALLAGHER, JR	T10	71-68-65-67	271	$28,750
GIL MORGAN	T10	70-67-63-71	271	$28,750
DUFFY WALDORF	T10	67-70-67-67	271	$28,750

BUICK OPEN
Warwick Hills G. & C.C.,
Grand Blanc, Michigan
August 4-7, 1994

FRED COUPLES	**1**	**72-65-65-68**	**270**	**$198,000**
COREY PAVIN	2	66-65-70-71	272	$118,800
GREG KRAFT	T3	71-72-67-66	276	$57,200
STEVE PATE	T3	71-67-69-69	276	$57,200
CURTIS STRANGE	T3	71-70-67-68	276	$57,200
KEITH CLEARWATER	T6	71-67-69-70	277	$38,225
BEN CRENSHAW	T6	72-68-69-68	277	$38,225
FRED FUNK	T8	65-70-71-72	278	$31,900
TOM LEHMAN	T8	71-67-70-70	278	$31,900
DUFFY WALDORF	T8	69-67-74-68	278	$31,900

PGA CHAMPIONSHIP
Southern Hills C.C.,
Tulsa, Oklahoma
August 11-14

NICK PRICE	**1**	**67-65-70-67**	**269**	**$310,000**
COREY PAVIN	2	70-67-69-69	275	$160,000
PHIL MICKELSON	3	68-71-67-70	276	$110,000
NICK FALDO	T4	73-67-71-66	277	$76,666
GREG NORMAN	T4	71-69-67-70	277	$76,666
JOHN COOK	T4	71-67-69-70	277	$76,666
STEVE ELKINGTON	T7	73-70-66-69	278	$57,500
JOSE MARIA OLAZABAL	T7	72-66-70-70	278	$57,500
BEN CRENSHAW	T9	70-67-70-72	279	$41,000
TOM KITE	T9	72-68-69-70	279	$41,000
LOREN ROBERTS	T9	69-72-67-71	279	$41,000
TOM WATSON	T9	69-72-67-71	279	$41,000
IAN WOOSNAM	T9	68-72-73-66	279	$41,000

For a complete summary of all players making the cut at the
PGA Championship, please refer to
"1994 Major Championships"

THE SPRINT INTERNATIONAL
Castle Pines G.C.,
Castle Pines, Colorado
August 18-21, 1994

STEVE LOWERY	1	----	**$252,000**
RICK FEHR	2	----	$151,200
DUFFY WALDORF	3	----	$95,200
ERNIE ELS	4	----	$67,200
TOM KITE	5	----	$56,000
JOHN ADAMS	T6	----	$48,650
CHRIS DIMARCO	T6	----	$48,650
MARK CALCAVECCHIA	T8	----	$42,000
DAVE STOCKTON, JR	T8	----	$42,000
PHIL MICKELSON	T10	----	$36,400
MIKE REID	T10	----	$36,400

Note: The Sprint International uses a modified Stableford system.

NEC WORLD SERIES OF GOLF
Firestone C.C. (South Course),
Akron, Ohio
August 25-28, 1994

JOSE-MARIA OLAZABAL	1	66-67-69-67 269	**$360,000**
SCOTT HOCH	2	71-64-65-70 270	$216,000
BRAD FAXON	T3	69-68-65-69 271	$116,000
STEVE LOWERY	T3	67-66-66-72 271	$116,000
JOHN HUSTON	T5	73-64-64-71 272	$76,000
MARK MCNULTY	T5	69-68-65-70 272	$76,000
MIKE HEINEN	7	71-67-65-70 273	$67,000
FRED COUPLES	T8	69-70-65-70 274	$60,000
GREG NORMAN	T8	67-67-68-72 274	$60,000
HALE IRWIN	T10	70-65-71-70 276	$52,000
NICK PRICE	T10	68-66-69-73 276	$52,000

GREATER MILWAUKEE OPEN
Brown Deer G.C.,
Franklin, Wisconsin
September 1-4, 1994

MIKE SPRINGER	1	69-67-65-67 268	**$180,000**
LOREN ROBERTS	2	70-63-68-68 269	$108,000
MARK CALCAVECCHIA	T3	67-68-64-71 270	$48,000
BOB ESTES	T3	67-66-65-72 270	$48,000
TOM PURTZER	T3	70-69-67-64 270	$48,000
JOEY SINDELAR	T3	67-68-66-69 270	$48,000

DAVE BARR	T7	69-64-70-68 271	$32,250
MARCO DAWSON	T7	68-66-69-68 271	$32,250
MARK O'MEARA	T9	68-69-67-68 272	$28,000
STEVE PATE	T9	68-70-65-69 272	$28,000

BELL CANADIAN OPEN
Glen Abbey G.C.,
Oakville, Ontario
September 8-11, 1994

NICK PRICE	1	67-72-68-68 275	**$234,000**
MARK CALCAVECCHIA	2	67-71-71-67 276	$140,400
TOM LEHMAN	3	69-69-70-69 277	$88,400
JAY DON BLAKE	T4	74-63-73-68 278	$57,200
MARK MCCUMBER	T4	74-65-67-72 278	$57,200
FULTON ALLEM	T6	69-69-71-70 279	$43,550
BRIAN KAMM	T6	71-71-69-68 279	$43,550
STEVE STRICKER	T6	69-70-69-71 279	$43,550
MARK O'MEARA	9	66-72-72-70 280	$37,700
BOB ESTES	T10	72-73-68-68 281	$32,500
GREG KRAFT	T10	72-70-70-69 281	$32,500
PAYNE STEWART	T10	68-72-72-69 281	$32,500

HARDEE'S GOLF CLASSIC
Oakwood G.C.,
Coal Valley, Illinois
September 15-18, 1994

MARK MCCUMBER	1	66-67-65-67 265	**$180,000**
KENNY PERRY	2	67-66-65-68 266	$108,000
MIKE DONALD	T3	70-66-64-67 267	$58,000
DAVID FROST	T3	68-67-67-65 267	$58,000
RUSS COCHRAN	5	67-66-70-65 268	$40,000
CURT BYRUM	T6	69-65-65-70 269	$32,375
JOHN HUSTON	T6	71-66-67-65 269	$32,375
TOM LEHMAN	T6	71-67-65-66 269	$32,375
ROBERT WRENN	T6	63-70-67-69 269	$32,375
MICHAEL BRADLEY	10	72-67-62-69 270	$23,000

B.C. OPEN
En-Joie G.C.,
Endicott, New York
September 22-25, 1994

MIKE SULLIVAN	1	65-67-68-66 266	**$162,000**

B.C. Open, continued

JEFF SLUMAN	2	63-68-67-72 270		$97,200
BRIAN CLAAR	T3	68-68-65-71 272		$52,200
MIKE HULBERT	T3	67-67-68-70 272		$52,200
RUSSELL BEIERSDORF	T5	69-66-68-70 273		$34,200
CURT BYRUM	T5	67-69-66-71 273		$34,200
BILL GLASSON	T7	70-65-68-71 274		$28,050
PAUL GOYDOS	T7	68-68-67-71 274		$28,050
BLAINE MCCALLISTER	T7	67-70-65-72 274		$28,050
ROBIN FREEMAN	T10	68-65-69-73 275		$22,500
MIKE HEINEN	T10	65-70-68-72 275		$22,500
P.H. HORGAN III	T10	68-67-69-71 275		$22,500

BUICK SOUTHERN OPEN
Callaway Gardens Resort,
Pine Mountain, Georgia
September 29-October 2, 1994

STEVE ELKINGTON	1	66-66-68	200	$144,000
STEVE RINTOUL	2	70-65-70	205	$86,400
BRAD BRYANT	3	70-68-69	207	$54,400
BUDDY GARDNER	T4	71-69-68	208	$33,066
STEVE PATE	T4	69-71-68	208	$33,066
GENE SAUERS	T4	72-67-69	208	$33,066
BLAINE MCCALLISTER	T7	69-71-69	209	$24,100
LARRY MIZE	T7	69-73-67	209	$24,100
JEFF SLUMAN	T7	69-70-70	209	$24,100
BOBBY WADKINS	T7	69-72-68	209	$24,100

WALT DISNEY WORLD/ OLDSMOBILE CLASSIC
Walt Disney World Resort,
Orlando, Florida
October 6-9, 1994

RICK FEHR	1	63-70-68-68 269		$198,000
CRAIG STADLER	T2	68-66-67-70 271		$96,800
FUZZY ZOELLER	T2	66-70-69-66 271		$96,800
TREVOR DODDS	T4	68-66-70-68 272		$48,400
STEVE STRICKER	T4	72-67-66-67 272		$48,400
ROBERT GAMEZ	6	68-69-68-68 273		$39,600
GLEN DAY	T7	65-68-72-69 274		$33,137
CONNIE HAMMOND	T7	68-72-67-67 274		$33,137
BRIAN KAMM	T7	69-69-68-68 274		$33,137
DOUG TEWELL	T7	69-66-71-68 274		$33,137

TEXAS OPEN
Oak Hills C.C.,
San Antonio, Texas
October 13-16, 1994

BOB ESTES	1	62-65-68-70 265		$180,000
GIL MORGAN	2	66-68-65-67 266		$108,000
DON POOLEY	3	69-65-65-68 267		$68,000
BRUCE LIETZKE	4	68-69-64-69 270		$48,000
CRAIG STADLER	T5	68-66-69-68 271		$36,500
MARK MCNULTY	T5	70-65-67-69 271		$36,500
JOHN WILSON	T5	66-68-67-70 271		$36,500
BEN CRENSHAW	T8	70-69-68-65 272		$25,000
BLAINE MCCALLISTER	T8	70-65-72-65 272		$25,000
MARK O'MEARA	T8	70-69-67-66 272		$25,000
DILLARD PRUITT	T8	70-68-67-67 272		$25,000
BRAD BRYANT	T8	66-67-70-69 272		$25,000
J.C. ANDERSON	T8	67-64-70-71 272		$25,000
BOB BURNS	T8	65-69-68-70 272		$25,000

LAS VEGAS INVITATIONAL
TPC at Summerlin,
Las Vegas, Nevada
October 13-16, 1994

BRUCE LIETZKE	1	66-67-68-66-65 332		$270,000
ROBERT GAMEZ	2	66-70-64-69-64 333		$162,000
PHIL MICKELSON	T3	70-66-66-70-63 335		$87,000
BILLY ANDRADE	T3	66-68-67-67-67 335		$87,000
PAUL STANKOWSKI	T5	70-66-66-65-66 336		$54,750
BILL GLASSON	T5	67-68-70-65-66 336		$54,750
JIM FURYK	T5	67-64-69-66-70 336		$54,750
SEAN MURPHY	T8	64-69-67-69-68 337		$42,000
SCOTT HOCH	T8	66-63-70-70-68 337		$42,000
GUY BOROS	T8	70-63-67-68-69 337		$42,000
KIRK TRIPLETT	T8	69-65-65-68-70 337		$42,000

THE TOUR CHAMPIONSHIP
Olympic Club (Lake),
San Francisco, California
October 27-30, 1994

MARK MCCUMBER	1	66-71-69-68 274		$540,000
FUZZY ZOELLER	2	71-69-66-68 274		$324,000
BRAD BRYANT	3	72-68-67-68 275		$207,000

The Tour Championship, continued

DAVID FROST	T4	66-69-75-66 276	$132,000
BILL GLASSON	T4	66-68-71-71 276	$132,000
JAY HAAS	6	69-71-71-66 277	$108,000
JEFF MAGGERT	7	72-66-70-70 278	$102,000
LOREN ROBERTS	T8	71-70-68-70 279	$93,000
STEVE LOWERY	T8	66-69-72-72 279	$93,000
BRUCE LIETZKE	T10	69-71-71-69 280	$81,000
COREY PAVIN	T10	69-69-70-72 280	$81,000
JOHN HUSTON	T10	74-68-66-72 280	$81,000

BOB CHARLES	T3	70-67-70	207	$52,800
J.C. SNEAD	T3	71-66-70	207	$52,800
GEORGE ARCHER	5	69-68-71	208	$38,400
SIMON HOBDAY	T6	75-69-65	209	$28,800
BOB MURPHY	T6	67-71-71	209	$28,800
TOM WARGO	T6	69-72-68	209	$28,800
TOMMY AARON	T9	69-71-70	210	$20,000
TERRY DILL	T9	73-73-64	210	$20,000
GARY PLAYER	T9	69-70-71	210	$20,000
CHI CHI RODRIGUEZ	T9	70-70-70	210	$20,000

Senior PGA TOUR

MERCEDES CHAMPIONSHIP
La Costa C.C.,
Carlsbad, California
January 6-9, 1994

JACK NICKLAUS	1	73-69-69-68	279	$100,000
BOB MURPHY	2	71-70-67-72	280	$60,000
DAVE STOCKTON	3	67-72-69-75	283	$48,000
RAY FLOYD	4	73-72-70-69	284	$40,000
JIM COLBERT	T5	71-74-70-70	285	$29,500
LEE TREVINO	T5	71-71-73-70	285	$29,500
BOB CHARLES	7	70-72-73-71	286	$24,000
AL GEIBERGER	8	72-73-71-72	288	$21,000
GEORGE ARCHER	T9	71-73-73-72	289	$18,250
SIMON HOBDAY	T9	73-74-71-71	289	$18,250

SENIOR SKINS GAME
Mauna Lani Resort,
Maui, Hawaii
January 29-30, 1994

RAY FLOYD		$240,000

ROYAL CARIBBEAN CLASSIC
The Links at Key Biscayne,
Key Biscayne, Florida
February 4-6, 1994

LEE TREVINO	1	66-73-66	205	$120,000
KERMIT ZARLEY	2	71-66-68	205	$70,400

SENIOR SLAM OF GOLF
Club Campestre de Queretaro
Queretaro, Mexico
February 7-8, 1994

TOM SHAW	1	70-69	139	$250,000
JIM COLBERT	2	70-71	141	$125,000
TOM WARGO	3	70-72	142	$75,000
JACK NICKLAUS	4	75-70	145	$50,000

GTE SUNCOAST CLASSIC
TPC of Tampa at Cheval,
Lutz, Florida
February 11-13, 1994

ROCKY THOMPSON	1	73-67-61	201	$105,000
RAY FLOYD	2	70-66-66	202	$61,600
LEE TREVINO	3	69-68-66	203	$50,400
ORVILLE MOODY	4	66-69-70	205	$42,000
MIKE HILL	T5	69-64-73	206	$30,800
RICHARD RHYAN	T5	70-70-66	206	$30,800
JIM COLBERT	7	68-74-65	207	$25,200
GEORGE ARCHER	T8	66-70-72	208	$19,250
BOB CHARLES	T8	71-70-67	208	$19,250
SIMON HOBDAY	T8	71-66-71	208	$19,250
J.C. SNEAD	T8	71-71-66	208	$19,250

THE INTELLINET CHALLENGE
The Vineyards,
Naples, Florida
February 18-20, 1994

MIKE HILL	1	69-69-63	201	$75,000

The Intellinet Challenge, continued

TOM WARGO	2	71-65-68	204	$44,000
GEORGE ARCHER	T3	67-67-71	205	$30,000
DICK GOETZ	T3	68-68-69	205	$30,000
DAVE STOCKTON	T3	69-67-69	205	$30,000
SIMON HOBDAY	T6	69-70-67	206	$18,000
JAY SIGEL	T6	65-71-70	206	$18,000
J.C. SNEAD	T6	68-71-67	206	$18,000
BOB CHARLES	T9	71-67-69	207	$13,500
RICHARD RHYAN	T9	68-71-68	207	$13,500

CHRYSLER CUP

TPC at Prestancia,
Sarasota, Florida
February 25-27, 1994

GEORGE ARCHER	1	68-63-72	203	$68,291
SIMON HOBDAY	2	67-67-69	203	$64,260
BOB CHARLES	T3	66-70-69	205	$51,888
TOM WEISKOPF	T3	71-67-67	205	$39,094
GARY PLAYER	T5	73-67-67	207	$43,833
BRUCE DEVLIN	T5	65-71-71	207	$43,583
AL GEIBERGER	T5	70-71-66	207	$32,495
GRAHAM MARSH	8	69-68-71	208	$42,094
TOMMY HORTON	T9	68-69-72	209	$38,734
DAVE STOCKTON	T9	69-72-68	209	$25,897
JIM COLBERT	T9	70-71-68	209	$25,727

GTE WEST CLASSIC

Ojai Valley Inn & C.C.,
Ojai, California
March 4-6, 1994

JAY SIGEL	1	70-66-62	198	$82,500
JIM COLBERT	2	62-64-72	198	$48,400
LARRY LAORETTI	T3	65-68-66	199	$36,300
BOB MURPHY	T3	67-66-66	199	$36,300
TOM WARGO	T5	66-64-70	200	$24,200
KERMIT ZARLEY	T5	67-65-68	200	$24,200
JIM ALBUS	T7	65-66-71	202	$17,600
BRUCE CRAMPTON	T7	68-67-67	202	$17,600
SIMON HOBDAY	T7	67-69-66	202	$17,600
GEORGE ARCHER	T10	67-70-66	203	$12,650
DON BIES	T10	69-66-68	203	$12,650
DALE DOUGLASS	T10	69-66-68	203	$12,650
RICHARD RHYAN	T10	65-69-69	203	$12,650

VANTAGE AT THE DOMINION

The Dominion C.C.,
San Antonio, Texas
March 11-13, 1994

JIM ALBUS	1	68-67-73	208	$97,500
GRAHAM MARSH	T2	72-67-70	209	$47,666
LEE TREVINO	T2	71-69-69	209	$47,666
GEORGE ARCHER	T2	69-69-71	209	$47,666
ROCKY THOMPSON	5	71-69-70	210	$31,200
JIM COLBERT	T6	71-70-70	211	$22,100
GIBBY GILBERT	T6	71-67-73	211	$22,100
J.C. SNEAD	T6	71-70-70	211	$22,100
TOM WARGO	T6	70-71-70	211	$22,100

DOUG SANDERS CELEBRITY CLASSIC

The Deerwood Club, Kingwood, Texas
March 25-27, 1994

TOM WARGO	1	71-66-72	209	$75,000
BOB MURPHY	2	75-69-66	210	$45,000
CHI CHI RODRIGUEZ	3	69-69-73	211	$37,000
JIMMY POWELL	4	72-70-70	212	$30,600
MIKE HILL	5	74-70-69	213	$24,600
GEORGE ARCHER	T6	72-72-70	214	$19,600
BOB CHARLES	T6	70-69-75	214	$19,600
HOMERO BLANCAS	T8	72-69-74	215	$15,600
WALTER ZEMBRISKI	T8	71-72-72	215	$15,600
JIM ALBUS	T10	70-73-73	216	$13,100
DALE DOUGLASS	T10	71-72-73	216	$13,100

THE TRADITION

Golf Club at Desert Mountain,
Scottsdale, Arizona
March 31-April 3, 1994

RAY FLOYD	1	65-70-68-68	271	$127,500
DALE DOUGLASS	2	68-68-69-66	271	$74,800
JIM COLBERT	3	70-66-68-70	274	$61,200
JACK NICKLAUS	T4	70-71-69-68	278	$41,933
JIMMY POWELL	T4	67-69-72-70	278	$41,933
TOM WEISKOPF	T4	68-70-70-70	278	$41,933
GIBBY GILBERT	T7	66-69-73-71	279	$28,900
MIKE HILL	T7	70-70-68-71	279	$28,900
ISAO AOKI	T9	67-69-71-73	280	$22,100

The Tradition, continued

DAVE STOCKTON	T9	68-70-72-70	280	$22,100
TOM WARGO	T9	68-75-65-72	280	$22,100

For a complete summary of all players making the cut at The Tradition, please refer to "1994 Major Championships"

PGA SENIORS CHAMPIONSHIP
PGA National G.C.,
Palm Beach Gardens, Florida
April 14-17, 1994

LEE TREVINO	**1**	**70-69-70-70**	**279**	**$115,700**
JIM COLBERT	2	68-71-74-67	280	$85,000
RAY FLOYD	T3	69-69-69-75	282	$57,500
DAVE STOCKTON	T3	70-69-71-72	282	$57,500
ISAO AOKI	T5	71-71-75-66	283	$32,500
DALE DOUGLASS	T5	70-71-70-72	283	$32,500
CHI CHI RODRIGUEZ	T5	73-72-69-69	283	$32,500
DEWITT WEAVER	T5	72-73-70-68	283	$32,500
JACK NICKLAUS	9	71-71-72-72	286	$20,500
BOB CHARLES	T10	69-74-71-73	287	$16,500
BOB MURPHY	T10	69-75-73-70	287	$16,500
TOM WARGO	T10	72-80-70-65	287	$16,500

For a complete summary of all players making the cut at the PGA Seniors , please refer to "1994 Major Championships"

DALLAS REUNION PRO-AM
Oak Cliff C.C.,
Dallas, Texas
April 21-24, 1994

LARRY GILBERT	**1**	**67-68-67**	**202**	**$75,000**
GEORGE ARCHER	T2	67-68-68	203	$40,000
ROCKY THOMPSON	T2	68-67-68	203	$40,000
JACK KIEFER	4	66-70-68	204	$30,000
BOB MURPHY	T5	68-66-71	205	$22,000
J.C.SNEAD	T5	65-71-69	205	$22,000
CHI CHI RODRIGUEZ	T7	67-68-71	206	$16,000
TOM SHAW	T7	70-71-65	206	$16,000
TOM WARGO	T7	69-67-70	206	$16,000
TERRY DILL	T10	70-68-69	207	$11,500
DICK HENDRICKSON	T10	68-70-69	207	$11,500
JOE JIMENEZ	T10	71-70-66	207	$11,500

LAS VEGAS SENIOR CLASSIC
TPC at Summerlin,
Las Vegas, Nevada
April 28-May 1, 1994

RAY FLOYD	**1**	**68-70-65**	**203**	**$135,000**
TOM WARGO	2	71-67-68	206	$80,100
JIM DENT	3	70-66-71	207	$65,700
LARRY GILBERT	4	66-73-70	209	$54,720
TOMMY AYCOCK	T5	72-67-71	210	$33,876
JIM COLBERT	T5	72-67-71	210	$33,876
JACK KIEFER	T5	68-70-72	210	$33,876
ROCKY THOMPSON	T5	70-70-70	210	$33,876
KERMIT ZARLEY	T5	66-72-72	210	$33,876
GEORGE ARCHER	T10	68-69-74	211	$22,500
CHI CHI RODRIGUEZ	T10	73-65-73	211	$22,500
LEE TREVINO	T10	72-67-72	211	$22,500

LIBERTY MUTUAL LEGENDS OF GOLF
Barton Creek C.C.,
Austin, Texas
May 5-8, 1994

DALE DOUGLASS-				
CHARLES COODY	**1**	**63-61-64**	**188**	**$200,000**
CHI CHI RODRIGUEZ-				
JIM DENT	T2	63-63-63	189	$82,500
BOB MURPHY-				
JIM COLBERT	T2	65-61-63	189	$82,500
HAROLD HENNING-				
GRAHAM MARSH	4	64-65-61	190	$55,000
LEE TREVINO-				
MIKE HILL	5	65-62-64	191	$45,000

PAINEWEBBER INVITATIONAL
TPC at Piper Glen,
Charlotte, North Carolina
May 13-15

LEE TREVINO	**1**	**70-65-68**	**203**	**$112,500**
JIM COLBERT	T2	68-70-66	204	$60,000
JIMMY POWELL	T2	69-66-69	204	$60,000

Painewebber Invitational, continued

GRAHAM MARSH	T4	71-68-66	205	$40,500
JERRY MCGEE	T4	69-66-70	205	$40,500
BUTCH BAIRD	6	66-70-70	206	$30,000
MIKE HILL	T7	71-68-68	207	$24,000
DICK LOTZ	T7	73-68-66	207	$24,000
LARRY ZIEGLER	T7	68-68-71	207	$24,000
RAY FLOYD	T10	70-69-69	208	$18,000
LARRY GILBERT	T10	69-68-71	208	$18,000
TOM SHAW	T10	67-69-72	208	$18,000

CADILLAC NFL GOLF CLASSIC
Upper Montclair C.C.,
Clinton, New Jersey
May 20-22, 1994

RAY FLOYD	**1**	**64-68-74**	**206**	**$133,000**
BOB MURPHY	T2	70-69-68	207	$72,000
GARY PLAYER	T2	71-67-69	207	$72,000
DAVE STOCKTON	T4	72-70-68	210	$48,600
LEE TREVINO	T4	70-69-71	210	$48,600
GEORGE ARCHER	6	67-70-74	211	$36,000
WALT ZEMBRISKI	7	70-72-70	212	$32,400
BOB CHARLES	T8	72-72-72	213	$25,800
LARRY GILBERT	T8	69-72-72	213	$25,800
JIM DENT	T8	70-75-68	213	$25,800

BELL ATLANTIC CLASSIC
Chester Valley G.C.,
Malvern, Pennsylvania
May 27-29, 1994

LEE TREVINO	**1**	**71-67-68**	**206**	**$105,000**
MIKE HILL	2	69-71-68	208	$61,600
TOMMY AARON	3	71-68-71	210	$50,400
TOM WARGO	T4	68-72-71	211	$34,533
JIM DENT	T4	68-71-72	211	$34,533
CHI CHI RODRIGUEZ	T4	69-71-71	211	$34,533
RAY FLOYD	T7	70-74-68	212	$23,800
JACK KIEFER	T7	74-67-71	212	$23,800
JIMMY POWELL	T9	73-70-70	213	$18,900
BOB MURPHY	T9	71-71-71	213	$18,900

BRUNO'S MEMORIAL CLASSIC
Greystone G.C.,
Birmingham, Alabama
June 2-5, 1994

JIM DENT	**1**	**66-68-67**	**201**	**$150,000**
LARRY GILBERT	T2	67-66-70	203	$73,333
BOB CHARLES	T2	66-66-71	203	$73,333
KERMIT ZARLEY	T2	67-68-68	203	$73,333
TOMMY AARON	T5	67-70-68	205	$39,000
JIM ALBUS	T5	64-71-70	205	$39,000
GEORGE ARCHER	T5	68-69-68	205	$39,000
DALE DOUGLASS	T5	68-68-69	205	$39,000
SIMON HOBDAY	T9	71-67-68	206	$26,000
JACK KIEFER	T9	69-67-70	206	$26,000
JAY SIGEL	T9	67-68-71	206	$26,000

NATIONWIDE CHAMPIONSHIP
CC of the South,
Alpharetta, Georgia
June 10-12, 1994

DAVE STOCKTON	**1**	**67-63-68**	**198**	**$172,500**
BOB MURPHY	2	67-64-68	199	$101,200
JIM ALBUS	T3	66-73-64	203	$75,900
JIM DENT	T3	72-64-67	203	$75,900
CHI CHI RODRIGUEZ	T5	71-65-68	204	$50,600
LEE TREVINO	T5	70-66-68	204	$50,600
JIMMY POWELL	T7	70-67-68	205	$39,100
JAY SIGEL	T7	70-67-68	205	$39,100
GIBBY GILBERT	T9	65-73-68	206	$31,050
TOM WARGO	T9	70-68-68	206	$31,050

SENIOR CLASSIC AT OPRYLAND
Springhouse G.C.,
Nashville, Tennessee
June 17-19, 1994

LEE TREVINO	**1**	**67-65-67**	**199**	**$157,500**
JIM ALBUS	T2	66-68-66	200	$84,000
DAVE STOCKTON	T2	62-69-69	200	$84,000
GIBBY GILBERT	4	71-65-66	202	$63,000

Senior Classic at Opryland, continued

GEORGE ARCHER	5	65-71-67	203	$50,400
TOM WARGO	T6	67-68-69	204	$39,900
RAY FLOYD	T6	70-66-68	204	$39,900
JIM DENT	T8	63-71-71	205	$28,875
GRAHAM MARSH	T8	69-68-68	205	$28,875
J.C. SNEAD	T8	68-67-70	205	$28,875
LARRY ZIEGLER	T8	68-69-68	205	$28,875

FORD SENIOR PLAYERS CHAMPIONSHIP

TPC of Michigan,
Dearborn, Michigan
June 24-26, 1994

DAVE STOCKTON	1	66-66-71-68	271	$210,000
JIM ALBUS	2	67-69-72-69	277	$123,200
ISAO AOKI	T3	67-70-73-68	278	$84,000
RAY FLOYD	T3	72-68-71-67	278	$84,000
LEE TREVINO	T3	66-69-74-69	278	$84,000
JIM DENT	T6	72-67-70-71	280	$50,400
HAROLD HENNING	T6	69-67-74-70	280	$50,400
JACK NICKLAUS	T6	68-72-73-67	280	$50,400
JAY SIGEL	9	67-71-73-70	281	$39,200
JERRY MCGEE	T10	69-69-74-70	282	$32,200
BOB MURPHY	T10	69-68-73-72	282	$32,200
TOM WARGO	T10	70-73-71-68	282	$32,200
TOM WEISKOPF	T10	65-71-74-72	282	$32,200

For a complete summary of all players making the cut at the Ford Senior Playerss, please refer to "1994 Major Championships"

U.S. SENIOR OPEN

Pinehurst C.C. (No. 2),
Pinehurst, North Carolina
June 30-July 3, 1994

SIMON HOBDAY	1	66-67-66-75	274	$145,000
JIM ALBUS	T2	66-69-66-74	275	$63,418
GRAHAM MARSH	T2	68-68-69-70	275	$63,418
DAVE STOCKTON	T4	74-67-68-68	277	$30,608
TOM WARGO	T4	69-70-68-70	277	$30,608
TOM WEISKOPF	T4	72-66-72-67	277	$30,608
BOB MURPHY	T7	71-70-71-67	279	$21,651
JACK NICKLAUS	T7	69-68-70-72	279	$21,651
JAY SIGEL	T7	73-66-70-70	279	$21,651
ISAO AOKI	10	69-71-73-67	280	$18,313

For a complete summary of all players making the cut at the Senior Open, please refer to "1994 Major Championships"

KROGER SENIOR CLASSIC

The Golf Center at Kings Island,
Mason, Ohio
July 8-10, 1994

JIM COLBERT	1	66-64-69	199	$127,500
RAY FLOYD	2	68-68-65	201	$74,800
MIKE HILL	T3	68-70-67	205	$46,750
BOB MURPHY	T3	71-65-69	205	$46,750
ROCKY THOMPSON	T3	66-70-69	205	$46,750
DEWITT WEAVER	T3	65-71-69	205	$46,750
BOB CHARLES	T7	71-69-67	207	$25,925
JIMMY POWELL	T7	71-71-65	207	$25,925
J.C. SNEAD	T7	68-70-69	207	$25,925
TOM WARGO	T7	68-70-69	207	$25,925

AMERITECH SENIOR OPEN

Stonebridge C.C.,
Aurora, Illinois
July 15-17, 1994

JOHN PAUL CAIN	1	66-67-69	202	$112,500
JIM COLBERT	T2	67-67-69	203	$60,000
SIMON HOBDAY	T2	66-69-68	203	$60,000
CHI CHI RODRIGUEZ	4	69-66-69	204	$45,000
JAY SIGEL	T5	70-69-66	205	$33,000
HARRY TOSCANO	T5	68-69-68	205	$33,000
TOMMY AARON	T7	72-67-67	206	$22,875
MIKE HILL	T7	70-64-72	206	$22,875
TOM WARGO	T7	71-67-68	206	$22,875
TOM WEISKOPF	T7	69-69-68	206	$22,875

SOUTHWESTERN BELL CLASSIC

Loch Loyd C.C.,
Belton, Missouri
July 22-24, 1994

JIM COLBERT	1	68-63-65	196	$105,000

Southwestern Bell Classic, continued

ISAO AOKI	T2	69-64-65	198	$56,000
LARRY GILBERT	T2	67-66-65	198	$56,000
GRAHAM MARSH	4	66-67-67	200	$42,000
DAVE STOCKTON	5	70-65-66	201	$33,600
LARRY LAORETTI	6	69-66-67	202	$28,000
ROCKY THOMPSON	7	68-68-67	203	$25,200
J.C. SNEAD	8	67-68-69	204	$22,400
KERMIT ZARLEY	9	69-69-67	205	$19,600
RAY FLOYD	T10	67-73-66	206	$17,500
BOB SMITH	T10	69-69-68	206	$17,500

NORTHVILLE LONG ISLAND CLASSIC
Meadow Brook Club,
Jericho, New York
July 29-31, 1994

LEE TREVINO	**1**	**66-69-65**	**200**	**$97,500**
JIM COLBERT	2	70-72-65	207	$57,200
JAY SIGEL	3	68-68-72	208	$46,800
ISAO AOKI	T4	69-69-72	210	$29,900
TERRY DILL	T4	71-72-67	210	$29,900
JERRY MCGEE	T4	71-66-73	210	$29,900
JIMMY POWELL	T4	66-73-71	210	$29,900
GEORGE ARCHER	T8	69-73-69	211	$19,500
HARRY TOSCANO	T8	67-71-73	211	$19,500
JIM ALBUS	T10	68-74-70	212	$14,430
BOB DICKSON	T10	67-73-72	212	$14,430
DAVE EICHELBERGER	T10	71-70-71	212	$14,430
RAY FLOYD	T10	69-73-70	212	$14,430
TOM WARGO	T10	72-70-70	212	$14,430

BANK OF BOSTON SENIOR GOLF CLASSIC
Nashawtuc C.C.,
Concord, Massachusetts
August 5-7, 1994

JIM ALBUS	**1**	**67-66-70**	**203**	**$112,500**
BOB BRUE	T2	67-73-65	205	$60,000
RAY FLOYD	T2	69-67-69	205	$60,000
.MIKE HILL	T4	73-68-66	207	$37,000
DICK LOTZ	T4	74-67-66	207	$37,000
LEE TREVINO	T4	70-67-70	207	$37,000

DAVE STOCKTON	T7	72-68-68	208	$25,500
TOM WARGO	T7	68-70-70	208	$25,500
BOB CHARLES	9	69-70-70	209	$21,000
BUTCH BAIRD	T10	70-67-73	210	$18,750
JOE JIMENEZ	T10	71-73-66	210	$18,750

FIRST OF AMERICA CLASSIC
Egypt Valley G.C.,
Ada, Michigan
August 12-14, 1994

TONY JACKLIN	**1**	**68-68**	**136**	**$97,500**
DAVE STOCKTON	2	67-70	137	$57,200
JIM ALBUS	T3	66-72	138	$42,900
LEE TREVINO	T3	72-66	138	$42,900
HARRY TOSCANO	T5	72-67	139	$28,600
TOM WARGO	T5	67-72	139	$28,600
JOHN PAUL CAIN	T7	69-71	140	$22,100
JIMMY POWELL	T7	66-74	140	$22,100
ROD CURL	T9	72-69	141	$17,550
LARRY MOWRY	T9	67-74	141	$17,550

BURNET SENIOR CLASSIC
Bunker Hills G.C.,
Coon Rapids, Minnesota
August 19-21, 1994

DAVE STOCKTON	**1**	**68-66-69**	**203**	**$157,500**
JIM ALBUS	2	69-66-69	204	$92,400
GEORGE ARCHER	T3	67-69-73	209	$53,760
JIM DENT	T3	68-72-69	209	$53,760
DAVE EICHELSERGER	T3	71-72-66	209	$53,760
LARRY GILBERT	T3	69-73-67	209	$53,760
CHI CHI RODRIGUEZ	T3	73-67-69	209	$53,760
DALE DOUGLASS	T8	73-69-68	210	$30,100
TOM WEISKOPF	T8	67-74-69	210	$30,100
KERMIT ZARLEY	T8	70-75-65	210	$30,100

FRANKLIN QUEST CHAMPIONSHIP
Park Meadows,
Park City, Utah
August 26-28, 1994

TOM WEISKOPF	**1**	**68-67-69**	**204**	**$75,000**

Franklin Quest Championship, continued

DAVE STOCKTON	2	68-66-70	204	$44,000
JACK KIEFER	T3	68-69-68	205	$33,000
BOB MURPHY	T3	69-66-70	205	$33,000
JIM ALBUS	T5	71-67-69	207	$22,000
GEORGE ARCHER	T5	72-66-69	207	$22,000
TOMMY AARON	T7	70-68-70	208	$16,000
TONY JACKLIN	T7	71-67-70	208	$16,000
JAY SIGEL	T7	69-69-70	208	$16,000
BOB SMITH	10	71-72-67	210	$13,000

GTE NORTHWEST CLASSIC

Inglewood G.C.,
Kenmore, Washington
September 2-4, 1994

SIMON HOBDAY	**1**	**70-69-70**	**209**	**$82,500**
JIM ALBUS	2	66-75-68	209	$48,400
TONY JACKLIN	T3	67-73-71	211	$33,000
LARRY LAORETTI	T3	72-70-69	211	$33,000
JAY SIGEL	T3	72-68-71	211	$33,000
BABE HISKEY	T6	69-75-68	212	$19,800
J.C. SNEAD	T6	73-70-69	212	$19,800
DAVE STOCKTON	T6	74-71-67	212	$19,800
BUTCH BAIRD	T9	72-72-69	213	$14,850
DAVE EICHELBERGER	T9	68-72-73	213	$14,850

QUICKSILVER CLASSIC

Quicksilver G.C.,
Midway, Pennsylvania
September 9-11, 1994

DAVE EICHELBERGER	**1**	**71-67-71**	**209**	**$157,500**
HOMERO BLANCAS	T2	71-71-69	211	$84,000
RAY FLOYD	T2	69-72-70	211	$84,000
BOB DICKSON	T4	69-72-71	212	$51,800
CHI CHI RODRIGUEZ	T4	72-71-69	212	$51,800
TOM WARGO	T4	73-70-69	212	$51,800
JIM COLBERT	T7	69-72-72	213	$33,600
JAY SIGEL	T7	73-71-69	213	$33,600
DAVE STOCKTON	T7	71-70-72	213	$33,600
JIM ALBUS	T10	70-71-73	214	$22,575
ISAO AOKI	T10	73-70-71	214	$22,575
JIM DENT	T10	74-70-70	214	$22,575
SIMON HOBDAY	T10	72-71-71	214	$22,575
GRAHAM MARSH	T10	71-68-75	214	$22,575
J.C. SNEAD	T10	72-69-73	214	$22,575

BANK ONE SENIOR CLASSIC

Kearney Hill Links,
Lexington, Kentucky
September 16-18, 1994

ISAO AOKI	**1**	**69-64-69**	**202**	**$82,500**
CHI CHI RODRIGUEZ	2	71-68-66	205	$48,400
GAY BREWER	T3	68-69-70	207	$33,000
JIM DENT	T3	69-72-66	207	$33,000
JACK KIEFER	T3	69-67-71	207	$33,000
JIM ALBUS	T6	66-68-74	208	$18,700
DAVE EICHELBERGER	T6	68-71-69	208	$18,700
JIMMY POWELL	T6	66-68-74	208	$18,700
DEWITT WEAVER	T6	67-69-72	208	$18,700
LARRY GILBERT	T10	72-67-70	209	$13,200
RIVES MCBEE	T10	69-70-70	209	$13,200
TOM WARGO	T10	69-69-71	209	$13,200

BRICKYARD CROSSING CHAMPIONSHIP

Brickyard Crossing,
Indianapolis, Indiana
September 23-25, 1994

ISAO AOKI	**1**	**66-67**	**133**	**$105,000**
JIMMY POWELL	T2	68-66	134	$56,000
TOM WARGO	T2	66-68	134	$56,000
JIM DENT	T4	65-70	135	$32,200
DAVE EICHELBERGER	T4	71-64	135	$32,200
SIMON HOBDAY	T4	66-69	135	$32,200
GRAHAM MARSH	T4	66-69	135	$32,200
JERRY MCGEE	8	70-66	136	$22,400
LARRY GILBERT	9	65-72	137	$19,600
BOB MURPHY	T10	69-69	138	$17,500
J.C. SNEAD	T10	67-71	138	$17,500

VANTAGE CHAMPIONSHIP

Tanglewood Park,
Clemmons, North Carolina
September 30-October 2, 1994

LARRY GILBERT	**1**	**66-66-66**	**198**	**$225,000**

Vantage Championship, continued

RAY FLOYD	2	70-64-65	199	$132,000
JIM DENT	T3	66-66-69	201	$99,000
DAVE STOCKTON	T3	63-74-64	201	$99,000
CALVIN PEETE	T5	72-66-66	204	$66,000
TOM WARGO	T5	70-66-68	204	$66,000
GEORGE ARCHER	T7	68-72-65	205	$45,750
JIM COLBERT	T7	68-70-67	205	$45,750
DICK GOETZ	T7	68-69-68	205	$45,750
JIMMY POWELL	T7	69-66-70	205	$45,750

THE TRANSAMERICA
Silverado C.C.,
Napa, California
October 7-9, 1994

KERMIT ZARLEY	1	70-68-66	204	$90,000
ISAO AOKI	2	69-72-63	204	$52,800
GARY PLAYER	T3	68-68-70	206	$36,000
J.C. SNEAD	T3	71-69-66	206	$36,000
DAVE STOCKTON	T3	71-69-66	206	$36,000
BUTCH BAIRD	T6	65-71-71	207	$18,600
BOB BRUE	T6	68-69-70	207	$18,600
JOHN PAUL CAIN	T6	69-69-69	207	$18,600
JIM DENT	T6	68-72-67	207	$18,600
JACK KIEFER	T6	70-69-68	207	$18,600
JAY SIGEL	T6	67-69-71	207	$18,600

RALEY'S SENIOR GOLD RUSH
Rancho Murieta C.C.,
Rancho Murieta, California
October 14-16, 1994

BOB MURPHY	1	69-71-68	208	$97,500
DAVE EICHELBERGER	2	68-69-71	208	$57,200
J.C. SNEAD	T3	71-76-63	210	$42,900
JIM ALBUS	T3	69-72-69	210	$42,900
LARRY GILBERT	T5	69-74-69	212	$26,867
BOB CHARLES	T5	71-72-69	212	$26,867
AL GEIBERGER	T5	72-69-71	212	$26,867
GARY PLAYER	8	72-71-70	213	$20,800
DAVE STOCKTON	T9	70-75-69	214	$16,250
TOMMY AYCOCK	T9	69-75-70	214	$16,250
BOB DICKSON	T9	71-72-71	214	$16,250
CHI CHI RODRIGUEZ	T9	70-70-74	214	$16,250

RALPH'S SENIOR CLASSIC
Rancho Park G.C.,
Los Angeles, California
October 21-23, 1994

JACK KIEFER	1	69-65-63	197	$112,500
DALE DOUGLASS	2	70-67-61	198	$66,000
JIM COLBERT	3	68-67-66	201	$54,000
JIM DENT	T4	68-63-71	202	$30,500
TONY JACKLIN	T4	65-72-65	202	$30,500
BOB MURPHY	T4	68-69-65	202	$30,500
JIMMY POWELL	T4	67-69-66	202	$30,500
BEN SMITH	T4	71-68-63	202	$30,500
KERMIT ZARLEY	T4	68-68-66	202	$30,500
DICK LOTZ	T10	68-68-67	203	$17,250
BOBBY NICHOLS	T10	64-71-68	203	$17,250
JAY SIGEL	T10	70-68-65	203	$17,250
J.C. SNEAD	T10	68-67-68	203	$17,250

KAANAPALI CLASSIC
Kaanapali G.C. (North),
Lahaina, Maui, Hawaii
October 28-30, 1994

BOB MURPHY	1	62-67-66	195	$82,500
JACK KIEFER	2	66-66-65	197	$48,400
DALE DOUGLASS	3	68-66-65	199	$39,600
GEORGE ARCHER	4	70-65-65	200	$33,000
LARRY MOWRY	5	68-65-68	201	$26,400
JERRY MCGEE	6	66-64-72	202	$22,000
HOMERO BLANCAS	T7	71-65-67	203	$17,600
HARRY TOSCANO	T7	70-67-66	203	$17,600
TOM WARGO	T7	68-64-71	203	$17,600
GIBBY GILBERT	T10	70-67-68	205	$13,200
LARRY GILBERT	T10	70-67-68	205	$13,200
ROCKY THOMPSON	T10	67-69-69	205	$13,200

LPGA TOUR

HEALTHSOUTH PALM BEACH CLASSIC
Wycliffe G. & C.C.,
Lake Worth, Florida
February 4-6, 1994

DAWN COE-JONES	1	67-69-65	201	$60,000

Healthsouth Palm Beach Classic, continued

LAURI MERTEN	2	71-67-64	202	$37,237
LAURA DAVIES	3	69-65-69	203	$27,173
LISA WALTERS	4	66-68-70	204	$21,134
DOTTIE MOCHRIE	5	70-67-69	206	$17,108
JAN STEPHENSON	6	70-68-69	207	$14,089
JULIE LARSEN	T7	71-69-68	208	$11,170
PAT BRADLEY	T7	68-69-71	208	$11,170
ROBIN WALTON	9	71-70-68	209	$8,527
CINDY FIGG-CURRIER	9	70-69-70	209	$8,527
TRACY KERDYK	9	68-70-71	209	$8,527

CUP O'NOODLES HAWAIIAN LADIES OPEN

Ko Olina G.C.,
Ewa Beach, Hawaii
February 17-19, 1994

MARTA FIGUERAS-DOTTI	1	68-70-71	209	$75,000
JANE GEDDES	2	69-70-71	210	$46,546
VICKI FERGON	T3	69-74-69	212	$27,256
TRACY KERDYK	T3	70-71-71	212	$27,256
VAL SKINNER	T3	67-71-74	212	$27,256
SHERRI STEINHAUER	T6	71-73-69	213	$11,377
JOAN PETCOCK	T6	72-71-70	213	$11,377
JENNY LIDBACK	T6	71-72-70	213	$11,377
BETH DANIEL	T6	72-70-71	213	$11,377
MARIANNE MORRIS	T6	71-71-71	213	$11,377
YUKO MORIGUCHI	T6	71-70-72	213	$11,377
MUFFIN SPENCER-DEVLIN	T6	68-73-72	213	$11,377
KATHRYN MARSHALL	T6	71-69-73	213	$11,377
NINA FOUST	T6	68-71-74	213	$11,377

CHRYSLER-PLYMOUTH TOURNAMENT OF CHAMPIONS

Grand Cypress Resort,
Orlando, Florida
March 2-5, 1994

DOTTIE MOCHRIE	1	72-75-71-69	287	$115,000
LAURI MERTEN	T2	71-78-70-70	289	$62,250
NANCY LOPEZ	T2	75-72-69-73	289	$62,250
MEG MALLON	4	75-76-71-68	290	$41,000
KRISTI ALBERS	5	75-77-70-69	291	$33,100
MISSIE BERTEOTTI	6	75-74-72-71	292	$27,200

DANA DORMANN	T7	75-76-71-71	293	$20,500
DONNA ANDREWS	T7	72-77-71-73	293	$20,500
BETSY KING	T7	72-71-74-76	293	$20,500
LAURA DAVIES	10	73-76-72-74	295	$16,350

PING/WELCH'S CHAMPIONSHIP

Randolph North G.C.,
Tucson, Arizona
March 10-13, 1994

DONNA ANDREWS	1	66-68-69-73	276	$63,750
JUDY DICKINSON	T2	71-71-69-68	279	$34,217
BRANDIE BURTON	T2	69-68-69-73	279	$34,217
MICHELLE MCGANN	T4	72-70-69-69	280	$20,316
SHERRI STEINHAUER	T4	66-70-72-72	280	$20,316
LAURI MERTEN	T6	73-70-67-71	281	$13,793
JAN STEPHENSON	T6	67-72-71-71	281	$13,793
HELEN ALFREDSSON	T8	74-71-68-69	282	$10,051
DALE EGGELING	T8	71-72-67-72	282	$10,051
DANA DORMANN	T8	67-74-67-74	282	$10,051

STANDARD REGISTER PING

Moon Valley C.C.,
Phoenix, Arizona
March 17-20, 1994

LAURA DAVIES	1	69-72-66-70	277	$105,000
BETH DANIE	T2	71-71-70-69	281	$56,359
ELAINE CROSBY	T2	73-69-66-73	281	$56,359
ALICE RITZMAN	T4	70-72-71-70	283	$30,527
HIROMI KOBAYASHI	T4	70-70-72-71	283	$30,527
KELLY ROBBINS	T4	68-70-71-74	283	$30,527
BRANDIE BURTON	7	71-69-72-72	284	$20,782
MICHELLE MCGANN	T8	75-68-72-70	285	$16,555
TERRY-JO MYERS	T8	71-72-71-71	285	$16,555
DOTTIE MOCHRIE	T8	72-70-70-73	285	$16,555

NABISCO DINAH SHORE

Mission Hills C.C.,
Rancho Mirage, California
March 24-27, 1994

DONNA ANDREWS	1	70-69-67-70	276	$105,000
LAURA DAVIES	2	70-68-69-70	277	$65,165

Nabisco Dinah Shore, continued

TAMMIE GREEN	3	70-72-69-68	279	$47,553
JAN STEPHENSON	4	70-69-70-71	280	$36,985
MICHELLE MCGANN	5	70-68-70-73	281	$29,940
GAIL GRAHAM	T6	73-71-71-68	283	$21,251
KELLY ROBBINS	T6	73-70-69-71	283	$21,251
BRANDIE BURTON	T6	73-73-65-72	283	$21,251
HOLLIS STACY	T9	72-72-70-70	284	$15,674
NANCY LOPEZ	T9	68-72-73-71	284	$15,674

For a complete summary of all players making the cut at the Dinah Shore, please refer to "1994 Major Championships"

ATLANTA WOMEN'S CHAMPIONSHIP
Eagle's Landing C.C.,
Stockbridge, Georgia
April 15-17, 1994

VAL SKINNER	1	70-68-68	206	$97,500
LISELOTTE NEUMANN	2	69-67-71	207	$60,510
BETH DANIEL	3	69-70-70	209	$44,156
JUDY DICKINSON	4	67-70-73	210	$34,344
DEBBIE MASSEY	T5	72-72-67	211	$23,331
HELEN ALFREDSSON	T5	68-74-69	211	$23,331
DOTTIE MOCHRIE	T5	71-69-71	211	$23,331
PATTY SHEEHAN	T8	73-71-68	212	$12,989
NANCY SCRANTON	T8	71-73-68	212	$12,989
MICHELE REDMAN	T8	74-68-70	212	$12,989
PAGE DUNLAP	T8	71-71-70	212	$12,989
KRISTI ALBERS	T8	71-71-70	212	$12,989
MELISSA MCNAMARA	T8	69-72-71	212	$12,989
JANE GEDDES	T8	69-72-71	212	$12,989

SPRINT SENIOR CHALLENGE
Indigo Lakes G. & T. Resort,
Daytona Beach, Florida
April 30-May 1, 1994

SANDRA PALMER	1	73-70	143	$40,000
MICKEY WRIGHT	2	73-74	147	$30,000
KATHY WHITWORTH	3	73-75	148	$20,000
MARLENE HAGGE	T4	75-76	151	$17,000

DONNA CAPONI	T4	74-77	151	$17,000
SANDRA HAYNIE	6	74-79	153	$14,000
JANE BLALOCK	7	80-77	157	$12,000
JUDY RANKIN	8	78-80	158	$11,000
CAROL MANN	9	80-81	161	$10,000
MARILYNN SMITH	10	79-86	165	$9,000

SPRINT CHAMPIONSHIP
Indigo Lakes G. & T. Resort
Daytona Beach, Florida
April 28-May 1, 1994

SHERRI STEINHAUER	1	68-68-67-70	273	$180,000
KELLY ROBBINS	2	68-68-70-68	274	$111,711
BARB BUNKOWSKY	3	68-72-68-70	278	$81,519
BETH DANIE	4	71-71-72-67	281	$63,404
ALICIA DIBOS	5	66-76-70-70	282	$51,326
FLORENCE DESCAMPE	T6	74-70-71-68	283	$36,431
CHRIS JOHNSON	T6	68-75-72-68	283	$36,431
TAMMIE GREEN	T6	71-71-70-71	283	$36,431
MARTHA NAUSE	T9	71-75-72-66	284	$23,550
DOTTIE MOCHRIE	T9	68-73-74-69	284	$23,550
DAWN COE-JONES	T9	72-71-71-70	284	$23,550
JUDY DICKINSON	T9	69-71-71-73	284	$23,550
SALLY LITTLE	T9	68-72-70-74	284	$23,550

SARA LEE CLASSIC
Hermitage G.C.,
Old Hickory, Tennessee
May 6-8, 1994

LAURA DAVIES	1	65-70-68	203	$78,750
MEG MALLON	2	65-70-69	204	$48,873
DEB RICHARD	3	71-71-64	206	$35,664
DINA AMMACCAPANE	T4	71-68-69	208	$22,895
AMY BENZ	T4	67-71-70	208	$22,895
JANE CRAFTER	T4	64-72-72	208	$22,895
BETSY KING	T7	71-71-67	209	$14,661
ROSIE JONES	T7	70-71-68	209	$14,661
DANIELLE AMMACCAPANE	T9	69-75-66	210	$11,183
TAMMIE GREEN	T9	71-70-69	210	$11,183
GAIL GRAHAM	T9	73-64-73	210	$11,183

MCDONALD'S LPGA CHAMPIONSHIP
Du Pont C.C.,
Wilmington, Delaware
May 12-15, 1994

LAURA DAVIES	1	**70-72-69-68**	**279**	**$165,000**
ALICE RITZMAN	2	68-73-71-70	282	$102,402
ELAINE CROSBY	T3	76-71-69-67	283	$54,660
PAT BRADLEY	T3	73-73-70-67	283	$54,660
HIROMI KOBAYASHI	T3	72-73-71-67	283	$54,660
LISELOTTE NEUMANN	T3	74-73-67-69	283	$54,660
SHERRI STEINHAUER	T7	75-70-72-68	285	$27,676
AMY ALCOTT	T7	71-75-70-69	285	$27,666
BETH DANIEL	T7	72-74-68-71	285	$27,676
PATTY SHEEHAN	T7	72-68-72-73	285	$27,676

For a complete summary of all players making the cut at the
McDonald's LPGA, please refer to "1994 Major Championships"

LADY KEYSTONE OPEN
Hershey C.C.,
Hershey, Pennsylvania
May 20-22, 1994

ELAINE CROSBY	1	**69-72-70**	**211**	**$60,000**
LAURA DAVIES	2	70-71-71	212	$37,237
VAL SKINNER	T3	70-71-72	213	$24,153
BETSY KING	T3	70-70-73	213	$24,153
NOELLE DAGHE	T5	69-74-71	214	$13,384
TINA BARRETT	T5	75-67-72	214	$13,384
MISSIE MCGEORGE	T5	74-68-72	214	$13,384
MISSIE BERTEOTTI	T5	66-75-73	214	$13,384
LAURIE BROWER	T9	76-69-70	215	$7,862
DONNA ANDREWS	T9	73-72-70	215	$7,862
DENISE BALDWIN	T9	74-69-72	215	$7,862
JAN STEPHENSON	T9	72-71-72	215	$7,862
PEARL SINN	T9	70-72-73	215	$7,862

LPGA CORNING CLASSIC
Corning C.C.,
Corning, New York
May 26-29, 1994

BETH DANIEL	1	**67-71-71-69**	**278**	**$75,000**
STEPHANIE FARWIN	T2	68-71-69-71	279	$40,256

NANCY RAMSBOTTOM	T2	64-71-71-73	279	$40,256
KELLY ROBBINS	T4	75-71-68-67	281	$20,065
TAMMIE GREEN	T4	72-73-67-69	281	$20,065
COLLEEN WALKER	T4	71-70-68-72	281	$20,065
MARTHA NAUSE	T4	68-69-72-72	281	$20,065
DONNA ANDREWS	T8	72-71-70-70	283	$12,454
DEB RICHARD	T8	71-71-71-70	283	$12,454
CHRIS JOHNSON	T10	72-73-73-66	284	$9,668
LAURA DAVIES	T10	70-74-68-72	284	$9,668
PAT BRADLEY	T10	65-73-70-76	284	$9,668

JCPENNEY/LPGA SKINS GAME
Stonebriar C.C.,
Frisco, Texas
May 28-29, 1994

PATTY SHEEHAN	1	**13 SKINS**	**$285,000**
BETSY KING	2	5 SKINS	$165,000
NANCY LOPEZ	T3	0 SKINS	
BRANDIE BURTON	T3	0 SKINS	

OLDSMOBILE CLASSIC
Walnut Hills C.C.,
East Lansing, Michigan
June 2-5, 1994

BETH DANIEL	1	**67-63-70-68**	**268**	**$90,000**
LISA KIGGENS	2	68-69-67-68	272	$55,855
AMY BENZ	3	68-67-70-68	273	$40,759
MEG MALLON	4	68-66-72-69	275	$31,702
TANIA ABITBOL	T5	72-69-67-69	277	$23,398
DONNA ANDREWS	T5	70-69-68-70	277	$23,398
MARIANNE MORRIS	7	68-70-69-71	278	$17,813
SHERRI TURNER	8	72-69-70-68	279	$15,700
DOTTIE MOCHRIE	T9	71-72-69-68	280	$13,435
COLLEEN WALKER	T9	75-67-68-70	280	$13,435

MINNESOTA LPGA CLASSIC
Edinburgh USA,
Brooklyn Park, MN
June 6-12, 1994

LISELOTTE NEUMANN	1	**68-71-66**	**205**	**$75,000**

Minnesota LPGA Classic, continued

HIROMI KOBAYASHI	2	72-70-65	207	$46,546
SHERRI STEINHAUER	3	72-70-66	208	$33,966
AMY ALCOTT	4	71-69-69	209	$26,418
KATIE PETERSON-PARKER	5	72-71-68	211	$21,386
JULIE LARSEN	6	70-73-69	212	$17,612
KELLY ROBBINS	T7	71-78-64	213	$11,447
TERRY-JO MYERS	T7	73-71-69	213	$11,447
MICHELLE MCGANN	T7	72-72-69	213	$11,447
DEB RICHARD	T7	71-73-69	213	$11,447
VAL SKINNER	T7	70-73-70	213	$11,447
CAROLINE PIERCE	T7	71-68-74	213	$11,447

ROCHESTER INTERNATIONAL
Locust Hill C.C.,
Pittsford, New York
June 16-19, 1994

LISA KIGGENS	1	67-69-71-66	273	$75,000
DAWN COE-JONES	2	69-67-71-67	274	$46,546
BETSY KING	3	66-68-72-69	275	$33,966
PATTY SHEEHAN	4	67-72-67-71	277	$26,418
KELLY ROBBINS	T5	68-69-73-69	279	$19,499
KRISTI ALBERS	T5	69-68-69-73	279	$19,499
TAMMIE GREEN	T7	71-70-69-70	280	$13,963
MICHELE REDMAN	T7	68-67-71-74	280	$13,963
HOLLIS STACY	T9	71-70-71-69	281	$10,659
HELEN ALFREDSSON	T9	69-70-70-72	281	$10,659

SHOPRITE LPGA CLASSIC
Greate Bay C.C.,
Somers Point, New Jersey
June 24-26, 1994

DONNA ANDREWS	1	67-66-74	207	$75,000
MICHELLE ESTILL	2	67-77-65	209	$46,546
CAROLINE PIERCE	T3	70-69-71	210	$24,845
KIM SAIKI	T3	68-71-71	210	$24,845
DOTTIE MOCHRIE	T3	69-68-73	210	$24,845
BARB BUNKOWSKY	T3	67-69-74	210	$24,845
JANET ANDERSON	T7	71-70-70	211	$13,250
PAT BRADLEY	T7	67-74-70	211	$13,250
HELEN ALFREDSSON	T7	71-68-72	211	$13,250
MEG MALLON	T10	74-68-70	212	$9,644
SALLY LITTLE	T10	68-73-71	212	$9,644
JUDY DICKINSON	T10	68-72-72	212	$9,644

YOUNGSTOWN-WARREN LPGA CLASSIC
Avalon Lakes G.C.,
Warren, OH
July 1-3, 1994

TAMMIE GREEN	1	67-69-70	206	$82,500
COLLEEN WALKER	2	68-69-71	208	$51,201
KIM SHIPMAN	T3	69-69-71	209	$33,211
DOTTIE MOCHRIE	T3	68-70-71	209	$33,211
BARB BUNKOWSKY	T5	74-68-68	210	$18,404
BETSY KING	T5	70-71-69	210	$18,404
KATIE PETERSON-PARKER	T5	69-71-70	210	$18,404
JEAN ZEDLITZ	T5	68-71-71	210	$18,404
JENNY LIDBACK	T9	71-72-68	211	$10,424
KELLY ROBBINS	T9	70-73-68	211	$10,424
PATTY SHEEHAN	T9	72-70-69	211	$10,424
LAURA BAUGH	T9	71-69-71	211	$10,424
DONNA ANDREWS	T9	71-69-71	211	$10,424

JAMIE FARR TOLEDO CLASSIC
Highland Meadows G.C.,
Sylvania, Ohio
July 8-10, 1994

KELLY ROBBINS	1	69-70-65	204	$75,000
TAMMIE GREEN	2	66-71-67	204	$46,546
MEG MALLON	3	67-70-69	206	$33,966
KRIS TSCHETTER	4	68-71-69	208	$26,418
BETH DANIEL	T5	71-71-67	209	$15,750
MICHELLE ESTILL	T5	71-70-68	209	$15,750
JUDY DICKINSON	T5	70-71-68	209	$15,750
DOTTIE MOCHRIE	T5	69-70-70	209	$15,750
LAURI MERTEN	T5	66-71-72	209	$15,750
DAWN COE-JONES	T10	71-71-68	210	$9,662
KIM WILLIAMS	T10	68-72-70	210	$9,662
AMY ALCOTT	T10	66-72-72	210	$9,662

JAL BIG APPLE CLASSIC
Wykagyl C.C.,
New Rochelle, New York
July 14-17, 1994

BETH DANIEL	1	70-69-66-71	276	$97,500
LAURA DAVIES	2	71-69-70-66	276	$60,510

JAL Big Apple Classic, continued

NANCY RAMSBOTTOM	T3	67-74-72-65	278	$39,250
NANCI BOWEN	T3	68-70-72-68	278	$39,250
PAT BRADLEY	5	70-67-72-70	279	$27,801
MISSIE BERTEOTTI	6	70-71-67-72	280	$22,895
CHRIS JOHNSON	7	73-68-73-67	281	$19,297
ALICIA DIBOS	T8	77-68-69-68	282	$16,190
MICHELE REDMAN	T8	69-71-71-71	282	$16,190
HELEN ALFREDSSON	T10	73-72-69-69	283	$11,736
MEG MALLON	T10	74-70-67-72	283	$11,736
LISA KIGGENS	T10	71-67-71-74	283	$11,736
DALE EGGELING	T10	69-68-72-74	283	$11,736
JULI INKSTER	T10	72-69-67-75	283	$11,736

U.S. WOMEN'S OPEN
Indianwood G. & C.C.,
Lake Orion, Michigan
July 21-24, 1994

PATTY SHEEHAN	1	66-71-69-71	277	$155,000
TAMMIE GREEN	2	66-72-69-71	278	$85,000
LISELOTTE NEUMANN	3	69-72-71-69	281	$47,752
TANIA ABITBOL	T5	72-68-73-70	283	$31,132
ALICIA DIBOS	T5	69-68-73-73	283	$31,132
MEG MALLON	T7	70-72-73-69	284	$21,486
AMY ALCOTT	T7	71-67-77-69	284	$21,486
BETSY KING	T7	69-71-72-72	284	$21,486
KELLY ROBBINS	T10	71-72-70-72	285	$16,445
DONNA ANDREWS	T10	67-72-70-76	285	$16,445
HELEN ALFREDSSON	T10	63-69-76-77	285	$16,445

For a complete summary of all players making the cut at the U.S.
Women's Opens, please refer to "1994 Major Championships"

PING/WELCH'S CHAMPIONSHIP
Blue Hill C.C.,
Canton, Massachusetts
July 28-31, 1994

HELEN ALFREDSSON	1	70-68-70-66	274	$67,500
PAT BRADLEY	T2	67-71-72-68	278	$36,230
JULI INKSTER	T2	68-69-72-69	278	$36,230
SHERRI STEINHAUER	T4	74-69-72-65	280	$21,511
PEARL SINN	T4	70-69-73-68	280	$21,511
ALICE MILLER	T6	74-69-71-67	281	$13,661
MELISSA MCNAMARA	T6	68-70-73-70	281	$13,661
GAIL GRAHAM	T6	72-70-68-71	281	$13,661
ROBIN WALTON	9	70-69-72-71	282	$10,642

JUDY DICKINSON	T10	71-71-72-69	283	$8,695
LAURI MERTEN	T10	70-71-72-70	283	$8,695
ANNIKA SORENSTAM	T10	70-68-71-74	283	$8,695

MCCALL'S LPGA CLASSIC AT STRATTON MOUNTAIN
Stratton Mountain C.C.,
Stratton Mountain, Vermont
August 4-7, 1994

CAROLYN HILL	1	69-72-65-69	275	$75,000
NANCY RAMSBOTTOM	2	69-69-70-70	278	$46,546
PAT BRADLEY	T3	73-73-71-66	283	$27,256
DEB RICHARD	T3	71-69-74-69	283	$27,256
JOAN PETCOCK	T3	73-68-68-74	283	$27,256
DOTTIE MOCHRIE	T6	73-69-72-70	284	$16,228
KRIS TSCHETTER	T6	70-69-72-73	284	$16,228
NANCY LOPEZ	T8	72-70-72-71	285	$11,825
DONNA ANDREWS	T8	68-71-73-73	285	$11,825
BETS KING	T8	64-73-72-76	285	$11,825

WEETABIX WOMEN'S BRITISH OPEN
Woburn G. & C.C.,
Milton Keynes, England
August 11-14, 1994

LISELOTTE NEUMANN	1	71-67-70-72	280	$80,325
DOTTIE MOCHRIE	T2	73-66-74-70	283	$41,693
ANNIKA SORENSTAM	T2	69-75-69-70	283	$41,693
LAURA DAVIES	T4	74-66-73-71	284	$22,376
CORINNE DIBNAH	T4	75-70-67-72	284	$22,376
CINDY FIGG-CURRIER	6	69-74-68-74	285	$16,448
HELEN ALFREDSSON	7	71-76-71-68	286	$14,153
TRACY HANSON	8	74-73-66-74	287	$12,240
SUZANNE STRUDWICK	T9	71-71-71-75	288	$9,563
VAL SKINNER	T9	77-71-66-74	288	$9,563
CAROLINE PIERCE	T9	70-75-71-72	288	$9,563

CHILDREN'S MEDICAL CENTER LPGA CLASSIC
C.C. of the North,
Dayton, Ohio
August 12-14, 1994

MAGGIE WILL	1	70-70-70	210	$52,500

Children's Medical Center LPGA Classicc, continued

JILL BRILES-HINTON	T2	68-72-70	210	$28,179
ALICIA DIBOS	T2	67-72-71	210	$28,179
TRACY KERDYK	T4	74-69-68	211	$16,731
BETH DANIEL	T4	70-70-71	211	$16,731
JUDY DICKINSON	6	69-75-68	212	$12,328
DEB RICHARD	T7	73-73-67	213	$ 8,805
ELLIE GIBSON	T7	70-72-71	213	$ 8,805
ROSIE JONES	T7	68-73-72	213	$ 8,805
SHELLEY HAMLIN	T7	72-68-73	213	$ 8,805

CHICAGO CHALLENGE

White Eagle G.C.,
Naperville, Illinois
August 18-21, 1994

JANE GEDDES	1	68-69-68-67	272	$75,000
ROBIN WALTON	T2	72-70-68-65	275	$40,256
DALE EGGELING	T2	70-67-71-67	275	$40,256
JUDY DICKINSON	4	70-70-71-67	278	$26,418
CATHY JOHNSTON-FORBES	T5	69-70-71-69	279	$17,947
BRANDIE BURTON	T5	71-72-66-70	279	$17,947
JANICE GIBSON	T5	70-67-71-71	279	$17,947
MISSIE MCGEORGE	T8	69-71-69-71	280	$12,454
MARGARET PLATT	T8	69-70-69-72	280	$12,454
MICHELLE MCGANN	T10	68-71-74-68	281	$9,650
KATIE PETERSEN-PARKER	T10	65-72-75-69	281	$9,650

du MAURIER LTD. CLASSIC

Ottawa Hunt and G.C.,
Ottawa, Ontario, Canada
August 25-28, 1994

MARTHA NAUSE	1	65-71-72-71	279	$120,000
MICHELLE MCGANN	2	66-71-71-72	280	$74,474
LISELOTTE NEUMANN	3	70-67-71-73	281	$54,346
JANE GEDDES	T4	74-67-70-72	283	$34,888
MEG MALLON	T4	70-72-68-73	283	$34,888
BETSY KING	T4	67-69-74-73	283	$34,888
DAWN COE-JONES	T7	72-70-71-71	284	$20,128
MARIANNE MORRIS	T7	69-72-70-73	284	$20,128
JUDY DICKINSON	T7	72-68-70-74	284	$20,128
KELLY ROBBINS	T7	66-70-73-75	284	$20,128

For a complete summary of all players making the cut at the
duMaurier Classic, please refer to "1994 Major Championships"

STATE FARM RAIL CLASSIC

Rail G.C.,
Springfield, Illinois
September 3-5, 1994

BARB MUCHA	1	67-69-67	203	$78,750
KIM SHIPMAN	2	68-67-69	204	$48,873
GAIL GRAHAM	T3	70-66-69	205	$31,701
SUZANNE STRUDWICK	T3	69-66-70	205	$31,701
LORI WEST	T5	70-69-67	206	$15,630
HIROMI KOBAYASHI	T5	69-70-67	206	$15,630
MICHELLE MCGANN	T5	70-68-68	206	$15,630
MEG MALLON	T5	66-72-68	206	$15,630
STEPHANIE FARWIG	T5	66-70-70	206	$15,630
KRISTI ALBERS	T5	66-70-70	206	$15,630

PING-CELLULAR ONE GOLF CHAMPIONSHIP

Columbia Edgewater C.C.
Portland, Oregon
September 9-11, 1994

MISSIE MCGEORGE	1	72-69-66	207	$75,000
BETSY KING	2	71-70-69	210	$46,546
CINDY RARICK	T4	72-71-68	211	$30,192
ALLISON FINNEY	T4	71-69-71	211	$30,192
SALLY LITTLE	T5	70-74-68	212	$14,886
DONNA ANDREWS	T5	73-69-70	212	$14,886
ELAINE CROSBY	T5	72-68-72	212	$14,886
ELLIE GIBSON	T5	68-72-72	212	$14,886
CHRIS JOHNSON	T5	72-67-73	212	$14,886
VAL SKINNER	T5	67-72-73	212	$14,886

SAFECO CLASSIC

Meridian Valley C.C.,
Kent, Washington
September 15-18, 1994

DEB RICHARD	1	71-68-70-67	276	$75,000
TAMMIE GREEN	T2	72-69-69-67	277	$32,079
ROSIE JONES	T2	70-69-70-68	277	$32,079
MICHELLE ESTILL	T2	68-70-69-70	277	$32,079
CHRIS JOHNSON	T2	68-71-67-71	277	$32,079
VICKI FERGON	T6	72-68-68-71	279	$15,179

Safeco LPGA Classic, continued

BETSY KING	T6	69-68-70-72	279	$15,179
ANNIKA SORENSTAM	T6	67-72-66-74	279	$15,179
KELLY ROBBINS	T9	73-68-68-71	280	$11,196
JULI INKSTER	T9	71-68-69-72	280	$11,196

HEARTLAND CLASSIC
Forest Hills C.C.,
St. Louis, Missouri
September 29-October 2, 1994

LISELOTTE NEUMANN	**1**	**70-71-67-70**	**278**	**$75,000**
ELAINE CROSBY	T2	71-71-69-70	281	$40,256
PEARL SINN	T2	67-70-72-72	281	$40,256
SHERRI TURNER	T4	73-72-71-67	283	$23,902
DEB RICHARD	T4	71-70-68-74	283	$23,902
CHRIS JOHNSON	T5	77-71-68-68	284	$16,228
JANE GEDDES	T5	70-73-70-71	284	$16,228
JOAN PETCOCK	T7	73-74-73-65	285	$13,083
CINDY SCHREYER	T8	73-71-76-66	286	$9,812
CAROLYN HILL	T8	74-72-72-68	286	$9,812
GAIL GRAHAM	T8	72-71-72-71	286	$9,812
NANCI BOWEN	T8	71-71-73-71	286	$9,812
COLLEEN WALKER	T8	71-70-73-72	286	$9,812

WORLD CHAMPIONSHIP OF WOMEN'S GOLF
Naples National G.C.,
Naples, Florida
October 13-16, 1994

BETH DANIEL	**1**	**68-70-71-65**	**274**	**$105,000**
ELAINE CROSBY	2	70-66-69-72	277	$55,000
LAURA DAVIES	3	68-73-67-71	279	$35,000
LISELOTTE NEUMANN	T4	71-67-72-70	280	$22,500
DOTTIE MOCHRIE	T4	67-69-73-71	280	$22,500
HELEN ALFREDSSON	6	71-72-68-71	282	$18,000
DONNA ANDREWS	T7	69-71-73-70	283	$16,000
SHERRI STEINHAUER	T7	67-71-75-70	283	$16,000
MARTHA NAUSE	T7	73-67-72-71	283	$16,000
VAL SKINNER	10	69-69-75-71	284	$14,000

NIKE TOUR

NIKE INLAND EMPIRE OPEN
Moreno Valley Ranch G.C.,
Moreno Valley, California
February 3-6, 1994

SKIP KENDALL	**1**	**65-67-65**	**191**	**$36,000**
EMLYN AUBREY	2	67-67-69	203	$22,700
BILL MURCHISON	3	66-68-71	205	$16,500
JEFF BARLOW	T4	69-68-69	206	$10,000
JACK FERENZ	T4	67-69-70	206	$10,000
BRYAN GORMAN	T4	68-67-71	206	$10,000
DAVID JACKSON	T4	70-71-65	206	$10,000
R.W. EAKS	T8	69-67-71	207	$5,100
JOHN ELLIOTT	T8	69-65-73	207	$5,100
JEFF HART	T8	67-70-70	207	$5,100
CHRIS PEDDICORD	T8	66-71-70	207	$5,100
MIKE SMITH	T8	73-67-67	207	$5,100

NIKE MONTERREY OPEN
Club Campestre,
Monterrey, Mexico
March 3-6, 1994

SCOTT GUMP	**1**	**67-67-68-67**	**269**	**$36,000**
BRIAN HENNINGER	2	67-70-66-67	270	$22,700
ROBERT FRIEND	3	68-65-68-70	271	$16,500
CLARK BURROUGHS	4	69-68-70-65	272	$12,500
TIM LOUSTALOT	T5	69-67-74-64	274	$7,583
CHRIS PERRY	T5	67-70-68-69	274	$7,583
J.P. HAYES	T5	68-68-68-70	274	$7,583
BILL PORTER	T5	66-68-69-71	274	$7,583
LARRY RENTZ	T5	70-64-69-71	274	$7,583
MONTE SCHEINBLUM	T5	69-68-66-71	274	$7,583

NIKE PENSACOLA CLASSIC
The Moors,
Milton, FL
March 31-April 3, 1994

BRUCE VAUGHAN	**1**	**68-66-66-71**	**271**	**$36,000**

NIKE Pensacola Open, continued

RON PHILO	2	62-70-69-71 272		$22,700
PAT BATES	T3	69-67-66-71 273		$14,500
SKIP KENDALL	T3	71-69-63-70 273		$14,500
WEBB HEINTZELMAN	T5	70-72-65-67 274		$7,583
HARRY RUDOLPH	T5	72-70-67-65 274		$7,583
DAVID DUVAL	T5	72-69-65-68 274		$7,583
ROBERT FRIEND	T5	71-67-68-68 274		$7,583
SCOTT GUMP	T5	70-66-70-68 274		$7,583
FRANKLIN LANGHAM	T5	68-65-69-72 274		$7,583

NIKE MISSISSIPPI GULF COAST CLASSIC
Windance G. & C.C.,
Gulfport, Mississippi
April 7-10, 1994

JOHN ELLIOTT	**1**	**68-71-68-69 276**		**$31,500**
CHRIS PERRY	2	67-69-71-69 276		$19,862
SKIP KENDALL	T3	70-67-67-73 277		$12,687
RICK PEARSON	T3	74-68-68-67 277		$12,687
CRAIG KANADA	T5	72-68-72-67 279		$7,546
TIM LOUSTALOT	T5	69-74-69-67 279		$7,546
BUDDY GARDNER	T5	67-71-72-69 279		$7,546
BOB WOLCOTT	T5	66-68-75-70 279		$7,546
JEFF COSTON	T9	70-69-72-69 280		$3 815
DAVID DUVAL	T9	72-67-72-69 280		$3,815
JIM FURYK	T9	70-70-69-71 280		$3,815
HUGH ROYER III	T9	73-70-69-68 280		$3,815
DAVE STOCKTON, JR.	T9	71-67-71-71 280		$3,815

NIKE PANAMA CITY BEACH CLASSIC
Hombre G.C.,
Panama City Beach, Florida
April 15-17, 1994

KEITH FERGUS	**1**	**66-64-72**	**202**	**$31,500**
TOMMY ARMOUR	2	67-68-69	204	$19,862
ROBERT FRIEND	3	68-66-72	206	$14,437
MIKE BRISKY	T4	71-67-69	207	$9,333
TOM BYRUM	T4	73-65-69	207	$9,333
SCOTT GUMP	T4	69-67-71	207	$9,333

WOODY AUSTIN	7	72-67-69	208	$7,000
PATRICK BURKE	T8	72-67-70	209	$3,987
JEFF GALLAGHER	T8	74-68-67	209	$3,987
JOHN MAGINNES	T8	70-69-70	209	$3,987
LEE RINKER	T8	72-66-71	209	$3,987
STEVE RINTOUL	T8	71-69-69	209	$3,987
CHRIS RULE	T8	69-68-72	209	$3,987
SONNY SKINNER	T8	62-62-71	209	$3,987

NIKE SHREVEPORT OPEN
Southern Trace C.C.,
Shreveport, Louisiana
April 21-24, 1994

OMAR URESTI	**1**	**65-71-63-71**	**270**	**$31,500**
PAT BATES	2	67-67-69-67	270	$19,862
TOMMY ARMOUR	3	71-68-67-66	272	$14,437
MIKE SCHUCIHART	4	70-66-70-67	273	$10,937
CHRIS PERRY	T5	69-68-68-69	274	$8,532
LANCE TEN BROECK	T5	69-66-71-68	274	$8,532
JAY COOPER	T7	72-68-70-66	276	$5,687
STEVE FORD	T7	66-71-69-70	276	$5,687
STEVE RINTOUL	T7	68-71-67-70	276	$5,687
BRUCE VAUGHAN	T7	68-70-73-65	276	$5,687

NIKE ALABAMA CLASSIC
Cherokee Ridge C.C.,
Union Grove, Alabama
April 28-May 1, 1994

TOMMY TOLLES	**1**	**66-69-70-69**	**274**	**$36,000**
CLARK BURROUGHS	2	69-71-66-69	275	$22,700
JEFF REHAUT	T3	67-70-72-67	276	$14,500
DAVID DUVAL	T3	73-66-65-72	276	$14,500
JERRY KELLY	5	69-67-71-70	277	$10,500
DAVID KIRKPATRICK	6	69-69-69-72	279	$9,000
GREG BRUCKNER	T7	70-68-70-72	280	$7,000
ROBERT FRIEND	T7	72-67-73-68	280	$7,000
TIM LOUSTALOT	T7	72-70-68-70	280	$7,000
BARRY FABYAN	T10	71-69-69-72	281	$3,950
JEFF GALLAGHER	T10	70-68-69-74	281	$3,950
PETER PERSONS	T10	67-68-72-74	281	$3,950
LEE RINKER	T10	72-65-72-72	281	$3,950

NIKE SOUTH CAROLINA CLASSIC
C.C. of South Carolina,
Florence, South Carolina
May 5-8, 1994

CHARLES RYMER	1	67-67-72-68	274	$31,500
PAT BATES	2	69-67-72-67	275	$19,862
CRAIG KANADA	T3	67-71-69-69	276	$12,687
BRUCE VAUGHAN	T3	65-71-73-67	276	$12,687
MIKE SCHUCHART	5	72-68-69-68	277	$9,187
TOMMY TOLLES	T6	66-71-73-68	278	$6,125
WOODY AUSTIN	T6	70-72-70-66	278	$6,125
TOM CARR	T6	68-71-75-64	278	$6,125
MIKE SPOSA	T6	68-71-70-69	278	$6,125

NIKE CENTRAL GEORGIA OPEN
River North C.C.,
Macon, Georgia
May 12-15, 1994

RICK PEARSON	1	71-68-65-69	273	$31,500
BILL MURCHISON	T2	65-72-67-69	273	$15,079
CHARLES RYMER	T2	73-66-65-69	273	$15,079
DANNY BRIGGS	T2	69-67-66-71	273	$15,079
EMLYN AUBREY	T5	67-72-70-65	274	$8,020
JIM SCHUMAN	T5	70-67-70-67	274	$8,020
TOMMY TOLLES	T5	69-71-66-68	274	$8,020
BARRY FABYAN	T8	69-68-70-68	275	$5,687
TIM LOUSTALOT	T8	66-69-68-71	275	$5,687
JERRY KELLY	T10	71-67-71-67	276	$3,937
HUGH ROYER, III	T10	68-69-68-71	276	$3,937

NIKE KNOXVILLE OPEN
Willow Creek G.C.,
Knoxville, Tennessee
May 19-22, 1994

VIC WILK	1	70-71-68-66	275	$36,000
BILL MURCHISON	2	72-66-70-68	276	$22,700
RICK PEARSON	3	71-70-66-70	277	$16,500
TOM GARNER	T4	73-65-70-70	278	$10,666
GARY RUSNAK	T4	69-69-70-70	278	$10,666
FRANK CONNER	T4	73-70-65-70	278	$10,666
EMLYN AUBREY	T7	72-69-67-71	279	$4,987
CLARK BURROUGHS	T7	70-73-70-66	279	$4,987
JOE DURANT	T7	74-70-67-68	279	$4,987
BARRY FABYAN	T7	73-69-67-70	279	$4,987
SCOTT GUMP	T7	69-70-69-71	279	$4,987
JERRY KELLY	T7	69-69-70-71	279	$4,987
JEFF KLEIN	T7	70-72-69-68	279	$4,987
THOMAS SCHERRER	T7	73-71-65-70	279	$4,987

NIKE GREATER GREENVILLE CLASSIC
Verdae Green G.C.,
Greenville, South Carolina
May 26-29, 1994

SCOTT GUMP	1	71-67-66-68	272	$31,500
TIM CONLEY	2	65-72-67-69	273	$19,865
RAFAEL ALARCON	3	70-68-67-69	274	$14,437
CHRIS TUCKER	T4	69-71-70-67	277	$9,333
TOMMY ARMOUR	T4	68-70-68-71	277	$9,333
THOMAS SCHERRER	T4	69-68-71-69	277	$9,333
ROB BOLDT	T7	71-67-70-70	278	$6,565
CRAIG KANADA	T7	69-69-72-68	278	$6,565
JOE HAMORSKI	T9	70-67-72-70	279	$4,375
SKIP KENDALL	T9	71-65-72-71	279	$4,375
KARL ZOLLER	T9	67-69-73-70	279	$4,375

NIKE MIAMI VALLEY OPEN
Heatherwoode G.C.,
Springboro, Ohio
June 2-5, 1994

TOMMY ARMOUR III	1	68-67-66-65	266	$36,000
JIM CARTER	2	69-69-66-65	269	$22,700
CLARK BURROUGHS	T3	69-68-63-70	270	$14,500
CHRIS PERRY	T3	69-69-64-68	270	$14,500
CRAIG KANADA	T5	70-61-72-68	271	$9,750
LEE RINKER	T5	68-68-67-68	271	$9,750
GLEN HNATIUK	T7	70-70-63-69	272	$7,500
JIM KANE	T7	69-69-65-69	272	$7,500
WOODY AUSTIN	T9	71-67-68-67	273	$5,000
TIM LOUSTALOT	T9	69-68-79-66	273	$5,000

NIKE CLEVELAND OPEN
Quail Hollow Resort,
Concord, Ohio
June 9-12, 1994

TOMMY ARMOUR III	**1**	**68-68-70-69 275**	**$36,000**
SCOTT GUMP	T2	72-70-64-69 275	$19,600
THOMAS SCHERRER	T2	70-69-69-67 275	$19,600
RUSSELL BEIERSDORF	T4	69-72-67-69 277	$11,500
BUDDY GARDNER	T4	67-71-66-73 277	$11,500
DANNY BRIGGS	6	70-65-76-67 278	$9,000
WEBB HEINTZELMAN	T7	71-70-70-68 279	$5,583
CHRIS PERRY	T7	73-68-72-66 279	$5,583
SAM RANDOLPH	T7	71-70-69-69 279	$5,583
LEE RINKER	T7	71-70-67-71 279	$5,583
HUGH ROYER III	T7	68-74-66-71 279	$5,583

NIKE DOMINION OPEN
The Dominion Club,
Glen Allen, Virginia
June 16-19, 1994

SONNY SKINNER	**1**	**70-65-67-69 271**	**$36,000**
JIM CARTER	2	65-68-68-70 271	$22,700
BARRY FABYAN	T3	72-68-69-63 272	$13,166
JOHN WILSON	T3	67-69-69-67 272	$13,166
JOHN RIEGGER	T3	70-69-65-68 272	$13,166
PETER PERSONS	T6	67-69-67-70 273	$8,500
JEFF WILSON	T6	69-72-66-66 273	$8,500
PAT BATES	8	68-70-66-70 274	$7,000
ROB BOLDT	T9	69-70-68-68 275	$3,974
GREG CESARIO	T9	65-70-70-70 275	$3,974
JERRY KELLY	T9	72-67-66-70 275	$3,974
FRANKLIN LANGHAM	T9	70-67-73-65 275	$3,974
BILL PORTER	T9	68-71-72-64 275	$3,974
DON REESE	T9	68-71-68-68 275	$3,974
BOB BURNS	T9	67-69-68-71 275	$3,974

NIKE CAROLINA CLASSIC
Prestonwood C.C.,
Cary, North Carolina
June 23-26, 1994

SKIP KENDALL	**1**	**65-72-70-69 276**	**$36,000**

PAT BATES	2	66-68-70-74 278	$22,700
EMLYN AUBREY	T3	67-73-69-70 279	$14,500
CHRIS PERRY	T3	70-70-70-69 279	$14,500
JEFF BARLOW	T5	68-72-67-73 280	$9,750
DAVID DUVAL	T5	70-69-69-72 280	$9,750
TRIPP ISENHOUR	T7	72-70-68-71 281	$7,000
THOMAS SCHERRER	T7	67-72-69-73 281	$7,000
BRUCE VAUGHAN	T7	71-71-71-68 281	$7,000
STEVE JONES	T10	68-71-71-72 282	$3,950
BILL MURCHISON	T10	69-71-70-72 282	$3,950
SONNY SKINNER	T10	69-69-71-73 282	$3,950
TOMMY TOLLES	T10	72-69-71-70 282	$3,950

NIKE GATEWAY CLASSIC
Lake Forest C.C.,
Lake Saint Louis, Missouri
July 21-24, 1994

BRAD FABEL	**1**	**70-68-71-70 279**	**$36,000**
JIM CARTER	T2	71-69-71-69 280	$19,600
CHRIS PERRY	T2	69-72-69-70 280	$19,600
JEFF COOK	T4	71-70-72-68 281	$9,400
SCOTT GUMP	T4	67-75-70-69 281	$9,400
CHRIS PATTON	T4	71-69-72-69 281	$9,400
LEE RINKER	T4	71-71-70-69 281	$9,400
TOMMY TOLLES	T4	70-68-73-70 281	$9,400
KEITH FERGUS	T9	72-68-70-72 282	$5,500
JERRY KELLY	T9	71-69-69-73 282	$5,500

NIKE WICHITA OPEN
Reflection Ridge G.C.,
Wichita, Kansas
July 28-31, 1994

DENNIS POSTLEWAIT	**1**	**66-66-69-70 271**	**$31,500**
CLARK BURROUGHS	2	67-68-71-66 272	$19,862
TOM CARR	T3	65-70-69-69 273	$12,687
TOMMY TOLLES	T3	68-65-69-71 273	$12,687
GREG BRUCKNER	T5	68-72-70-64 274	$8,020
HUGH ROYER III	T5	68-71-67-68 274	$8,020
BRUCE VAUGHAN	T5	63-71-69-71 274	$8,020
PAT BATES	T8	68-70-68-69 275	$5,250
JEFF FREEMAN	T8	64-70-70-71 275	$5,250
MIKE SPOSA	T8	67-68-72-68 275	$5,250

NIKE DAKOTA DUNES OPEN
Dakota Dunes C.C.,
Dakota Dunes, South Dakota
August 4-7, 1994

PAT BATES	**1**	**74-68-69-65**	**276**	**$36,000**
REX CALDWELL	T2	71-70-69-68	278	$19,600
GARY WEBB	T2	73-69-72-64	278	$19,600
JEFF BREHAUT	T4	71-70-69-69	279	$11,500
VIC WILK	T4	70-70-72-67	279	$11,500
TIM LOUSTALOT	6	69-67-71-73	280	$9,000
SCOTT GUMP	7	70-70-70-71	281	$8,000
GREG BRUCKNER	T8	66-72-74-70	282	$6,500
SONNY SKINNER	T8	71-70-70-71	282	$6,500
JEFF BARLOW	T10	69-70-75-69	283	$4,166
THOMAS SCHERRER	T10	73-66-75-69	283	$4,166
DON REESE	T10	67-72-72-72	283	$4,166

NIKE OZARKS OPEN
Highland Springs C.C.,
Springfield, Missouri
August 11-14, 1994

JERRY HAAS	**1**	**69-65-69-69**	**272**	**$36,000**
FRANK CONNER	2	68-71-70-64	273	$22,700
PAT BATES	T3	66-70-70-68	274	$14,500
DAVID DUVAL	T3	69-66-67-72	274	$14,500
CHARLES RYMER	T5	71-70-69-65	275	$7,583
SONNY SKINNER	T5	71-69-69-66	275	$7,583
CLARK BURROUGHS	T5	68-67-67-73	275	$7,583
BUDDY GARDNER	T5	71-69-66-69	275	$7,583
DAVID JACKSON	T5	67-71-67-70	275	$7,583
VIC WILK	T5	66-66-72-71	275	$7,583

NIKE TEXARKANA OPEN
Texarkana C.C.,
Texarkana, Texas
August 18-21, 1994

MIKE BRISKY	**1**	**66-65-68-67**	**266**	**$36,000**
SONNY SKINNER	2	67-66-68-72	273	$22,700
DAVID DUVAL	T3	69-69-69-67	274	$14,500
DAVID KIRKPATRICK	T3	68-65-72-69	274	$14,500
RALPH HOWE III	T5	68-67-70-70	275	$8,625
FRANKLIN LANGHAM	T5	70-69-72-64	275	$8,625

JOHN MAGINNES	T5	71-66-72-66	275	$8,625
TRAY TYNER	T5	69-67-66-73	275	$8,625
JIM CARTER	T9	71-66-67-72	276	$4,625
ROBERT FRIEND	T9	70-67-68-71	276	$4,625
THOMAS SCHERRER	T9	70-70-66-70	276	$4,625
TOMMY TOLLES	T9	67-68-68-73	276	$4,625

NIKE PERMIAN BASIN OPEN
The Club at Mission Dorado,
Odessa, Texas
August 25-28, 1994

BRUCE VAUGHAN	**1**	**68-67-67-67**	**269**	**$31,500**
GARY RUSNAK	T2	67-68-70-68	273	$17,150
BOB WOLCOTT	T2	71-64-70-68	273	$17,150
CHRIS PERRY	T4	70-72-67-65	274	$9,333
JEFF BARLOW	T4	68-66-69-71	274	$9,333
GENE JONES	T4	70-67-69-68	274	$9,333
BILL PORTER	T7	67-67-72-69	275	$6,562
ZORAN ZORKIC	T7	69-68-68-70	275	$6,562
GREG CESARIO	T9	69-68-68-71	276	$3,815
RICK DALPOS	T9	73-67-66-70	276	$3,815
R.W. EAKS	T9	70-70-69-67	276	$3,815
RICKY GONZALEZ	T9	70-70-68-68	276	$3,815
JERRY HAAS	T9	70-68-70-68	276	$3,815

NIKE NEW MEXICO CHARITY CLASSIC
Valle Grande G.C.,
Bernalillo, New Mexico
September 1-4, 1994

JIM CARTER	**1**	**69-66-71-66**	**272**	**$31,500**
EMLYN AUBREY	T2	65-71-71-66	273	$17,150
CHAD GINN	T2	67-71-71-64	273	$17,150
DAVID DUVAL	4	65-74-69-66	274	$10,937
BRUCE VAUGHAN	T5	69-71-71-64	275	$8,020
R.W. EAKS	T5	70-70-66-69	275	$8,020
CHRIS PERRY	T5	67-68-71-69	275	$8,020
WOODY AUSTIN	T8	69-72-68-67	276	$4,200
KEITH FERGUS	T8	69-71-68-68	276	$4,200
JOHN MAGINNES	T8	71-71-68-66	276	$4,200
MATT PETERSON	T8	71-71-66-68	276	$4,200
BILL PORTER	T8	67-73-68-68	276	$4,200

NIKE UTAH CLASSIC
Riverside C.C.,
Provo, Utah
September 9-11, 1994

CHRIS PERRY	1	69-68-68	205	$31,500
DAVID DUVAL	2	70-65-71	206	$19,862
TOM GARNER	3	68-71-69	208	$14,437
JIM CARTER	4	72-68-69	209	$10,937
JEFF BARLOW	T5	71-71-68	210	$8,020
BUDDY GARDNER	T5	70-69-71	210	$8,020
JERRY KELLY	T5	68-71-71	210	$8,020
CRAIG KANADA	8	74-71-66	211	$6,125
CLARK BURROUGHS	T9	72-71-69	212	$4,046
GARY RUSNAK	T9	69-74-69	212	$4,046
DON REESE	T9	68-68-76	212	$4,046

NIKE BOISE OPEN
Hillcrest C.C.,
Boise, Idaho
September 16-18, 1994

KEITH FERGUS	1	65-69-64	198	$36,000
BILL MURCHISON	2	66-64-68	198	$22,700
WOODY AUSTIN	T3	68-71-61	200	$13,166
SCOTT GUMP	T3	67-68-65	200	$13,166
J.P. HAYES	T3	69-61-70	200	$13,166
LEE RINKER	6	66-71-64	201	$9,000
JOHN MAGINNES	7	68-68-66	202	$8,000
EMLYN AUBREY	T8	68-67-68	203	$5,500
JERRY HAAS	T8	67-67-69	203	$5,500
JERRY KELLY	T8	69-70-64	203	$5,500

NIKE TRI-CITIES CLASSIC
Meadow Springs C.C.,
Richland, Washington
September 23-25, 1994

JERRY HAAS	1	69-67-67	203	$31,500
BRAD FABEL	2	70-66-68	204	$19,862
LEE RINKER	3	67-68-70	205	$14,437
JIM CARTER	T4	69-67-71	207	$7,729
JEFF COOK	T4	70-70-67	207	$7,729
CHARLES RYMER	T4	69-66-72	207	$7,729
KEVIN SUTHERLAND	T4	70-70-67	207	$7,729
DAVID DUVAL	T4	68-66-73	207	$7,729
HARRY RUDOLPH	T4	67-67-73	207	$7,729
STEVE HASKINS	10	74-65-69	208	$4,375

NIKE SONOMA COUNTY OPEN
Windsor C.C.,
Windsor, California
September 29-October 2, 1994

JERRY HAAS	1	67-68-71-71	277	$31,500
WOODY AUSTIN	2	68-68-69-74	279	$19,862
KEITH FERGUS	T3	70-76-69-65	280	$11,520
LEE RINKER	T3	70-67-71-72	280	$11,520
MIKE SCHUCHART	T3	74-68-69-69	280	$11,520
JOHN DOWDALL	T6	70-76-66-69	281	$7,000
DAVID JACKSON	T6	67-71-71-72	281	$7,000
CHRISTIAN PENA	T6	70-72-66-73	281	$7,000
EMLYN AUBREY	T9	70-74-70-69	283	$4,046
BOB WOLCOTT	T9	73-70-71-69	283	$4,046
JERRY KELLY	T9	66-73-72-72	283	$4,046
DAVE SUTHERLAND	T9	77-65-69-72	283	$4,046

NIKE TOUR CHAMPIONSHIP
Pumpkin Ridge G.C.,
Cornelius, Oregon
October 13-16, 1994

MIKE SCHUCHART	1	69-67-68-73	277	$40,500
EMLYN AUBREY	T2	72-69-67-70	278	$19,762
JEFF COOK	T2	73-70-67-68	278	$19,762
LEE RINKER	T2	69-70-69-70	278	$19,762
JOHN MAGINNES	5	68-69-68-74	279	$12,375
JIM CARTER	T6	69-68-71-72	280	$9,562
DAVID DUVAL	T6	67-73-69-71	280	$9,562
BRAD FABEL	8	68-74-69-70	281	$7,875
KEITH FERGUS	T9	69-73-72-68	282	$5,625
J.P. HAYES	T9	70-72-69-71	282	$5,625
TIM LOUSTALOT	T9	71-72-74-65	282	$5,625

European TOUR

MADEIRA ISLAND OPEN
Madeira Santo da Serra, Madeira Island
January 13-16, 1994

MATS LANNER		70-67-69	206	£41,660

DUBAI DESERT CLASSIC
Emirates G.C.,
Dubai, United Arab Emirates
January 27-30, 1994

ERNIE ELS   61-69-67-71 268   £75,000

MOROCCAN OPEN
Golf Royal de Agadir, Agadir, Morocco
January 20-23, 1994

ANDERS FORSBRAND   70-68-69-69 276   £58,330

JOHNNIE WALKER CLASSIC
Blue Canyon C.C., Phuket, Thailand
February 3-6, 1994

GREG NORMAN   75-70-64-68 277   £100,000

TURESPANA OPEN DE TENERIFE
Golf del Sur,
Santa Cruz de Tenerife, Canary Islands
February 10-13, 1994

DAVID GILFORD   72-70-66-70 278   £41,660

OPEN DE EXTREMADURA
Golf del Guadiana, Badajoz, Spain
February 17-20, 1994

PAUL RIALES   72-69-69-71 281   £41,660

TURESPANA MASTERS OPEN
Andalucia, Spain
February 24-27, 1994

CARL MASON   67-70-71-70 278   £50,535

TURESPANA OPEN MEDITERRIANIA
Villa Martin G.C., Torrevieja, Spain
March 3-6, 1994

JOSE-MARIA OLAZABAL   70-65-71-70 276   £50,000

TURESPANA OPEN DE BALEARES
Island of Majorca, Spain
March 10-13, 1994

BARRY LANE   64-70-66-69 269   £41,616

PORTUGUESE OPEN
Penha Longa G.C., Sintra, Portugal
March 17-20, 1994

PHILLIP PRICE   64-71-73-72 278   £50,000

OPEN V33
Golf de Villette d'Anthon, Lyon, France
April 1-4, 1994

STEPHEN AMES   70-67-71-74 282   £37,500

TOURNOI PERRIER DE PARIS
Paris, France
April 14-17, 1994

PETER BAKER/
DAVID RUSSELL   58-68-65-69 260   £35,000

HEINECKEN OPEN CATALONIA
Pals G.C., Gerona, Spain
April 21-24, 1994

JOSE COCERES   70-69-67-69 275   £50,000

AIR FRANCE CANNES OPEN
Cannes Mougains G.C., Cannes, France
April 28-May 1, 1994

IAN WOOSNAM   72-70-63-66 271   £50,000

BENSON AND HEDGES INTERNATIONAL OPEN
St. Mellion G. & C.C.,
Plymouth, England
May 5-8, 1994

SEVE BALLESTEROS   69-70-72-70 281   £108,330

PEUGEOT OPEN DE ESPANA
Club de Campo, Madrid, Spain
May 12-15, 1994

COLIN MONTGOMERIE   70-71-66-70 277   £83,330

VOLVO PGA
Wentworth Club (West), Surrey, England
May 27-30, 1994

JOSE-MARIA OLAZABAL   67-68-71-65 271   £133,330

ALFRED DUNHILL OPEN
Royal Zoute G.C.,
Knokke-le-Heist, Belgium
June 2-5, 1994

NICK FALDO   67-74-67-71 279   £100,000

HONDA OPEN
Gut Kaden C.C., Alveslohe, Germany
June 9-12, 1994

ROBERT ALLENBY   72-67-68-69 276   £83,330

JERSEY EUROPEAN AIRWAYS OPEN
La Moye (Nicklaus), St. Brelade, England
June 16-19, 1994

PAUL CURRY   73-62-68-63 266   £58,330

PEUGEOT OPEN DE FRANCE
Le Golf National, Versailles, France
June 23-26, 1994

MARK RON   70-71-67-66 274   £91,660

MURPHY'S IRISH OPEN
Mount Juliet C.C.,
County Kilkenny, Ireland
June 30-July 3, 1994

BERNHARD LANGER   70-68-70-67 275   £98,765

BELL'S SCOTTISH OPEN
Gleneagles (King's),
Auchterarder, Scotland
July 6-9, 1994

CARL MASON   67-69-61-68 265   £100,000

BRITISH OPEN
Turnberry (Ailsa), Turneberry, Scotland
July 14-17, 1994

NICK PRICE   1   69-66-67-66 268   £110,000

HEINEKEN DUTCH OPEN
Hilversumsche G.C.,
Hilversum, Netherlands
July 21-24, 1994

MIGUAL-ANGEL JIMENEZ   65-68-67-70 270   £108,330

SCANDANAVIAN MASTERS
Drottningholm G.C.,
Drottningholm, Sweden
July 28-31, 1994

VIJAY SINGH   68-67-69-64 268   £108,330

BMW INTERNATIONAL OPEN
Germany
August 4-7, 1994

MARK MCNULTY   70-71-68-65 274   £87,500

HOHE BRUKE OPEN
Austria
August 11-14, 1994

MARK DAVIS   68-69-69-64 270   £41,660

MURPHY'S ENGLISH OPEN
Forrest of Arden G.C.,
Warwickshire, England
August 18-21, 1994

COLIN MONTGOMERIE   70-67-68-69 274   £100,000

VOLVO GERMAN OPEN
Hubbelrath G.C., Dusseldorf, Germany
August 25-28, 1994

COLIN MONTGOMERIE   65-68-66-70 269 £108,330

CANON EUROPEAN MASTERS
G.C. Crans-sur-Sierre, Switzerland
September 1-4, 1994

EDUARDO ROMERO   64-68-66-68 266 £112,190

EUROPEAN OPEN
East Sussex National G.C.,
Uckfield, England
September 8-11, 1994

DAVID GILFORD   70-68-70-67 275 £100,000

DUNHILL BRITISH MASTERS
Woburn G. & C.C. (Duke's),
Buckinghamshire, England
September 15-18, 1994

IAN WOOSNAM   71-70-63-67 272 £108,330

TROPHEE LANCOME
St. Nom-la-Breteche, Versailles, France
September 22-25, 1994

VIJAY SINGH   65-63-69-66 263 £100,000

MERCEDES GERMAN MASTERS
Motzner See G. & C.C.,
Motzen, Germany
September 29-October 2, 1994

SEVE BALLESTEROS   68-70-65-67 270 £104,125

CHEMAPOL TROPHY CZECH OPEN
Czech Republic
October 20-23, 1994

PER-ULRIK JOHANSSON   61-56-54-66 237 £83,330

Women's Pro Golf European Tour

FORD CLASSIC
Woburn G. & C.C. (Duchess),
Milton Keynes, England
April 28-May 1, 1994

CATRIN NILSMARK   73-66-73-73 284 £15,000

COSTA AZUL LADIES'
Costa Azul, Portugal
May 19-22, 1994

SANDRINE MENDIBURU   70-70 140 £7,500

OVB DAMEN OPEN
Europa-Sportregion,
Zell am See, Austria
June 16-19, 1994

FLORENCE DESCAMPE   70-70-69-68 277 £25,000

BMW EUROPEAN MASTERS
Golf du Bercuit,
Grez-Doiceau, Belgium
June 23-26, 1994

HELEN WADSWORTH   69-66-70-73 278 £24,000

HENNESSEY LADIES' CUP
Koln G. & L.C.,
Gladbach, Germany
June 30-July 3, 1994

LISELOTTE NEUMANN   69-71-70-66 276 £33,000

WOMEN'S IRISH HOLIDAYS OPEN
Ireland
July 28-31, 1994

LAURA DAVIES   70-72-69-71 282 £10,500

SCOTTISH OPEN
Dalmahoy Hotel G. & C.C.,
Edinburgh, Scotland
August 4-7, 1994

| LAURA DAVIES | 69-69-68-72 278 | £11,250 |

TRYGG HANSA LADIES' OPEN
Haninge G.C.,
Haninge, Sweden
August 18-21, 1994

| LISELOTTE NEUMANN | 69-67-71-67 274 | £15,000 |

WATERFORD LADIES' ENGLISH OPEN
Tytherington C.,
Macclesfield, England
September 1-4, 1994

| PATRICIA MAUNIER | 73-74-70-71 288 | £9,000 |

SEWS LADIES' DUTCH OPEN
Het Rik van Nijmegan,
Groesbeck, Netherlands
September 9-11, 1994

| LIZ WEINA | 74-68-72 214 | £8,250 |

BMW ITALIAN LADIES' OPEN
Lignano G.C.,
Venice, Italy
September 22-25, 1994

| CORINNE DIBNAH | 73-67-71-66 277 | £10,500 |

LA MANGA CLUB SPANISH OPEN
La Mange G.C.,
Cartagena, Spain
September 29-October 2, 1994

| MARIE LAURA DE LORENZI | 71-72-68-71 282 | £9,000 |

VAR OPEN DE FRANCE FEMININ
St. Edreoul, France
October 13-16, 1994

| JULIE FORBES | 73-70-70 213 | £8,250 |

Japanese Tour
* Total purse. Winner's share information not available.

TOUKEN CORPORATION CUP
Kedoin G.C.
March 10-13, 1994

| C. WARREN | 208 | ¥18,000,000 |

DAIDO-DRINKO SHIZUOKA OPEN
Shizuoka C./Hamaoka C.
March 17-20, 1994

| T. NAKAJIMA | 280 | ¥18,000,000 |

UNITED AIRLINES KSB OPEN
Kinojou G.C.
March 24-27, 1994

| K. TAKAMI | 281 | ¥12,600,000 |

DESCENTE CLASSIC MUNSINGWEAR OPEN
Century Miki G.C.
March 31-April 3, 1994

| B. WATTS | 280 | ¥14,400,000 |

POCARISWEAT OPEN
Hakuryuko C.C.
April 7-10, 1994

| Y. MIZUMAKI | 203 | ¥14,400,000 |

TSURUYA OPEN
Sports Shinkou C.C.
April 14-17, 1994

| T. NAKAJIMA | 279 | ¥18,000,000 |

DUNLOP OPEN
Ibaraki G.C.
April 21-24, 1994

| M. OZAKI | 274 | ¥18,000,000 |

THE CROWNS
Nagoya G.C./Wago C.
April 28-May 1, 1994

| R. MACKAY | 269 | ¥21,600,000 |

FUJI-SANKEI CLASSIC
Kawana Hotel G.C./Fuji C.
May 5-8, 1994

| K. MUROTA | 284 | ¥21,600,000 |

PGA CHAMPIONSHIP
Lake Green G.C.
May 12-15, 1994

| H. GODA | 279 | ¥18,000,000 |

PEPSI-UBEKOUSAN
La Costa Resort, La Costa, California
May 19-22, 1994

| T. NAKAJIMA | 268 | ¥14,400,000 |

MITSUBISHI GALANT
Hokkaido Hayakita C.C.
May 26-29, 1994

| K. TOMORI | 205 | ¥18,000,000 |

JCB CLASSIC SENDAI
Omotezaoukokokusai G.C.
June 2-5, 1994

| M. KURAMOTO | 271 | ¥18,000,000 |

SAPPORO TOKYU OPEN
Sapporokokusai C.C./Shimamatsu C.
June 9-12, 1994

| Y. MIZUMAKI | 277 | ¥18,000,000 |

YOMIURI OPEN
Yomiuri G.C.
June 16-19, 1994

| T. WATNABE | 270 | ¥18,000,000 |

MIZUNO OPEN
Tokinodai C.C.
June 23-26, 1994

| B. WATTS | 280 | ¥18,000,000 |

PGA PHILANTHROPY
Golden Valley G.C.
June 30-July 3, 1994

| T. HAMILTON | 278 | ¥18,000,000 |

NGA OPEN
Easthill G.C.
July 5-6, 1994

| S. OGAWA | 135 | *¥5,000,000 |

YONEX OPEN HIROSHIMA
Hiroshima C.C./Happonmatsu C.
July 7-10, 1994

| M. OZAKI | 274 | ¥14,400,000 |

IBAREKI OPEN
Mito Green C.C./Yamagata
July 12-13, 1994

| M. KUSAKABE | 136 | *¥20,000,000 |

TOYAMA OPEN
Kureha C.C.
July 15-16, 1994

| M. KAWAMURA | 138 | *¥30,000,000 |

BRIDGESTONE CUP HYOGO OPEN
Daitakarazuka G.C.
July 15-16, 1994

| M. KANAYAMA | 134 | *¥15,000,000 |

NIKKEI CUP- PETE NAKAMURA MEMORIAL
Mitsuikankotomakomai G.C.
July 21-24, 1994

| T. SUZUKI | 268 | ¥14,400,000 |

NST NIIGATA OPEN
Kakajo G.C.
July 28-31, 1994

| P. IZUMIKAWA | 276 | ¥10,800,000 |

KYOTO-SHIGA OPEN
Ujitawara C.C.
August 2, 1994

| T. NISHINO | 68 | *¥10,000,000 |

CHIBA OPEN
Sodegaura C.C./Shinsode C.
August 2-3, 1994

| H. MAKINO | 135 | *¥15,000,000 |

NISSAN CUP TOCHIGI OPEN
Shiobara C.C.
August 2-3, 1994

| F. IRINO | 137 | *¥30,000,000 |

SANKO GRANDSUMMER
Sanko 72 C.C.
August 4-7, 1994

| T. SUZUKI | 272 | *¥70,000,000 |

GIFU OPEN
Kagamigahara C.C.
August 6-7, 1994

| Y. SUGAWARA | 135 | *¥15,000,000 |

ACOM INTERNATIONAL
Seve Ballesteros G.C.
August 11-14

| N. OZAKI | 41PTS | ¥18,000,000 |

MARUMAN OPEN
Narita Springs C.C.
August 18-21, 1994

| D. ISHII | 279 | ¥21,600,000 |

HISAMITSU KBC AUGUSTA
Keya G.C.
August 25-28, 1994

| B. WATTS | 271 | ¥18,000,000 |

PGA MATCH PLAY CHAMPIONSHIP
Nidom Classic C.
September 1-4, 1994

| T. HAMILTON | 8&7 | ¥14,400,000 |

HOKKAIDO OPEN
Emuzu G.C.
September 1-4, 1994

| T. OYAMA | 284 | *¥15,000,000 |

TOHUKU OPEN
Green Academy C.C.
September 1-4, 1994

| Y. NIIZEKI | 276 | *¥15,000,000 |

KANTO OPEN
Tsuga C.C.
September 1-4, 1994

| H. SASKAI | 277 | *¥30,000,000 |

CHUBU OPEN
Shinyo C.C.
September 1-4, 1994

| E. MIZOGUCHI | 285 | *¥20,000,000 |

KANSAI OPEN
Asahikokusai Tojo C.C.
September 1-4, 1994

| K. KANAYAMA | 281 | *¥25,000,000 |

CHU-SHIKOKU OPEN
Kamo C.C.
September 1-4, 1994

| H. SHIRAKATA | 279 | *¥20,000,000 |

KYUSYU OPEN
Nishinihon C.C.
September 1-4, 1994

M. KUSAKABE	281	*¥20,000,000

SUNTORY OPEN
Narashino C.C.
September 8-11, 1994

D. ISHII	277	¥18,000,000

ANA OPEN
Sapporo G.C. (Wattu)
September 15-18, 1994

M. OZAKI	268	¥18,000,000

CRAINE CUP MANIWA OPEN
Maniwa C.C.
September 21-22, 1994

Y. AKITOMI	133	*¥20,000,000

GENE SARAZEN CLASSIC
Rope Club
September 22-25, 1994

C. FRANCO	272	¥19,800,000

JAPAN OPEN
Yokkaichi C.C.
September 29-October 2, 1994

M. OZAKI	268	¥18,000,000

TOKAI CLASSIC
Miyoshi C.C. (West)
July 12-13, 1994

C. PAVIN	277	¥19,800,000

ASIHI BEER GOLF DIGEST
Tomei C.C.
October 13-16, 1994

E. MIZOGUCHI	265	¥27,000,000

ZENRIN FUKUOKA OPEN
Asouiizuka G.C.
October 15-16, 1994

M. HARADA	139	*¥30,000,000

BRIDGESTONE OPEN
Sodegaura C.C. (Sodegaura)
October 20-23, 1994

B. WATTS	274	¥36,000,000

PHILIP MORRIS CHAMPIONSHIP
ABC G.C.
October 27-30, 1994

B. WATTS	276	¥36,000,000

MITSUBISHI OIL CUP/ M. HIRAO PRO-AM CHARITY
Shinchiba C.C.
October 31, 1994

Y. KANEKO	66	*¥7,555,000

Japanese Senior Tour

AMERICAN EXPRESS GRAND SLAM GOLF CHAMPIONSHIP
Oakhills C.C.
March 25-27, 1994

L. TREVINO	207	¥60,000,000

TPC STARTS SENIOR
Garden G.C.
April 7-10, 1994

S. KANAI	282	¥50,000,000

DAIICHI SEIMEI CUP
Tomisato G.C.
May 20-22, 1994

| H. ISHII | 203 | *¥50,000,000 |

MIZUNO SENIOR
Taiei C.C.
May 27-29, 1994

| T. UEDA | 204 | *¥30,000,000 |

JAPAN PRO SENIOR CHAMPIONSHIP
Shimoakima C.C.
June 2-5, 1994

| S. UCHIDA | 281 | *¥50,000,000 |

KOMATSU OPEN
Sawara Springs C.C.
June 10-12, 1994

| R. ODA | 208 | *¥30,000,000 |

HTB SENIOR CLASSIC
Chitose Airport C.C.
July 1-3, 1994

| M. AMANO | 208 | *¥30,000,000 |

NAGOYA TV CUP
Hananoki G.C.
September 16-18, 1994

| S. KANAI | 207 | *¥40,000,000 |

NOBORU GOTCH MEMORIAL TOKYU CUP
Groundoak G.C.
September 23-25, 1994

| N. MATSUMOTO | 202 | *¥35,000,000 |

HOUOU CUP
Houou C.C.
October 28-30, 1994

| S. KANAI | 202 | *¥35,000,000 |

Asian Tour

MANILA SOUTHWOODS PHILIPPINE OPEN GOLF CHAMPIONSHIP
Manila Southwoods G. & C.C. (Masters)
Manila, Philippines
February 17-20, 1994

| CARLOS FRANCO | 72-69-68-71 280 | $51,646 |

KENT HONG KONG OPEN GOLF CHAMPIONSHIP
Royal Hong Kong G.C. (Composite)
New Territories, Fanling, Hong Kong
February 24-27, 1994

| DAVID FROST | 69-69-69-67 274 | $49,980 |

CLASSIC INDIAN OPEN GOLF CHAMPIONSHIP
Royal Calcutta G.C.,
Calcutta, India
March 4-7, 1994

| EMLYN AUBREY | 69-70-76-70 285 | $33,320 |

THAI INTERNATIONAL THAILAND OPEN GOLF CHAMPIONSHIP
Thana City C.C.,
Bangkok, Thailand
March 10-13

| BRANDT JOBE | 65-72-69-70 276 | $49,980 |

BENSON & HEDGES MALAYSIA OPEN
Royal Selangor G.C.,
Kuala Lumpur, Malaysia
March 17-20, 1994

| JOAKIM HAEGGMAN | 71-67-72-69 279 | $41,650 |

SAMPOERNA INDONESIA OPEN GOLF CHAMPIONSHIP
Damai Indah G. & C.C.,
Jakarta, Indonesia
March 24-27, 1994

FRANK NOBILO   69-67-68-69 273 $41,650

SABAH MASTERS GOLF CHAMPIONSHIP
Sabah G. & C.C.,
Kota Kinabalu, Sabah, Malaysia
March 31-April 3, 1994

CRAIG MCCLELLAN   75-71-71-67 284 $43,316

CHING FONG REPUBLIC OF CHINA OPEN GOLF CHAMPIONSHIP
Taiwan G. & C.C. (Tamsui),
Taipei County, Taiwan
April 7-10, 1994

CHAI-YUH HONG   70-65-73-68 276 $0 (AM)

MAEKYUNG BANDO FASHION OPEN GOLF CHAMPIONSHIP
Nam Seoul G.C.,
Sungnam, Kyungki-Do, Korea
April 14-17, 1994

JONG DUK KIM   74-72-70-68 284 $49,980

DUNLOP OPEN GOLF CHAMPIONSHIP
Ibaraki G.C. (East),
Kojimashinden, Ibaraki Prefecture, Japan
April 21-24, 1994

MASASHI OZAKI   67-68-70-69 274 $172,000

Australian Tour

VICTORIAN OPEN
Woodland C., Melbourne, Victoria
November 4-7, 1993

LUCAS PARSONS   72-69-65-70 276   N/A

AUSTRALIAN OPEN
Metropolitan G.C., Melbourne, Victoria
November 25-28, 1994

BRAD FAXON   65-74-66-70 275 $153,000

GREG NORMAN HOLDEN CLASSIC
Lakes C., Sydney, New South Wales
December 2-5, 1993

CURTIS STRANGE   68-67-69-70 274 $126,000

AIR NEW ZEALAND-SHELL OPEN
The Grange, New Zealand
December 9-12, 1994

TERRY PRICE   71-72-68-66 277 $29,800

COOLUM CLASSIC
Hyatt Coolum Resort,
Coolum, Queensland
December 16-19, 1994

DAVID DIAZ   68-68-72-67 275 $24,120

PLAYERS CHAMPIONSHIP
Kingston Heath, Melbourne, Victoria
January 20-23, 1994

PATRICK BURKE   69-67-72-72 280 $37,800

AUSTRALIAN SKINS GAME
Turtle Point G.C., Queensland
February 12-13, 1994

DAVID GRAHAM $69,840

AUSTRALIAN MASTERS
Huntingdale G.C., Melbourne, Victoria
February 17-20, 1994

CRAIG PARRY   74-70-70-68 282   N/A

CANON CHALLENGE
Castle Hill C.C.,
Sydney, New South Wales
February 24-27, 1994

PETER SENIOR   68-67-72-69 276 $38,880

South
American Tour

ABIERTO DE LA REPUBLICA DEL PARAGUAY
Yacht & Golf Club, Asuncion, Paraguay
November 11-14, 1993

RAUL FRETES   74-71-69-68 282 $10,800

ABIERTO DE URUGUAY
Club de Golf del Uruguay,
Montevideo, Uruguay
November 18-21, 1993

CARLOS FRANCO   73-71-68-67 279 $10,800

ABIERTO DE LOS LEONES
Club de Golf Los Leones, Santiago, Chile
November 25-28, 1993

CARLOS FRANCO   71-67-68-65 271 $14,400

ABIERTO DE PRINCE OF WALES
Prince of Wales C.C., Santiago, Chile
December 2-5, 1993

MIGUEL FERNANDEZ   65-69-71-70 275 $21,600

ABIERTO DE BOGOTA
C.C. de Bogota, Bogota, Colombia
September 29-October 2

MIGUEL GUZMAN   66-69-71-70 276 $14,400

LOS ANDES OPEN
Copa Club Colombia, Bogota, Colombia
October 6-9, 1994

RON WUENSCHE   74-70-67-67 278   N/A

T.C. ECUADORIAN OPEN
Guayaquil C.C., Guayaquil, Ecuador
October 20-23, 1994

MAURICIO MOLINA   68-72-69-71 280 $18,000

TOUR PRIZE MONEY & STATISTICS FOR 1994

OVERVIEW: *Key statistics and the official money lists for the PGA TOUR, Senior PGA TOUR, LPGA and the NIKE TOUR. Please note that, at press time, the Senior Tour and LPGA had tournaments yet to play.*

PGA TOUR

SCORING LEADERS

1	GREG NORMAN	68.81
2	FRED COUPLES	69.28
3	NICK PRICE	69.39
4	TOM LEHMAN	69.46
5	MARK MCCUMBER	69.56
6	LOREN ROBERTS	69.61
7	COREY PAVIN	69.6
8	PHIL MICKELSON	69.6
9	HALE IRWIN	69.7
10	BOB ESTES	69.7
	PGA TOUR AVG.	**71.1**

DRIVING LEADERS

I	DAVIS LOVE III	283.8
2	DENNIS PAULSON	283.0
3	FRED COUPLES	279.9
4	TODD BARRANGER	279.1
5	ROBERT GAMEZ	278.4
T6	KELLY GIBSON	277.5
T6	NICK PRICE	277.5
T8	BILL GLASSON	277.1
T8	GREG NORMAN	277.1
10	MIKE HEINEN	275.3
	PGA TOUR AVG.	**261.8**

DRIVING ACCURACY

1	DAVID EDWARDS	91.6
2	FRED FUNK	80.1
T3	JOHN MAHAFFEY	79.0
T3	DOUG TEWELL	79.0
5	LARRY NIZE	78.8
6	HALE IRWIN	78.0
7	DAVID OGRIN	77.9
T8	BRUCE FLEISHER	77.7
T8	TOM GARNER	77.7
10	D.A. WEIBRING	77.6
	PGA TOUR AVG.	**69.2**

GREENS IN REGULATION

1	BILL GLASSON	73.0
2	FUZZY ZOELLER	72.8
3	HAL SUTTON	72.2
4	MARK MCCUMBER	71.3
5	DAN FORSMAN	71.2
T6	DAVE BARR	70.9
T6	BOB ESTES	70.9
8	TOM LEHMAN	70.8
9	3 Tied With	70.6
	PGA TOUR AVG.	**65.9**

ALL AROUND

1	BOB ESTES	227
2	JOHN HUSTON	250
3	BILL GLASSON	257
4	GREG NORMAN	293
5	NICK PRICE	298
6	TON LEHMAN	312
7	LENNIE CLEMENTS	332
8	JAY HAAS	345
9	DONNIE HAMMOND	351
10	KIRK TRIPLETT	359
	PGA TOUR AVG.	**707**

TOTAL DRIVING

1	NICK PRICE	43
2	BILL GLASSON	48
3	GREG NORMAN	51
4	FUZZY ZOELLER	54
5	TOM WATSON	63
6	GIL MORGAN	67
7	DAN FORSMAN	75
8	HAL SUTTON	77
T9	BRUCE LIETZKE	80
T9	MIKE HEINEN	80
	PGA TOUR AVG.	**179**

PUTTING LEADERS

1	LOREN ROBERTS	1.737
2	BEN CRENSHAW	1.739
3	DAVID FROST	1.742
T4	PHIL NICKELSON	1.744
T4	MARR WURTZ	1.744
6	GREG NORMAN	1.747
7	COREY PAVIN	1.749
8	BLAINE MCCALLISTER	1.750
9	GREG KRAFT	1.751
10	STEVE STRICKER	1.752
	PGA TOUR AVG.	**1.794**

BIRDIE LEADERS

1	BRAD BRYANT	397
2	JAY HAAS	374
3	MARK BROOKS	372
4	TED TRYBA	365
5	HAL SUTTON	360
6	STEVE STRICKER	358
7	CLARK DENNIS	357
8	KENNY PERRY	355
9	BOB ESTES	352
10	PAUL GOYDOS	346
	PGA TOUR AVG.	**265**

EAGLE LEADERS

1	DAVIS LOVE III	18
2	MARK BROOKS	15
3	GUY BOROS	14
T4	ROBIN FREEMAN	13
T4	MIKE STANDLY	13
6	ROBERT GAMEZ	12
T7	JAY DELSING	11
T7	KELLY GIBSON	11
T7	TOM LEHMAN	11
T7	GLEN DAY	11
	PGA TOUR AVG.	**5**

SAND SAVES %

1	COREY PAVIN	65.4
2	BEN CRENSHAW	63.1
3	STAN UTLEY	62.8
4	KIRK TRIPLETT	61.6
5	BRIAN KAMM	61.4
T6	BOB ESTES	60.4
T6	PAYNE STEWART	60.4
T8	SCOTT HOCH	60.3
T8	RICHARD ZOKOL	60.3
10	J0HN INMAN	59.9
	PGA TOUR AVG.	**51.5**

Senior PGA TOUR

SCORING LEADERS

1	RAY FLOYD	69.13
2	DAVE STOCKTON	69.39
3	LEE TREVINO	69.55
4	TOM WARGO	69.98
5	GEORGE ARCHER	69.89
6	JIM ALBUS	69.91
7	JIM COLBERT	69.99
8	ISAO AOKI	70.03
9	BOB MURPHY	70.05
10	TOM WEISKOPF	70.09
	SR. TOUR AVG.	**72.08**

DRIVING LEADERS

1	JIM DENT	275.8
2	TOM WEISKOPF	273.2
3	JAY SIGEL	272.4
4	TERRY DILL	271.7
5	ROCKY THOMPSON	268.3
6	RAY FLOYD	267.7
7	TOMMY AYCOCK	266.6
8	BOB CARSON	266.3
9	JIM ALBUS	265.5
10	J.C. SNEAD	264.4
	SR. TOUR AVG.	**252.4**

DRIVING ACCURACY

1	CALVIN PEETE	84.1
2	CHARLES SIFFORD	81.8
3	JOHN PAUL CAIN	81.5
4	HOWIE JOHNSON	79.1
5	WALTER ZEMBRISKI	77.8
6	LEE ELDER	77.4
7	BOB MURPHY	77.3
T8	BOB CHARLES	77.2
T8	ROBERT ZIMMERMAN	77.2
10	GRAHAM MARSH	76.9
	SR. TOUR AVG.	**60.9**

GREENS IN REGULATION

1	RAY FLOYD	76.3
2	LARRY GILBERT	75.2
3	BOB CHARLES	75.0
4	DAVE STOCKTON	74.9
5	BOB MURPHY	74.7
6	TOM WEISKOPF	74.6
7	JIM ALBUS	74.3
8	ISAO AOXI	73.8
9	DALE DOUGLASS	73.4
10	TOM WARGO	73.1
	SR. TOUR AVG.	**66.5**

ALL AROUND

1	DAVE STOCKTON	82
2	TOM WARGO	83
3	JIM ALBUS	93
4	JIM COLBERT	118
5	LARRY GILBERT	125
6	ISAO AOKI	129
7	RAY FLOYD	133
8	BOB MURPHY	137
9	LEE TREVINO	142
10	JIM DENT	159
	SR. TOUR AVG.	**365**

TOTAL DRIVING

1	LARRY GILBERT	23
2	JIM ALBUS	27
3	RAY FLOYD	29
T4	GRAHAM MARSH	38
T4	JAY SIGEL	38
6	TOM WARGO	39
7	ISAO AOKI	44
T8	J.C. SNEAD	52
T8	LEE TREVINO	52
10	TOM WEISKOPF	55
	SR. TOUR AVG.	**92**

BIRDIE LEADERS

1	JIM ALBUS	432
2	DAVE STOCKTON	425
3	TOM WARGO	418
4	JIM COLBERT	402
5	JIM DENT	386
6	BOB MURPHY	350
7	JACK KIEFER	346
8	ROCKY THOMPSON	345
T9	GEORGE ARCHER	339
T9	SIMON HOBDAY	339
	SR. TOUR AVG.	**237**

PUTTING LEADERS

1	DAVE STOCKTON	1.732
2	JIM COLBERT	1.737
T3	RAY FLOYD	1.741
T3	LEE TREVINO	1.741
5	JIM DENT	1.744
6	GEORGE ARCHER	1.750
7	ISAO AOKI	1.753
T8	JIM ALBUS	1.762
T8	TOM WARGO	1.762
10	JIMMY POWELL	1.764
	SR. TOUR AVG.	**1.811**

EAGLE LEADERS

1	J.C. SNEAD	14
T2	TOM SHAW	12
T2	TOM WARGO	12
4	JIM ALBUS	11
5	TERRY DILL	10
T6	JIM DENT	9
T6	LARRY GILBERT	9
T6	JERRY MCGEE	9
9	3 Tied with	8
	SR. TOUR AVG.	**3**

SAND SAVES   %

1	LEE TREVINO	62.9
2	CHI CHI RODRIGUEZ	62.3
T3	DALE DOUGLASS	57.5
T3	DAVE STOCKTON	57.5
5	TOM WEISKOPF	57.4
6	BOB MURPHY	55.4
7	JIM COLBERT	55.0
8	TOMMY AARON	54.5
9	SIMON HOBDAY	54.3
10	KERMIT ZARLEY	54.1
	SR. TOUR AVG.	**45.7**

LPGA TOUR

SCORING LEADERS

1	BETH DANIEL	70.82
2	LAURA DAVIES	70.96
3	DOTTIE MOCHRIE	70.98
4	DONNA ANDREWS	71.18
5	MICHELLE MCGANN	71.43
6	MEG MALLON	71.45
7	LISELOTTE NEUMANN	71.46
8	BETSY KING	71.61
9	SHERRI STEINHAUER	71.63
10	PATTY SHEEHAN	71.65

DRIVING LEADERS

1	LAURA DAVIES	253.1
2	KELLY ROBBINS	252.7
3	MICHELLE MCGANN	246.8
4	FLORENCE DESCAMPE	246.3
5	CHRIS JOHNSON	245.8
6	JILL BRILES-HINTON	245.4
7	HELEN ALFREDSSON	245.3
8	KIM SHIPMAN	244.5
9	SUSAN THIELBAR	243.8
10	MICHELLE ESTILL	243.7

DRIVING ACCURACY

1	JODY ANSCHUTZ	.830
2	NANCY RAMSBOTTOM	.813
3	MARTA FIGUERAS-DOTTI	.804
4	MEG MALLON	.799
5	AMY FRUHWIRTH	.793
6	JENNY LIDBACK	.793
7	CAROLINE PIERCE	.792
8	DONNA ANDREWS	.789
9	LYNN CONNELLY	.788
10	BARB BUNKOWSKY	.787

GREENS IN REGULATION

1	BETH DANIEL	.740
2	DONNA ANDREWS	.736
3	BETSY KING	.729
4	SHERRI STEINHAUER	.719
5	DOTTIE MOCHRIE	.711
6	MICHELLE MCGANN	.706
7	NANCY RAMSBOTTOM	.704
8	VAL SKINNER	.703
9	LAURA DAVIES	.701
10	MEG MALLON	.697

PUTTING LEADERS

1	SHARON BARRETT	29.00
2	VICKI GOETZE	29.33
3	CINDY SCHREYER	29.46
4	JANE CRAFTER	29.49
T5	CAROLINE PIERCE	29.50
T5	STEPHANIE MAYNOR	29.50
7	JODI FIGLEY	29.55
8	ELAINE CROSBY	29.61
9	LUCIANA BEMVENUTI	29.62
10	FLORENCE DESCAMPE	29.63

BIRDIE LEADERS

1	DOTTIE MOCHRIE	310
2	KELLY ROBBINS	300
3	BETSY KING	295
4	SHERRI STEINHAUER	293
T5	MEG MALLON	287
T5	MICHELLE MCGANN	287
7	CHRIS JOHNSON	280
8	BETH DANIEL	274
9	ELAINE CROSBY	273
10	LAURA DAVIES	267

EAGLE LEADERS

1	LAURA DAVIES	15

2	MICHELLE MCGANN	9
T3	DONNA ANDREWS	7
T3	LAUREL KEAN	7
T5	JILL BRILES-MINTON	6
T5	CHRIS JOHNSON	6
	SEVEN TIED WITH	5

SAND SAVES   %

1	BETH DANIEL	.589
2	LISA WALTERS	.580
3	JOAN PETCOCK	.560
4	JULI INKSTER	.559
5	SHIRLEY FURLONG	.550
6	JUDY DICKINSON	.542
7	KIM BAUER	.516
T8	ALLISON FINNEY	.512
T8	DOTTIE MOCHRIE	.512
10	MICHELE REDMAN	.507

PGA 1994 MONEY LEADERS

1	NICK PRICE	$1,499,927
2	GREG NORMAN	$1,330,307
3	MARK MCCUMBER	$1,208,209
4	TOM LEHMAN	$1,031,144
5	FUZZY ZOELLER	$1,016,804
6	LOREN ROBERTS	$1,015,671
7	JOSE MARIA OLAZABAL	$969,900
8	COREY PAVIN	$906,305
9	JEFF MAGGERT	$814,475
10	HALE IRWIN	$814,436
11	SCOTT HOCH	$804,559
12	STEVE LOWERY	$794,048
13	MIKE SPRINGER	$770,717
14	BOB ESTES	$765,360
15	PHIL MICKELSON	$748,316
16	JOHN HUSTON	$731,499
17	BILL GLASSON	$689,110
18	BRAD BRYANT	$687,803
19	ERNIE ELS	$684,440
20	DAVID FROST	$671,683
21	BEN CRESHAW	$659,252
22	TOM KITE	$658,689
23	FRED COUPLES	$625,654
24	BRAD FAXON	$612,847
25	JAY HAAS	$593,386
26	KENNY PERRY	$585,941
27	RICK FEHR	$573,963
28	BRUCE LITZKE	$564,926
29	HAL SUTTON	$540,162
30	MARK CALCAVECCHIA	$533,201
31	MARK BROOKS	$523,285
32	CRAIG STADLER	$474,831
33	DAVIS LOVE III	$474,219
34	DAVID EDWARDS	$458,845
35	LEE JANZEN	$442,588
36	ANDREW MAGEE	$431,041
37	JOHN COOK	$429,725
38	KIRK TRIPLETT	$422,171
39	LENNIE CLEMENTS	$416,880

PGA 1994 Money Leaders, continued

40	MIKE HEINEN	$390,963
41	CURTIS STRANGE	$390,881
42	LARRY MIZE	$386,029
43	TOM WATSON	$380,373
44	ROBERT GAMEZ	$380,353
45	GLEN DAY	$357,236
46	CRAIG PARRY	$354,602
47	BLAINE MCCALLISTER	$351,554
48	BILLY ANDRADE	$342,208
49	JOHN DALY	$340,034
50	STEVE STRICKER	$334,409
51	JIM GALLAGHER, JR.	$325,976
52	VIJAY SINGH	$325,959
53	DAVE BARR	$314,885
54	GIL MORGAN	$309,690
55	JAY DON BLAKE	$309,351
56	SCOTT SIMPSON	$307,884
57	DICKY PRIDE	$305,769
58	NEAL LANCASTER	$305,038
59	JEFF SLUMAN	$301,178
60	MIKE SULLIVAN	$298,586
61	DONNIE HAMMOND	$295,436
62	STEVE ELKINGTON	$294,943
63	BRIAN HENNINGER	$294,075
64	STEVE PATE	$291,651
65	CLARK DENNIS	$289,065
66	BRETT OGLE	$284,495
67	FRED FUNK	$281,905
68	CHIP BECK	$281,131
69	GREG KRAFT	$279,901
70	NOLAN HENKE	$278,419
71	DUFFY WALDORF	$274,971
72	D.A. WEIBRING	$255,757
73	GENE SAUERS	$250,654
74	TED TRYBA	$246,481
75	PAUL GOYDOS	$241,107
76	GUY BOROS	$240,775
77	RUSS COCHRAN	$239,827
78	JIM FURYK	$236,603
79	JIM MCGOVERN	$227,764
80	BOB LOHR	$225,048
81	JOHNNY MILLER	$225,000
82	GARY HALLBERG	$224,965
83	NICK FALDO	$221,146
84	MIKE HULBERT	$221,007
85	CHRIS DIMARCO	$216,839
86	MARK O'MEARA	$214,070
87	COLIN MONTGOMERIE	$213,828
88	PETER JACOBSEN	$211,762
89	BOBBY WADKINS	$208,358
90	KEITH CLEARWATER	$203,549
91	WAYNE LEVI	$200,476
92	DAVID OGRIN	$199,199
93	MARK CARNEVALE	$192,653
94	TOM PURTZER	$187,307
95	JIM THORPE	$185,714
96	DAVE STOCKTON, JR.	$185,209
97	SCOTT VERPLANK	$183,015
98	BRIAN KAMM	$181,884
99	MIKE STANDLY	$179,850
100	DAVID FEHERTY	$178,501
101	BOB BURNS	$178,168
102	DOUG TEWELL	$177,388
103	ROBIN FREEMAN	$177,044
104	MICHAEL BRADLE	$175,137
105	DILLARD PRUITT	$171,866
106	PAUL STANKOWSKI	$170,393
107	YOSHINORI MIZUMAKI	$168,450
108	ED HUMENIK	$168,332
109	FULTON ALLEM	$166,144
110	BRIAN CLAAR	$165,370
111	BRANDEL CHAMBLEE	$161,018
112	DAN FORSMAN	$160,805
113	BILLY MAYFAIR	$158,159
114	MARK MCNULTY	$157,700
115	STEVE RINTOUL	$157,618
116	KEN GREEN	$155,156
117	JOHN WILSON	$155,058
118	BOB GILDER	$154,868
119	MIKE REID	$154,441
120	JESPER PARNEVIK	$148,816
121	JOE OZAKI	$147,308
122	JOHN MORSE	$146,137
123	PAYNE STEWART	$145,687
124	JAY DELSING	$143,738
125	DENNIS PAULSON	$142,515

LPGA 1994 MONEY LEADERS

1	LAURA DAVIES	$667,652
2	BETH DANIEL	$656,687
3	LISELOTTE NEUMANN	$505,701
4	DOTTIE MOCHRIE	$472,728
5	DONNA ANDREWS	$429,015
6	TAMMIE GREEN	$418,969
7	SHERRI STEINHAUER	$398,604
8	KELLY ROBBINS	$396,778
9	MEG MALLON	$341,627
10	ELAINE CROSBY	$338,043
11	BETSY KING	$325,074
12	PATTY SHEEHAN	$323,562
13	VAL SKINNER	$297,494
14	MICHELLE MCGANN	$269,936
15	JANE GEDDES	$257,045
16	DEB RICHARD	$251,513
17	HELEN ALFREDSSON	$247,444
18	JUDY DICKINSON	$246,879
19	PAT BRADLEY	$236,274
20	DAWN COE-JONES	$223,696
21	HIROMI KOBAYASHI	$222,774
22	MARTHA NAUSE	$210,825
23	CHRIS JOHNSON	$205,489
24	LAURI MERTEN	$202,002
25	ALICE RITZMAN	$186,715
26	LISA KIGGENS	$183,279
27	MISSIE MCGEORGE	$181,281
28	ALICIA DIBOS	$180,374
29	NANCY RAMSBOTTOM	$179,325
30	BRANDIE BURTON	$172,821
31	BARB BUNKOWSKY	$167,039
32	DALE EGGELING	$157,196
33	NANCY LOPEZ	$150,399
34	AMY ALCOTT	$150,000
35	BARB MUCHA	$147,238
36	MICHELLE ESTILL	$147,150
37	COLLEEN WALKER	$141,200
38	KRISTI ALBERS	$136,834

39	MISSIE BERTEOTTI	$121,856
40	GAIL GRAHAM	$121,812
41	MARTA FIGUERAS-DOTTI	$119,330
42	ANNIKA SORENSTAM	$118,934
43	AMY BENZ	$118,742
44	ROSIE JONES	$115,166
45	JULI INKSTER	$113,829
46	CAROLYN HILL	$111,543
47	KRIS TSCHETTER	$111,180
48	MICHELE REDMAN	$108,471
49	SHERRI TURNER	$108,282
50	JOAN PETCOCK	$108,043
51	VICKI FERGON	$102,943
52	DANA DORMANN	$101,715
53	ROBIN WALTON	$101,048
54	JAN STEPHENSON	$99,766
55	SALLY LITTLE	$97,190
56	HOLLIS STACY	$95,146
57	KIM SHIPMAN	$95,060
58	PEARL SINN	$91,499
59	JULIE LARSEN	$90,875
60	KATIE PETERSON-PARKER	$87,167
61	NANCI BOWEN	$86,338
62	MAGGIE WILL	$85,343
63	TINA BARRETT	$84,729
64	TRACY KERDYK	$84,145
65	CAROLINE PIERCE	$83,451
66	CINDY RARICK	$81,923
67	MARIANNE MORRIS	$78,630
68	JENNY LIDBACK	$75,036
69	TANIA ABITBOL	$72,586
70	STEPHANIE FARWIG	$72,454
71	CINDY FIGG-CURRIER	$72,158
72	SHELLEY HAMLIN	$71,864
73	LISA WALTERS	$71,732
74	ALLISON FINNEY	$69,132
75	JANE CRAFTER	$65,730
76	DANIELLE AMMACCAPANE	$61,964
77	SUZANNE STRUDWICK	$61,951
78	KIM WILLIAMS	$61,703
79	KAREN LUNN	$61,152
80	MUFFIN SPENCER-DEVLIN	$59,294
81	JANICE GIBSON	$58,156
82	VICKI GOETZE	$57,311
83	TERRY-JO MYERS	$57,053
84	LORI WEST	$56,594
85	ELLIE GIBSON	$56,279
86	JOANNE CARNER	$55,474
87	PAGE DUNLAP	$55,048
88	CATHY JOHNSTON-FORBES	$53,950
89	SUSIE REDMAN	$53,168
90	FLORENCE DESCAMPE	$53,020
91	DINA AMMACCAPANE	$52,453
92	KRIS MONAGHAN	$51,847
93	KIM SAIKI	$50,817
94	ALICE MILLER	$50,563
95	JILL BRILES-HINTON	$50,532
96	DENISE BALDWIN	$46,246
97	NANCY SCRANTON	$45,413
98	CINDY SCHREYER	$44,994
99	MELISSA MCNAMARA	$43,337
100	LEIGH ANN MILLS	$43,286
101	BARB THOMAS	$42,769
102	TRISH JOHNSON	$42,750
103	MARDI LUNN	$42,016
104	STEPHANIE MAYNOR	$41,570
105	MARY BETH ZIMMERMAN	$41,543
106	JENNIFER WYATT	$40,323
107	NOELLE DAGHE	$39,626
108	JEAN ZEDLITZ	$39,123
109	AMY HILL READ	$38,731
110	JANET ANDERSON	$37,968
111	ALISON NICHOLAS	$37,651
112	JODI FIGLEY	$35,585
113	PAMELA WRIGHT	$35,561
114	NANCY HARVEY	$35,552
115	CAROLINE KEGGI	$33,097
116	BECKY IVERSON	$32,146
117	KATHRYN MARSHALL	$29,957
118	NINA FOUST	$28,246
119	AYAKO OKAMOTO	$26,871
120	PENNY HAMMEL	$26,545
121	KATHY GUADAGNINO	$26,318
122	LYNN CONNELLY	$26,050
123	DEBBIE MASSEY	$24,638
124	MITZI EDGE	$23,724
125	CONNIE CHILLEMI	$23,019

SENIOR 1994 MONEY LEADERS

1	DAVE STOCKTON	$1,338,419
2	LEE TREVINO	$1,202,369
3	RAY FLOYD	$1,142,762
4	JIM ALBUS	$1,096,128
5	JIM COLBERT	$996,615
6	TOM WARGO	$928,344
7	BOB MURPHY	$855,862
8	JIM DENT	$854,891
9	LARRY GILBERT	$831,244
10	GEORGE ARCHER	$684,944
11	ISAO AOKI	$632,975
12	SIMON HOBDAY	$606,621
13	J.C. SNEAD	$564,314
14	CHI CHI RODRIGUEZ	$556,098
15	JIMMY POWELL	$555,745
16	MIKE HILL	$532,521
17	JAY SIGEL	$519,130
18	DALE DOUGLASS	$518,186
19	KERMIT ZARLEY	$517,724
20	DAVE EICHELBERGER	$516,487
21	JACK KIEFER	$509,117
22	ROCKY THOMPSON	$487,373
23	BOB CHARLES	$473,237
24	GRAHAM MARSH	$459,768
25	JERRY MCGEE	$350,119
26	TOMMY AARON	$339,815
27	GIBBY GILBERT	$324,242
28	GARY PLAYER	$309,776
29	TOM WEISKOPF	$298,624
30	DEWITT WEAVER	$295,037
31	JOHN PAUL CAIN	$274,568
32	HOD DICKSON	$254,532
33	WALTER ZEMBRISKI	$246,412
34	JACK NICKLAUS	$239,278
35	TOM SHAW	$229,119
36	TERRY DILL	$224,885
37	TONY JACKLIN	$221,384
38	LARRY LAORETTI	$220,001
39	CHARLES COODY	$219,295
40	TOMMY AYCOCK	$212,660

Senior PGA 1994 Money Leaders, continued

41	RICHARD RHYAN	$210,183
42	ORVILLE MOODY	$208,490
43	HARRY TOSCANO	$207,508
44	DICK GOETE	$202,657
45	HOMERO BLANCAS	$193,550
46	LARRY ZIEGLER	$185,644
47	BOB BRUE	$184,693
48	BEN SMITH	$180,943
49	BUTCH BAIRD	$177,031
50	CALVIN PEETE	$175,432
51	DICK LOTZ	$167,152
52	RIVES MCBEE	$166,177
53	DICK HENDRICKSON	$153,155
54	GAY BREWER	$151,314
55	DON JANUARY	$147,976
56	DON BIES	$137,185
57	LARRY MOWRY	$135,923
58	BOBBY NICHOLS	$131,695
59	HAROLD HENNING	$126,894
60	MILLER BARBER	$126,327
61	BILL HALL	$125,352
62	BOB SMITH	$123,957
63	JIM FERREE	$119,963
64	MARION HECK	$110,097
65	BRUCE CRAMPTON	$103,860
66	JOE JIMENEZ	$103,106
67	ROBERT ZIMMERMAN	$82,882
68	ROBERT GAONA	$74,873
69	AL GEIBERGER	$72,729
70	RANDY PETRI	$70,669
71	BABE HISKEY	$68,720
72	GENE LITTLER	$66,592
73	RICHARD BASSETT	$62,869
74	MIKE JOYCE	$58,155
75	DAVE HILL	$57,757
76	ROD CURL	$57,176
77	FRED RULZ	$52,986
78	GEORGE SHORTRIDGE	$50,014
79	BOB CARSON	$45,528
80	BOB REITH	$45,078
81	KEN STILL	$44,991
82	BOB GOALBY	$44,904
83	BILLY CASPER	$43,970
84	BOB BETLEY	$42,683
85	LEE ELDER	$42,070
86	BOB WYNN	$40,523
87	BRUCE DEVLIN	$40,224
88	AL KELLEY	$39,304
89	BOB PANASIK	$39,020
90	CHARLES SIFFORD	$35,325
91	ARNOLD PALMER	$34,471
92	ED SNEED	$30,256
93	WALTER MORGAN	$27,444
94	LOU GRAHAM	$24,153
95	DON MASSENGALE	$23,595
96	BRUCE SUMMERHAYS	$20,711
97	RON SKILES	$18,926
98	TOMMY HORTON	$18,119
99	BOB IRVING	$16,958
100	GENE BOREK	$16,475
101	ROBERT RAWLINS	$14,795
102	ART PROCTOR	$14,743
103	BOB LEAVER	$13,869
104	JOHN BRODIE	$12,996
105	ROGER KENNEDY	$12,680
106	BRUCE LEHNHARD	$11,116
107	BUNKY HENRY	$10,993
108	TERRY SMALL	$10,706
109	JESSE VAUGHN	$10,609
110	HOWIE JOHNSON	$ 9,774
111	BILLY MAYWELL	$ 9,550
112	MIKE FETCHICK	$9,473
113	KIKUO ARAI	$8,500
114	ROGER STERN	$8,198
115	QUINTON GRAY	$8,118
116	BOB MENNE	$7,533
117	PAT O'BRIEN	$7,435
118	JIM O'HERN	$7,378
119	RANDY GLOVER	$7,369
120	SNELL LANCASTER	$7,194
121	DOUG DALELEL	$7,140
122	DOUG FORD	$6,259
123	DOW FINSTERWALD	$6,196
124	BOB VERWEY	$6,184
125	TOM ULOZAS	$6,155

NIKE 1994 MONEY LEADERS

1	CHRIS PERRY	$167,148
2	SCOTT GUMP	$161,035
3	PAT BATES	$155,469
4	JIM CARTER	$142,750
5	SKIP KENDALL	$131,067
6	BRUCE VAUGHAN	$129,617
7	TOMMY ARMOUR III	$126,620
8	DAVID DUVAL	$126,430
9	JERRY HAAS	$116,583
10	EMLYN AUBREY	$113,919
11	SONNY SKINNER	$112,178
12	LEE RINKER	$108,229
13	KEITH FERGUS	$107,053
14	BILL MURCHISON	$104,765
15	CLARK BURROUGHS	$102,998
16	TOMMY TOLLES	$98,618
17	MIKE SCHUCHART	$97,546
18	BRAD FABEL	$95,138
19	THOMAS SCHERRER	$87,131
20	BILL PORTER	$82,599
21	CHARLES RYMER	$75,658
22	RICK PEARSON	$75,292
23	WOODY AUSTIN	$72,206
24	VIC WILK	$68,145
25	ROBERT FRIEND	$65,009
26	JERRY KELLY	$60,928
27	TIM LOUSTALOT	$57,995
28	GARY RUSNAK	$57,003
29	CRAIG KANADA	$56,516
30	OMAR URESTI	$53,987
31	JEFF BARLOW	$53,214
32	FRANK CONNER	$50,243
33	BUDDY GARDNER	$50,033
34	JEFF COOK	$50,030
35	JOHN MAGINNES	$48,381
36	BOB WOLCOTT	$47,785
37	MIKE BRISKY	$46,938
38	JOHN ELLIOTT	$45,525
39	DANNY BRIGGS	$44,145
40	J.P. HAYES	$42,066
41	DENNIS POSTLEWAIT	$41,641
42	DAVID JACKSON	$40,870
43	DAVID KIRKPATRICK	$38,802
44	GREG BRUCKNER	$37,084
45	JEFF BREHAUT	$36,598

NIKE 1994 Money Leaders, continued

46	TOM CARR	$36,105	39	TIM SIMPSON	$3,348,787
47	MIKE SPOSA	$32,772	40	JEFF SLUMAN	$3,296,749
48	CHAD GINN	$31,928	41	LARRY NELSON	$3,273,248
49	REX CALDWELL	$31,703	42	STEVE ELKINGTON	$3,271,135
50	HARRY FABYAN	$31,604	43	ANDY BEAN	$3,243,075
51	RON PHILO	$31,187	44	KEN GREEN	$3,174,225
52	HUGH ROYER III	$30,059	45	LOREN ROBERTS	$3,131,398
53	MATT PETERSON	$29,993	46	TOM PURTZER	$3,130,116
54	TOM GARNER	$29,708	47	JOHN HUSTON	$3,113,443
55	FRANKLIN LANGHAM	$27,957	48	D.A. WEIBRING	$3,095,307
56	TIM CONLEY	$25,140	49	BRAD FAXON	$3,065,652
57	PETER PERSONS	$25,040	50	MIKE REID	$3,029,011
58	STEVE HASKINS	$24,672	51	BOB TWAY	$3,028,191
59	BRIAN HENNINGER	$23,905	52	MARK BROOKS	$2,933,316
60	MIKE SMITH	$23,723	53	DAN FORSMAN	$2,845,611
61	WEBB HEINTZELMAN	$23,180	54	BILL GLASSON	$2,818,132
62	R.W. EAKS	$23,123	55	JODIE MUDD	$2,763,755
63	HARRY RUDOLPH	$22,935	56	JOHNNY MILLER	$2,745,424
64	JEFF GALLAGHER	$22,595	57	DAN POHL	$2,742,851
65	SAM RANDOLPH	$22,585	58	GENE SAUERS	$2,690,997
66	TRAY TYNER	$22,540	59	DON POOLEY	$2,584,319
67	GARY WEBB	$22,373	60	HUBERT GREEN	$2,580,463
68	TOM BYRUM	$21,120	61	ANDREW MAGEE	$2,575,955
69	JIM SCHUKAN	$20,974	62	MIKE HULBERT	$2,566,972
70	RICH PARKER	$20,610	63	LEE JANZEN	$2,531,430

PGA TOUR CAREER MONEY

			64	HOWARD TWITTY	$2,524,478
			65	RUSS COCHRAN	$2,523,319
1	TOM KITE	$9,159,418	66	BOB GILDER	$2,497,111
2	GREG NORMAN	$7,937,669	67	RICK FEHR	$2,472,430
3	FRED COUPLES	$6,889,149	68	BLAINE MCCALLISTER	$2,439,597
4	PAUL AZINGER	$6,774,728	69	DONNIE HAMMOND	$2,426,578
5	TOM WATSON	$6,751,328	70	DOUG TEWELL	$2,378,598
6	NICK PRICE	$6,726,418	71	CALVIN PEETE	$2,302,363
7	PAYNE STEWART	$6,523,260	72	BOBBY WADKINS	$2,281,686
8	CURTIS STRANGE	$6,433,442	73	ROCCO MEDIATE	$2,261,620
9	BEN CRENSHAW	$6,107,759	74	TOM WEISKOPF	$2,241,687
10	LANNY WADKINS	$5,931,370	75	JEFF MAGGERT	$2,225,845
11	CORY PAVIN	$5,835,444	76	J.C. SNEAD	$2,219,171
12	HAL IRWIN	$5,654,063	77	DAVE BARR	$2,152,105
13	CRAIG STADLER	$5,606,436	78	BRAD BRYANT	$2,142,399
14	CHIP BECK	$5,585,763	79	MARK WIEBE	$2,136,907
15	BRUCE LIETZKE	$5,440,868	80	ROGER MALTBIE	$2,102,415
16	JACK NICKLAUS	$5,372,176	81	TOM LEHMAN	$2,072,026
17	MARK O'MEARA	$5,212,337	82	KENNY PERRY	$2,070,684
18	RAY FLOYD	$5,129,013	83	BILLY ANDRADE	$2,034,796
19	DAVID FROST	$5,100,514	84	GARY HALLBERG	$2,028,979
20	MARK CALCAVECCHIA	$5,023,163	85	KEITH CLEARWATER	$2,021,787
21	FUZZY ZOELLER	$4,748,065	86	IAN BAKER-FINCH	$1,998,077
22	GIL MORGAN	$4,735,568	87	NOLAN HENKE	$1,978,048
23	SCOTT HOCH	$4,673,254	88	FULTON ALLEM	$1,977,016
24	JAY HAAS	$4,604,562	89	BOBLOHR	$1,972,842
25	DAVIS LOVE III	$4,511,891	90	JAY DON BLAKE	$1,943,438
26	MARK MCCUMBER	$4,423,778	91	MIKE DONAL	$1,933,004
27	LARRY MIZE	$4,294,710	92	MIKE SULLIVAN	$1,909,914
28	JOHN COOK	$4,274,977	93	ARNOLD PALMER	$1,904,667
29	WAYNE LEVI	$4,191,292	94	BOB ESTE	$1,898,407
30	SCOTT SIMPSON	$3,973,157	95	STEVE JONES	$1,894,679
31	HAL SUTTON	$3,931,853	96	DAVID GRAHAM	$1,874,780
32	JOHN MAHAFFEY	$3,671,400	97	JIM THORPE	$1,860,830
33	STEVE PATE	$3,571,833	98	BILLY MAYFAIR	$1,854,433
34	JIM GALLAGHER, JR.	$3,526,698	99	ED FIORI	$1,831,823
35	LEE TREVINO	$3,478,449	100	GARY PLAYER	$1,814,950
36	PETER JACOBSEN	$3,472,507	101	WAYNE GRADY	$1,808,421
37	DAVID EDWARDS	$3,420,417	102	MARK LYE	$1,800,654
38	JOEY SINDELAR	$3,362,503	103	LEONARD THOMPSON	$1,782,683
			104	GREG BURNS	$1,763,208
			105	BILL RITTON	$1,736,642

PGA Career Money Leaders, continued

106	DAVE RUMMELS	$1,723,929
107	DAVID PEOPLES	$1,709,103
108	MORRIS HATALSKY	$1,693,447
109	BILLY CASPER	$1,691,583
110	BOB MURPHY	$1,642,861
111	PHIL BLACKMAR	$1,636,584
112	GARY KOCH	$1,613,407
113	MILLER BARBER	$1,602,408
114	LON HINKLE	$1,600,247
115	KENNY KNOX	$1,595,087
116	DUFFY WALDORF	$1,587,825
117	GENE LITTLER	$1,578,625
118	ROBERT GAMEZ	$1,574,214
119	TED SCHULZ	$1,571,878
120	BILY RAY BROWN	$1,570,170
121	JERY PATE	$1,556,872
122	JIM COLBERT	$1,553,135
123	BOB EASTWOOD	$1,551,414
124	ACE RENNER	$1,548,764
125	PHIL MICKELSON	$1,547,984

LPGA CAREER MONEY

1	BETSY KING	$4,827,708
2	PAT BRADLEY	$4,772,115
3	BETH DANIEL	$4,489,352
4	PATTY SHEEHAN	$4,455,399
5	NANCY LOPEZ	$4,017,249
6	AMY ALCOTT	$3,060,706
7	JOANNE CARNER	$2,840,071
8	AYAKO OKAMOTO	$2,710,231
9	DOTTIE MOCHRIE	$2,574,716
10	JAN STEPHENSON	$2,275,075
11	JANE GEDDES	$2,252,699
12	ROSIE JONES	$2,184,531
13	JULI INKSTER	$2,070,418
14	HOLLIS STACY	$2,004,109
15	COLLEEN WALKER	$1,991,323
16	JUDY DICKINSON	$1,990,807
17	MEG MALLON	$1,850,301
18	KATHY WHITWORTH	$1,726,597
19	TAMMIE GREEN	$1,715,863
20	DEB RICHARD	$1,669,243
21	LAURA DAVIES	$1,666,108
22	SALLY LITTLE	$1,647,285
23	DANIELLE AMMACCAPANE	$1,631,836
24	CHRIS JOHNSON	$1,550,927
25	DAWN COE-JONES	$1,522,483
26	SHERRI STEINHAUER	$1,453,252
27	DONNA CAPONI	$1,387,919
28	KATHY POSTLEWAIT	$1,381,510
29	LISELOTTE NEUMANN	$1,364,478
30	ALICE RITZMAN	$1,362,909
31	CINDY RARICK	$1,345,708
32	SANDRA PALMER	$1,331,999
33	JANE BLALOCK	$1,290,943
34	BRANDIE BURTON	$1,286,545
35	DEBBIE MASSEY	$1,267,042
36	VAL SKINNER	$1,231,828
37	SHERRI TURNER	$1,196,401
38	DONNA ANDREWS	$1,189,041
39	DALE EGGELING	$1,174,494
40	ELAINE CROSBY	$1,165,291
41	LAURI MERTEN	$1,112,217
42	MARTHA NAUSE	$1,111,220
43	VICKI FERGON	$1,106,649
44	AMY BENZ	$1,098,729
45	PATTI RIZZO	$1,072,650
46	NANCY SCRANTON	$1,057,097
47	SANDRA HAYNIE	$1,055,874
48	MARTA FIGUERAS-DOTTI	$1,040,292
49	ALICE MILLER	$1,025,608
50	MICHELLE MCGANN	$993,107
51	KRISTI ALBERS	$952,311
52	MISSIE BERTEOTTI	$938,090
53	SHELLEY HAMLIN	$921,460
54	JANE CRAFTER	$918,059
55	HELEN ALFREDSSON	$914,479
56	DONNA WHITE	$908,589
57	LORI GARBACZ	$897,700
58	MISSIE MCGEORGE	$894,381
59	JUDY RANKIN	$887,858
60	BARB BUNKOWSKY	$847,766
61	JODY ANSCHUTZ	$835,652
62	CATHY GERRING	$821,185
63	MUFFIN SPENCER-DEVLIN	$791,022
64	CATHY MORSE	$771,694
65	HIROMI KOBAYASHI	$771,592
66	SANDRA POST	$746,714
67	LAURIE RINKER-GRAHAM	$740,486
68	ROBIN WALTON	$729,130
69	TINA BARRETT	$726,455
70	PENNY HAMMEL	$709,086
71	DANA DORMANN	$696,917
72	KELLY ROBBINS	$687,927
73	MARY BETH ZIMMERMAN	$685,156
74	BARB MUCHA	$681,469
75	CAROLINE KEGGI	$676,670
76	LAURA BAUGH	$663,843
77	KRIS TSCHETTER	$660,435
78	OK HEE KU	$644,445
79	LISA WALTERS	$637,303
80	JO ANN WASHAM	$634,055
81	MYRA BLACKWELDER	$629,814
82	JANET COLES	$628,282
83	ALLISON FINNEY	$615,486
84	JANET ANDERSON	$612,552
85	SHIRLEY FURLONG	$606,221
86	KRIS MONAGHAN	$598,281
87	TRISH JOHNSON	$593,153
88	CINDY FIGG-CURRIER	$588,793
89	CAROLYN HILL	$584,482
90	JERILYN BRITZ	$563,352
91	SANDRA SPUZICH	$560,878
92	PENNY PULZ	$540,401
93	BONNIE LAUER	$539,876
94	DEBBIE AUSTIN	$532,972
95	LYNN ADAMS	$529,428
96	ANNE-MARIE PALLI	$528,975
97	KATHY GUADAGNINO	$514,620
98	BECKY PEARSON	$511,548
99	SILVIA BERTOLACCINI	$511,395
100	CAROL MANN	$506,666
101	DOT GERMAIN	$505,704
102	PAMELA WRIGHT	$481,896
103	MARLENE HAGGE	$481,031
104	NANCY RAMSBOTTOM	$476,446
105	MICHELLE ESTILL	$472,452
106	MAGGIE WILL	$459,732
107	MITZI EDGE	$451,953
108	CINDY HILL	$442,977
109	LYNN CONNELLY	$432,746
110	JOAN PETCOCK	$430,978

LPGA Career Money Leaders, continued

111	JILL BRILES-HINTON	$401,108
112	PAT MEYERS	$397,488
113	LENORE RITTENHOUSE	$397,258
114	CATHY MARINO	$386,703
115	CATHY JOHNSTON-FORBES	$377,542
116	KIM SHIPMAN	$373,225
117	TRACY KERDYK	$371,750
118	JO ANN PRENTICE	$370,292
119	MICKEY WRIGHT	$368,770
120	DEEDEE LASKER	$364,297
121	GAIL GRAHAM	$364,132
122	BETH SOLOMON	$362,529
123	STEPHANIE FARWIG	$357,335
124	SUSAN SANDERS	$350,163
125	TERRY-JO MYERS	$345,548

SENIOR CAREER MONEY

1	BOB CHARLES	$5,162,605
2	LEE TREVINO	$5,108,902
3	CHI CHI RODRIGUEZ	$5,095,222
4	MIKE HILL	$4,506,499
5	GEORGE ARCHER	$4,319,452
6	DALE DOUGLASS	$4,087,677
7	BRUCE CRAMPTON	$3,604,534
8	JIM DENT	$3,522,605
9	JIM COLBERT	$3,483,021
10	GARY PLAYER	$3,466,026
11	MILLER BARBER	$3,393,652
12	DAVE STOCKTON	$3,183,785
13	AL CEIBERGER	$3,101,060
14	ORVILLE MOODY	$3,057,323
15	HAROLD HENNING	$2,942,073
16	DON JANUARY	$2,827,192
17	CHARLES COODY	$2,692,028
18	JIM ALBUS	$2,444,543
19	WALTER ZEMBRISKI	$2,374,676
20	RAY FLOYD	$2,292,920
21	ROCKY THOMPSON	$2,254,004
22	JIM FERREE	$2,126,146
23	DAVE HILL	$2,067,259
24	GENE LITTLER	$2,044,991
25	SIMON HOBDAY	$2,028,075
26	GIBBY GILBERT	$1,981,602
27	DON BIES	$1,901,353
28	JIMMY POWELL	$1,789,840
29	J.C. SNEAD	$1,785,293
30	BOBBY NICHOLS	$1,637,662
31	BILLY CASPER	$1,625,173
32	BOB MURPHY	$1,624,605
33	GAY BREWER	$1,622,645
34	LARRY MOWRY	$1,596,470
35	TOMMY AARON	$1,557,620
36	DEWITT WEAVER	$1,553,669
37	ARNOLD PALMER	$1,535,247
38	BUTCH BAIRD	$1,531,290
39	ISAO AOKI	$1,513,292
40	TOM SHAW	$1,493,504
41	TOM WARGO	$1,485,614
42	BEN SMITH	$1,464,139
43	LEE ELDER	$1,415,430
44	LARRY LAORETTI	$1,387,540
45	RIVES MCBEE	$1,357,402
46	LARRY GILBERT	$1,347,034
47	DICK HENDRICKSON	$1,345,636
48	KERMIT ZARLEY	$1,280,944
49	JACK NICKLAUS	$1,243,588
50	TERRY DILL	$1,219,753
51	JACK KIEFER	$1,187,106
52	BOB BRUE	$1,164,087
53	DON MASSENGALE	$1,163,954
54	JOE JIMENEZ	$1,152,943
55	RICHARD RHYAN	$1,144,580
56	PETER THOMSON	$1,061,118
57	JOHN PAUL CAIN	$1,020,023
58	LARRY ZIEGLER	$941,910
59	HOMERO BLANCAS	$911,742
60	CHARLES SIFFORD	$903,005
61	AL KELLEY	$846,272
62	KEN STILL	$837,824
63	FRANK BEARD	$779,684
64	BOB BETLEY	$711,760
65	CHARLES OWENS	$708,090
66	LOU GRAHAM	$699,810
67	BOB GOALBY	$692,553
68	JOHN BRODIE	$688,305
69	BRUCE DEVLIN	$674,489
70	MIKE FETCHICK	$670,321
71	DOUG DALZIEL	$625,493
72	TOMMY AYCOCK	$614,517
73	BOB ERICKSON	$609,416
74	TOM WEISKOPF	$595,152
75	DOUG SANDERS	$534,117
76	HOWIE JOHNSON	$531,759
77	DAVE EICHELBERGER	$528,414
78	MIKE JOYCE	$527,423
79	JAY SIGEL	$519,130
80	BABE HISKEY	$514,238
81	JIM O'HERN	$512,947
82	J.C. GOOSIE	$496,221
83	BOB WYNN	$489,766
84	JERRY MCGEE	$463,310
85	GRAHAM MARSH	$459,768
86	JACK FLECK	$453,450
87	BILLY MAXWELL	$447,195
88	PHIL RODGERS	$426,329
89	HARRY TOSCANO	$420,507
90	ROBERTO DE VICENZO	$406,858
91	GORDON JONES	$401,867
92	ART WALL	$399,733
93	BILL COLLINS	$396,542
94	DICK LOTZ	$369,071
95	JIM KING	$347,116
96	DOUG FORD	$342,145
97	FRED HAWKINS	$332,688
98	BILL JOHNSTON	$325,566
99	DICK GOETZ	$318,442
100	BOB REITH	$308,479
101	CHICK EVANS	$292,843
102	QUINTON GRAY	$291,913
103	GARDNER DICKINSON	$284,066
104	ROBERT GAONA	$281,700
105	ROBERT RAWLINS	$280,023
106	WALTER MORGAN	$277,610
107	PAUL HARNEY	$269,152
108	DAN MORGAN	$261,200
109	BOB DICKSON	$254,532
110	BOB TOSKI	$252,435
111	JIM COCHRAN	$242,178
112	AL BALDING	$241,632
113	GEORGE BAYER	$240,338
114	AL CHANDLER	$235,513
115	TONY JACKLIN	$221,384

Senior PGA Career Money Leaders, continued

116	ART SILVESTRONE	$219,610
117	BOB BOLDT	$218,673
118	PAUL MORAN	$214,303
119	DOW FINSTERWALD	$214,283
120	BOB STONE	$198,876
121	GARY COWAN	$185,663
122	FRED HAAS	$183,373
123	CALVIN PEETE	$182,408
124	AGIM BARDHA	$177,171
125	RAFE BOTTS	$172,929

SONY RANKINGS—TOP 50

(As of 10/23/94)

1	NICK PRICE, ZIM	21.54
2	GREG NORMAN, AUS	21.06
3	NICK FALDO, ENG	15.79
4	JOSE-MARIA OLAZABAL, SP	15.27
5	BERNHARD LANGER, GER	15.07
6	FRED COUPLES, USA	14.04
7	ERNIE ELS, SA	13.66
8	COLIN MONTGOMERIE, EUR	12.78
9	COREY PAVIN, USA	11.02
10	DAVID FROST, SA	10.22
11	MASAHI OZAKI, JAP	9.69
12	TOM KITE, USA	9.53
13	MARK MCNULTY, ZIM	8.58
14	VIJAY SINGH, FIJ	8.53
15	IAN WOOSNAM, WAL	8.47
16	TOM LEHMAN, USA	8.34
17	FUZZY ZOELLER, USA	8.32
18	SEVE BALLESTEROS, SP	8.29
19	PHIL MICKELSON, USA	7.58
20	PAUL AZINGER, USA	7.44
21	LOREN ROBERTS, USA	7.42
22	DAVIS LOVE III, USA	7.08
23	LARRY MIZE, USA	6.81
24	BRAD FAXON, USA	6.75
25	JOHN COOK, USA	6.72
26	TOM WATSON, USA	6.20
27	HALE LRWIN, USA	6.12
28	LEE JANZEN, USA	5.93
29	FRANK NOBILO, NZ	5.87
30	JEFF MAGGERT, USA	5.82
31	DAVID GIFFORD, EUR	5.64
32	STEVE ELKINGTON, AUS	5.63
33	BARRY LANE, EUR	5.56
34	JOHN HUSTON, USA	5.38
35	JESPER PARNEVIK, EUR	5.38
36	SCOTT HOCH, USA	5.36
37	TOMMY NAKAJIMA, JAP	5.34
38	SAM TORRANCE, EUR	5.33
39	BEN CRENSHAW, USA	5.27
40	PETER SENIOR, AUS	5.20
41	DAVID EDWARDS, USA	5.17
42	BRUCE LIETZKE, USA	5.17
43	MARK MCCUMBER, USA	5.15
44	CRAIG PARRY, AUS	5.13
45	CURTIS STRANGE, USA	5.07
46	MIGUEL JIMENEZ, EUR	5.03
47	JAY HAAS, USA	4.91
48	BOB ESTES, USA	4.88
49	RICK FEHR, USA	4.84
50	MARK ROE, EUR	4.84

PING LEADERBOARD—TOP 50

(As of 10/23/94)

1	LAURA DAVIES, ENG	316.22
2	LISELOTTE NEUMANN, SWE	227.65
3	BETSY KING, USA	181.55
4	DONNA ANDREWS, USA	176.03
5	DOTTIE MOCHRIE, USA	173.45
6	HELEN AFREDSSON, SWE	169.05
7	BETH DANIEL, USA	159.58
8	TAMMIE GREEN, USA	157.98
9	PATTY SHEEHAN, USA	157.17
10	BRANDIE BURTON, USA	132.88
11	JANE GEDDES, USA	124.53
12	MEG MALLON, USA	119.40
13	KELLY ROBBINS, USA	115.78
14	SHERRIE STEINHAUER, USA	110.11
15	LAUD MERTEN, USA	98.78
16	MICHELLE MCGANN, USA	98.39
17	M. HIRASE, JAP	97.55
18	AYAKO OKAMOTO, JAP	96.55
19	DEB RICHARD, USA	94.85
20	HIROMO KOBAYASHI, JAP	92.69
21	MICHIKO HATTORI, JAP	90.00
22	JAE-SOOK WON, KOR	89.60
23	D. COE-JONES, CAN	89.40
24	ELAINE CROSBY, USA	85.70
25	TRISH JOHNSON, ENG	80.67
26	TOSHIMI KIMURA, JAP	77.30
27	PAT BRADLEY, USA	76.99
28	ANNIKA SORESTAM, SWE	76.38
29	JUDY DICKINSON, USA	75.69
30	IKUYO SHIOTANI, JAP	74.70
31	KIMINO HIYOSHI, JAP	70.80
32	A. FUKUSHIMA, JAP	70.50
33	CORINNE DIBNAH, AUS	67.75
34	NANCY LOPEZ, USA	65.82
35	VAL SKINNER, USA	65.65
36	YUKO MORIGUCHI, JAP	61.70
37	JULI INKSTER, USA	58.90
38	ROSIE JONES, USA	56.63
39	MISSIE MCGEORGE, USA	55.68
40	NANCY RAMSBOTTOM, USA	55.32
41	LISA KIGGENS, USA	55.30
42	ALICE RITZMAN, USA	54.59
43	M. DE LORENZI, FR	54.25
44	M. MURAI, JAP	53.10
45	LORA FAIRCLOUGH, ENG	52.00
46	CHRIS JOHNSON, USA	51.50
47	MARTHA NAUSE, USA	51.15
48	DALE EGGELING, USA	49.77
49	A. YAMAOKA, JAP	49.00
50	TRACY HANSON, USA	48.60

PERSONALITIES

OVERVIEW: *Biographies and career summaries of leading players, administrators, and members of the media.*

PGA TOUR

JOHN ADAMS

Birthdate: May 5,1954
Birthplace: Altus, OK
Exempt Status: 151st on 1994 money list.
PGA TOUR Victories: None.
Other Victories: 1975 Arizona State Amateur.
National/International Teams: None.

PGA TOUR CAREER SUMMARY

Year	Money	Rank
1978	$2,025	196
1979	$1,785	224
1980	$19,895	123
1981	$17,898	138
1982	$54,014	85
1983	$59,287	87
1984	$73,567	80
1985	$9,613	181
1986	$64,906	124
1987	$51,976	149
1988	$64,341	140
1989	$104,824	120
1990	$126,733	122
1991	$117,549	125
1992	$173,069	89
1993	$221,753	78
1994	$106,689	151
Career	$1,272,924	144

FULTON ALLEM

Birthdate: September 15, 1957
Birthplace: Kroonstad, South Africa
Exempt Status: 1993 Tournament Winner.
PGA TOUR Victories: (3) 1991 Independent Insurance Agent Open, 1993 Southwestern Bell Colonial, NEC World Series of Golf.
Other Victories: None.
National/International Teams: None.

PGA TOUR CAREER SUMMARY

Year	Money	Rank
1987	$88,734	105
1988	$163,911	73
1989	$134,706	104
1990	$134,493	116
1991	$229,702	71
1992	$208,981	74
1993	$851,345	9
1994	$166,144	109
Career	$1,977,017	**88**

MICHAEL ALLEN

Birthdate: January 31, 1959
Birthplace: San Mateo, CA
Exempt Status: 162nd on 1994 money list.
PGA TOUR Victories: None.
Other Victories: 1989 Bell Scottish Open.
National/International Teams: None.

PGA TOUR CAREER SUMMARY

Year	Money	Rank
1990	$95,319	14
1991	$47,626	177
1992	$11,455	233
1993	$23,107	273
1994	$91,191	162
Career	$476,663	239

BILLY ANDRADE

Birthdate: January 25, 1964
Birthplace: Fall River, MA
Exempt Status: Top 125 on 1994 money list.
PGA TOUR Victories: 1991 Kemper Open, Buick Classic.
Other Victories: None.
National/International Teams: 1986 World Amateur Cup, 1987 Walker Cup.

PGA TOUR CAREER SUMMARY

Year	Money	Rank
1988	$74,950	134
1989	$202,242	69
1990	$231,362	64
1991	$615,765	14
1992	$202,509	76

Year	Money	Rank
1993	$365,759	40
1994	$342,208	48
Career	$2,034,796	83

PAUL AZINGER

Birthdate: January 6,1960
Birthplace: Holyoke, MA
Exempt Status: Winner, 1993 PGA.
PGA TOUR Victories: (11)**1987** Phoenix Open, Panasonic-Las Vegas Invitational, Canon-Sammy Davis Jr. Greater Hartford Open. **1988** Hertz Bay Hill Classic. **1989** Canon Greater Hartford Open. **1990** MONY Tournament of Champions. **1991** AT&T Pebble Beach National Pro-Am. **1992** Tour Championship. **1993** Memorial Tournament, New England Classic, PGA Championship.
Other Victories: 1988 Fred Meyer Challenge (with Bob Tway), **1990** BMW Open, **1991** Fred Meyer Challenge (with Ben Crenshaw) **1992** BMW Open.
National/International Teams: 1989 Ryder Cup, World Cup. **1991** Ryder Cup. **1993** Ryder Cup.

PGA TOUR CAREER SUMMARY

Year	Money	Rank
1982	$10,655	171
1983	DNP	---
1984	$27,821	144
1985	$81,179	93
1986	$254,019	29
1987	$822,481	2
1988	$594,850	11
1989	$951,649	3
1990	$944,731	4
1991	$685,603	9
1992	$929,863	7
1993	$1,458,456	2
1994	$13,422	242
Career	$6,774,728	4

IAN BAKER-FINCH

Birthdate: October 24, 1960
Birthplace: Nambour, Australia
Exempt Status: Winner, 1991 British Open.
PGA TOUR Victories: (1) **1989** Southwestern Bell Colonial.
Other Victories: 1988 Australian Masters. **1991** British Open.
National/International Teams: 1985 Australian World Cup, Australia/New Zealand Kirin Cup. **1986,1987,1988** Kirin Cup. **1989, 1990, 1991** Four Tours World Championship of Golf.

PGA TOUR CAREER SUMMARY

Year	Money	Rank
1988	$75,640	133
1989	$253,309	53
1990	$611,492	16
1991	$649,513	13
1992	$261,816	58
1993	$140,621	114
1994	$81,326	167
Career	$1,998,077	86

SEVE BALLESTEROS

Birthdate: April 9,1957
Birthplace: Pedrena, Santander, Spain
Exempt Status: Non-Exempt.
PGA TOUR Victories: (6) **1978** Greater Greensboro Open. **1980** Masters. **1983** Masters, Manufacturers Hanover Westchester Classic. **1985** USF&G Classic. **1988** Manufacturers Hanover Westchester Classic.
Other Victories: 1976 Swiss Open Japanese Open Dunlop Phoenix (Japan) Lancome Trophy Swiss Open. **1977** French Open. **1978** Swiss Open, German Open, Japanese Open, Kenya Open, Lancome Trophy. **1980** Dutch Open, Madrid Open. **1981** World Match Play, Madrid Open, Dunlop Phoenix (Japan), Australian PGA, Spanish Open. **1982** World Match Play, French Open. **1983** Irish Open, British PGA, Lancome Trophy. **1984** British Open, World Match Play. **1985** French Open, World Match Play, Spanish Open, Irish Open,1986 French Open, Irish Open, British Masters, Dutch Open, Lancome Trophy. **1988** Taiheiyo Masters (Japan), British Open, German Open, Dunlop Phoenix (Japan), Lancome Trophy. **1989** Swiss Open, Madrid Open. **1991** Volvo PGA, British Masters.**1992** Dubai Desert Classic, Turespana Open de Balearas.
National/International Teams: 1975, 1976, 1977,1992 World Cup. **1979, 1983,1985, 1987, 1989, 1991, 1993** Ryder Cup. **1986,1988** Dunhill Cup.

PGA TOUR CAREER SUMMARY

Year	Money	Rank
1983	$210,933	18
1984	$132,660	52
1985	$206,638	18
1986	$45,877	141
1987	$305,058	32
1988	$165,202	71
1989	$138,094	101
1990	$84,584	144
1991	$64,320	160

Year	Money	Rank
1992	$39,206	184
1993	$34,850	193
1994	$49,245	189
Career	$1,476,667	N/A

DAVE BARR

Birthdate: March 1, 1952
Birthplace: Kelowna, British Columbia
Exempt Status: Top 125 on 1994 money list.
PGA TOUR Victories: (2) 1981 Quad Cities Open. **1987** Georgia-Pacific Atlanta Golf Classic.
Other Victories: 1983 World Cup Individual Title. **1985** World Cup Team Title (with Dan Halldorson). **1994** Alfred Dunhill Cup.
National/International Teams: 1972 Canadian World Amateur Cup. **1977,1978, 1982, 1983, 1984, 1985, 1987, 1988, 1989, 1990, 1991, 1993** World Cup. **1986, 1987, 1988, 1989, 1990, 1993, 1994** Dunhill Cup.

PGA TOUR CAREER SUMMARY

Year	Money	Rank
1978	$11,897	133
1979	$13,022	142
1980	$14,664	141
1981	$46,214	90
1982	$12,474	166
1983	$52,800	96
1984	$113,336	62
1985	$126,177	65
1986	$122,181	70
1987	$202,241	54
1988	$291,244	33
1989	$190,480	75
1990	$197,979	80
1991	$144,389	108
1992	$118,859	119
1993	$179,264	96
1994	$314,885	53
Career	$2,152,105	77

CHIP BECK

Birthdate: September 12, 1956
Birthplace: Fayetteville, NC
Exempt Status: 68th on 1994 money list..
PGA TOUR Victories: (4) 1988 Los Angeles Open, USF&G Classic. **1990** Buick Open. **1992** Freeport-McMoran Classic.
Other Victories: 1989, 1992 Merrill Lynch Shoot-Out Championships.
National/International Teams: 1988 Kirin Cup.**1989** Asahi Glass Four Tours World

Championship of Golf. **1989, 1991, 1993** Ryder Cup.

PGA TOUR CAREER SUMMARY

Year	Money	Rank
1980	$17,109	131
1981	$30,034	110
1982	$57,608	76
1983	$149,909	33
1984	$177,289	34
1985	$76,036	97
1986	$215,140	39
1987	$523,003	9
1988	$918,818	2
1989	$894,087	9
1990	$571,816	17
1991	$578,535	16
1992	$689,703	17
1993	$803,376	25
1994	$281,131	68
Career	$5,585,764	14

RONNIE BLACK

Birthdate: May 26,1958
Birthplace: Hobbs, NM
Exempt Status: 137th on 1994 money list.
PGA TOUR Victories: (2) 1983 Southern Open. **1984** Anheuser-Busch Classic.
Other Victories: None.
National/International Teams: None.

PGA TOUR CAREER SUMMARY

Year	Money	Rank
1982	$6,329	91
1983	$87,524	63
1984	$172,636	35
1985	$ 61,684	109
1986	$166,761	56
1987	$144,158	77
1988	$100,603	112
1989	$264,988	51
1990	$34,011	90
1991	$135,865	113
1992	$129,386	11
1993	$120,041	125
1994	$123,404	137
Career	$1,547,380	126

JAY DON BLAKE

Birthdate: October 28, 1958
Birthplace: St. George, UT
Exempt Status: 55th on 1994 money list.
PGA TOUR Victories: 1991 Shearson Lehman Brothers Open.

Other Victories: None.
National/International Teams: None.

PGA TOUR CAREER SUMMARY

Year	Money	Rank
1987	$ 87,634	106
1988	$131,937	90
1989	$200,499	71
1990	$148,384	106
1991	$563,854	21
1992	$299,298	51
1993	$202,482	86
1994	$309,351	55
Career	$1,943,438	90

BRAD BRYANT

Birthdate: December 11, 1954
Birthplace: Amarillo, TX
Exempt Status: 18th on 1994 money list.
PGA TOUR Victories: None.
Other Victories: 1988 Utah State Open.
National/International Teams: None.

PGA TOUR CAREER SUMMARY

Year	Money	Rank
1978	$ 4,350	173
1979	$ 63,013	67
1980	$ 56,115	68
1981	$ 52,070	80
1982	$ 99,576	37
1983	$ 93,021	61
1984	$ 36,605	127
1985	$ 1,683	231
1986	$ 11,290	202
1987	$ 17,090	191
1988	$ 62,614	141
1989	$174,393	84
1990	$189,795	86
1991	$152,202	99
1992	$227,529	69
1993	$230,139	74
1994	$687,803	18
Career	$2,142,399	78

MARK BROOKS

Birthdate: March 25, 1961
Birthplace: Fort Worth, TX
Exempt Status: 1994 Tournament Winner.
PGA TOUR Victories: (4) 1988 Canon
Sammy Davis, Jr. Greater Hartford Open.
1991 Kmart Greater Greensboro Open,
Greater Milwaukee Open. 1994 Kemper Open.
Other Victories: None.
National/International Teams: None.

PGA TOUR CAREER SUMMARY

Year	Money	Rank
1984	$40,438	122
1985	$32,094	141
1986	$47,264	140
1987	$42,100	165
1988	$280,636	36
1989	$112,834	115
1990	$307,948	45
1991	$667,263	11
1992	$629,754	21
1993	$249,697	66
1994	$523,285	31
Career	$2,933,316	52

MARK CALCAVECCHIA

Birthdate: June 12, 1960
Birthplace: Laurel, NE
Exempt Status: 30th on 1994 money list.
PGA TOUR Victories: (6) 1986 Southwest
Golf Classic. 1987 Honda Classic. 1988 Bank
of Boston Classic. 1989 Phoenix Open,
Nissan Los Angeles Open. 1992 Phoenix
Open.
Other Victories: 1988 Australian Open.
National/International Teams: 1987 Kirin
Cup. 1987, 1989, 1991 Ryder Cup. 1989,
1990 Asahi Glass Four Tours World
Championship of Golf. 1989, 1990 Dunhill
Cup.

PGA TOUR CAREER SUMMARY

Year	Money	Rank
1981	$404	253
1982	$25,064	134
1983	$16,313	161
1984	$29,660	140
1985	$15,957	162
1986	$155,012	58
1987	$522,423	10
1988	$751,912	6
1989	$807,741	5
1990	$834,281	7
1991	$323,621	50
1992	$377,234	39
1993	$630,366	21
1994	$533,201	30
Career	$5,023,183	20

BRIAN CLAAR

Birthdate: July 29, 1959
Birthplace: Santa Monica, CA
Exempt Status: 110th on 1994 money list.
PGA TOUR Victories: None.
Other Victories: 1989 Hong Kong Open,
Thailand Open.

National/International Teams: None.

PGA TOUR CAREER SUMMARY

Year	Money	Rank
1986	$117,355	7
1987	$ 43,111	162
1988	$ 30,276	172
1989	$ 88,010	133
1990	$161,356	98
1991	$251,309	67
1992	$192,255	78
1993	$202,624	85
1994	$165,370	110
Career	$1,221,389	148

KEITH CLEARWATER

Birthdate: September 1,1959
Birthplace: Long Beach, CA
Exempt Status: 90th on 1994 money list.
PGA TOUR Victories: (2) **1987** Colonial National Invitation, Centel Classic.
Other Victories: **1985** Alaska State Open.
National/International Teams: None.

PGA TOUR CAREER SUMMARY

Year	Money	Rank
1987	$320,007	31
1988	$82,876	127
1989	$87,490	136
1990	$130,103	118
1991	$239,727	69
1992	$609,273	22
1993	$348,763	44
1994	$203,549	90
Career	$2,021,787	85

LENNIE CLEMENTS

Birthdate: January 20, 1957
Birthplace: Cherry Point, NC
Exempt Status: 39th on 1994 money list.
PGA TOUR Victories: None.
Other Victories: **1982** Timex Open. **1983** Sahara Nevada Open. **1988** Spalding Invitational.
National/International Teams: None.

PGA TOUR CAREER SUMMARY

Year	Money	Rank
1981	$7,786	178
1982	$44,796	97
1983	$44,455	110
1984	$25,712	146
1985	$49,383	120
1986	$112,642	79
1987	$124,989	83

1988	$86,332	120
1989	$69,399	147
1990	$80,095	146
1991	$62,827	163
1992	$30,121	198
1993	$141,526	115
1994	$416,880	39
Career	$1,296,925	141

RUSS COCHRAN

Birthdate: October 31, 1958
Birthplace: Paducah, KY
Exempt Status: 77th on 1994 money list.
PGA TOUR Victories: (1) **1991** Centel Western Open.
Other Victories: **1983** Magnolia Classic, Greater Baltimore Open.
National/International Teams: None.

PGA TOUR CAREER SUMMARY

Year	Money	Rank
1983	$7,986	188
1984	$133,342	51
1985	$87,331	87
1986	$89,817	92
1987	$148,110	74
1988	$148,960	80
1989	$132,678	107
1990	$230,278	65
1991	$684,851	10
1992	$326,290	46
1993	$293,868	59
1994	$239,827	77
Career	$2,523,320	65

JOHN COOK

Birthdate: October 2, 1957
Birthplace: Toledo, OH
Exempt Status: 37th on 1994 money list.
PGA TOUR Victories: (6) **1981** Bing Crosby National Pro-Am. **1983** Canadian Open. **1987** The International. **1992** Bob Hope Chrysler Classic, United Airlines Hawaiian Open, Las Vegas Invitational.
Other Victories: **1978** U.S. Amateur. **1982** Sao Paulo Brazilian Open. **1983** World Cup Team Title (with Rex Caldwell).
National/International Teams: **1979** World Amateur Cup. **1983** World Cup. **1993** Ryder Cup.

PGA TOUR CAREER SUMMARY

Year	Money	Rank
1980	$43,316	78
1981	$127,608	25

Year	Money	Rank
1982	$57,483	77
1983	$216,868	16
1984	$65,710	89
1985	$53,573	106
1986	$255,126	27
1987	$333,184	29
1988	$139,916	84
1989	$39,445	172
1990	$448,112	28
1991	$646,984	26
1992	$1,165,606	3
1993	$342,321	45
1994	$429,725	37
Career	$4,274,977	28

FRED COUPLES

Birthdate: October 3, 1959
Birthplace: Seattle, WA
Exempt Status: winner, 1992 Masters.
PGA TOUR Victories: (10) **1983** Kemper Open. **1984** Tournament Players Championship. **1987** Byron Nelson Golf Classic. **1990** Nissan Los Angeles Open. **1991** Federal Express St. Jude Classic, B.C. Open. **1992** Nissan Los Angeles Open, Nestle Invitational, Masters. **1993** Honda Classic.
Other Victories: 1991 Johnnie Walker World Championship of Golf in Jamaica. **1990** RMCC invitational (with Ray Floyd), Sazale Classic (with Mike Donald). **1992, 1993** World Cup (with Davis Love III).
National/International Teams: 1984 U.S. vs. Japan. **1989, 1991, 1993** Ryder Cup. **1990, 1991** Asahi Glass Four Tours World Championship of Golf. **1992, 1993** Dunhill Cup. **1992, 1993** World Cup.

PGA TOUR CAREER SUMMARY

Year	Money	Rank
1981	$78,939	53
1982	$77,606	53
1983	$209,733	19
1984	$334,573	7
1985	$171,272	38
1986	$116,065	76
1987	$441,025	19
1988	$489,822	21
1989	$693,944	11
1990	$757,999	9
1991	$791,749	3
1992	$1,364,188	1
1993	$796,579	10
1994	$625,654	23
Career	$6,889,149	3

BEN CRENSHAW

Birthdate: January 11,1952
Birthplace: Austin, TX
Exempt Status: 1994 Tournament winner.
PGA TOUR Victories: (17) **1973** San Antonio-Texas Open. **1976** Bing Crosby National Pro-Am, Hawaiian Open, Kings Island Open. **1977** Colonial National Invitational. **1979** Phoenix Open, Walt Disney World Team Championship (with George Burns). **1980** Anheuser-Busch Classic. **1983** Byron Nelson Classic. **1984** Masters. **1986** Buick Open, Vantage Championship. **1987** USF&G Classic. **1988** Doral Ryder Open. **1990** Southwestern Bell Colonial. **1992** Centel Western Open. **1993** Nestle Invitational.
Other Victories: 1976 Irish Open. **1980** Texas State Open. **1988** World Cup Individual Title.
National/International Teams: 1981, 1983, 1987 Ryder Cup. **1983** U.S. vs. Japan. **1987, 1988** World Cup. **1988** Kirin Cup.

PGA TOUR CAREER SUMMARY

Year	Money	Rank
1980	$237,727	8
1981	$151,038	20
1982	$54,277	83
1983	$275,474	7
1984	$270,989	16
1985	$25,814	149
1986	$388,169	8
1987	$638,194	3
1988	$696,895	8
1989	$433,095	21
1990	$351,193	33
1991	$224,563	75
1992	$439,071	31
1993	$318,605	51
1994	$659,252	21
Career	$6,107,759	9

JOHN DALY

Birthdate: April 28, 1966
Birthplace: Sacramento, CA
Exempt Status: winner, **1991** PGA Championship.
PGA TOUR Victories: (3) **1991** PGA Championship. **1992** B.C. Open. 1994 Bell South Classic.
Other Victories:1987 Missouri Open.**1990** Ben Hogan Utah Classic.
National/International Teams: 1992, 1993 Dunhill Cup.

PGA TOUR CAREER SUMMARY

Year	Money	Rank
1991	$574,783	17
1992	$387,455	37
1993	$225,591	76
1994	$340,034	49
Career	$1,527,862	128

GLEN DAY

Birthdate: November 16, 1965
Birthplace: Mobile, AL
Exempt Status: 45th on 1994 money list.
PGA TOUR Victories: None.
Other Victories: 1989 Malaysian Open.
National/International Teams: None.

PGA TOUR CAREER SUMMARY

Year	Money	Rank
1994	$357,236	45
Career	$357,236	N/A

JAY DELSING

Birthdate: October 17, 1960
Birthplace: St. Louis, MO
Exempt Status: 124th on 1994 money list.
PGA Tour Victories: None.
Other Victories: None.
National/International Teams: None.

Year	Money	Rank
1985	$46,480	125
1986	$65,407	123
1987	$58,657	136
1988	$45,504	152
1989	$26,565	187
1990	$207,740	74
1991	$149,775	100
1992	$296,740	52
1993	$233,484	71
1994	$143,738	124
Career	$1,274,533	143

ED DOUGHERTY

Birthdate: November 4,1947
Birthplace: Chester, PA
Exempt Status: 157th on 1994 money list.
PGA TOUR Victories: None.
Other Victories: 1985 Club Pro Player of the Year, Club Pro Championship.
National/International Teams: None.

PGA TOUR CAREER SUMMARY

Year	Money	Rank
1975	$ 9,374	129
1976	$17,333	113
1977	$17,606	113
1978	$ 9,936	141
1979	$24,802	115
1980	$9,113	168
1981	DNP	---
1982	$27,948	128
1982-86	DNP	---
1987	$76,705	115
1988	$22,455	195
1989	$1,800	267
1990	$124,505	123
1991	$201,958	82
1992	$237,525	66
1993	$167,651	99
1994	$96,987	157
Career	$1,075,417	162

DAVID EDWARDS

Birthdate: April 18,1956
Birthplace: Neosho, MO
Exempt Status: 1993 tournament winner.
PGA TOUR Victories: (4) **1980** Walt Disney World Team Championship (with Danny Edwards). **1984** Los Angeles Open. **1992** Memorial Tournament. **1993** MCI Heritage Classic.
Other Victories: 1973 Oklahoma State Junior Title. **1978** NCAA Championship.
National/International Teams: None.

PGA TOUR CAREER SUMMARY

Year	Money	Rank
1980	$35,810	93
1981	$68,211	65
1982	$49,896	91
1983	$114,037	48
1984	$236,061	23
1985	$21,506	157
1986	$122,079	71
1987	$148,217	73
1988	$151,513	76
1989	$239,906	57
1990	$166,028	95
1991	$396,695	38
1992	$515,070	27
1993	$653,087	20
1994	$458,845	34
Career	$3,420,418	37

STEVE ELKINGTON

Birthdate: December 8,1962
Birthplace: Inverell, Australia
Exempt Status: winner, 1991 Players Championship.
PGA TOUR Victories: (3) **1990** Kmart Greater Greenboro Open.

1991 THE PLAYERS Championship. **1992** Infiniti Tournament of Champions.
Other Victories: 1992 Australian Open.
National/International Teams: None.

PGA TOUR CAREER SUMMARY

Year	Money	Rank
1987	$75,738	118
1988	$149,972	79
1989	$231,062	61
1990	$548,564	18
1991	$549,120	25
1992	$746,352	12
1993	$675,383	17
1994	$294,943	62
Career	$3,271,135	42

BOB ESTES

Birthdate: February 2,1966
Birthplace: Graham, TX
Exempt Status: 1994 Tournament winner.
PGA TOUR Victories: None
Other Victories: 1988 Bogey Hills Invitational.
National/International Teams: None.

PGA TOUR CAREER SUMMARY

Year	Money	Rank
1988	$5,968	237
1989	$135,628	102
1990	$212,090	69
1991	$147,364	105
1992	$190,778	80
1993	$447,187	32
1994	$765,360	14
Career	$1,898,407	94

NICK FALDO

Birthdate: July 18,1957
Birthplace: Hertfordshire, England
Exempt Status: Winner, 1989 Masters.
PGA TOUR Victories: (3) 1984 Sea Pines Heritage Classic.**1989** Masters. **1990** Masters.
Other Victories: 1987 British Open. **1990** British Open. **1992** British Open.
National/International Teams: 1977, 1979, 1981, 1985, 1987, 1989, 1991, 1993 Ryder Cup. **1977, 1991** World Cup. **1985, 1988, 1987, 1991** Dunhill Cup. **1986** Nissan Cup.**1987** Kirin Cup. **1990** Four Tours Championship.

PGA TOUR CAREER SUMMARY

Year	Money	Rank
1981	$23,320	119
1982	$56,667	79

1983	$67,851	79
1984	$116,845	38
1985	$54,060	117
1986	$52,965	135
1987	$36,281	169
1988	$179,120	84
1989	$327,981	31
1990	$345,262	37
1991	$127,156	117
1992	$345,188	41
1993	$188,886	91
1994	$221,146	83
Career	$2,142,708	78

BRAD FAXON

Birthdate: August 1,1961
Birthplace: Oceanport, NJ
Exempt Status: 24th on 1994 money list.
PGA TOUR Victories: (4) 1986 Provident Classic. **1991** Buick Open. **1992** New England Classic, The International.
Other Victories: 1979, 1980 Rhode Island Amateur.
National/International Teams: 1983 Walker Cup.

PGA TOUR CAREER SUMMARY

Year	Money	Rank
1984	$71,688	82
1985	$46,813	124
1986	$92,716	90
1987	$113,534	90
1988	$162,656	74
1989	$222,076	63
1990	$197,118	81
1991	$422,088	34
1992	$812,093	8
1993	$312,023	55
1994	$612,847	24
Career	$3,065,651	49

RICK FEHR

Birthdate: August 28,1962
Birthplace: Seattle, WA
Exempt Status: 1994 Tournament winner.
PGA TOUR Victories: (3) 1986 B.C. Open. **1994** B.C. Open, Walt Disney World/Oldsmobile.
Other Victories: 1982 Western Amateur.
National/International Teams: 1983 Walker Cup.

PGA TOUR CAREER SUMMARY

Year	Money	Rank
1985	$40,101	133

Year	Money	Rank
1986	$151,162	61
1987	$106,808	94
1988	$79,080	130
1989	$93,142	131
1990	$149,867	105
1991	$288,983	55
1992	$433,003	33
1993	$556,322	28
1994	$573,963	27
Career	$2,472,430	67

JOHN FLANNERY

Birthdate: April 11, 1962
Birthplace: Salinas, CA
Exempt Status: 159th on 1994 money list.
PGA TOUR Victories: None.
Other Victories: 1987 California State Open.
National/International Teams: None.

PGA TOUR CAREER SUMMARY

Year	Money	Rank
1993	$161,234	102
1994	$94,105	159
Career	$255,339	N/A

BRUCE FLEISHER

Birthdate: October 16, 1948
Birthplace: Union City, TN
Exempt Status: 163rd on 1994 money list.
PGA TOUR Victories: 1991 New England Classic.
Other Victories: 1989 Club Pro Championship.1990 Jamaica Open, Bahamas Open, Brazilian Open.
National/International Teams: None.

PGA TOUR CAREER SUMMARY

Year	Money	Rank
1972	$9,019	---
1973	$14,610	---
1974	$33,975	77
1975	$7,773	141
1976	$11,295	137
1977	$9,101	155
1978	$8,347	154
1979	$11,420	149
1980	$13,649	149
1981	$69,221	64
1982	$36,659	110
1983	$50,285	102
1984	$30,186	138
1985	DNP	---
1986	$7,866	213
1987	$2,405	254

1988	$2,198	268
1989	DNP	---
1990	$ 10,626	227
1991	$219,335	76
1992	$236,516	68
1993	$214,279	81
1994	$88,680	163
Career	$1,093,056	161

DAN FORSMAN

Birthdate: July 15, 1958
Birthplace: Rhinelander, WI
Exempt Status: 112th on 1994 money list.
PGA TOUR Victories: (4) 1985 Lite Quad Cities Open. 1986 Hertz Bay Hill Classic. 1990 Shearson Lehman Hutton Open. 1992 Buick Open.
Other Victories: None.
National/International Teams: None.

PGA TOUR CAREER SUMMARY

Year	Money	Rank
1983	$37,859	118
1984	$52,152	105
1985	$150,334	53
1986	$169,445	54
1987	$157,727	63
1988	$269,440	40
1989	$141,174	99
1990	$319,160	43
1991	$214,175	78
1992	$763,190	10
1993	$410,150	36
1994	$160,805	112
Career	$2,845,611	53

DAVID FROST

Birthdate: September 11,1959
Birthplace: Cape Town, South Africa
Exempt Status: winner, 1989 World Series.
PGA TOUR Victories: (8) 1988 Southern Open, Northern Telecom Tucson Open. 1989 NEC World Series of Golf. 1990 USF&G Classic. 1992 Buick Classic, Hardee's Golf Classic. 1993 Canadian Open, Hardee's Golf Classic.
Other Victories: 1983 Gordon's Gin Classic. 1984 Cannes Open. 1987 South African Masters, Merrill Lynch Shootout. 1989 Sun City Million Dollar Challenge. 1990 Sun City Million Dollar Challenge.
National/International Teams: None.

PGA TOUR CAREER SUMMARY

Year	Money	Rank
1985	$118,537	70

Year	Money	Rank
1986	$187,944	48
1987	$518,072	11
1988	$691,500	9
1989	$620,430	11
1990	$372,485	32
1991	$171,262	93
1992	$717,884	15
1993	$1,030,717	5
1994	$671,683	20
Career	$5,100,514	19

FRED FUNK

Birthdate: June 14,1956
Birthplace: Takoma Park, MD
Exempt Status: 67th on 1994 money list.
PGA TOUR Victories: (1) **1992** Shell Houston Open.
Other Victories: **1993** Mexican Open.
National/International Teams: None.

PGA TOUR CAREER SUMMARY

Year	Money	Rank
1989	$59,695	157
1990	$179,346	91
1991	$226,915	73
1992	$416,930	34
1993	$309,435	56
1994	$281,905	67
Career	$1,474,226	130

JIM GALLAGHER, JR.

Birthdate: March 24,1961
Birthplace: Johnstown, PA
Exempt Status: winner, 1993 TOUR Championship.
PGA TOUR Victories: (3) **1990** Greater Milwaukee Open. **1993** Anheuser-Busch Golf Classic, THE TOUR Championship.
Other Victories: **1982** Indiana State Open (as an Amateur). **1983** Indiana State Open.
National/International Teams: **1991** Four Tours World Championship of Golf. **1993** Ryder Cup.

PGA TOUR CAREER SUMMARY

Year	Money	Rank
1984	$22,249	148
1985	$19,061	159
1986	$79,967	107
1987	$39,402	166
1988	$83,766	124
1989	$265,809	50
1990	$476,706	25
1991	$570,627	18

1992	$638,314	19
1993	$1,078,870	4
1994	$325,976	51
Career	$3,526,698	34

ROBERT GAMEZ

Birthdate: July 21,1968
Birthplace: Las Vegas, NV
Exempt Status: 44th on 1994 money list.
PGA TOUR Victories: (2) **1990** Northern Telecom Tucson Open, Nestle Invitational.
Other Victories: **1990** PGA TOUR Rookie of the year. **1989** Porter Cup.
National/International Teams: **1989** Walker Cup.

PGA TOUR CAREER SUMMARY

Year	Money	Rank
1989	$4,827	237
1990	$461,407	27
1991	$280,349	59
1992	$215,648	72
1993	$236,458	70
1994	$380,353	44
Career	$1,574,214	118

BOB GILDER

Birthdate: December 31, 1950
Birthplace: Corvallis, OR
Exempt Status: 118th on 1994 money list.
PGA TOUR Victories: (6) **1976** Phoenix Open. **1980** Canadian Open. **1982** Byron Nelson Classic, Manufacturers Hanover Westchester Classic, Bank of Boston Classic. **1983** Phoenix Open.
Other Victories: **1974** New Zealand Open. **1982** Bridgestone International. **1988** Kapakua International, Acom Team Title (with Doug Tewell).
National/International Teams: **1982** World Cup, U.S. vs. Japan. **1983** Ryder Cup.

PGA TOUR CAREER SUMMARY

Year	Money	Rank
1976	$101,262	24
1977	$ 36,844	72
1978	$ 72,515	36
1979	$134,428	22
1980	$152,597	19
1981	$ 74,756	59
1982	$308,648	6
1983	$139,125	39
1984	$ 23,313	147
1985	$ 47,152	123
1986	$ 98,181	85
1987	$ 94,310	100

Year	Money	Rank
1988	$144,523	82
1989	$187,910	78
1990	$154,934	102
1991	$251,683	66
1992	$170,761	91
1993	$148,496	108
1994	$154,868	118
Career	$2,497,111	66

1987	$237,271	36
1988	$779,181	4
1989	$304,754	37
1990	$267,172	54
1991	$263,034	65
1992	$360,398	41
1993	$229,750	75
1994	$155,156	116
Career	$3,174,225	44

BILL GLASSON

Birthdate: April 29,1960
Birthplace: Fresno,CA
Exempt Status: 1994 Tournament winner.
PGA TOUR Victories: (5) **1985** Kemper Open. **1988** B.C. Open, Centel Classic. **1989** Doral-Ryder Open. **1992** Kemper Open.
Other Victories: None.
National/International Teams: None.

PGA TOUR CAREER SUMMARY

Year	Money	Rank
1984	$17,845	162
1985	$195,449	29
1986	$121,516	72
1987	$151,701	69
1988	$380,651	30
1989	$474,511	19
1990	$156,791	100
1991	$46,995	178
1992	$283,765	54
1993	$299,799	57
1994	$689,110	17
Career	$2,818,133	54

KEN GREEN

Birthdate: July 23,1958
Birthplace: Danbury, CT
Exempt Status: 116th on 1994 money list.
PGA TOUR Victories: (5) **1985** Buick Open. **1986** The International. **1988** Canadian Open, Greater Milwaukee Open. **1989** Kmart Greater Greensboro Open.
Other Victories: **1985** Connecticut Open. **1988** Dunlop Phoenix in Japan. **1990** Hong Kong Open. **1992** Connecticut Open.
National/International Teams: **1989** Ryder Cup, Four Tours World Championship of Golf.

PGA TOUR CAREER SUMMARY

Year	Money	Rank
1982	$11,899	167
1983	$40,263	114
1984	$20,160	158
1985	$151,355	52
1986	$317,835	16

JAY HAAS

Birthdate: December 2,1953
Birthplace: St. Louis, MO
Exempt Status: 1993 Tournament winner.
PGA TOUR Victories: (9) **1978** Andy Williams-San Diego Open. **1981** Greater Milwaukee Open, B.C. Open. **1982** Hall of Fame Classic, Texas Open. **1987** Big "I" Houston Open. **1988** Bob Hope Chrysler Classic. **1992** Federal Express St. Jude Classic. **1993** H-E-B Texas Open.
Other Victories: **1976** Southwestern Open, Missouri Open. **1991** Mexican Open.
National/International Teams: 1975 Walker Cup. **1983** Ryder Cup.

PGA TOUR CAREER SUMMARY

Year	Money	Rank
1980	$114,102	35
1981	$181,894	15
1982	$229,748	13
1983	$191,735	23
1984	$148,514	45
1985	$121,488	69
1986	$189,204	45
1987	$270,347	37
1988	$490,409	20
1989	$248,830	54
1990	$180,023	89
1991	$200,637	84
1992	$632,627	20
1993	$601,603	26
1994	$593,386	25
Career	$4,604,561	24

GARY HALLBERG

Birthdate: May 31,1958
Birthplace: Berwyn, IL
Exempt Status: 82nd on 1994 money list.
PGA TOUR Victories: (3) **1983** Isuzu-Andy Williams-San Diego Open. **1987** Greater Milwaukee Open. **1992** Buick Southern Open.
Other Victories: **1982** Chunichi Crowns in Japan. **1986** Chrysler Team Championship (with Scott Hoch). **1988** Jerry Ford Invitational.

National/International Teams: None.

PGA TOUR CAREER SUMMARY

Year	Money	Rank
1980	$64,244	63
1981	$45,793	91
1982	$36,192	111
1983	$120,140	45
1984	$187,260	30
1985	$108,872	75
1986	$68,479	121
1987	$210,786	48
1988	$28,551	179
1989	$146,833	95
1990	$128,954	121
1991	$273,546	62
1992	$236,629	67
1993	$147,706	111
1994	$224,965	82
Career	$2,028,979	84

DONNIE HAMMOND

Birthdate: April 1,1957
Birthplace: Frederick, MD
Exempt Status: 61st on 1994 money list.
PGA TOUR Victories: (2) **1986** Bob Hope Chrysler Classic. **1989** Texas Open Presented by Nabisco.
Other Victories: 1982 Florida Open. **1989** Co-winner Jerry Ford Invitational. **1990** Co-winner Jerry Ford Invitational.
National/International Teams: None.

PGA TOUR CAREER SUMMARY

Year	Money	Rank
1983	$41,336	112
1984	$67,874	86
1985	$102,709	77
1986	$254,987	28
1987	$157,480	64
1988	$256,019	44
1989	$458,741	20
1990	$151,811	104
1991	$102,668	135
1992	$197,065	77
1993	$340,432	47
1994	$295,436	61
Career	$2,426,578	69

DUDLEY HART

Birthdate: August 4,1968
Birthplace: Rochester, NY
Exempt Status: 135th on 1994 money list.
PGA TOUR Victories: None.
Other Victories: 1990 Florida Open, Louisiana Open.

National/International Teams: None.

PGA TOUR CAREER SUMMARY

Year	Money	Rank
1991	$126,217	120
1992	$254,903	61
1993	$316,750	52
1994	$126,313	135
Career	$824,183	190

MIKE HEINEN

Birthdate: January 17, 1967
Birthplace: Rayne, LA
Exempt Status: 40th on 1994 money list..
PGA TOUR Victories: (3) **1990** B.C. Open.
1991 Phoenix Open. **1993** Bell South Classic.
Other Victories: None.
National/International Teams: None.

PGA TOUR CAREER SUMMARY

Year	Money	Rank
1994	$390,963	40
Career	$390,963	N/A

NOLAN HENKE

Birthdate: November 25, 1964
Birthplace: Battle Creek, MI
Exempt Status: 1993 tournament winner.
PGA TOUR Victories: (3) **1990** B.C. Open.
1991 Phoenix Open. **1993** Bell South Classic.
Other Victories: None.
National/International Teams: None.

PGA TOUR CAREER SUMMARY

Year	Money	Rank
1989	$59,465	159
1990	$294,592	48
1991	$518,811	28
1992	$326,387	45
1993	$502,375	31
1994	$278,419	70
Career	$1,978,048	87

BRIAN HENNINGER

Birthdate: October 19, 1963
Birthplace: Sacramento, CA
Exempt Status: 1994 Tournament winner.
PGA TOUR Victories: (1) **1994** Deposit Guaranty Classic.
Other Victories: 1992 Ben Hogan South Texas, Ben Hogan Macon Open, Ben Hogan Knoxville Open.
National/International Teams: None.

PGA TOUR CAREER SUMMARY

Year	Money	Rank
1993	$112,811	130
1994	$294,075	63
Career	$306,886	N/A

SCOTT HOCH

Birthdate: November 24,1955
Birthplace: Raleigh, NC
Exempt Status: 1994 Tournament winner.
PGA TOUR Victories: (4) **1980** Quad Cities Open. **1982** USF&G Classic. **1984** Lite Quad Cities Open. **1989** Las Vegas Invitational. **1994** Bob Hope Chrysler.
Other Victories: 1982 Pacific Masters, Casio World Open. **1986** Casio World Open. **1990** Korean Open. **1991** Korean Open.
National/International Teams:1978 World Amateur Cup. 1979 Walker Cup.

PGA TOUR CAREER SUMMARY

Year	Money	Rank
1980	$45,800	75
1981	$49,606	85
1982	$193,882	16
1983	$144,605	37
1984	$224,345	27
1985	$186,020	35
1986	$222,077	36
1987	$391,747	20
1988	$397,599	26
1989	$670,680	10
1990	$333,978	40
1991	$520,038	27
1992	$84,798	146
1993	$403,742	37
1994	$804,559	11
Career	$4,673,254	23

MIKE HULBERT

Birthdate: April 14, 1958
Birthplace: Elmira, NY
Exempt Status: 84Th on 1994 money list.
PGA TOUR Victories: (3) **1986** Federal Express-St Jude Classic. **1989** B.C. Open. **1991** Anheuser Busch Golf Classic.
Other Victories: None.
National/International Teams: None.

PGA TOUR CAREER SUMMARY

Year	Money	Rank
1985	$18,368	161
1986	$276,687	21
1987	$204,375	49
1988	$127,752	94
1989	$477,621	16
1990	$216,002	67
1991	$551,750	24
1992	$279,577	55
1993	$193,833	89
1994	$221,007	84
Career	$2,566,972	62

JOHN HUSTON

Birthdate: June 1,1961
Birthplace: Mt. Vernon, IL
Exempt Status: 1994 Tournament winner.
PGA TOUR Victories: (2) **1990** Honda Classic. **1992** Walt Disney World/Oldsmobile Classic.
Other Victories: 1988 JC Penney Classic (with Amy Benz). **1985** Florida Open.
National/International Teams: None.

PGA TOUR CAREER SUMMARY

Year	Money	Rank
1988	$150,301	78
1989	$203,207	68
1990	$435,690	30
1991	$395,853	40
1992	$515,452	26
1993	$681,441	15
1994	$731,499	16
Career	$3,113,442	47

JOHN INMAN

Birthdate: November 26, 1962
Birthplace: Greensboro, NC
Exempt Status: 1993 Tournament winner.
PGA TOUR Victories: (2) **1987** Provident Classic. **1993** Buick Southern Open.
Other Victories: 1984 Fred Haskins Award.
National/International Teams: None.

PGA TOUR CAREER SUMMARY

Year	Money	Rank
1987	$148,386	72
1988	$66,305	137
1989	$99,378	178
1990	$85,289	143
1991	$84,501	167
1992	$173,828	87
1993	$242,140	69
1994	$117,356	144
Career	$1,017,182	171

HALE IRWIN

Birthdate: June 3, 1945
Birthplace: Joplin, MO

Exempt Status: winner, 1990 U.S. Open.
PGA TOUR Victories: (19) **1971** Heritage
Classic. **1973** Heritage Classic. **1974** U.S.
Open. **1975** Western Open, Atlanta Classic.
1976 Glen Campbell Los Angeles Open,
Florida Citrus Open. **1977** Atlanta Classic,
Hall of Fame Classic, San Antonio Texas
Open. **1979** U.S. Open. **1981** Hawaiian Open,
Buick Open. **1982** Honda Inverrary Classic.
1983 Memorial Tournament. **1984** Bing
Crosby Pro-Am. **1985** Memorial Tournament.
1990 U.S. Open, Buick Classic.
Other Victories: 1978 Australian PGA. **1979**
South African PGA, World Cup Individual Title.
1981 Bridgestone Classic. **1982** Brazilian Open.
1986 Bahamas Classic. **1987** Fila Classic.
National/International Teams: 1974, 1979
World Cup. **1975, 1977, 1979, 1981, 1991**
Ryder Cup. **1983** U.S. vs. Japan.

PGA TOUR CAREER SUMMARY

Year	Money	Rank
1980	$109,810	38
1981	$276,499	7
1982	$173,719	19
1983	$232,567	13
1984	$183,364	31
1985	$195,007	31
1986	$59,983	128
1987	$100,825	96
1988	$164,996	72
1989	$150,977	93
1990	$836,249	6
1991	$422,652	33
1992	$98,208	131
1993	$252,686	65
1994	$814,436	10
Career	$5,654,062	12

PETER JACOBSEN

Birthdate: March 4,1954
Birthplace: Portland, OR
Exempt Status: 88th on 1994 money list.
PGA TOUR Victories: (4) **1980** Buick-
Goodwrench Open. **1984** Colonial National
Invitation, Sammy Davis Jr. Greater Hartford
Open. **1990** Bob Hope Chrysler Classic.
Other Victories: 1976 Oregon Open,
Northern California Open. **1979** Western
Australian Open. **1981** Johnny Walker Cup.
1982 Johnny Walker Cup. **1986** Fred Meyer
Challenge (with Curtis Strange).
National/International Teams: None.

PGA TOUR CAREER SUMMARY

Year	Money	Rank
1980	$138,562	26
1981	$85,624	50
1982	$145,832	25
1983	$158,765	29
1984	$295,025	10
1985	$214,959	23
1986	$112,984	78
1987	$79,924	111
1988	$526,765	16
1989	$267,241	48
1990	$547,280	19
1991	$263,180	84
1992	$106,100	127
1993	$222,291	77
1994	$211,762	88
Career	$3,472,507	36

LEE JANZEN

Birthdate: August 28,1964
Birthplace: Austin, MN
Exempt Status: winner, 1993 U.S. Open.
PGA TOUR Victories: (3) **1992** Northern
Telecom Open. **1993** Phoenix Open, U.S.
Open.
Other Victories: None.
National/International Teams: 1993 Ryder
Cup.

PGA TOUR CAREER SUMMARY

Year	Money	Rank
1990	$132,986	115
1991	$228,242	72
1992	$795,279	9
1993	$932,335	7
1994	$442,588	35
Career	$2,531,430	63

TOM KITE

Birthdate: December 9,1949
Birthplace: Austin, TX
Exempt Status: winner, 1992 U.S. Open.
PGA TOUR Victories: (19) **1976** IVB-
Bicentennial Golf Classic. **1978** B.C.
Open.**1981** American Motors-Inverrary
Classic.**1982** Bay Hill Classic. **1983** Bing
Crosby National Pro-Am. **1984** Doral-Eastern
Open, Georgia-Pacific Atlanta Classic. **1985**
MONY Tournament of Champions. **1986**
Western Open. **1987** Kemper Open. **1989**
Nestle Invitational, THE PLAYERS
Championship, Nabisco Championships. **1990**
Federal Express St. Jude Classic. **1991** Infiniti
Tournament of Champions. **1992** BellSouth
Classic, U.S. Open. **1993** Bob Hope Chrysler
Classic, Nissan Los Angeles Open.
Other Victories: 1980 European Open. **1981,**

1982 Vardon Trophy.
National/International Teams: None.

PGA TOUR CAREER SUMMARY

Year	Money	Rank
1980	$152,490	20
1981	$375,699	1
1982	$341,061	3
1983	$257,086	9
1984	$348,840	5
1985	$258,793	14
1986	$394,184	7
1987	$525,516	8
1988	$760,405	5
1989	$1,395,27	8
1990	$658,202	15
1991	$396,580	39
1992	$957,444	6
1993	$887,811	8
1994	$658,689	22
Career	$9,159,418	1

GREG KRAFT

Birthdate: April 4,1964
Birthplace: Detroit, MI
Exempt Status: 69th on 1994 money list.
PGA TOUR Victories: None.
Other Victories: 1993 Deposit Guaranty Golf Classic.
National/International Teams: None.

PGA TOUR CAREER SUMMARY

Year	Money	Rank
1992	$88,824	140
1993	$290,581	60
1994	$279,901	69
Career	$659,306	209

NEAL LANCASTER

Birthdate: September 13,1960
Birthplace: Smithfield, NC
Exempt Status: 1994 Tournament winner.
PGA TOUR Victories: None.
Other Victories: 1989 Pine Tree Open, Utah State Open.
National/International Teams: None.

PGA TOUR CAREER SUMMARY

Year	Money	Rank
1990	$85,769	142
1991	$180,037	90
1992	$146,967	103
1993	$149,381	107
1994	$305,038	58
Career	$867,092	187

BERNHARD LANGER

Birthdate: August 27, 1957
Birthplace: Anhausen, Germany
Exempt Status: Winner, 1993 Masters.
PGA TOUR Victories: 1985 The Masters, Sea Pines Heritage Classic. **1993** The Masters.
Other Victories: 1980 Dunlop Masters, Colombian Open. **1981** German Open, Bob Hope British Classic. **1982** German Open. **1983** Italian Open, Glasgow Classic, TPC at St. Mellion, Johnnie Walker Tournament, Caslo World (Japan). **1984** Irish Open, Dutch Open, French Open. **1985** German Open, Australian Masters, The Masters, European Open, Sun City Challenge, Lancome Trophy. **1986** German Open. **1987** Irish Open, Co-winner Lancome Trophy, British PGA Championship, Belgian Classic. **1988** European Epson Match Play. **1989** Peugeot Spanish Open, German Masters. **1990** Madrid Open, Austrian Open. **1991** Sun City Million Dollar Challenge, Mercedes German Masters, Hong Kong Open, Benson & Hedges Open. **1992** Heineken Dutch Open, Honda Open. **1993** Volvo PGA Championship, The Masters, Volvo German Open.
National/International Teams:
1976 ,1977 ,1978 ,1979, 1980, 1990, 1991 World Cup. **1981, 1983, 1985, 1987, 1989, 1991, 1993** Ryder Cup. **1986, 1993,** Nissan Cup (captain both years). **1987** Kirin Cup (captain). **1989** Four Tours World Championship (captain).

PGA TOUR CAREER SUMMARY

Year	Money	Rank
1984	$82,465	75
1985	$271,044	13
1986	$379,800	10
1987	$366,430	23
1988	$100,635	111
1989	$195,973	73
1990	$35,150	187
1991	$112,539	129
1992	$41,211	181
1993	$626,938	23
1994	$118,241	142
Career	$2,330,426	N/A

TOM LEHMAN

Birthdate: March 7,1959
Birthplace: Austin, MN
Exempt Status: 4th on 1994 money list.
PGA TOUR Victories: None.
Other Victories: 1991 Ben Hogan Tour

Player of the Year, Ben Hogan Mississippi Classic, Ben Hogan South Carolina Classic.
National/International Teams: None.

PGA TOUR CAREER SUMMARY

Year	Money	Rank
1983	$9,413	183
1984	$9,382	184
1985-91	DNP	---
1992	$579,093	24
1993	$422,761	33
1994	$1,031,144	4
Career	$2,072,025	81

WAYNE LEVI

Birthdate: February 22, 1952
Birthplace: Little Falls, NY
Exempt Status: 91st on 1994 money list.
PGA TOUR Victories: (12) **1978** Walt Disney World National Team Play (with Bob Mann). **1979** Houston Open. **1980** Pleasant Valley Jimmy Fund Classic. **1982** Hawaiian Open, LaJet Classic. **1983** Buick Open. **1984** B. C. Open. **1985** Georgia-Pacific Atlanta Classic. **1990** BellSouth Atlanta Classic, Centel Western Open, Canon Greater Hartford Open, Canadian Open.
Other Victories: 1988 Chrysler Team Championship (with George Burns).
National/International Teams: 1990 Four Tours World Championship. **1991** Ryder Cup.

PGA TOUR CAREER SUMMARY

Year	Money	Rank
1977	$8,136	159
1978	$25,039	99
1979	$141,612	20
1980	$120,145	32
1981	$62,177	69
1982	$280,681	8
1983	$193,252	22
1984	$252,921	20
1985	$221,425	22
1986	$154,777	59
1987	$203,322	53
1988	$190,073	61
1989	$499,292	16
1990	$1,024,647	2
1991	$195,861	87
1992	$237,935	65
1993	$179,521	95
1994	$200,476	91
Career	$4,191,292	29

BRUCE LIETZKE

Birthdate: July 18,1951

Birthplace: Kansas City, KS
Exempt Status: 1994 Tournament winner
PGA TOUR Victories: (12) **1977** Joe Garagiola-Tucson Open, Hawaiian Open. 1978 Canadian Open. **1979** Joe Garagiola-Tucson Open. **1980** Colonial National Invitation. **1981** Bob Hope Desert Classic, Wickes-Andy Williams-San Diego Open, Byron Nelson Classic. **1982** Canadian Open. **1984** Honda Classic. **1988** GTE Byron Nelson Classic. **1992** Southwestern Bell Colonial.
Other Victories: 1971 Texas State Amateur.
National/International Teams: 1981 Ryder Cup. **1984** U.S. vs. Japan.

PGA TOUR CAREER SUMMARY

Year	Money	Rank
1980	$183,884	16
1981	$343,446	4
1982	$217,447	14
1983	$153,255	32
1984	$342,853	6
1985	$136,992	59
1986	$183,761	47
1987	$154,383	68
1988	$500,815	19
1989	$307,987	36
1990	$329,294	41
1991	$568,272	19
1992	$703,605	16
1993	$163,241	101
1994	$564,926	28
Career	$5,440,868	15

ROBERT LOHR

Birthdate: November 2,1960
Birthplace: Cincinnati, OH
Exempt Status: 80th on 1994 money list.
PGA TOUR Victories: (1) **1988** Walt Disney World Oldsmobile Classic.
Other Victories: 1990 Mexican Open.
National/International Teams: None.

PGA TOUR CAREER SUMMARY

Year	Money	Rank
1985	$93,651	81
1986	$85,949	99
1987	$137,108	80
1988	$315,536	32
1989	$144,242	98
1990	$141,260	109
1991	$386,759	41
1992	$128,307	112
1993	$314,982	54
1994	$225,048	80
Career	$1,972,842	89

DAVIS LOVE III

Birthdate: April 13,1964
Birthplace: Charlotte, NC
Exempt Status: 1993 Tournament winner.
PGA TOUR Victories: (8) **1987** MCI Heritage
Classic. **1990** The International. **1991** MCI
Heritage Classic. **1992** THE PLAYERS
Championship, MCI Heritage Classic, Kmart
Greater Greensboro Open. **1993** Infiniti
Tournament of Champions, Las Vegas
Invitational.
Other Victories: 1992 World Cup (with Fred
Couples), Lincoln Mercury Kapalua
International.
National/International Teams: 1985 Walker
Cup. **1992** Dunhill Cup. **1992**, **1993** World
Cup. **1993** Ryder Cup.

PGA TOUR CAREER SUMMARY

Year	Money	Rank
1986	$113,245	77
1987	$297,378	33
1988	$156,068	75
1989	$278,760	44
1990	$537,172	20
1991	$686,360	8
1992	$1,191,630	2
1993	$777,059	12
1994	$474,219	33
Career	$4,511,891	25

STEVE LOWERY

Birthdate: October 12, 1960
Birthplace: Birmingham, AL
Exempt Status: 1994 Tournament winner.
PGA TOUR Victories: (1) **1994** Sprint
International.
Other Victories: 1992 Ben Hogan Tulsa
Open.
National/International Teams: None.

PGA TOUR CAREER SUMMARY

Year	Money	Rank
1988	$44,327	157
1989	$38,699	174
1990	$68,524	159
1991	$87,597	143
1992	$22,608	207
1993	$188,287	92
1994	$794,048	12
Career	$1,205,391	150

ANDREW MAGEE

Birthdate: May 22, 1962

Birthplace: Paris, France
Exempt Status: 1994 Tournament winner.
PGA TOUR Victories: (4) **1988** Pensacola
Open. **1991** Nestle Invitational, Las Vegas
Invitational. **1994** Northern Telecom Open.
Other Victories: None.
National/International Teams: None.

PGA TOUR CAREER SUMMARY

Year	Money	Rank
1985	$75,593	99
1986	$69,478	120
1987	$94,598	99
1988	$261,954	43
1989	$126,770	109
1990	$210,507	71
1991	$750,082	5
1992	$285,947	53
1993	$269,988	62
1994	$431,041	25
Career	$2,575,955	61

JEFF MAGGERT

Birthdate: February 20, 1964
Birthplace: Columbia, MO
Exempt Status: 1993 tournament winner.
PGA TOUR Victories: (1) **1993** Walt Disney
World/Oldsmobile Classic.
Other Victories: 1990 Ben Hogan Tour
Player of the Year. Ben Hogan Knoxville
Open, Ben Hogan Buffalo Open.
National/International Teams: None.

PGA TOUR CAREER SUMMARY

Year	Money	Rank
1990	$2,080	277
1991	$240,940	68
1992	$377,408	38
1993	$793,023	11
1994	$814,475	8
Career	$2,225,846	75

ROGER MALTBIE

Birthdate: June 30,1951
Birthplace: Modesto, CA
Exempt Status: Winner, 1985 NEC World
Series of Golf.
PGA TOUR Victories: (5) **1975** Ed
McMahon-Quad Cities Open, Pleasant Valley
Classic. **1976** Memorial Tournament. **1985**
Manufacturers Hanover Westchester Classic,
NEC World Series of Golf.
Other Victories: 1974 California State Open,
1980 Magnolia Classic.

National/International Teams: None.

Year	Money	Rank
1975	$81,035	23
1976	$117,736	18
1977	$51,727	59
1978	$12,440	129
1979	$9,796	155
1980	$38,626	84
1981	$75,009	58
1982	$77,067	55
1983	$75,751	70
1984	$118,128	56
1985	$360,554	8
1986	$213,206	40
1987	$157,023	65
1988	$150,602	77
1989	$134,333	105
1990	$58,536	169
1991	$37,962	188
1992	$109,742	125
1993	$155,454	103
1994	$67,686	174
Career	$2,102,416	80

DICK MAST

Birthdate: March 23,1951
Birthplace: Bluffton, OH
Exempt Status: 131st on 1994 money list.
PGA TOUR Victories: None.
Other Victories: 1990 Mississippi Gulf Coast Classic, Pensacola Open, Fort Wayne Open.
National/International Teams: None.

PGA TOUR CAREER SUMMARY

Year	Money	Rank
1974	$7,108	156
1975	$280	276
1976	DNP	---
1977	$4,387	182
1978	DNP	---
1979	$5,715	180
1980-84	DNP	---
1985	$2,887	219
1986	$79,389	109
1987	$90,768	103
1988	$128,568	56
1989	$38,955	173
1990	$4,200	252
1991	$17,274	216
1992	$150,847	98
1993	$210,125	82
1994	$129,822	131
Career	$866,125	188

BILLY MAYFAIR

Birthdate: August 6, 1966
Birthplace: Phoenix, AZ
Exempt Status: 1993 tournament winner.
PGA TOUR Victories: (1) 1993 Greater Milwaukee Open.
Other Victories: None.
National/International Teams: None.

PGA TOUR CAREER SUMMARY

Year	Money	Rank
1989	$111,996	116
1990	$893,658	12
1991	$185,668	89
1992	$191,878	79
1993	$513,072	30
1994	$158,159	113
Career	$1,854,433	98

BLAINE McCALLIST.ER

Birthdate: October 17,1958
Birthplace: Fort Stockton, TX
Exempt Status: 1993 tournament winner.
PGA TOUR Victories: (5) 1988 Hardee's Golf Classic. 1989 Honda Classic, Bank of Boston Classic. 1991 H-E-B. Texas Open. 1993 B.C. Open.
Other Victories: None.
National/International Teams: None.

PGA TOUR CAREER SUMMARY

Year	Money	Rank
1982	$7,894	80
1983	$5,218	201
1984-85	DNP	---
1986	$88,732	94
1987	$120,005	87
1988	$225,680	49
1989	$593,891	15
1990	$152,048	103
1991	$412,975	36
1992	$261,187	59
1993	$290,434	61
1994	$351,554	47
Career	$2,439,597	68

MARK McCUMBER

Birthdate: September 7,1951
Birthplace: Jacksonville, FL
Exempt Status: Winner, 1994 TOUR Championship.
PGA TOUR Victories: (9) 1979 Doral-Eastern Open. 1983 Western Open, Pensacola Open. 1985 Doral-Eastern Open. 1987 Anheuser-Busch Classic. 1988 THE PLAYERS

Championship. **1989** Beatrice Western Open.
1994 Anheuser-Busch Open, THE TOUR
Championship.
Other Victories: None.
National/International Teams: 1988, 1989
World Cup. **1989** Ryder Cup.

PGA TOUR CAREER SUMMARY

Year	Money	Rank
1980	$38,985	86
1981	$33,363	103
1982	$31,684	119
1983	$288,294	8
1984	$133,445	50
1985	$192,752	32
1986	$110,442	80
1987	$390,865	22
1988	$559,111	13
1989	$548,587	14
1990	$163,413	97
1991	$173,852	92
1992	$136,653	108
1993	$363,289	41
1994	$1,208,209	3
Career	$4,423,778	26

JIM McGOVERN

Birthdate: February 2,1965
Birthplace: Teaneck, NJ
Exempt Status: 79th on 1994 money list.
PGA TOUR Victories: (1) **1993** Shell
Houston Open.
Other Victories: 1988 Metropolitan Open.
1990 Hogan Lake City Classic, Texarkana
Open, New Haven Open.
National/International Teams: None.

PGA TOUR CAREER SUMMARY

Year	Money	Rank
1991	$88,867	141
1992	$169,889	92
1993	$587,495	27
1994	$227,764	79
Career	$1,074,015	163

ROCCO MEDIATE

Birthdate: December 17,1962
Birthplace: Greensburg, PA
Exempt Status: 1993 tournament winner.
PGA TOUR Victories: (2) **1991** Doral-Ryder
Open. **1993** Kmart Greater Greensboro Open.
Other Victories: 1984 South Florida
Invitational. **1992** Perrier French Open.
National/International Teams: None.

PGA TOUR CAREER SUMMARY

Year	Money	Rank
1986	$20,670	174
1987	$112,099	91
1988	$129,829	92
1989	$132,501	108
1990	$240,825	62
1991	$597,438	15
1992	$301,896	49
1993	$680,623	16
1994	$45,940	193
Career	$2,261,620	73

PHIL MICKELSON

Birthdate: June 16,1970
Birthplace: San Diego, CA
Exempt Status: 1994 tournament winner.
PGA TOUR Victories: (4) **1991** Northern
Telecom Open. **1993** Buick Invitational of
California, The International.**1994** Mercedes
Championships.
Other Victories: 1990 U.S. Amateur.
National/International Teams: 1989, 1991
Walker Cup.

PGA TOUR CAREER SUMMARY

Year	Money	Rank
1991	$0	---
1992	$171,713	90
1993	$628,735	22
1994	$748,316	15
Career	$1,548,764	124

LARRY MIZE

Birthdate: September 23,1958
Birthplace: Augusta, GA
Exempt Status: Winner, 1987 Masters
PGA TOUR Victories: (4) **1983** Danny
Thomas-Memphis Classic. **1987** Masters.
1993 Northern Telecom Open, Buick Open.
Other Victories: 1993 Johnny Walker World
Championship.
National/International Teams: 1987 Ryder
Cup.

PGA TOUR CAREER SUMMARY

Year	Money	Rank
1982	$28,787	124
1983	$146,325	35
1984	$172,513	36
1985	$231,041	17
1986	$314,051	17
1987	$561,407	6
1988	$187,823	62
1989	$278,388	45

Year	Money	Rank
1990	$668,198	14
1991	$279,081	60
1992	$316,428	47
1993	$724,680	12
1994	$386,029	42
Career	$4,294,710	27

GIL MORGAN

Birthdate: September 25,1946
Birthplace: Wewoka, OK
Exempt Status: 54th on 1994 money list.
PGA TOUR Victories: (7) **1977** B.C. Open.
1978 Glen Campbell Los Angeles Open,
World Series of Golf. **1979** Danny Thomas
Memphis Classic. **1983** Joe Garagiola Tucson
Open, Glen Campbell Los Angeles Open.
1990 Kemper Open.
Other Victories: 1978 Pacific Masters.
National/International Teams: 1979, 1983
Ryder Cup.

PGA TOUR CAREER SUMMARY

Year	Money	Rank
1980	$135,308	28
1981	$171,184	18
1982	$139,652	26
1983	$306,133	5
1984	$281,948	13
1985	$133,941	62
1986	$98,770	84
1987	$133,980	81
1988	$286,002	34
1989	$300,395	39
1990	$702,629	11
1991	$232,912	70
1992	$272,959	56
1993	$810,312	24
1994	$309,690	54
Career	$4,735,868	22

JODIE MUDD

Birthdate: April 23,1960
Birthplace: Louisville, KY
Exempt Status: Winner, 1990 The Players
Championship.
PGA TOUR Victories: (4) **1988** Federal
Express St. Jude Classic. **1989** GTE Byron
Nelson Golf Classic. **1990** The Players
Championship, Nabisco Championships.
Other Victories: None.
National/International Teams: 1981 Walker
Cup. **1990** World Cup, Four Tours World
Championship of Golf.

PGA TOUR CAREER SUMMARY

Year	Money	Rank
1982	$34,216	114
1983	$21,515	145
1984	$42,244	114
1985	$186,648	34
1986	$182,812	48
1987	$203,923	51
1988	$422,022	23
1989	$404,860	26
1990	$911,746	5
1991	$148,453	102
1992	$88,081	141
1993	$89,366	150
1994	$27,868	214
Career	$2,763,755	55

GREG NORMAN

Birthdate: February 10,1955
Birthplace: Queensland, Australia
Exempt Status: Winner, 1993 British Open.
PGA TOUR Victories: (12) **1984** Kemper
Open, Canadian Open. **1986** Panasonic Las
Vegas Invitational, Kemper Open. **1988** MCI
Heritage Classic. **1989** The International,
Greater Milwaukee Open. **1990** Doral-Ryder
Open, The Memorial Tournament. **1992**
Canadian Open. **1993** Doral-Ryder Open.
1994 The Players Championship.
Other Victories: 1976 Lakes Classic in
Australia. **1977** Martini International. **1978**
New South Wales Open, Fiji Open. **1979**
Martini International, Hong Kong Open. **1980**
French Open, World Match Play,
Scandanavian Enterprise Open, Australian
Open, Australian Masters. **1981** Martini
International, Dunlop Masters, Australian
Masters. **1982** Dunlop Masters, State Express
Classic, Benson & Hedges International
Open. **1983** Australian Masters, Queensland
Open, New South Wales Open, Cannes
Invitational, Kapalua International, Hong Kong
Open, World Match Play. **1984** Australian
Masters, Victoria Open. **1986** British Open,
European Open, Suntory World Match Play,
Queensland Open, New South Wales Open,
South Australian Open, Western Australian
Open. **1987** Australian Open, Australian
Masters. **1993** British Open, PGA Grand Slam
of Golf. **1994** Johnnie Walker Classic.
National/International Teams: 1976, 1978
World Cup. **1985, 1986** Australian Nissan
Cup. **1985, 1986, 1987, 1988, 1989, 1990,**
1992 Dunhill Cup. **1987** Australian Kirin Cup.
1989 Australian Four Tours.

PGA TOUR CAREER SUMMARY

Year	Money	Rank
1983	$71,411	74
1984	$310,230	9
1985	$165,458	42
1986	$653,296	1
1987	$535,450	7
1988	$514,854	17
1989	$835,096	4
1990	$1,165,477	1
1991	$320,196	53
1992	$876,443	18
1993	$1,359,653	3
1994	$1,330,307	2
Career	$7,937,869	2

BRETT OGLE

Birthdate: July 14, 1964
Birthplace: Paddington, Australia
Exempt Status: 1994 tournament winner.
PGA TOUR Victories: (2) **1993** AT&T Pebble Beach National Pro-Am **1994** Hawaiian Open.
Other Victories: **1985** Australian Junior Championship. **1989** Mirage Queensland Open. **1990** Australian Open.
National/International Teams: **1992** World Cup.

PGA TOUR CAREER SUMMARY

Year	Money	Rank
1993	$337,373	49
1994	$284,495	66
Career	$621,868	215

JOSE MARIA OLAZABAL

Birthdate: February 5, 1966
Birthplace: Fuentenabia, Spain
Exempt Status: Not a PGA TOUR member.
PGA TOUR Victories: (4) **1990** NEC World Series of Golf. **1991** The International. **1994** Masters, NEC World Series of Golf.
Other victories: **1983** Italian Amateur, Spanish Amateur. **1986** European Masters, Swiss Open, Sanyo Open. **1988** Belgian Open, German Masters. **1989** Tenerife Open, Dutch Open. **1990** Benson & Hedges International, Irish Open, Lancome Trophy, Visa Taiheyo Club Masters. **1991** Catalonia Open. **1992** Turespana Open de Tenerife, Open Mediterrania. **1994** Volvo PGA.
National/International Teams: **1986**, **1987**, **1988**, **1989**, **1992** Dunhill Cup. **1987**, **1989**, **1991**, **1993** Ryder Cup. **1989** World Cup. **1987** Kirin Cup. **1989**, **1990** Four Tours World

Championship.

PGA TOUR CAREER SUMMARY

Year	Money	Rank
1987	$7,470	215
1988	DNP	---
1989	$56,039	160
1990	$337,837	38
1991	$382,124	43
1992	$63,429	161
1993	$60,160	174
1994	$969,900	7
Career	$1,876,959	N/A

MARK O'MEARA

Birthdate: January 13, 1957
Birthplace: Goldsboro, NC
Exempt Status: 86th on 1994 money list.
PGA TOUR Victories: (8) **1984** Greater Milwaukee Open. **1985** Bing Crosby Pro-Am, Hawaiian Open. **1989** AT&T Pebble Beach National Pro-Am. **1990** AT&T Pebble Beach National Pro-Am, H-E-B Texas Open. **1991** Walt Disney World/Oldsmobile Classic. **1992** AT&T Pebble Beach National Pro-Am.
Other Victories: None.
National/International Teams: **1984** U.S. vs. Japan. **1985** Nissan Cup. **1985**, **1989**, **1991** Ryder Cup.

PGA TOUR CAREER SUMMARY

Year	Money	Rank
1981	$76,083	55
1982	$31,711	118
1983	$69,354	76
1984	$465,873	2
1985	$340,840	10
1986	$252,827	30
1987	$327,250	30
1988	$438,311	22
1989	$815,804	13
1990	$707,175	10
1991	$583,896	20
1992	$759,648	11
1993	$349,516	43
1994	$214,070	86
Career	$5,212,337	17

CRAIG PARRY

Birthdate: December 1, 1966
Birthplace: Sunshine, Australia
Exempt Status: 46th on 1994 money list.
PGA TOUR Victories: None.
Other Victories: **1987** Canadian Tournament Players Championship. **1989** Wang Four Stars National Pro-Celebrity, German Open,

Bridgestone ASO (Japan). **1991** Lancia
Martini Italian Open, Bell's Scottish Open.
1994 Australian Masters.
National/International Teams: 1988 Kirin
Cup. **1989, 1990, 1991** Four Tours World
Championship of Golf.

PGA TOUR CAREER SUMMARY

Year	Money	Rank
1989	$1,650	282
1990	$43,351	181
1991	$83,767	162
1992	$241,901	64
1993	$323,068	50
1994	$354,602	46
Career	$919,571	181

STEVE PATE

Birthdate: May 26, 1961
Birthplace: Ventura, CA
Exempt Status: 64th on 1994 money list.
PGA TOUR Victories: (5) **1987** Southwest
Classic. **1988** MONY Tournament of
Champions, Shearson Lehman Hutton Andy
Williams Open. **1991** Honda Classic. **1992**
Buick Invitational of California.
Other Victories: None.
National/International Teams: 1988 Kirin
Cup. **1991** Ryder Cup.

PGA TOUR CAREER SUMMARY

Year	Money	Rank
1985	$89,358	86
1986	$176,100	51
1987	$335,728	26
1988	$582,473	12
1989	$306,554	35
1990	$334,505	39
1991	$727,997	6
1992	$472,626	30
1993	$254,841	84
1994	$291,651	64
Career	$3,571,832	33

COREY PAVIN

Birthdate: November 16,1959
Birthplace: Oxnard, CA
Exempt Status: 1991 leading money winner.
PGA TOUR Victories: (11) **1984** Houston
Coca-Cola Open. **1985** Colonial National
Invitation. **1986** Hawaiian Open, Greater
Milwaukee Open. **1987** Bob Hope Chrysler
Classic, Hawaiian Open. **1988** Texas Open
presented by Nabisco. **1991** Bob Hope
Chrysler Classic, BellSouth Atlanta Classic.

1992 Honda Classic. **1994** Nissan Los
Angeles Open.
Other Victories: 1993 Toyota World Match
Play.
National/International Teams: 1981 Walker
Cup. **1985** Nissan Cup. **1991, 1993** Ryder
Cup.

PGA TOUR CAREER SUMMARY

Year	Money	Rank
1984	$250,536	18
1985	$387,508	6
1986	$304,558	19
1987	$498,406	15
1988	$216,768	50
1989	$177,084	82
1990	$468,830	26
1991	$979,430	1
1992	$980,934	5
1993	$675,087	18
1994	$906,305	8
Career	$5,835,443	11

KENNY PERRY

Birthdate: August 10, 1960
Birthplace: Elizabethtown, KY
Exempt Status: 1994 tournament winner.
PGA TOUR Victories: (2) **1991** Memorial
Tournament.**1994** New England Classic.
Other Victories: None.
National/International Teams: None.

PGA TOUR CAREER SUMMARY

Year	Money	Rank
1987	$107,239	93
1988	$139,421	85
1989	$202,099	70
1990	$279,881	50
1991	$368,784	44
1992	$190,455	81
1993	$196,863	88
1994	$585,941	26
Career	$2,070,685	82

NICK PRICE

Birthdate: January 28,1957
Birthplace: Durban, South Africa
Exempt Status: Winner, 1992 PGA
Championship.
PGA TOUR Victories: (14) **1983** World
Series of Golf. **1991** GTE Byron Nelson
Classic, Canadian Open. **1992** PGA
Championship, H-E-B Texas Open. **1993** The
Players Championship, Canon Greater
Hartford Open, Sprint Western Open, Federal

Express St. Jude Classic. **1994** Honda
Classic, Southwestern Bell Colonial, Motorola
Open, PGA Championship, Canadian Open.
Other Victories: 1979 Asseng International.
1980 Swiss Open. **1981** South African
Masters, Italian Masters. **1982** Vaal Reefs
Open. **1985** Lancome Trophy, ICL
International. **1992** PGA Grand Slam of Golf,
Air New Zealand Shell Open. **1993** ICL
International. **1994** British Open.
National/International Teams: 1993 Dunhill
Cup. **1978, 1993** World Cup.

PGA TOUR CAREER SUMMARY

Year	Money	Rank
1983	$49,435	103
1984	$109,480	66
1985	$96,069	80
1986	$225,373	35
1987	$334,169	28
1988	$266,300	42
1989	$296,170	42
1990	$520,777	22
1991	$714,389	7
1992	$1,135,773	4
1993	$1,478,557	1
1994	$1,499,927	1
Career	$6,726,418	6

DICKY PRIDE

Birthdate: July 15, 1969
Birthplace: Tuscaloosa, AL
Exempt Status: 1994 Tournament winner.
PGA TOUR Victories: (1) 1994 Federal
Express St.Jude Memorial Classic.
Other Victories: None.
National/International Teams: None.

PGA TOUR CAREER SUMMARY

Year	Money	Rank
1994	$305,769	57
Career	$305,729	N/A

TOM PURTZER

Birthdate: Dec. 5,1951
Birthplace: Des Moines, IA
Exempt Status: Winner 1991 NEC World
Series of Golf.
PGA TOUR Victories: (5) 1977 Glen
Campbell Los Angeles Open. **1984** Phoenix
Open. **1988** Gatlin Brothers Southwest
Classic. **1991** Southwestern Bell Colonial,
NEC World Series of Golf.
Other Victories: None.
National/International Teams: 1979 U.S. vs.
Japan.
PGA TOUR CAREER SUMMARY

Year	Money	Rank
1975	$2,093	194
1976	$26,682	82
1977	$79,337	37
1978	$58,618	55
1979	$113,270	30
1980	$118,185	34
1981	$122,812	27
1982	$100,118	36
1983	$103,261	55
1984	$164,244	39
1985	$49,979	119
1986	$218,281	37
1987	$123,287	85
1988	$197,740	5
1989	$154,868	8
1990	$285,176	49
1991	$750,568	4
1992	$166,722	9
1993	$107,570	136
1994	$187,307	94
Career	$3,130,116	46

LOREN ROBERTS

Birthdate: June 24,1955
Birthplace: San Luis Obispo, CA
Exempt Status: 1994 Tournament winner.
PGA TOUR Victories: (1) 1994 Nestle Bay
Hill Invitational.
Other Victories: None.
National/International Teams: None.

PGA TOUR CAREER SUMMARY

Year	Money	Rank
1981	$8,935	172
1982	DNP	---
1983	$7,724	189
1984	$87,515	87
1985	$92,761	83
1986	$53,655	133
1987	$87,489	138
1988	$138,890	89
1989	$275,862	46
1990	$478,522	24
1991	$281,173	56
1992	$338,673	43
1993	$316,508	53
1994	$1,015,671	6
Career	$3,131,398	45

DAVE RUMMELLS

Birthdate: January 26, 1958
Birthplace: Cedar Rapids, IA
Exempt Status: 138th on 1994 money list.
PGA TOUR Victories: None.
Other Victories: None.

National/International Teams: None.

PGA TOUR CAREER SUMMARY

Year	Money	Rank
1986	$83,227	103
1987	$154,720	67
1988	$274,800	38
1989	$419,979	24
1990	$111,539	131
1991	$213,627	79
1992	$95,203	134
1993	$247,963	67
1994	$122,872	138
Career	$1,723,930	106

GENE SAUERS

Birthdate: August 22, 1962
Birthplace: Savannah,GA
Exempt Status: 73rd on 1994 money list.
PGA TOUR Victories: (2) **1986** Bank of Boston Classic. **1989** Hawaiian Open.
Other Victories: None.
National/International Teams: None.

PGA TOUR CAREER SUMMARY

Year	Money	Rank
1984	$36,537	128
1985	$48,526	121
1986	$199,044	42
1987	$244 655	38
1988	$280,719	35
1989	$303,669	38
1990	$374,485	31
1991	$400,535	37
1992	$434,566	32
1993	$117,608	128
1994	$250,654	73
Career	$2,690,998	58

TOM SIECKMANN

Birthdate: January 14, 1955
Birthplace: York, NE
Exempt Status: 184th on 1994 money list.
PGA TOUR Victories: (1) **1988** Anheuser-Busch Classic.
Other Victories: None.
National/International Teams: None.

PGA TOUR CAREER SUMMARY

Year	Money	Rank
1985	$30,052	143
1986	$63,395	125
1987	$52,259	146
1988	$209,151	54
1989	$97,465	128
1990	$141,241	110
1991	$278,598	61
1992	$173,424	88
1993	$201,429	87
1994	$55,304	184
Career	$1,302,657	140

SCOTT SIMPSON

Birthdate: September 17,1955
Birthplace: San Diego, CA
Exempt Status: winner, 1987 U.S. Open.
PGA TOUR Victories: (6) **1980** Western Open. **1984** Manufacturers Hanover Westchester Classic. **1987** Greater Greensboro Open, U.S. Open. **1989** BellSouth Atlanta Classic. **1993** GTE Byron Nelson Classic.
Other Victories: None.
National/International Teams: **1977** Walker Cup. **1987** Ryder Cup.

PGA TOUR CAREER SUMMARY

Year	Money	Rank
1979	$53,084	74
1980	$141,323	24
1981	$108,793	34
1982	$146,903	24
1983	$144,172	38
1984	$248,581	22
1985	$171,245	39
1986	$202,223	41
1987	$621,032	4
1988	$108,301	106
1989	$298,920	40
1990	$235,309	63
1991	$322,936	51
1992	$155,284	97
1993	$707,166	14
1994	$307,884	56
Career	$3,973,157	30

JOEY SINDELAR

Birthdate: March 30, 1958
Birthplace: Fort Knox, KY
Exempt Status: 145th on 1994 money list.
PGA TOUR Victories: (6) **1985** Greater Greensboro Open, B.C. Open. **1987** B.C. Open. **1988** Honda Classic, The International. **1990** Hardee's Golf Classic.
Other Victories: None.
National/International Teams: **1988** Kirin Cup. **1990** World Cup.

PGA TOUR CAREER SUMMARY

Year	Money	Rank
1984	$116,528	59

Year	Money	Rank
1985	$282,762	12
1986	$341,231	14
1987	$235,033	40
1988	$813,732	3
1989	$196,092	72
1990	$307,207	46
1991	$168,352	94
1992	$395,354	35
1993	$391,649	38
1994	$114,563	145
Career	$3,342,503	38

VIJAY SINGH

Birthdate: February 22,1963
Birthplace: Lautoka, Fiji
Exempt Status: 1993 tournament winner.
PGA TOUR Victories: (1) **1993** Buick Classic.
Other Victories: 1984 Malaysian PGA Championship. **1984** Volvo German Open. **1988, 1989** Nigerian Open. **1990** Turespana Masters. **1992** Volvo German Open.
National/International Teams: None.

PGA TOUR CAREER SUMMARY

Year	Money	Rank
1993	$657,831	19
1994	$325,959	52
Career	$983,790	178

MIKE SPRINGER

Birthdate: November 3,1965
Birthplace: San Francisco, CA
Exempt Status: 1994 tournament winner.
PGA TOUR Victories: (1) **1994** Greater Milwaukee Open.
Other Victories: None.
National/International Teams: None.

PGA TOUR CAREER SUMMARY

Year	Money	Rank
1991	$178,587	91
1992	$144,316	104
1993	$214,729	79
1994	$770,717	13
Career	$1,308,349	139

JEFF SLUMAN

Birthdate: September 11,1957
Birthplace: Rochester, NY
Exempt Status: Winner, 1988 PGA Championship.
PGA TOUR Victories: (1) **1988** PGA Championship.

Other Victories: 1985 Tallahassee Open.
National/International Teams: None.

PGA TOUR CAREER SUMMARY

Year	Money	Rank
1983	$13,643	171
1984	$603	281
1985	$100,523	78
1986	$154,129	60
1987	$335,590	27
1988	$503,321	18
1989	$154,507	89
1990	$264,012	56
1991	$552,979	23
1992	$729,027	14
1993	$187,841	93
1994	$301,178	59
Career	$3,296,749	40

CRAIG STADLER

Birthdate: June 2,1953
Birthplace: San Diego, CA
Exempt Status: Winner, 1992 World Series of Golf.
PGA TOUR Victories: (11) **1980** Bob Hope Desert Classic, Greater Greensboro Open. **1981** Kemper Open. **1982** Joe Garagiola Tucson Open, The Masters, Kemper Open, World Series of Golf. **1984** Byron Nelson Classic. **1991** THE TOUR Championship. **1992** NEC World Series of Golf. **1994** Buick Invitational of California.
Other Victories: None.
National/International Teams: 1982 U.S. vs. Japan. **1975** Walker Cup. **1983, 1985** Ryder Cup.

PGA TOUR CAREER SUMMARY

Year	Money	Rank
1980	$206,291	8
1981	$218,829	8
1982	$446,462	1
1983	$214,496	17
1984	$324,241	8
1985	$297,926	11
1986	$170,076	53
1987	$235,831	39
1988	$276,313	37
1989	$409,419	25
1990	$278,482	52
1991	$827,628	2
1992	$487,460	28
1993	$553,622	29
1994	$474,831	32
Career	$5,606,436	13

MIKE STANDLY

Birthdate: May 19, 1964
Birthplace: Abilene, TX
Exempt Status: 1993 tournament winner.
PGA TOUR Victories: (1) **1993** Freeport-McMoRan Classic.
Other Victories: 1984 Boone Links Invitational.
National/International Teams: None.

PGA TOUR CAREER SUMMARY

Year	Money	Rank
1991	$55,846	171
1992	$213,712	73
1993	$323,886	49
1994	$179,850	99
Career	$773,294	196

PAYNE STEWART

Birthdate: January 30, 1957
Birthplace: Springfield, MO
Exempt Status: Winner, 1991 U.S. Open.
PGA TOUR Victories: (8) **1982** Quad Cities Open. **1983** Walt Disney World Classic. **1987** Hertz Bay Hill Classic. **1989** MCI Heritage Classic, PGA Championship. **1990** MCI Heritage Classic, GTE Byron Nelson Classic. **1991** U.S. Open.
Other Victories: 1981 India Open.
National/International Teams: 1986 Nissan Cup. **1987** Kirin Cup. **1987, 1989, 1991, 1993** Ryder Cup. **1987, 1990** World Cup. **1989, 1990** Asahi Glass Four Tours World Championship of Golf.

PGA TOUR CAREER SUMMARY

Year	Money	Rank
1981	$13,400	157
1982	$98,686	38
1983	$178,809	25
1984	$288,795	11
1985	$225,729	19
1986	$535,389	3
1987	$511,026	12
1988	$553,571	14
1989	$1,201,301	2
1990	$976,281	3
1991	$476,971	31
1992	$334,738	44
1993	$982,876	6
1994	$145,687	123
Career	$6,523,260	7

CURTIS STRANGE

Birthdate: January 30, 1955

Birthplace: Norfolk, VA
Exempt Status: Winner, 1988 U.S. Open.
PGA TOUR Victories: (17) **1979** Pensacola Open. **1980** Michelob-Houston Open, Manufacturers Hanover Westchester Classic. **1983** Sammy Davis, Jr. Greater Hartford Open. **1984** LaJet Classic. **1985** Honda Classic, Panasonic Las Vegas Invitational, Canadian Open. **1986** Houston Open. **1987** Canadian Open, Federal Express St. Jude Classic, NEC World Series of Golf. **1988** Independent Insurance Agent Open, Memorial Tournament, U.S. Open, Nabisco Championships. **1989** U.S. Open.
Other Victories: 1989 Greg Norman Holden Classic. **1993** Greg Norman Holden Classic.
National/International Teams: 1974 World Amateur Cup. **1975** Walker Cup. **1983, 1985, 1987, 1989** Ryder Cup. **1985** Nissan Cup. **1987, 1988** Kirin Cup. **1987, 1988, 1989, 1991** Dunhill Cup. **1989** Four Tours Championship.

PGA TOUR CAREER SUMMARY

Year	Money	Rank
1980	$271,888	3
1981	$201,513	9
1982	$263,378	10
1983	$200,116	21
1984	$276,773	14
1985	$542,321	1
1986	$237,700	32
1987	$925,941	1
1988	$1,147,644	1
1989	$752,587	7
1990	$277,172	53
1991	$336,333	48
1992	$150,639	99
1993	$262,697	63
1994	$390,881	41
Career	$6,433,442	8

STEVE STRICKER

Birthdate: February 23, 1967
Birthplace: Edgerton, WI
Exempt Status: 50th on 1994 money list.
PGA TOUR Victories: None.
Other Victories: 1993 Canadian PGA.
National/International Teams: None.

PGA TOUR CAREER SUMMARY

Year	Money	Rank
1990	$3,973	255
1992	$5,550	261
1993	$46,171	186
1994	$334,409	50
Career	$390,624	N/A

HAL SUTTON

Birthdate: April 28,1958
Birthplace: Shreveport, LA
Exempt Status: 29th on 1994 money list.
PGA TOUR Victories: (7) **1982** Walt Disney World Golf Classic. **1983** Tournament Players Championship, PGA Championship. **1985** St. Jude Memphis Classic, Southwest Classic. **1986** Phoenix Open, Memorial Tournament.
Other Victories: 1985 Chrysler Team Championship (with Ray Floyd).
National/International Teams: 1983 U.S. vs. Japan. **1985, 1987** Ryder Cup.

PGA TOUR CAREER SUMMARY

Year	Money	Rank
1982	$237,434	11
1983	$426,668	1
1984	$227,949	26
1985	$365,340	7
1986	$429,434	6
1987	$477,996	16
1988	$137,296	88
1989	$422,703	23
1990	$207,084	75
1991	$346,411	47
1992	$39,234	185
1993	$74,144	161
1994	$540,162	29
Career	$3,931,854	31

DOUG TEWELL

Birthdate: August 27, 1949
Birthplace: Baton Rouge, LA
Exempt status: 102nd on 1994 money list.
PGA TOUR victories: (2) **1986** Los Angeles Open. **1987** Pensacola Open.
Other Victories: 1988 Acom Team title (with Bob Gilder). **1978** South Central PGA.
National/International Teams: None.

PGA TOUR CAREER SUMMARY

Year	Money	Rank
1975	$1,812	201
1976	$3,640	185
1977	$33,162	76
1978	$16,629	113
1979	$84,500	43
1980	$161,684	17
1981	$41,540	94
1982	$78,770	52
1983	$112,367	49
1984	$117,988	57
1985	$137,426	58
1986	$310,285	18
1987	$150,116	71
1988	$209,196	53

1989	$174,607	83
1990	$137,795	112
1991	$137,360	111
1992	$159,856	96
1993	$132,478	117
1994	$177,388	102
Career:	$2,378,598	70

KIRK TRIPLETT

Birthdate: March 29,1962
Birthplace: Moses Lake, WA
Exempt Status: 38th on 1994 money list.
PGA TOUR Victories: None.
Other Victories: 1988 Alberta Open, Nevada Open, Ft. McMurray Classic.
National/International Teams: None.

PGA TOUR CAREER SUMMARY

Year	Money	Rank
1990	$183,464	88
1991	$137,302	112
1992	$175,868	85
1993	$189,418	90
1994	$422,171	38
Career	$1,108,222	159

BOB TWAY

Birthdate: May 4,1959
Birthplace: Oklahoma City, OK
Exempt Status: Winner,1986 PGA Championship.
PGA TOUR Victories: (6) **1986** Shearson Lehman Bros. Andy Williams Open, Manufacturers Hanover Westchester Classic, Georgia Pacific Atlanta Classic, PGA Championship. **1989** Memorial Tournament. **1990** Las Vegas Invitational.
Other Victories: 1983 Sandpiper Santa Barbara Open. **1986** Fred Meyer Challenge (with Paul Azinger). **1987** Oklahoma State Open, Chrysler Team Championship (with Mike Hulbert).
National/International Teams: 1980 World Amateur Cup. **1986** Nissan Cup.

PGA TOUR CAREER SUMMARY

Year	Money	Rank
1985	$164,023	45
1986	$652,780	2
1987	$212,362	47
1988	$381,966	29
1989	$488,340	17
1990	$495,862	23
1991	$322,931	52
1992	$47,632	179

Year	Money	Rank
1993	$148,120	109
1994	$114,176	114
Career	$3,028,192	51

HOWARD TWITTY

Birthdate: January 15,1949
Birthplace: Phoenix, AZ
Exempt Status: 1993 Tournament winner.
PGA TOUR Victories: (3) **1979** B.C. Open.
1980 Sammy Davis Jr. Greater Hartford
Open. **1993** United Airlines Hawaiian Open.
Other Victories: None.
National/International Teams: None.

PGA TOUR CAREER SUMMARY

Year	Money	Rank
1980	$165,190	14
1981	$52,183	79
1982	$57,355	78
1983	$20,000	150
1984	$51,971	106
1985	$92,958	82
1986	$156,119	57
1987	$169,442	61
1988	$87,985	119
1989	$107,200	119
1990	$129,444	120
1991	$226,426	74
1992	$284,042	57
1993	$416,833	34
1994	$131,408	130
Career	$2,524,478	64

LANNY WADKINS

Birthdate: December 5,1949
Birthplace: Richmond, VA
Exempt Status: 185th on 1994 money list.
PGA TOUR Victories: (21) **1972** Sahara
Invitational. **1973** Byron Nelson Classic, USI
Classic. **1977** PGA Championship, World
Series of Golf. **1979** Glen Campbell Los
Angeles Open, Tournament Players
Championship. **1982** Phoenix Open, MONY
Tournament of Champions, Buick Open. **1983**
Greater Greensboro Open, MONY
Tournament of Champions. **1985** Bob Hope
Classic, Los Angeles Open, Walt Disney
World/Oldsmobile Classic. **1987** Doral-Ryder
Open. **1988** Hawaiian Open, Colonial National
Invitation. **1990** Anheuser-Busch Golf Classic.
1991 United Hawaiian Open. **1992** Canon
Greater Hartford Open.
Other Victories: **1970** U.S. Amateur, Western
Amateur. **1978** Canadian PGA, Garden State
PGA (Australia).**1979** Bridgestone Open. **1984**

World Nissan Championship. **1990** Fred
Meyer Challenge (with Bobby Wadkins).
National/International Teams: 1969, 1971
Walker Cup. **1970** World Amateur Cup. **1982,
1983** U.S. vs. Japan. **1985** Nissan Cup. **1987**
Kirin Cup.**1977, 1979, 1983, 1985, 1987,
1989, 1991, 1993** Ryder Cup. **1977, 1984,
1985** World Cup.

PGA TOUR CAREER SUMMARY

Year	Money	Rank
1980	$67,778	58
1981	$51,704	81
1982	$306,827	7
1983	$319,271	3
1984	$198,996	29
1985	$446,893	2
1986	$264,931	23
1987	$501,727	13
1988	$616,596	10
1989	$233,363	60
1990	$673,433	13
1991	$651,495	12
1992	$366,837	40
1993	$244,643	68
1994	$54,114	185
Career	$5,931,370	10

GRANT WAITE

Birthdate: August 11,1964
Birthplace: Palmerston, New Zealand
Exempt Status: 1993 tournament winner.
PGA TOUR Victories: 1993 Kemper Open.
Other Victories: 1992 New Zealand Open.
National/International Teams: None.

PGA TOUR CAREER SUMMARY

Year	Money	Rank
1990	$60,076	177
1991-92	DNP	---
1993	$411,405	35
1994	$71,695	172
Career	$533,176	226

DUFFY WALDORF

Birthdate: August 20, 1962
Birthplace: Los Angeles, CA
Exempt Status: 71st on 1994 money list.
PGA TOUR Victories: None.
Other Victories: 1984 California State
Amateur. **1984** Broadmoor Invitational. **1985**
Rice Planters.
National/International Teams: None.

PGA TOUR CAREER SUMMARY

Year	Money	Rank
1987	$53,175	148

Year	Money	Rank
1988	$55,221	143
1989	$149,945	94
1990	$71,673	157
1991	$196,081	86
1992	$582,120	23
1993	$202,638	84
1994	$274,971	71
Career	$1,587,825	116

TOM WATSON

Birthdate: September 4,1949
Birthplace: Kansas City, MO
Exempt Status: 43rd on 1994 money list.
PGA TOUR Victories: (32) **1974** Western
Open. **1975** Byron Nelson Golf Classic. **1977**
Bing Crosby National Pro-Am, Wickes Andy
Williams San Diego Open, Masters, Western
Open. **1978** Joe Garagiola Tucson Open, Bing
Crosby National Pro-Am, Byron Nelson Golf
Classic, Colgate Hall of Fame Classic,
Anheuser-Busch Classic. **1979** Sea Pines
Heritage Classic, Tournament of Champions,
Byron Nelson Golf Classic, Memorial
Tournament, Colgate Hall of Fame Classic.
1980 Andy Williams San Diego Open, Glen
Campbell Los Angeles Open, MONY
Tournament of Champions, New Orleans
Open, Byron Nelson Classic, World Series of
Golf. **1981** Masters, USF&G New Orleans
Open, Atlanta Classic. **1982** Glen Campbell
Los Angeles Open, Sea Pines Heritage
Classic, U.S. Open. **1984** Seiko-Tucson
Match Play, MONY Tournament of
Champions, Western Open. **1987** Nabisco
Championships of Golf.
Other Victories: **1975** British Open. **1977**
British Open. **1980** Dunlop Phoenix, British
Open. **1982** British Open. **1983** British Open.
1992 Hong Kong Open.
National/International Teams: **1977, 1981,
1983, 1989** Ryder Cup. **1982, 1984** USA vs.
Japan.

PGA TOUR CAREER SUMMARY

Year	Money	Rank
1971	$2,185	224
1972	$31,081	79
1973	$74,973	35
1974	$135,474	10
1975	$153,795	7
1976	$138,202	12
1977	$310,653	1
1978	$382,429	1
1979	$462,636	1
1980	$530,808	1
1981	$347,660	3

1982	$316,483	5
1983	$237,519	12
1984	$476,260	1
1985	$226,778	18
1986	$278,338	20
1987	$616,351	5
1988	$273,216	39
1989	$185,398	80
1990	$213,988	88
1991	$364,877	45
1992	$299,818	50
1993	$342,023	46
1994	$380,378	43
Career	$6,751,327	5

D.A. WEIBRING

Birthdate: May 25, 1953
Birthplace: Quincy, IL
Exempt Status: 72nd on 1994 money list.
PGA TOUR Victories: (3) **1979** Quad Cities
Open. **1987** Beatrice Western Open. **1991**
Hardee's Golf Classic.
Other Victories: **1985** Polaroid Cup, Shell-Air
New Zealand Open. **1989** Family House
Invitational.
National/International Teams: None.

PGA TOUR CAREER SUMMARY

Year	Money	Rank
1980	$78,611	53
1981	$92,388	45
1982	$117,941	31
1983	$61,831	84
1984	$110,325	65
1985	$153,079	50
1986	$167,602	55
1987	$391,363	21
1988	$186,677	63
1989	$98,688	127
1990	$156,235	101
1991	$558,648	22
1992	$253,018	62
1993	$299,294	58
1994	$255,757	72
Career	$3,095,307	48

IAN WOOSNAM

Birthdate: March 2, 1958
Birthplace: Oswestry, Wales
PGA TOUR Victories: (2) **1991** USF&G
Classic, Masters.
Other Victories: **1979** News of the World
under-23 Match-play Championship. **1982**
Swiss Open, Cacherel under-25
Championship. **1983** Silk Cut Masters. **1984**

Scandinavian Enterprise Open. **1985** Zambian Open. **1986** Lawrence Batley TPC, "555" Kenya Open. **1987** Jersey Open, Cespa Madrid Open, Bell's Scottish Open, Lancome Trophy, Million Dollar Challenge, Suntory World Match Play Championship, Hong Kong Open, International Trophy (World Cup individual). **1988** Volvo PGA Championship, Carrolls Irish Open, Panasonic European Open. **1989** Carrolls Irish Open. **1990** Amex Mediterranean Open, Monte Carlo Open, Bell's Scottish Open, Epson Grand Prix, Suntory World Match Play Championship. **1991** Mediterranean Open, Monte Carlo Open, PGA Grand Slam. **1992** European Monte Carlo. **1993** Murphy's English Open, Lancome Trophy.
National/International Teams: 1980, 1982, 1983, 1984, 1985,1987, 1990, 1991, 1992, 1993 World Cup. **1983, 1985, 1987, 1989, 1991, 1993** Ryder Cup. **1985, 1986, 1988, 1989, 1990, 1991, 1993** Dunhill Cup. **1985, 1986** Nissan Cup. **1987** Kirin Cup. **1989,1993** Four Tours World Championship of Golf.

PGA TOUR CAREER SUMMARY

Year	Money	Rank
1986	$4,000	233
1987	$3,980	236
1988	$6,484	219
1989	$146,323	97
1990	$72,138	156
1991	$485,023	23
1992	$52,046	171
1993	$55,426	176
1994	$51,895	188
Career	$879,295	N/A

FUZZY ZOELLER

Birthdate: November 11,1951
Birthplace: New Albany, IN
Exempt Status: 5th on 1994 money list.
PGA TOUR Victories: (10) **1979** Wickes Andy Williams San Diego Open, Masters. **1981** Colonial National Invitational. **1983** Sea Pines Heritage Classic, Las Vegas Pro-Celebrity Classic. **1984** U.S. Open. **1985** Hertz Bay Hill Classic. **1986** AT&T Pebble Beach National Pro-Am, Sea Pines Heritage Classic, Anheuser-Busch Golf Classic.
Other Victories: 1985 Skins Game. **1986** Skins Game. **1987** Merrill Lynch Shootout Championships.
National/International Teams: 1979, 1983, 1985 Ryder Cup.

PGA TOUR CAREER SUMMARY

Year	Money	Rank
1980	$95,531	46
1981	$151,571	19
1982	$128,512	28
1983	$417,597	2
1984	$157,460	40
1985	$244,003	15
1986	$358,115	13
1987	$222,921	44
1988	$209,584	51
1989	$217,742	65
1990	$199,629	79
1991	$385,139	42
1992	$125,003	114
1993	$378,175	39
1994	$1,016,804	5
Career	$4,748,085	21

RICHARD ZOKOL

Birthdate: August 21, 1958
Birthplace: Kitimat, B.C., Canada
Exempt Status: 169th on 1994 money list.
PGA TOUR Victories: 1992 Greater Milwaukee Open.
Other Victories: 1981 Canadian Amateur. **1982** British Columbia Open. **1984** Utah Open. **1992** Deposit Guaranty Golf Classic.
National/International Teams: 1980 World Amateur Cup. **1992** World Cup.

PGA TOUR CAREER SUMMARY

Year	Money	Rank
1982	$15,110	156
1983	$38,107	117
1984	$56,605	97
1985	$71,192	102
1986	$37,888	152
1987	$114,406	89
1988	$142,153	83
1989	$51,323	163
1990	$191,634	84
1991	$78,426	149
1992	$311,909	48
1993	$214,419	80
1994	$78,074	169
Career	$1,401,247	131

LPGA
PERSONALITIES

OVERVIEW: *Career victories, earnings, and current playing status for the leading members of the LPGA Tour Division.*

KRISTI ALBERS

Birthdate: December 7, 1963
Birthplace: El Paso, TX
Exempt Status: Exempt
LPGA Victories: (1) **1993** Sprint Classic.

LPGA TOUR CAREER SUMMARY

Year	Money	Rank
1986	$9,230	122
1987	$17,569	104
1988	$27,609	81
1989	$72,900	44
1990	$111,515	35
1991	$139,982	31
1992	$173,189	30
1993	$815,477	17
1994	$136,834	38
Career	$952,311	51

HELEN ALFREDSSON

Birthdate: April 9, 1965
Birthplace: Goteborg, Sweden
Exempt Status: Exempt
LPGA Victories: (2) **1993** Nabisco Dinah Shore. **1994** Ping/Welch's Championship.

LPGA TOUR CAREER SUMMARY

Year	Money	Rank
1992	$262,115	16
1993	$402,685	5
1994	$247,444	17
Career	$914,479	55

DANIELLE AMMACCAPANE

Birthdate: November 27, 1965
Birthplace: Babylon, NY
Exempt Status: Exempt
LPGA Victories: (4) **1991** Standard Register PING. **1992** Standard Register PING, Centel Classic, Lady Keystone Open.

LPGA TOUR CAREER SUMMARY

Year	Money	Rank
1988	$71,105	44
1989	$135,109	23
1990	$300,231	9
1991	$361,925	6
1992	$513,639	3
1993	$187,862	28
1994	$61,964	76
Career	$1,631,836	23

DONNA ANDREWS

Birthdate: April 12, 1967
Birthplace: Lynchburg, VA
Exempt Status: Exempt
LPGA Victories: (4) **1993** Ping-Cellular One LPGA Golf Championship. **1994** Ping/Welch's Championship, Nabisco Dinah Shore, ShopRite LPGA Classic.

LPGA TOUR CAREER SUMMARY

Year	Money	Rank
1990	$52,430	75
1991	$73,472	65
1992	$299,839	13
1993	$334,285	9
1994	$429,015	5
Career	$1,189,041	38

TINA BARRETT

Birthdate: June 5, 1966
Birthplace: Baltimore, MD
Exempt Status: Exempt
LPGA Victories: (1) **1989** Mitsubishi Motors Ocean State Open.

LPGA TOUR CAREER SUMMARY

Year	Money	Rank
1989	$39,776	69
1990	$17,867	121
1991	$138,232	32
1992	$184,719	28
1993	$261,491	19
1994	$84,729	63
Career	$726,455	69

AMY BENZ

Birthdate: May 12, 1962
Birthplace: Rochester, NY
Exempt Status: Exempt
LPGA Victories: None
Other Victories: (1) **1988** JCPenney Classic (with John Huston).

LPGA TOUR CAREER SUMMARY

Year	Money	Rank
1983	$13,143	95
1984	$41,014	54
1985	$62,260	31
1986	$72,407	31
1987	$42,870	57
1988	$117,059	24
1989	$98,129	35
1990	$128,216	29
1991	$96,248	51
1992	$141,673	40
1993	$166,968	35
1994	$118,742	43
Career	$1,072,650	44

MISSIE BERTEOTTI

Birthdate: September 22, 1963
Birthplace: Pittsburgh, PA
Exempt Status: Exempt
LPGA Victories: (1) **1993** PING/WELCH'S Championship.

LPGA TOUR CAREER SUMMARY

Year	Money	Rank
1986	$34,092	65
1987	$62,446	45
1988	$69,441	45
1989	$38,493	71
1990	$107,030	38
1991	$106,459	47
1992	$213,720	22
1993	$184,553	31
1994	$121,856	39
Career	$938,090	52

PAT BRADLEY

Birthdate: March 24,1951
Birthplace: Westford, MA
Exempt Status: Exempt
LPGA Victories: (30) **1976** Girl Talk Classic. **1977** Bankers Trust Classic. **1978** Lady Keystone, Hoosier Classic, Rail Charity Classic. **1980** Greater Baltimore Classic, Peter Jackson Classic. **1981** Women's Kemper Open, U.S. Women's Open. **1983** Mazda Classic of Deer Creek, Chrysler-Plymouth Charity Classic, Columbia Savings Classic, Mazda Japan Classic. **1985** Rochester International, du Maurier Classic, LPGA National Pro-Am. **1986** Nabisco Dinah Shore, S&H Golf Classic, LPGA Championship, du Maurier Classic, Nestle World Championship. **1987** Standard Register Turquoise Classic. **1989** Al Star/Centinela Hospital Classic.
1990 Oldsmobile LPGA Classic, Standard Register Turquoise Classic, LPGA Corning Classic. **1991** Centel Classic, Rail Charity Golf Classic, SAFECO Classic, MBS LPGA Classic.
Other Victories: (4) **1975** Colgate Far East Open. **1978** JCPenney Classic (with Lon Hinkle). **1989** JCPenney Classic (with Bill Glasson). **1992** JCPenney/LPGA Skins Game.

LPGA TOUR CAREER SUMMARY

Year	Money	Rank
1974	$10,839	39
1975	$28,293	14
1976	$84,288	6
1977	$78,709	8
1978	$118,057	2
1979	$132,428	4
1980	$183,377	6
1981	$197,050	3
1982	$113,089	11
1983	$240,207	3
1984	$220,478	4
1985	$387,378	2
1986	$492,021	1
1987	$140,132	15
1988	$15,965	109
1989	$423,714	4
1990	$480,018	5
1991	$763,118	1
1992	$238,541	19
1993	$188,135	27
1994	$236,274	19
Career	$4,772,115	2

BARB BUNKOWSKY

Birthdate: October 13, 1958
Birthplace: Toronto, Ontario
Exempt Status: Exempt
LPGA Victories: (1) **1984** Chrysler-Plymouth Charity Classic.

LPGA TOUR CAREER SUMMARY

Year	Money	Rank
1983	$28,747	60

Year	Money	Rank
1984	$71,682	24
1985	$28,887	76
1986	$25,295	80
1987	$64,365	42
1988	$35,989	71
1989	$4,648	154
1990	$48,064	79
1991	$150,719	28
1992	$79,424	64
1993	$142,907	39
1994	$167,039	31
Career	$835,652	60

BRANDIE BURTON

Birthdate: January 8, 1972
Birthplace: San Bernardino, CA
Exempt Status: Exempt
LPGA Victories: (4) **1992** Ping/Welch's Championship. **1993** Jamie Farr Toledo Classic, du Maurier Ltd. Classic, SAFECO Classic.

LPGA TOUR CAREER SUMMARY

Year	Money	Rank
1991	$176,412	22
1992	$419,571	4
1993	$517,741	3
1994	$172,821	30
Career	$1,286,545	34

JOANNE CARNER

Birthdate: April 4, 1939
Birthplace: Kirkland, WA
Exempt Status: Exempt
LPGA Victories: (42) **1970** Wendell West Open. **1971** U.S. Women's Open, Bluegrass Invitational. **1974** Bluegrass Invitational, Hoosier Classic, Desert Inn Classic, St. Paul Open, Dallas Civitan, Portland Classic. **1975** American Defender Classic, All-American Classic, Peter Jackson Classic. **1976** Orange Blossom Classic, Lady Tara Classic, Hoosier Classic, U.S. Women's Open. **1977** Talk Tournament, Borden Classic, National Jewish Hospital Open. **1978** Peter Jackson Classic, Borden Classic. **1979** Honda Civic Classic, Women's Kemper Open.**1980** Whirlpool Championship of Deer Creek, Bent Tree Ladies Classic, Sunstar '80, Honda Civic Classic, Lady Keystone Open. **1981** S&H Golf Classic, Lady Keystone Open, Columbia Savings LPGA Classic, Rail Charity Golf Classic. **1982** Elizabeth Arden Classic, McDonald's LPGA Kids' Classic, Chevrolet World Championship of Women's Golf, Henredon Classic, Rail Charity Golf Classic. **1983** Chevrolet World Championship of Women's Golf, Portland Ping Championship. **1984** Corning Classic. **1985** Elizabeth Arden Classic, SAFECO Classic.
Other Victories: (4) **1977** LPGA Team Championship (with Judy Rankin). **1978** Colgate Triple Crown. **1979** Colgate Triple Crown. **1982** JCPenney Classic (with John Mahaffey).

LPGA TOUR CAREER SUMMARY

Year	Money	Rank
1970	$14,551	11
1971	$21,604	6
1972	$18,902	15
1973	$19,688	25
1974	$87,094	1
1975	$64,843	2
1976	$103,275	3
1977	$113,712	2
1978	$108,093	4
1979	$98,219	9
1980	$185,916	5
1981	$206,648	2
1982	$310,399	1
1983	$291,404	1
1984	$144,900	9
1985	$141,941	11
1986	$82,802	26
1987	$66,601	41
1988	$121,218	21
1989	$97,888	36
1990	$87,218	48
1991	$86,874	56
1992	$175,880	29
1993	$134,956	41
1994	$55,474	86
Career	$2,840,071	7

DAWN COE-JONES

Birthdate: October 19, 1960
Birthplace: Campbell River, B.C.
Exempt Status: Exempt
LPGA Victories: (2) **1992** Women's Kemper Open. 1994 Healthsouth Palm Beach Classic.
Other Victories: (1) **1992** Pizza-La LPGA Matchplay Championship.

LPGA TOUR CAREER SUMMARY

Year	Money	Rank
1984	$19,603	91
1985	$34,864	68

Year	Money	Rank
1986	$54,332	47
1987	$72,045	33
1988	$52,659	58
1989	$143,423	19
1990	$240,478	11
1991	$158,013	25
1992	$251,392	17
1993	$271,978	16
1994	$223,696	20
Career	$1,522,483	25

JANE CRAFTER

Birthdate: December 14, 1955
Birthplace: Perth, Australia
Exempt Status: Exempt
LPGA Victories: (1) **1990** Phar-Mor at Inverrary.
Other Victories: (1) **1987** JCPenney Classic (with Steve Jones).

LPGA TOUR CAREER SUMMARY

Year	Money	Rank
1981	$1,617	135
1982	$7,472	108
1983	$37,433	43
1984	$48,729	46
1985	$60,884	32
1986	$79,431	28
1987	$59,876	48
1988	$32,733	73
1989	$35,086	77
1990	$112,840	34
1991	$34,168	101
1992	$155,485	35
1993	$187,190	29
1994	$65,730	75
Career	$918,059	54

ELAINE CROSBY

Birthdate: June 6, 1958
Birthplace: Birmingham, MI
Exempt Status: Exempt
LPGA Victories: (2) **1989** Mazda Japan Classic. **1994** Lady Keystone Open.

LPGA TOUR CAREER SUMMARY

Year	Money	Rank
1985	$10,133	122
1986	$5,533	146
1987	$31,024	74
1988	$15,655	112
1989	$126,899	28
1990	$169,543	18

1991	$181,610	21
1992	$109,125	50
1993	$177,726	33
1994	$338,043	10
Career	$1,165,291	40

BETH DANIEL

Birthdate: October 14, 1956
Birthplace: Charleston, SC
Exempt Status: Exempt
LPGA Victories: (31) **1979** Patty Berg Classic. **1980** Golden Lights Championship, Patty Berg Classic, Columbia Savings Classic, Chevrolet World Championship of Women's Golf. **1981** Florida Lady Citrus, Chevrolet World Championship of Women's Golf. **1982** Bent Tree Ladies Classic, American Express Sun City Classic, Birmingham Classic, Columbia Savings Classic, WUI Classic. **1983** McDonald's LPGA Kids Classic. **1985** Kyocera Inamori Classic. **1989** Greater Washington Open, Rail Charity Golf Classic, SAFECO Classic, Konica San Jose Classic. **1990** Orix Hawaiian Ladies Open, Women's Kemper Open, Phar-Mor in Youngstown, Mazda LPGA Championship, Northgate Classic, Rail Charity Golf Classic, Centel Classic. **1991** Phar-Mor at Inverrary, McDonald's Championship.
Other Victories: (4) **1979** World Ladies. **1981** JCPenney Classic (with Tom Kite). **1988** Nichirei Ladies Cup US-Japan Team Championship. **1990** JCPenney Classic (with Davis Love III). **1991** Konica World Ladies. **1994** LPGA Corning Classic, Oldsmobile Classic, JAL Big Apple Classic, World Championship of Women's Golf.

LPGA TOUR CAREER SUMMARY

Year	Money	Rank
1979	$97,027	10
1980	$231,000	1
1981	$206,977	1
1982	$223,634	5
1983	$167,403	6
1984	$94,204	16
1985	$177,235	8
1986	$103,547	21
1987	$83,308	29
1988	$140,635	17
1989	$504,851	2
1990	$863,578	1
1991	$469,501	4
1992	$329,681	11
1993	$140,001	40

Year	Money	Rank
1994	$656,687	2
Career	$4,489,352	3

LAURA DAVIES

Birthdate: October 5, 1973
Birthplace: Coventry, England
Exempt Status: Exempt
LPGA Victories: (7) **1988** Circle K LPGA Tucson Open, Jamie Farr Toledo Classic. **1989** Lady Keystone Open. **1991** Inamori Classic. **1993** McDonald's Championship. **1994** Standard Register Ping, Sara Lee Classic, McDonald's LPGA Championship.

LPGA TOUR CAREER SUMMARY

Year	Money	Rank
1988	$160,382	15
1989	$181,574	13
1990	$64,863	64
1991	$200,831	20
1992	$150,163	39
1993	$240,643	20
1994	$667,652	1
Career	$1,666,108	21

ALICIA DIBOS

Birthdate: March 1, 1960
Birthplace: Lima, Peru
Exempt Status: Exempt.
LPGA Victories: None.

LPGA TOUR CAREER SUMMARY

Year	Money	Rank
1993	$28,721	117
1994	$180,374	28
Career	$209,095	175

JUDY DICKINSON

Birthdate: May 4, 1950
Birthplace: Akron, OH
Exempt Status: Exempt
LPGA Victories: (4) **1985** Boston Five Classic. **1986** Rochester International, SAFECO Classic. **1992** Inamori Classic.

LPGA TOUR CAREER SUMMARY

Year	Money	Rank
1978	$5,330	83
1979	$24,561	48
1980	$30,648	46
1981	$42,570	36
1982	$47,187	29
1983	$69,091	23
1984	$85,479	18
1985	$167,809	9
1986	$195,834	10
1987	$19,602	96
1988	$160,440	14
1989	$23,460	96
1990	$80,784	52
1991	$251,018	14
1992	$351,559	10
1993	$186,317	30
1994	$246,879	18
Career	$1,990,807	16

DALE EGGELING

Birthdate: April 21, 1954
Birthplace: Statesboro, GA
Exempt Status: Exempt
LPGA Victories: (1) **1980** Boston Five Classic.

LPGA TOUR CAREER SUMMARY

Year	Money	Rank
1976	$321	113
1977	$5,859	70
1978	$9,690	68
1979	$21,333	55
1980	$45,335	27
1981	$50,594	23
1982	$57,691	26
1983	$52,967	29
1984	$53,355	37
1985	$34,894	67
1986	$52,684	50
1987	$33,203	71
1988	$32,203	74
1989	$56,108	55
1990	$147,990	24
1991	$78,386	61
1992	$138,781	41
1993	$145,789	38
1994	$157,196	32
Career	$1,017,298	37

JANE GEDDES

Birthdate: February 5, 1960
Birthplace: Huntington, NY
Exempt Status: Exempt
LPGA Victories: (11) **1986** U.S. Women's Open, Boston Five Classic. **1987** Women's Kemper Open, GNA/ Glendale Federal Classic, Mazda LPGA Championship, Jamie Farr Toledo Classic, Boston Five Classic. **1991** The Jamaica Classic, Atlantic City

Classic. **1993** Oldsmobile Classic. **1994** Chicago Challenge.

LPGA TOUR CAREER SUMMARY

Year	Money	Rank
1983	$13,7559	4
1984	$53,682	3
1985	$108,971	17
1986	$221,255	5
1987	$396,818	3
1988	$90,298	33
1989	$186,485	12
1990	$181,874	16
1991	$315,240	10
1992	$164,127	32
1993	$263,149	18
1994	$257,045	15
Career	$1,995,654	12

GAIL GRAHAM

Birthdate: January 16, 1964
Birthplace: Vanderhoof, BC
Exempt Status: Exempt
LPGA Victories: None.

LPGA TOUR CAREER SUMMARY

Year	Money	Rank
1990	$10,948	143
1991	$46,386	90
1992	$58,938	79
1993	$126,048	45
1994	$121,812	40
Career	$364,132	121

TAMMIE GREEN

Birthdate: December 17, 1959
Birthplace: Somerset, OH
Exempt Status: Exempt
LPGA Victories: (4) 1989 du Maurier Ltd. Classic. **1993** HEALTHSOUTH Palm Beach Classic, Rochester International.**1994** Youngstown-Warren LPGA Classic.

LPGA TOUR CAREER SUMMARY

Year	Money	Rank
1987	$68,346	39
1988	$120,271	22
1989	$204,143	8
1990	$155,756	22
1991	$237,073	15
1992	$154,717	37
1993	$356,579	7
1994	$418,969	6
Career	$1,715,863	19

SHELLEY HAMLIN

Birthdate: May 28, 1949
Birthplace: San Mateo, CA
Exempt Status: Exempt
LPGA Victories: (3) 1978 Patty Berg Classic. **1992** The Phar-Mor at Inverrary. **1993** ShopRite LPGA Classic.
Other Victories: (1) 1975 Japan Classic.

LPGA TOUR CAREER SUMMARY

Year	Money	Rank
1972	$12,845	24
1973	$22,831	19
1974	$28,276	18
1975	$15,980	27
1976	$14,960	43
1977	$12,069	55
1978	$34,494	29
1979	$41,739	26
1980	$50,843	23
1981	$32,798	46
1982	$32,878	47
1983	$19,486	77
1984	$9,923	120
1985	$18,564	94
1986	$20,035	93
1987	$85,466	26
1988	$28,521	77
1989	$47,254	61
1990	$17,701	122
1991	$16,170	138
1992	$157,327	34
1993	$129,447	44
1994	$71,864	72
Career	$921,460	53

JULI INKSTER

Birthdate: June 24, 1960
Birthplace: Santa Cruz, CA
Exempt Status: Exempt
LPGA Victories: (15) 1983 SAFECO Classic. **1984** Nabisco Dinah Shore, du Maurier Classic. **1985** Lady Keystone Open. **1986** Women's Kemper Open, McDonald's Championship, Lady Keystone Open, Atlantic City Classic. **1988** Crestar Classic, Atlantic City Classic, SAFECO Classic. **1989** Nabisco Dinah Shore, Crestar Classic. **1991** LPGA Bay State Classic. **1992** JAL Big Apple Classic.
Other Victories: (1) 1986 JCPenney Classic (with Tom Purtzer).

LPGA TOUR CAREER SUMMARY

Year	Money	Rank
1983	$52,220	30

Year	Money	Rank
1984	$186,501	6
1985	$99,651	19
1986	$285,293	3
1987	$140,739	14
1988	$235,344	10
1989	$180,848	14
1990	$54,251	73
1991	$213,096	17
1992	$392,063	7
1993	$116,583	47
1994	$113,829	45
Career	$2,070,418	13

CHRIS JOHNSON

Birthdate: April 25, 1958
Birthplace: Arcata, CA
Exempt Status: Exempt
LPGA Victories: (6) **1984** Samaritan Turquoise Classic, Tucson Conquistadores Open. **1986** GNA/Glendale Federal Classic. **1987** Columbia Savings LPGA National Pro-Am. **1990** Atlantic City Classic. **1991** Ping/Welch's Championship.

LPGA TOUR CAREER SUMMARY

Year	Money	Rank
1980	$2,827	123
1981	$25,182	55
1982	$60,449	24
1983	$37,967	42
1984	$70,979	25
1985	$67,123	29
1986	$200,648	8
1987	$197,722	8
1988	$46,219	61
1989	$97,195	37
1990	$187,486	14
1991	$135,416	33
1992	$105,197	53
1993	$111,027	50
1994	$205,489	22
Career	$1,550,927	24

TRISH JOHNSON

Birthdate: January 17, 1966
Birthplace: Bristol, England
Exempt Status: Exempt
LPGA Victories: (2) **1993** Las Vegas LPGA at Canyon Gate, Atlanta Women's Championship.

LPGA TOUR CAREER SUMMARY

Year	Money	Rank
1988	$23,972	89
1989	$17,215	115
1990	$58,729	71
1991	$85,639	57
1992	$33,103	112
1993	$331,745	10
1994	$42,750	102
Career	$593,153	87

ROSIE JONES

Birthdate: November 13, 1959
Birthplace: Santa Ana, CA
Exempt Status: Exempt
LPGA Victories: (5) **1987** Rail Charity Golf Classic. **1988** USX Golf Classic, Nestle World Championship, Santa Barbara Open. **1991** Rochester International.

LPGA TOUR CAREER SUMMARY

Year	Money	Rank
1982	$2,869	127
1983	$64,955	27
1984	$81,793	19
1985	$66,665	30
1986	$71,399	33
1987	$188,000	10
1988	$323,392	3
1989	$110,671	32
1990	$353,832	6
1991	$281,089	12
1992	$204,096	25
1993	$320,964	11
1994	$115,166	44
Career	$2,184,531	12

LISA KIGGENS

Birthdate: August 13, 1972
Birthplace: Salinas, CA
Exempt Status: Exempt
LPGA Victories: None.
Other Victories: None.

LPGA TOUR CAREER SUMMARY

Year	Money	Rank
1992	$5,401	171
1993	$64,851	72
1994	$183,279	26
Career	$253,531	157

BETSY KING

Birthdate: August 13, 1955
Birthplace: Reading, PA
Exempt Status: Exempt
LPGA Victories: (29) **1984** Women's Kemper

Open, Freedom Orlando Classic, Columbia Savings Classic. **1985** Samaritan Turquoise Classic, Rail Charity Classic. **1986** Henredon Classic, Rail Charity Classic. **1987** Circle K LPGA Tucson Open, Nabisco Dinah Shore, McDonald's Championship, Atlantic City Classic. **1988** Women's Kemper Open, Rail Charity Golf Classic, Cellular One Ping Golf Championship. **1989** Jamaica Classic, Women's Kemper Open, USX Golf Classic, McDonald's Championship, U.S. Women's Open, Nestle World Championship. **1990** Nabisco Dinah Shore, U.S. Women's Open, JAL Big Apple Classic. **1991** LPGA Corning Classic, JAL Big Apple Classic. **1992** Mazda LPGA Championship, The Phar-Mor in Youngstown, Mazda Japan Classic. **1993** Toray Japan Queens Cup.

Other Victories: (4) **1981** Itsuki Charity Classic (Japan). **1985** Ladies British Open. **1990** Itoman World Match Play Championship. **1993** JCPenney/LPGA Skins Game.

LPGA TOUR CAREER SUMMARY

Year	Money	Rank
1977	$4,008	83
1978	$44,092	20
1979	$53,900	19
1980	$28,480	50
1981	$51,029	22
1982	$50,563	28
1983	$94,767	14
1984	$266,771	1
1985	$214,411	6
1986	$290,195	2
1987	$460,385	2
1988	$256,957	8
1989	$654,132	1
1990	$543,844	3
1991	$341,784	9
1992	$551,320	2
1993	$595,992	1
1994	$325,074	10
Career	$4,827,708	1

HIROMI KOBAYASHI

Birthdate: January 8, 1963
Birthplace: Fukushima, Japan
Exempt Status: Exempt
LPGA Victories: (2) **1993** JAL Big Apple Classic, Minnesota LPGA Classic.

LPGA TOUR CAREER SUMMARY

Year	Money	Rank
1990	$66,325	60
1991	$76,582	63
1992	$58,851	80
1993	$347,060	8
1994	$222,774	21
Career	$771,592	65

NANCY LOPEZ

Birthdate: January 6, 1957
Birthplace: Torrance, CA
Exempt Status: Exempt
LPGA Victories: (47) **1978** Bent Tree Ladies Classic, Sunstar Classic, Greater Baltimore Classic, Coca-Cola Classic, Golden Lights Championship, LPGA Championship, Bankers Trust Classic, Colgate European Open, Colgate Far East Open. **1979** Sunstar Classic, Sahara National Pro-Am, Women's International, Coca-Cola Classic, Golden Lights Championship, Lady Keystone Open, Colgate European Open, Mary Kay Classic. **1980** Women's Kemper Open, Sarah Coventry, Rail Charity Classic. **1981** Arizona Copper Classic, Colgate Dinah Shore, Sarah Coventry. **1982** J&B Scotch Pro-Am, Mazda Japan Classic. **1983** Elizabeth Arden Classic, J&B Scotch Pro-Am. **1984** Uniden LPGA Invitational, Chevrolet World Championship of Women's Golf. **1985** Chrysler/ Plymouth Charity Classic, LPGA Championship, Mazda Hall of Fame Championship, Henredon Classic, Portland Ping Championship. **1987** Sarasota Classic, Cellular One Ping Golf Championship. **1988** Mazda Classic, Al Star/ Centinela Hospital Classic, Chrysler Plymouth Classic. **1989** Mazda LPGA Championship, Atlantic City Classic, Nippon Travel - MBS Classic. **1990** MBS LPGA Classic. **1991** Sara Lee Classic. **1992** Rail Charity Golf Classic, Ping Cellular One LPGA Golf Championship. **1993** Youngstown-Warren LPGA Classic.

Other Victories: (3) **1980** JCPenney Classic (with Curtis Strange). **1987** Mazda Champions (with Miller Barber). **1992** Wendy's Three-Tour Challenge (with Dottie Mochrie and Patty Sheehan).

LPGA TOUR CAREER SUMMARY

Year	Money	Rank
1977	$23,138	31
1978	$189,813	1
1979	$197,488	1
1980	$209,078	4
1981	$165,679	6
1982	$166,474	6
1983	$91,477	15

Year	Money	Rank
1984	$183,756	7
1985	$416,472	1
1986	$67,700	35
1987	$204,823	7
1988	$322,154	4
1989	$487,153	3
1990	$301,262	8
1991	$153,772	26
1992	$382,128	8
1993	$304,480	14
1994	$150,399	33
Career	$4,017,249	5

MEG MALLON
Born: April 14, 1963
Birthplace: Natick, MA
Exempt Status: Exempt
LPGA Victories: (6) 1991 Oldsmobile LPGA Classic, Mazda LPGA Championship, U.S. Women's Open, Dakyo World Championship. **1993** PING/WELCH'S Championship, Sara Lee Classic.
Other Victories: 1983 Michigan Amateur.

LPGA TOUR CAREER SUMMARY

Year	Money	Rank
1987	$1,572	175
1988	$25,002	87
1989	$42,574	67
1990	$129,381	27
1991	$633,802	2
1992	$400,052	6
1993	$276,291	15
1994	$341,627	9
Career	$1,850,301	17

MISSIE McGEORGE
Birthdate: August 20, 1959
Birthplace: Pueblo, CO
Exempt Status: Exempt
LPGA Victories: (1) 1994 Ping Cellular One Golf Championship.

LPGA TOUR CAREER SUMMARY

Year	Money	Rank
1983	$4,596	133
1984	$20,117	89
1985	$21,563	87
1986	$23,436	83
1987	$63,259	44
1988	$93,397	31
1989	$68,493	48
1990	$93,721	45
1991	$113,959	46
1992	$30,248	118
1993	$180,311	32
1994	$181,281	27
Career	$894,381	58

MICHELLE McGANN
Birthdate: December 30, 1969
Birthplace: West Palm Beach, FL
Exempt Status: Exempt
LPGA Victories: None.
Other Victories: 1988 Doherty Cup Championship.

LPGA TOUR CAREER SUMMARY

Year	Money	Rank
1989	$11,679	130
1990	$34,846	98
1991	$121,663	40
1992	$239,062	18
1993	$315,921	12
1994	$269,936	14
Career	$993,107	50

LAURI MERTEN
Birthdate: July 6, 1960
Birthplace: Waukesha, WI
Exempt Status: Exempt
LPGA Victories: (3) 1983 Rail Charity Golf Classic. **1984** Jamie Farr Toledo Classic. **1993** U.S. Women's Open.

LPGA TOUR CAREER SUMMARY

Year	Money	Rank
1983	$51,930	31
1984	$108,920	13
1985	$39,597	55
1986	$45,967	55
1987	$63,492	43
1988	$36,772	70
1989	$42,832	66
1990	$47,263	82
1991	$25,494	112
1992	$53,204	86
1993	$394,744	6
1994	$202,002	24
Career	$1,112,217	41

DOTTIE MOCHRIE
Birthdate: August 17, 1965
Birthplace: Saratoga Springs, NY
Exempt Status: Exempt
LPGA Victories: (8) 1989 Oldsmobile LPGA

Classic. **1990** Crestar Classic. **1992** Nabisco Dinah Shore, Sega Women's Championship, Welch's Classic, Sun-Times Challenge. **1993** World Championship of Women's Golf. **Other Victories: (1) 1992** JCPenney Classic (with Dan Forsman), Wendy's Three-Tour Challenge (with Patty Sheehan and Nancy Lopez). **1994** Chrysler-Plymouth Tournament of Champions.

LPGA TOUR CAREER SUMMARY

Year	Money	Rank
1988	$137,293	20
1989	$130,830	27
1990	$231,410	12
1991	$477,767	3
1992	$693,335	1
1993	$429,118	4
1994	$472,728	4
Career	$2,574,716	9

KRIS MONAGHAN

Born: August 24, 1960
Birthplace: Spokane, WA
Exempt Status: Exempt
LPGA Victories: None

LPGA TOUR CAREER SUMMARY

Year	Money	Rank
1985	$17,942	96
1986	$19,756	94
1987	$21,937	91
1988	$19,670	101
1989	$17,639	112
1990	$65,725	61
1991	$134,753	36
1992	$40,025	102
1993	$208,987	23
1994	$51,847	92
Career	$598,281	86

MARTHA NAUSE

Born: September 10, 1954
Birthplace: Sheboygan, WI
Exempt Status: Exempt
LPGA Victories: (1) 1994 Du Maurier Ltd. Classic.

LPGA TOUR CAREER SUMMARY

Year	Money	Rank
1978	$2,646	99
1979	$5,151	97
1980	$10,019	82
1981	$30,866	47
1982	$27,206	57
1983	$41,760	37
1984	$39,169	55
1985	$25,211	79
1986	$37,850	63
1987	$69,412	38
1988	$138,490	19
1989	$138,639	21
1990	$83,383	50
1991	$143,702	30
1992	$64,810	71
1993	$42,090	94
1994	$210,825	24
Career	$1,111,220	42

LISELOTTE NEUMANN

Birthdate: May 20, 1966
Birthplace: Finspang, Sweden
Exempt Status: Exempt
LPGA Victories: (1) 1994 Minnesota LPGA Classic.

LPGA TOUR CAREER SUMMARY

Year	Money	Rank
1988	$188,729	12
1989	$119,915	30
1990	$82,323	51
1991	$151,367	27
1992	$225,667	21
1993	$90,776	57
1994	$505,701	3
Career	$1,364,478	29

NANCY RAMSBOTTOM

Birthdate: August 19, 1962
Birthplace: Birmingham, AL
Exempt Status: Exempt
LPGA Victories: None.

LPGA TOUR CAREER SUMMARY

Year	Money	Rank
1985	$16,997	97
1986	$17,300	98
1987	$24,490	83
1988	$10,834	131
1989	$16,493	116
1990	$31,974	101
1991	$22,294	120
1992	$63,385	73
1993	$93,354	55
1994	$179,325	29
Career	$476,446	104

CINDY RARICK

Birthdate: September 12, 1959
Birthplace: Glenwood, MN
Exempt Status: Exempt
LPGA Victories: (5) **1987** Tsumura Hawaiian Ladies Open, LPGA Corning Classic. **1989** Chrysler-Plymouth Classic. **1990** Planters Pat Bradley International. **1991** Northgate Computer Classic.

LPGA TOUR CAREER SUMMARY

Year	Money	Rank
1985	$22,094	86
1986	$29,093	72
1987	$162,073	11
1988	$63,699	49
1989	$196,611	11
1990	$259,163	10
1991	$201,342	19
1992	$155,303	36
1993	$174,407	34
1994	$81,923	66
Career	$1,345,708	31

DEB RICHARD

Birthdate: June 3, 1963
Birthplace: Abbeville, LA
Exempt Status: Exempt
LPGA Victories: (3) **1987** Rochester International. **1991** Women's Kemper Open, The Phar-Mor in Youngstown.
Other Victories: (2) **1991** JBP Cup Match Play. **1994** Safeco Classic.

LPGA TOUR CAREER SUMMARY

Year	Money	Rank
1986	$98,451	22
1987	$83,225	30
1988	$112,647	26
1989	$70,594	47
1990	$186,464	15
1991	$376,640	5
1992	$266,427	15
1993	$223,282	22
1994	$251,513	16
Career	$1,669,243	20

ALICE RITZMAN

Birthdate: March 1, 1952
Birthplace: Kalispell, MT
Exempt Status: Exempt
LPGA Victories: None

LPGA TOUR CAREER SUMMARY

Year	Money	Rank
1978	$2,504	102
1979	$24,647	47
1980	$38,024	38
1981	$44,664	33
1982	$31,406	49
1983	$39,285	41
1984	$33,604	60
1985	$47,046	50
1986	$84,443	25
1987	$62,312	46
1988	$59,420	53
1989	$177,507	15
1990	$112,840	33
1991	$102,576	49
1992	$201,922	26
1993	$113,992	48
1994	$186,715	25
Career	$1,362,909	30

KELLY ROBBINS

Birthdate: September 29, 1969
Birthplace: Mt. Pleasant, MI
Exempt Status: Exempt
LPGA Victories: (2) **1993** LPGA Corning Classic. **1994** Jamie Farr Toledo Classic.

LPGA TOUR CAREER SUMMARY

Year	Money	Rank
1992	$90,405	59
1993	$200,744	24
1994	$396,778	7
Career	$687,927	72

PATTY SHEEHAN

Birthdate: October 27, 1956
Birthplace: Middlebury, VT
Exempt Status: Exempt
LPGA Victories: (32) **1981** Mazda Japan Classic. **1982** Orlando Lady Classic, SAFECO Classic, Inamori Classic. **1983** Corning Classic, LPGA Championship, Henredon Classic, Inamori Classic. **1984** Elizabeth Arden Classic, LPGA Championship, McDonald's Kids Classic, Henredon Classic. **1985** Sarasota Classic, J&B Scotch Pro-Am. **1986** Sarasota Classic, Kyocera Inamori Classic, Konica San Jose Classic. **1988** Sarasota Classic, Mazda Japan Classic. **1989** Rochester International. **1990** The Jamaica Classic, McDonald's Championship, Rochester International, Ping Cellular One

Golf Championship, SAFECO Classic. **1991** Orix Hawaiian Ladies Open. **1992** Rochester International, Jamie Farr Toledo Classic, U.S. Women's Open. **1993** Standard Register Ping, Mazda LPGA Championship.**1994** U.S. Women's Open.

Other Victories: (2) **1992** Weetabix Women's British Open, Wendy's Three-Tour Challenge (with Dottie Mochrie and Nancy Lopez).

LPGA TOUR CAREER SUMMARY

Year	Money	Rank
1980	$17,139	63
1981	$118,463	11
1982	$225,022	4
1983	$250,399	2
1984	$255,185	2
1985	$227,908	5
1986	$214,281	7
1987	$208,107	6
1988	$326,171	2
1989	$253,605	5
1990	$732,618	2
1991	$342,204	8
1992	$418,622	5
1993	$540,547	2
1994	$323,563	11
Career	$4,455,399	4

VAL SKINNER

Birthdate: October 16, 1960
Birthplace: Hamilton, MT
Exempt Status: Exempt
LPGA Victories: (5) **1985** Konica San Jose Classic. **1986** Mazda Classic. **1987** MasterCard International.**1993** Lady Keystone Open. **1994** Atlanta Women's Championship.

LPGA TOUR CAREER SUMMARY

Year	Money	Rank
1983	$29,485	57
1984	$23,021	79
1985	$132,307	14
1986	$165,243	11
1987	$122,039	18
1988	$60,334	52
1989	$102,089	34
1990	$66,577	59
1991	$61,923	74
1992	$41,651	100
1993	$129,665	43
1994	$297,494	13
Career	$1,231,828	36

HOLLIS STACY

Birthdate: March 16, 1954
Birthplace: Savannah, GA
Exempt Status: Exempt
LPGA Victories: (18) **1977** Rail Charity Golf Classic, Lady Tara Classic, U.S. Women's Open. **1978** U.S. Women's Open, Birmingham Classic. **1979** Mayflower Classic. **1980** CPC International. **1981** West Virginia LPGA Classic, Inamori Classic. **1982** Whirlpool Championship of Deer Creek, S&H Golf Classic, West Virginia LPGA Classic. **1983** S&H Golf Classic, CPC International, Peter Jackson Classic. **1984** U.S. Women's Open. **1985** Mazda Classic of Deer Creek. **1991** Crestar-Farm Fresh Classic.

LPGA TOUR CAREER SUMMARY

Year	Money	Rank
1974	$5,071	60
1975	$14,409	33
1976	$34,842	16
1977	$89,155	5
1978	$95,800	6
1979	$81,265	11
1980	$89,913	11
1981	$138,908	9
1982	$161,379	8
1983	$149,036	9
1984	$87,106	17
1985	$100,592	18
1986	$104,286	19
1987	$86,261	24
1988	$34,091	72
1989	$134,460	24
1990	$64,074	65
1991	$114,731	45
1992	$132,323	44
1993	$191,257	26
1994	$95,146	56
Career	$2,004,109	14

SHERRI STEINHAUER

Birthdate: December 27, 1962
Birthplace: Madison, WI
Exempt Status: Exempt
LPGA Victories: (2) **1992** du Maurier Ltd. Classic. **1994** Sprint Championship.

LPGA TOUR CAREER SUMMARY

Year	Money	Rank
1986	$7,733	131
1987	$45,741	54

Year	Money	Rank
1988	$54,262	57
1989	$44,825	64
1990	$109,407	37
1991	$165,568	24
1992	$315,145	12
1993	$311,967	13
1994	$398,604	8
Career	$1,453,252	26

JAN STEPHENSON

Birthdate: December 22, 1951
Birthplace: Sydney, Australia
Exempt Status: Exempt
LPGA Victories: (16) **1976** Sarah Coventry
Naples Classic, Birmingham Classic. **1978**
Women's International. **1980** Sun City
Classic. **1981** Peter Jackson Classic, Mary
Kay Classic, United Virginia Bank Classic.
1982 LPGA Championship, Lady Keystone.
1983 Tucson Conquistadores LPGA Open,
Lady Keystone Open, U.S. Women's Open.
1985 GNA Classic. **1987** Santa Barbara
Open, SAFECO Classic, Konica San Jose
Classic.
Other Victories: (7) **1973** Australian Open.
1977 Australian Open. **1981** World Ladies.
1983 JCPenney Mixed Team (with Fred
Couples). **1985** Nichirei Ladies Cup,
Hennessy French Open. **1990**
JCPenney/LPGA Skins Game.

LPGA TOUR CAREER SUMMARY

Year	Money	Rank
1974	$16,270	28
1975	$20,066	21
1976	$64,827	8
1977	$65,820	11
1978	$66,033	13
1979	$69,519	15
1980	$41,318	34
1981	$180,528	5
1982	$133,212	10
1983	$193,364	4
1984	$101,215	14
1985	$148,030	10
1986	$165,238	12
1987	$227,303	4
1988	$236,739	9
1989	$71,550	45
1990	$31,070	105

1991	$49,467	88
1992	$132,634	42
1993	$161,123	36
1994	$99,766	54
Career	$2,275,075	10

KRIS TSCHETTER

Birthdate: December 30, 1964
Birthplace: Detroit, MI
Exempt Status: Exempt
LPGA Victories: (1) **1992** Northgate
Computer Classic.
Other Victories: (1) **1991** JCPenney Classic
(with Billy Andrade).

LPGA TOUR CAREER SUMMARY

Year	Money	Rank
1988	$7,590	145
1989	$18,315	109
1990	$39,469	91
1991	$129,532	38
1992	$157,436	33
1993	$196,913	25
1994	$111,180	47
Career	$660,435	77

LISA WALTERS

Birthdate: January 9, 1960
Birthplace: Prince Rupert, B.C.
Exempt Status: Exempt
LPGA Victories: (2) **1992** Itoki Hawaiian
Ladies Open. **1993** Itoki Hawaiian Ladies
Open.

LPGA TOUR CAREER SUMMARY

Year	Money	Rank
1984	$37,568	56
1985	$32,080	70
1986	$53,411	48
1987	$72,024	34
1988	$22,665	94
1989	$21,979	100
1990	$36,047	94
1991	$32,380	105
1992	$108,157	51
1993	$149,260	37
1994	$71,732	73
Career	$637,303	79

SENIOR PGA TOUR PERSONALITIES

OVERVIEW: *Biographies and career summaries of leading Senior PGA TOUR players, including 1994 statistical summaries and career highlights.*

TOMMY AARON

Birthdate: February 22, 1937
Birthplace: Gainesville, GA
Exempt Status: 26th on 1994 money list.
PGA TOUR Victories: (2) **1970** Atlanta Classic. **1973** Masters.
Senior PGA TOUR Victories: (1) **1992** Kaanapaii Classic.
Other Victories: 1969 Canadian Open. **1960** Western Amateur.
National/International Teams: 1959 Walker Cup. **1969**, **1973** Ryder Cup.

SENIOR PGA TOUR CAREER SUMMARY

Year	Money	Rank
1987	$98,421	29
1988	$81,829	41
1989	$51,800	60
1990	$107,651	46
1991	$152,443	43
1992	$459,230	12
1993	$266,611	34
1994	$339,815	26
Sr. Career	$1,557,620	35

JIM ALBUS

Birthdate: June 18,1940
Birthplace: Staten Island, NY
Exempt Status: 4th on 1994 money list.
PGA TOUR Victories: None
Senior PGA TOUR Victories: (4) **1991** MAZDA Presents THE SENIORS PLAYERS Championship. **1993** GTE Suncoast Classic. **1994** Vantage at the Dominion, Bank of Boston Senior Golf Classic.
Other Victories: 1970 Metropolitan Open Championship. **1985** Metropolitan Open Championship.
National/International Teams: None.

SENIOR PGA TOUR CAREER SUMMARY

Year	Money	Rank
1990	$14,433	95

Year	Money	Rank
1991	$301,406	20
1992	$404,693	16
1993	$627,883	12
1994	$1,096,128	4
Sr. Career	$2,444,543	18

ISAO AOKI

Birthdate: August 31, 1942
Birthplace: Abiko, Chiba, Japan
Exempt Status: 11th on 1994 money list.
Senior PGA TOUR Victories: (2) **1992** Nationwide Championship. **1994** Bank One Senior Classic.
Other Victories: 1991 Bridgestone Tournament.
National/International Teams:1982, 1983, 1984 Japanese National Team. **1985, 1987, 1988** Kirin Cup.

SENIOR PGA TOUR CAREER SUMMARY

Year	Money	Rank
1992	$324,650	26
1993	$557,667	15
1994	$632,975	11
Sr. Career	$1,515,292	39

TOMMY AYCOCK

Birthdate: September 2, 1941
Birthplace: Edinburg, TX
Exempt Status: 40th on 1994 money list.
PGA TOUR Victories: None.
Senior PGA TOUR Victories: None.
Other Victories: South Texas PGA Championship (6 times).
National/International Teams: None.

SENIOR PGA TOUR CAREER SUMMARY

Year	Money	Rank
1992	$190,030	38
1993	$211,826	39
1994	$212,660	40
Sr. Career	$614,517	72

GEORGE ARCHER

Birthdate: October 1,1939
Birthplace: San Francisco, CA
Exempt Status: 10th on 1994 money list.
PGA TOUR Victories: (12) **1965** Lucky International. **1967** Greensboro. **1968** Pensacola, New Orleans. **1969** Williams San Diego, Hartford. **1972** Glen Campbell Los Angeles, Greensboro Open. **1976** Del Webb Sahara Invitational. **1984** Bank of Boston Classic.
Senior PGA TOUR Victories: (16) **1989** Gatlin Brothers Southwest Classic. **1990** MONY Tournament of Champions, Northville Long Island Classic, GTE Northwest Classic, Gold Rush at Rancho Mudeta. **1991** Northville Long Island Classic, GTE North Classic, Raley's Senior Gold Rush. **1992** MurataReunion Pro-Am, Northville Long Island Classic, Bruno's Memorial Classic. **1993** Ameritech Senior Open, First of America Classic, Raley's Senior Gold Rush, PING Kaanapaii Classic. **1994** The Chrysler Cup.
Other Victories: **1963** Trans-Mississippi Amateur. **1963** Northern California Open. **1968** PGA National Team Championship (with Bobby Nichols). **1969** Argentine Masters. **1981** Colombian Open. **1982** Philippines Open.
National/International Teams: **1990**, **1991**, **1992**, **1993** U.S. DuPont Cup Team.

SENIOR PGA TOUR CAREER SUMMARY

Year	Money	Rank
1989	$ 98,063	45
1990	$749,691	4
1991	$963,455	2
1992	$860,175	2
1993	$963,124	3
1994	$684,944	10
Sr. Career	$4,319,452	5

MILLER BARBER

Birthdate: March 31, 1931
Birthplace: Shreveport, LA
Exempt Status: 11th on all-time money list.
PGA TOUR Victories: (11) **1964** Cajun Classic. **1967** Oklahoma City Open. **1968** Byron Nelson Classic. **1969** Kaiser International. **1970** New Orleans Open, Phoenix Open. **1972** Tucson Open. **1973** World Open. **1974** Ohio Kings Island Open. **1977** Anheuser-Busch Classic. **1978** Phoenix Open.
Senior PGA TOUR Victories: (24) **1981** Peter Jackson Champions, Suntree Senior Classic, PGA Seniors Championship. **1982** U.S. Senior Open, Suntree Senior Classic, and T1 Hilton Head Senior, International (last two rounds rained out). **1983** Senior TPC, Merrill Lynch/ Golf Digest Commemorative, United Virginia Bank, Hilton Head Seniors International. **1984** Roy Clark Senior Challenge, U.S. Senior Open, Greater Syracuse Seniors, Denver Post Champions. **1985** Sunrise Senior Classic, U.S. Senior Open, PaineWebber World Seniors Invitational. **1986** MONY Tournament of Champions. **1987** Showdown Classic, Newport Cup. **1988** Showdown Classic, Fairfield-Barnett Classic. **1989** .MONY Tournament of Champions, Vintage Chrysler Invitational.
Other Victories: **1985** Shootout at Jeremy Ranch (with Ben Crenshaw). **1985** Coca Cola Grand Slam. **1987** Mazda Champions (with Nancy Lopez). **1991** Fuji Electric Grandslam.
National/International Teams: **1969**, **1971** Ryder Cup. **1991**, **1992** Chrysler Cup. **1991**, **1992** DuPont Cup.

SENIOR PGA TOUR CAREER SUMMARY

Year	Money	Rank
1981	$83,136	1
1982	$106,890	1
1983	$231,008	2
1984	$299,099	2
1985	$241,999	4
1986	$204,837	9
1987	$347,571	5
1988	$329,833	9
1989	$370,229	11
1990	$274,184	21
1991	$288,753	21
1992	$170,798	40
1993	$318,986	30
1994	$126,327	60
Sr. Career	$3,393,652	11

BOB BETLEY

Birthdate: February 1, 1940
Birthplace: Butte, MT
Exempt Status: Non-exempt.
PGA TOUR Victories: None.
Senior PGA TOUR Victories: (1) **1993** Bank of Boston Senior Golf Classic.
Other Victories: **1972** Nevada Open. **1974** Idaho Open. **1976** Frontier Airlines Invitational, Arizona Open. **1977** Nevada Open, Utah Open. **1978** Frontier Airlines Invitational, Izod International,

Arizona Open. **1990** Colorado Open.
National/International Teams: None.

SENIOR PGA TOUR CAREER SUMMARY

Year	Money	Rank
1991	$ 84,262	59
1992	$ 78,012	70
1993	$407,300	24
1994	$42,683	84
Sr. Career	$711,760	64

DON BIES

Birthdate: December 10, 1937
Birthplace: Cottonwood, ID
Exempt Status: 27th on all-time money list.
PGA TOUR Victories: (2)**1975** Sammy Davis, Jr.
Greater Hartford Open.
SENIOR PGA TOUR Victories: (6) **1988** Northville
Invitational, GTE Kaanapali Classic. **1989** Murata
Seniors Reunion, The Traditional Desert Mountain,
GTE Kaanapali Classic. **1992** PaineWebber Invitational.
Other Victories: 1989 Air New Zealand Shell
Open.
National/International Teams: None.

SENIOR PGA TOUR CAREER SUMMARY

Year	Money	Rank
1988	$293,552	11
1989	$421,769	8
1990	$265,275	2
1991	$191,174	3
1992	$352,618	21
1993	$239,781	36
1994	$137,185	56
Sr. Career	$1,901,353	27

BOB CHARLES

Birthdate: March 14, 1936
Birthplace: Carterton, New Zealand
Exempt Status: 23rd on 1994 money list.
PGA TOUR Victories: (5) **1963** Houston Open.
1965 Tucson Open.**1967** Atlanta Classic.**1968**
Canadian Open.**1974** Greater Greensboro Open.
Senior PGA TOUR Victories: (21) **1987** Vintage
Chrysler Invitational, GTE Classic, Sunwest
Bank/Charley Pride Golf Classic. **1988**
NYNEX/Golf Digest Commemorative, Sunwest
Bank/Charley Pride Classic, Rancho Murieta
Senior Gold Rush, Vantage Presents Bank One
Classic, Pepsi Senior Challenge. **1989** GTE
Suncoast Classic, NYNEX/Golf Digest
Commemorative, Digital Seniors Classic, Sunwest
Bank/Charley Pride Classic, Fairfield Barnett
Space Coast Classic.**1990** Digital Seniors Classic,
GTE Kaanapali Classic. **1991** GTE Suncoast
Classic. **1992** Raley's Senior Gold
Rush,Transamerica Senior Golf Classic. **1993**
Doug Sanders Celebrity Classic, Bell Atlantic
Classic, Quicksilver Classic.
Other Victories: 1954, 1966, 1970, 1973 New
Zealand Open. **1961, 1979, 1980** New Zealand
PGA. **1962, 1974** Swiss Open. **1963** British Open.
1969 Picadilly Match Play. **1972** Dunlop Masters.
1972 John Player Classic. **1973** Scandinavian
Open, South African Open. **1978** Air New Zealand
Shell open. **1983** Tallahassee Open.
National/International Teams: None.

SENIOR PGA TOUR CAREER SUMMARY

Year	Money	Rank
1986	$261,160	7
1987	$389,437	3
1988	$533,929	1
1989	$725,887	1
1990	$584,318	7
1991	$673,910	6
1992	$473,903	1
1993	$1,046,823	2
1994	$473,237	23
Sr. Career	$5,162,605	1

JIM COLBERT

Birthdate: March 9,1941
Birthplace: Elizabeth, NJ
Exempt Status: 5th on 1994 money list.
PGA TOUR Victories: (8) **1969** Monsanto Open.
1972 Greater Milwaukee Open. **1973** Greater
Jacksonville Open. **1974** American Golf Classic.
1975 Walt Disney World Team Championship (with
Dean Refram). **1980** Joe Garagiola Tucson Open.
1983 Colonial National Invitation, Texas Open.
Senior PGA TOUR Victories: (9) **1991**
Southwestern Bell Classic, Vantage Championship,
First Development Kaanapali Classic. **1992** GTE
Suncoast Classic, Vantage Championship. **1993**
Royal Caribbean Classic, Ford Senior Players
Championship.**1994** Kroger Senior Classic,
Southwestern Bell Classic.
Other Victories: 1987 Jerry Ford Invitational.
National/International Teams: 1992, 1993 DuPont
Cup.

SENIOR PGA TOUR CAREER SUMMARY

Year	Money	Rank
1991	$880,749	3
1992	$825,768	3
1993	$779,889	7
1994	$996,615	5
Sr. Career	$3,483,021	9

CHARLES COODY

Birthdate: July 13,1937
Birthplace: Stamford, TX
Exempt Status: 17th on all time money list.
PGA TOUR Victories: (3) **1964** Dallas Open. **1969** Cleveland Open. **1971** Masters.
Senior PGA TOUR Victories: (4) **1989** General Tire Las Vegas Classic. **1990** Vantage Championship. **1991** NYNEX Commemorative, Transamerica Senior Golf Championship.
Other Victories: 1971 World Series of Golf. **1973** John Player Classic. **1994** Liberty Mutual Legends of Golf (with Dale Douglass).
National/International Teams: 1971 Ryder Cup. **1989**, **1990** DuPont Cup.

SENIOR PGA TOUR CAREER SUMMARY

Year	Money	Rank
1987	$93,064	31
1988	$161,286	20
1989	$403,880	10
1990	$762,901	3
1991	$543,326	8
1992	$286,294	28
1993	$221,982	37
1994	$219,215	39
Sr. Career	$2,692,028	17

BRUCE CRAMPTON

Birthdate: September 28,1935
Birthplace: Sydney, Australia
Exempt Status: 7th on all-time money list.
PGA TOUR Victories: (14) **1961** Milwaukee Open. **1962** Motor City Open. **1964** Texas Open.**1965** Bing Crosby National Pro Am, Colonial NIT, "500" Festival Open. **1969** Hawaiian Open. **1970** Westchester Classic. **1971** Western Open. **1973** Phoenix Open, Tucson Open, Houston Open, American Golf Classic. **1976** Houston Open.
Senior PGA TOUR Victories: (19) **1986** Benson & Hedges Invitational at the Dominion, MONY Syracuse Senior Classic, GTE Northwest Classic, PaineWebber World Seniors Invitational, Pepsi Senior Challenge, Las Vegas Senior Classic, Shearson Lehman Brothers Seniors. **1987** Denver Champions of Golf, Greenbrier/American Express Championship, MONY Syracuse Seniors Classic, Vantage Presents Bank One Seniors. **1988** United Hospitals Classic, GTE Northwest Classic. **1989** MONY Arizona Classic, Ameritech Senior Open. **1990** PaineWebber Invitational, Gatlin Brothers Southwest Senior Classic. **1991** Infinite Senior Tournament of Champions. **1992** GTE West Classic.
Other Victories: 1956 Australian Open. **1959** Far East Open. **1961** Milwaukee Open. **1987**, **1988** Liberty Mutual Legends of Golf(with Orville Moody).
National/International Teams: None.

SENIOR PGA TOUR CAREER SUMMARY

Year	Money	Rank
1985	$14,250	57
1986	$454,299	1
1987	$437,904	2
1988	$332,927	8
1989	$443,582	7
1990	$464,569	11
1991	$514,509	11
1992	$471,873	11
1993	$366,762	25
1994	$103,860	65
Sr. Career	$3,604,534	7

JIM DENT

Birthdate: May 9,1939
Birthplace: Augusta, GA
Exempt Status: 8th on 1994 money list.
Senior PGA TOUR Victories: (8) **1989** MONY Syracuse Senior Classic, Newport Cup. **1990** Vantage at The Dominion, MONY Syracuse Senior Classic, Kroger Senior Classic, Crestar Classic. **1992** Newport Cup. **1994** Bruno's Memorial Classic.
Other Victories: 1976, **1977**, **1978** Florida PGA Championship.
National/International Teams: 1990, **1991** DuPont Cup.

SENIOR PGA TOUR CAREER SUMMARY

Year	Money	Rank
1989	$337,691	12
1990	$693,214	6
1991	$529,315	9
1992	$593,979	9
1993	$513,515	1
1994	$854,891	8
Sr. Career	$3,522,605	8

DALE DOUGLASS

Birthdate: March 5,1936
Birthplace: Wewoka, OK
Exempt Status: 18th on 1994 money list.
PGA TOUR Victories: (3) **1969** Azalea Open, Kemper Open. **1970** Phoenix Open.
Senior PGA TOUR Victories: (10) **1986** Vintage Invitational, Johnny Mathis Senior Classic, U.S. Senior Open, Fairfield Barnett Senior Classic. **1988** GTE Suncoast Classic. **1990** Bell Atlantic Classic. **1991** Showdown Classic. **1992** NYNEX Commemorative, Ameritech Senior Open. **1993** Ralphs Senior Classic.
Other Victories: **1990** Liberty Mutual Legends of Golf (with Charles Coody). **1994** Liberty Mutual Legends of Golf (with Charles Coody).
National/International Teams: **1969** Ryder Cup. **1989**, **1990**, **1991**, **1992** DuPont Cup.

SENIOR PGA TOUR CAREER SUMMARY

Year	Money	Rank
1986	$309,760	3
1987	$296,429	7
1988	$280,457	12
1989	$313,275	14
1990	$568,198	8
1991	$606,949	7
1992	$694,564	6
1993	$499,858	19
1994	$518,186	18
Sr. Career	$4,087,677	6

JIM FERREE

Birthdate: June 10,1931
Birthplace: Pine Bluff, NC
Exempt Status: 22nd on all-time money list.
PGA TOUR Victories: (1) **1958** Vancouver Centennial.
Senior PGA TOUR Victories: (2) **1986** Greater Grand Rapids Open. **1991** Bell Atlantic Classic.
Other Victories: **1961** Jamaica Open. **1962** Panama Open. **1963** Maracaibo Open. **1964** Children's Memorial Hospital Classic. **1981**, **1982** Tri-State Senior PGA.
National/International Teams: **1993** DuPont Cup.

SENIOR PGA TOUR CAREER SUMMARY

Year	Money	Rank
1981	$16,694	15
1982	$16,455	30
1983	$69,547	11
1984	$103,717	13
1985	$153,087	9
1986	$184,667	11
1987	$111,858	23
1988	$112,137	30
1989	$194,992	24
1990	$144,680	40
1991	$279,384	23
1992	$194,633	37
1993	$424,333	22
1994	$119,963	63
Sr. Career	$2,126,146	22

RAYMOND FLOYD

Birthdate: September 4,1942
Birthplace: Fort Bragg, NC
Exempt Status: 3rd on 1994 money list.
PGA TOUR Victories: (22) **1963** St. Petersburg Open. **1966** St. Paul Open. **1969** Jacksonville Open, American Golf Classic, PGA Championship. **1975** Kemper Open. **1976** Masters, World Open. **1977** Byron Nelson Classic, Pleasant Valley Classic. **1979** Greensboro Open. **1980** Doral Eastern Open. **1981** Doral Eastern Open, Tournament Players Championship, Manufacturers Hanover Western Classic. **1982** Memorial Tournament, Danny Thomas Memphis Classic, PGA Championship. **1985** Houston Open. **1986** U.S. Open, Walt Disney/Oldsmobile Classic. **1992** Doral-Ryder Open.
Senior PGA TOUR Victories: (8) **1992** GTE North Classic, Ralphs Senior Classic, Senior TOUR Championship. **1993** Gulfstream Aerostream Invitational, Northville Long Island Classic. **1994** The Tradition, Las Vegas Senior Classic, Cadillac NFL Golf Classic.
Other Victories: **1978** Brazilian Open. **1979** Costa Rica Cup. **1981** Canadian PGA. **1985** Chrysler Team Championship (with Hal Sutton). **1988** Skins game. **1990** RMCC Invitational (with Fred Couples). **1993** Franklin Funds Shark Shootout (with Steve Elkington).
National/International Teams: **1969**, **1975**, **1977**, **1981**, **1983**, **1985**, **1991**, **1993** Ryder Cup.

SENIOR PGA TOUR CAREER SUMMARY

Year	Money	Rank
1992	$436,991	14
1993	$713,168	9
1994	$1,142,762	3
Sr. Career	$2,292,920	20

AL GEIBERGER

Birthdate: September 1, 1937
Birthplace: Red Bluff, CA

Exempt Status: 13th on all-time money list.
PGA TOUR Victories: (11) **1962** Ontario Open.
1963 Almaden Open. **1965** American Golf Classic.
1966 PGA Championship. **1974** Sahara
Invitational. **1975** Tournament of Champions,
Tournament Players Championship. **1976** Greater
Greensboro Open, Western Open. **1977** Danny
Thomas Memphis Classic. **1979** Colonial National
Invitational.
Senior PGA TOUR Victories: (9) **1987** Vantage
Championship, Hilton Head Seniors International,
Las Vegas Senior Classic. **1988** Pointe/Del E.
Webb Arizona Classic. **1989** GTE Northwest
Classic. **1991** Kroger Senior Classic. **1992** Infinite
Tournament of Champions.**1993** Infinite
Tournament of Champions, GTE West Classic.
Other Victories: **1989** Liberty Mutual Legends of
Golf (with Harold Henning).
National/International Teams: **1967**, **1975** Ryder
Cup. **1991**, **1993** DuPont Cup.

SENIOR PGA TOUR CAREER SUMMARY

Year	Money	Rank
1987	$264,798	9
1988	$348,735	6
1989	$527,033	3
1990	$373,624	1
1991	$519,926	10
1992	$385,339	19
1993	$608,877	13
1994	$72,729	69
Sr. Career	$3,028,331	13

GIBBY GILBERT

Birthdate: January 14,1941
Birthplace: Chattanooga, TN
Exempt Status: 27th on1993 money list.
PGA TOUR Victories: (3) **1970** Houston
Champion International. **1976** Danny Thomas
Memphis Classic. **1977** Walt Disney World National
Team Championship (with Grier Jones).
Senior PGA TOUR Victories: (4) **1992**
Southwestern Bell Classic, First of America
Classic, Kroger Senior Classic. **1993** Las Vegas
Senior Classic.
Other Victories: **1988**, **1989**, **1990** Tennessee
Opens.
National/International Teams: **1993** Dupont Cup.

SENIOR PGA TOUR CAREER SUMMARY

Year	Money	Rank
1991	$392,351	14
1992	$603,630	8
1993	$661,378	11
1994	$324,242	27
Sr. Career	$1,981,602	26

LARRY GILBERT

Birthdate: November 19,1942
Birthplace: Fort Knox, KY
Exempt Status: 9th on1994 money list.
PGA TOUR Victories: None.
Senior PGA TOUR Victories: (2) **1994** Dallas
Reunion Pro-Am, Vantage Championship.
Other victories: **1981**, **1982**, **1991** PGA Club
Professional Championship.
National/International Teams: None.

SENIOR PGA TOUR CAREER SUMMARY

Year	Money	Rank
1993	$515,790	17
1994	$831,244	9
Sr. Career	$1,347,034	46

DICK HENDRICKSON

Birthdate: January 22, 1935
Birthplace: St. Louis, MO
Exempt Status: Non-exempt.
PGA TOUR Victories: None
Senior PGA TOUR Victories: None.
Other Victories: **1972** Philadelphia PGA
Championship, Mini Byron.
National/International Teams: None.

SENIOR PGA TOUR CAREER SUMMARY

Year	Money	Rank
1985	$1,463	114
1986	$5,069	79
1988	$83,076	38
1989	$144,739	31
1990	$159,070	34
1991	$281,863	22
1992	$270,025	31
1993	$243,262	35
1994	$153,155	53
Sr. Career	$1,345636	47

HAROLD HENNING

Birthdate: October 3,1934
Birthplace: Johannesburg, South Africa
Exempt Status: 15th on all-time money list.
PGA TOUR Victories: (1) **1966** Texas Open
Senior PGA TOUR Victories: (3) **1985**
Seiko/Tucson Match Play Championship. **1988**
GTE Classic. **1991** First of America Classic.
Other Victories: **1989** Liberty Mutual Legends of

Golf. **1970** Tallahassee Open. **1965** World Cup (with Gary Player).
National/International Teams: 1961,1965,1966, 1967, 1970, 1971 World Cup.

SENIOR PGA TOUR CAREER SUMMARY

Year	Money	Rank
1984	$6,500	72
1985	$197,624	6
1986	$173,034	12
1987	$151,986	17
1988	$366,230	5
1989	$453,163	6
1990	$409,879	12
1991	$394,803	13
1992	$347,857	22
1993	$314,104	31
1994	$126,894	59
Sr. Career	$2,942,073	15

MIKE HILL

Birthdate: January 27, 1939
Birthplace: Jackson, MI
Exempt Status: 16th on 1994 money list.
PGA TOUR Victories: (3) **1970** Doral Eastern Open. **1972** San Antonio Texas Open. **1977** Ohio Kings Island Open.
Senior PGA TOUR Victories: (16) **1990** GTE Suncoast Classic, GTE North Classic, Fairfield Barnett Space Coast Classic, Security Pacific Senior Classic, New York Life Champions. **1991** Doug Sanders Kingwood Celebrity Classic, Ameritech Senior Open, GTE Northwest Classic, Nationwide Championship, New York Life Champions. **1992** Vintage ARCO Invitational, Doug Sanders Kingwood Celebrity Classic. **1994** The Intellinet Challenge.
Other Victories: 1989 Mazda Champions (with Patti Rizzo).
National/International Teams: 1990, 1991, 1992, 1993 Dupont Cup.

SENIOR PGA TOUR CAREER SUMMARY

Year	Money	Rank
1989	$412,104	9
1990	$895,678	2
1991	$1,065,657	1
1992	$802,423	4
1993	$798,116	6
1994	$532,521	16
Sr. Career	$4,506,499	4

SIMON HOBDAY

Birthdate: June 23,1940
Birthplace: Mareking, South Africa
Exempt Status: 12th on 1994 money list.
Senior PGA TOUR Victories: (4) **1993** Senior Classic, Hyatt Senior TOUR Championship. **1994** U.S. Senior Open, GTE Northwest Classic.
Other Victories: 1971 South African Open. **1976** German Open, Rhodesian Open. **1977** Rhodesian Open. **1979** Madrid Open. **1985** TrustBank Tournament.
National/International Teams: 1966 Eisenhower Trophy (representing Zambia).

SENIOR PGA TOUR CAREER SUMMARY

Year	Money	Rank
1991	$353,654	16
1992	$397,382	18
1993	$670,417	1
1994	$606,621	12
Sr. Career	$2,028,075	25

DON JANUARY

Birthdate: November 20,1929
Birthplace: Plainview, TX
Exempt Status: 16th on all-time money list.
PGA TOUR Victories: (10) **1956** Dallas Centennial Open. **1960** Tucson Open. **1961** St. Paul Open. **1963** Tucson Open. **1966** Philadelphia Classic. **1967** PGA Championship. **1968** Tournament of Champions, Jacksonville Open. **1975** San Antonio Texas Open. **1976** MONY Tournament of Champions.
Senior PGA TOUR Victories: (22) **1980** Atlantic City Senior International. **1981** Michelob-Egypt Temple, Eureka Federal Savings. **1982** Michelob Classic, PGA Seniors Championship. **1983** Gatlin Brothers Senior Classic, Peter Jackson Champions, Marlboro Classic, Denver Post Champions, Citizen's Union Senior Classic, Suntree Seniors Classic. **1984** Vintage Invitational, du Maurier Champions, Digital Middlesex Classic. **1985** Senior TOUR Roundup, The Dominion Seniors, United Hospitals Senior Golf Championship, Greenbrier/American Express Championship. **1986** Senior Players Reunion Pro-Am, Greenbrier/American Express Championship, Seiko/Tucson Match Play Championship. **1987** MONY Senior Tournament of Champions.
Other Victories: 1956 Apple Valley Clambake. **1959** Valencia Open. **1979** PGA Seniors

Championship. **1980** Australian Seniors. **1984** Shootout at Jeremy Ranch. **1985** Legends of Golf, Mazda Champions (with Alice Miller). **1986** Legends of Golf.
National/International Teams: 1965,1977 Ryder Cup.

SENIOR PGA TOUR CAREER SUMMARY

Year	Money	Rank
1981	$68,075	2
1982	$99,508	2
1983	$237,671	1
1984	$328,597	1
1985	$247,006	3
1986	$299,795	4
1987	$116,685	21
1988	$82,013	40
1989	$59,813	58
1990	$216,243	28
1991	$262,437	28
1992	$328,896	25
1993	$274,338	33
1994	$147, 976	55
Sr. Career	$2,827,192	16

JACK KIEFER

Birthdate: January 1, 1940
Birthplace: Columbia, PA
Exempt Status: 21st on 1994 money list.
SENIOR PGA TOUR Victories: (1) 1994 Ralph's Senior Classic.
Other Victories: 1971 Pennsylvania State Open. **1975** New Jersey Open. **1976** New Jersey Open. **1983** New Jersey Open. **1985** Dodge Open. **1990** New Jersey Senior Open, New Jersey Senior PGA Championship.
National/International Teams: None.

SENIOR PGA TOUR CAREER SUMMARY

Year	Money	Rank
1990	$21,930	87
1991	$119,453	54
1992	$203,095	36
1993	$333,511	27
1994	$509,117	21
Sr. Career	$1,187,106	51

LARRY LAORETTI

Birthdate: July 11, 1939
Birthplace: Mahopac, NY
Exempt Status: Non-exempt.

Senior PGA TOUR Victories: (1) 1992 U.S. Senior Open.
Other Victories: None.
National/International Teams: 1992 DuPont Cup.

SENIOR PGA TOUR CAREER SUMMARY

Year	Money	Rank
1989	$3,025	110
1990	$165,339	32
1991	$371,097	15
1992	$444,385	13
1993	$183,694	46
1994	$220,001	38
Sr. Career	$1,387,540	44

DICK LOTZ

Birthdate: October 15,1942
Birthplace: Oakland, CA
Exempt Status: Non-exempt.
PGA TOUR Victories: (3) 1969 Alameda Open. **1970** Kemper Open, Pensacola Open.
Senior PGA TOUR Victories: None.
Other Victories: None.
National/International Teams: None.

SENIOR PGA TOUR CAREER SUMMARY

Year	Money	Rank
1993	$199,244	44
1994	$167,152	51
Sr. Career	$369,071	94

RIVES McBEE

Birthdate: October 31, 1938
Birthplace: Denton, TX
Exempt Status: Non-exempt.
PGA TOUR Victories: None
Senior PGA TOUR Victories: (3) 1989 RJR Bank One Classic. **1990** Showdown Classic,Vantage Bank One Classic.
Other Victories: 1973 PGA Club Professional Championship.
National/International Teams: 1989, 1990 DuPont Cup.

SENIOR PGA TOUR CAREER SUMMARY

Year	Money	Rank
1989	$258,487	18
1990	$480,329	10
1991	$141,745	47
1992	$128,862	42
1993	$181,803	47
1994	$166,177	52
Sr. Career	$1,357,402	45

ORVILLE MOODY

Birthdate: December 9,1933
Birthplace: Chickasha, OK
Exempt Status: 14th on all-time money list.
PGA TOUR Victories: (1) **1969** U.S. Open.
Senior PGA TOUR Victories: (11) **1984** Daytona Beach Seniors Classic, MONY Tournament of Champions. **1987** Rancho Murieta Senior Gold Rush, GTE Kaanapali Classic. **1988** Vintage Chrysler Invitational, Senior Players Reunion, Greater Grand Rapids Open. **1989** Mazda Senior TPC, U.S. Senior Open. **1991** PaineWebber Invitational. **1992** Franklin Showdown Classic.
Other Victories: 1958 All-Army Championship. **1962** All-Service Championship. **1969** World Cup (with Lee Trevino), World Series of Golf. **1971** Hong Kong Open, Morocco Grand Prix. **1977** International Caribbean Open. **1984** Viceroy Panama Open. **1986** Australian PGA. **1987** Australian PGA, Liberty Mutual Legends of Golf (with Bruce Crampton). **1988** Liberty Mutual Legends of Golf (with Bruce Crampton).
National/International Teams: 1969 World Cup (with Trevino).

SENIOR PGA TOUR CAREER SUMMARY

Year	Money	Rank
1984	$183,920	5
1985	$134,643	12
1986	$128,755	16
1987	$355,793	16
1988	$411,859	4
1989	$647,985	2
1990	$273,224	22
1991	$227,826	3
1992	$288,263	2
1993	$196,565	4
1994	$208,490	42
Sr. Career	$ 3,057,323	14

LARRY MOWRY

Birthdate: October 20, 1936
Birthplace: San Diego, CA
Exempt Status: Non-exempt.
PGA TOUR Victories: None.
Senior PGA TOUR Victories: (5) **1987**Crestar Classic, Pepsi Senior Challenge. **1988** General Tire Las Vegas Classic. **1989** General Foods PGA Seniors Championship, RJR at The Dominion.
Other Victories: 1968 Rebel Yell Classic. **1969** Magnolia Classic. **1979** Florida Open, Florida PGA, Colorado Open. **1983** Florida Open.

National/International Teams: None.

SENIOR PGA TOUR CAREER SUMMARY

Year	Money	Rank
1986	$2,563	96
1987	$200,151	13
1988	$275,466	13
1989	$322,788	13
1990	$314,657	17
1991	$ 67,899	62
1992	$ 96,322	60
1993	$180,703	49
1994	$135,923	57
Sr. Career	$1,596,470	34

BOB MURPHY

Birthdate: February 14, 1943
Birthplace: Brooklyn, NY
Exempt Status: 7th on 1994 money list.
PGA TOUR Victories: (5) **1968** Philadelphia Classic, Thunderbird Classic. **1970** Greater Hartford Open. **1975** Jackie Gleason Inverrary Classic. **1986** Canadian Open.
Senior PGA TOUR Victories: (4) **1993** Bruno's Memorial Classic, GTE North Classic. **1994** Raley's Senior Gold Rush, Kaanapali Classic.
Other Victories: 1965 U.S. Amateur. **1966** NCAA. **1967** Florida Open. **1979** Jerry Ford Invitational.
National/International Teams: 1966 Eisenhower Trophy. **1967** Walker Cup. **1975** Ryder Cup. **1993** DuPont Cup.

SENIOR PGA TOUR CAREER SUMMARY

Year	Money	Rank
1993	$768,743	8
1994	$855,862	7
Sr. Career	$1,624,605	32

BOBBY NICHOLS

Birthdate: April 14,1936
Birthplace: Louisville, KY
Exempt Status: 30th on all time money list.
PGA TOUR Victories: (11) **1962** St. Petersburg Open, Houston Classic. **1963** Seattle Open. **1964** PGA Championship, Carling World Open. **1965** Houston Classic, **1966** Minnesota Classic. **1970** Dow Jones Open. **1973** Westchester Classic. **1974** Andy Williams San Diego Open, Canadian Open.
Senior PGA TOUR Victories: (1) **1989** Southwestern Bell Classic.
Other Victories: 1968 PGA Team Championship (with George Archer). **1986** Showdown Classic (with Curt Byrum).

National/International Teams: 1967 Ryder Cup.

SENIOR PGA TOUR CAREER SUMMARY

Year	Money	Rank
1986	$56,676	36
1987	$196,698	14
1988	$226,936	14
1989	$210,097	22
1990	$158,144	35
1991	$252,764	29
1992	$223,218	32
1993	$181,433	48
1994	$131,695	58
Sr. Career	$1,637,662	30

JACK NICKLAUS

Birthdate: January 21, 1940
Birthplace: Columbus, OH
Exempt Status: Non-exempt.
PGA TOUR Victories: (70) **1962** U.S.Open, Seattle World's Fair, Portland. **1963** Palm Springs, Masters, Tournament of Champions, PGA Championship, Sahara. **1964** Portland, Tournament of Champions, Phoenix, Whitemarsh. **1965** Portland, Masters, Memphis, Thunderbird, Philadelphia. **1966** Masters, Sahara. **1967** U.S. Open, Sahara, Bing Crosby, Western, Westchester. **1968** Western, American Golf Classic. **1969** Sahara, Kaiser, San Diego. **1970** Byron Nelson, National Four Ball (with Arnold Palmer). **1971** PGA Championship, Tournament of Champions, Byron Nelson, National Team (with Arnold Palmer), Disney World. **1972** Bing Crosby, Doral Eastern, Masters, U.S. Open, Westchester, Match Play, Disney. **1973** Bing Crosby, New Orleans, Tournament of Champions, Atlanta, PGA Championship, Ohio Kings Island, Walt Disney. **1974** Hawaii, Tournament Players Championship. **1975** Doral Eastern, Heritage, Masters, PGA Championship, World Open. **1976** Tournament Players Championship, World Series of Golf. **1977** Gleason Inverrary, Tournament of Champions, Memorial. **1978** Gleason Inverrary, Tournament Players Championship, IVB Philadelphia. **1980** U.S. Open, PGA Championship. **1982** Colonial National Invitation. **1984** Memorial. **1986** Masters.
Senior PGA TOUR Victories: (6) **1990** The Tradition at Desert Mountain, Mazda Senior TPC. **1991** The Tradition at Desert Mountain, PGA Seniors Championship, U.S. Senior Open. **1993** U.S. Senior Open. **1994** Mercedes Championships.
Other Victories: 1959 U.S. Amateur. **1961** U.S. Amateur, NCAA. **1962** World Series of Golf. **1963**

World Series of Golf, World Cup, International Trophy (World Cup individual). **1964** Australian Open, World Cup (with Arnold Palmer), International Trophy (World Cup individual). **1966** World Cup (with Arnold Palmer). **1967** World Cup (with Arnold Palmer). **1971** World Cup (with Lee Trevino), International Trophy (World Cup individual). **1973** World Cup (with Johnny Miller). **1983** Chrysler Team (with Johnny Miller).
National/International Teams: 1959, 1961 Walker Cup. **1963, 1964, 1966, 1967, 1971, 1973** World Cup. **1969, 1971, 1973, 1975, 1977, 1981, 1983, 1987** Ryder Cup.

SENIOR PGA TOUR CAREER SUMMARY

Year	Money	Rank
1990	$340,000	15
1991	$343,734	17
1992	$114,548	53
1993	$206,028	42
1994	$239,278	34
Sr. Career	$1,243,588	49

GARY PLAYER

Birthdate: November 1, 1935
Birthplace: Johannesburg, South Africa
Exempt Status: 28th on 1994 money list.
PGA TOUR Victories: (21) **1958** Kentucky Derby Open. **1961** Lucky International, Sunshine, Masters. **1962** PGA Championship. **1963** San Diego. **1964** "500" Festival, Pensacola. **1965** U.S. Open. **1969** Tournament of Champions. **1970** Greater Greensboro. **1971** Jacksonville, Tournament National Airlines. **1972** New Orleans, PGA Championship. **1973** Southern. **1974** Masters, Danny Thomas Memphis. **1978** Masters, Tournament of Champions, Houston Open.
Senior PGA TOUR Victories: (17) **1985** Quadel Seniors Classic. **1986** General Foods PGA Seniors Championship, United Hospital Classic, Denver Post Champions. **1987** Mazda Senior TPC, U.S. Senior Open, PaineWebber World Seniors Invitational. **1988** General Foods PGA Seniors Championship, Aetna Challenge, Southwestern Bell Classic, U.S. Senior Open, GTE North Classic. **1989** GTE North Classic, RJR Championship. **1990** PGA Seniors Championship, **1991** Royal Caribbean Classic, **1993** Bank One Classic.
Other Victories: South African Open (13 times). Australian Open (7 times). **1957** Australian PGA. **1959** British Open. **1965** Suntory World Match

Play, World Cup (with Harold Henning), International Trophy (World Cup individual), World Series of Golf. **1966** Suntory World Match Play. **1968** British Open, Suntory World Match Play, World Series of Golf. **1971** Suntory World Match Play. **1972** World Series of Golf, Brazilian Open. **1973** Suntory World Match Play. **1974** Brazilian Open. **1976** South African Dunlop Masters. **1977** International Trophy (World Cup individual). **1980** Chile Open. **1984** Johnnie Walker.

National/International Teams: 1956, 1957, 1958, 1959, 1960, 1962, 1963, 1964, 1965, 1966, 1967, 1968, 1971, 1972, 1973, 1977 World Cup.

SENIOR PGA TOUR CAREER SUMMARY

Year	Money	Rank
1985	$30,000	44
1986	$291,190	5
1987	$333,439	6
1988	$435,914	2
1989	$514,116	4
1990	$507,268	9
1991	$337,253	18
1992	$346,798	23
1993	$360,272	26
1994	$309,776	28
Sr. Career	$3,466,026	10

DICK RHYAN

Birthdate: November 28, 1934
Birthplace: Columbus, OH
Exempt Status: Non-exempt.
PGA TOUR Victories: None.
Senior PGA TOUR Victories: None.
Other Victories: 1966 Northern Ohio PGA Section, North Florida PGA Seniors.
National/International Teams: None.

SENIOR PGA TOUR CAREER SUMMARY

Year	Money	Rank
1987	$1,300	T150
1988	$147,423	23
1989	$109,933	41
1990	$156,868	37
1991	$179,486	36
1992	$131,013	48
1993	$203,374	41
1994	$210,183	41
Sr. Career	$1,144,580	55

CHI CHI RODRIGUEZ

Birthdate: October 23, 1935
Birthplace: Bayamon, Puerto Rico

Exempt Status: 14th on 1994 money list.
PGA TOUR Victories: (8) **1963** Denver Open. **1964** Lucky International, Western Open, **1967** Texas Open. **1968** Sahara Invitational. **1972** Byron Nelson Classic. **1973** Greater Greensboro Open. **1979**Tallahassee 0pen.
Senior PGA TOUR Victories: (22) **1986** Senior TPC, Digital Seniors Classic, United Virginia Bank Seniors. **1987** General Foods PGA Seniors Championship, Vantage at The Dominion,United Hospitals Classic, Silver Pages Classic, Senior Players Reunion, Digital Seniors Classic, GTE Northwest Classic. **1988** Doug Sanders Kingwood Classic, Digital Seniors Classic. **1989** Crestar Classic. **1990** Las Vegas Senior Classic, Ameritech Senior Open, Sunwest Bank/Charley Pride Senior Golf Classic.**1991** GTE West Classic, Vintage ARGO Invitational, Las Vegas Senior Classic, Murata Reunion Pro-Am.**1992** Ko Olina Senior Invitational, **1993** Burnet Senior Classic.
Other Victories: 1976 Pepsi Mixed Team Championship (with JoAnn Washam).
National/International Teams: 1961, 1962, 1963, 1964, 1965, 1966, 1967, 1968, 1971, 1974, 1976 World Cup. **1973** Ryder Cup.

SENIOR PGA TOUR CAREER SUMMARY

Year	Money	Rank
1985	$7,700	71
1986	$399,172	2
1987	$509,145	1
1988	$313,940	10
1989	$275,414	17
1990	$729,788	5
1991	$794,013	4
1992	$711,095	5
1993	$798,857	5
1994	$556,098	14
Sr. Career	$5,095,222	3

TOM SHAW

Birthdate: December 13, 1938
Birthplace: Wichita, KS
Exempt Status: Non-exempt.
PGA TOUR Victories: (5) **1969** Doral Open, AVCO Golf Classic. **1971** Bing Crosby National Pro Am, Hawaiian Open.
Senior PGA TOUR Victories: (3) **1989** Showdown Classic. **1993** The Tradition. **1994** Senior Slam of Golf.
Other Victories: None.
National/International Teams: 1989 DuPont Cup.

SENIOR PGA TOUR CAREER SUMMARY

Year	Money	Rank
1989	$281,393	16
1990	$235,683	26
1991	$278,103	24
1992	$144,821	45
1993	$324,385	29
1994	$229,119	35
Sr. Career	$1,493,504	40

BEN SMITH

Birthdate: May 7, 1934
Birthplace: Atlanta, GA
Exempt Status: Non-exempt.
Senior PGA TOUR Victories: None.
Other Victories: 1982 Center Invitational.
National/International Teams: None.

SENIOR PGA TOUR CAREER SUMMARY

Year	Money	Rank
1984	$3,475	87
1985	$78,303	17
1986	$103,863	18
1987	$93,227	30
1988	$160,363	22
1989	$133,920	34
1990	$201,223	31
1991	$178,258	37
1992	$121,138	50
1993	$209,427	40
1994	$180,943	48
Sr. Career	$1,464,139	42

J.C. SNEAD

Birthdate: October 14, 1940
Birthplace: Hot Springs, VA
Exempt Status: 13th on 1994 money list.
PGA TOUR Victories: (8) 1971 Tucson Open, Doral Eastern Open. 1972 Philadelphia Classic. 1975 Wickes Andy Williams San Diego Open. 1976 Andy Williams San Diego Open, Kaiser International. 1981 Southern Open. 1987 Manufacturers Hanover Westchester Classic.
Senior PGA TOUR Victories: (1) 1993 Vantage.
Other Victories: 1973 Australian Open. 1980 Jerry Ford Invitational (co-winner).
National/International Teams: 1971, 1973, 1975 Ryder cup.

SENIOR PGA TOUR CAREER SUMMARY

Year	Money	Rank
1990	$47,494	74
1991	$302,287	19
1992	$383,698	2
1993	$487,500	2
1994	$564,314	13
Sr. Career	$1,785,293	29

DAVE STOCKTON

Birthdate: November 2,1941
Birthplace: San Bernardino, CA
Exempt Status: 1st on 1994 money list.
PGA TOUR Victories: (11) 1967 Colonial National Foursome (with Laurie Hammer). 1968 Cleveland Open, Greater PGA Championship. 1971 Massachusetts Classic. 1973 Greater Milwaukee Open. 1974 Glen Campbell Los Angeles Open, Quad Cities Open, Sammy Davis Jr. Greater Hartford Open. 1976 PGA Championship.
Senior PGA TOUR Victories: (9) 1992 MAZDA Presents THE SENIOR PLAYERS Championship.1993 Muratec Reunion Pro Am, Southwestern Bell Classic, Franklin Quest Championship, GTE Northwest Classic, The Transamerica. 1994 Nationwide Championship, Ford Senior Players Championship, Burnet Senior Classic.
Other Victories: 1992 Senior TOUR Rookie of the Year.
National/International Teams: 1970, 1976 World Cup. 1971, 1977, 1991 Ryder Cup. 1993 DuPont Cup.

SENIOR PGA TOUR CAREER SUMMARY

Year	Money	Rank
1991	$12,965	94
1992	$ 656,458	7
1993	$1,175,944	1
1994	$1,338,419	1
Sr. Career	$1,183,785	12

ROCKY THOMPSON

Birthdate: October 14,1939
Birthplace: Shreveport, LA
Exempt Status: 22nd on 1994 money list.
Senior PGA TOUR Victories: (3) 1991 MONY Syracuse Senior Classic, Digital Seniors Classic. 1994 GTE Suncoast Classic.
Other Victories: None.
National/International Teams: 1991 DuPont Cup.

SENIOR PGA TOUR CAREER SUMMARY

Year	Money	Rank
1989	$17,300	84
1990	$308,915	18
1991	$435,794	12

Year	Money	Rank
1992	$432,778	15
1993	$571,844	14
1994	$487,373	22
Sr. Career	$2,254,004	21

HARRY TOSCANO

Birthdate: April 1, 1942
Birthplace: New Castle, PA
Exempt Status: Non-exempt.
PGA TOUR Victories: None.
Senior PGA TOUR Victories: None.
National/International Teams: None.

SENIOR PGA TOUR CAREER SUMMARY

Year	Money	Rank
1992	$11,849	98
1993	$201,150	43
1994	$207,508	43
Sr. Career	$420,507	89

LEE TREVINO

Birthdate: December 1,1939
Birthplace: Dallas, TX
Exempt Status: 2nd on 1994 money list.
PGA TOUR Victories: (27) **1968** U.S. Open, Hawaiian Open. **1969** Tucson Open. **1970** Tucson Open, National Airlines Open. **1971** Tallahassee Open, Danny Thomas Memphis Classic, U.S. Open, Canadian Open, Sahara Invitational. **1972** Danny Thomas Memphis Classic, Greater Hartford Open, Greater St. Louis Classic. **1973** Jackie Gleason Inverrary, Doral Eastern Open. **1974** New Orleans Open, PGA Championship. **1975** Florida Citrus Open. **1976** Colonial National Invitational. **1977** Canadian Open. **1978** Colonial National Invitational. **1979** Canadian Open. **1980** Tournament Players Championship, Danny Thomas Memphis Classic, San Antonio Texas Open. **1981** MONY Tournament of Champions. **1984** PGA Championship.
Senior PGA TOUR Victories: (24) **1990** Royal Caribbean Classic, Aetna Challenge, Vintage Chrysler Invitational, Doug Sanders Kingwood Celebrity Classic, NYNEX Commemorative, U.S. Senior Open, Transamerica Senior Golf Championship. **1991** Aetna Challenge, Vantage at The Dominion, Sunwest Bank/Charley Pride Senior Classic. **1992** Vantage at The Dominion, The Tradition, PGA Seniors Championship, Las Vegas Senior Classic, Bell Atlantic Classic. **1993** Cadillac NFL Classic, Nationwide Championship,

Vantage Championship.**1994** Royal Caribbean Classic, PGA Seniors Championship, Painewebber Invitational, Bell Atlantic Classic, Senior Classic at Opryland, Northville Long Island Classic.
Other Victories: 1969 International Trophy (World Cup individual). **1971** British Open. **1972** British Open. **1974** World Series of Golf. **1975** Mexican Open. **1977** Morocco Grand Prix. **1978** Benson & Hedges, Lancome Trophy. **1979** Canadian PGA. 1983 Canadian PGA. **1987** Skins Game.
National/International Teams: 1968, 1969, 1970, 1971, 1974 World Cup. **1969, 1971, 1973, 1975, 1979, 1981, 1985** Ryder Cup.

SENIOR PGA TOUR CAREER SUMMARY

Year	Money	Rank
1989	$9,258	93
1990	$1,190,518	1
1991	$723,163	5
1992	$1,027,000	2
1993	$956,591	4
1994	$1,202,369	2
Sr. Career	$5,108,902	2

TOM WARGO

Birthdate: September 16,1942
Birthplace: Marlette, MI
Exempt Status: 6th on 1994 money list.
Senior PGA TOUR Victories: (2) **1993** PGA Senior's Championship. **1994** Doug Sanders Celebrity Classic.
Other Victories: 1990 PGA Club Professional Stroke Play Championship. **1992** Gateway PGA Sectional Championship.
National/International Teams: None.

SENIOR PGA TOUR CAREER SUMMARY

Year	Money	Rank
1993	$557,270	16
1994	$928,344	6
Sr. Career	$1,485,614	41

DEWITT WEAVER

Birthdate: September 14,1939
Birthplace: Danville, KY
Exempt Status: 30th on 1994 money list.
PGA TOUR Victories: (2) **1971** U.S. Professional Match Play. **1972** Southern Open.
Senior PGA TOUR Victories: (1) **1991** Bank One Senior Classic.
Other Victories: Georgia Open (4).
National/International Teams: None.

SENIOR PGA TOUR CAREER SUMMARY

Year	Money	Rank
1989	$4,133	105
1990	$118,555	45
1991	$264,569	27
1992	$399,155	17
1993	$472,220	21
1994	$295,037	30
Sr. Career	$1,553,669	36

TOM WEISKOPF

Birthdate: November 9,1942
Birthplace: Massillon, OH
Exempt Status: Non-exempt.
PGA TOUR Victories: (15) **1968** Andy Williams San Diego Open, Buick Open. **1971** Kemper Open, IVB Philadelphia Classic. **1972** Jackie Gleason Inverrary Classic. **1973** Colonial National Invitation, Kemper Open, IVS Philadelphia Classic, Canadian Open. **1976** Greater Greensboro Open, Canadian Open. **1977** Kemper Open. **1978** Doral Eastern Open. **1981** LaJet Classic. **1982** Western Open.
Senior PGA TOUR Victories: (1) **1994** Franklin Quest Championship.
Other Victories: **1972** Picadilly World Match Play. **1973** British Open, World Series of Golf, South African PGA. **1979** Argentina Open.
National/International Teams: **1972** World Cup. **1973**, **1975** Ryder Cup.

SENIOR PGA TOUR CAREER SUMMARY

Year	Money	Rank
1992	$15,296	221
1993	$296,528	32
1994	$298,624	29
Sr. Career	$595,152	74

KERMIT ZARLEY

Birthdate: September 29,1941
Birthplace: Seattle, WA
Exempt Status: 19th on 1994 money list.
PGA TOUR Victories: (2) **1968** Kaiser International. **1970** Canadian Open.
Senior PGA TOUR Victories: (1) **1994** The Transamerica.
Other Victories: **1972** National team championship (with Babe Hiskey).
National/International Teams: None.

SENIOR PGA TOUR CAREER SUMMARY

Year	Money	Rank
1991	$6,858	113
1992	$341,647	24
1993	$414,715	23
1994	$517,724	19
Sr. Career	$1,280,944	48

WALT ZEMBRISKI

Birthdate: May 24,1935
Birthplace: Mahwah, NJ
Exempt Status: 19th on all-time money list.
Senior PGA TOUR Victories: (3) **1988** Newport Cup, Vantage Championship. **1989** GTE West Classic.
Other Victories: **1965** New Jersey Amateur.
National/International Teams: None.

SENIOR PGA TOUR CAREER SUMMARY

Year	Money	Rank
1985	$47,023	35
1986	$103,551	19
1987	$189,403	15
1988	$348,531	7
1989	$291,861	15
1990	$276,292	20
1991	$265,951	26
1992	$273,087	30
1993	$331,960	28
1994	$246,412	33
Sr. Career	$2,374,070	19

LARRY ZIEGLER

Birthdate: August 12,1939
Birthplace: St. Louis, MO
Exempt Status: Non-exempt.
PGA TOUR Victories: (3) **1969** Michigan Classic. **1975** Greater Jacksonville Open. **1976** First NBC New Orleans Open.
Senior PGA TOUR Victories: (1) **1991** Newport Cup.
Other Victories: **1974** Morocco International Grand Prix. **1978** South and Central American Open.
National/International Teams: None.

SENIOR PGA TOUR CAREER SUMMARY

Year	Money	Rank
1989	$133,339	35
1990	$102,152	49
1991	$169,686	38
1992	$135,015	47
1993	$216,073	38
1994	$185,644	46
Sr. Career	$941,910	58

FOREIGN PLAYERS

OVERVIEW: *Biographies and career summaries of leading foreign players, including Tour currently played, and career highlights.*

ROBERT ALLENBY
Birthdate: July 12,1971
Birthplace: Melbourne, Australia
Tour: Australia/New Zealand
Career Highlights: Leader of Australian Order of Merit **1992**, **1993**. **1993** Optus Players Championship. **1992** Johnnie Walker Classic (Aus), Perak Masters (Malaysia). **1991** Victoria Open. **1990** Victoria Amateur.
National/International Teams: **1993** World Cup, Dunhill Cup.

PETER BAKER
Birthdate: October 7,1967
Birthplace: Shifnal, England
Tour: Europe
Career Highlights: **1988** Benson & Hedges International. **1990** UAP under-25 Championship. **1993** Dunhill British Masters, Scandinavian Masters. Seventh, **1993** PGA European Tour Order of Merit.
National/International Teams:
1985 Walker Cup. **1993** Ryder Cup, Dunhill Cup.

SEVE BALLESTEROS
Birthdate: April 9,1957
Birthplace: Pedrena, Santander, Spain
Career Highlights: **1976** Swiss Open, Japanese Open, Dunlop Phoenix (Japan), Lancome Trophy, Swiss Open. **1977** French Open. **1978** Swiss Open, German Open, Japanese Open, Kenya Open, Lancome Trophy. **1980** Dutch Open, Madrid Open, Masters. **1981** World Match Play, Madrid Open, Dunlop Phoenix (Japan), Australian PGA, Spanish Open. **1982** World Match Play, French Open. **1983** Irish Open, Masters, British PGA, Lancome Trophy. **1984** British Open, World Match Play. **1985** USF&G Classic, French Open, World Match Play, Spanish Open, Irish Open.**1986** French Open, Irish Open, British Masters, Dutch Open, Lancome Trophy. **1988** Taiheiyo Masters (Japan), British Open, German Open, Dunlop Phoenix (Japan), Lancome Trophy. **1989** Swiss Open, Madrid Open. **1991** Volvo PGA, British Masters.**1992** Dubai Desert Classic, Turespana Open de Balearas.
National/International Teams: **1975**, **1976**, **1977**,**1992** World Cup. **1979**, **1983**,**1985**, **1987**, **1989**, **1991**, **1993** Ryder Cup. **1986**,**1988** Dunhill Cup.

LUIS CARBONETTI
Birthdate: April 23, 1953
Birthplace: Buenos Aires
Career Highlights: 1st place, Argentine Tour Order of Merit **1985-1986.**
National/International Teams: **1993** World Cup

RODGER DAVIS
Birthdate: May 18, 1951
Birthplace: Sydney, Australia
Career Highlights: **1978** West Australia Open, Netherlands Masters. **1979** Victoria Open. **1981** State Express Classic. **1985** Victoria PGA Championship. **1986** Whyte & Mackay PGA Championship, New Zealand Open, Air New Zealand Open, Australian Open. **1988** Bi-Centennial Classic, Wang Pro-Celebrity. **1989** Ford New South Wales Open. **1990** Wang Pro-Celebrity, Peugeot Spanish Open, Palm Meadows Cup. **1991** Volvo Masters, AMP New Zealand Open, Sanctuary Cove Classic. **1992** Sanctuary Cove Classic. **1993** Air France Cannes Open.

ERNIE ELS
Birthdate: October 17,1969
Birthplace: Johannesburg, South Africa
Career Highlights: **1986** South African Amateur Championship. **1989** South African Stroke Play Championship (AM). **1990** Amatola Sun Classic. **1992** Protea Assurance South African Open,

Lexington PGA Championship, South African Masters, Hollard Royal Swazi Sun Classic, First National Bank Players Championship and Goodyear Classic. **1991-1992** Leader, Sunshine Tour Order of Merit.
National/International Teams: 1992 Dunhill Cup.**1993** World Cup.

NICK FALDO
Birthdate: July 18,1957
Birthplace: Hertfordshire, England
Career Highlights: 1977 European Tour Rookie of the Year. **1978** British PGA Championship Winner. **1984** Car Care Plan International (England). **1980** British PGA Championship. **1981** British PGA Championship. **1983** Leading money winner, European Tour. **1984** Sea Pines Heritage Classic. **1987** British Open, Peugeot Spanish Open, named Member of the British Empire. **1988** Volvo Masters, Peugeot French Open. **1989** Suntory World Match-Play Championship, Peugeot French Open, Dunhill British Masters, Volvo PGA Championship, Masters. **1990** Johnnie Walker Classic British Open, Masters. **1991** Carroll's Irish Open. **1992** Johnnie Walker World Championship, Toyota World Match-Play Championship, PGA European Open, Scandinavian Masters, Open Championship, Carroll's Irish Open, leading money winner, European Tour. **1993** Johnnie Walker Classic (Singapore), Carroll's Irish Open (play-off).
National/International Teams: 1977, 1979, 1981, 1985, 1987, 1989, 1991, 1993 Ryder Cup. **1977, 1991** World Cup. **1985, 1988, 1987, 1991** Dunhill Cup. **1986** Nissan Cup.**1987** Kirin Cup. **1990** Four Tours Championship.

ANDERS FORSBRAND
Birthdate: April 1, 1961
Birthplace: Filipstad, Sweden
Career Highlights: 1982 Swedish PGA Championship. **1983** Stiab GP. **1984** Swedish International, Gevalia Open. **1987** Ebel European Masters-Swiss Open. **1991** Volvo Open di Firenze, Benson & Hedges Trophy (with Helen Alfredsson). **1992** Volvo Open di Firenze, Credit Lyonnais Cannes Open, Equity & Law Challenge.
National/International Teams: 1984, 1985, 1988, 1991, 1993 World Cup. **1984** Kirin Cup. **1985, 1986, 1987, 1991** Dunhill Cup.

JOAKIM HAEGGMAN
Birthdate: August 28, 1969

Birthplace: Kalmar, Sweden
Career Highlights: Placed 15th on **1993** PGA European Tour Order of Merit. **1990** Wermland Open. **1992** SI Compaq Open. **1993** Peugeot Spanish Open.
National/International Teams:
1993 Ryder Cup, World Cup, Dunhill Cup.

MARK JAMES
Birthdate: October 28, 1953
Birthplace: Manchester
Career Highlights: 1988 Peugeot Spanish Open, South African TPC. **1989** NM English Open, AGF Open, Karl Litten Desert Classic. **1990** NM English Open, Dunhill British Masters. **1993** Madeira Island Open, Turespana Iberia-Open de Canarias.

KANG-SUN LEE
Birthdate: September 18, 1949
Birthplace: Seoul, Korea
Career Highlights: 1990 Maung Korean Open, Shin Han Dong Hae Open. **1993** Korean PGA Championship.
National/International Teams: 1993 World Cup.

BARRY LANE
Birthdate: June 21, 1960
Birthplace: Hayes, England
Career Highlights: 5th, European Tour Order of Merit, **1992**. 10th, **1993. 1983** Jamaica Open. **1987** Equity & Law Challenge. **1988** Bell's Scottish Open. **1992** Mercedes German Masters. **1993** Canon European Masters.
National/International Teams:
1988 World Cup, Dunhill Cup. **1993** Ryder Cup.

BERNHARD LANGER
Birthdate: August 27,1957
Birthplace: Anhausen, Germany
Career Highlights: Leader, European Tour Order of Merit, **1981** and **1984. 1980** Dunlop Masters, Colombian Open. **1981** German Open, Bob Hope British Classic. **1982** German Open. **1983** Italian Open, Glasgow Classic, TPC at St. Mellion, Johnnie Walker Tournament, Caslo World (Japan). **1984** Irish Open, Dutch Open, French Open. **1985** German Open, Australian Masters, The Masters, European Open, Sun City Challenge, Lancome Trophy. **1986** German Open. **1987** Irish Open, Co-winner Lancome Trophy, British PGA Championship, Belgian Classic. **1988** European

Epson Match Play. **1989** Peugeot Spanish Open, German Masters. **1990** Madrid Open, Austrian Open. **1991** Sun City Million Dollar Challenge, Mercedes German Masters, Hong Kong Open, Benson & Hedges Open. **1992** Heineken Dutch Open, Honda Open. **1993** Volvo PGA Championship, Masters, Volvo German Open.
National/International Teams:
1976 ,**1977** ,**1978** ,**1979**, **1980**, **1990**, **1991** World Cup. **1981**, **1983**, **1985**, **1987**, **1989**, **1991**, **1993** Ryder Cup. **1986**, **1993** Nissan Cup (captain both years). **1987** Kirin Cup (captain). **1989** Four Tours World Championship (captain).

LIANG-HSI CHEN
Birthdate: October 18, 1959
Birthplace: Tamsui, Taiwan
Career Highlights: Leader, Taiwan Order of Merit, **1989**, **1990**. **1986** Johor Classic, Taiwan Linkou Open. **1987** Mercuries Cup of Taiwan Master, Korea Open, Sarak Open. **1988** Taiwan 747 Classic, Hwa Lain Open, Kaohsiung Open. **1989** Taiwan Yuan An Open. **1990** Republic of China PGA Championship, Peral Height Open, Tamsui Open. **1991** Indonesia Open. **1992** Taiwan Chang Hwa Open.
National/International Teams: **1990**,**1993** World Cup.

SANDY LYLE
Birthdate: February 9,1958
Birthplace: Shrewsbury, England
Career Highlights: **1978** Nigerian Open. **1979** Scandinavian Open, European Open. **1981** French Open. **1983** Madrid Open. **1984** Italian Open, Lancome Trophy, Kapalua International, Casio World (Japan). **1985** British Open. **1987** German Masters, Masters. **1988** Dunhill Masters, Suntory World Match Play. **1991** BMW International Open. **1992** Lancia Martini Italian Open.
National/International Teams:
1977 Walker Cup. **1979**, **1981**, **1983**, **1985**, **1987** Ryder Cup. **1979**,**1980**, **1987** World Cup (medalist in 1980). **1985**, **1986**, **1987**, **1988**, **1989**, **1990** Dunhill Cup. **1985**, **1986** Nissan Cup (medalist in 1985). **1987**, **1988** Kirin Cup.

MARK McNULTY
Birthdate: October 25,1953
Birthplace: Zimbabwe
Career Highlights: Twice finished runner-up in the PGA European Tour Order of Merit, in **1987** and

1990. **1987** Million Dollar Challenge, German Open, Dunhill British Masters, London Standard 4-Stars Pro Celebrity, Trustbank Tournament of Champions, Swazi Sun Pro-Am, AECI Charity Classic, South African Open. **1988** Benson & Hedges Trophy (with Marie Laure de Lorenzi), Cannes Open. **1989** Torras Monte Carlo Open. **1990** Volvo German Open, Credit Lyonnais Cannes Open. **1991** Volvo German Open. **1992** Zimbabwe Open. **1993** Lexington PGA Championship.
National/International Teams: **1993** World Cup.

COLIN MONTGOMERIE
Birthdate: June 23,1963
Birthplace: Glasgow, Scotland
Career Highlights: **1988** European Tour Rookie of the Year. Leader, **1993** Europeon Tour Order of Merit. **1985** Scottish Stroke Play. **1987** Scottish Amateur Championship. **1989** Portuguese Open. **1991** Scandinavian Masters. **1993** Heineken Dutch Open, Volvo Masters.
National/International Teams:
1985, **1987** Walker Cup. **1988**, **1991** World Cup. **1988**, **1991**, **1992** Dunhill Cup. **1991**, **1993** Ryder Cup.

TOMMY NAKAJIMA
Birthdate: October 24,1954
Birthplace: Gunma, Japan
Career Highlights: **1992** Pepsi Ube Kusan, NST Niigata Open, Japan Match Play Championship. Four Japan Opens, three Japan PGA Championships, three Japan Match Play Championships and one Japan Series Championship.

NAM-SIN PARK
Birthdate: April 14, 1959
Birthplace: Kyungki-Do
Career Highlights: **1986** Fantom Seoul Open. **1987** Que-Nam Open. **1988** Que-Nam Open, Korea Dong-Hae Open. **1990** Astra Korean PGA Championship, Cambridge Members Open. **1992** Fantom Seoul Open. **1993** Maekyung Korea Open, Fantom Open.
National/International Teams: **1988**, **1989**, **1990**, **1991**, **1992**, **1993** World Cup.

FRANK NOBILO
Birthdate: May 14,1960
Birthplace: Aucland, New Zealand
Career Highlights: **1978** New Zealand Amateur.

1979 New Zealand Under-25 Stroke Play Championship. **1982** New South Wales PGA. **1985** New Zealand PGA. **1987** New Zealand PGA. **1988** PLM Open. **1991** Lancome Trophy. **1993** Turespana Mediterranean Open.
National/International Teams: 1978 World Amateur Team. **1982, 1987, 1988, 1990, 1991, 1992, 1993** World Cup. **1985, 1986, 1987, 1989, 1990, 1992, 1993** Dunhill Cup.

Scandinavian Enterprise Open, Volvo Masters. **1990** Melbourne Classic, PLM Open, Ebel European Masters. **1992** Portuguese Open, Daikyo Palm Meadows Cup. **1993** Austrian Open.
National/International Teams: 1983, 1984, 1987, 1988, 1990, 1991 World Cup. **1986, 1987, 1988, 1989, 1990, 1991, 1992** Dunhill Cup. **1988** Kirin Cup. **1989** Ryder Cup. **1989, 1990, 1991** Four Tours World Championship of Golf.

JOSE MARIA OLAZABAL
Birthdate: February 5, 1966
Birthplace: Fuenterrabia, Spain
PGA TOUR Victories: (2) **1990** NEC World Series of Golf. **1991** The International.
Career Highlights:
1983 Italian Amateur, Spanish Amateur. **1986** European Masters, Swiss Open, Sanyo Open. **1988** Belgian Open, German Masters. **1989** Tenerife Open, Dutch Open. **1990** Benson & Hedges International, Irish Open, Lancome Trophy, Visa Taiheyo Club Masters. **1990** NEC World Series of Golf. **1991** Catalonia Open, The International. **1992** Turespana Open de Tenerife, Open Mediterrania. **1994** Masters, NEC World Series of Golf.
National/International Teams: 1986, 1987, 1988, 1989, 1992 Dunhill Cup. **1987, 1989, 1991, 1993** Ryder Cup. **1989** World Cup. **1987** Kirin Cup. **1989, 1990** Four Tours World Championship.

MASASHI "JUMBO" OZAKI
Birthdate: January 27,1947
Birthplace: Tokushima, Japan
Career Highlights: Six-time leading money winner, JPGA. **1990** Yonex Hiroshima Open, Maruman Open, Daiwa KBC Augusta. **1992** Dunlop Open, Chunichi Crowns, Philanthropy Cup, All Nippon Airways Open, Japan Open, Visa Taiheyo Masters.

RONAN RAFFERTY
Birthdate: January 13, 1964
Birthplace: Newry, N. Ireland
Career Highlights: Leader, **1989** PGA European Tour Order of Merit. **1979** British Boys Championship. **1980** English Open Amateur Strokeplay Championship. **1982** Venezuelan Open, Daiko Palm Meadows Cup, Portuguese Open. **1987** South Australian Open, New Zealand Open. **1988** Australian Match-Play Championship, Equity & Law Challenge. **1989** Lancia Italian Open,

STEVEN RICHARDSON
Birthdate: July 24,1966
Birthplace: Windsor, England
Career Highlights:
1989 English Amateur Championship. **1991** Girona Open, Portuguese Open. **1993** German Masters.
National/International Teams:
1989 Walker Cup. **1991** Ryder Cup. **1991, 1992** Dunhill Cup. **1991** Four Tours World Championship of Golf.

JOSE RIVERO
Birthdate: September 20, 1955
Birthplace: Spain
Career Highlights:
1984 Lawrence Batley International. **1987** Peugeot French Open. **1988** Monte Carlo Open. **1992** Open Catalonia.
National/International Teams:
1984,1987, 1988, 1990, 1991,1992,1993 World Cup.

COSTANTINO ROCCA
Birthdate: December 4, 1956
Birthplace: Bergamo, Italy
Career Highlights: 1988 Rolex Pro-Am. **1989** Index Open (Italy), Italian Native, Italian PGA Championship.**1993** Open V33 du Grand Lyon, Peugeot French Open.
National/International Teams:
1988, 1990, 1991, 1992, 1993 World Cup. **1993** Ryder Cup.

EDUARDO ROMERO
Birthdate: July 12, 1954
Birthplace: Cordoba, Argentina
Career Highlights: 1983 Argentine PGA. **1984** Chile Open. **1986** Argentine PGA, Chile Open. **1989** Argentine Open, Lancome Trophy. **1990** Volvo Open di Firenze. **1991** Peugeot Spanish Open, Peugeot French Open.

National/International Teams: 1983,1984, 1987, 1988, 1991, 1993 World Cup.

ANDERS SORENSEN
Birthdate: June 20, 1962
Birthplace: Helsingor, Denmark
Career Highlights: 1982 Danish Amateur Stroke-Play Championship. **1985** Danish. **1986** Toms Open, Amateur Stroke-Play Championship. **1987** Nescafe Cup (Sweden), Volvo Albatross Open.
National/International Teams: 1987, 1988, 1989, 1990, 1991, 1992, 1993 World Cup.

STEEN TINNING
Birthdate: October 7, 1962
Birthplace: Copenhagen, Denmark
Career Highlights: 1983 Danish Amateur Close Championship. **1986** European Junior Championship. **1989** Tomj Open (Denmark).
National/International Teams: 1987, 1988, 1989, 1990, 1993 World Cup.

SAM TORRANCE
Birthdate: August 24, 1953
Birthplace: Largs, Scotland
Career Highlights: 1980 Scottish PGA Championship, Australian PGA Championship. **1981** Carroll's Irish Open. **1982** Portuguese Open, Spanish Open. **1983** Portuguese Open, Scandinavian Enterprise Open. **1984** Sanyo Open, Bensen & Hedges International, Tunisian Open. **1985** Johnnie Walker Monte Carlo Open, Scottish PGA Championship. **1987** Lancia Italian Open. **1990** Mercedes German Masters. **1991** Jersey European Airways Open, Scottish PGA Championship. **1993** Honda Open, Scottish PGA Championship, Heineken Open Catatonia, Kronenbourg Open.
National/International Teams: 1976, 1978, 1982, 1984, 1985, 1987, 1989, 1990, 1991, 1993 World Cup. **1981, 1983, 1985, 1987, 1989, 1991, 1993** Ryder Cup,

JEAN VAN DE VELDE
Birthdate: May 29, 1966
Birthplace: Mont de Marsan, France

Career Highlights: 1985 French Youth Championship. **1986** French Amateur Championship, French Youth Championship. **1988** UAP Under-25s European Open Championship. **1993** Rome Masters.
National/International Teams: 1989, 1990, 1991, 1992, 1993 World Cup.

IAN WOOSNAM
Birthdate: March 2,1958
Birthplace: Oswestry, Wales
Career Highlights: 1979 News of the World under-23 Match-play Championship. **1982** Swiss Open, Cacherel under-25 Championship. **1983** Silk Cut Masters. **1984** Scandinavian Enterprise Open. **1985** Zambian Open. **1986** Lawrence Batley TPC, "555" Kenya Open. **1987** Jersey Open, Cespa Madrid Open, Bell's Scottish Open, Lancome Trophy, Million Dollar Challenge, Suntory World Match Play Championship, Hong Kong Open, International Trophy (World Cup individual). **1988** Volvo PGA Championship, Carrol's Irish Open, Panasonic European Open. **1989** Carrolls Irish Open. **1990** Amex Mediterranean Open, Monte Carlo Open, Bell's Scottish Open, Epson Grand Prix, Suntory World Match Play Championship. **1991** Mediterranean Open, Monte Carlo Open, USF&G Classic, Masters, PGA Grand Slam. **1992** European Monte Carlo. **1993** Murphy's English Open, Lancome Trophy.
National/International Teams: 1980, 1982, 1983, 1984, 1985, 1987, 1990, 1991, 1992, 1993 World Cup. **1983, 1985, 1987, 1989, 1991, 1993** Ryder Cup. **1985, 1986, 1988, 1989, 1990, 1991, 1993** Dunhill Cup. **1985, 1986** Nissan Cup. **1987** Kirin Cup. **1989, 1993** Four Tours World Championship of Golf.

YU-SHU HSIEH
Birthdate: November 5, 1960
Birthplace: Taiwan
Career Highlights: Winner Taiwan Circuit Order of Merit **1991, 1988, 1987, 1986, 1985. 1985** Taiwan Taichung Open, Linkou Open. **1986** Taiwan King Grapes Open. **1988** General Choutze-Jou Memorial Open, Taiwan Open, Chia Yi Open, Miller Beer Open, Taiwan BMW Open, Indonesia Open. **1991** Taiwan Chanh-Hwa Open. **1993** Taiwan Taichung Open, Mercuries Cup of Taiwan Master.

HALL OF FAME

OVERVIEW: *Dates and short career biographies of the leading players of the past (omitting those covered in the Personalities chapters) since 1870, including the British and European tours, the PGA TOUR, the LPGA, as well as prominent professionals from Asia, Africa, and Australia/New Zealand.*

WILLIE ANDERSON
1878-1910
Emigrant to the United States became the first to win four U.S. Opens (1901, 1903, 1904, 1905).

TOMMY ARMOUR
1896-1968
Won the 1927 U.S. Open, 1930 PGA Championship, and the 1931 British Open. His brilliant 1930 campaign was overshadowed by Bobby Jones' Grand Slam, and Armour has been unjustly overlooked. His *How to Play Your Best Golf All the Time* became a best-seller and for many years was the biggest-selling book ever authored on golf.

JOHN BALL
Dec. 24, 1861-1940
Prominent English amateur of the late 19th and early 20th century. After winning the British Amateur in 1888, Ball became the first English-born player to win the British Open in 1890, and in the same year won his second Amateur, the first to win both titles in the same year. Ball subsequently won the 1892, 1894, 1899, 1907, 1910, and 1912 Amateurs, a record seven titles in all in addition to two runner-up finishes. Ball was also runner-up in the 1892 British Open.

JIM BARNES
April 8, 1886 -May 26, 1966
Won 1916, 1919 PGA Championship; 1921 U.S. Open, 1925 British Open.

PATTY BERG
Born Feb. 13, 1918
Leading player on the LPGA Tour during the 1940s, 1950s and 1960s. Patty Berg first came to national attention by reaching the final of the 1935 U.S. Women's Amateur, losing to Glenna Collett Vare in Vare's final Amateur victory. Berg reached the final in 1937 and won the Amateur in 1938 at Westmoreland. A fixture on the fledgling Women's Professional Golf Association circuit, she won the inaugural U.S. Women's Open. Berg, a founder of the LPGA, won a total of 41 events on the LPGA and WPGA circuit, and was runner-up in the 1957 Open at Winged Foot. She was runner-up in the 1956 and 1959 LPGA Championships. In addition, Berg won the 1953, 1957, and 1958 Western Opens, the 1955 and 1957 Titleholders, both considered majors at the time. Her last victory came in 1962.

JULIUS BOROS
Born March 3, 1920
Won 18 PGA Tour events, including 1952, 1963 U.S. Open, 1968 PGA Championship. Oldest player ever to win a major championship. Member, Ryder Cup team 1959, 1963, 1965, 1967. PGA Player of Year, 1952, 1963. Career PGA Tour earnings, $1,004,861.

JAMES BRAID
Feb. 6, 1870-Nov. 27, 1950
The Scottish-born member of the Great Triumvirate of Braid, Taylor and Vardon—Braid won five British Opens in all and was the first to achieve this feat. His victories came in 1901, 1905, 1906, 1908, and 1910. In addition Braid won four Brish PGA championships in 1903, 1905, 1907 and 1911 as well as the 1910 French Open title. Braid was runner-up in the British Open in 1897 and 1909.

MIKE BRADY
April 15, 1887 -Dec. 3, 1972

Lost to Walter Hagen in a celebrated playoff in the 1919 U.S. Open. Also was runner-up in 1911. Hagen promptly resigned his club pro job after winning in 1919 and Oakland Hills promptly hired Brady. Brady subsequently won the 1922 Western Open at Oakland Hills.

BILLY BURKE

Dec. 14, 1902 -April 19, 1972
Greatest season was 1931, when he won the U.S. Open, reached the semi-finals of the PGA Championship, and won four events on the professional circuit, plus appeared on the Ryder Cup team where he was undefeated in two matches. Subsequently selected for the 1933 Ryder Cup team and won his only match.

JACK BURKE, JR.

Born Jan. 29, 1923
First rose to prominence with two lopsided victories in the 1951 Ryder Cup matches. Subsequently selected for the 1953 and 1955 sides, and in 1957 was named captain of the team. Also served as non-playing captain in the 1973 matches. Won 15 PGA tournaments in his career, including the 1956 Masters and PGA Championships. Perhaps his most famous match was his nine-hour, 40-hole quarterfinal loss to Cary Middlecoff in the 1955 PGA. Selected PGA Player of the Year in 1956, and subsequently challenged in the PGA Championship (fourth, 1958).

JOANNE CARNER

Born April 4, 1939
Prominent LPGA professional of the 1970s and 1980s following an outstanding amateur career in the 1950s and 1960s. Carner first broke into the headlines in 1956 when, as a 17-year-old, she reached the finals of the U.S. Women's Amateur in the same year she won the Girls Junior Amateur. She went on to win the Amateur five times (in 1957, 1960, 1962, 1966, and 1968) and reach the final round a total of seven times. Carner competed four times on the Curtis Cup team (1958, 1960, 1962, and 1964) and was undefeated in five singles matches. After winning the Burdine's Invitational on the LPGA Tour as an amateur in 1969, Carner made the decision to turn pro in 1970 and has since won an astonishing 42 victories on the LPGA Tour, including the U.S. Women's Open in 1971 and 1976. Carner led the money list in 1974, 1982, and in 1983 at the age of 44.

HARRY COOPER

Born August 6, 1904
Prominent PGA Tour professional of the 1920s and 1930s. Perennial U.S. Open contender (with seven top ten finishes and second place in 1927 and 1936), he also placed second in the 1936 Masters as well as reaching the quarterfinals of the PGA on several occasions. His greatest successes were across the border— he won the Canadian Open in 1932 and 1937. Cooper won 321 PGA Tour titles in all and the inaugural Vardon Trophy in 1937. Subsequently was active as a senior golfer, placing sixth in the 1955 PGA Seniors Championship.

HENRY COTTON

Born Jan. 26, 1907
Prominent English player of the 1930s. Cotton almost single-handedly upheld the prestige of British golf in the 1930s with three victories in the British Open (1934, 1937, and 1948). In additon he captured many titles on the European Continent in the 1930s. His greatest year was 1937 when he won the British, French and Czechoslovakian Opens and was selected fort he 1937 Ryder Cup matches. Cotton served as captain of the Ryder Cup team in 1947 and 1953.

BOBBY CRUICKSHANK

Nov 16. 1894-Aug. 27, 1975
Prominent player on the PGA circuit from the early 1920s to the early 1930s. Of Scottish birth, he first rose to prominence in reaching the finals of the 1922 and 1923 PGA Championships, losing both times to eventual champion Gene Sarazen. Also was runner-up in the 1923 and 1932 U.S. Opens, and won 20 tour events in his career. His greatest year was 1927, when he won the Los Angeles and Texas Opens and finished as the leading money winner for the year. He last won on tour in 1935.

JIMMY DEMARET

May 24, 1910-Dec. 28, 1983
Perhaps the all-time character of the PGA Tour, he also won 31 events in a long career between 1935 and 1957 and was the first three-time winner of the Masters. Demaret reached his peak in the late 1940s with wins in the Masters in 1947, runner-up to Ben Hogan in both the 1948 U.S. Open and PGA Championsip, and leading money winner status in 1947. He reached the the semi-finals of the PGA Championship four times in all but never won. Selected on the 1951 Ryder Cup team, his career declined in the 1950s although he managed several

key wins including the 1952 Crosby. Known for his outrageous humor and outrageously colorful outfits, he was the original host of Shell's Wonderful World of Golf in the early 1960s, and was introduced to a new generation of golf fans. The over-70s groupings on the PGA Senior Tour are known as the Friends of Demaret in his honor.

ROBERTO DE VICENZO
Born April 14, 1923
Perhaps the archetypal international golfer of the 1950s, he won an astonishing 230 tournaments worldwide in his career, including four on the PGA Tour and the 1967 British Open. The Argentine-born golfer had the misfortune to sign an incorrect scorecard in the 1968 Masters (after tying Bob Goalby), and was disqualified. DeVicenzo subsequently found great success in the early days of the PGA Senior Tour, winning the Liberty Mutual Legends of Golf three times and the inaugural U.S. Senior Open in 1980. Also won the 1974 PGA Seniors Championship, and represented Argentina 17 times in the Canada and World Cups (leading Argentina to victory in 1953).

LEO DIEGEL
April 27, 1899-May 5, 1951
Prominent player of the 1920s and early 1930s who won 11 PGA Circuit events, and was a four-time winner of the Canadian Open (1924-25, 1928-29). Selected for the inaugural 1927 Ryder Cup team and went on to play on the 1929, 1931 and 1933 teams as well. Diegel's great year was 1928 when he won the Canadian Open and, in winning the 1928 PGA Championship, stopped the four-year winning streak of Walter Hagen (defeating him in the quarter-final to avenge defeats by Hagen in the 1925 quarter-finals and the 1926 final). Diegel achieved the rare double of defending both titles successfully in 1929, this time defeating Hagen in the semi-finals and finishing off The Haig's career. Diegel was runner-up to Bobby Jones at the British Open in 1930, but subsequently did not challenge at any major championships.

ED DUDLEY
Feb. 19, 1901-Oct. 25, 1963
Leading tour player of the late 1920s and 1930s, Dudley was a 13-time winner on the Tour. After winning both the Los Angeles and Western Opens in 1931, Dudley had his best year in 1933 when he was a quarter-finalist in the PGA Championship

and won selection to the Ryder Cup team. Won two key matches in the 1937 Ryder Cup matches to help the United States win for the first time in England.

OLIN DUTRA
Jan. 17, 1901-May 5, 1983
Played on the PGA Tour in the late 1920s and 1930s, winning 19 tournaments in all. Was most prominent in the early 1930s, winning the 1932 PGA Championship, the 1934 U.S. Open at Merion and playing in the 1933 and 1935 Ryder Cup matches. In the 1932 PGA Championship, Dutra played 196 holes and finished an astounding 19 under par, including finishing as low qualifier and winning his matches 9&8, 5&3, 5&4, 3&2, and 4&3.

CHICK EVANS
July 18, 1890-Nov. 6, 1979
Ranked just below Bobby Jones among U.S. Amateur golfers of the 1920s. Evans was the first amateur to win the U.S. Open and U.S. Amateur in one year, a feat he achieved in 1916 . Evans went on to win the U.S. Amateur in 1920, while finishing runner-up three times. Selected to the Walker Cup team in 1922, 1924, and 1928, Evans competed in a record 50 consecutive U.S. Amateurs in his long career.

JOHNNY FARRELL
Born April 1, 1901
Prominent PGA Tour player of the 1920s and early 1930s who won 22 events in his career. Reached the semi-finals of the 1926 PGA Championship, but his best year was 1927 when he won eight tournaments in all. In 1928 he won the U.S. Open at Olympia Fields by defeating Bobby Jones in a 36-hole playoff. In 1929 he was runner-up at both the British Open and the PGA Championship. Farrell was a key member of the first Ryder Cup team in 1927, and subsequently played in the 1929 and 1931 Matches. His career declined in the 1930s, but Farrell reappeared in the 1950s when he competed in several PGA Seniors Championships.

DOUG FORD
Born August 6, 1922
Top-ranked player of the 1950s and early 1960s, Ford won 19 PGA Tour titles in his career including the 1955 PGA Championship and the 1957 Masters. Ford had his greatest year in 1957, winning the Los

Angeles Open, the Western Open, and a spot on the Ryder Cup team in addition to the Masters. Ford continued to be a strong threat on tour through the early 1960s, winning the Canadian Open in 1959 and 1963, the 1962 Crosby, and finishing fifth in the 1961 and 1962 PGA Championships. Ford was on the Ryder Cup team between 1955-61, and was named PGA Player of the Year in 1955. Ford managed several top-20 finishes in the PGA Seniors Championship in the 1970s and won two unofficial Seniors events in 1981, but by the mid-80s was finding only limited success on the Tour.

VIC GHEZZI

Oct. 19, 1912-May 30, 1976
Top-ranked PGA Tour player of the late 1930s and 1940s. First rose to prominence at 22 with a victory in the 1935 Los Angeles Open. Ghezzi won the 1941 PGA Championship at Cherry Hills, and after World War II made a brief comeback, finishing runner-up in the 1946 U.S. Open and reaching the semi-finals of the 1947 PGA Championship. Ghezzi was selected for the 1939 and 1941 Ryder Cup teams but the matches were cancelled due to the war. Ghezzi played in the PGA Seniors Championship in the 1960s, finishing as high as seventh in 1964.

RALPH GULDAHL

Born Nov. 22, 1911
Leading player on the PGA Tour in the 1930s and early 1940s, winning 14 tournaments overall. He first rose to prominence with a runner-up finish in the 1933 U.S. Open at the age of 20 (losing to Johnny Goodman, also 20 at the time). His career reached a peak in the late 1930s when he won three consecutive Western Opens (considered a quasi-major championship at the time) in 1936-38, and then won back-to-back U.S. Opens in 1937 and 1938. Guldahl also was a key member of the 1937 Ryder Cup team in winning both his matches. Guldahl also had a stellar 1939 campaign winning the Masters and the Greensboro Open and reached the semi-finals of the PGA Championship in 1940. But after reaching the quarter-finals in the 1941 PGA Championship he did not have significant success in major golf tournaments.

WALTER HAGEN

Dec. 21, 1892-Oct. 6, 1969
One of the great characters of golf and the greatest professional player of the 1920s, Hagen is known today not only for his eleven major championships but his successful efforts to raise the status of the touring golf professional. Hagen first came to national attention as a minor-league baseball pitching prospect but turned to golf full-time after his astonishing victory in the 1914 U.S. Open (at the age of 21). Hagen won the Western Open in 1916 and reached the semi-finals of the inaugural PGA Championship that year at Siwanoy, and returned to the victor's circle at the U.S. Open in 1919 when it resumed following the First World War. But his successes of the 1910s are overshadowed by his play in the 1920s. A runner-up finish in the 1921 U.S. Open, plus victories in the Western Open and that year's PGA Championship touched off a fabulous decade in which he won nine major championships, numerous tournaments on the PGA Circuit, and earned riches giving golf exhibitions worldwide. Hagen won an incredible 33 consecutive matches in the PGA Championship between 1924 and 1928 in winning four consecutive PGA Championships. Walter Hagen also became the first American to win the British Open, and won the affection of the British public in four dashing championships won in 1922, 1924, 1928 and 1929. Hagen was the first American golfer to earn a living as a touring professional, and it was the respect in which golfers such as Hagen and Harry Vardon were held that led the Inverness Club to open the clubhouse to professionals in the 1920 U.S. Open. Hagen was also the first professional golfer to found his own equipment company, and started his own informal tour of exhibition matches and appearances. One of his most celebrated triumphs was a 12 and 11 victory over Bobby Jones in a 72-hole exhibition in 1926, but he could be beaten quite handily as well, losing 18 and 17 to an unknown British professional at the start of one of his exhibition tours. His manager Bob Harlow became the first manger of the PGA Tour Circuit in the 1930s, after The Haig's career went into eclipse. But Hagen continued to be a force throughout the 1930s, winning the 1932 Western Open and serving as captain of the U.S. Ryder Cup team between 1927-37.

CHICK HARBERT

Born Feb. 20, 1915
Prominent PGA Tour pro in the 1940s and 1950s. Masterful match player, Harbert first rose to prominence with a victory in the 1942 Texas Open, but became a leading player after the Second World War by reaching the final of the 1947 PGA Championship. He earned a slot on the 1949 Ryder Cup team and won his only match. After another loss in the finals of the 1952 PGA, Harbert finally

broke through with a victory in 1954 which included match victories over Jerry Barber, Tommy Bolt, and defending champion Walter Burkemo. Harbert, who won a total of nine PGA Tour titles between 1941 and 1958, was named captain of the victorious 1955 Ryder Cup team. He continued to compete in the PGA Championship throughout the 1960s, but switched to the Senior circuit in the late 1960s and finished in the top five of the PGA Seniors Championships several times.

CHANDLER HARPER

Born March 10, 1914.
Leading player on the PGA Tour in the 1940s and 1950s, amassing a total of 20 PGA Tour victories including the 1950 PGA Championship. Harper finished fifth in the 1946 U.S. Open but had his greatest success in the 1950s, with a career best in 1955 when he won the Colonial and was selected to the Ryder Cup team. After concluding his Tour career, Harper had great success as a senior golfer, winning the U.S. National Senior Open and the 1968 PGA Seniors Championship.

E.J. (DUTCH) HARRISON

March 29, 1910-June 19, 1982
Feared competitor on Tour from the 1930s to the 1950s. Harrison first rose to prominence by reaching the semi-finals of the 1939 PGA Championship. Harrison won fifteen events between 1937 and 1958, including the 1949 Canadian Open, the 1953 Western Open, and the 1954 Crosby. Harrison was a regular in the Ryder Cup line-up after the Second World War, and finished third in the U.S. Open as late as 1960. Harrison went on to even greater success as a senior, winning the U.S. National Senior Open four times in a row between 1962 and 1965, as well as managing four top-five finishes in the PGA Seniors Championship.

SANDRA HAYNIE

Born June 4, 1943
Leading LPGA player of the 1960s and 1970s. Haynie won the 1957 and 1958 Texas amateurs, and the 1960 Trans-Mississippi as an amateur, and turned pro in 1961. Haynie won the U.S. Women's Open in 1974 and the LPGA Championship in 1965 and 1974. As there were only two designated major championships in 1974, Haynie is considered along with Babe Zaharias to have achieved the LPGA Grand Slam. Haynie won a total of 42 LPGA tournaments in her career, including a final major

championship in the 1982 Peter Jackson Classic. Haynie led the Tour in victories in 1974 and 1975.

BEN HOGAN

Born Aug. 13, 1912
The leading PGA Tour professional of the 1940s and 1950s, and some still call Hogan the greatest player of all time. Won a total of 62 PGA Tour events between 1938 and 1953, including victories in every major championship. Hogan was plagued by a snap-hook early in his career and was overshadowed in major championship play by fellow Texan Byron Nelson despite leading the tour in prize money 1940-42 and winning the Vardon Trophy in 1940 and 1941. In 1942 Hogan won six Tour victories and finished runner-up in the Masters, but it was immediately after the war that he made his mark, with 13 victories in 1946 including the PGA Championship, his first major. Hogan dominated golf in the late 1940s, with victories in the 1948 PGA Championship and U.S. Open, and a leading role in the 1947 Ryder Cup victory in Portland. Hogan suffered massive injuries in a near-fatal auto accident in 1949 and his career was thought to be finished. But after serving as nonplaying captain in the 1949 Ryder Cup matches, he staged the most spectacular comeback in the history of golf by achieving even greater success in the 1950s, including a victory in the 1950 U.S. Open just weeks after returning to competitive golf. His injuries prevented him from competing in the PGA Championship, but Hogan still amassed nine major championships in all, including the first three legs of the modern Grand Slam in 1953. He won the U.S. Open four times in all, a record never bettered, and wrote one of the enduring classics of golf instruction in *Five Lessons*. Hogan finished runner-up in the 1955 and 1956 U.S. Opens and finished third in 1960, but after that his career went into decline (except for a spectacular run at the 1967 Masters). He did not choose to compete on the senior circuit, but instead concentrated on the management of the fabulously successful Ben Hogan Co., a major golf equipment manufacturing concern. Hogan has served as host at Colonial since the 1940s and continues to fulfill that function today. Hogan served as non-playing captain of the 1967 Ryder Cup team.

DOROTHY CAMPBELL HURD HOWE

1883-1946
Prominent amateur golfer of the early 20th centruy. The Scot first gained notice as a three-time winner

of the Scottish amateur from 1903 to 1905. Her finest year was 1909 when she won both the U.S. and British amateur titles. She successfully defended in the U.S. Women's Amateur in 1910 and added the Canadian Ladies Amateur—becoming the first woman to win these three national amateur championships. She continued to be a force in amateur golf in the 1910s, winning the 1911 British and Canadian titles and the 1912 Canadian championship. After the First World War she reached the finals of the U.S. Women's Amateur in 1920, losing to Alexa Stirling, but came back to win the title a third time in 1924.

JOCK HUTCHINSON
June 6, 1884-Sept. 28, 1977
Scottish-born, Hutchinson achieved his greatest successes in the United States, first breaking through with runner-up finishes in both the 1916 PGA and U.S. Open. His most successful campaign was 1920, when he won the PGA Championship and the Western Open, and finished runner-up to Ted Ray in the U.S. Open. Hutchinson went on to win the 1921 British Open at St. Andrews, his hometown. Hutchinson became the dominant player in the early years of the PGA Seniors Championship, winning victories in 1937 and 1947, and finishing runner-up six times.

BETTY JAMESON
Born May 19, 1919
A prominent amateur of the 1930s and 1940s and a leading LPGA/WPGA player of the 1940s. Jameson won back-to-back titles in the U.S. Women's Amateur in 1939 and 1940. Jameson won ten LPGA titles in the 1940s and 1950s after turning professional in 1945. Her biggest triumph was a victory in the 1947 U.S. Women's Open. Jameson was much less prominent during the 1950s but did finish runner-up in the 1952 Open and as victor in the 1954 Western Open, considered a major championship at the time. After winning three titles in 1955, she did not figure prominently in LPGA events.

ROBERT T. JONES
March 17, 1902-Dec. 18, 1971
A golfing prodigy who, after conquerng a terrfic temper, went on to become the most popular golfer of his time as well as a celebrated author and founder of both the Augusta National Golf Club and the Masters. Jones was a teenage golfing phenomenon the likes of which golf had not yet seen,

winning entry into the U.S. Amateur at 14 years, five months in 1916. The USGA did not stage competitions in 1917-18 due to the First World War, but in 1919 Jones reached the final of the Amateur, and in 1920 was medalist in the stroke-play phase of the Amateur as well as winner of the Southern Amateur. By 1922 Jones' game had blossomed and he finished runner-up in the U.S. Open at Skokie, and then won his first U.S. Open in 1923 at Inwood. His 1924 campaign brought him the Amateur Championship at Merion and a runner-up finish in the Open at Oakland Hills. By 1925 Jones was regarded as the finest golfer in the country with the possible exception of Walter Hagen (and this at 23 years of age), and he solidified his reputation with another Amateur Championship and second-place in the Open. In 1926 Jones had his greatest year to date, winning the U.S. and British Opens before losing in the final of the U.S. Amateur to George Von Elm at Baltusrol. Jones, a lifelong amateur, began a career as an Atlanta lawyer, but continued his assualt on golf's records each summer, winning the British Open at St. Andrews and storming to an 8 & 7 victory over Charles Evans in the final of the U.S. Amateur at Minkahda. His 1928 campaign was likewise successful, with a runner-up finish in the U.S. Open followed by a smashing 10 & 9 victory in the Amateur over Phillip Perkins. His 1929 campaign brought him a victory in the U.S. Open at Winged Foot, where after finishing in a tie after 72 holes he proceeded to defeat Al Espinosa by 23 strokes in a 36-hole playoff—but Jones did not fare well in the British Open and after finishing as medalist in the Amateur at Pebble Beach lost to 19-year old Johnny Goodman in the first round of match play. He made use of the time by playing the new Cypress Point course and, impressed with the design, asked architect Alister MacKenzie to collaborate with him on the design for the Augusta National Golf Club. Jones' final summer of major championship golf, in 1930, was a frank assault on the "Impregnable Quadrilateral," the Open and Amateur Championships of the United States and Great Britain. He defeated Mac Smith by two strokes in both the U.S. Open at Interlachen and the British Open ay Hoylake. He faltered somewhat at St. Andrews in his first British Amateur, winning a fourth-round match over Cyril Tolley with the aid of a crucial stymie before cruising to victory in the final. He completed the Grand Slam, as it became known, by finishing as medallist at the Amateur and cruising to victory including an 8 & 7 margin in the final over Eugene Homans. Jones subsequently retired from competitive golf, although he continued to write, and played exhibitions as late as the Second World War to raise money for the war effort. He founded Augusta National Golf

Club in 1932 and the Masters in 1933. He suffered from a crippling disease for the last 20 years of his life, but continued to play host at the Masters through 1967. His book *Down the Fairway* is considered one of the game's enduring classics.

LAWSON LITTLE

June 23, 1910-Feb. 1, 1968
The leading amateur of the 1930s and later a successful touring professional. Little rose to prominence in 1934 by winning both the British and U.S. Amateur Championships, and by the astounding feat of defending both titles successfully in 1935. After 1935 Little joined the PGA Tour circuit as a professional—the first prominent amateur to turn professional and presaging prominent defections by Arnold Palmer and Jack Nicklaus from the amateur ranks in later years. Little's decision paid off immediately with a victory in the 1936 Canadian Open, but he did not fulfill the expectations of many despite winning the 1940 U.S. Open and several PGA Tour events, including the 1940 Los Angeles Open and the 1941 Texas Open.

BOBBY LOCKE

Born 1917
Prominent South African golfer of the 1940s and 1950s. Locke first gained attention before the Second World War in winning the New Zealand Open, but after the war quickly established himself as a force in the United States and Europe with a runner-up finish in the 1946 British Open to Sam Snead, a third place finish in the 1947 U.S. Open, and victory in the 1949 British Open. Locke also won 11 events on the PGA Tour between 1947-50, including the 1947 Tournament of Champions and Canadian Open and the 1948 Phoenix Open. In maintaining a presence on the PGA Tour, in South African golf, and in Britain, Locke became the first golfer to fashion his own world-wide tour, presaging the career of Gary Player in the 1960s and 1970s, and Greg Norman in the 1980s and 1990s. Locke's career continued to blossom in the 1950s, crowned by three more victories in the British Open in 1950, 1952 and 1957. He also took home the national championships of South Africa, Germany, France, Switzerland and Egypt during this decade. He was allowed to compete for England in the 1953 Canada Cup, but afterwards represented South Africa and was not allowed to compete on the Ryder Cup team. His final Canada Cup appearance was in 1960, after which he ceased to be a prominent figure in world golf.

NANCY LOPEZ

Born Jan. 6, 1957
Dominant LPGA player of the late 1970s, and a prominent player of the 1980s and 1990s. Lopez won the 1972 and 1974 U.S. Girls Junior Amateur, the 1976 Women's NCAA Championship and was undefeated on the 1976 Curtis Cup team, but her career took off in the late 1970s after she turned professional. After winning Rookie of the Year honors in 1977, Lopez won nine tournaments in 1978 including five out of six and a total of seven by mid-June. She won another eight in 1979 and three more in 1980. She has won the LPGA Championship three times (1978, 1985 and 1990), and her 47 career wins place her sixth on the all-time LPGA list.

LLOYD MANGRUM

Aug. 1, 1914-Nov. 17, 1973
Prominent member of the PGA Tour from the 1930s to the 1950s who enjoyed his greatest success in the ten years after the Second World War. Mangrum first won on the Tour in 1940 and gained notice with a runner-up finish in the Masters that year, but after reaching the semi-finals of the 1941 PGA and winning the New Orleans Open and the Crosby in 1942 he was considered one of the leading golfers in the country. Mangrum won the 1946 U.S. Open at Canterbury in a celebrated playoff with Vic Ghezzi and Byron Nelson in which all three tied after the eighteen-hole playoff—Mangrum went on to shoot 72 in the second playoff to win by one. In the late 1940s Mangrum was, after Hogan and Snead, the leading golfer on the Tour, winning a spot on the 1947 and 1949 Ryder Cup teams. In 1951 he finished as leading money-winner and won the Vardon Trophy, and had another outstanding season in 1953 winning four tournaments and the Vardon Trophy. He served as non-playing captain of the victorious 1955 Ryder Cup team, after which his career went into decline, although he did win the 1956 Los Angeles Open and had a victory as late as 1958 on Tour.

CAROL MANN

Born February 3, 1941
Leading LPGA Tour player of the 1960s and 1970s. Mann started out on the junior amateur circuit, and turned professional in the early 1960s. She won 38 tournaments in all, including the 1965 U.S. Women's Open. Her greatest year was in 1968, when she won ten tournaments (including three

consecutive weeks. She led the tour in victories two other times (1969 and 1975) and won the 1968 Vare Trophy. She won the 1958 Western and Chicago Juniors and the 1960 Chicago Amateur.

JOHN McDERMOTT
Aug. 12, 1891-Aug. 1, 1971
McDermott, rather than Francis Ouimet, was the first American-born golfer to win the U.S. Open, a feat he achieved in 1911 at Chicago Golf Club, in a playoff with Mike Brady and George Smith. McDermott had lost a playoff to Alex Smith for the Open title in 1910. McDermott successfully defended his title in 1912, the last American professional to do so until Ralph Guldahl in 1938.

FRED McLEOD
April 25, 1882-May 5, 1976
Prominent player of the 1900s to the 1920s, McLeod won the U.S. Open in a playoff with Willie Smith in 1908 at Myopia Hunt Club. After the First World War he returned to prominence, finishing as runner-up in the 1921 U.S. Open and the 1919 PGA Championship. McLeod was a leading figure in the early days of senior competition, finishing runner-up in the 1937 PGA Seniors Championship, and returning to win the 1938 title at Augusta National.

CARY MIDDLECOFF
Born Jan. 6, 1921
Leading player of the late 1940s and 1950s. Middlecoff began his Tour career with a bang, winning his first tournament in 1947, finishing runner-up in the Masters in 1948, and winning the U.S. Open and seven Tour events in 1949. In 1951 he won another six tournaments including Colonial, and by 1953 he was a member of the Ryder Cup squad. Middlecoff had his best year in 1955, winning six tournaments including the Masters and the Western Open, reached the finals of the PGA Championship, and again won a spot on the Ryder Cup team. In 1956 he won his second U.S. Open, and finished runner-up in 1957, but by the late 50s his game was in decline and, despite a selection to the 1959 Ryder Cup team, he had lost his spot in the forefront of golf to the likes of Palmer and Nicklaus. His final Tour victory was at Memphis in 1961, giving him a career total of 40 titles.

TOM MORRIS, JR.
1851-Dec. 25, 1875
Dominant player of the late 1860s and early 1870s.

Young Tom, son of St. Andrews greenkeeper Old Tom Morris, not only dominanted golf—he practically re-invented it as well as setting new standards of achievement. Morris won the first of four successive British Open Championships in 1868 at the age of 17. His streak included an 11-stroke victory in 1869 and a 12-stroke victory in 1870 (in a 36-hole format). His 149 in the 1870 British Open over 36 holes was a stroke average that was not equalled until the invention of the rubber-cored ball. After his third consecutive victory, the Championship Belt became his property and the Open was discontinued until a cup was offered as a prize in 1872, whereupon Morris promptly won a fourth consecutive championship. Young Tom introduced the use of the niblick (five-iron) for approach shots. But Young Tom's career was cut tragically short when he died on Christmas Day, 1875, shortly after the death of his young wife in childbirth.

TOM MORRIS, SR.
June 16, 1821-1908
Leading professional, greenkeeper, and course architect of the mid-to-late 19th century. Father of Young Tom Morris, Old Tom was the proprietor of the St. Andrews golf shop, greenkeeper (professional and superintendent), as well as a club maker, course architect, and like son Tom a four-time winner of the British Open. Morris was famous in golf from the early 1840s due to a series of great victories paired with his mentor Allen Robertson against Willie and Jamie Dunn. After serving as apprentice to Robertson, Morris became the greenkeeper at Prestwick in 1851 and remained there through his first three Open Championships, returning to become greenkeeper at St. Andrews where he remained the rest of his life. After the death of Robertson in 1859, Morris became the dominant player in the early years of the British Open, with victories in 1861, 1862, 1864, and 1871. In addition to his four victories, he was four times runner-up in the Open, including finishing second to his son in 1868-69, a unique achievement in golf. Morris laid out many golf courses of the late 19th century and remodeled others, including Royal Dornoch. His apprentices included Donald Ross and Charles Balir Macdonald, and thus his influence has been felt in American golf course architecture.

BYRON NELSON
Born Feb. 4, 1912
The dominant player of the mid-1940s, Nelson won 53 titles in all during his short career on the Tour,

which lasted only from 1935-1946. Nelson shot to stardom in 1937 when he won the Masters in the spring and defeated major championship winners Leo Diegel, Johnny Farrell, and Craig Wood at the PGA Championship before losing in the quarterfinals. He also was selected for the 1937 Ryder Cup team which was the first to win on British soil. After a quiet 1938, Nelson won the U.S. Open in 1939, in addition to several tour victories including the Phoenix and Western Opens. Nelson continued his strong play into the 1940s with wins in the 1940 PGA Championship and the 1942 Masters. Not eligible for military service, Nelson devoted the war years to golf (including a number of war-bond rally exhibitions), and was the dominant player of the time, winning eight tournaments in 1944 and a PGA Tour record 18 in 1945, including the PGA Championship and a record 11 straight tournaments during the winter and spring. Nelson won the Vardon Trophy in 1945 and was voted Athlete of the Year by the Associated Press in recognition of his achievement. Nelson reduced his schedule in 1946 and retired from full-time competition after the 1946 season, although he played on the 1947 Ryder Cup team and occasionally appeared in Tour events during the 1950s (such as his victorious appearance in the 1951 Crosby). He declined to compete on the Senior circuit in later years, restricting himself to serving as non-playing captain of the 1965 Ryder Cup team, and hosting the Byron Nelson Classic annually since 1968.

JACK NICKLAUS

Born Jan. 21, 1940
Dominant PGA Tour player of the late 1960s and early 1970s. Nicklaus was a golfing prodigy in his native Ohio, playing at Scioto, and under the tutelage of Jack Grout rose rapidly to the front rank of American golf, finishing as runner-up in the U.S. Open at the age of 20, and winning both the NCAA Championship and the U.S. Amateur at 21. He closed his amateur career with his second Walker Cup appearance in 1961.

The second phase of his career began with his decision to turn professional in 1962, and his subsequent victory in the 1962 U.S. Open. Nicklaus' crewcut and chubby features proved unpopular with golfers when he defeated all the crowd favorites in tournament after tournament and, by 1966, had supplanted Arnold Palmer as the leading golfer of the day. But seven major championship victories in the 1960s (the 1962 and 1967 U.S. Opens, the 1966 British Open, the 1963-64 and 1966 Masters, and the 1963 PGA) and several popular victories in the Canada and World Cups (paired with Arnold Palmer) earned Nicklaus the respect

of golf fans everywhere. Nicklaus closed his decade with his first Ryder Cup appearance in 1969. His concession of Tony Jacklin's two-foot putt gave Britain a tie in the matches (after five straight losses) and showed the public a magnanimous side of his personality.

The third phase of his career began with a British Open victory in 1970, and during a decade when many golfers expect their games to go into steep decline, Nicklaus won eight more major championships, including his historic 1972 run at the Grand Slam, where he took the first two legs of the Slam at Augusta and Pebble Beach before finishing second to Lee Trevino at Muirfield in the British Open. Nicklaus added two more World Cup appearances, four Ryder Cups, four Australian Opens and the 1970 World Match Play Championship to his portfolio.

The fourth phase of his career began in 1980 with Nicklaus winning both the U.S. Open and the PGA Championship and silencing critics who had begun to suggest that Nicklaus' best days were gone. With golf fans now on his side, he won a hugely popular eighteenth major championship and sixth Masters title in 1986, and continued to show flashes of his old form. He also captained two Ryder Cup teams in 1983 and 1987 to take a spectator's role for the first time in golf.

Although his Tour career had faded by 1990, he proved reluctant to play the PGA Senior Tour and instead has played a limited schedule on both the senior and regular Tours since then, he has had very conspicuous success on the Senior Tour with victories in the Senior Open, the Senior Players Championship, and The Tradition.

FRANCIS OUIMET

May 8, 1893-Sept. 2, 1967
The first American golf celebrity and the dominant amateur until the rise of Bobby Jones. Ouimet was assured of a place in golf's annals after his astonishing playoff victory in the 1913 U.S. Open over Harry Vardon and Ted Ray, considered the best players in the world at the time. Ouimet followed up his upset of the century with a victory in the 1914 Amateur before having his amateur status revoked because of a business association with a sporting goods concern. The outcry over Ouimet's banishment forced the USGA to rescind the ban in 1918, and Ouimet returned to amateur competition. He reached the finals of the Amateur in 1920 and won the Amateur a second time in 1931. In addition, Ouimet played on eight Walker Cup teams between 1922 and 1934, and served as non-playing captain of the Walker Cup team five times between 1936 and 1949. Ouimet subsequently was elected

captain of the Royal & Ancient, the first American to hold the post.

ARNOLD PALMER

Born 1929

Dominant PGA Tour professional of the early 1960s. Palmer first appeared on the national golfing map in 1954 when he captured the U.S. Amateur. Promptly turning professional, he struggled in his early years but captured key championships such as the 1955 Canadian Open and the 1956 Eastern Open before winning the Masters and his first money-title in 1958.

After a solid campaign in 1959 with three victories, Palmer began to dominate the Tour in 1960 when he won eight tournaments (six before July) including the Masters and the U.S. Open before finishing second in the British Open to Kel Nagle, foiling his bid for the Grand Slam. Palmer's commitment to the British Open is credited with reviving interest in the championship in the United States. Palmer continued to dominate the headlines from 1961-64, winning two more Masters titles and two British Opens in addition to two Ryder Cups and four World Cup selections. In the second half of the decade he continued to be successful on Tour with 12 more wins, although more major championships eluded him.

In the 1970s Palmer faded as a major championship contender after a third-place finish at the 1973 U.S. Open, but he continued to win infrequently in the United States and more so in foreign tournaments (he won the Spanish Open and the British PGA, for example, in this period).

In 1980 Palmer became eligible for the fledgling PGA Senior Tour and promptly recaptured the public's imagination in winning the PGA Seniors Championship in 1980, the U.S. Senior Open in 1981, a second PGA Seniors Championship and the Senior TPC in 1983, and a Senior TPC in 1985. In addition to these major senior titles, Palmer won five other titles between 1981 and 1988.

Palmer continues to compete in Senior and regular Tour events in the 1990s, and has had conspicuous success in the unofficial Senior Skins match, which he has won three times in this decade.

HENRY PICARD

Born Nov. 28, 1907

Prominent PGA Tour player of the late 1930s. Picard was a leading Tour player by the mid-1930s, winning five tournaments in 1935, but he turned in his first outstanding major championship performance with a fifth-place finish in the 1936 U.S.

Open, and subsequently won two key points in the 1937 Ryder Cup matches. He broke into the front-rank of American golfers in 1938 with a victory in the Masters in addition to reaching the semi-finals in the PGA Championship. He followed 1938 with a better 1939, winning the PGA Championship in addition to seven other Tour titles and another Ryder Cup appearance. Picard's career quickly declined thereafter and he won his last PGA Tour title in 1941, bringing his career total to 26.

BETSY RAWLS

Born May 4, 1928

Prominent LPGA Tour player of the 1950s, 1960s, and 1970s. Rose through the amateur ranks in the late 1940s and after winning the 1949 Trans-National she finished runner-up to Babe Zharias in the 1950 U.S. Women's Open. Turning pro in 1951, she won her first Open Championship. By 1952 she was in the top rank of the LPGA, winning the Western Open in addition to five other tournaments.

Throughout the 1950s she was a consistent winner on the Tour, with major championship victories in the 1953 Open and the 1957 Open, and closed out the decade with victories in the 1959 Western Open and LPGA Championship.

After a strong start in the 1960s with a record fourth win in the Open in 1960, Rawls was not able to continue her blazing 1950s form. Yet she managed to regain her form to win another major championship in the 1969 LPGA Championship.

JOHNNY REVOLTA

Born April 5, 1911

Prominent PGA Tour player of the 1930s and 1940s, later renowned as an instructor. Revolta burst onto the PGA Tour circuit with a splash, winning five tournaments in 1935 (at age 24) including the PGA Championship. He was the leading money-winner in 1935 and played in the Ryder Cup. Revolta never equalled 1935, although he played on the 1937 Ryder Cup team and won tournaments as late as 1947. Revolta wrote golf instruction books and became a celebrated teacher later in life, and several present-day LPGA players are former students.

PAUL RUNYAN

Born July 12, 1908

Prominent PGA Tour player of the 1930s. Runyan was a young phenom in the early 30s, winning the

PGA Championship by the age of 24 (in 1933) and making the Ryder Cup team. Runyan won nine events in total during 1933, and seven more in 1934, when he finished as leading money-winner for the Tour. Runyan's career declined in the mid-30s, but revived on the strength of his victory in the 1938 PGA Championship, which led to selection for the phantom 1939 and 1941 Ryder Cup teams. Runyan had a fine run as a senior player, finishing runner-up in the PGA Seniors in 1959-1960, and winning in 1961-62.

GENE SARAZEN

Born Feb. 27, 1902

One of the youngest players ever to win the U.S. Open, Sarazen arrived with a thump in international golf with victories in the 1922 U.S. Open and PGA, plus a successful title defense in 1923 of his PGA crown. Sarazen, in the 1923 PGA, was the last golfer to beat Hagen in a PGA Championship match until 1928. Sarazen's fine play in the 1920s was overshadowed by the successes of Bobby Jones and Walter Hagen, but Sarazen did finish as runner-up in the 1928 British Open in addition to many tour victories in the period. Following the retirement of Jones and the aging of Hagen, Sarazen emerged as a dominant player, winning eight Tour events in 1930, as well as the British and U.S. Opens in 1932. Sarazen also won the 1933 PGA Championship at Blue Mound for a sixth major championship. Sarazen's final total became seven majors after he won the 1935 Masters with "The shot heard round the world," a double-eagle on the 15th hole that is still considered one of the most exciting events in the modern game. With his victory in the Masters Sarazen also became the first golfer to win the career Grand Slam. Sarazen was a steady Tour circuit player during these years, winning 15 other tournaments and the 1930 leading money-winner title. Sarazen repeated as British Open champion in 1932 and was selected for the Ryder Cup team six consecutive times between 1927 and 1937. In later years Sarazen was an active golf personality, winning fame with a new generation of golfers via his role as host of Shell's Wonderful World of Golf—and through his senior play. Sarazen won the 1954 and 1958 PGA Seniors Championship. Late in life, in 1973 at Troon, The Squire, as he was known for his courtly manner, managed to score a rare hole-in-one at the famed Postage Stamp hole, a feat discussed even more than the plus-fours he continued to wear for golf attire. In the early 1990s he became associated with the Sarazen World Championship of Golf, a tournament played at Chateu Elan in Georgia, where he is a course design consultant.

DENNY SHUTE

Oct. 25, 1904-May 13, 1974

Leading PGA Tour player of the 1930s. Shute had a meteoric career on the Tour circuit, winning selection to the Ryder Cup team in 1931 and subsequently taking the British Open title in 1933 in addition to serving again on the Ryder Cup squad. Shute's career rose to a crescendo in 1936-38, winning the 1936 PGA Championship and defending the title successfully in 1937, as well as winning selection to the Ryder Cup team. As late as 1939 Shute was still a major force in profesional golf, losing in a play-off for the U.S. Open. He had a successful run in senior golf, finishing runner-up in the 1955 and 1959 PGA Seniors Championship.

ALEX SMITH

1880-April 20, 1931

Prominent professional of the early 20th century and older brother of Mac Smith. The Scottish native moved to the United States in his teens and at the age of 18 he finished runner-up in the first 72-hole U.S. Open at Myopia Hunt Club. During the early 1900s he was consistently on the leaderboard at the U.S. Open, finishing as runner-up again in 1902 and 1905 before winning in 1906 at Onwentsia and in 1910 at Philadelphia Cricket Club. Also finished third in the U.S. Open three times in addition to victories in the 1903 and 1906 Western Opens.

HORTON SMITH

May 22, 1908-Oct. 15, 1963

Leading player on the embryonic PGA Tour Circuit of the 1930s. Grabbed the attention of the golfing world when he reached the semi-finals of the 1928 PGA Championship as a 20-year-old. Smith won eight tour events in 1929 and qualified for the Ryder Cup team where he was one of two Americans to win a singles match. Smith finished third in the 1930 U.S. Open, and reached the quarterfinals of the PGA Championship. In 1931 Smith again reached the quarters of the PGA and played on the Ryder Cup team. In late 1933 Smith entered the peak of his career with a key win in the Ryder Cup singles, followed by a victory in the inaugural Masters in spring 1934. Smith had his greatest year in 1936, leading the PGA Tour money list, reaching the quarterfinals of the PGA and winning a second Masters Championship. In all Smith won 31 tournaments, his last great season coming in 1940 when he had his last victory and finished third in the U.S. Open. He was selected to eight Ryder Cup teams in all (three series were cancelled due to the

Second World War) and remained undeafeated in Ryder Cup play.

MAC SMITH

March 18, 1890-Nov. 3, 1949

Widely regarded as the greatest player never to win a major, Smith was a perennial contender from the 1910s to the 1930s who managed many classic victories. The younger brother of U.S. Open champion Alex Smith, Mac first gained notice when he tied his brother (along with John J. McDermott) in the 1910 U.S. Open at Philadelphia Cricket Club, only to lose in the play-off. Smith won the 1912 Western Open, but disappeared from the leaderboards for several years, only to come strongly in the 1920s during the golf boom of the roaring 20s. Smith won the 1925 Western Open, and had an outstanding season in 1926 when he won five tournaments highlighted by victory in the Texas and Canadian Opens. Smith won the lucrative Los Angeles Open four times, in 1928, 1929, 1932, and 1934, but perhaps his great claim to fame was as an asterisk to history, since he finished as runner-up to Bobby Jones on both legs of Jones' 1930 Grand Slam that were open to professionals—the British and U.S. Opens. Smith had success in the early 1930s but by 1940 his star had dimmed.

SAM SNEAD

Born May 27, 1912

The all-time leading tournament winner for the PGA Tour (81 in all, and a total of 135 tournaments worldwide) who was a leading player from the 1930s to the 1970s on the Tour. Snead was a late bloomer for the period, winning his first tournament in 1936 and joining the Tour in 1937. He won five victories in all in 1937 including the Crosby, played on the Ryder Cup team and finished third on the money-winning list. His 1938 campaign was even more spectacular, with eight victories including the Crosby and the Canadian Open, and the first of four runner-up finishes in the U.S. Open. Snead won the Vardon Trophy and was the leading money-winner for the year. His career took a back seat to the meteoric rise of Byron Nelson and Ben Hogan in the late 1930s and early 1940s, but he won twelve more tournaments in 1939-41 including another Crosby and two Canadian Opens. Snead finally won a major championship in 1942 with a victory in the PGA , but his appearances were limited throughout the war.

In 1945 Snead returned to an active schedule and he won six tournaments in '45 and another five in 1946 plus the only British Open he ever competed in, at St. Andrews. After off-years in 1947 and 1948, Snead shook off his slump with the finest year of his career in 1949, winning the Vardon Trophy, playing on the winning Ryder Cup team, and winning two major championships (his first Masters and second PGA Championship) in addition to a runner-up finish in the U.S. Open and victories in four regular tour events. He continued his strong form into 1950 with 11 Tour victories (a total not equaled since), including his fourth Crosby and runner-up finish in the PGA Championship.

He remained at the pinnacle of golf throughout the 1950s, especially with the fading of such long-time rivals as Ben Hogan and Byron Nelson. Snead took the 1951 PGA as well as the 1952 and 1954 Masters to reach a total of seven major championship victories. He represented the United States in the 1953 and 1955 Ryder Cup matches and paired with Ben Hogan to win the 1956 Canada Cup. By the late 1950s, however, his age was beginning to show in the week-to-week Tour grind as he slipped to 45th on the money list by the end of the decade. Snead also captained the winning 1959 Ryder Cup team and was undeafeated in two matches.

Snead's place in golf during the 1960s was very unusual, as he became the first golfer to maintain an active and successful presence in both senior and regular competition. He scored a PGA Tour-record eighth victory in the Greater Greensboro Open in 1965, fully six months after his first senior victories in the PGA Senior Championship and the World Seniors. Snead also represented the United States in three consecutive Canada Cup victories in 1960-1962, winning the individual title at Dorado in Puerto Rico in 1961. Later in the decade Snead won two more PGA Seniors Championships in 1965 and 1967, and he captained the United States team to the historic tie in the 1969 Ryder Cup matches.

In the 1970s, Snead did not play a major role on the world golfing scene, but he continued to make headlines with several outstanding performances. In 1973 he won the PGA Seniors Championship by an amazing fifteen strokes over Julius Boros, and in 1974 finished third in the PGA Championship behind Lee Trevino and Jack Nicklaus. In 1979 he shot his age in the Quad Cities Open (67), and then bettered it in the next round with a 66. But 1979 was the last year he won money in a Tour event.

Snead was active in the early years of the 1980s on the fledgling PGA Senior Tour, and won the 1980 Golf Digest Commemorative and the 1982 Legends of Golf paired with Don January. During the late 1980s his appearances were limited to the Senior Tour and the Masters. Snead surprised crowds with a playoff loss in the par-three tournament at the 1992 Masters, at the age of 80.

LOUISE SUGGS

Born Sept. 7, 1923

Prominent amateur of the late 1940s and a leading LPGA Tour player of the 1950s and 1960s. Suggs shocked women's golf in 1946 by winning two major championships—the Titleholders and the Western Open—as an 18-year-old amateur. She won the 1947 Women's Amateur after finishing as medalist in qualifying, and after three North and South Amateur titles, decided to try her luck in the pro ranks. She found almost immediate success in the embryonic WPGA with major championships in the 1947 and 1949 Western Opens and became a founder of the LPGA after winning the 1949 Open.

Suggs hit a peak in the 1950s with six more major championships (the 1952 Open, 1957 LPGA, 1953 Western, and the 1954, 1956, and 1959 Titleholders). During the decade she was also a three-time runner-up in the Open, and a multiple tournament winner on the regular LPGA Tour circuit, in addition to taking the Vare Trophy in 1957.

Suggs was one of the few 1950s standouts to build a successful career in the 1960s—Suggs won an average of two tournaments a year for the first half of the decade. Her career dwindled in the late 1960s and by the 1970s she was rarely in contention.

JOHN H. TAYLOR

March 19, 1871-February, 1963.

Leading British professional of the 1890s, 1900s and 1910s. Taylor was one of the Great Triumvirate of Harry Vardon, Taylor and James Braid that dominated golf between 1900 and the First World War. Taylor was the first of the trio to achieve national golfing success, winning the 1894 British Open and repeating his success in 1895. He finished runner-up to Harry Vardon in 1896 and did not challenge for the title in the remainder of the decade.

In the 1900s Taylor found his greatest success—despite the vigorous competition between Braid, Vardon and Taylor, J.H. won the 1900 and 1909 championships and was runner-up four times, from 1904-07. In addition he won the 1904 and 1907 British PGA as well as the 1907 and 1909 French Open.

In the 1910s Taylor's age began to tell, but he managed to win the 1913 British Open and finish runner-up to Vardon in the 1914 events. He also won the 1912 German Open. He concluded his active career as a player with the First World War.

PETER THOMSON

Born Aug. 23, 1929

Prominent Australian golfer of the 1950s and 1960s, active on both the PGA and European Tours. Thomson's great achievement was in the British Open, where he first leapt into the spotlight in 1952, at the age of 22, with a runner-up finish to Bobby Locke. After another runner-up finish in 1953, Thomson won the first of his Open titles at Royal Birkdale. After successfully defending his crown at St. Andrews in 1955, Thomson became the first player in 70 years to win three consecutive titles with an Open title in 1956. Thomson also won the Texas Open in 1956 and had a career-best fourth place finish in the U.S. Open. After a runner-up finish in 1957, Thomson won a fourth title in 1958 at Royal Lytham.

Thomson's career slowed significantly in the 1960s, but Thomson managed a fifth victory in the British Open with a 1965 win at Southport. He was not heard much of after this time except as an administrator, until the birth of the PGA Senior Tour.

He joined the Tour soon after turning 50 but waited until 1985 and age 55 to have his greatest year, with a record nine victories. In addition to his major championship and Senior victories, Thomson won three Australian Opens, nine New Zealand Opens, and the national championships of an assortment of colonies and nations, including Germany, Hong Kong, Holland, Spain and Italy.

JEROME S. TRAVERS

May 19, 1887-March 30, 1951

Leading amateur of the 1900s and 1910s. Travers had his first successes in the U.S. Amateur, winning in 1907 and 1908 at Euclid and Garden City, respectively. Travers won back-to-back Amateurs again in 1912-13, becoming the first player to win four Amateur titles. After losing in the final of the 1914 Amateur to Francis Ouimet, Travers had his greatest season in golf in 1915 when he became one of the few amateurs ever to win the U.S. Open. Travers set a record for widest victory margin in the first round of the 1915 Amateur (14 & 13 over 36 holes) but could not complete the rare Amateur/Open double.

WALTER TRAVIS

1862-1927

Australian-born amateur who was the dominant force in amateur golf during the 1900s. Travis won the 1900, 1901 and 1903 Amateurs to become the first player to ever win the title three times. Travis finished second to Laurie Aucterlonie in the 1902 U.S. Open, just missing that rare double. But Travis achieved a rare double of his own by becoming the first golfer to win the British and U.S. Amateurs with his British Amateur victory in 1904.

HARRY VARDON
May 9, 1870-March 20, 1937
Leading British professional of the 1890s, 1900s, and 1910s. Vardon was the best player and best known of the Great Triumvirate that dominated golf between 1900 and 1914.

Vardon became well-known after breaking J.H. Taylor's lock on the British Open with a victory in 1896. He continued his great success with back-to-back victories in the 1898-99 British Open, and crowned his success by taking the 1900 U.S. Open title during an exhibition tour of the United States.

Vardon became the first professional golfer to attract such a following that he could sustain himself as a full-time professional and live off his prize earnings and from exhibition fees throughout the world. In this respect he presaged the globe-trotting Walter Hagen and wandering foreign players such as Bobby Locke, Peter Thomson, and Gary Player. Vardon popularized the modern overlapping grip (usually known as the Vardon grip) and the modern golf swing which took fullest advantage of the flight characteristics of the rubber-cored ball.

After two more British Open Championships in 1900 and 1903 plus runner-up finishes in 1901-02, Vardon was severely affected by a bout of tuberculosis and by the putting yips (so severe that he once whiffed a putt in competition), and he was not a factor for the remainder of the decade. But he regained his health and form in the 1910s and won two more British Opens (in 1911 and 1914) and had runner-up finishes in the 1912 British Open and the 1913 U.S. Open. After the First World War his age began to tell and, except for a runner-up finish in the 1920 U.S. Open at Inverness, he did not figure again at the top of major championship leaderboards.

GLENNA COLLETT VARE
Born June 20, 1903
Dominant woman player in the United States during the 1920s and early 1930s. She began her career in the 1920s with four U.S. Women's Amateurs, in 1922, 1925, 1928, and 1929 and also won the 1923 and 1924 Canadian Ladies.

In the 1930s she continued to win championships, with two more victories in the U.S. Women's Amateur (the last in 1935), as well as three appearances for the USA on the Curtis Cup squad.

In addition to these national championships, Vare was a six-time champion of the prestigious North and South championship, and served as captain of the Curtis Cup team in 1948 and as non-playing captain in 1950.

JOYCE WETHERED
Born Nov. 7, 1901
Dominant English female amateur of the early 1920s. Wethered had a brief but extremely active career in golf, first winning the English Ladies Championship in 1920. In 1921 she repeated her victory in the English Amateur, but had her greatest success in 1922 and 1924 when she won both the British Ladies Amateur and the English Ladies Amateur. Wethered won two more British Ladies Amateurs in 1925 and 1929 in addition to the 1923 English Ladies Amateur.

KATHY WHITWORTH
Born Sept. 27, 1939
Dominant player of the 1960s and 1970s on the LPGA Tour. After a solid amateur career in the 1950s, Whitworth turned pro at age 19 in 1958 and won her first LPGA victory in 1962. From 1965 until the end of the decade, Whitworth was the dominant player on the Tour, never winning fewer than seven tournaments in a year and taking home four major championships, including the 1965-66 Titleholders, and the 1967 Western Open and LPGA Championship. She also won the 1965-67 and 1969 Vare Trophies.

Whitworth picked up in 1970 where she left off in 1969 and steamrolled to twenty-eight tour victories in the decade, including the 1970 and 1975 LPGA Championships. After winning the Vare Trophy from 1970-72, however, Whitworth's successes began to be spaced further and further apart.

The 1980s began strongly for Whitworth with at least one victory per season from 1981-85. In addition, Whitworth became the first woman to earn $1 million in prize money, one of two women selected for the Legends of Golf, and a Hall of Famer. She has not won since 1985 but her LPGA-sanctioned victories totaled eighty-eight wins, a record that still stands in all of professional golf.

CRAIG WOOD
Nov. 18, 1901-May 8, 1968
Prominent PGA Tour player of the 1930s and 1940s, Wood still holds the record for the longest drive

ever hit in major championship play (430 yards on the fifth hole at St. Andrews in the British Open). Wood arrived late on the Tour but gained attention in 1929 when he reached the quarterfinals of the PGA Championship. Wood earned a selection to the victorious 1931 Ryder Cup team. He won 3 tournaments in 1932 and in 1933 lost the British Open in a playoff to Denny Shute. His 1934 season was his most successful to date. Wood played Ryder Cup and repeated his runner-up finish at Augusta in the 1935 Masters, while in 1936 he reached the semi-finals of the 1936 PGA—but he didn't recapture top form until 1941, when he won the U.S. Open. In 1942 he won his second major, the Masters, as well as the 1942 Canadian Open. After the war Wood disappeared from the tour golfing scene, and did not play on any senior circuit.

MICKEY WRIGHT

Born Feb. 14, 1935

Dominant LPGA Tour player of the early 1960s. Wright first gained attention for winning the 1952 U.S. Girls Junior Amateur. After losing in the finals of the 1954 Women's Amateur, Wright turned professional in 1956 and won a total of 82 LPGA events in her career. She won the 1958 Women's Open and the LPGA Championship to enter the front rank of LPGA players, and closed out the 1950s with five wins in 1959 including a second U.S. Open.

Her greatest years were in the 1960s, however, and she began the decade with six wins in 1960 including the LPGA Championship. In 1961 she was the leading money winner and won three of the four major championships, failing to win only the LPGA. In 1962 she won the money-title and an astonishing ten events, including four in a row, and her eighth and ninth majors in the Titleholders and the Western Open. Her 1963 campaign was the most spectacular of all, with thirteen wins and two more majors in the LPGA and the Western Open. Her 1964 results were only slightly less spectacular, with the money title, eleven victories, and a twelfth major at the U.S. Women's Open. Wright tied Betsy Rawls' record for most victories in the Open. Plagued by injuries, she sharply reduced her schedule in 1965 and never again played more than 22 events on Tour in a year. Consequently she was less

of a dominant player, although a thirteenth major victory in the 1967 Western Open plus at least one win per year throughout the decade proved she was still a force to be reckoned with.

Beginning in 1970, Wright became a part-time player on Tour—hence, she rarely won, although she stayed in the top-50 on the money list as late as 1977. In 1979 she made one last run at a title but lost to Nancy Lopez in the Coca Cola Classic.

Wright's playing schedule in the 1980s was limited to just three official events, and she did not play a decisive role in any of them. But her U.S. Open record of four wins still stands, and her record of 82 wins has been eclipsed to date only by Kathy Whitworth.

BABE ZAHARIAS

June 26, 1911-September 27, 1956

America's first female golf celebrity and leading player of the 1940s and 1950s. Zaharias first came to national attention as a track and field star, winning a record five gold medals at the 1932 Olympic Games in Los Angeles. Turning to golf, her national fame as an athlete brought a new level of awareness to women's golf. Although originally classified as a professional, she won back her amateur status during the Second World War and won the 1946-47 U.S. Women's Amateur as well as the 1947 British Amateur and three Western Open victories. Formally turning professional in 1947, she dominated the WPGA and later the LPGA (of which she was a founding member) until illness shortened her career in the mid-1950s. She won the 1947 Titleholders and the 1948 U.S. Women's Open for her fourth and fifth major championships.

Zaharias had her greatest year in 1950 when she completed the Grand Slam of the Women's Open, the Titleholders, and the Western Open, in addition to leading the money-list. She was the leading money-winner again in 1951 and in 1952 took another major with a Titleholders victory, but illness prevented her from playing a full schedule in 1952-53. She made a comeback in 1954 and took the Vare Trophy and her tenth and final major with a U.S. Women's Open championship. Her cancer reappeared in 1955 and limited her schedule to eight events, but she managed two wins which were her final ones in competitive golf. Cancer took its toll and Zaharias died in 1956 while still in the top rank of female American golfers.

MAJOR CHAMPIONSHIP WINNERS OF THE PAST

OVERVIEW: *Winners, runners-up and prize money for the four major championships on the PGA TOUR, Senior PGA TOUR, and the LPGA Tour.*

Men's Major Championships

THE MASTERS

Augusta National Golf Club, Augusta, GA

YEAR	WINNER	SCORE	RUNNER-UP
1934	Horton Smith	284	Craig Wood
1935	*Gene Sarazen	282	Craig Wood
1936	Horton Smith	285	Harry Cooper
1937	Byron Nelson	283	Ralph Guldahl
1938	Henry Picard	285	Ralph Guldahl
			Harry Cooper
1939	Ralph Guldahl	279	Sam Snead
1940	Jimmy Demaret	280	Lloyd Mangrum
1941	Craig Wood	280	Byron Nelson
1942	*Byron Nelson	280	Ben Hogan
1943	*No Tournament*	—	————
1944	*No Tournament*	—	————
1945	*No Tournament*	—	————
1946	Herman Keiser	282	Ben Hogan
1947	Jimmy Demaret	281	Byron Nelson
			Frank Stranahan
1948	Claude Harmon	279	Cary Middlecoff
1949	Sam Snead	282	Johnny Bulla
			Lloyd Mangrum
1950	Jimmy Demaret	283	Jim Ferrier
1951	Ben Hogan	280	Skee Riegel
1952	Sam Snead	286	Jack Burke, Jr.
1953	Ben Hogan	274	Ed Oliver, Jr.
1954	*Sam Snead	289	Ben Hogan
1955	Cary Middlecoff	279	Ben Hogan
1956	Jack Burke, Jr.	289	Ken Venturi
1957	Doug Ford	282	Sam Snead
1958	Arnold Palmer	284	Doug Ford
			Fred Hawkins

* Won in playoff

YEAR	WINNER,	SCORE	RUNNER-UP
1959	Art Wall, Jr.	284	Cary Middlecoff
1960	Arnold Palmer	282	Ken Venturi
1961	Gary Player	280	Charles Coe
			Arnold Palmer
1962	*Arnold Palmer	280	Gary Player
			Dow Finsterwald
1963	Jack Nicklaus	286	Tony Lema
1964	Arnold Palmer	276	Dave Marr
			Jack Nicklaus
1965	Jack Nicklaus	271	Arnold Palmer
			Gary Player
1966	*Jack Nicklaus	288	Tommy Jacobs
			Gay Brewer, Jr.
1967	Gay Brewer, Jr.	280	Bobby Nichols
1968	Bob Goalby	277	Roberto DeVicenzo
1969	George Archer	281	Billy Casper
			George Knudson
			Tom Weiskopf
1970	*Billy Casper	279	Gene Littler
1971	Charles Coody	279	Johnny Miller
			Jack Nicklaus
1972	Jack Nicklaus	286	Bruce Crampton
			Bobby Mitchell
			Tom Weiskopf
1973	Tommy Aaron	283	J.C. Snead
1974	Gary Player	278	Tom Weiskopf
			Dave Stockton
1975	Jack Nicklaus	276	Johnny Miller
			Tom Weiskopf
1976	Ray Floyd	271	Ben Crenshaw
1977	Tom Watson	276	Jack Nicklaus
1978	Gary Player	277	Hubert Green
			Rod Funseth
			Tom Watson
1979	*Fuzzy Zoeller	280	Ed Sneed
			Tom Watson
1980	Seve Ballesteros	275	Gibby Gilbert
			Jack Newton
1981	Tom Watson	280	Johnny Miller
			Jack Nicklaus
1982	*Craig Stadler	284	Dan Pohl
1983	Seve Ballesteros	280	Ben Crenshaw
			Tom Kite
1984	Ben Crenshaw	277	Tom Watson

* Won in playoff

YEAR	WINNER	SCORE	RUNNER-UP
1985	Bernhard Langer	282	Curtis Strange
			Seve Ballesteros
			Ray Floyd
1986	Jack Nicklaus	279	Greg Norman
			Tom Kite
1987	*Larry Mize	285	Seve Ballesteros
			Greg Norman
1988	Sandy Lyle	281	Mark Calcavecchia
1989	*Nick Faldo	283	Scott Hoch
1990	*Nick Faldo	278	Ray Floyd
1991	Ian Woosnam	277	JoseMaria Olazabal
1992	Fred Couples	275	Ray Floyd
1993	Bernhard Langer	277	Chip Beck
1994	Jose Maria Olazabal	279	Tom Lehman

The United States Open Championship

DATE	WINNER	SCORE	RUNNER-UP	SITE
1895	Horace Rawlins	173	Willie Dunn	Newport G. C., Newport, RI
1896	James Foulis	152	Horace Rawlins	Shinnecock Hills G. C., Southampton, NY
1897	Joe Lloyd	162	Willie Anderson	Chicago G. C., Wheaton, IL
1898	Fred Herd	328	Alex Smith	Myopia Hunt Club, S. Hamilton, MA
1899	Willie Smith	315	George Low	Baltimore C. C.
			Val Fitzjohn	(Roland Park Course),
			W.H. Way	Baltimore, MD
1900	Harry Vardon	313	J.H. Taylor	Chicago G. C., Wheaton, IL
1901	*Willie Anderson	331	Alex Smith	Myopia Hunt Club, S. Hamilton, MA
1902	Laurence Auchterlonie	307	Stewart Gardner	Garden City G. C.,
			Walter J. Travis	Garden City, NY
1903	*Willie Anderson	307	David Brown	Baltusrol G. C. (original course), Springfield, NJ
1904	Willie Anderson	303	Gilbert Nicholls	Glen View Club, Golf, IL
1905	Willie Anderson	314	Alex Smith	Myopia Hunt Club, S. Hamilton, MA
1906	Alex Smith	295	William Smith	Onwentsia Club, Lake Forest, IL

Won in playoff

DATE	WINNER	SCORE	RUNNER-UP	SITE
1907	Alex Ross	302	Gilbert Nicholls	Philadelphia Cricket C. (St. Martin's Course), Philadelphia, PA
1908	*Fred McLeod	322	Willie Smith	Myopia Hunt Club, S. Hamilton, MA
1909	George Sargent	290	Tom McNamara	Englewood G. C., Englewood, NJ
1910	*Alex Smith	298	John J. McDermott Macdonald Smith	Philadelphia Cricket C. (St. Martin's Course), Philadelphia, PA
1911	*John J. McDermott	307	Michael J. Brady George O. Simpson	Chicago G. C., Wheaton, IL
1912	John J. McDermott	294	Tom McNamara	C. C. of Buffalo, Buffalo, NY
1913	*Francis Ouimet	304	Harry Vardon Edward Ray	The Country Club (Original Course), Brookline, MA
1914	Walter Hagen	290	Charles Evans, Jr.	Midlothian C. C. Blue Island, IL
1915	Jerome D. Travers	297	Tom McNamara	Baltusrol G. C., (Revised Course), Springfield, NJ
1916	Charles Evans, Jr.	286	Jock Hutchison	Minikahda Club, Minneapolis, MN
1917	*No Championship*			
1918	*No Championship*			
1919	*Walter Hagen	301	Michael J. Brady	Brae Burn C. C., West Newton, MA
1920	Edward Ray	295	Harry Vardon Jack Burke, Sr. Leo Diegel Jock Hutchison	Inverness Club, Toledo, OH
1921	James M. Barnes	289	Walter Hagen Fred McLeod	Columbia C. C., Chevy Chase, MD
1922	Gene Sarazen	288	Robert T. Jones, Jr John L. Black	Skokie C. C., Glencoe, IL
1923	*Robert T. Jones, Jr.	296	Bobby Cruickshank	Inwood C. C., Inwood, NY
1924	Cyril Walker	297	Robert T. Jones, Jr.	Oakland Hills C. C. (South Course), Birmingham, MI
1925	William Macfarlane	291	Robert T. Jones, Jr.	Worcester C. C., Worcester, MA
1926	Robert T. Jones, Jr.	293	Joe Turnesa	Scioto C. C., Columbus, OH

*Won in playoff

DATE	WINNER	SCORE	RUNNER-UP	SITE
1927	*Tommy Armour	301	Harry Cooper	Oakmont C. C., Oakmont, PA
1928	*Johnny Farrell	294	Robert T. Jones, Jr.	Olympia Fields C. C. (North Course), Matteson, IL
1929	*Robert T. Jones, Jr.	294	Al Espinosa	Winged Foot G. C. (West Course), Mamaroneck, NY
1930	Robert T. Jones, Jr.	287	Macdonald Smith	Interlachen C. C., Minneapolis, MN
1931	*Billy Burke	292	George Von Elm	Inverness Club, Toledo, OH
1932	Gene Sarazen	286	Bobby Cruickshank T. Philip Perkins	Fresh Meadow C. C., Flushing, NY
1933	John Goodman	287	Ralph Guldahl	North Shore G. C., Glenview, IL
1934	Olin Dutra	293	Gene Sarazen	Merion Cricket C. (East Course), Ardmore, PA
1935	Sam Parks, Jr.	299	Jimmy Thomson	Oakmont C. C., Oakmont, PA
1936	Tony Manero	282	Harry Cooper	Baltusrol G. C. (Upper Course), Springfield, NJ
1937	Ralph Guldahl	281	Sam Snead	Oakland Hills C. C. (South Course), Birmingham, MI
1938	Ralph Guldah	284	Dick Metz	Cherry Hills Club, Englewood, CO
1939	*Byron Nelson	284	Craig Wood Denny Shute	Philadelphia C. C. (Spring Mill Course), West Conshohocken, PA
1940	*Lawson Little	287	Gene Sarazen	Canterbury G. C., Cleveland, OH
1941	*Craig Wood	284	Denny Shute	Colonial Club, Fort Worth, TX
1942	*No championship*			
1943	*No championship*			
1944	*No championship*			
1945	*No championship*			
1946	*Lloyd Mangrum	284	Byron Nelson Vic Ghezzi	Canterbury G. C., Cleveland, OH
1947	*Lew Worsham	282	Sam Snead	St. Louis C. C., Clayton, MO

Won in playoff

DATE	WINNER	SCORE	RUNNER-UP	SITE
1948	Ben Hogan	276	Jimmy Demaret	Riviera C. C., Los Angeles, CA
1949	Cary Middlecoff	286	Sam Snead Clayton Heafner	Medinah C. C. (No. 3 Course), Medinah, IL
1950	*Ben Hogan	287	Lloyd Mangrum George Fazio	Merion G. C. (East Course), Ardmore, PA
1951	Ben Hogan	287	Clayton Heafner	Oakland Hills C. C. (South Course), Birmingham, MI
1952	Julius Boros	281	Ed S. Oliver	Northwood Club, Dallas, TX
1953	Ben Hogan	283	Sam Snead	Oakmont C. C., Oakmont, PA
1954	Ed Furgol	284	Gene Littler	Baltusrol G. C. (Lower Course), Springfield, NJ
1955	*Jack Fleck	287	Ben Hogan	Olympic Club (Lake Course), San Francisco, CA
1956	Cary Middlecoff	281	Julius Boros Ben Hogan	Oak Hill C. C. (East Course), Rochester, NY
1957	*Dick Mayer	282	Cary Middlecoff	Inverness Club, Toledo, OH
1958	Tommy Bolt	283	Gary Player	Southern Hills C. C., Tulsa, OK
1959	Bill Casper, Jr.	282	Bob Rosburg	Winged Foot G. C. (West Course), Mamaroneck, NY
1960	Arnold Palmer	280	Jack Nicklaus	Cherry Hills C. C., Englewood, CO
1961	Gene Littler	281	Doug Sanders Bob Goalby	Oakland Hills C. C. (South Course), Birmingham, MI
1962	*Jack Nicklaus	283	Arnold Palmer	Oakmont C. C., Oakmont, PA
1963	*Julius Boros	293	Jacky Cupit Arnold Palmer	The Country Club (Championship Course), Brookline, MA
1964	Ken Venturi	278	Tommy Jacobs	Congressional C. C. (Composite Course), Washington, D.C.

* *Won in playoff*

DATE	WINNER	SCORE	RUNNER-UP	SITE
1965	*Gary Player	282	Kel Nagle	Bellerive C. C., St. Louis, MO
1966	*Bill Casper, Jr.	278	Arnold Palmer	Olympic Club (Lake Course), San Francisco, CA
1967	Jack Nicklaus	275	Arnold Palmer	Baltusrol G. C. (Lower Course), Springfield, NJ
1968	Lee Trevino	275	Jack Nicklaus	Oak Hill C. C. (East Course), Rochester, NY
1969	Orville Moody	281	Deane Beman Al Geiberger Bob Rosburg	Champions G. C. (Cypress Creek Course), Houston, TX
1970	Tony Jacklin	281	Dave Hill	Hazeltine National G. C., Chaska, MN
1971	*Lee Trevino	280	Jack Nicklaus	Merion G. C. (East Course), Ardmore, PA
1972	Jack Nicklaus	290	Bruce Crampton	Pebble Beach G. L., Pebble Beach, CA
1973	John Miller	279	John Schlee	Oakmont C. C., Oakmont, PA
1974	Hale Irwin	287	Forrest Fezler	Winged Foot G. C. (West Course), Mamaroneck, NY
1975	*Lou Graham	287	John Mahaffey	Medinah C. C. (No. 3 Course), Medinah, IL
1976	Jerry Pate	277	Tom Weiskopf Al Geiberger	Atlanta Athletic C. (Highlands Course), Duluth, GA
1977	Hubert Green	278	Lou Graham	Southern Hills C. C., Tulsa, OK
1978	Andy North	285	J.C. Snead Dave Stockton	Cherry Hills C. C., Englewood, CO
1979	Hale Irwin	284	Gary Player Jerry Pate	Inverness Club, Toledo, OH
1980	Jack Nicklaus	272	Isao Aoki	Baltusrol G. C. (Lower Course), Springfield, NJ
1981	David Graham	273	Bill Rogers George Burns	Merion G. C. (East Course), Ardmore, PA

Won in playoff

DATE	WINNER	SCORE	RUNNER-UP	SITE
1982	Tom Watson	282	Jack Nicklaus	Pebble Beach G. L., Pebble Beach, CA
1983	Larry Nelson	280	Tom Watson	Oakmont C. C., Oakmont, PA
1984	*Fuzzy Zoeller	276	Greg Norman	Winged Foot G. C. (West Course), Mamaroneck, NY
1985	Andy North	279	Denis Watson / Dave Barr	Oakland Hills C. C. (South Course), Birmingham, MI
1986	Raymond Floyd	279	Lanny Wadkins / Chip Beck	Shinnecock Hills G. C., Southampton, NY
1987	Scott Simpson	277	Tom Watson	The Olympic Club (Lake Course), San Francisco, CA
1988	*Curtis Strange	278	Nick Faldo	The Country Club (Championship Course), Brookline, MA
1989	Curtis Strange	278	Ian Woosnam / Mark McCumber / Chip Beck	Oak Hill C. C. (East Course), Rochester, NY
1990	*Hale Irwin	280	Mike Donald	Medinah C. C. (No. 3 Course), Medinah, IL
1991	*Payne Stewart	282	Scott Simpson	Hazeltine National G. C., Chaska, MN
1992	Tom Kite	285	Jeff Sluman	Pebble Beach G. L., Pebble Beach, CA
1993	Lee Janzen	272	Payne Stewart	Baltusrol G. C. (Lower Course), Springfield, NJ
1994	*Ernie Els	279	Colin Montgomerie / Loren Roberts	Oakmont C. C., Oakmont, PA

The Open Championship (British Open)

Rotates annually between (at present) The Old Course at St. Andrews (Scotland), Muirfield (Scotland), Royal Troon (Scotland), Turnberry (Scotland), Royal Birkdale (England), Royal Lytham & St. Anne's (England), and Royal St. George's (England).

DATE	WINNER	SCORE	RUNNER-UP	SITE
1860	Willie Park	174	Tom Morris, Sr.	Prestwick
1861	Tom Morris, Sr.	163	Willie Park	Prestwick
1862	Tom Morris, Sr.	163	Willie Park	Prestwick
1863	Willie Park	168	Tom Morris, Sr.	Prestwick

* Won in playoff

DATE	WINNER	SCORE	RUNNER-UP	SITE
1864	Tom Morris, Sr.	160	Andrew Strath	Prestwick
1865	Andrew Strath	162	Willie Park	Prestwick
1866	Willie Park	169	David Park	Prestwick
1867	Tom Morris, Sr.	170	Willie Park	Prestwick
1868	Tom Morris, Jr.	154	Tom Morris, Sr.	Prestwick
1869	Tom Morris, Jr.	157	Tom Morris, Sr.	Prestwick
1870	Tom Morris, Jr.	149	David Strath	Prestwick
			Bob Kirk	
1871	*No Championship*			
1872	Tom Morris, Jr.	166	David Strath	Prestwick
1873	Tom Kidd	179	Jamie Anderson	St. Andrews
1874	Mungo Park	159	Unknown	Musselburgh
1875	Willie Park	166	Bob Martin	Prestwick
1876	Bob Marlin	176	David Strath	St. Andrews
1877	Jamie Anderson	160	R. Pringle	Musselburgh
1878	Jamie Anderson	157	Robert Kirk	Prestwick
1879	Jamie Anderson	169	A. Kirkaldy	St. Andrews
			J. Allan	
1880	Robert Ferguson	162	Unknown	Musselburgh
1881	Robert Ferguson	170	Jamie Anderson	Prestwick
1882	Robert Ferguson	171	Willie Fernie	St. Andrews
1883	*Willie Fernie	159	Robert Ferguson	Musselburgh
1884	Jack Simpson	160	D. Rolland	Prestwick
			Willie Fernie	
1885	Bob Martin	171	Archie Simpson	St. Andrews
1886	David Brown	157	Willie Campbell	Musselburgh
1887	Willie Park, Jr.	161	Bob Martin	Prestwick
1888	Jack Burns	171	B. Sayers	St. Andrews
			D. Anderson	
1889	*Willie Park, Jr.	155	Andrew Kirkaldy	Musselburgh
1890	John Ball	164	Willie Fernie	Prestwick
1891	Hugh Kirkaldy	166	Andrew Kirkaldy	St. Andrews
			Willie Fernie	
1892	Harold H. Hilton	305	John Ball	Muirfield
			Hugh Kirkaldy	
1893	William Auchterlonie	322	John E. Laidlay	Prestwick
1894	John H. Taylor	326	Douglas Rolland	Royal St. George's
1895	John H. Taylor	322	Alexander Herd	St. Andrews
1896	*Harry Vardon	316	John H. Taylor	Muirfield
1897	Harold H. Hilton	314	James Braid	Hoylake
1898	Harry Vardon	307	Willie Park, Jr.	Prestwick
1899	Harry Vardon	310	Jack White	Royal St. George's
1900	John H. Taylor	309	Harry Vardon	St. Andrews
1901	James Braid	309	Harry Vardon	Muirfield
1902	Alexander Herd	307	Harry Vardon	Hoylake

* Won in playoff

DATE	WINNER	SCORE	RUNNER-UP	SITE
1903	Harry Vardon	300	Tom Vardon	Prestwick
1904	Jack White	296	John H. Taylor	Royal St. George's
1905	James Braid	318	John H. Taylor	St. Andrews
			Rolland Jones	
1906	James Braid	300	John H. Taylor	Muirfield
1907	Arnaud Massy	312	John H. Taylor	Hoylake
1908	James Braid	291	Tom Ball	Prestwick
1909	John H. Taylor	295	James Braid	Deal
			Tom Ball	
1910	James Braid	299	Alexander Herd	St. Andrews
1911	Harry Vardon	303	Arnaud Massy	Royal St. George's
1912	Edward (Ted) Ray	295	Harry Vardon	Muirfield
1913	John H. Taylor	304	Edward Ray	Hoylake
1914	Harry Vardon	306	John H. Taylor	Prestwick
1915	*No Championship*			
1916	*No Championship*			
1917	*No Championship*			
1918	*No Championship*			
1919	*No Championship*			
1920	George Duncan	303	Alexander Herd	Deal
1921	*Jock Hutchison	296	Roger Wethered	St. Andrews
1922	Walter Hagen	300	George Duncan	Royal St. George's
				James M. Barnes
1923	Arthur G. Havers	295	Walter Hagen	Troon
1924	Walter Hagen	301	Ernest Whitcombe	Hoylake
1925	James M. Barnes	300	Archie Compston	Prestwick
			Ted Ray	
1926	Robert T. Jones, Jr.	291	Al Watrous	Royal Lytham
1927	Robert T. Jones, Jr.	285	Aubrey Boomer	St. Andrews
1928	Walter Hagen	292	Gene Sarazen	Royal St. George's
1929	Walter Hagen	292	Johnny Farrell	Muirfield
1930	Robert T. Jones, Jr.	291	Macdonald Smith	Hoylake
			Leo Diegel	
1931	Tommy D. Armour	296	J. Jurado	Carnoustie
1932	Gene Sarazen	283	Macdonald Smith	Prince's
1933	*Denny Shute	292	Craig Wood	St. Andrews
1934	Henry Cotton	283	S. F. Brews	Royal St. George's
1935	Alfred Perry	283	Alfred Padgham	Muirfield
1936	Alfred Padgham	287	James Adams	Hoylake
1937	Henry Cotton	290	R. A. Whitcombe	Carnoustie
1938	R. A. Whitcombe	295	James Adams	Royal St. George's
1939	Richard Burton	290	Johnny Bulla	St. Andrews
1940	*No Championship*			
1941	*No Championship*			
1942	*No Championship*			

* *Won in playoff*

DATE	WINNER	SCORE	RUNNER-UP	SITE
1943	*No Championship*			
1944	*No Championship*			
1945	*No Championship*			
1946	Sam Snead	290	Bobby Locke	St. Andrews
			Johnny Bulla	
1947	Fred Daly	293	R. W. Horne	Hoylake
			Frank Stranahan	
1948	Henry Cotton	294	Fred Daly	Muirfield
1949	*Bobby Locke	283	Harry Bradshaw	Royal St. George's
1950	Bobby Locke	279	Roberto DeVicenzo	Troon
1951	Max Faulkner	285	A. Cerda	Portrush
1952	Bobby Locke	287	Peter Thomson	Royal Lytham
1953	Ben Hogan	282	Frank Stranahan	Carnoustie
			Dai Rees	
			Peter Thomson	
			A. Cerda	
1954	Peter Thomson	283	S.S. Scott	Royal Birkdale
			Dai Rees	
			Bobby Locke	
1955	Peter Thomson	281	John Fallon	St. Andrews
1956	Peter Thomson	286	Flory Van Donck	Hoylake
1957	Bobby Locke	279	Peter Thomson	St. Andrews
1958	*Peter Thomson	278	Dave Thomas	Royal Lytham
1959	Gary Player	284	Fred Bullock	Muirfield
			Flory Van Donck	
1960	Kel Nagle	278	Arnold Palmer	St. Andrews
1961	Arnold Palmer	284	Dai Rees	Royal Birkdale
1962	Arnold Palmer	276	Kel Nagle	Troon
1963	*Bob Charles	277	Phil Rodgers	Royal Lytham
1964	Tony Lema	279	Jack Nicklaus	St. Andrews
1965	Peter Thomson	285	Brian Huggett	Southport
			Christy O'Connor	
1966	Jack Nicklaus	282	Doug Sanders	Muirfield
			Dave Thomas	
1967	Roberto DeVicenzo	278	Jack Nicklaus	Hoylake
1968	Gary Player	289	Jack Nicklaus	Carnoustie
			Bob Charles	
1969	Tony Jacklin	280	Bob Charles	Royal Lytham
1970	*Jack Nicklaus	283	Doug Sanders	St. Andrews
1971	Lee Trevino	278	Lu Liang Huan	Royal Birkdale
1972	Lee Trevino	278	Jack Nicklaus	Muirfield
1973	Tom Weiskopf	276	Johnny Miller	Troon
1974	Gary Player	282	Peter Oosterhuis	Royal Lytham
1975	*Tom Watson	279	Jack Newton	Carnoustie
1976	Johnny Miller	279	Jack Nicklaus	Royal Birkdale
*Won in playoff			Seve Ballesteros	

DATE	WINNER	SCORE	RUNNER-UP	SITE
1977	Tom Watson	268	Jack Nicklaus	Turnberry
1978	Jack Nicklaus	281	Ben Crenshaw	St. Andrews
			Tom Kite	
			Ray Floyd	
			Simon Owen	
1979	Seve Ballesteros	283	Ben Crenshaw	Royal Lytham
			Jack Nicklaus	
1980	Tom Watson	271	Lee Trevino	Muirfield
1981	Bill Rogers	276	Bernhard Langer	Royal St. George's
1982	Tom Watson	284	Nick Price	Royal Troon
			Peter Oosterhuis	
1983	Tom Watson	275	Andy Bean	Royal Birkdale
1984	Seve Ballesteros	276	Tom Watson	St. Andrews
			Bernhard Langer	
1985	Sandy Lyle	282	Payne Stewart	Royal St. George's
1986	Greg Norman	280	Gordon Brand	Turnberry
1987	Nick Faldo	279	Paul Azinger	Muirfield
			Rodger Davis	
1988	Seve Ballesteros	273	Nick Price	Royal Lytham
1989	*Mark Calcavecchia	275	Wayne Grady	Royal Troon
			Greg Norman	
1990	Nick Faldo	270	Payne Stewart	St. Andrews
			Mark McNulty	
1991	Ian Baker-Finch	272	Mike Harwood	Royal Birkdale
1992	Nick Faldo	272	John Cook	Muirfield
1993	Greg Norman	267	Nick Faldo	Royal St. George's
1994	Nick Price	268	Jesper Parnevik	Turnberry

The PGA Championship

DATE	WINNER	SCORE	RUNNER UP	SITE
1916	James M. Barnes	1 up	Jock Hutchison	Siwanoy C. C., Bronxville, NY
1917	*No Championship*			
1918	*No Championship*			
1919	James M. Barnes	6 & 5	Fred McLeod	Engineers C. C., Roslyn, NY
1920	Jock Hutchison	1 up	J. Douglas Edgar	Flossmoor C. C., Flossmoor, IL
1921	Walter Hagen	3 & 2	James M. Barnes	Inwood C. C., Far Rockaway, NY
1922	Gene Sarazen	4 & 3	Emmet French	Oakmont C. C., Oakmont, PA
1923	Gene Sarazen	1 up	Walter Hagen	Pelham C. C., Pelham, NY

DATE	WINNER	SCORE	RUNNER-UP	SITE
1924	Walter Hagen	2 up	James M. Barnes	French Lick C. C., French Lick, IN
1925	Walter Hagen	6 & 5	William Mehlhorn	Olympia Fields C. C., Olympia Fields, IL
1926	Walter Hagen	5 & 3	Leo Diegel	Salisbury G. C., Westbury, NY
1927	Walter Hagen	1 up	Joe Turnesa	Cedar Crest C. C., Dallas, TX
1928	Leo Diegel	6 & 5	Al Espinosa	Five Farms C. C., Baltimore, MD
1929	Leo Diegel	6 & 4	Johnny Farrell	Hillcrest C. C., Los Angeles, CA
1930	Tommy Armour	1 up	Gene Sarazen	Fresh Meadow C. C., Flushing, NY
1931	Tom Creavy	2 & 1	Denny Shute	Wannamoisett C. C., Rumford, RI
1932	Olin Dutra	4 & 3	Frank Walsh	Keller G. C., St. Paul, MN
1933	Gene Sarazen	5 & 4	Willie Goggin	Blue Mound C. C., Milwaukee, WI
1934	Paul Runyan	1 up	Craig Wood	Park C. C., Williamsville, NY
1935	Johnny Revolta	5 & 4	Tommy Armour	Twin Hills C. C., Oklahoma City, OK
1936	Denny Shute	3 & 2	Jimmy Thomson	Pinehurst C. C., Pinehurst, NC
1937	Denny Shute	1 up	Harold McSpaden	Pittsburg G. C., Aspinwall, PA
1938	Paul Runyan	8 & 7	Sam Snead	Shawnee C. C., Shawnee, Pa.
1939	Henry Picard	1 up	Byron Nelson	Pomonok C. C., Flushing, NY
1940	Byron Nelson	1 up	Sam Snead	Hershey C. C., Hershey, PA
1941	Vic Ghezzi	1 up	Byron Nelson	Cherry Hills C. C., Denver, CO
1942	Sam Snead	2 & 1	Jim Turnesa	Seaview C. C., Atlantic City, NJ
1943	*No Championship*			
1944	Bob Hamilton	1 up	Byron Nelson	Manito G. & C. C., Spokane, WA
1945	Byron Nelson	4 & 3	Sam Byrd	Morraine C. C., Dayton, OH
1946	Ben Hogan	6 & 4	Ed Oliver	Portland G. C., Portland, OR

DATE	WINNER	SCORE	RUNNER-UP	SITE
1947	Jim Ferrier	2 & 1	Chick Harbert	Plum Hollow C. C., Detroit, MI
1948	Ben Hogan	7 & 6	Mike Turnesa	Norwood Hills C. C., St. Louis, MO
1949	Sam Snead	3 & 2	Johnny Palmer	Hermitage C. C., Richmond, VA
1950	Chandler Harper	4 & 3	Henry Williams, Jr.	Scioto C. C., Columbus, OH
1951	Sam Snead	7 & 6	Walter Burkemo	Oakmont C. C., Oakmont, PA
1952	Jim Turnesa	1 up	Chick Harbert	Big Spring C. C., Louisville, KY
1953	Walter Burkemo	2 & 1	Felice Torza	Birmingham C. C., Birmingham, MI
1954	Chick Harbert	4 & 3	Walter Burkemo	Keller G. C., St. Paul, MN
1955	Doug Ford	4 & 3	Cary Middlecoff	Meadowbrook C. C., Detroit, MI
1956	Jack Burke, Jr.	3 & 2	Ted Kroll	Blue Hill C. C., Boston, MA
1957	Lionel Hebert	2 & 1	Dow Finsterwald	Miami Valley C. C., Dayton, OH
1958	Dow Finsterwald	276	Billy Casper	Llanerch C. C., Havertown, PA
1959	Bob Rosburg	277	Jerry Barber Doug Sanders	Minneapolis G. C., St. Paul, MN
1960	Jay Hebert	281	Jim Ferrier	Firestone C. C., Akron, OH
1961	*Jerry Barber	277	Don January	Olympia Fields C. C., Olympia Fields, IL
1962	Gary Player	278	Bob Goalby	Aronomink G. C., Newtown Square, PA
1963	Jack Nicklaus	279	Dave Ragan, Jr.	Dallas A. C., Dallas, TX
1964	Bobby Nichols	271	Jack Nicklaus Arnold Palmer	Columbus C. C., Columbus, OH
1965	Dave Marr	280	Billy Casper Jack Nicklaus	Laurel Valley C. C., Ligonier, PA
1966	Al Geiberger	280	Dudley Wysong	Firestone C. C., Akron, OH
1967	*Don January	281	Don Massengale	Columbine C. C., Littleton, CO
1968	Julius Boros	281	Bob Charles Arnold Palmer	Pecan Valley C. C., San Antonio, TX
1969	Ray Floyd	276	Gary Player	NCR C. C., Dayton, OH

*Won in playoff

DATE	WINNER	SCORE	RUNNER-UP	SITE
1970	Dave Stockton	279	Arnold Palmer Bob Murphy	Southern Hills C. C., Tulsa, OK
1971	Jack Nicklaus	281	Billy Casper	PGA National G. C., Palm Beach Gdns, FL
1972	Gary Player	281	Tommy Aaron Jim Jamieson	Oakland Hills C. C., Birmingham, MI
1973	Jack Nicklaus	277	Bruce Crampton	Canterbury G. C., Cleveland, OH
1974	Lee Trevino	276	Jack Nicklaus	Tanglewood G. C., Winston-Salem, NC
1975	Jack Nicklaus	276	Bruce Crampton	Firestone C. C., Akron, OH
1976	Dave Stockton	281	Ray Floyd Don January	Congressional C. C., Bethesda, MD
1977	*Lanny Wadkins	282	Gene Littler	Pebble Beach G. L., Pebble Beach, CA
1978	*John Mahaffey	276	Jerry Pate Tom Watson	Oakmont C. C., Oakmont, PA
1979	*David Graham	272	Ben Crenshaw	Oakland Hills C. C., Birmingham, MI
1980	Jack Nicklaus	274	Andy Bean	Oak Hill C. C., Rochester, NY
1981	Larry Nelson	273	Fuzzy Zoeller	Atlanta A. C., Duluth, GA
1982	Raymond Floyd	272	Lanny Wadkins	Southern Hills C. C., Tulsa, OK
1983	Hal Sutton	274	Jack Nicklaus	Riviera C. C., Pacific Palisades, CA
1984	Lee Trevino	273	Gary Player Lanny Wadkins	Shoal Creek C. C., Birmingham, AL
1985	Hubert Green	278	Lee Trevino	Cherry Hills C. C., Denver, CO
1986	Bob Tway	276	Greg Norman	Inverness C. C., Toledo, OH
1987	*Larry Nelson	287	Lanny Wadkins	PGA National G. C., Palm Beach Grdns, FL
1988	Jeff Sluman	272	Paul Azinger	Oak Tree G. C., Edmond, OK
1989	Payne Stewart	276	Mike Reid	Kemper Lakes G. C., Hawthorn Woods, IL
1990	Wayne Grady	282	Fred Couples	Shoal Creek C. C., Birmingham, AL
1991	John Daly	276	Bruce Lietzke	Crooked Stick G. C., Carmel, IN

*Won in playoff

DATE	WINNER	SCORE	RUNNER-UP	SITE
1992	Nick Price	278	John Cook	Bellerive C. C.,
			Jim Gallagher	St. Louis, MO
			Gene Sauers	
			Nick Faldo	
1993	*Paul Azinger	272	Greg Noman	Inverness Club,
				Toledo, OH
1994	Nick Price	269	Corey Pavin	Southern Hills C.C.,
				Tulsa, OK

Women's Major Championships

The United States Women's Open Championship

DATE	WINNER	SCORE	RUNNER UP	SITE
1946	Patty Berg	5 & 4	Betty Jameson	Spokane C. C.,
				Spokane, WA
1947	Betty Jameson	295	Sally Sessions	Starmount Forest C. C,
			Polly Riley	Greensboro, NC
1948	Babe Zaharias	300	Betty Hicks	Atlantic City C. C.,
				Northfield, NJ
1949	Louise Suggs	291	Babe Zaharias	Prince Georges G. & C. C.,
				Landover, MD
1950	Babe Zaharias	291	Betsy Rawls	Rolling Hills C. C.,
				Wichita, KS
1951	Betsy Rawls	293	Louise Suggs	Druid Hills G. C.,
				Atlanta, GA
1952	Louise Suggs	284	Marlene Bauer	Bala G. C.,
			Betty Jameson	Philadelphia, PA
1953	*Betsy Rawls	302	Jacqueline Pung	C. C. of Rochester,
				Rochester, NY
1954	Babe Zaharias	291	Betty Hicks	Salem C. C.,
				Peabody, MA
1955	Fay Crocker	299	Louise Suggs	Wichita C. C.,
			Mary Lena Faulk	Wichita, KS
1956	*Kathy Cornelius	302	Barbara McIntire	Northland C. C.,
				Duluth, MN
1957	Betsy Rawls	299	Patty Berg	Winged Foot G. C.
				(East Course),
				Mamaroneck, NY
1958	Mickey Wright	290	Louise Suggs	Forest Lake C. C.,
				Bloomfield Hills, MI
1959	Mickey Wright	287	Louise Suggs	Churchill Valley C. C.,
				Pittsburgh, PA
1960	Betsy Rawls	292	Joyce Ziske	Worcester C. C.,
				Worcester, MA

*Won in playoff

DATE	WINNER	SCORE	RUNNER-UP	SITE
1961	Mickey Wright	293	Betsy Rawls	Baltusrol G.C. (Lower Course), Springfield, NJ
1962	Murle Lindstrom	301	Ruth Jessen JoAnn Prentice	Dunes G. & B. Club, Myrtle Beach, SC
1963	Mary Mills	289	Sandra Haynie Louise Suggs	Kenwood C. C., Cincinnati, OH
1964	*Mickey Wright	290	Ruth Jessen	San Diego C. C., Chula Vista, CA
1965	Carol Mann	290	Kathy Cornelius	Atlantic City C. C., Northfield, NJ
1966	Sandra Spuzich	297	Carol Mann	Hazeltine Nat. G. C., Chaska, MN
1967	Catherine Lacoste	294	Susie Maxwell Beth Stone	Virginia Hot Springs G. & T. C. (Cascades), Hot Springs, VA
1968	Susie Maxwell Berning	289	Mickey Wright	Moselem Springs G. C., Fleetwood, PA
1969	Donna Caponi	294	Peggy Wilson	Scenic Hills C. C., Pensacola, FL
1970	Donna Caponi	287	Sandra Haynie Sandra Spuzich	Muskogee C. C, Muskogee, OK
1971	JoAnne Carner	288	Kathy Whitworth	Kahkwa Club, Erie, PA
1972	Susie Maxwell Berning	299	Kathy Ahern Pam Barnett Judy Rankin	Winged Foot G. C., (East Course), Mamaroneck, NY
1973	Susie Maxwell Berning	290	Shelly Hamlin Gloria Ehret	C. C. of Rochester, Rochester, NY
1974	Sandra Haynie	295	Beth Stone Carol Mann	La Grange C. C., La Grange, IL
1975	Sandra Palmer	295	Nancy Lopez JoAnne Carner Sandra Post	Atlantic City C. C., Northfield, NJ
1976	*JoAnne Carner	292	Sandra Palmer	Rolling Green G. C., Springfield, PA
1977	Hollis Stacy	292	Nancy Lopez	Hazeltine Nat. G. C., Chaska, MN
1978	Hollis Stacy	289	JoAnne Carner Sally Little	C. C. of Indianapolis, Indianapolis, IN
1979	Jerilyn Britz	284	Debbie Massey Sandra Palmer	Brooklawn C. C., Fairfield, CT
1980	Amy Alcott	280	Hollis Stacy	Richland C. C., Nashville, TN
1981	Pat Bradley	279	Beth Daniel	La Grange C. C., La Grange, IL

*Won in playoff

DATE	WINNER	SCORE	RUNNER-UP	SITE
1982	Janet Alex	283	Sandra Haynie Donna H. White JoAnne Carner Beth Daniel	Del Paso C.C., Sacramento, CA
1983	Jan Stephenson	290	JoAnne Carner Patty Sheehan	Cedar Ridge C. C., Tulsa, OK
1984	Hollis Stacy	290	Rosie Jones	Salem C. C., Peabody, MA
1985	Kathy Guadagnino	280	Judy Clark	Baltusrol G. C. (Upper Course), Springfield, NJ
1986	*Jane Geddes	287	Sally Little	NCR C. C., Kettering, OH
1987	*Laura Davies	285	Ayako Okamoto JoAnne Carner	Plainfield C. C., Edison, NJ
1988	Liselotte Neumann	277	Patty Sheehan	Baltimore C. C., (Five Farms East), Baltimore, MD
1989	Betsy King	278	Nancy Lopez	Indianwood G. & C. C. (Old/East Course), Lake Orion, MI
1990	Betsy King	284	Patty Sheehan	Atlanta A. C. (Riverside Course), Duluth, GA
1991	Meg Mallon	283	Pat Bradley	Colonial C. C ., Fort Worth, TX
1992	*Patty Sheehan	280	Juli Inkster	Oakmont C. C., Oakmont, PA
1993	Laurie Merten	280	Helen Alfredsson	Crooked Stick G. C., Carmel, IN
1994	Patty Sheehan	277	Tammie Green	Iandianwood G. & C. C. (Old/East Course), Lake Orion, MI

Mazda LPGA Championship

DATE	WINNER	SCORE	RUNNER-UP	SITE
1955	Beverly Hanson	220 (4 &3)	Louise Suggs	Orchard Ridge C. C., Ft. Wayne, IN
1956	Marlene Hagge	291	Patty Berg	Forest Lake C. C., Detroit, MI
1957	Louise Suggs	285	Wiffi Smith	Churchill Valley C. C., Pittsburgh, PA
1958	Mickey Wright	288	Fay Crocker	Churchill Valley C. C., Pittsburgh, PA

*Won in playoff

DATE	WINNER	SCORE	RUNNER-UP	SITE
1959	Betsy Rawls	288	Patty Berg	Sheraton Hotel C. C., French Lick, IN
1960	Mickey Wright	292	Louise Suggs	Sheraton Hotel C. C., French Lick, IN
1961	Mickey Wright	287	Louise Suggs	Stardust C. C., Las Vegas, NV
1962	Judy Kimball	282	Shirley Spork	Stardust C. C., Las Vegas, NV
1963	Mickey Wright	294	Mary Lena Faulk Mary Mills Louise Suggs	Stardust C. C., Las Vegas, NV
1964	Mary Mills	278	Mickey Wright	Stardust C. C., Las Vegas, NV
1965	Sandra Haynie	279	Clifford A. Creed	Stardust C. C., Las Vegas, NV
1966	Gloria Ehret	282	Mickey Wright	Stardust C. C., Las Vegas, NV
1967	Kathy Whitworth	284	Shirley Englehorn	Pleasant Valley C. C., Sutton, MA
1968	*Sandra Post	294	Kathy Whitworth	Pleasant Valley C. C., Sutton, MA
1969	Betsy Rawls	293	Susie Berning Carol Mann	Concord G. C., Kiamesha Lake, NY
1970	Shirley Englehorn	285	Kathy Whitworth	Pleasant Valley C. C., Sutton, MA
1971	Kathy Whitworth	288	Kathy Ahern	Pleasant Valley C. C., Sutton, MA
1972	Kathy Ahern	293	Jane Blalock	Pleasant Valley C. C., Sutton, MA
1973	Mary Mills	288	Betty Burfeindt	Pleasant Valley C. C., Sutton, MA
1974	Sandra Haynie	288	JoAnne Carner	Pleasant Valley C. C., Sutton, MA
1975	Kathy Whitworth	288	Sandra Haynie	Pine Ridge G. C., Baltimore, MD
1976	Betty Burfeindt	287	Judy Rankin	Pine Ridge G. C., Baltimore, MD
1977	Chako Higuchi	279	Pat Bradley Sandra Post Judy Rankin	Bay Tree Golf Plantation, N. Myrtle Beach, SC
1978	Nancy Lopez	275	Amy Alcott	Jack Nicklaus G. C., Kings Island, OH
1979	Donna Caponi	279	Jerilyn Britz	Jack Nicklaus G. C., Kings Island, OH
1980	Sally Little	285	Jane Blalock	Jack Nicklaus G. C., Kings Island, OH

*Won in playoff

DATE	WINNER	SCORE	RUNNER-UP	SITE
1981	Donna Caponi	280	Jerilyn Britz	Jack Nicklaus G. C., Kings Island, OH
1982	Jan Stephenson	279	JoAnne Carner	Jack Nicklaus G. C., Kings Island, OH
1983	Patty Sheehan	279	Sandra Haynie	Jack Nicklaus G. C., Kings Island, OH
1984	Patty Sheehan	272	Beth Daniel Pat Bradley	Jack Nicklaus G. C., Kings Island, OH
1985	Nancy Lopez	273	Alice Miller	Jack Nicklaus G. C., Kings Island, Oh
1986	Pat Bradley	277	Patty Sheehan	Jack Nicklaus G. C., Kings Island, OH
1987	Jane Geddes	275	Betsy King	Jack Nicklaus G. C., Kings Island, OH
1988	Sherri Turner	281	Amy Alcott	Jack Nicklaus G. C., Kings Island, OH
1989	Nancy Lopez	274	Ayako Okamoto	Bethesda C. C., Bethesda, MD
1990	Beth Daniel	280	Rosie Jones	Bethesda C. C., Bethesda, MD
1991	Meg Mallon	274	Pat Bradley Ayako Okamoto	Bethesda C. C., Bethesda, MD
1992	Betsy King	267	JoAnne Carner Karen Noble Liselotte Neumann	Bethesda C. C., Bethesda, MD
1993	Patty Sheehan	275	Lauri e Merten	Bethesda C. C., Bethesda, MD
1994	Laura Davies	279	Alice Ritzman	DuPont C. C., Wilmington, DE

NABISCO Dinah Shore

Mission Hills Country Club, Rancho Mirage, CA
Previously known as the Colgate Dinah Shore (1972-1981)
(Designated Major Commencing 1983.)

DATE	WINNER	SCORE	RUNNER-UP
1972	Jane Blalock	213	Carol Mann Judy Rankin
1973	Mickey Wright	284	Joyce Kazmierski
1974	*Jo Ann Prentice	289	Jane Blalock Sandra Haynie
1975	Sandra Palmer	283	Kathy McMullen
1976	Judy Rankin	285	Betty Burfeindt

Won in playoff

DATE	WINNER	SCORE	RUNNER-UP
1977	Kathy Whitworth	289	JoAnne Carner
			Sally Little
1978	*Sandra Post	283	Penny Pulz
1979	Sandra Post	276	Nancy Lopez
1980	Donna Caponi	275	Amy Alcott
1981	Nancy Lopez	277	Carolyn Hill
1982	Sally Little	278	Hollis Stacy
			Sandra Haynie
1983	Amy Alcott	282	Beth Daniel
			Kathy Whitworth
1984	*Juli Inkster	280	Pat Bradley
1985	Alice Miller	275	Jan Stephenson
1986	Pat Bradley	280	Val Skinner
1987	*Betsy King	283	Patty Sheehan
1988	Amy Alcott	274	Colleen Walker
1989	Juli Inkster	279	Tammie Green
	JoAnne Carner		
1990	Betsy King	283	Kathy Postlewait
			Shirley Furlong
1991	Amy Alcott	273	Dottie Mochrie
1992	*Dottie Mochrie	279	Juli Inkster
1993	Helen Alfredsson	284	Amy Benz
			Tina Barrett
1994	Donna Andrews	276	Laura Davies

Du Maurier Ltd. Classic

(Previously known as La Canadienne (1973), and the Peter Jackson Classic
(1974-1982). Designated Major commencing 19 79.)

DATE	WINNER	SCORE	RUNNER-UP	SITE
1973	*Jocelyne Bourassa	214	Sandra Haynie	Montreal G. C.,
			Judy Rankin	Montreal
1974	Carole Jo Callison	208	Jo Anne Carner	Candiac G. C.,
				Montreal
1975	*JoAnne Carner	214	Carol Mann	St. George's C. C.,
				Toronto
1976	*Donna Caponi	212	Judy Rankin	Cedar Brae G. & C. C.,
				Toronto
1977	Judy Rankin	214	Pat Meyers	Lachute G. & C. C.,
			Sandra Palmer	Montreal
1978	JoAnne Carner	278	Hollis Stacy	St. George's C. C.,
				Toronto
1979	Amy Alcott	285	Nancy Lopez	Richelieu Valley C. C.,
				Montreal

*Won in playoff

DATE	WINNER	SCORE	RUNNER-UP	SITE
1980	Pat Bradley	277	JoAnne Carner	St. George's C. C., Toronto, Ontario
1981	Jan Stephenson	278	Nancy Lopez	Summerlea C. C., Dorion, Quebec
1982	Sandra Haynie	280	Beth Daniel	St. George's C. C., Toronto, Ontario
1983	Hollis Stacy	277	JoAnne Carner Alice Miller	Beaconsfield G. C., Montreal, Quebec
1984	Juli Inkster	279	Ayako Okamoto	St. George's G. & C. C., Toronto, Ontario
1985	Pat Bradley	278	Jane Geddes	Beaconsfield C. C., Montreal, Quebec
1986	*Pat Bradley	276	Ayako Okamoto	Board of Trade C. C., Toronto, Ontario
1987	Jody Rosenthal	272	Ayako Okamoto	Islemere G. C., Laval, Quebec
1988	Sally Little	279	Laura Davies	Vancouver G. C., Coquitlam, B.C.
1989	Tammie Green	279	Pat Bradley Betsy King	Beaconsfield G. C., Montreal, Quebec
1990	Cathy Johnston	276	Patty Sheehan	Westmount G. & C. C., Kitchener, Ontario
1991	Nancy Scranton	279	Debbie Massey	Vancouver G. C., Coquitlam, B. C.,
1992	Sherri Steinhauer	277	Judy Dickinson	St. Charles C. C., Winnipeg, Manitoba
1993	*Brandie Burton	277	Betsy King	London Hunt and C. C., London, Ontario
1994	Martha Nause	279	Michelle McGann	Ottawa Hunt & G. C., Ottawa, Ontario

Senior Men's Major Championships

The United States Senior Open

DATE	WINNER	SCORE	RUNNER-UP	SITE
1980	Roberto De Vicenzo	285	William C. Campbell	Winged Foot G. C. (East Course), Mamaroneck, NY
1981	*Arnold Palmer	289	Bob Stone Billy Casper	Oaklånd Hills C. C. (South Course), Birmingham, MI
1982	Miller Barber	282	Gene Littler Dan Sikes	Portland G. C., Portland, OR
1983	*Billy Casper	288	Rod Funseth	Hazeltine National G. C., Chaska, MN

*Won in playoff

DATE	WINNER	SCORE	RUNNER-UP	SITE
1984	Miller Barber	286	Arnold Palmer	Oak Hills C. C. (East Course), Rochester, NY
1985	Miller Barber	285	Roberto DeVicenzo	Edgewood Tahoe G. C., Stateline, NV
1986	Dale Douglass	279	Gary Player	Scioto C. C., Columbus, OH
1987	Gary Player	270	Doug Sanders	Brooklawn C. C., Fairfield, CT
1988	*Gary Player	288	Bob Charles	Medinah C. C. (No. 3 Course), Medinah, IL
1989	Orville Moody	279	Frank Beard	Laurel Valley G. C., Ligonier, PA
1990	Lee Trevino	275	Jack Nicklaus	Ridgewood C. C. (Center and West nines), Paramus, NJ
1991	*Jack Nicklaus	282	Chi Chi Rodriguez	Oakland Hills C. C. (South Course), Birmingham, MI
1992	Larry Laoretti	275	Jim Colbert	Saucon Valley C. C. (Old Course), Bethlehem, PA
1993	Jack Nicklaus	278	Tom Weiskopf	Cherry Hills C. C., Englewood, CO
1994	Simon Hobday	274	Graham Marsh	Pinehurst C. C., Pinehurst, NC

PGA Seniors' Championship

(Played at Augusta National G.C., 1937-38; North Shore C. C. & Bobby Jones G. C., 1940; Sarasota Bay C. C. & Bobby Jones G. C., 1941; Ft. Myers G. & C. C., 1942; PGA National, 1945-62 [Dunedin], 1964, 1966-1973 [JDM CC], 1982-present [Champions Course]; Port St. Lucie C. C., 1963, 1974; Ft. Lauderdale C. C., 1965; Walt Disney World [Magnolia], 1975-79; Turnberry Isle C. C. [South Course], 1979-1981.)

DATE	WINNER	SCORE	RUNNER-UP
1937	Jock Hutchinson	223	George Gordon
1938	*Fred McLeod	154	Otto Hackbarth
1939	*No Championship*		
1940	*Otto Hackbarth	146	Jock Hutchinson
1941	Jack Burke, Sr.	142	Eddie Williams

* *Won in playoff*

DATE	WINNER	SCORE	RUNNER-UP
1942	Eddie Williams	138	Jock Hutchinson
1943	*No Championship*		
1944	*No Championship*		
1945	Eddie Williams	148	Jock Hutchinson
1946	*Eddie Williams	146	Jock Hutchinson
1947	Jock Hutchinson	145	Ben Richter
1948	Charles McKenna	141	Ben Richter
1949	Marshall Crichton	145	Louis Chiapetta
			Jock Hutchinson
			George Smith
1950	Al Watrous	142	Bill Jeliffe
1951	*Al Watrous	142	Jock Hutchinson
1952	Ernie Newnham	146	Al Watrous
1953	Harry Schwab	142	Charles McKenna
			Gene Sarazen
1954	Gene Sarazen	214	Perry Del Vecchio
			Al Watrous
1955	Mortie Dutra	213	Mike Murra
			Gene Sarazen
			Denny Shute
1956	Pete Burke	215	Ock Willoweit
1957	*Al Watrous	210	Bob Stupple
1958	Gene Sarazen	288	Charles Sheppard
1959	Willie Goggin	284	Leland Gibson
			Paul Runyan
			Denny Shute
1960	Dick Metz	284	Tony Longo
			Paul Runyan
1961	Paul Runyan	278	Jimmy Demaret
1962	Paul Runyan	278	Errie Ball
			Dutch Harrison
			Joe Brown
1963	Herman Barron	272	John Barnum
1964	Sam Snead	279	John Barnum
1965	Sam Snead	278	Joe Lopez , Sr.
1966	Freddie Haas	286	John Barnum
			Dutch Harrison

* *Won in playoff*

DATE	WINNER	SCORE	RUNNER-UP
1967	Sam Snead	279	Bob Hamilton
1968	Chandler Harper	279	Sam Snead
1969	Tommy Bolt	278	Pete Fleming
1970	Sam Snead	290	Freddie Haas
1971	Julius Boros	285	Tommy Bolt
1972	Sam Snead	286	Tommy Bolt
			Julius Boros
1973	Sam Snead	268	Julius Boros
1974	Roberto DeVicenzo	273	Julius Boros
			Art Wall
1975	*Charlie Sifford	280	Fred Wampler
1976	Pete Cooper	283	Fred Wampler
1977	Julius Boros	283	Freddie Haas
1978	*Joe Jimenez	286	Joe Cheves
			Manuel de la Torre
1979	*Jack Fleck	289	Bob Erickson
			Bill Johnson
1979	Don January	270	George Bayer
1980	*Arnold Palmer	289	Paul Harney
1981	Miller Barber	281	Arnold Palmer
1982	Don January	288	Julius Boros
1983	*No Championship*		
1984	Arnold Palmer	282	Don January
1984	Peter Thomson	286	Don January
1985	*No Championship*		
1986	Gary Player	281	Lee Elder
1987	Chi Chi Rodriguez	282	Dale Douglass
1988	Gary Player	284	Chi Chi Rodriguez
1989	Larry Mowry	281	Miller Barber
			Al Geiberger
1990	Gary Player	281	Chi Chi Rodriguez
1991	Jack Nicklaus	271	Bruce Crampton
1992	Lee Trevino	278	Mike Hill
1993	*Tom Wargo	275	Bruce Crampton
1994	Lee Trevino	279	Jim Colbert

The Tradition

(Played at Desert Mountain G. C.—Cochise Course.)

DATE	WINNER	SCORE
1989	Don Bies	275
1990	Jack Nicklaus	206
1991	Jack Nicklaus	277
1992	Lee Trevino	274
1993	Tom Shaw	269
1994	*Raymond Floyd	271

* *Won in playoff*

FORD Senior Players Championship

(Previously known as the Senior Tour Players Championship, 1983-86; and the Mazda Senior Tournament Players Championship. Played at: Canterbury G.C., Cleveland, Ohio, 1983-1986; Sawgrass C.C., Ponte Vedra, Fla., 1986; Players Club at Sawgrass (Valley), Ponte Vedra, Fla., 1988-89; and Dearborn C.C., Dearborn, MI 1990-present.)

DATE	WINNER	SCORE
1983	Miller Barber	278
1984	Arnold Palmer	276
1985	Arnold Palmer	274
1986	Chi Chi Rodriguez	206
1987	Gary Player	280
1988	Billy Casper	278
1989	Orville Moody	271
1990	Jack Nicklaus	261
1991	Jim Albus	279
1992	Dave Stockton	277
1993	Jim Colbert	278
1994	Dave Stockton	271

TEAM EVENTS—
PROFESSIONAL
INTERNATIONALS

OVERVIEW: *Prominent international team events involving touring professionals.*

THE RYDER CUP

USA vs. Great Britain through 1971. USA vs. Great Britain & Ireland through 1977. USA vs. Europe since 1979. 12-man teams in a three-day format with foursome, best ball, and singles play.

YEAR	WINNER	SCORE	SITE
1927	USA	9.5-2.5	Worcester C. C., USA
1929	Great Britain	7-5	Moortown G. C., England
1931	USA	9-3	Scioto C. C., USA
1933	Great Britain	6.5-5.5	Southport & Ainsdale G. C., England
1935	USA	9-3	Ridgewood C. C., USA
1937	USA	8-4	Southport & Ainsdale G. C., England
1947	USA	11-1	Portland G. C., USA
1949	USA	7-5	Ganton G. C., England
1951	USA	9.5-2.5	Pinehurst C. C., USA
1953	USA	6.5-5.5	Wentworth G. C., England
1955	USA	8-4	Thunderbird G. & C. C., USA
1957	Great Britain	7.5-4.5	Lindrick G. C., England
1959	USA	8.5-3.5	Eldorado C. C., USA
1961	USA	14.5-9.5	Royal Lytham & St. Annes, England
1963	USA	23-9	East Lake C. C., USA
1965	USA	19.5-12.5	Royal Birkdale G. C., England
1967	USA	23.5-8.5	Champions G. C., USA
1969	Tie	16-16	Royal Birkdale G. C., England
1971	USA	18.5-13.5	Old Warson C. C., USA
1973	USA	19-13	Muirfield, Scotland
1975	USA	21-11	Laurel Valley G. C., USA
1977	USA	12.5-7.5	Royal Lythan & St. Anne's, England
1979	USA	17-11	The Greenbrier, USA
1981	USA	18.5-9.5	Walton Heath G. C., England
1983	USA	14.5-13.5	PGA National G. C., USA
1985	Europe	16.5-11.5	The Belfry, England
1987	Europe	15-13	Muirfield Village G. C., USA
1989	Tie	14-14	The Belfry, England
1991	USA	14.5-13.5	The Ocean Course, USA
1993	USA	15-13	The Belfry, England

THE SOLHEIM CUP

USA vs. Europe. 10-woman teams in a three-day
format with foursome, best ball, and singles play.

YEAR	WINNER	SCORE	LOSER	SITE
1990	USA	284	Europe	Lake Nona G. C., Orlando, Florida, USA
1992	Europe	282	USA	Dalmahoy G. & C. C., Edinburgh, Scotland
1994	USA	13-7	Europe	The Greenbrier G. C., White Sulphur Springs, West Virginia, USA

THE WORLD CUP

Two-man national teams competing in a combined stroke-play championship.
Known as the Canada Cup until 1966.

—TEAM TROPHY—

YEAR	WINNER	TEAM MEMBERS	SITE
1953	Argentina	Roberto de Vicenzo/Antonio Cerda	Montreal
1954	Australia	Peter Thompson/Kel Nagle	Canada
1955	United States	Ed Furgol/Chick Harbert	Washington, DC
1956	United States	Ben Hogan/Sam Snead	Wentworth (UK)
1957	Japan	Torakichi Nakamura/Koichi Ono	Tokyo
1958	Ireland	Harry Bradshaw/Christy O'Connor	Mexico City
1959	Australia	Peter Thompson/Kel Nagle	Melbourne
1960	United States	Sam Snead/Arnold Palmer	Dublin
1961	United States	Sam Snead/Jimmy Demaret	Dorado (Puerto Rico)
1962	United States	Sam Snead/Arnold Palmer	Buenos Aires
1963	United States	Jack Nicklaus/Arnold Palmer	Paris
1964	United States	Jack Nicklaus/Arnold Palmer	Maui
1965	South Africa	Gary Player/Harold Henning	Madrid
1966	United States	Jack Nicklaus/Arnold Palmer	Tokyo
1967	United States	Jack Nicklaus/Arnold Palmer	Mexico City
1968	Canada	Al Balding/George Knudson	Rome
1969	United States	Lee Trevino/Orville Moody	Singapore
1970	Australia	David Graham/Bruce Devlin	Buenos Aires
1971	United States	Jack Nicklaus/Lee Trevino	Palm Beach (USA)
1972	Rep. of China	Hsieh Min-Nan/Lu Liang-Huan	Melbourne
1973	United States	Johnny Miller/Jack Nicklaus	Marbella, Spain
1974	South Africa	Bobby Cole/Dale Hayes	Caracas
1975	United States	Johnny Miller/Lou Graham	Bangkok
1976	Spain	Manuel Pinero/Seve Ballesteros	Palm Springs
1977	Spain	Antonio Garrido/Seve Ballesteros	Manila
1978	United States	John Mahaffey/Andy North	Kauai
1979	United States	John Mahaffey/Hale Irwin	Athens
1980	Canada	Dan Halldorson/Jim Nelford	Bogota
1981	No Tournament		

YEAR	WINNER	TEAM MEMBERS	SITE
1982	Spain	Manuel Pinero/Jose Canizares	Acapulco
1983	United States	Rex Caldwell/John Cook	Jakarta
1984	Spain	Jose Canizares/Jose Rivero	Rome
1985	Canada	Dave Barr/Dan Halldorson	La Quinta, USA
1986	No Tournament		
1987	Wales	Ian Woosnam/David Llewellyn	Maui
1988	United States	Ben Crenshaw/Mark McCumber	Melbourne
1989	Australia	Peter Fowler/Wayne Grady	Marbella, Spain
1990	Germany	Bernhard Langer/Torsten Giedeon	Orlando
1991	Sweden	Per-Ulrik Johansson/Anders Forsbrand	Rome
1992	United States	Fred Couples/Davis Love III	Madrid
1993	United States	Fred Couples/Davis Love III	Orlando

—INTERNATIONAL (INDIVIDUAL TITLE) TROPHY—

YEAR	WINNER	COUNTRY
1953	Antonio Cerda	Argentina
1954	Stan Leonard	Canada
1955	Ed Furgol	United States
1956	Ben Hogan	United States
1957	Torakichi Nakamura	Japan
1958	Angel Miguel	Spain
1959	Stan Leonard	Canada
1960	Flory Van Donck	Belgium
1961	Sam Snead	United States
1962	Roberto de Vicenzo	Argentina
1963	Jack Nicklaus	United States
1964	Jack Nicklaus	United States
1965	Gary Player	South Africa
1966	George Knudson	Canada
1967	Arnold Palmer	United States
1968	Al Balding	Canada
1969	Lee Trevino	United States
1970	Roberto de Vicenzo	Argentina
1971	Jack Nicklaus	United States
1972	Hsieh Min-Nan	Rep. of China
1973	Johnny Miller	United States
1974	Bobby Cole	South Africa
1975	Johnny Miller	United States
1976	Emesto Acosta	Mexico
1977	Gary Player	South Africa
1978	John Mahaffey	United States
1979	Hale Irwin	United States
1980	Sandy Lyle	Scotland

YEAR	WINNER	COUNTRY
1981	No Tournament	
1982	Manuel Pinero	Spain
1983	Dave Barr	Canada
1984	Jose Canizares	Spain
1985	Howard Clark	England
1986	No Tournament	
1987	Ian Woosnam	Wales
1988	Ben Crenshaw	United States
1989	Peter Fowler	Australia
1990	Payne Stewart	United States
1991	Ian Woosnam	Wales
1992	Brett Ogle	Australia
1993	Bernhard Langer	Germany

THE ALFRED DUNHILL CUP

The Old Course at St. Andrews, Scotland

Three-man national teams competing in round-robin matches.

YEAR	WINNER	RUNNER-UP
1985	Australia	USA
1986	Australia	Japan
1987	England	Scotland
1988	Ireland	Australia
1989	USA	Japan
1990	Ireland	England
1991	Sweden	South Africa
1992	England	Scotland
1993	USA	England
1994	Canada	USA

THE PRESIDENT'S CUP

USA vs. an International team from Asia, Africa, and Australasia.
12-man teams in a three-day format with foursome, best ball, and singles play.

YEAR	WINNER	SCORE	RUNNER-UP	SITE
1994	USA	20-12	International	Robert Trent Jones G. C., Manssas, Virginia, USA

TOUR WINNERS
OF THE PAST

OVERVIEW: *Past winners, locations, and winning scores of all current PGA TOUR , LPGA Tour, and Senior PGA TOUR events. Winners of major championships are not included. Playoff winners are marked with an asterisk.*

PGA TOUR

INFINITI TOURNAMENT OF CHAMPIONS
LaCosta C.C.,
Carlsbad, CA (1969-present).

TOURNAMENT OF CHAMPIONS

1953	Al Besselink	280
1954	Art Wall	278
1955	Gene Littler	280
1956	Gene Littler	281
1957	Gene Littler	285
1958	Stan Leonard	275
1959	Mike Souchak	281
1960	Jerry Barber	268
1961	Sam Snead	273
1962	Arnold Palmer	276
1963	Jack Nicklaus	273
1964	Jack Nicklaus	279
1965	Arnold Palmer	277
1966	*Arnold Palmer	283
1967	Frank Beard	278
1968	Don January	276
1969	Gary Player	284
1970	Frank Beard	273
1971	Jack Nicklaus	279
1972	*Bobby Mitchell	280
1973	Jack Nicklaus	276
1974	Johnny Miller	280

MONY TOURNAMENT OF CHAMPIONS

1975	*Al Geiberger	277
1976	Don January	277
1977	*Jack Nicklaus	281
1978	Gary Player	281
1979	Tom Watson	275
1980	Tom Watson	276
1981	Lee Trevino	273
1982	Lanny Wadkins	280
1983	Lanny Wadkins	280
1984	Tom Watson	274
1985	Tom Kite	275
1986	Calvin Peete	267
1987	Mac O'Grady	278
1988	Steve Pate	202
1989	Steve Jones	279

INFINITI TOURNAMENT OF CHAMPIONS

1990	Paul Azinger	272
1991	Tom Kite	272
1992	*Steve Elkington	279
1993	Davis Love III	272
1994	Phil Mickelson	276

UNITED AIRLINES HAWAIIAN OPEN
Waialae C.C.,
Honolulu, HI (1965-present).

HAWAIIAN OPEN

1965	*Gay Brewer	281
1966	Ted Makalena	271
1967	*Dudley Wysong	284
1968	Lee Trevino	272
1969	Bruce Crampton	274
1970	No Tournament	
1971	Tom Shaw	273
1972	*Grier Jones	274
1973	John Schlee	273
1974	Jack Nicklaus	271
1975	Gary Groh	274
1976	Ben Crenshaw	270
1977	Bruce Lietzke	273
1978	*Hubert Green	274

United Airlines Hawaiian Open continued

1979	Hubert Green	267
1980	Andy Bean	266
1981	Hale Irwin	265
1982	Wayne Levi	277
1983	Isao Aoki	268
1984	*Jack Renner	271
1985	Mark O'Meara	267
1986	Corey Pavin	272
1987	*Corey Pavin	270
1988	Lanny Wadkins	271
1989	Gene Sauers	197
1990	David Ishii	279

UNITED HAWAIIAN OPEN

1991	Lanny Wadkins	270

UNITED AIRLINES HAWAIIAN OPEN

1992	John Cook	265
1993	Howard Twitty	269
1994	Brett Ogle	269

NORTHERN TELECOM OPEN

TPC at StarPass,
Tucson, AZ (1987-present).

TUCSON OPEN

1945	Ray Mangrum	268
1946	Jimmy Demaret	268
1947	Jimmy Demaret	264
1948	Skip Alexander	264
1949	Lloyd Mangrum	263
1950	Chandler Harper	267
1951	Lloyd Mangrum	269
1952	Henry Williams	274
1953	Tommy Bolt	265
1954	No Tournament	
1955	Tommy Bolt	265
1956	Ted Kroll	264
1957	Dow Finsterwald	269
1958	Lionel Hebert	265
1959	Gene Littler	266
1960	Don January	271

HOME OF THE SUN INVITATIONAL

1961	*Dave Hill	269

TUCSON OPEN

1962	Phil Rodgers	263
1963	Don January	266
1964	Jack Cupit	274
1965	Bob Charles	271

1966	*Joe Campbell	278
1967	Arnold Palmer	273
1968	George Knudson	273
1969	Lee Trevino	271
1970	*Lee Trevino	275
1971	J.C. Snead	273
1972	Miller Barber	273

DEAN MARTIN TUCSON OPEN

1973	Bruce Crampton	277
1974	Johnny Miller	272
1975	Johnny Miller	263

NBC TUCSON OPEN

1976	Johnny Miller	274

JOE GARAGIOLA TUCSON OPEN

1977	*Bruce Lietzke	275
1978	Tom Watson	276
1979	Bruce Lietzke	265
1980	Jim Colbert	270
1981	Johnny Miller	265
1982	Craig Stadler	266
1983	*Gil Morgan	271

SEIKO-TUCSON MATCH PLAY CHAMPIONSHIPS

1984	Tom Watson	2&1
1985	Jim Thorpe	4&3
1986	Jim Thorpe	67

SEIKO-TUCSON OPEN

1987	Mike Reid	268

NORTHERN TELECOM TUCSON OPEN

1988	David Frost	266
1989	No tournament	
1990	Robert Gamez	270

NORTHERN TELECOM OPEN

1991	Phi Mickelson	272
1992	Lee Janzen	270
1993	Larry Mize	271
1994	Andrew Magee	270

PHOENIX OPEN

TPC of Scottsdale,
Scottsdale, AZ (1987-present).

1935	Ky Laffoon	281
1936	No Tournament	
1937	No Tournament	
1938	No Tournament	
1939	Byron Nelson	198
1940	Ed Oliver	205

Phoenix Open continued

Year	Winner	Score
1941	No Tournament	
1942	No Tournament	
1943	No Tournament	
1944	*Harold McSpaden	273
1945	Byron Nelson	274
1946	*Ben Hogan	273
1947	Ben Hogan	270
1948	Bobby Locke	268
1949	*Jimmy Demaret	278
1950	Jimmy Demaret	269
1951	Lew Worsham	272
1952	Lloyd Mangrum	274
1953	Lloyd Mangrum	272
1954	*Ed Furgol	272
1955	Gene Littler	275
1956	Cary Middlecoff	276
1957	Billy Casper	271
1958	Ken Venturi	274
1959	Gene Littler	268
1960	*Jack Fleck	273
1961	*Arnold Palmer	270
1962	Arnold Palmer	269
1963	Arnold Palmer	273
1964	Jack Nicklaus	271
1965	Rod Funseth	274
1966	Dudley Wysong	278
1967	Julius Boros	272
1968	George Knudson	272
1969	Gene Littler	263
1970	Dale Douglass	271
1971	Miller Barber	261
1972	Homero Blancas	273
1973	Bruce Crampton	268
1974	Johnny Miller	271
1975	Johnny Miller	260
1976	Bob Gilder	268
1977	*Jerry Pate	277
1978	Miller Barber	272
1979	Ben Crenshaw	199
1980	Jeff Mitchell	272
1981	David Graham	268
1982	Lanny Wadkins	263
1983	*Bob Gilder	271
1984	Tom Purtzer	268
1985	Calvin Peete	270
1986	Hal Sutton	267
1987	Paul Azinger	268

Year	Winner	Score
1988	*Sandy Lyle	269
1989	Mark Calcavecchia	263
1990	Tommy Armour III	267
1991	Nolan Henke	268
1992	Mark Calcavecchia	264
1993	Lee Janzen	273
1994	Bill Glasson	268

AT&T PEBBLE BEACH NATIONAL PRO-AM

Pebble Beach G.L., Monterey Peninsula, CA (1947-present); Spyglass Hill G.C., Monterey Peninsula, CA (1967-present); Poppy Hills G.C., Monterey Peninsula (1991-present).

BING CROSBY PROFESSIONAL-AMATEUR

Year	Winner	Score
1937	Sam Snead	68
1938	Sam Snead	139
1939	Dutch Harrison	138
1940	Ed Oliver	135
1941	Sam Snead	136
1942	Lloyd Mangrum	
	Leland Gibson	133
1943	No Tournament	
1944	No Tournament	
1945	No Tournament	
1946	No Tournament	
1947	Ed Furgol	
	George Fazio	213
1948	Lloyd Mangrum	205
1949	Ben Hogan	208
1950	Sam Snead	
	Jack Burke, Jr	
	Smiley Quick	
	Dave Douglas	214
1951	Byron Nelson	209
1952	Jimmy Demaret	145

BING CROSBY PROFESSIONAL-AMATEUR INVITATIONAL

Year	Winner	Score
1953	Lloyd Mangrum	204
1954	Dutch Harrison	210
1955	Cary Middlecoff	209

BING CROSBY PROFESSIONAL-AMATEUR GOLF CHAMPEIONSHIP

Year	Winner	Score
1956	Cary Middlecoff	202
1957	Jay Hebert	213
1958	Billy Casper	277

AT&T National Pro-Am continued

1959	Art Wall	279
1960	Ken Venturi	286
1961	Bob Rosburg	282
1962	*Doug Ford	286
1963	Billy Casper	285

BING CROSBY NATIONAL PROFESSIONAL-AMATEUR

1964	Tony Lema	284
1965	Bruce Crampton	284
1966	Don Massengale	283
1967	Jack Nicklaus	284
1968	*Johnny Pott	285
1969	George Archer	283
1970	Bert Yancey	278
1971	Tom Shaw	278
1972	*Jack Nicklaus	284
1973	*Jack Nicklaus	282
1974	Johnny Miller	208
1975	Gene Littler	280
1976	Ben Crenshaw	281
1977	Tom Watson	273
1978	*Tom Watson	280
1979	Lon Hinkle	284
1980	George Burns	280
1981	*John Cook	209
1982	Jim Simons	274
1983	Tom Kite	276
1984	*Hale Irwin	278
1985	Mark O'Meara	283

AT&T PEBBLE BEACH NATIONAL PRO-AM

1986	Fuzzy Zoeiler	205
1987	Johnny Miller	278
1988	*Steve Jones	280
1989	Mark O'Meara	277
1990	Mark O'Meara	281
1991	Paul Azinger	274
1992	*Mark O'Meara	275
1993	Brett Ogle	276
1994	Johnny Miller	281

BOB HOPE CHRYSLER CLASSIC

Played at:
Bermuda Dunes C.C., Palm Springs, CA (1960-present). Indian Wells C.C., Indian Wells, CA, (1960-present).Tamarisk C.C. Palm Springs, CA, (1960-present). La Quinta C.C., La Quinta, CA (1964-present). PGA West/Palmer Course, La Quinta, CA (1989-present).

PALM SPRINGS GOLF CLASSIC

1960	Arnold Palmer	338
1961	Billy Maxwell	345
1962	Arnold Palmer	342
1963	*Jack Nicklaus	345
1964	*Tommy Jacobs	348

BOB HOPE DESERT CLASSIC

1965	Billy Casper	348
1966	*Doug Sanders	349
1967	Tom Nieporte	349
1968	*Arnold Palmer	348
1969	Billy Casper	345
1970	Bruce Devlin	339
1971	Arnold Palmer	342
1972	Bob Rosburg	344
1973	Arnold Palmer	343
1974	Hubert Green	341
1975	Johnny Miller	339
1976	Johnny Miller	344
1977	Rik Massengale	337
1978	Bill Rogers	339
1979	John Mahaffey	343
1980	Craig Stadler	343
1981	Bruce Lietzke	335
1982	*Ed Fiori	335
1983	*Keith Fergus	335

BOB HOPE CLASSIC

1984	*John Mahaffey	340
1985	*Lanny Wadkins	333

BOB HOPE CHRYSLER CLASSIC

1986	*Donnie Hammond	335
1987	Corey Pavin	341
1988	Jay Haas	338
1989	*Steve Jones	343
1990	Peter Jacobsen	339
1991	*Corey Pavin	331
1992	*John Cook	336
1993	Tom Kite	325
1994	Scott Hoch	334

BUICK INVITATIONAL OF CALIFORNIA

Torrey Pines G.C.,
San Diego, CA (1968-present).

Buick Invitational of California continued

SAN DIEGO OPEN

1952	Ted Kroll	276
1953	Tommy Bolt	274
1954	Gene Littler	274

CONVAIR-SAN DIEGO OPEN

1955	Tommy Bolt	274
1956	Bob Rosburg	270

SAN DIEGO OPEN INVITATIONAL

1957	Arnold Palmer	271
1958	No Tournament	
1959	Marty Furgol	274
1960	Mike Souchak	269
1961	*Arnold Palmer	271
1962	*Tommy Jacobs	277
1963	Gary Player	270
1964	Art Wall	274
1965	*Wes Ellis	267
1966	Billy Casper	268
1967	Bob Goalby	269

ANDY WILLIAMS-SAN DIEGO OPEN INVITATIONAL

1968	Tom Weiskopf	273
1969	Jack Nicklaus	284
1970	*Pete Brown	275
1971	George Archer	272
1972	Paul Harney	275
1973	Bob Dickson	278
1974	Bobby Nichols	275
1975	*J. C. Snead	279
1976	J. C. Snead	272
1977	Tom Watson	269
1978	Jay Haas	278
1979	Fuzzy Zoeller	282
1980	*Tom Watson	275

WICKE ANDY WILLIAMS SAN DIEGO OPEN

1981	*Bruce Lietzke	278
1982	Johnny Miller	270

ISUZU/ANDY WILLIAMS SAN DIEGO OPEN

1983	Gary Hallberg	271
1984	*Gary Koch	272
1985	*Woody Blackburn	269

SHEARSON LEHMAN BROTHERS ANDY WILLIAMS OPEN

1986	*Bob Tway	204
1987	George Burns	266

SHEARSON LEHMAN HUTTON ANDY WILLIAMS OPEN

1988	Steve Pate	269

SHEARSON LEHMAN HUTTON OPEN

1989	Greg Twiggs	271
1990	Dan Forsman	275

SHEARSON LEHMAN BROTHERS OPEN

1991	Jay Don Blake	268

BUICK INVITATIONAL OF CALIFORNIA

1992	Steve Pate	200
1993	Phil Mickelson	278
1994	Craig Stadler	268

NISSAN LOS ANGELES OPEN

Riviera C.C.,
Pacific Palisades, CA (1973-present).

LOS ANGELES OPEN

1926	Harry Cooper	279
1927	Bobby Cruikshank	282
1928	Mac Smith	284
1929	Mac Smith	285
1930	Densmore Shute	296
1931	Ed Dudley	285
1932	Mac Smith	281
1933	Craig Wood	281
1934	Mac Smith	280
1935	*Vic Ghezzi	285
1936	Jimmy Hines	280
1937	Harry Cooper	274
1938	Jimmy Thomson	273
1939	Jimmy Demaret	274
1940	Lawson Little	282
1941	Johnny Bulla	281
1942	*Ben Hogan	282
1943	No Tournament	
1944	Harold McSpaden	278
1945	Sam Snead	283
1946	Byron Nelson	284
1947	Ben Hogan	280
1948	Ben Hogan	275
1949	Lloyd Mangrum	284
1950	*Sam Snead	280
1951	Lloyd Mangrum	280
1952	Tommy Bolt	289

Nissan Los Angeles Open continued

1953	Lloyd Mangrum	280
1954	Fred Wampler	281
1955	Gene Littler	276
1956	Lloyd Mangrum	272
1957	Doug Ford	280
1958	Frank Stranahan	275
1959	Ken Venturi	278
1960	Dow Finsterwald	280
1961	Bob Goalby	275
1962	Phil Rodgers	268
1963	Arnold Palmer	274
1964	Paul Harney	280
1965	Paul Harney	276
1966	Arnold Palmer	273
1967	Arnold Palmer	269
1968	Billy Casper	274
1969	*Charles Sifford	276
1970	*Billy Casper	276

GLEN CAMPBELL LOS ANGELES OPEN

1971	*Bob Lunn	274
1972	*George Archer	270
1973	Rod Funseth	276
1974	Dave Stockton	276
1975	Pat Fitzsimons	275
1976	Hale Irwin	272
1977	Tom Purtzer	273
1978	Gil Morgan	278
1979	Lanny Wadkins	276
1980	TomWatson	276
1981	Johnny Miller	270
1982	*Tom Watson	271
1983	Gil Morgan	270

LOS ANGELES OPEN

1984	David Edwards	279
1985	Lanny Wadkins	264
1986	Doug Tewell	270

LOS ANGELES OPEN PRESENTED BY NISSAN

1987	*Tze-Chung Chen	275
1988	Chip Beck	267

NISSAN LOS ANGELES OPEN

1989	Mark Calcavecchia	272
1990	Fred Couples	266
1991	Ted Schulz	272
1992	*Fred Couples	269
1993	Tom Kite	206
1994	Corey Pavin	271

DORAL RYDER OPEN

Doral C.C. (Blue),
Miami, FL (1962-present).

DORAL C.C. OPEN INVITATIONAL

1962	Billy Casper	283
1963	Dan Sikes	283
1964	Billy Casper	277
1965	Doug Sanders	274
1966	Phil Rodgers	278
1967	Doug Sanders	275
1968	Gardner Dickinson	275
1969	Tom Shaw	276

DORAL-EASTERN OPEN INVITATIONAL

1970	Mike Hill	279
1971	J.C. Snead	275
1972	Jack Nicklaus	276
1973	Lee Trevino	276
1974	Brian Allin	272
1975	Jack Nicklaus	276
1976	Hubert Green	270
1977	Andy Bean	277
1978	Tom Weiskopf	272
1979	Mark McCumber	279
1980	*Raymond Floyd	279
1981	Raymond Floyd	273
1982	Andy Bean	278
1983	Gary Koch	271
1984	Tom Kite	272
1985	Mark McCumber	284
1986	*Andy Bean	276

DORAL RYDER OPEN

1987	Lanny Wadkins	277
1988	Ben Crenshaw	274
1989	Bill Glasson	275
1990	*Greg Norman	273
1991	*Rocco Mediate	276
1992	Raymond Floyd	271
1993	Greg Norman	265
1994	John Huston	274

HONDA CLASSIC

Weston Hills G&C.C.,
Fort Lauderdale, FL (1992-present).

JACKIE GLEASON'S INVERRARY CLASSIC

1972	Tom Weiskopf	278

JACKIE GLEASON'S INVERRARY

Honda Open continued

NATIONAL AIRLINES CLASSIC

1973	Lee Trevino	279

JACKIE GLEASON'S
INVERRARY CLASSIC

1974	Leonard Thompson	278
1975	Bob Murphy	273
1976	Hosted Tournament Players Championship	
1977	Jack Nicklaus	275
1978	Jack Nicklaus	276
1979	Larry Nelson	274
1980	Johnny Miller	274

AMERICAN MOTORS
INVERRARY CLASSIC

| 1981 | Tom Kite | 274 |

HONDA INVERRARY CLASSIC

| 1982 | Hale Irwin | 269 |
| 1983 | Johnny Miller | 278 |

HONDA CLASSIC

1984	*Bruce Lietzke	280
1985	*Curtis Strange	275
1986	Kenny Knox	287
1987	Mark Calcavecchia	279
1988	Joey Sindelar	276
1989	Blaine McCallister	266
1990	John Huston	282
1991	Steve Pate	279
1992	*Corey Pavin	273
1993	*Fred Couples	207
1994	Nick Price	276

THE NESTLE INVITATIONAL

Bay Hill Club,
Orlando, FL (1979-present).

FLORIDA CITRUS OPEN
INVITATIONAL

1966	Lionel Hebert	279
1967	Julius Boros	274
1968	Dan Sikes	274
1969	Ken Still	278
1970	Bob Lunn	271
1971	Arnold Palmer	270
1972	Jerry Heard	276
1973	Brian Allin	265
1974	Jerry Heard	273
1975	Lee Trevino	276
1976	*Hale Irwin	270
1977	Gary Koch	274

| 1978 | Mac McLendon | 271 |

BAY HILL CITRUS CLASSIC

1979	*Bob Byman	278
1980	Dave Eichelberger	279
1981	Andy Bean	266
1982	*Tom Kite	278
1983	*Mike Nicolette	283
1984	*Gary Koch	272

HERTZ BAY HILL CLASSIC

1985	Fuzzy Zoeller	275
1986	Dan Forsman	202
1987	Payne Stewart	264
1988	Paul Azinger	271

THE NESTLE INVITATIONAL

1989	*Tom Kite	278
1990	Robert Gamez	274
1991	Andrew Magee	203
1992	Fred Couples	269
1993	Ben Crenshaw	280
1994	Loren Roberts	275

THE PLAYERS CHAMPIONSHIP

TPC at Sawgrass,
Ponte Vedra, FL (1982-present).

TOURNAMENT PLAYERS
CHAMPIONSHIP

1974	Jack Nicklaus	272
1975	Al Geiberger	270
1976	Jack Nicklaus	269
1977	Mark Hayes	289
1978	Jack Nicklaus	289
1979	Lanny Wadkins	283
1980	Lee Trevino	278
1981	*Raymond Floyd	285
1982	Jerry Pate	280
1983	Hal Sutton	283
1984	Fred Couples	277
1985	Calvin Peete	274
1986	John Mahaffey	275
1987	*Sandy Lyle	274

THE PLAYERS CHAMPIONSHIP

1988	Mark McCumber	273
1989	Tom Kite	279
1990	Jodie Mudd	278
1991	Steve Elkington	276
1992	Davis Love III	273
1993	Nick Price	270
1994	Greg Norman	264

FREEPORT-MCMORAN CLASSIC

English Tum G&C.C.,
New Orleans, LA (1989-present).

GREATER NEW ORLEANS OPEN

1938	Harry Cooper	285
1939	Henry Picard	284
1940	Jimmy Demaret	286
1941	Henry Picard	276
1942	Lloyd Mangrum	281
1943	No Tournament	
1944	Sammy Byrd	285
1945	*Byron Nelson	284
1946	Byron Nelson	277
1947	No Tournament	
1948	Bob Hamilton	280
1949-57	No Tournaments	
1958	*Billy Casper	278
1959	Bill Collins	280
1960	Dow Finsterwald	270
1961	Doug Sanders	272
1962	Bo Wininger	281
1963	Bo Wininger	279
1964	Mason Rudolph	283
1965	Dick Mayer	273
1966	Frank Beard	276
1967	George Knudson	277
1968	George Archer	271
1969	*Larry Hinson	275
1970	*Miller Barber	278
1971	Frank Beard	276
1972	Gary Player	279
1973	*Jack Nicklaus	280
1974	Lee Trevino	267

FIRST NBC NEW ORLEANS OPEN

1975	Billy Casper	271
1976	Larry Ziegler	274
1977	Jim Simons	273
1978	Lon Hinkle	271
1979	Hubert Green	273

GREATER NEW ORLEANS OPEN

1980	Tom Watson	273

USF&G NEW ORLEANS OPEN

1981	Tom Watson	270

USF&G CLASSIC

1982	Scott Hoch	206
1983	Bill Rogers	274
1984	Bob Eastwood	272
1985	Seve Ballesteros	205
1986	Calvin Peete	269
1987	Ben Crenshaw	268
1988	Chip Beck	262
1989	Tim Simpson	274
1990	David Frost	276
1991	*Ian Woosnam	275

FREEPORT-MCMORAN CLASSIC

1992	Chip Beck	276
1993	Mike Standly	281
1994	Ben Crenshaw	273

MCI HERITAGE CLASSIC

Harbour Town G.L.,
Hilton Head, SC (1969-present).

HERITAGE CLASSIC

1969	Arnold Palmer	283
1970	Bob Goalby	280

SEA PINES HERITAGE CLASSIC

1971	Hale Irwin	279
1972	Johnny Miller	281
1973	Hale Irwin	272
1974	Johnny Miller	276
1975	Jack Nicklaus	271
1976	Hubert Green	274
1977	Graham Marsh	273
1978	Hubert Green	277
1979	Tom Watson	270
1980	*Doug Tewell	280
1981	Bill Rogers	278
1982	*Tom Watson	280
1983	Fuzzy Zoeller	275
1984	Nick Faldo	270
1985	*Bernhard Langer	273
1986	Fuzzy Zoeller	276

MCI HERITAGE CLASSIC

1987	Davis Love III	271
1988	Greg Norman	271
1989	Payne Stewart	268
1990	*Payne Stewart	276
1991	Davis Love III	271
1992	Davis Love III	269
1993	David Edwards	273
1994	Hale Irwin	266

KMART GREATER GREENSBORO OPEN

Forest Oaks C.C.,
Greensboro, NC (1977-present).

Freeport-McMoRan Classic continued

GREATER GREENSBORO OPEN

1938	Sam Snead	272
1939	Ralph Guldahl	280
1940	Ben Hogan	270
1941	Byron Nelson	276
1942	Sam Byrd	279
1943	No Tournament	
1944	No Tournament	
1945	Byron Nelson	271
1946	Sam Snead	270
1947	Vic Ghezzi	286
1948	Lloyd Mangrum	278
1949	*Sam Snead	276
1950	Sam Snead	269
1951	Art Doering	279
1952	Dave Douglas	277
1953	*Earl Stewart	275
1954	*Doug Ford	283
1955	Sam Snead	273
1956	*Sam Snead	279
1957	Stan Leonard	276
1958	Bob Goalby	275
1959	Dow Finsterwald	278
1960	Sam Snead	270
1961	Mike Souchak	276
1962	Billy Casper	275
1963	Doug Sanders	270
1964	*Julius Boros	277
1965	Sam Snead	273
1966	*Doug Sanders	276
1967	George Archer	267
1968	Billy Casper	267
1969	*Gene Littler	274
1970	Gary Player	271
1971	*Bud Allin	275
1972	*George Archer	272
1973	Chi Chi Rodriguez	267
1974	Bob Charles	270
1975	Tom Weiskopf	275
1976	Al Geiberger	268
1977	Danny Edwards	276
1978	Seve Ballesteros	282
1979	Raymond Floyd	282
1980	Craig Stadler	275
1981	*Larry Nelson	281
1982	Danny Edwards	285
1983	Lanny Wadkins	275

1984	Andy Bean	280
1985	Joey Sindelar	285
1986	Sandy Lyle	275
1987	Scott Simpson	282
1988	*Sandy Lyle	271
1989	Ken Green	277
1990	Steve Elkington	282
1991	*Mark Brooks	275
1992	Davis Love III	272
1993	*Rocco Mediate	281
1994	Mike Springer	275

SHELL HOUSTON OPEN

TPC at The Woodlands,
The Woodlands, TX (1985-present).

TOURNAMENT OF CHAMPIONS

1946	Byron Nelson	274
1947	Bobby Locke	277
1948	No Tournament	
1949	John Palmer	272

HOUSTON OPEN

1950	Cary Middlecoff	277
1951	Marty Furgol	277
1952	Jack Burke, Jr.	277
1953	*Cary Middlecoff	283
1954	Dave Douglas	277
1955	Mike Souchak	273
1956	Ted Kroll	277
1957	Arnold Palmer	279
1958	Ed Oliver	281

HOUSTON CLASSIC

1959	*Jack Burke, Jr.	277
1960	*Bill Collins	280
1961	*Jay Hebert	276
1962	*Bobby Nichols	278
1963	Bob Charles	268
1964	Mike Souchak	278
1965	Bobby Nichols	273

HOUSTON CHAMPION INTERNATIONAL

1966	Arnold Palmer	275
1967	Frank Beard	274
1968	Roberto De Vicenzo	274
1969	Hosted U.S. Open	
1970	*Gibby Gilbert	282
1971	*Hubert Green	280

HOUSTON OPEN

1972	Bruce Devlin	278

Shell Houston Open continued

1973	Bruce Crampton	277
1974	Dave Hill	276
1975	Bruce Crampton	273
1976	Lee Elder	278
1977	Gene Littler	276
1978	Gary Player	270
1979	Wayne Levi	268

MICHELOB HOUSTON OPEN

1980	*Curtis Strange	266
1981	Ron Streck	198
1982	*Ed Sneed	275

HOUSTON COCA-COLA OPEN

1983	David Graham	275
1984	Corey Pavin	274

HOUSTON OPEN

1985	Raymond Floyd	277
1986	*Curtis Strange	274

BIG I HOUSTON OPEN

1987	*Jay Haas	276

INDEPENDENT INSURANCE AGENT OPEN

1988	*Curtis Strange	270
1989	Mike Sullivan	280
1990	*Tony Sills	204
1991	Fulton Allem	273

SHELL HOUSTON OPEN

1992	Fred Funk	272
1993	*Jim McGovern	199
1994	Mike Heinen	272

BELLSOUTH CLASSIC

Atlanta C.C.,
Marietta, GA (1967-present).

ATLANTA CLASSIC

1967	Bob Charles	282
1968	Bob Lunn	280
1969	*Bert Yancey	277
1970	Tommy Aaron	275
1971	*Gardner Dickinson	275
1972	Bob Lunn	275
1973	Jack Nicklaus	272
1974	Hosted TPC	
1975	Hale Irwin	271
1976	Hosted U.S. Open	
1977	Hale Irwin	273
1978	Jerry Heard	269
1979	Andy Bean	265
1980	Larry Nelson	270

1981	*Tom Watson	277

GEORGIA-PACIFIC ATLANTA GOLF CLASSIC

1982	*Keith Fergus	273
1983	*Calvin Peete	206
1984	Tom Kite	269
1985	*Wayne Levi	273
1986	Bob Tway	269
1987	Dave Barr	265
1988	Larry Nelson	268

BELLSOUTH ATLANTA GOLF CLASSIC

1989	*Scott Simpson	278
1990	Wayne Levi	275
1991	*Corey Pavin	272

BELLSOUTH CLASSIC

1992	Tom Kite	272
1993	Nolan Henke	271
1994	John Daly	274

GTE BYRON NELSON CLASSIC

TPC at Las Colinas,
Irving, TX (1986-present).

DALLAS OPEN

1944	Byron Nelson	276
1945	Sam Snead	276
1946	Ben Hogan	284
1947-55	No Tournaments	
1956	Don January	268
1956A	*Peter Thomson	267
1957	Sam Snead	264
1958	*Sam Snead	272
1959	Julius Boros	274
1960	*Johnny Pott	275
1961	Earl Stewart, Jr.	278
1962	Billy Maxwell	277
1963	No Tournament	
1964	Charles Coody	271
1965	No Tournament	
1966	Roberto De Vicenzo	276
1967	Bert Yancey	274

BYRON NELSON GOLF CLASSIC

1968	Miller Barber	270
1969	Bruce Devlin	277
1970	*Jack Nicklaus	274
1971	Jack Nicklaus	274
1972	*Chi Chi Rodriquez	273
1973	*Lanny Wadkins	277
1974	Brian Allin	269

GTE Byron Nelson Classic continued

1975	Tom Watson	269
1976	Mark Hayes	273
1977	Raymond Floyd	276
1978	Tom Watson	272
1979	*Tom Watson	275
1980	Tom Watson	274
1981	*Bruce Lietzke	281
1982	Bob Gilder	266
1983	Ben Crenshaw	273
1984	Craig Stadler	276
1985	*Bob Eastwood	272
1986	Andy Bean	269
1987	*Fred Couples	266

GTE BYRON NELSON GOLF CLASSIC

1988	*Bruce Lietzke	271
1989	*Jodie Mudd	265
1990	Payne Stewart	202
1991	Nick Price	270
1992	*Billy Ray Brown	199
1993	Scott Simpson	270
1994	Neal Lancaster	132

KEMPER OPEN

TPC at Avenel,
Potomac, MD (1987-present).

KEMPER OPEN

1968	Arnold Palmer	276
1969	Dale Douglass	274
1970	Dick Lotz	278
1971	*Tom Weiskopf	277
1972	Doug Sanders	275
1973	Tom Weiskopf	271
1974	*Bob Menne	270
1975	Raymond Floyd	278
1976	Joe Inman	277
1977	Tom Weiskopf	277
1978	Andy Bean	273
1979	Jerry McGee	272
1980	John Mahaffey	275
1981	Craig Stadler	270
1982	Craig Stadler	275
1983	*Fred Couples	287
1984	Greg Norman	280
1985	Bill Glasson	278
1986	*Greg Norman	277
1987	Tom Kite	270

1988	*Morris Hatalsky	274
1989	Tom Byrum	268
1990	Gil Morgan	274
1991	*Billy Andrade	263
1992	Bill Glasson	276
1993	Grant Waite	275
1994	Mark Brooks	271

SOUTHWESTERN BELL COLONIAL

Colonial C.C.,
Fort Worth, TX (1946-present).

COLONIAL NATIONAL INVITATION TOURNAMENT

1946	Ben Hogan	279
1947	Ben Hogan	279
1948	Clayton Heafner	272
1949	No Tournament	
1950	Sam Snead	277
1951	Cary Middlecoff	282
1952	Ben Hogan	279
1953	Ben Hogan	282
1954	Johnny Palmer	280
1955	Chandler Harper	276
1956	Mike Souchak	280
1957	Roberto DeVicenzo	284
1958	Tommy Bolt	282
1959	*Ben Hogan	285
1960	Julius Boros	280
1961	Doug Sanders	281
1962	*Arnold Palmer	281
1963	Julius Boros	279
1964	Billy Casper	279
1965	Bruce Crampton	276
1966	Bruce Devlin	280
1967	Dave Stockton	278
1968	Billy Casper	275
1969	Gardner Dickinson	278
1970	Homero Blancas	273
1971	Gene Littler	283
1972	Jerry Heard	275
1973	Tom Weiskopf	276
1974	Rod Curl	276
1975	Hosted TPC	
1976	Lee Trevino	273
1977	Ben Crenshaw	272
1978	Lee Trevino	268

Southwestern Bell Colonial Open continued

1979	Al Geiberger	274
1980	Bruce Lietzke	271
1981	Fuzzy Zoeller	274
1982	Jack Nicklaus	273
1983	*Jim Colbert	278
1984	*Peter Jacobsen	270
1985	Corey Pavin	266
1986	*Dan Pohl	205
1987	Keith Clearwater	266
1988	Lanny Wadkins	270

SOUTHWESTERN BELL COLONIAL

1989	Ian Baker-Finch	270
1990	Ben Crenshaw	272
1992	*Bruce Lietzke	267
1993	Fulton Allem	264
1994	Nick Price	266

THE MEMORIAL TOURNAMENT
Muirfield Village G.C.,
Dublin, OH (1976-present).

1976	*Roger Maltbie	288
1977	Jack Nicklaus	281
1978	Jim Simons	284
1979	Tom Watson	285
1980	David Graham	280
1981	Keith Fergus	284
1982	Raymond Floyd	281
1983	Hale Irwin	281
1984	*Jack Nicklaus	280
1985	Hale Irwin	281
1986	Hal Sutton	271
1987	Don Pooley	272
1988	Curtis Strange	274
1989	Bob Tway	277
1990	Greg Norman	216
1991	*Kenny Perry	273
1992	*David Edwards	273
1993	Paul Azinger	274
1994	Tom Lehman	268

BUICK CLASSIC
Westchester C.C.,
Harrison, NY (1967-present).
WESTCHESTER CLASSIC

1967	Jack Nicklaus	272

1968	Julius Boros	272
1969	Frank Beard	275
1970	Bruce Crampton	273
1971	Arnold Palmer	270
1972	Jack Nicklaus	270
1973	*Bobby Nichols	272
1974	Johnny Miller	269
1975	*Gene Littler	271

AMERICAN EXPRESS WESTCHESTER CLASSIC

1976	David Graham	272
1977	Andy North	272
1978	Lee Elder	274

MANUFACTURERS HANOVER WESTCHESTER CLASSIC

1979	Renner Jack	277
1980	Curtis Strange	273
1981	Raymond Floyd	275
1982	Bob Gilder	261
1983	Seve Ballesteros	276
1984	Scott Simpson	269
1985	*Roger Maltbie	275
1986	Bob Tway	272
1987	*J.C. Snead	276
1988	*Seve Ballesteros	276
1989	*Wayne Grady	277

BUICK CLASSIC

1990	Hale Irwin	269
1991	Billy Andrade	273
1992	David Frost	268
1993	Vijay Singh	280
1994	Lee Janzen	268

CANON GREATER HARTFORD OPEN
TPC at River Highlands,
Cromwell, CT (1991-present).
INSURANCE CITY OPEN

1952	Ted Kroll	273
1953	Bob Toski	269
1954	*Tommy Bolt	271
1955	Sam Snead	269
1956	*Arnold Palmer	274
1957	Gardner Dickinson	272
1958	Jack Burke, Jr.	268
1959	Gene Littler	272
1960	*Arnold Palmer	270

Canon Greater Hartford Open continued

1961	*Billy Maxwell	271
1962	*Bob Goalby	271
1963	Billy Casper	271
1964	Ken Venturi	273
1965	*Billy Casper	274
1966	Art Wall	266

GREATER HARTFORD OPEN INVITATIONAL

1967	Charlie Sifford	272
1968	Billy Casper	266
1969	*Bob Lunn	268
1970	Bob Murphy	267
1971	*George Archer	268
1972	*Lee Trevino	269

SAMMY DAVIS JR. GREATER HARTFORD OPEN

1973	Billy Casper	264
1974	Dave Stockton	268
1975	*Don Bies	267
1976	Rik Massengale	266
1977	Bill Kratzert	265
1978	Rod Funseth	264
1979	Jerry McGee	267
1980	*Howard Twitty	266
1981	Hubert Green	264
1982	Tim Norris	259
1983	Curtis Strange	268
1984	Peter Jacobsen	269
1985	*Phil Blackmar	271

CANON SAMMY DAVIS JR. GREATER HARTFORD OPEN

1986	*Mac O'Grady	269
1987	Paul Azinger	269
1988	*Mark Brooks	269

CANON GREATER HARTFORD OPEN

1989	Paul Azinger	267
1990	Wayne Levi	267
1991	*Billy Ray Brown	271
1992	Lanny Wadkins	274
1993	Nick Price	271
1994	David Frost	268

MOTOROLA WESTERN OPEN

Cog Hill C.C. (Dubsdread),
Lemont, IL (1991-present).

WESTERN OPEN

| 1899 | *Willie Smith | 156 |

1900	No Tournament	
1901	Laurie Auchterlonie	160
1902	Willie Anderson	299
1903	Alex Smith	318
1904	Willie Anderson	304
1905	Arthur Smith	278
1906	Alex Smith	306
1907	Robert Simpson	307
1908	Willie Anderson	299
1909	Willie Anderson	288
1910	Chick Evans, Jr.	6&5
1911	Robert Simpson	2&1
1912	Mac Smith	299
1913	John McDermott	295
1914	Jim Barnes	293
1915	Tom McNamara	304
1916	Walter Hagen	286
1917	Jim Barnes	283
1918	No Tournament	
1919	Jim Barnes	283
1920	Jock Hutchinson	296
1921	Walter Hagen	287
1922	Mike Brady	291
1923	Jock Hutchinson	281
1924	Bill Mehlhorn	293
1925	Mac Smith	281
1926	Walter Hagen	279
1927	Walter Hagen	281
1928	Abe Espinosa	291
1929	Tommy Armour	273
1930	Gene Sarazen	278
1931	Ed Dudley	280
1932	Walter Hagen	287
1933	Mac Smith	282
1934	*Harry Cooper	274
1935	John Revolta	290
1936	Ralph Guldahl	274
1937	*Ralph Guldahl	288
1938	Ralph Guldahl	279
1939	Byron Nelson	281
1940	*Jimmy Demaret	293
1941	Ed Oliver	275
1942	Herman Barron	276
1943	No Tournament	
1944	No Tournament	
1945	No Tournament	
1946	Ben Hogan	271
1947	Johnny Palmer	270
1948	*Ben Hogan	281

Motorola Western Open continued

1949	Sam Snead	268
1950	Sam Snead	282
1951	Marty Furgol	270
1952	Lloyd Mangrum	274
1953	Dutch Harrison	278
1954	*Lloyd Mangrum	277
1955	Cary Middlecoff	272
1956	*Mike Fetchick	284
1957	*Doug Ford	279
1958	Doug Sanders	275
1959	Mike Souchak	272
1960	*Stan Leonard	278
1961	Arnold Palmer	271
1962	Jacky Cupit	281
1963	*Arnold Palmer	280
1964	Chi Chi Rodriguez	268
1965	Billy Casper	270
1966	Billy Casper	283
1967	Jack Nicklaus	274
1968	Jack Nicklaus	273
1969	Billy Casper	276
1970	Hugh Royer	273
1971	Bruce Crampton	279
1972	Jim Jamieson	271
1973	Billy Casper	272
1974	Tom Watson	287
1975	Hale Irwin	283
1976	Al Geiberger	288
1977	Tom Watson	283
1978	*Andy Bean	282
1979	*Larry Nelson	286
1980	Scott Simpson	281
1981	Ed Fiori	277
1982	Tom Weiskopf	276
1983	Mark McCumber	284
1984	*Tom Watson	280
1985	Scott Verplank	279
1986	*Tom Kite	286

BEATRICE WESTERN OPEN

1987	D. A. Weibring	207
1988	Jim Benepe	278
1989	*Mark McCumber	275

CENTEL WESTERN OPEN

1990	Wayne Levi	275
1991	Russ Cochran	275
1992	Ben Crenshaw	276

SPRINT WESTERN OPEN

1993	Nick Price	269

MOTOROLA WESTERN OPEN

1994	Nick Price	277

ANHEUSER-BUSCH GOLF CLASSIC

Kingsmill G.C.,
Kingsmill, VA (1981-present).

KAISER INTERNATIONAL OPEN INVITATIONAL

1968	Kermit Zarley	273
1969	Miller Barber	135
1969A	*Jack Nicklaus	273
1970	*Ken Still	278
1971	Billy Casper	269
1972	George Knudson	271
1973	*Ed Sneed	275
1974	Johnny Miller	271
1975	Johnny Miller	272
1976	J. C. Snead	274

ANHEUSER-BUSCH GOLF CLASSIC

1977	Miller Barber	272
1978	Tom Watson	270
1979	John Fought	277
1980	Ben Crenshaw	272
1981	John Mahaffey	276
1982	Calvin Peete	203
1983	Calvin Peete	276
1984	Ronnie Black	267
1985	*Mark Wiebe	273
1986	Fuzzy Zoeller	274
1987	Mark McCumber	267
1988	*Tom Sieckmann	270
1989	*Mike Donald	268
1990	Lanny Wadkins	266
1991	Mike Hulbert	266
1992	David Peoples	271
1993	Jim Gallagher	269
1994	Mark McCumber	267

DEPOSIT GUARANTY GOLF CLASSIC

Hattiesburg C.C., Hattiesburg, MS (1968-present).

MAGNOLIA STATE CLASSIC

1968	*B.R. McLendon	269

Deposit Guaranty Classic continued

1969	Larry Mowry	272
1970	Chris Blocker	271
1971	Roy Pace	270
1972	Mike Morey	269
1973	Dwight Nevil	268
1974	Dwight Nevil	133
1975	Bob Wynn	270
1976	Dennis Meyer	271
1977	Mike McCullough	269
1978	Craig Stadler	268
1979	Bobby Walzel	272
1980	*Roger Maltbie	65
1981	*Tom Jones	268
1982	Payne Stewart	270
1983	Russ Cochran	203
1984	*Lance Ten Broeck	201
1985	*Jim Gallagher, Jr.	131

DEPOSIT GUARANTY CLASSIC

1986	Dan Halldorson	263
1987	David Ogrin	267
1988	Frank Conner	267
1989	*Jim Booros	199
1990	Gene Sauers	268
1991	*Larry Silveira	266
1992	Richard Zokol	267
1993	Greg Kraft	267
1994	Brian Henninger	135
Note:	1983-85 TPS Event	

NEW ENGLAND CLASSIC

Pleasant Valley C.C.,
Sutton,MA (1965-present).

CARLING WORLD OPEN

1965	Tony Lema	279

KEMPER OPEN

1968	Arnold Palmer	276

AVCO GOLF CLASSIC

1969	Tom Shaw	280
1970	Billy Casper	277

MASSACHUSETTS CLASSIC

1971	Dave Stockton	275

USI CLASSIC

1972	Bruce Devlin	275
1973	Lanny Wadkins	279

PLEASANT VALLEY CLASSIC

1974	Victor Regalado	278

1975	Roger Maltbie	276
1976	Bud Allin	277
1977	Raymond Floyd	271

AMERICAN OPTICAL CLASSIC

1978	John Mahaffey	270
1979	Lou Graham	275

PLEASANT VALLEY JIMMY FUND CLASSIC

1980	*Wayne Levi	273
1981	Jack Renner	273

BANK OF BOSTON CLASSIC

1982	Bob Gilder	271
1983	Mark Lye	273
1984	George Archer	270
1985	George Burns	267
1986	*Gene Sauers	274
1987	Sam Randolph	199
1988	Mark Calcavecchia	274
1989	Blaine McCallister	271
1990	Morris Hatalsky	275

NEW ENGLAND CLASSIC

1991	*Bruce Fleisher	268
1992	Brad Faxon	268
1993	Paul Azinger	268
1994	Kenny Perry	268

FEDEX ST. JUDE CLASSIC

TPC at Southwind,
Germantown, TN (1989-present).

MEMPHIS INVITATIONAL OPEN

1958	Billy Maxwell	267
1959	*Don Whitt	272
1960	*Tommy Bolt	273
1961	Cary Middlecoff	266
1962	*Lionel Hebert	267
1963	*Tony Lema	270
1964	Mike Souchak	270
1965	*Jack Nicklaus	271
1966	Bert Yancey	265
1967	Dave Hill	272
1968	Bob Lunn	268
1969	Dave Hill	265

DANNY THOMAS MEMPHIS CLASSIC

1970	Dave Hill	267
1971	Lee Trevino	268
1972	Lee Trevino	281
1973	Dave Hill	283

Fed Ex St. Jude Classic continued

1974	Gary Player	273
1975	Gene Littler	270
1976	Gibby Gilbert	273
1977	Al Geiberger	273
1978	*Andy Bean	277
1979	*Gil Morgan	278
1980	Lee Trevino	272
1981	Jerry Pate	274
1982	Raymond Floyd	271
1983	Larry Mize	274
1984	Bob Eastwood	280

ST. JUDE MEMPHIS CLASSIC

1985	*Hal Sutton	279

FEDERAL EXPRESS ST. JUDE CLASSIC

1986	Mike Hulbert	280
1987	Curtis Strange	275
1988	Jodie Mudd	273
1989	John Mahaffey	272
1990	*Tom Kite	269
1991	Fred Couples	269
1992	Jay Haas	263
1993	Nick Price	266
1994	Dicky Pride	267

BUICK OPEN

Warwick Hills C.C.,
Grand Blanc, MI (1978-present).

BUICK OPEN INVITATIONAL

1958	Billy Casper	285
1959	Art Wall	282
1960	Mike Souchak	282
1961	Jack Burke, Jr.	284
1962	Bill Collins	284
1963	Julius Boros	274
1964	Tony Lema	277
1965	Tony Lema	280
1966	Phil Rodgers	284
1967	Julius Boros	283
1968	Tom Weiskopf	280
1969	Dave Hill	277
1970	No Tournament	
1971	No Tournament	

VERN PARSELL BUICK OPEN

1972	Gary Groh	273

LAKE MICHIGAN CLASSIC

1973	Wilf Homenuik	215

FLINT ELKS OPEN

1974	Bryan Abbott	135
1975	Spike Kelley	208
1976	Ed Sabo	279
1977	Bobby Cole	271

BUICK GOODWRENCH OPEN

1978	*Jack Newton	280
1979	*John Fought	280
1980	Peter Jacobsen	276

BUICK OPEN

1981	*Hale Irwin	277
1982	Lanny Wadkins	273
1983	Wayne Levi	272
1984	Denis Watson	271
1985	Ken Green	268
1986	Ben Crenshaw	270
1987	Robert Wrenn	262
1988	Scott Verplank	268
1989	Leonard Thompson	273
1990	Chip Beck	272
1991	*Brad Faxon	271
1992	*Dan Forsman	276
1993	Larry Mize	272
1994	Fred Couples	270

THE INTERNATIONAL

Castle Pines G.C.,
Castle Rock, CO (1986-present).

1986	Ken Green	Plus 12
1987	John Cook	Plus 11
1988	Joey Sindelar	Plus 17
1989	Greg Norman	Plus 13
1990	Davis Love III	Plus 14
1991	Jose M. Olazabal	Plus 10
1992	Brad Faxon	Plus 14
1993	Phil Mickelson	45

SPRINT INTERNATIONAL

1994	Steve Lowery	$252,000

GREATER MILWAUKEE OPEN

Tuckaway C.C.,
Franklin, WS (1973-present).

1968	Dave Stockton	275
1969	Ken Still	277
1970	Deane Beman	276
1971	Dave Eichelberger	270

Greater Milwaukee Open continued

Year	Winner	Score
1972	Jim Colbert	271
1973	Dave Stockton	276
1974	Ed Sneed	276
1975	Art Wall	271
1976	Dave Hill	270
1977	Dave Eichelberger	278
1978	*Lee Elder	275
1979	Calvin Peete	269
1980	Bill Kratzert	266
1981	Jay Haas	274
1982	Calvin Peete	274
1983	*Morris Hatalsky	275
1984	Mark O'Meara	272
1985	Jim Thorpe	274
1986	*Corey Pavin	272
1987	Gary Hallberg	269
1988	Ken Green	268
1989	Greg Norman	269
1990	*Jim Gallagher, Jr.	271
1991	Mark Brooks	270
1992	Richard Zokol	269
1993	Billy Mayfair	270
1994	Mike Springer	268

CANADIAN OPEN

Glen Abbey G.C.,
Oakville, Ontario (1981-present).

Year	Winner	Score
1904	J. H. Oke	156
1905	George Cumming	148
1906	Charles Murray	170
1907	Percy Barrett	306
1908	Albert Murray	300
1909	Karl Keller	309
1910	Daniel Kenny	303
1911	Charles Murray	314
1912	George Sargent	299
1913	Albert Murray	295
1914	Karl Keller	300
1915	No Tournament	
1916	No Tournament	
1917	No Tournament	
1918	No Tournament	
1919	J. Douglas Edgar	278
1920	*J. Douglas Edgar	298
1921	W. H. Trovinger	293
1922	Al Watrous	303
1923	C. W. Hackney	295
1924	Leo Diegel	285
1925	Leo Diegel	295
1926	Mac Smith	283
1927	Tommy Armour	288
1928	Leo Diegel	282
1929	Leo Diegel	274
1930	*Tommy Armour	273
1931	*Walter Hagen	292
1932	Harry Cooper	290
1933	Joe Kirkwood	282
1934	Tommy Armour	287
1935	Gene Kdnes	280
1936	Lawson Little	271
1937	Harry Cooper	285
1938	*Sam Snead	277
1939	Harold McSpaden	282
1940	*Sam Snead	281
1941	Sam Snead	274
1942	Craig Wood	275
1943	No Tournament	
1944	No Tournament	
1945	Byron Nelson	280
1946	*George Fazio	278
1947	Bobby Locke	268
1948	C. W. Congdon	280
1949	Dutch Harrison	271
1950	Jim Ferrier	271
1951	Jim Ferrier	273
1952	John Palmer	263
1953	Dave Douglas	273
1954	Pat Fletcher	280
1955	Arnold Palmer	265
1956	Doug Sanders	273
1957	George Bayer	271
1958	Wesley Ellis, Jr.	267
1959	Doug Ford	276
1960	Art Wall, Jr.	269
1961	Jacky Cupit	270
1962	Ted Kroll	278
1963	Doug Ford	280
1964	Kel Nagle	277
1965	Gene Littler	273
1966	Don Massengale	280
1967	*Billy Casper	279
1968	Bob Charles	274
1969	*Tommy Aaron	275
1970	Kermit Zarley	279

Canadian Open continued

1971	*Lee Trevino	275
1972	Gay Brewer	275
1973	Tom Weiskopf	278
1974	Bobby Nichols	270
1975	*Tom Weiskopf	274
1976	Jerry Pate	267
1977	Lee Trevino	280
1978	Bruce Lietzke	283
1979	Lee Trevino	281
1980	Bob Gilder	274
1981	Peter Oosterhuis	280
1982	Bruce Lietzke	277
1983	*John Cook	277
1984	Greg Norman	278
1985	Curtis Strange	279
1986	Bob Murphy	280
1987	Curtis Strange	276
1988	Ken Green	275
1989	Steve Jones	271
1990	Wayne Levi	278
1991	Nick Price	273
1992	*Greg Norman	280
1993	David Frost	279
1994	Nick Price	275

HARDEE'S GOLF CLASSIC
Oakwood C.C.,
Coal Valley, IL (1975-present).
QUAD CITIES OPEN

1972	Deane Beman	279
1973	Sam Adams	268
1974	Dave Stockton	271

ED MCMAHON-JAYCEES
QUAD CITY OPEN

1975	Roger Maltbie	275
1976	John Lister	268
1977	Mike Morley	267
1978	Victor Regalado	269
1979	D. A. Weibring	266

QUAD CITIES OPEN

| 1980 | Scott Hoch | 266 |
| 1981 | *Dave Barr | 270 |

MILLER HIGH-LIFE QUAD CITIES OPEN

1982	Payne Stewart	268
1983	*Danny Edwards	266
1984	Scoff Hoch	266

LITE QUAD CITIES OPEN

| 1985 | Dan Forsman | 267 |

HARDEE'S GOLF CLASSIC

1986	Mark Wiebe	268
1987	Kenny Knox	265
1988	Blaine McCallister	261
1989	Curt Byrum	268
1990	*Joey Sindelar	268
1991	D. A. Weibring	267
1992	David Frost	266
1993	David Frost	259
1994	Mark McCumber	265

B. C. OPEN
En Joie G.C.,
Endicott, NY (1971- present).
BROOME COUNTY OPEN

| 1971 | *Claude Harmon, Jr. | 69 |

B. C. OPEN

1972	Bob Payne	136
1973	Hubert Green	266
1974	*Richie Karl	273
1975	Don Iverson	274
1976	Bob Wynn	271
1977	Gil Morgan	270
1978	Tom Kite	267
1979	Howard Twitty	270
1980	Don Pooley	271
1981	Jay Haas	270
1982	Calvin Peete	265
1983	Pat Lindsey	268
1984	Wayne Levi	275
1985	Joey Sindelar	274
1986	Rick Fehr	267
1987	Joey Sindelar	266
1988	Bill Glasson	268
1989	*Mike Hulbert	268
1990	Nolan Henke	268
1991	Fred Couples	269
1992	John Daly	266
1993	Blaine McCallister	271
1994	Mike Sullivan	266

BUICK SOUTHERN OPEN
Callaway Gardens Resort,
Pine Mountain, GA (1991-present).

GREEN ISLAND OPEN INVITATIONAL

1970	Mason Rudolph	274

SOUTHERN OPEN INVITATIONAL

1971	Johnny Miller	267
1972	*DeWitt Weaver	276
1973	Gary Player	270
1974	Forrest Fezler	271
1975	Hubert Green	264
1976	Mac McClendon	274
1977	Jerry Pate	266
1978	Jerry Pate	269
1979	*Ed Fiori	274
1980	Mike Sullivan	269
1981	*J. C. Snead	271
1982	Bobby Clampett	266
1983	*Ronnie Black	271
1984	Hubert Green	265
1985	Tim Simpson	264
1986	Fred Wadsworth	269
1987	Ken Brown	266
1988	*David Frost	270
1989	Ted Schulz	266

BUICK SOUTHERN OPEN

1990	*Kenny Knox	265
1991	David Peoples	276
1992	Gary Hallberg	206
1993	*John Inman	278
1994	Steve Elkington	200

LAS VEGAS INVITATIONAL

Rotates among Las Vegas C.C., Las Vegas; Desert Inn C.C., LasVegas; and TPC at Summerlin, Las Vegas (1992-present).

PANASONIC LAS VEGAS CLASSIC

1983	Fuzzy Zoeller	340
1984	Denis Watson	341
1985	Curtis Strange	338
1986	Greg Norman	333
1987	Paul Azinger	271
1988	Gary Koch	274

LAS VEGAS INVITATIONAL

1989	*Scott Hoch	336
1990	*Bob Tway	334
1991	*Andrew Magee	329
1992	John Cook	334
1993	John Inman	331
1994	Bruce Leitzke	332

WALT DISNEYWORLD/ OLDSMOBILE CLASSIC

Rotates among Palm, Magnolia, Lake Buena Vista C.C., Lake Buena Vista, FL (1971-present).

WALT DISNEY WORLD OPEN

1971	Jack Nicklaus	273
1972	Jack Nicklaus	267
1973	Jack Nicklaus	275

WALT DISNEY WORLD NATIONAL TEAM CHAMPIONSHIP

1974	Hubert Green/ Mac McClendon	255
1975	Jim Colbert/ Dean Refram	252
1976	*Woody Blackburn/ Bill Kratzert	260
1977	Gibby Gilbert/ GrierJones	253
1978	Wayne Levi/ Bob Mann	254
1979	George Burns/ Ben Crenshaw	255
1980	Danny Edwards/ Dave Edwards	253
1981	Vance Heafner/ Mike Holland	275

WALT DISNEY WORLD GOLF CLASSIC

1982	*Hal Sutton	269
1983	Payne Stewart	269
1984	Larry Nelson	266

WALT DISNEY WORLD OLDSMOBILE CLASSIC

1985	Lanny Wadkins	267
1986	*Ray Floyd	275
1987	Larry Nelson	268
1988	*Bob Lohr	263
1989	Tim Simpson	272
1990	Tim Simpson	264
1991	Mark O'Meara	267
1992	John Huston	262
1993	Jeff Maggert	265
1994	Rick Fehr	269

H-E-B TEXAS OPEN

Oak Hills C.C., San Antonio, TX (1977-present).

TEXAS OPEN

Year	Winner	Score
1922	Bob MacDonald	281
1923	Walter Hagen	279
1924	Joe Kirkwood	279
1925	Joe Turnesa	284
1926	Mac Smith	288
1927	Bobby Cruikshank	272
1928	Bill Mehlhorn	297
1929	Bill Mehlhorn	277
1930	Denny Shute	277
1931	Abe Espinosa	281
1932	Clarence Clark	287
1933	No Tournament	
1934	Witty Cox	283
1935-38	No Tournaments	
1939	Dutch Harrison	271
1940	Byron Nelson	271
1941	Lawson Little	273
1942	*Chick Harbert	272
1943	No Tournament	
1944	Johnny Revolta	273
1945	Sam Byrd	268
1946	Ben Hogan	264
1947	Ed Oliver	265
1948	Sam Snead	264
1949	Dave Douglas	268
1950	Sam Snead	265
1951	*Dutch Harrison	265
1952	Jack Burke, Jr.	260
1953	Tony Holguin	264
1954	Chandler Harper	259
1955	Mike Souchak	257
1956	Gene Littler	276
1957	Jay Hebert	271
1958	Bill Johnston	274
1959	Wes Ellis	276
1960	Arnold Palmer	276
1961	Arnold Palmer	270
1962	Arnold Palmer	273
1963	Phil Rodgers	268
1964	Bruce Crampton	273
1965	Frank Beard	270
1966	Harold Henning	272
1967	Chi Chi Rodriquez	277
1968	No Tournament	
1969	*Deane Beman	274

SAN ANTONIO TEXAS OPEN
| 1970 | Ron Cerrudo | 273 |

1971	No Tournament	
1972	Mike Hill	273
1973	Ben Crenshaw	270
1974	Terry Diehl	269
1975	*Don January	275
1976	*Hutch Baird	273
1977	Hale Irwin	266
1978	Ron Streck	265
1979	Lou Graham	268
1980	Lee Trevino	265

TEXAS OPEN
1981	*Bill Rogers	266
1982	Jay Haas	262
1984	Calvin Peete	266
1985	*John Mahaffey	268

VANTAGE CHAMPIONSHIP
| 1986 | Ben Crenshaw | 196 |

NABISCO CHAMPIONSHIPS OF GOLF
| 1987 | Tom Watson | 268 |

TEXAS OPEN PRESENTED BY NABISCO
| 1988 | Corey Pavin | 259 |
| 1989 | Donnie Hammond | 258 |

H-E-B TEXAS OPEN
1990	Mark O'Meara	261
1991	*Blaine McCallister	269
1992	*Nick Price	263
1993	Jay Haas	269
1994	Bob Estes	265

THE TOUR CHAMPIONSHIP
The Olympic Club,
San Francisco, CA (1993-present).

VANTAGE CHAMPIONSHIP
| 1986 | Ben Crenshaw | 196 |

NABISCO CHAMPIONSHIP OF GOLF
| 1987 | Tom Watson | 268 |

NABISCO GOLF CHAMPIONSHIPS
| 1988 | *Curtis Strange | 279 |

NABISCO CHAMPIONSHIPS
| 1989 | *Tom Kite | 276 |
| 1990 | *Jodie Mudd | 273 |

THE TOUR CHAMPIONSHIP
1991	*Craig Stadler	279
1992	Paul Azinger	276
1993	Jim Gallagher	277
1994	Mark McCumber	274

LINCOLN-MERCURY KAPALUA INTERNATIONAL

Plantation Course, Kapalua G.C.,
Maui, HI (1991-present).

KAPALUA INTERNATIONAL

| 1983 | Greg Norman | 268 |
| 1984 | Sandy Lyle | 266 |

ISUZU KAPALUA INTERNATIONAL

1985	Mark O'Meara	275
1986	Andy Bean	278
1987	Andy Bean	267
1988	Bob Gilder	266
1989	*Peter Jacobsen	270
1990	David Peoples	264

PING KAPALUA INTERNATIONAL

| 1991 | *Mike Hulbert | 276 |

LINCOLN-MERCURY KAPALUA INTERNATIONAL

1992	Davis Love III	275
1993	Fred Couples	274
1994	Not Available at press time	

FRANKLIN FUNDS SHARK SHOOTOUT

Sherwood C.C.,
Thousand Oaks, CA (1989-present)

RMCC INVITATIONAL

| 1989 | Curtis Strange/
Mark O'Meara | 190 |
| 1990 | Ray Floyd/
Fred Couples | 182 |

SHARK SHOOTOUT BENEFITING RMCC

| 1991 | Tom Purtzer/
Lanny Wadkins | 189 |

FRANKLIN FUNDS SHARK SHOOTOUT

1992	Davis Love III/ Tom Kite	191
1993	Steve Elkington/ Ray Floyd	188
1994	Not available at press time.	

SKINS GAME

Bighom G.C., Palm Desert, CA

1983	Gary Player	$170,000
1984	Jack Nicklaus	$240,000
1985	Fuzzy Zoeller	$255,000

1986	Fuzzy Zoeller	$370,000
1987	Lee Trevino	$310,000
1988	Ray Floyd	$290,000
1989	Curtis Strange	$265,000
1990	Curtis Strange	$225,000
1991	Payne Stewart	$260,000
1992	Payne Stewart	$220,000
1993	Payne Stewart	$280,000
1994	Not available at press time.	

JCPENNEY CLASSIC

Innisbrook Resort,
Tarpon Springs, FL (1990-present).

HAIG & HAIG SCOTCH FOURSOME

1960	*Jim Turnesa/ Gloria Armstrong	139
1961	Dave Ragan/ Mickey Wright	272
1962	Mason Rudolph/ Kathy Whitworth	272
1963	Dave Ragan/ Mickey Wright	273
1964	Sam Snead/ Shirley Englehorn	272
1965	Gardner Dickinson/ Ruth Jessen	281
1966	Jack Rule/ Sandra Spuzich	276

PEPSI-COLA MIXED TEAM

| 1976 | Chi Chi Rodriguez/
JoAnn Washam | 275 |
| 1977 | Jerry Pate/
Hollis Stacy | 270 |

JCPENNEY CLASSIC

1978	*Lon Hinkle/ Pat Bradley	267
1979	Dave Eichelberger/ Murle Breer	268
1980	Curtis Strange/ Nancy Lopez	268
1981	Tom Kite/ Beth Daniel	270
1982	John Mahaffey/ JoAnne Carner	268
1983	Fred Couples/ Jan Stephenson	264

1984	Mike Donald/			1971	Charles Coody	(141)
	Vicki Alvarez	270		1972	Gary Player	(142)
1985	Larry Rinker/			1973	Tom Weiskopf	(137)
	Laurie Rinker	267		1974	Lee Trevino	(139)
1986	Tom Purtzer/			1975	Tom Watson	(140)
	Juli Inkster/	267		1976	Jack Nicklaus	275
1987	Steve Jones/			1977	Lanny Wadkins	267
	Jane Crafter	268		1978	*Gil Morgan	278
1988	John Huston/			1979	Lon Hinkle	272
	Amy Benz	269		1980	Tom Watson	270
1989	*Bill Glasson/			1981	Bill Rogers	275
	Pat Bradley	267		1982	*Craig Stadler	278
1990	Davis Love III/			1983	Nick Price	270
	Beth Daniel	266		1984	Denis Watson	271
1991	*Billy Andrade/			1985	Roger Maltbie	268
	Kris Tschetter	266		1986	Dan Pohl	277
1992	Dan Forsman/			1987	Curtis Strange	275
	Dottie Mochrie	264		1988	*Mike Reid	275
1993	Mike Spring/			1989	*David Frost	276
	Melissa McNamara 265			1990	Jose-Maria Olazabal 262
1994	Not available at press time.			1991	*Tom Purtzer	279
				1992	Craig Stadler	273

MERRILL LYNCH SHOOT-OUT FINALS
Rotated annually (1987-93).

| 1993 | Fulton Allem | 270 |
| 1994 | Jose Marie Olazabal 269 |

1987	Fuzzy Zoeller
1988	David Frost
1989	Chip Beck
1990	John Mahaffey
1991	Davis Love III
1992	Chip Beck
1993	Vijay Singh
1994	Not available at press time.

LPGA TOUR

HEALTHSOUTH PALM BEACH CLASSIC
Wycliffe G&C.C., Lake Worth,Fla.
WHIRLPOOL CHAMPIONSHIP OF DEER CREEK

NEC WORLD SERIES OF GOLF
Firestone Country Club, South Course, Akron, OH (From1962-1975, played as a four-man, 36 hole exhibition.)

1980	JoAnneCarner	282
1981	Sandra Palmer	284
1982	*Hollis Stacy	282

MAZDA CLASSIC OF DEER CREEK

1962	Jack Nicklaus	(135)
1963	Jack Nicklaus	(140)
1964	Tony Lema	(138)
1965	Gary Player	(139)
1966	Gene Littler	(143)
1967	Jack Nicklaus	(144)
1968	Gary Player	(143)
1969	Orville Moody	(141)
1970	Jack Nicklaus	(136)

1983	Pat Bradley	272
1984	Silvia Bertolaccini	280
1985	Hollis Stacy	280

MAZDA CLASSIC

1986	Val Skinner	280
1987	*Kathy Postlewait	286
1988	Nancy Lopez	283

OLDSMOBILE LPGA CLASSIC

1989	*Dottie Mochrie	279
1990	*Pat Bradley	281
1991	Meg Mallon	276

HealthSouth Palm Beach Classic continued

1992   *Colleen Walker   279

HEALTHSOUTH PALM BEACH CLASSIC

1993	*Tammie Green	208
1994	Dawn Coe-Jones	201

CUP NOODLES HAWAIIAN LADIES OPEN

Ko Olina G.C., Ewa Beach,
Oahu, HI(1990-present).

TSUMURA LADIES OPEN

1987	Cindy Rarick	207

ORIENT LEASING HAWAIIAN LADIES OPEN

1988	Ayako Okamoto	213

ORIX HAWAIIAN LADIES OPEN

1989	Sherri Turner	205
1990	Beth Daniel	210
1991	Patty Sheehan	207

ITOKI HAWAIIAN LADIES OPEN

1992	Lisa Walters	208
1993	Lisa Walters	210
1994	Marta Figueras-Dotti	209

CHRYSLER-PLYMOUTH TOURNAMENT OF CHAMPIONS

Grand Cypress Resort,
Orlando, FL (1994-present).

1994	Dottie Mochrie	287

PING/WELCH'S CHAMPIONSHIP

Randolph Park North,
Tucson, AZ (1981-present).

ARIZONA COPPER CLASSIC

1981	Nancy Lopez	278
1982	*Ayako Okamoto	281

TUCSON CONQUISTADORES OPEN

1983	Jan Stephenson	207
1984	Chris Johnson	272

CIRCLE K LPGA TUCSON OPEN

1985	Amy Alcott	279
1986	Penny Pulz	276
1987	Betsy King	281
1988	Laura Davies	278
1989	Lori Garbacz	274

1990	Colleen Walker	276

PING/WELCH'S CHAMPIONSHIP (Tucson)

1991	Chris Johnson	273
1992	Brandie Burton	277
1993	Meg Mallon	272
1994	Donna Andrews	276

STANDARD REGISTER PING

Moon Valley C.C.,
Phoenix, AZ (1987-present).

SUN CITY CLASSIC

1980	Jan Stephenson	275
1981	Patty Hayes	277
1982	*Beth Daniel	278

SAMARITAN TURQUOISE CLASSIC

1983	Anne-Marie Palli	205
1984	Chris Johnson	276
1985	*Betsy King	280

STANDARD REGISTER TURQUOISE CLASSIC

1986	M. B. Zimmerman	278
1987	Pat Bradley	286
1988	Ok-Hee Ku	281
1989	Allison Finney	282
1990	Pat Bradley	280

STANDARD REGISTER PING

1991	Danielle Ammaccapane	283
1992	Danielle Ammaccapane	279
1993	Patty Sheehan	275
1994	Laura Davies	277

ATLANTA WOMEN'S CHAMPIONSHIP

Eagle's Landing C.C.,
Stockbridge, GA (1992-present).

SEGA WOMEN'S CHAMPIONSHIP

1992	Dottie Mochrie	277

ATLANTA WOMEN'S CHAMPIONSHIP

1993	Trish Johnson	282
1994	Val Skinner	206

SPRINT CLASSIC

Killeam C.C. & Inn,
Tallahassee, FL (1990-present).

CENTEL CLASSIC

1990	Beth Daniel	271

Spring Championship continued

1991	Pat Bradley	278
1992	Danielle Ammaccapane	208

SPRINT CLASSIC

1993	Kristi Albers	279

SPRINT CHAMPIONSHIP

1994	Sherri Steinhauer	273

SARA LEE CLASSIC

Hermitage G.C.,
Old Hickory, TN (1988-present).

1988	*Patti Rizzo	207
1989	Kathy Postlewait	203
1990	Ayako Okamoto	210
1991	Nancy Lopez	206
1992	*Maggie Will	207
1993	*Meg Mallon	205
1994	Laura Davies	203

McDONALD'S CHAMPIONSHIP

Du Pont C.C.,
Wilmington, DE (1987-present).

McDONALD'S KIDS CLASSIC

1981	Sandra Post	282
1982	JoAnne Carner	276
1983	*Beth Daniel	286
1984	Patty Sheehan	281

McDONALD'S CHAMPIONSHIP

1985	Alice Miller	272
1986	Juli Inkster	281
1987	Betsy King	278
1988	Kathy Postlewait	276
1989	Betsy King	272
1990	Patty Sheehan	275
1991	Beth Daniel	273
1992	Ayako Okamoto	205
1993	Laura Davies	277
1994	Laura Davies	279

LADY KEYSTONE OPEN

Hershey C.C.,
Hershey, PA (1978-present).

1975	Susie Berning	142
1976	Susie Berning	215
1977	Sandra Spuzich	201

1978	Pat Bradley	206
1979	Nancy Lopez	212
1980	JoAnne Carner	207
1981	JoAnne Carner	203
1982	Jan Stephenson	211
1983	Jan Stephenson	205
1984	Amy Alcott	208
1985	Juli Inkster	209
1986	*Juli Inkster	210
1987	Ayako Okamoto	208
1988	*Shirley Furlong	205
1989	Laura Davies	207
1990	Cathy Gerring	208
1991	Colleen Walker	207
1992	Danielle Ammaccapane	208
1993	Val Skinner	210
1994	Elaine Crosby	211

LPGA CORNING CLASSIC

Corning C.C.,
Corning, NY (1979-present).

1979	Penny Pulz	284
1980	Donna Caponi	281
1981	Kathy Hite	282
1982	Sandra Spuzich	280
1983	Patty Sheehan	272
1984	JoAnne Carner	281
1985	Patti Rizzo	272
1986	Laurie Rinker	278
1987	Cindy Rarick	275
1988	Sherri Turner	273
1989	Ayako Okamoto	272
1990	Pat Bradley	274
1991	Betsy King	273
1992	Colleen Walker	276
1993	*Kelly Robbins	277
1994	Beth Daniel	278

JCPENNEY LPGA SKINS GAME

Stonebriar C.C.,
Frisco, TX (1990-present).

1990	Jan Stephenson	6 skins
1991	No Tournament	
1992	Pat Bradley	8 skins
1993	Betsy King	7 skins
1994	Patty Sheehan	13 skins

OLDSMOBILE CLASSIC

Walnut Hills C.C.,
East Lansing, MI (1992-present).

1992	Barb Mucha	276
1993	Jane Geddes	277
1994	Beth Daniel	268

MINNESOTA LPGA CLASSIC

Edinburgh USA G.C.,
Brooklyn Park, MN (1990-present).

NORTHGATE CLASSIC

1990	Beth Daniel	203

NORTHGATE COMPUTER CLASSIC

1991	*Cindy Rarick	211
1992	Kris Tschetter	211
1993	Hiromi Kobayashi	205
1994	Liselotte Neumann	205

ROCHESTER INTERNATIONAL

Locust Hill C.C.,
Pittsford, NY (1977-present).

BANKERS TRUST CLASSIC

1977	Pat Bradley	213
1978	Nancy Lopez	214

SARAH COVENTRY

1979	Jane Blalock	280
1980	Nancy Lopez	283
1981	Nancy Lopez	285

ROCHESTER INTERNATIONAL

1982	*Sandra Haynie	276
1983	Ayako Okamoto	282
1984	*Kathy Whitworth	281
1985	Pat Bradley	280
1986	Judy Dickinson	281
1987	Deb Richard	280
1988	*Mei-Chi Cheng	287
1989	*Patty Sheehan	278
1990	Patty Sheehan	271
1991	Rosie Jones	276
1992	Patty Sheehan	269
1993	Tammie Green	276
1994	Lisa Kiggens	273

SHOPRITE LPGA CLASSIC

Greate Bay Resort & C.C.,
Somers Point, NJ (1991-present).

ATLANTIC CITY CLASSIC

1986	Juli Inkster	209
1987	Betsy King	207
1988	*Juli Inkster	206
1989	Nancy Lopez	206
1990	Chris Johnson	275
1991	Jane Geddes	208

SHOPRITE LPGA CLASSIC

1992	Anne-Marie Palli	207
1993	Shelley Hamlin	204
1994	Donna Andrews	207

YOUNGSTOWN-WARREN LPGA CLASSIC

Squaw Creek C.C.,
Warren, OH (1990-present).

PHAR-MOR IN YOUNGSTOWN

1990	*Beth Daniel	207
1991	*Deb Richard	207
1992	*Betsy King	209

YOUNGSTOWN-WARREN LPGA CLASSIC

1993	Nancy Lopez	203
1994	Tammie Green	206

JAMIE FARR TOLEDO CLASSIC

Highland Meadows G.C.,
Sylvania, OH (1989-present).

1984	Lauri Peterson	278
1985	Penny Hammel	278
1986	No Tournament	
1987	Jane Geddes	280
1988	Laura Davies	277
1989	Penny Hammel	206
1990	Tina Purizer	205
1991	*Alice Miller	205
1992	Patty Sheehan	209
1993	Brandie Burton	201
1994	*Kelly Robbins	204

JAL BIG APPLE CLASSIC

Wykagyl C.C.,
New Rochelle, NY (1990-present).

1990	Betsy King	273
1991	Betsy King	279
1992	Juli Inkster	273

JAL Big Apple Classic continued

| 1993 | Hiromi Kobayashi | 278 |
| 1994 | *Beth Daniel | 276 |

PING/WELCH'S CHAMPIONSHIP

Blue Hill C.C.,
Canton, MA (1992-present).

BOSTON FIVE CLASSIC

1980	Dale Eggering	276
1981	Donna Caponi	276
1982	Sandra Palmer	281
1983	Patti Rizzo	277
1984	Laurie Rinker	286
1985	Judy Dickinson	280
1986	Jane Geddes	281
1987	Jane Geddes	277
1988	Colleen Walker	274
1989	Amy Alcott	272
1990	*Barb Mucha	277

LPGA BAY STATE CLASSIC

| 1991 | Juli Inkster | 275 |

WELCH'S CLASSIC

| 1992 | Dottie Mochrie | 278 |

PING/WELCH'S CHAMPIONSHIP (Boston)

| 1993 | *Missie Berteotti | 276 |
| 1994 | Helen Alfredsson | 274 |

MCCALL'S LPGA CLASSIC AT STRATTON MOUNTAIN

Stratton Mountain C.C.,
Stratton Mountain, VT (1990-present).

STRATTON MOUNTAIN LPGA CLASSIC

| 1990 | *Cathy Gerring | 281 |
| 1991 | M. McNamara | 278 |

MCCALL'S LPGA CLASSIC AT STRATTON MOUNTAIN

1992	F. Descampe	278
1993	D. Lofland-Dormann	275
1994	Carolyn Hill	275

SUN-TIMES CHALLENGE

Eagle C.C.,
Naperville, IL (1992-present).

CHICAGO SUN-TIMES SHOOT-OUT

| 1991 | Martha Nause | 275 |

SUN-TIMES CHALLENGE

1992	*Dottie Mochrie	216
1993	Cindy Schreyer	272
1994	Jane Geddes	272

STATE FARM RAIL CHARITY GOLF CLASSIC

Rail G.C.,
Springfield, IL (1976-present).

JERRY LEWIS MUSCULAR DYSTROPHY CLASSIC

| 1976 | *Sandra Palmer | 213 |

STATE FARM RAIL CHARITY GOLF CLASSIC

1977	Hollis Stacy	271
1978	Pat Bradley	276
1979	Jo Ann Washam	275
1980	Nancy Lopez	275
1981	JoAnne Carner	205
1982	JoAnne Carner	202
1983	Lauri Peterson	210
1984	Cindy Hill	207
1985	Betsy King	205
1986	*Betsy King	205
1987	Rosie Jones	208
1988	Betsy King	207
1989	Beth Daniel	203
1990	Beth Daniel	203
1991	Pat Bradley	197
1992	*Nancy Lopez	199
1993	*Helen Dobson	203
1994	Barb Mucha	203

PING-CELLULAR ONE GOLF CHAMPIONSHIP

Rotated among Portland G.C., Columbia Edgewater C.C., and Riverside G & C.C., Portland, OR (1972-present).

PORTLAND CLASSIC

1972	Kathy Whitworth	212
1973	Kathy Whitworth	144
1974	JoAnne Carner	211
1975	Jo Ann Washam	215
1976	Donna Caponi	217

PING-Cellular One Championship continued

PORTLAND PING TEAM
CHAMPIONSHIP (Unofficial event)

1977	*JoAnne Carner/ Judy Rankin	202
1978	*Donna Caponi/ Kathy Whitworth	203
1979	Nancy Lopez/ Jo Ann Washam	198
1980	Donna Caponi/ Kathy Whitworth	195
1981	*Donna Caponi/ Kathy Whitworth	203
1982	*Sandra Haynie/ Kathy McMullen	196

PORTLAND PING CHAMPIONSHIP

1983	*JoAnne Carner	212
1984	Amy Alcott	212
1985	Nancy Lopez	215

PING-CELLULAR ONE GOLF
CHAMPIONSHIP

1986	Ayako Okamoto	207
1987	Nancy Lopez	210
1988	Betsy King	213
1989	Muffin Spencer-Devlin	214
1990	Patty Sheehan	208
1991	Michelle Estill	208
1992	*Nancy Lopez	209
1993	Donna Andrews	208
1994	Missie McGeorge	207

SAFECO CLASSIC

Meridian Valley C.C.,
Kent, WA (1982-present).

1982	Patty Sheehan	276
1983	Juli Inkster	283
1984	Kathy Whitworth	279
1985	JoAnne Carner	279
1986	Judy Dickinson	274
1987	Jan Stephenson	277
1988	Juli Inkster	278
1989	Beth Daniel	273
1990	Patty Sheehan	270
1991	*Pat Bradley	280
1992	Colleen Walker	277
1993	Brandie Burton	274
1994	Deb Richard	276

WORLD CHAMPIONSHIP
OF WOMEN'S GOLF

Moved annually (1980-present).

CHEVROLET WORLD CHAMPIONSHIP OF WOMEN'S GOLF

1980	Beth Daniel	282
1981	Beth Daniel	284
1982	JoAnne Carner	284
1983	JoAnne Carner	282
1984	Nancy Lopez	281

NESTLE WORLD CHAMPIONSHIP

1985	Amy Alcott	274
1986	Pat Bradley	279
1987	Ayako Okamoto	282
1988	Rosie Jones	279
1989	Betsy King	275

TROPHEE URBAN-WORLD CHAMPIONSHIP OF WOMEN'S GOLF

1990	Cathy Gerring	278

DAIKYO WORLD CHAMPIONSHIP OF WOMEN'S GOLF

1991	Meg Mallon	216

WORLD CHAMPIONSHIP OF WOMEN'S GOLF

1992	No Tournament	
1993	Dottie Mochrie	283
1994	Beth Daniel	274

NICHIREI INTERNATIONAL

Moved annually.

PIONEER CUP

	Individual	Team
1979	Yuko Moriguchi	USA
1980	Amy Alcott	USA
1981	Chako Higuchi	Japan
1982	Nayako Yoshikawa	USA

SPORTS NIPPON TEAM MATCH

1983	Chako Higuchi	USA

NICHIREI INTERNATIONAL
US-JAPAN TEAM CHAMPIONSHIP

1984	Hollis Stacy	Japan
1985	Jan Stephenson	USA
1986	Ayako Okamoto	USA
1987	Fukumi Tani	USA
1988	Beth Daniel	USA
1989	Colleen Walker	USA
1990	-------	USA

Nichirei International continued

1991	-------	USA
1992	-------	USA
1993	-------	USA
1994	-------	USA

TORAY QUEENS CUP

Musashigaoka G.C.,
Japan (1993-present).

LPGA JAPAN CLASSIC

1973	Jan Ferraris	216
1974	Chako Higuchi	218
1975	Shelley Hamlin	218

MIZUNO JAPAN CLASSIC

1976	Donna Caponi	217
1977	Debbie Massey	220
1978	*Michiko Okada	216
1979	Amy Alcott	211

MAZDA JAPAN CLASSIC

1980	Tatsuko Ohsako	213
1981	Patty Sheehan	213
1982	Nancy Lopez	207
1983	Pat Bradley	206
1984	Nayoko Yoshikawa	210
1985	Jane Blalock	206
1986	*Ai-Yu Tu	213
1987	Yuko Moriguchi	206
1988	*Patty Sheehan	206
1989	Elaine Crosby	205
1990	Debbie Massey	133
1991	Liselofte Neumann	211
1992	*Betsy King	205

TORAY QUEENS CUP

1993	Betsy King	205
1994	Not available at press time.	

JCPENNEY CLASSIC

Innisbrook Resort,
Tarpon Springs, FL (1990-present).
(Unofficial event)

HAIG & HAIG SCOTCH FOURSOME

1960	*Jim Turnesa/	
	Gloria Armstrong	139
1961	Dave Ragan/	
	Mickey Wright	272
1962	Mason Rudolph/	

	Kathy Whitworth	272
1963	Dave Ragan/	
	Mickey Wright	273
1964	Sam Snead/	
	Shirley Englehorn	272
1965	Gardner Dickinson/	
	Ruth Jessen	281
1966	Jack Rule/	
	Sandra Spuzich	276

PEPSI-COLA MIXED TEAM

1976	Chi Chi Rodriguez/	
	JoAnn Washam	275
1977	Jerry Pate/	
	Hollis Stacy	270

JCPENNEY CLASSIC

1978	*Lon Hinkle/	
	Pat Bradley	267
1979	Dave Eichelberger/	
	Murle Breer	268
1980	Curtis Strange/	
	Nancy Lopez	268
1981	Tom Kite/	
	Beth Daniel	270
1982	John Mahaffey/	
	JoAnne Carner	268
1983	Fred Couples/	
	Jan Stephenson	264
1984	Mike Donald/	
	Vicki Alvarez	270
1985	Larry Rinker/	
	Laurie Rinker	267
1986	Tom Purtzer/	
	Juli Inkster	267
1987	Steve Jones/	
	Jane Crater	268
1988	John Huston/	
	Amy Benz	269
1989	*Bill Glasson/	
	Pat Bradley	267
1990	Davis Love III/	
	Beth Daniel	266
1991	*Billy Andrade/	
	Kris Tschetter	266
1992	Dan Forsman/	
	Dottie Mochrie	264
1993	Mike Spring/	
	Melissa McNamara	265
1994	Not available at press time.	

INAMORI CLASSIC

StoneRidge C.C.,
Poway, CA (1988-present).

INAMORI CLASSIC

1980	Amy Alcott	280
1981	*Hollis Stacy	286
1982	Patty Sheehan	277
1983	Patty Sheehan	209
1984	No Tournament	

KYOCERA INAMORI GOLF CLASSIC

1985	Beth Daniel	286
1986	Patty Sheehan	278
1987	Ayako Okamoto	275

SAN DIEGO INAMORI GOLF CLASSIC

1988	Ayako Okamoto	272

RED ROBIN KYOCERA INAMORI CLASSIC

1989	Patti Rizzo	277
1990	Kris Monaghan	276

INAMORI CLASSIC

1991	Laura Davies	277
1992	Judy Dickinson	277
1993	Kris Monaghan	275

Tournament discontinued.

LAS VEGAS LPGA AT CANYON GATE

Desert Inn C.C.,
Las Vegas, NV (1990-93).

DESERT INN LPGA INTERNATIONAL

1990	Maggie Will	214
1991	Penny Hammel	211

LAS VEGAS LPGA INTERNATIONAL

1992	Dana Lofland	212

LAS VEGAS LPGA AT CANYON GATE

1993	Trish Johnson	209
1994	No Tournament.	

LPGA MATCH PLAY CHAMPIONSHIP

Waikolo Beach G.C.,
Waikoloa, Hawaii (1992-present).

ITOMAN LPGA WORLD MATCH PLAY CHAMPIONSHIP

1990	Betsy King

JBP CUP LPGA MATCH PLAY CHAMPIONSHIP

1991	Deb Richard

PIZZA-LA LPGA MATCH PLAY CHAMPIONSHIP

1992	Dawn Coe-Jones
1993	No Tournament
1994	Not available at press time.

Senior PGA TOUR

MERCEDES CHAMPIONSHIPS

LaCosta C.C.,
Carlsbad, CA (1984-present).

MONY SENIOR TOURNAMENT OF CHAMPIONS

1984	Orville Moody	288
1985	Peter Thomson	284
1986	Miller Barber	282
1987	*Don January	287
1988	Dave Hill	211
1989	Miller Barber	280
1990	George Archer	283

INFINITI SENIOR TOURNAMENT OF CHAMPIONS

1991	Bruce Crampton	279
1992	Al Geiberger	282
1993	Al Geiberger	280
1994	Jack Nicklaus	279

SENIOR SKINS GAME

Mauna Lani Resort,
Kohala Coast, HI (1990-93).
(Unofficial event.)

1988	Chi Chi Rodriguez	$300,000
1989	Chi Chi Rodriguez	$120,000
1990	Arnold Palmer	$240,000
1991	Jack Nicklaus	$310,000
1992	Arnold Palmer	$205,000
1993	Arnold Palmer	$190,000
1994	Ray Floyd	$240,000

ROYAL CARIBBEAN CLASSIC

Links at Key Biscayne,
Key Biscayne, FL (1987-present).

GUS MACHADO SENIOR CLASSIC

1987	Gene Littler	207

Royal Caribbean Classic continued

| 1988 | Lee Elder | 202 |
| 1989 | No Tournament | |

ROYAL CARIBBEAN CLASSIC

1990	Lee Trevino	206
1991	Gary Player	200
1992	Don Massengale	205
1993	Jim Colbert	199
1994	Lee Trevino	205

GTE SUNCOAST CLASSIC

TPC of Tampa Bay at Cheval,
Tampa, FL (1992-present).

GTE SUNCOAST SENIORS CLASSIC

| 1988 | Dale Douglass | 210 |
| 1989 | *Bob Charles | 207 |

GTE SUNCOAST CLASSIC

1990	Mike Hill	207
1991	Bob Charles	210
1992	*Jim Colbert	200
1993	Jim Albus	206
1994	Rocky Thompson	201

THE CHALLENGE

The Vineyards G&C.C. (South),
Naples, FL (1991-present).

AETNA CHALLENGE

1988	Gary Player	207
1989	Gene Littler	209
1990	Lee Trevino	200
1991	Lee Trevino	205
1992	Jimmy Powell	197
1993	Mike Hill	202

THE INTELLINET CHALLENGE

| 1994 | Mike Hill | 201 |

CHRYSLER CUP

TPC at Prestancia,
Sarasota, FL (1987-present).

1986	United States	68.5
1987	International	59.9
1988	United States	55.0
1989	United States	71.0
1990	United States	53.5
1991	United States	58.5
1992	United States	54.0
1993	United States	-44
1994	International	-58

GTE WEST CLASSIC

Ojai Valley Inn & C.C.,
Ojai, CA (1989-present).

**AMERICAN GOLF CARTA
BLANCA/JOHNNY MATHIS CLASSIC**

| 1985 | Peter Thomson | 205 |

JOHNNY MATHIS SENIOR CLASSIC

| 1986 | Dale Douglass | 202 |

GTE CLASSIC

| 1987 | Bob Charles | 208 |
| 1988 | Harold Henning | 214 |

GTE WEST CLASSIC

1989	Walter Zembriski	197
1990	No Tournament	
1991	Chi Chi Rodriguez	132
1992	Bruce Crampton	195
1993	Al Geiberger	198
1994	Jay Sigel	198

VANTAGE AT THE DOMINION

Dominion C.C.,
San Antonio, TX (1985-present).

THE DOMINION SENIORS

| 1985 | Don January | 206 |

BENSON & HEDGES INVITATIONAL

| 1986 | Bruce Crampton | 202 |

VANTAGE AT THE DOMINION

| 1987 | Chi Chi Rodriguez | 203 |
| 1988 | Billy Casper | 205 |

RJR AT THE DOMINION

| 1989 | Larry Mowry | 201 |

VANTAGE AT THE DOMINION

1990	Jim Dent	205
1991	Lee Trevino	137
1992	Lee Trevino	201
1993	J.C. Snead	214
1994	Jim Albus	208

GULFSTREAM AEROSPACE INVITATIONAL

Vintage Club (Mountain), IndianWells, CA

Gulfstream Aerospace Invitational continued
(Desert), IndianWells, CA
VINTAGE CLASSIC
1981   Gene Liftler   271
VINTAGE INVITATIONAL
1982   Miller Barber   282
1983   Gene Liftler   280
1984   Don January   280
1985   Peter Thomson   280
1986   Dale Douglass   272
VINTAGE CHRYSLER INVITATIONAL
1987   Bob Charles   285
1988   Orville Moody   263
1989   Miller Barber   281
1990   LeeTrevino   205
VINTAGE ARCO INVITATIONAL
1991   Chi Chi Rodriguez   206
1992   *Mike Hill   203
GULFSTREAM AEROSPACE INVITATIONAL
1993   Ray Floyd   194
Tournament Discontinued.

**DOUG SANDERS KINGWOOD
CELEBRITY CLASSIC**
Deerwood Club,
Houston, TX (1988-present).
1988   Chi Chi Rodriguez   208
1989   Homero Blancas   208
1990   Lee Trevino   203
1991   Mike Hill   203
1992   Mike Hill   134
1993   Bob Charles   208
1994   Tom Wargo   209

MURATEC REUNION PRO-AM
Stonebriar C.C.,
Frisco, TX (1989-present).
SENIOR PLAYERS REUNION PRO-AM
1985   Peter Thomson   202
1986   Don January   203
1987   Chi Chi Rodriguez   201
1988   *Orville Moody   206
MURATA SENIORS REUNION
1989   Don Bies   208
MURATA REUNION PRO-AM
1990   Frank Beard   207

1991   *Chi Chi Rodriguez 208
1992   *George Archer   211
1993   Dave Stockton   211
DALLAS REUNION PRO-AM
1994   Larry Gilbert   202

LAS VEGAS SENIOR CLASSIC
Desert Inn C.C.,
Las Vegas, NV (1986-present).
LAS VEGAS SENIOR CLASSIC
1986   Bruce Crampton   206
1987   Al Geiberger   203
**GENERAL TIRE
LAS VEGAS CLASSIC**
1988   Larry Mowry   204
1989   *Charles Coody   205
LAS VEGAS SENIOR CLASSIC
1990   Chi Chi Rodriguez   204
1991   Chi Chi Rodriguez   204
1992   Lee Trevino   206
1993   Gibby Gilbert   204
1994   Ray Floyd   203

**LIBERTY MUTUAL
LEGENDS OF GOLF**
Barton Creek C.C.,
Austin, TX (1990-present).
(Unofficial event.)
LEGENDS OF GOLF
1978   Sam Snead/
        Gardner Dickinson 193
1979   Julius Boros/
        Roberto De Vicenzo 195
LIBERTY MUTUAL LEGENDS OF GOLF
1980   Tommy Bolt/
        Art Wall   187
1981   Gene Littler/
        Bob Rosburg   257
1982   Sam Snead/
        Don January   183
1983   Rod Funseth/
        Roberto DeVicenzo   258
1984   Billy Casper/
        Gay Brewer   258
1985   Don January/
        Gene Littler   257

Liberty Mutual Legends of Golf continued

1986	Don January/	
	Gene Littler	255
1987	Bruce Crampton/	
	Orville Moody	251
1988	*Bruce Crampton/	
	Orville Moody	254
1989	Harold Henning/	
	Al Geiberger	251
1990	Dale Douglass/	
	Charles Coody	249
1991	Lee Trevino/	
	Mike Hill	252
1992	Lee Trevino/	
	Mike Hill	251
1993	*Harold Henning	204
1994	Dale Douglass	
	Charles Coody	188

PAINEWEBBER INVITATIONAL

TPC at Piper Glen,
Charlotte, NC (1989-present).
WORLD SENIORS INVITATIONAL

1980	*Gene Littler	211
1981	Miller Barber	282
1982	Gene Littler	280
1983	Doug Sanders	283

WBTV WORLD SENIORS INVITATIONAL

1984	Peter Thomson	281

PAINEWEBBER WORLD SENIORS INVITATIONAL

1985	Miller Barber	277
1986	Bruce Crampton	279
1987	*Gary Player	207

PAINEWEBBER INVITATIONAL

1988	Dave Hill	206
1989	No Tournament	
1990	Bruce Crampton	205
1991	Orville Moody	207
1992	Don Bies	203
1993	Mike Hill	204
1994	Lee Trevino	203

CADILLAC/NFL GOLF CLASSIC

Upper Montclair C.C.,
Clinton, NJ (1993-present).

1993	Lee Trevino	209
1994	Ray Floyd	206

BELL ATLANTIC CLASSIC

Chester Valley G.C.,
Malvem, PA (1985-present).
UNITED HOSPITALS SENIOR GOLF CHAMPIONSHIP

1985	Don January	135
1986	Gary Player	206
1987	Chi Chi Rodriguez	202

UNITED HOSPITALS CLASSIC

1988	*Bruce Crampton	205

BELL ATLANTIC/ST. CHRISTOPHER'S CLASSIC

1989	*Dave Hill	206

BELL ATLANTIC CLASSIC

1990	*Dale Douglass	204
1991	Jim Ferree	208
1992	Lee Trevino	205
1993	Bob Charles	204
1994	Lee Trevino	206

BRUNO'S MEMORIALCLASSIC

Greystone G.C.,
Birmingham, AL (1992-present).

1992	George Archer	208
1993	Bob Murphy	203
1994	Jim Dent	201

NATIONWIDE CHAMPIONSHIP

C.C. of the South,
Alpharetta, GA (1991-present).

1991	Mike Hill	212
1992	Isao Aoki	208
1993	Lee Trevino	205
1994	Dave Stockton	198

KROGER SENIOR CLASSIC

Jack Nicklaus Sports Center (Grizzly),
Kings Island, OH (1990-present).

1990	Jim Dent	133
1991	Al Geiberger	203
1992	*Gibby Gilbert	203
1993	Simon Hobday	202
1994	Jim Colbert	199

AMERITECH SENIOR OPEN

Stonebridge C.C.,
Aurora, IL (1991-present).

1989	Bruce Crampton	205
1990	Chi Chi Rodriguez	203
1991	Mike Hill	200
1992	Dale Douglass	201
1993	George Archer	133
1994	John Paul Cain	202

SOUTHWESTERN BELL CLASSIC

Loch Lloyd C.C.,
Belton, MO (1991-present).

SILVER PAGES CLASSIC

1987	Chi Chi Rodriguez	200

SOUTHWESTERN BELL CLASSIC

1988	*Gary Player	203
1989	*Bobby Nichols	209
1990	Jimmy Powell	208
1991	Jim Colbert	201
1992	Gibby Gilbert	193
1993	Dave Stockton	204
1994	Jim Colbert	196

NORTHVILLE LONG ISLAND CLASSIC

Meadow Brook Club,
Jericho, NY (1988-present).

THE NORTHVILLE INVITATIONAL

1988	Don Bies 202	

NORTHVILLE LONG ISLAND CLASSIC

1989	*Butch Baird	183
1990	George Archer	208
1991	George Archer	204
1992	George Archer	205
1993	Ray Floyd	208
1994	Lee Trevino	200

BANK OF BOSTON CLASSIC

Nashawtuc C.C.,
Concord, MA (1984-present).

MARLBORO CLASSIC

1981	Bob Goalby	208
1982	Arnold Palmer	276

1983	Don January	273

DIGITAL MIDDLESEX CLASSIC

1984	Don January	209

DIGITAL SENIORS CLASSIC

1985	*Lee Elder	208
1986	Chi Chi Rodriguez	203
1987	Chi Chi Rodriguez	198
1988	Chi Chi Rodriguez	202
1989	Bob Charles	200
1990	Bob Charles	203
1991	Rocky Thompson	205
1992	*Mike Hill	136

BANK OF BOSTON CLASSIC

1993	Bob Betley	204
1994	Jim Albus	203

FIRST OF AMERICA CLASSIC

The Highlands,
Grand Rapids, MI (1990-present).

GREATER GRAND RAPIDS OPEN

1986	*Jim Ferree	204
1987	Billy Casper	200
1988	Orville Moody	203
1989	John Paul Cain	203
1990	Don Massengale	134

FIRST OF AMERICA CLASSIC

1991	*Harold Henning	202
1992	Gibby Gilbert	202
1993	*George Archer	199
1994	Tony Jacklin	136

BURNET SENIOR CLASSIC

Bunker Hills G.C.,
Coon Rapids, MN (1993-present.)

1993	Chi Chi Rodriguez	201
1994	Dave Stockton	203

FRANKLIN QUEST CHAMPIONSHIP

Jeremy Ranch G.C.,
Park City, UT (1982-present).

THE SHOOTOUT AT JEREMY RANCH

1982	Billy Casper	279
1983	Bob Goalby/	
	Mike Reid	256

Franklin Showdown Classic continued

1984	Don January/	
	Mike Sullivan	250
1985	Miller Barber/	
	Ben Crenshaw	257

SHOWDOWN CLASSIC

1986	Bobby Nichols/	
	Curt Byrum	249
1987	Miller Barber	210
1988	Miller Barber	207
1989	Tom Shaw	207
1990	Rives McBee	202
1991	Dale Douglass	209

FRANKLIN SHOWDOWN CLASSIC

1992	*Orville Moody	137
1993	Dave Stockton	197
1994	Tom Weiskopf	204

GTE NORTHWEST CLASSIC
Inglewood C.C.,
Kenmore, WA (1987-present).

1986	Bruce Crampton	210
1987	Chi Chi Rodriguez	206
1988	Bruce Crampton	207
1989	Al Geiberger	204
1990	George Archer	205
1991	Mike Hill	198
1992	Mike Joyce	204
1993	Dave Stockton	200
1994	Simon Hobday	209

GTE NORTH CLASSIC
Broadmoor C.C.,
Indianapolis, IN (1988-1993).

1988	Gary Player	201
1989	Gary Player	135
1990	*Mike Hill	201
1991	George Archer	199
1992	Ray Floyd	199
1993	Bob Murphy	134
1994	No Tournament	

QUICKSILVER CLASSIC
Quicksilver C.C.,
Midway, PA (1993-present).

1993	Bob Charles	207
1994	Dave Eichelberger	209

BANK ONE SENIOR CLASSIC
Keamey Hill Links,
Lexington, KY (1990-present).

CITIZENS UNION SENIOR GOLF CLASSIC

1983	Don January	269
1984	Gay Brewer	204
1985	Lee Elder	135

BANK ONE SENIOR GOLF CLASSIC

1986	*Gene Littler	201
1987	Bruce Crampton	197
1988	Bob Charles	200

RJR BANK ONE CLASSIC

1989	Rives McBee	202

VANTAGE BANK ONE CLASSIC

1990	Rives McBee	201

BANK ONE SENIOR CLASSIC

1991	*DeWitt Weaver	207
1992	Terry Dill	203
1993	Gary Player	202
1994	Isao Aoki	202

VANTAGE CHAMPIONSHIP
Tanglewood Park,
Clemmons, NC (1987-present).

VANTAGE CHAMPIONSHIP

1987	Al Geiberger	206
1988	Walt Zembriski	278

RJR CHAMPIONSHIP

1989	Gary Player	207

VANTAGE CHAMPIONSHIP

1990	Charles Coody	202
1991	Jim Colbert	205
1992	Jim Colbert	132
1993	Lee Trevino	198
1994	Larry Gilbert	198

THE TRANSAMERICA
Silverado C.C. (South),
Napa, CA (1989-present).

TRANSAMERICA SENIOR
GOLF CHAMPIONSHIP

1989	Billy Casper	207

The Transamerica continued

1990	LeeTrevino	205
1991	Charles Coody	204
1992	Bob Charles	200
1993	Dave Stockton	203
1994	Kermit Zarley	204

RALEY'S SENIOR GOLD RUSH

Rancho Murieta C.C. (North)
Rancho Murieta, CA (1987-present).

RANCHO MURIETA SENIOR GOLD RUSH

1987	Orville Moody	205
1988	Bob Charles	207
1989	Dave Hill	207

GOLD RUSH AT RANCHO MURIETA

| 1990 | George Archer | 204 |

RALEY'S SENIOR GOLD RUSH

1991	George Archer	206
1992	Bob Charles	201
1993	George Archer	202
1994	Bob Murphy	208

RALPH'S SENIOR CLASSIC

Rancho Park G.C.,
Los Angeles, CA (1900-present).

SECURITY PACIFIC SENIOR CLASSIC

| 1990 | Mike Hill | 201 |
| 1991 | *John Brodie | 200 |

RALPHS SENIOR CLASSIC

1992	Ray Floyd	195
1993	*Dale Douglas	196
1994	Jack Kiefer	197

KAANAPALI CLASSIC

Royal Kaanapali G.C. (North),
Maui, HI (1987-present).

GTE KAANAPALI CLASSIC

1987	Orville Moody	132
1988	Don Bies	204
1989	Don Bies	132
1990	Bob Charles	206

FIRST DEVELOPMENT KAANAPALI CLASSIC

| 1991 | Jim Colbert | 195 |

KAANAPALI CLASSIC

1992	Tommy Aaron	198
1993	George Archer	199
1994	Bob Murphy	195

DUPONT CUP
JAPAN VS. USA
SENIOR GOLF MATCH

Kitaura G.C.,
Ibaragi, Japan (1993).

1989	United States	1,493
1990	United States	20-12
1991	United States	24-8
1992	United States	22-10
1993	United States	26-6
1994	Not available at press time.	

SENIOR TOUR CHAMPIONSHIP

HyattDorado Beach (East)
Dorado, Puerto Rico (1988-present).

MAZDA CHAMPIONS

1985	Don January/ Alice Miller	127
1986	Bob Charles/ Amy Alcott	193
1987	Miller Barber/ Nancy Lopez	191
1988	Dave Hill/ Colleen Walker	186
1989	Mike Hill/ Patti Rizzo	191

NEW YORK LIFE CHAMPIONS

| 1990 | *Mike Hill | 201 |

SENIOR TOUR CHAMPIONSHIP

1991	Mike Hill	202
1992	Ray Floyd	197
1993	Simon Hobday	199
1994	Not available at press time.	

CLUB PRO CHAMPIONS

OVERVIEW: *Top-five finishers, scores and prize money for the primary club professional tournaments. Club pros have had their own "Tour" for many years, featuring winter tournaments (typically in Florida around the time of the PGA Merchandise Show); prize money is low but the quality of competition often high with several former and future PGA TOUR players competing. Although no full-time club pro has won a major championship since Claude Harmon in the 1948 Masters, several club professionals such as Jim Albus, Larry Laoretti and Tom Wargo have found fame and fortune on the PGA Senior TOUR.*

PGA Club Professional Tournament

Oaks Course (Par 71), Robert Trent Jones Course (Par 71) and North Port National G.C. (Par 72), Oage Beach and Lake Ozark, Missouri, Oct. 6-10

Sammy Rachels	**1**	**68-72-71-73**	**284**	**$32,000**
Darrell Kestner	T2	70-71-73-70	284	$19,500
Ronald McDougal	T2	72-65-76-71	284	$19,500
Bruce Zabriski	4	73-69-71-72	285	$14,000
Wayne DeFrancesco	T5	73-71-74-68	286	$10,500
Denny Hepler	T5	74-71-72-69	286	$10,500
Larry Emery	T5	74-72-69-71	286	$10,500
Drue Johnson	T5	70-70-76-70	286	$10,500
Stephen Keppler	T9	77-72-71-67	287	$7,250
Mark Mielke	T9	74-72-70-71	287	$7,250
Gary Trivisomno	T9	72-71-71-73	287	$7,250
Gary Groh	T9	66-76-71-74	287	$7,250

PGA Senior Club Professional Tournament

Ibis G. & C.C. (Par 72)
West Palm Beach, Florida, Oct. 18-21

Roger Kennedy	**1**	**72-69-70-72**	**283**	**$14,000**
Bill Garrett	2	75-70-70-69	284	$11,000
Patrick O'Brien	3	72-70-74-70	286	$9,000

Tom Joyce	4	71-77-71-68	287	$7,500
Bob Irving	5	71-73-72-74	290	$6,500
Bobby Mitchell	T6	73-74-75-69	291	$4,625
Gene Borek	T6	73-72-74-72	291	$4,625
Rocky Nelson	T6	72-77-71-71	291	$4,625
Gary Groh	T6	73-72-69-77	291	$4,625
Joe Carr	T10	79-71-71-71	292	$3,625
Art Proctor	T10	76-74-70-72	292	$3,625

Titleist/Foot-Joy PGA Assistant Professional Championship

PGA West—Nicklaus Private Course (Par 72), La Quinta, California, Dec. 14-17, 1993

Steve Brady	**1**	**71-73-69-71**	**284**	**$6,000**
Rob McNamara	2	68-75-72-73	288	$4,500
John Dal Corobbo	3	73-72-71-74	290	$3,500
John Mazza	4	72-76-74-69	291	$3,250
Joe Meade	T5	74-75-75-72	296	$2,758
Dan Hornig	T5	76-74-74-72	296	$2,758
Mike Taylor	T5	70-74-74-78	296	$2,758

Langert PGA Stroke Play Championship

PGA National GC (Par 72)
Palm Beach Gardens, Florida, Jan. 23-26

Dana Quigley	**1**	**70-66-72-69**	**277**	**$6,000**

Jerry Impellittiere	2	71-72-65-70	278	$4,500
Jim Estes	3	70-68-70-73	281	$3,500
Terence R. Hughes	T4	71-70-70-71	282	$2,600
Michael Zinni	T4	71-72-69-70	282	$2,600
Cary Hungate	T4	67-72-70-73	282	$2,600

Langert PGA Match Play Championship

PGA National GC (Par 72)
Miami, Florida, Mar 3-6

QUARTER-FINALS
Rick Vershure def. Bruce Summerhays, 3 and 2
Tom Dolby def. Bruce Zabriski, 2 and 1
Tom Cleaver dewf. Mike Baker, 7 and 5
Ron McDougal def. Larry Rentz, 1 up (19)

SEMI-FINALS
McDougal def. Vershure, 3 and 2
Cleaver def. Dolby, 5 and 4

FINALS
Cleaver def. McDougal, 5 and 3

Langert PGA Quarter Century Championship

PGA National G.C. (Estate—Par 72)
Palm Beach Gardens, Florida, Jan. 4-5

Under 50			
Michael Limback	75-75	150	$344
Age 50-54			
Tom Joyce	71-69	140	$800
Age 55-59			
Steve Bull	70-69	139	$1,000
Age 60-64			
Bob Ross	71-70	141	$800
Age 65-69			
Ray Montgomery	75-72	147	$800
Age 70-74			
Bob Duden	76-70	146	$800

Age 75-79			
Henry Williams	78-82	160	$800
Age 80-84			
Ralph Bond	86-85	171	$500
Age 85-89			
Tommy Shannon	94-97	191	$400

Langert PGA Senior Stroke Play Championship

PGA National G.C. (Par 72)
Palm Beach Gardens, Florida, Jan. 7-9

Age 50-54			
Gene Carello	75-71-70	216	$1,000
Age 55-59			
Larry Mancour	72-73-72	217	$1,100
Age 60-64			
Bob Ross	74-76-71	221	$800
Age 65-69			
Ray Montgomery	66-71	137	$800
Age 70-74			
Joe Taylor	72-75	147	$700
Age 75-79			
Philip Friel Jr.	76-77	153	$700
Age 80-84			
Ralph Bond	75-68	143	$600
Age 85-89			
Ted Lockie	77-78	155	$400

Langert PGA Senior-Junior Championship

PGA National G.C.
(Haig and Estate—Par 72)
Palm Beach Gardens, Florida, Jan. 15-17

Lloyd Monroe/Gary Hardin	1	204	$10,000
Bill Kennedy/Nic Borojevich	2	204	$7,000
Marion Heck/Charles Stucklen	T3	205	$4,166
Dick Sarta/Bruce Zabriski	T3	205	$4,166
Paul Barkhouse/Gene Fieger	T3	205	$4,166

PGA Cup Matches

1973 USA 7, Great Britain & Ireland 1   Pinehurst No. 2, USA

1974 USA 11-1/2, Great Britain & Ireland 4-1/2   Pinehurst No. 2, USA

1975 USA 9-1/2, Great Britain & Ireland 6-1/2   Hillside G.C., England

1976 USA 9-1/2, Great Britain & Ireland 6-1/2   Moortown G.C., England

1977 USA 8-1/2, Great Britain & Ireland 8-1/2   Mission Hills C.C., USA

1978 Great Britain & Ireland 10-1/2, USA 6-1/2   St. Mellion G. & C.C., England

1979 Great Britain & Ireland 12-1/2, USA 4-1/2   Castletown Links, Isle of Man

1980 USA 15, Great Britain & Ireland 6   Oak Tree G.C., USA

1981 USA 10-1/2, Great Britain & Ireland 10-1/2   Turnberry Isle C.C., USA

1982 USA 13-1/2, Great Britain & Ireland 7-1/2   Halston Hills Club, USA

1983 Great Britain & Ireland 14-1/2, USA 6-1/2   Muirfield, Scotland

1984 Great Britain & Ireland 12-1/2, USA 8-1/2   Turnberry, Scotland

1986 USA 16, Great Britain & Ireland 9   Knollwood C.C., USA

1988 USA 15-1/2, Great Britain & Ireland 10-1/2   The Belfry, England

1990 USA 19, Europe 7   Turtle Point G.C., USA

1992 USA 12, Europe 11   Kildare C.C., Ireland

1994 USA 15, Europe 11   PGA National G.C., USA

PGA Tournament Series (Florida), 1993-94

Dates	Winner	Score	Money	Site
Nov. 15-16	Bruce Zabriski	138	$3,300	Cobblestone CC, Palm City
Nov. 17-18	Bruce Zabriski	137	$3,400	Monarch CC, Stuart
Nov. 22-23	Steve Brady	140	$3,300	Wellington Club West, Wellington
Nov. 29-30	John Mattuci	141	$3,200	St. Lucie West C.C., Port St. Lucie
Dec. 2-3	Steve Brady	136	$3,400	Winston Trails C.C., Lake Worth
Dec. 5-6	Earl Puckett	139	$1,700	BallenIsles of JDM, Palm Beach Gardens
Dec. 6-7	Darrell Kestner	139	$3,500	The Reserve G. & T.C., Ft. Pierce
Dec. 8-9	Bill Hall	141	$1,500	Cub Med at Village of Sandpiper, Port St. Lucie
Dec. 9-10	Bruce Zabriski	137	$3,500	Breakers West C.C., West Palm Beach
Dec. 12-13	Butch Grattan	137	$3,500	BallenIsles C.C. of JDM, Palm Beach Gardens

Dec. 13-14— (Sr.) Austin Straub   141 $1,700   St. Lucie West C.C

  (Super Sr.) Mal McMullen   144 $900

Dec. 16-17— Bruce Zabriski   143 $3,500   Binks Forest C.C., Wellington

  (Sr.) Charlie Huckaby   140 $1,700   Palm Beach Gardens M.C.

  (Super Sr.) Buck Adams   145 $800

Feb. 9-10— (Sr.) Steve Bull   138 $1,800   PGA National G.C. (Estate), Lake Park

  (Super Sr.) Ray Montgomery   134 $900

Feb. 11-12— Mike San Filippo   132 $3,500   PGA National G.C. (Estate), Lake Park

Feb. 13-14— (Sr.) Jim Ferriel Jr.   134 $1,700   PGA National (Estate), Lake Park

  (Super Sr.) Walker Inman Jr.   141 $900

Feb. 15-16— Pete Oakley   139 $3,500   PGA National G.C. (Haig), Palm Beach Gardens

Feb. 17-18— (Sr.) Herb Rose   67 $1,700   PGA National G.C. (Haig), Palm Beach Gardens

  (Super Sr.) Ray Montgomery   70 $850

Feb. 21-22— Brian Fogt   134 $3,300   Club Med at Village of Sandpiper, Port St. Lucie

Feb. 23-24— (Sr.) Dennis Bradley 138 $1,700   Club Med at Village of Sandpiper, Port St. Lucie

  (Super Sr.) Ken Weiler   139 $850

Feb. 25-26— Chris Caulfield   134 $3,150   PGA National G.C. (Estate), Lake Park

PGA Club Professional Tournament

1968 Howell Fraser   272 $8,000   Century C.C.

1969 Bob Rosburg   275 $8,000   San Marcos C.C.

1970 Rex Baxter   285 $8,000   Sunol Valley C.C.

1971 Sam Snead   275 $15,000   Pinehurst C.C.

1972 Don Massengale   280 $15,000   Pinehurst C.C.

1973 Rives McBee   282 $16,500   Pinehurst C.C.

1974 Roger Watson   284 $16,500   Pinehurst C.C.

1975 Roger Watson   279 $16,500   Callaway Gardens Resort

1976 Bob Galloway   280 $16,500   Callaway Gardens Resort

1977 Laurie Hammer   282 $16,500   Callaway Gardens Resort

1978 John Gentile   276 $17,000   Callaway Gardens Resort

1979 Buddy Whitten   278 $20,000   Callaway Gardens Resort

Year	Name	Score	Prize	Venue
1980	John Traub	283	$20,000	PGA National G.C.
1981	Larry Gilbert	285	$20,000	PGA National G.C.
1982	Larry Gilbert	284	$20,000	PGA National G.C.
1983	Larry Webb	283	$20,000	La Quinta Hotel G.C.
1984	Bill Schumaker	284	$25,000	PGA National G.C.
1985	Ed Dougherty	277	$27,500	La Quinta Hotel G.C./Mission Hills
1986	Bob Lendzion	284	$30,000	PGA West/La Quinta Hotel/Mission Hills
1987	Jay Lumpkin	279	$30,000	PGA West/La Quinta Hotel/Mission Hills
1988	Bob Boyd	287	$30,000	Pinehurst C.C.
1989	Bruce Fleisher	277	$30,000	PGA West/La Quinta Hotel/Mission Hills
1990	Brett Upper	275	$32,000	PGA West/La Quinta Hotel/Mission Hills
1991	Larry Gilbert	267	$32,000	Doral C.C.
1992	Ron McDougal	273	$32,000	PGA West/La Quinta Hotel/Mission Hills
1993	Jeffrey Roth	275	$32,000	PGA National G.C.
1994	Sammy Rachels	284	$32,000	Osage Beach and Lake Ozark, MO

Foot-Joy PGA Assistant Professional Championship

Year	Name	Score	Prize	Venue
1977	Mike Zack	209	$3,000	Thorny Lea G.C.
1978	Larry Griffin	209	$3,000	Thorny Lea G.C.
1979	Loren Roberts	212	$3,000	Thorny Lea G.C.
1980	John Jackson	205	$3,000	Thorny Lea G.C.
1981	Ted O'Rourke	210	$3,300	Thorny Lea G.C.
1982	Darrell Kestner	213	$3,500	Thorny Lea G.C.
1983	Victor Tortorici	214	$4,000	Thorny Lea G.C.
1984	Fred Funk	206	$4,000	Thorny Lea G.C.
1985	Jon Fiedler	211	$4,000	Thorny Lea G.C.
1986	Robert Thompson	209	$5,000	Thorny Lea G.C.
1987	Darrell Kestner	210	$5,000	Thorny Lea G.C.
1988	Webb Heintzelman	205	$5,000	Thorny Lea G.C.
1989	Mike West	210	$5,500	Thorny Lea G.C.
1990	Steve Gotsche	205	$5,500	Thorny Lea G.C.
1991	Kim Thompson	278	$6,000	PGA West (Nicklaus Private)
1992	Bill Loeffler	283	$6,000	PGA West (Nicklaus Private)
1993	Steve Brady	284	$6,000	PGA West (Nicklaus Private)

AMATEUR GOLF

OVERVIEW: *Winners of national amateur championships since inception, plus annual amateur rankings, Curtis and Walker Cup results through the years and prominent 1994 amateur results.*

U.S. Men's Amateur

Year	Winner	Site	Year	Winner	Site
1895	Charles Blair MacDonald	Newport	1939	Marvin H. Ward	North Shore
1896	H.J. Whigham	Shinnecock	1940	Richard D. Chapman	Winged Foot (West)
1897	H.J. Whigham	Chicago	1941	Marvin H. Ward	Omaha Field
1898	Findlay S. Douglas	Morris County	1942	*No tournament*	
1899	H.M. Harriman	Onwentsia	1943	*No tournament*	
1900	Walter J. Travis	Garden City	1944	*No tournament*	
1901	Walter J. Travis	CC of Atlantic City	1945	*No tournament*	
1902	Louis N. James	Glen View	1946	Ted Bishop	Baltusrol (Lower)
1903	Walter J. Travis	Nassau	1947	Skee Riegel	Pebble Beach
1904	H. Chandler Egan	Baltusrol	1948	William P. Turnesa	Memphis
1905	H. Chandler Egan	Chicago	1949	Charles R. Coe	Oak Hill (East)
1906	Eben M. Byers	Englewood	1950	Sam Urzetta	Minneapolis
1907	Jerome D. Travers	Euclid	1951	Billy Maxwell	Saucon Valley (Old)
1908	Jerome D. Travers	Garden City	1952	Jack Westland	Seattle
1909	Robert A. Gardner	Chicago	1953	Gene Littler	Oklahoma City
1910	Wiliam C. Fownes Jr.	The Country Club	1954	Arnold Palmer	CC of Detroit
1911	Harold H. Hilton	Apawamis	1955	E. Harvie Ward Jr.	CC of Virginia (James R.)
1912	Jerome D. Travers	Chicago	1956	E. Harvie Ward	Knollwood
1913	Jerome D. Travers	Garden City	1957	Hillman Robbins Jr.	The Country Club
1914	Francis Ouimet	Ekwanok	1958	Charles R. Coe	Olympic (Lake)
1915	Robert A. Gardner	CC of Detroit	1959	Jack Nicklaus	Broadmoor (East)
1916	Chick Evans	Merion	1960	Deane Beman	St. Louis
1917	*No tournament*		1961	Jack Nicklaus	Pebble Beach
1918	*No tournament*		1962	Labron E. Harris Jr.	Pinehurst (No.2)
1919	S. Davidson Herron	Oakmont	1963	Deane Beman	Wakonda
1920	Chick Evans	Engineers	1964	Wilaim C. Campbell	Canterbury
1921	Jesse P. Guilford	St. Louis	1965	Robert J. Murphy Jr.	Southern Hills
1922	Jess W. Sweetser	The Country Club	1966	Gary Cowan	Merion (East)
1923	Max R. Marston	Rossmoor	1967	Robert B. Dickson	Broadmoor (West)
1924	Robert T. Jones Jr.	Merion	1968	Bruce Fleisher	Scioto
1925	Robert T. Jones Jr.	Oakmont	1969	Steven N. Melnyk	Oakmont
1926	George Von Elm	Baltusrol	1970	Lanny Wadkins	Waverly
1927	Robert T. Jones Jr.	Minikahda	1971	Gary Cowan	Wilmington (South)
1928	Robert T. Jones Jr.	Brae Burn	1972	Marvin Giles III	Charlotte
1929	Harrison R. Johnston	Pebble Beach	1973	Craig Stadler	Inverness
1930	Robert T. Jones Jr.	Merion	1974	Jerry Pate	Ridgewood
1931	Francis Ouimet	Beverly	1975	Fred Ridley	CC of Virginia (James R.)
1932	C. Ross Somerville	Baltimore	1976	Bill Sander	Bel Air
1933	George T. Dunlap Jr.	Kenwood	1977	John Fought	Aronimink
1934	W. Lawson Little Jr.	The Country Club	1978	John Cook	Plainfield
1935	W. Lawson Little Jr.	The Country Club (O.)	1979	Mark O'Meara	Canterbury
1936	John W. Fischer	Garden City	1980	Hal Sutton	CC of N. Carolina
1937	John Goodman	Alderwood	1981	Nathaniel Crosby	Olympic (Lake)
1938	William P. Turnesa	Oakmont	1982	Jay Sigel	The Country Club

Year	Winner	Site
1983	Jay Sigel	North Shore
1984	Scott Verplank	Oak Tree
1985	Sam Randolph	Montclair
1986	Buddy Alexander	Shoal Creek
1987	Bill Mayfair	Jupiter Hills
1988	Eric Meeks	Va. Hot Spr. (Cascades)
1989	Chris Patton	Merion (East)
1990	Phil Mickelson	Cherry Hills
1991	Mitch Voges	The Honors
1992	Justin Leonard	Muirfield Village
1993	John Harris	Champions (Cypress Cr.)
1994	Eldrick (Tiger) Woods	TPC at Sawgrass

U.S. Men's Mid-Amateur

Year	Winner	Site
1981	Jim Holtgrieve	Bellerive
1982	William Hoffer	Knollwood
1983	Jay Sigel	Cherry Hills
1984	Michael Podolak	Atlanta A.C.
1985	Jay Sigel	The Vintage C.
1986	Bill Loeffler	Annandale
1987	Jay Sigel	Brook Hollow
1988	David Eger	Prairie Dunes
1989	James Taylor	Crooked Stick
1990	Jim Stuart	Troon
1991	Jim Stuart	Long Cove
1992	Danny Yates	Detroit
1993	Jeff Thomas	Eugene
1994	Tim Jackson	Hazeltine National

U.S. Men's Senior Amateur

Year	Winner	Site
1955	J. Wood Platt	Belle Meade
1956	Frederick J. Wright	Somerset
1957	J. Clark Espie	Ridgewood
1958	Thomas C. Robbins	Monterey Peninsula
1959	J. Clark Espie	Memphis
1960	Michael Cestone	Oyster Harbours
1961	Dexter H. Dabiels	Southern Hills
1962	Merrill L. Carlsmith	Evanston
1963	Merrill L. Carlsmith	Sea Island
1964	William D. Higgins	Waverly
1965	Robert B. Kiersky	Fox Chapel
1966	Dexter H. Daniels	Tucson National
1967	Ray Palmer	Shinnecock Hills
1968	Curtis Person Sr.	Atlanta C.C.
1969	Curtis Person Sr.	Wichita
1970	Gene Andrews	California
1971	Tom Draper	Sunnybrook
1972	Lewis W. Oehmig	Sharon
1973	William Hyndman III	Onwentsia
1974	Dale Morey	Harbour Town
1975	William F. Colm	Carmel Valley
1976	Lewis W. Oehmig	Cherry Hills
1977	Dale Morey	Salem
1978	Keith K. Compton	Pine Tree

Year	Winner	Site
1979	William C. Campbell	Chicago
1980	William C. Campbell	Va. Hot Springs
1981	Edgar R. Updegraff	Seattle
1982	Alton Duhon	Tucson
1983	William Hyndman III	Crooked Stick
1984	Robert Rawlins	Birmingham (Mich.)
1985	Lewis W. Oehmig	Wild Dunes
1986	R.S. Williams	Interlachen
1987	John Richardson	Saucon Valley
1988	Clarence Moore	Milwaukee
1989	R.S. Williams	Lochinvar
1990	Jackie Cummings	Desert Forest
1991	Bill Bosshard	Crystal Downs
1992	Clarence Moore	Loxahatchee
1993	Joe Ungvary	Farmington
1994	O. Gordon Brewer	Champions

U.S. Men's Amateur Public Links

Year	Winner	Site
1922	Edmund R. Held	Ottawa Park
1923	Richard J. Walsh	E. Potomac Park
1924	Joseph Coble	Community
1925	Raymond J. McAuliffe	Salisbury
1926	Lester Bolstad	Grover Cleveland Pk.
1927	Carl F. Kauffmann	Ridgewood
1928	Carl F. Kauffman	Cobb's Creek
1929	Carl F. Kauffman	Forest Park
1930	Robert E. Wingate	Jacksonville Muni.
1931	Charles Ferrara	Keller
1932	R.L. Miller	Shawnee
1933	Charles Ferrara	Eastmoreland
1934	David A. Mitchell	S. Park Allegheny
1935	Frank Strafaci	Coffin Muni.
1936	B. Patrick Abbott	Bethpage
1937	Bruce N. McCormick	Harding Park
1938	Al Leach	Highland Park
1939	Andrew Swedko	Mt. Pleasant Pk.
1940	Robert C. Clark	Rackham
1941	William M. Welch Jr.	Indian Canyon
1942	*No tournament*	
1943	*No tournament*	
1944	*No tournament*	
1945	*No tournament*	
1946	Smiley L. Quick	Wellshire
1947	Wilfred Crossley	Meadowbrook
1948	Michael Ferentz	N. Fulton Park
1949	Kenneth J. Towns	Rancho
1950	Stan Bielat	Seneca
1951	Dave Stanley	Brown Deer Park
1952	Omer L. Bogan	Miami
1953	Ted Richards Jr.	West Seattle
1954	Gene Andrews	Cedar Crest
1955	Sam Kocsis	Coffin Muni.
1956	James H. Buxbaum	Harding Park
1957	Don Essig III	Hershey Park
1958	Daniel D. Sikes Jr.	Silver Lake
1959	William A. Wright	Wellshire

Year	Winner	Site
1960	Verne Callison	Ala Wai
1961	Richard H. Sikes	Rackham
1962	Richard H. Sikes	Sheridan Park
1963	Robert Lunn	Haggin Oaks
1964	William McDonald	Francis A. Gross
1965	Arne Dokka	North Park
1966	Lamont Kaiser	Brown Deer Park
1967	Verne Callsion	Jefferson Park
1968	Gene Towry	Tenison Memorial
1969	John M. Jackson Jr.	Downing
1970	Robert Risch	Cog Hill (No. 4)
1971	Fred Haney	Papago
1972	Bob Allard	Coffin Muni.
1973	Stan Stopa	Flanders Valley
1974	Charles Barenaba Jr.	Brookside
1975	Randy Barenaba	Wailua
1976	Eddie Mudd	Bunker Hills
1977	Jerry Vidovic	Brown Deer Park
1978	Dean Prince	Bangor Muni.
1979	Dennis Walsh	West Delta
1980	Jodie Mudd	Edgewood Tahoe
1981	Jodie Mudd	Bear Creek Golf World
1982	Billy Tuten	Eagle Creek
1983	Billy Tuten	Hominy Hill
1984	Bill Malley	Indian Canyon
1985	Jim Sorenson	Wailua
1986	Bill Mayfair	Tanglewood Park
1987	Kevin Johnson	Glenview
1988	Ralph Howe III	Jackson Hole
1989	Tim Hobby	Cog Hill (No. 4)
1990	Michael Combs	Eastmoreland
1991	David Berganio Jr.	Otter Creek
1992	Warren Schutte	Edinburgh USA
1993	David Berganio Jr.	Riverside Dunes
1994	Guy Yamamoto	Eagle Bend

U.S. Amateur Public Links Team

Year	Winner	Site
1923	Chicago	E. Potomac Park
1924	Washington	Community
1925	New York	Salisbury
1926	Chicago	Grover Cleveland Pk.
1927	Pittsburgh	Ridgewood
1928	Pittsburgh	Cobb's Creek
1929	New York	Forest Park
1930	Brooklyn	Jacksonville Muni.
1931	San Francisco	Keller
1932	Louisville, Ky.	Shawnee
1933	Los Angeles	Eastmoreland
1934	Los Angeles	S. Park Allegheny
1935	San Antonio	Coffin Muni.
1936	Seattle	Bethpage
1937	Sacramento	Harding Park
1938	Los Angeles	Highland Park
1939	Los Angeles	Mt. Pleasant Pk.

Year	Winner	Site
1940	San Francisco	Rackham
1941	Detroit	Indian Canyon
1942	*No tournament*	
1943	*No tournament*	
1944	*No tournament*	
1945	*No tournament*	
1946	Long Beach, Calif	Wellshire
1947	Atlanta	Meadowbrook
1948	Raleigh	N. Fulton Park
1949	San Francisco	Rancho
1950	Los Angeles	Seneca
1951	Dayton	Brown Deer Park
1952	Chicago	Miami
1953	Jacksonville	West Seattle
1954	Dallas	Cedar Crest
1955	Miami	Coffin Muni.
1956	Memphis	Harding Park
1957	Honolulu	Hershey Park
1958	St. Paul	Silver Lake
1959	Dallas	Wellshire
1960	Pasadena, Calif.	Ala Wai
1961	Honolulu	Rackham
1962	Seattle	Sheridan Park
1963	Toledo	Haggin Oaks
1964	Los Angeles	Francis A. Gross
1965	Phoenix	North Park
1966	Pittsburgh	Brown Deer Park
1967	Dayton	Jefferson Park
1968	Dallas	Tenison Memorial
1969	Pasadena, Calif.	Downing
1970	Chicago	Cog Hill (No. 4)
1971	Portland	Papago
1972	Portland	Coffin Muni.
1973	Seattle	Flanders Valley
1974	San Francisco	Brookside
1975	Honolulu	Wailua
1976	Detroit	Bunker Hills
1977	Tacoma, Wash.	Brown Deer Park
1978	Louisville, Ky.	Bangor Muni.
1979	Phoenix	West Delta
1980	Los Angeles	Edgewood Tahoe
1981	Chicago	Bear Creek Golf World
1982	Phoenix	Eagle Creek
1983	Los Angeles	Hominy Hill
1984	Phoenix	Indian Canyon
1985	Phoenix	Wailua
1986	Clemmons, N.C.	Tanglewood Park
1987	San Francisco	Glenview
1988	Sacramento	Jackson Hole
1989	Las Vegas	Cog Hill (No. 4)
1990	Portland	Eastmoreland
1991	San Diego	Otter Creek
1992	Los Angeles	Edinburgh USA
1993	San Diego	Riverside Dunes
1994	Las Vegas	Eagle Bend

Walker Cup
Bi-annual amateur men's competition between the United States and Great Britain & Ireland

Year   Score, Site

1922 USA 8, Great Britain & Ireland 4
National Golf Links of America

1923 USA 6, Great Britain 5
St. Andrews (Old)

1924 USA 9, Great Britain & Ireland 3
Garden City G.C.

1926 USA 6, Great Britain & Ireland 5
St. Andrews (Old)

1928 USA 11, Great Britain & Ireland 1
Chicago G.C.

1930 USA 10, Great Britain & Ireland 2
Royal St. George's G.C.

1932 USA 8, Great Britain 1
The Country Club (Mass.)

1934 USA 9, Great Britain & Ireland 2
St. Andrews (Old)

1936 USA 9, Great Britain & Ireland 0
Pine Valley G.C.

1938 Great Britain & Ireland 7, USA 4
St. Andrews (Old)

1940-46 *No competition*

1947 USA 8, Great Britain & Ireland 4
St. Andrews (Old)

1949 USA 10, Great Britain & Ireland 2
Winged Foot G.C. (West)

1951 USA 6, Great Britain & Ireland 3
Birkdale G.C.

1953 USA 9, Great Britain & Ireland 3
The Kittansett Club

1955 USA 10, Great Britain & Ireland 2
St. Andrews (Old)

1957 USA 8, Great Britain & Ireland 3
Minikahda Club

1959 USA 9, Great Britain & Ireland 3
Muirfield

1961 USA 11, Great Britain & Ireland 1
Seattle G.C.

1963 USA 12, Great Britain & Ireland 8
Turnberry (Ailsa)

1965 USA 11, Great Britain & Ireland 11
Baltimore C.C. (Five Farms)

1967 USA 13, Great Britain & Ireland 7
Royal St. George's G.C.

1969 USA 10, Great Britain & Ireland 8
Milwaukee C.C.

1971 Great Britain & Ireland 13, USA 11
St. Andrews (Old)

1973 USA 14, Great Britain & Ireland 10
The Country Club (Mass.)

1975 USA 15-1/2, Great Britain & Ireland 8-1/2
St. Andrews (Old)

1977 USA 16, Great Britain & Ireland 8
Shinnecock Hills

1979 USA 15-1/2, Great Britain & Ireland 8-1/2
Muirfield

1981 USA 15, Great Britain & Ireland 9
Cypress Point Club

1983 USA 13-1/2, Great Britain & Ireland 10-1/2
Royal Liverpool G.C.

1985 USA 13, Great Britain & Ireland 11
Pine Valley G.C.

1987 USA 16-1/2, Great Britain & Ireland 7-1/2
Sunningdale G.C.

1989 Great Britain & Ireland 12-1/2, USA 11-1/2
Peachtree G.C.

1991 USA 14, Great Britain & Ireland 10
Portmarnock G.C.

1993 USA 19, Great Britain 5
Interlachen C.C.

U.S. Men's Amateur Rankings

1955
1. Harvie Ward
2. Joe Conrad
3. Doug Sanders
4. Hillman Robbins
5. Eddie Merrins

1956
1. Harvie Ward
2. Ken Venturi
3. Arnold Blum
4. Doug Sanders
5. Billy Joe Patton

1957
1. Hillman Robbins
2. Dr. F. Taylor
3. Rex Baxter
4. Billy Joe Patton
5. Billy Campbell

1958
1. Charles Coe
2. Bill Hyndman
3. Dick Chapman
4. Billy Joe Patton
5. Phil Rodgers

1959
1. Jack Nicklaus
2. Charles Coe
3. Deane Beman

4. Bill Hyndman
5. Dick Crawford

1960
1. Jack Nicklaus
2. Deane Beman
3. Charlie Smith
4. Bob Cochran
5. Tommy Aaron

1961
1. Jack Nicklaus
2. Bill Hyndman
3. Charles Coe
4. Deane Beman
5. Bob Gardner

1962
1. Labron Harris
2. Billy Joe Patton
3. R.H. Sikes
4. Deane Beman
5. Dr. Ed Updegraff

1963
1. Deane Beman
2. R.H. Sikes
3. George Archer
4. Charles Coe
5. Billy Joe Patton

1964
1. Bill Campbell
2. Deane Beman
3. Dale Morey
4. Ed Tutwiler
5. Steve Opperman

1965
1. George Bouteil
2. Bob Murphy
3. Don Allen
4. Jim Wiechers
5. Deane Beman

1966
1. Gary Cowan
2. Jim Wiechers
3. Marty Fleckman
4. Ron Cerrudo
5. Deane Beman

1967
1. Bob Dickson
2. Bob Smith
3. Hal Underwood
4. Marty Fleckman
5. Bill Campbell

1968
1. Vinny Giles
2. Jack Lewis
3. Bruce Fleisher
4. Bill Hyndman
5. Bill Barbarossa

1969
1. Steve Melnyk
2. Allen Miller
3. Vinny Giles
4. Joe Inman
5. Lanny Wadkins

1970
1. Lanny Wadkins
2. Allen Miller
3. Howard Twitty
4. Gary Cowan
5. Tom Kite

1971
1. Gary Cowan
2. Eddie Pearce
3. Ben Crenshaw
4. Vinny Giles
5. Allen Miller

1972
1. Ben Crenshaw
2. Vinny Giles
3. Mark Hayes
4. Danny Edwards
5. Gary Sanders

1973
1. Ben Crenshaw
2. Vinny Giles
3. Craig Stadler
4. Gary Koch
5. Dick Siderowf

1974
1. Jerry Pate
2. Curtis Strange
3. George Burns
4. Bill Hyndman
5. Gary Koch

1975
1. Andy Bean
2. Fred Ridley
3. Curtis Strange
4. Vinny Giles
5. Phil Hancock

1976
1. Scott Simpson

2. Bob Byman
3. Bill Sander
4. Jay Sigel
5. Dick Siderowf

1977
1. John Fought
2. Gary Hallberg
3. Jim Nelford
4. Scott Simpson
5. John Cook

1978
1. Bobby Clampett
2. John Cook
3. Vance Heafner
4. Scott Hoch
5. Jay Sigel

1979
1. John Cook
2. Mark O'Meara
3. Hal Sutton
4. Rafael Alarcon
5. Jay Sigel

1980
1. Hal Sutton
2. Jay Sigel
3. Fred Couples
4. Jay Don Blake
5. Bobby Clampett

1981
1. Jodie Mudd
2. Frank Fuhrer
3. Nathaniel Crosby
4. Corey Pavin
5. Jay Sigel

1982
1. Jay Sigel
2. Rick Fehr
3. Nathaniel Crosby
4. Brad Faxon
5. John Slaughter

1983
1. Jay Sigel
2. Billy Tuten
3. Scott Verplank
4. Brandel Chamblee
5. Dillard Pruitt

1984
1. Scott Verplank
2. John Inman
3. Jay Sigel

4. Davis Love III
5. Danny Mijovic

1985
1. Scott Verplank
2. Sam Randolph
3. Jay Sigel
4. Clark Burroughs
5. Peter Persons

1986
1. Stewart Alexander
2. Scott Verplank
3. Sam Randolph
4. Chris Kite
5. Bill Andrade

1987
1. Bill Mayfair
2. Jay Sigel
3. Brian Watts
4. Kevin Johnson
5. Hugh Royer

1988
1. Eric Meeks
2. Jay Sigel
3. Ralph Howe
4. David Eger
5. Bill Mayfair

1989-1991
Not available

1992
1. Justin Leonard
2. David Duval
3. Allen Doyle
4. David Howser
5. John Harris

1993
1. Justin Leonard
2. Todd Demsey
3. John Harris
4. Allen Doyle
5. Brian Gay

1994
1. Allen Doyle
2. Eldrick (Tiger) Woods
3. Chris Riley
4. Gary Simpson
5. Alan Bratton

U.S. Women's Amateur

Year	Winner	Site	Year	Winner	Site
1895	Mrs. Charles S. Brown	Meadow Brook	1951	Dorothy Kirby	Town & Country
1896	Beatrix Hoyt	Morris County	1952	Jacqueline Pung	Waverly
1897	Beatrix Hoyt	Essex County	1953	Mary Lena Faulk	Rhode Island
1898	Beatrix Hoyt	Ardsley	1954	Barbara Romack	Allegheny
1899	Ruth Underhill	Philadelphia	1955	Patricia Lesser	Myers Park
1900	Frances C. Griscom	Shinnecock Hills	1956	Marlene Stewart	Meridian Hills
1901	Genevieve Hecker	Baltusrol	1957	JoAnne Gunderson	Del Paso
1902	Genevieve Hecker	The Country Club	1958	Anne Quast	Wee Burn
1903	Bessie Anthony	Chicago	1959	Barbara McIntire	Congressional
1904	Georgianna M. Bishop	Merion	1960	JoAnne Gunderson	Tulsa
1905	Pauline Mackay	Morris County	1961	Anne Quast Decker	Tacoma
1906	Harriot S. Curtis	Brae Burn	1962	JoAnne Gunderson	C.C. of Rochester
1907	Margaret Curtis	Midlothian	1963	Anne Quast Welts	Taconic
1908	Katherine C. Harley	Chevy Chase	1964	Barbara McIntire	Prairie Dunes
1909	Dorothy I. Campbell	Merion	1965	Jean Ashley	Lakewood
1910	Dorothy I. Campbell	Homewood	1966	JoAnne Carner	Birmingham
1911	Margaret Curtis	Baltusrol	1967	Mary Lou Dill	Annandale
1912	Margaret Curtis	Essex County	1968	JoAnne Carner	Birmingham
1913	Gladys Ravenscroft	Wilmington	1969	Catherina Lacoste	Las Colinas
1914	Katherine Jackson	Nassau	1970	Martha Wilkinson	Wee Burn
1915	Florence Vanderbeck	Onwentsia	1971	Laura Baugh	Atlanta C.C.
1916	Alexa Stirling	Belmont Springs	1972	Mary Budke	St. Louis
1917	*No tournament*		1973	Carol Semple	Montclair
1918	*No tournament*		1974	Cynthia Hill	Broadmoor
1919	Alexa Stirling	Shawnee	1975	Beth Daniel	Brae Burn
1920	Alexa Stirling	Mayfield	1976	Donna Horton	Del Paso
1921	Marion Hollins	Hollywood	1977	Beth Daniel	Cincinatti
1922	Glenna Collett	Greenbrier	1978	Cathy Sherk	Sunnybrook
1923	Edith Cummings	Westchester-Biltmore	1979	Carolyn Hill	Memphis
1924	Dorothy C. Hurd	Rhode Island	1980	Juli Inkster	Prairie Dunes
1925	Glenna Collett	St. Louis	1981	Juli Inkster	Waverly
1926	Helen Stetson	Merion	1982	Juli Inkster	Broadmoor
1927	Miriam Burns Horn	Cherry Valley	1983	Joanne Pacillo	Canoe Brook
1928	Glenna Collett	Va. Hot Springs	1984	Deb Richard	Broadmoor
1929	Glenna Collett	Oakland Hills	1985	Mickiko Hattori	Fox Chapel
1930	Glenna Collett	Los Angeles	1986	Kay Cockerill	Pasatiempo
1931	Helen Hicks	CC of Buffalo	1987	Kay Cockerill	Rhode Island
1932	Virginia Van Wie	Salem	1988	Pearl Sinn	Minikahda
1933	Virginia Van Wie	Exmoor	1989	Vicki Goetze	Pinehurst No. 2
1934	Virginia Van Wie	Whitemarsh Valley	1990	Pat Hurst	Canoe Brook
1935	Glenna Collett Vare	Interlachen	1991	Amy Fruhwirth	Prairie Dunes
1936	Pamela Barton	Canoe Brook	1992	Vicki Goetze	Kemper Lakes
1937	Estelle Lawson Page	Memphis	1993	Jill McGill	San Diego
1938	Patty Berg	Westmoreland	1994	Wendy Ward	Cascades
1939	Betty Jameson	Wee Burn			
1940	Betty Jameson	Pebble Beach			
1941	Elizabeth Hicks Newell	The Country Club			
1942	*No tournament*				
1943	*No tournament*				
1944	*No tournament*				
1945	*No tournament*				
1946	Babe Zaharias	Southern Hills			
1947	Louise Suggs	Franklin Hills			
1948	Grace S. Lenczyk	Pebble Beach			
1949	Dorothy Porter	Merion			
1950	Beverly Hanson	Atlanta A.C.			

U.S. Women's Mid-Amateur

Year	Winner	Site
1987	Cindy Scholefield	Southern Hills
1988	Martha Lang	Amelia Island
1989	Robin Weiss	The Hills of Lakeway
1990	Carol Semple Thompson	Allegheny
1991	Sarah LeBrun Ingram	Desert Highlands
1992	Marion Maney-McInerny	Old Marsh
1993	Sarah LeBrun Ingram	Rochester
1994	Maria Jemsek	Tacoma

U.S. Women's Senior Amateur

Year	Winner	Site
1962	Maureen Orcutt	Manufacturers'
1963	Marion Choate	CC of Florida
1964	Lorna Smith	Del Paso
1965	Lorna Smith	Exmoor
1966	Maureen Orcutt	Lakewood
1967	Marge Mason	Atlantic City
1968	Carolyn Cudone	Monterey Peninsula
1969	Carolyn Cudone	Ridgelea
1970	Carolyn Cudone	Coral Ridge
1971	Carolyn Cudone	Sea Island
1972	Carolyn Cudone	Manufacturers'
1973	Gwen Hibbs	San Marcos
1974	Justine B. Cushing	Lakewood
1975	Alberta Bower	Rhode Island
1976	Cecile Maclaurin	Monterey Peninsula
1977	Dorothy Porter	Dunes Club
1978	Alice Dye	Rancho Bernardo
1979	Alice Dye	Herdscrabble
1980	Dorothy Porter	Sea Island
1981	Dorothy Porter	Spring Lake
1982	Edean Ihlanfeldt	Kissing Camels
1983	Dorothy Porter	Gulph Mills
1984	Constance Guthrie	Tacoma
1985	Marlene Street	Sheraton Savannah
1986	Constance Guthrie	Lakewood
1987	Anne Sander	Manufacturers'
1988	Lois Hodge	Sea Island
1989	Anne Sander	TPC at The Woodlands
1990	Anne Sander	Del Rio
1991	Phyllis Preuss	Pine Needles
1992	Rosemary Thompson	Tucson
1993	Anne Sander	Preakness Hills
1994	Nancy Fitzgerald	Sea Island

U.S. Women's Amateur Public Links

1977	Kelly Fuiks	Yahara Hills
1978	Kelly Fuiks	Myrtlewood
1979	Lori Castillo	Braemar
1980	Lori Castillo	Center Square
1981	Mary Enright	Emerald Valley
1982	Nancy Taylor	Alvamar
1983	Kelli Antolock	Ala Wai
1984	Heather Farr	Meadowbrook
1985	Danielle Ammaccapane	Flanders Valley
1986	Cindy Schreyer	SentryWorld
1987	Tracy Kerdyk	Cog Hill No. 4
1988	Pearl Sinn	Page Belcher
1989	Pearl Sinn	Indian Canyon
1990	Cathy Mockett	Hyland Hills
1991	Tracy Hanson	Birdwood
1992	Amy Fruwirth	Haggin Oaks
1993	Connie Masterson	Jackson Hole
1994	Jill McGill	Tam O'Shanter

U.S. Women's Amateur Public Links Team

Year	Winner	Site
1977	Phoenix	Yahara Hills
1978	Miami	Myrtlewood
1979	Chicago	Braemar
1980	Chicago	Center Square
1981	Phoenix	Emerald Valley
1982	Portland	Alvamar
1983	Chicago	Ala Wai
1984	Athens, Ga.	Meadowbrook
1985	Phoenix	Flanders Valley
1986	Phoenix	SentryWorld
1987	Miami	Cog Hill No. 4
1988	Tulsa	Page Belcher
1989	Phoenix	Indian Canyon
1990	Albuquerque	Hyland Hills
1991	Spokane	Birdwood
1992	Sacramento	Haggin Oaks
1993	Cocoa Beach, Fla.	Jackson Hole
1994	Miami	Tam O'Shanter

Curtis Cup

Bi-annual amateur women's competition between the United States and Great Britain & Ireland

Year	Score, Site
1932	USA 5-1/2, Great Britain & Ireland 3-1/2 Wentworth
1934	USA 6-1/2, Great Britain & Ireland 2-1/2 Chevy Chase
1936	USA 4-1/2, Great Britain & Ireland 4-1/2 Gleneagles
1938	USA 5-1/2, Great Britain & Ireland 3-1/2 Essex
1940-46	*No competition*
1948	USA 6-1/2, Great Britain & Ireland 2-1/2 Birkdale
1950	USA 7-1/2, Great Britain & Ireland 1-1/2 C.C. of Buffalo
1952	USA 5, Great Britain & Ireland 4 Muirfield
1954	USA 6, Great Britain & Ireland 3 Merion
1956	USA 5, Great Britain & Ireland 4 Prince's
1958	USA 4-1/2, Great Britain & Ireland 4-1/2 Brae Burn
1960	USA 6-1/2, Great Britain & Ireland 2-1/2 Lindrick
1962	USA 8, Great Britain & Ireland 1 Broadmoor
1964	USA 10-1/2, Great Britain & Ireland 7-1/2 Royal Porthcawl

Year	Score, Site
1966	USA 13, Great Britain & Ireland 5 Virginia Hot Springs
1968	USA 10-1/2, Great Britain & Ireland 7-1/2 Royal County Down
1970	USA 11-1/2, Great Britain & Ireland 6-1/2 Brae Burn
1972	USA 10, Great Britain & Ireland 8 Western Gailes
1974	USA 13, Great Britain & Ireland 5 San Francisco
1976	USA 11-1/2, Great Britain & Ireland 6-1/2 Royal Lytham & St. Anne's
1978	USA 12, Great Britain & Ireland 6 Apawamis Club
1980	USA 13, Great Britain & Ireland 5 St. Pierre
1982	USA 14-1/2, Great Britain & Ireland 3-1/2 Denver
1984	USA 9-1/2, Great Britain & Ireland 8-1/2 Muirfield
1986	Great Britain & Ireland 13, USA 5 Prairie Dunes
1988	Great Britain & Ireland 11, USA 7 Royal St. George's
1990	USA 14, Great Britain 4 Somerset Hills
1992	Great Britain & Ireland 10, USA 8 Royal Liverpool

U.S. Women's Amateur Rankings

1955
1. Pat Lesser
2. Wiffi Smith
3. Jackie Yates
4. Polly Riley
5. Barbara Romack

1956
1. Marlene Stewart
2. JoAnne Gunderson
3. Wiffi Smith
4. Anne Quast
5. Wanda Sanches

1957
1. JoAnne Gunderson
2. Ann C. Johnstone
3. Barabara McIntire
4. Anne Richardson
5. Mary Ann Downey

1958
1. Anne Quast

2. Barbara McIntire
3. Barbara Romack
4. JoAnne Gunderson
5. Carolyn Cudone

1959
1. Barbara McIntire
2. Ann C. Johnstone
3. Joanne Goodwin
4. JoAnne Gunderson
5. Anne Quast

1960
1. JoAnne Gunderson
2. Barbara McIntire
3. Ann C. Johnstone
4. Judy Eller
5. Anne Quast

1961
1. Anne Quast Decker
2. Barbara McIntire
3. Phyllis Preuss
4. Judy Bell
5. Barbara Williams

1962
1. JoAnne Gunderson
2. Clifford Ann Creed
3. Phyllis Preuss
4. Ann C. Johnstone
5. Carol Sorenson

1963
1. Anne Quast Welts
2. Nancy Roth
3. JoAnne Gunderson
4. Peggy Conley
5. Janis Ferraris

1964
1. Barbara McIntire
2. Carol Sorenson
3. Barbara Boddie
4. Nancy Roth
5. Phyllis Preuss

1965
1. Nancy Roth Syms
2. Marlene Streit
3. Jean Ashley
4. Phyllis Preuss
5. Barbara McIntire

1966
1. JoAnne Carner
2. Nancy Roth
3. Shelley Hamlin
4. Roberta Albers

1967
1. Mary Lou Dill
2. Phyllis Preuss
3. Jane Bastanchury
4. Martha Wilkinson
5. Dorothy Porter

1968
1. JoAnne Carner
2. Catherina LaCoste
3. Alice Dye
4. Jane Bastanchury
5. Phyllis Preuss

1969
1. Catherine LaCoste
2. Jane Bastanchury
3. JoAnne Carner
4. Barbara McIntire
5. Phyllis Preuss

1970
1. Martha Wilkinson
2. Jane Bastanchury
3. Cynthia Hill
4. Lancy Smith
5. Hollis Stacy

1971
1. Laura Baugh
2. Beth Barry
3. Phyllis Preuss
4. Lancy Smith
5. Barbara McIntire

1972
1. Jane Booth
2. Mary Budke
3. Mickey Walker
4. Debbie Massey
5. Beth Barry

1973
1. Carol Semple
2. Jane Booth
3. Beth Barry
4. Liana Zambresky
5. Anne Sander

1974
1. Debbie Massey
2. Cynthia Hill
3. Lancy Smith
4. Carol Semple
5. Marlene Streit

1975
1. Debbie Massey
2. Beth Daniel
3. Cynthia Hill
4. Nancy Lopez
5. Nancy Roth Syms

1976
1. Nancy Lopez
2. Donna Horton
3. Debbie Massey
4. Carol Semple
5. Marianne Bretton

1977
1. Beth Daniel
2. Cathy Reynolds
3. Cynthia Hill
4. Marcia Dolan
5. Lancy Smith

1978
1. Cathy Sherk
2. Beth Daniel
3. Nancy Syms
4. Judith Oliver
5. Carolyn Hill

1979
1. Carolyn Hill
2. Lancy Smith
3. Brenda Goldsmith
4. Mary Hafeman
5. Julie Gumlia

1980
1. Patti Rizzo
2. Juli Inkster
3. Carol Semple
4. Lori Castillo
5. Kathy Baker

1981
1. Juli Inkster
2. Patti Rizzo
3. Amy Benz
4. Leslie Shannon
5. Mary Hafeman

1982
1. Juli Inkster
2. Kathy Baker
3. Amy Benz
4. Cathy Hanlon
5. Anne Sander

1983
1. Penny Hammel
2. Jody Rosenthal
3. Joanne Pacillo
4. Anne Sander
5. Tammy Wellborn

1984
1. Claire White
2. Leslie Shannon
3. Deb Richard
4. Jody Rosenthal
5. Danielle Ammaccapane

1985
1. Danielle Ammaccapane
2. Kim Williams
3. Michiko Hattori
4. Kathleen McCarthy
5. Leslie Shannon

1986
1. Leslie Shannon
2. Kay Cockerill
3. Carol Semple Thompson
4. Lancy Smith
5. Cindy Scholefield

1987
1. Kay Cockerill
2. Cindy Scholefield
3. Tracy Kerdyk
4. Carol Semple Thompson
5. Caroline Keggi

1988
1. Pearl Sinn
2. Caroline Keggi
3. Anne Sander
4. Michiko Hattori
5. Tracy Kerdyk

1989-1991
Not available.

1992
1. Vicki Goetze
2. Carol Semple Thompson
3. Sarah Ingram
4. Robin Weiss
5. Moira Dunn

1993
1. Sarah Ingram
2. Emilee Klein
3. Carol Semple Thompson
4. Jill McGill
5. Stephanie Sparks

1994
1. Stephanie Neill
2. Sarah Ingram
3. Wendy Ward
4. Robin Weiss
5. Page Marsh Lea

Men's World Amateur Team Championship

Bi-annual amateur men's competition between 4-man national teams.

Year	Winner, Site
1958	Australia St. Andrews, Scotland
1960	USA Merion G.C., USA
1962	USA Fuji G.C., Japan
1964	Gr. Britain & Ireland Olgiata G.C., Italy
1966	Australia Club de Golf, Mexico
1968	USA Royal Melbourne, Australia
1970	USA Real Club de la Purta de Hierro, Spain
1972	USA Olivos G.C., Argentina
1974	USA Campo de Golf, Dominican Rep.
1976	Gr. Britain & Ireland Pennina G.C., Portugal
1978	USA Pacific Harbour G.&C.C., Fiji
1980	USA Pinehurst, USA
1982	USA Lausanne G.C., Switzerland
1984	Japan Royal Hong Kong G.C., Hong Kong
1986	Canada Laguinta, Venezuela
1988	Gr. Britain & Ireland Ullna G.C., Sweden
1990	Sweden Christchurch G.C., New Zealand
1992	New Zealand Capilano G.&C.C., Canada
1994	USA La Boulie

Women's World Amateur Team Championship

Bi-annual amateur women's competition between 4-woman national teams.

Year   Winner, Site
1964   France
    St. Germain G.C., France
1966   USA
    Mexico City C.C., Mexico
1968   USA
    Victoria G.C., Australia.
    Southampton, NY
1970   USA
    RSHE Club de Campo, Spain
1972   USA
    The Hindu C.C., Argentina
1974   USA
    Campo de Golf, Dominican Rep.
1976   USA
    Vilamoura G.C., Portugal
1978   Australia
    Pacific Harbour G.&C.C.
1980   USA
    Pinehurst, USA
1982   USA
    Geneva G.C., Switzerland
1984   USA
    Royal Hong Kong G.C., Hong Kong
1986   Spain
    Lagunita C.C., Venezuela
1988   USA
    Drottningholm G.C., Sweden
1990   USA
    Russley G.C., New Zealand
1992   Spain
    Marine Drive G.C., Canada
1994   USA
    La Boulie

Oldsmobile Scramble

Annual amateur men's competition between club teams competing with a club pro and a PGA Tour pro, with the final played in Orlando, FL.

1984
(GROSS)   Little Turtle C.C.,
    Westerville, OH

1985
(GROSS)   Buena Vista G.C.,
    Taft, Calif.

1986
(GROSS)   Hickory Hills G.C.,
    Grove City, Ohio

1987
(GROSS)   Sun Air C.C.,
    Haines City, Fla.
1988
(GROSS)   Fox Bend G.C.,
    Oswego, Ill.
1989
(GROSS)   TPC at The Woodlands,
    The Woodlands, Tx.
(NET)   Fox Bend G.C.,
    Oswego, Ill.
1990
(GROSS)   Walt Disney World G.C.,
    Lake Buena Vista, Fla.
(NET)   Shady Valley G.C.,
    Arlington, Tex.
1991
(GROSS)   Aquia Harbour
    Stafford, Va.
(NET)   Lochmoor C.C.,
    North Ft. Myers, Fla.
1992
(GROSS)   Jaycee G.C.,
    Chillicothe, Ohio
(NET)   Karsten G.C.,
    Tempe, Ariz.
1993
(GROSS)   PGA West,
    La Quinta, Calif.
(NET)   Valleywood G.C.,
    Swanton, Ohio

Miscellaneous 1994 Amateur Champions (Non-USGA events)

Eastern Amateur (Portsmouth Manor G.C.):
Steve Liebler

Northern Amateur (Sand Creek C.C.):
John Bernalovicz

Northwest Amateur (Spencer G. & C.C.):
Chris Vandell

Northeast Amateur (Wannamoisett C.C.)
G. Simpson

Porter Cup (Niagara Falls C.C.):
Allen Doyle

Southern Amateur (Lake Nona G.C.):
Trey Sones

Pacific Northwest Amateur (Royal Oaks G.C.):
Tiger Woods

Commonwealth National Invitational:
Robin McCool

1994 COLLEGIATE GOLF

OVERVIEW: *Significant 1994 tournament results, plus All-American team selections since 1965, Men's Division I, II and III individual and team champions plus Women's individual and team champions, since the start of competition.*

1994 Collegiate Results

MEN

NCAA East Regional
Team: Clemson
Indiv: Mark Swygert, Clemson

NCAA West Regional
Team: Univ. of Nevada—Las Vegas
Indiv: Edward Fryatt, UNLV

NCAA Central Regional
Team: Texas
Indiv: Dean Larson, Houston

Atlantic Coast Conference
Team: Georgia Tech
Indiv: Mikko Rantanen, Georgia Tech

Big Eight
Team: Oklahoma State
Indiv: Bob Kalinowski, Colorado

Southwest Conference
Team: Texas
Indiv: Justin Leonard, Texas

West Coast Conference
Team: Pepperdine
Indiv: Russ Humphrey, USF

Southland Conference
Team: Sam Houston St.
Indiv: Dean Choate, Sam Houston St.

Pacific 10 Conference
Team: Stanford
Indiv: Jason Gore, Arizona

Big West Conference
Team: Nevada-Las Vegas
Indiv: Chris Riley, UNLV

WAC
Team: Fresno State
Indiv: Joe Alcosta, Fresno State

Atlantic 10 Conference
Team: Rhode Island
Indiv: Mike Harrington, URI

Southern Conference
Team: East Tennessee
Indiv: Garrett Willis, East Tennessee

Metro Conference
Team: Virginia Tech
Indiv: Lance Combrink, Tulane

Patriot League
Team: Army
Indiv: Rick Gregson, Army

Ohio Valley Conference
Team: Middle Tennessee
Indiv: Caine Fitzgerald, SE Missouri

Atlantic Coast Conference
Team: Georgia Tech
Indiv: Mikko Rantanen

WOMEN

NCAA West Regional
Team: San Jose State
Indiv: Charlotta Eliasson, Okla. St.

NCAA East Regional
Team: Wake Forest
Indiv: Erika Wolff, Indiana

Southwest Conference
Team: Georgia Tech
Indiv: Mikko Rantanen

Pacific 10
Team: Arizona State
Indiv: Jennifer Biehn, USC

WAC
Team: New Mexico
Indiv: Brittany Schaff, New Mexico

Big Eight
Team: Oklahome State
Indiv: Charlotta Eliasson, OSU

Big Ten Conference
Team: Wisconsin
Indiv: Erika Wicoff, Indiana

Southeastern Conference
Team: Georgia
Indiv: Katharina Larson, Tennessee

Big West
Team: San Jose State
Indiv: Janice Moodie, San Jose State

Southwest Conference
Team: Texas
Indiv: Nadine Ash, Texas

Atlantic Coast Conference
Team: Georgia Tech
Indiv: Mikko Rantanen

NCAA Division I Champions -Men
Team (Italics), Individual
1897 *Yale Univ.*
Louis Bayard Jr., Princeton
1898 *Harvard Univ., Yale Univ.*
John Reid Jr., Yale
James Curtis, Harvard
1899 *Harvard*
Percy Pyne, Princeton
1900 *No Meeting*
1901 *Harvard Univ.*
H. Lindsley, Harvard
1902 *Yale Univ., Harvard Univ.*
Charles Hitchcock Fr., Yale
Chandler Egan, Harvard
1903 *Harvard Univ.*
F.O. Reinhart, Princeton
1904 *Harvard Univ.*
A.L. White, Harvard
1905 *Yale Univ.*
Robert Abbott, Yale
1906 *Yale Univ.*
W.E. Clow Jr., Yale
1907 *Yale Univ.*
Ellis Knowles, Yale
1908 *Yale Univ.*
H.H. Wilder, Harvard
1909 *Yale Univ.*
Albert Seckel, Princeton
1910 *Yale Univ.*
Robert Hunter, Yale
1911 *Yale Univ.*
George Stanley, Yale
1912 *Yale Univ.*
F.C. Davison, Harvard
1913 *Yale Univ.*
Nathaniel Wheeler, Yale
1914 *Princeton Univ.*
Edward Allis, Harvard

1915 *Yale Univ.*
Francis Blossom, Yale
1916 *Harvard Univ.*
J.W. Hubbell, Harvard
1917 *No Meeting*
1918 *No Meeting*
1919 *Princeton Univ.*
A.L. Walker Jr., Columbia
1920 *Princeton Univ.*
Jess Sweetser, Yale
1921 *Dartmouth Univ.*
Simpson Dean, Princeton
1922 *Princeton Univ.*
Pollack Boyd, Dartmouth
1923 *Princeton Univ.*
Dexter Cummings, Yale
1924 *Yale Univ.*
Dexter Cummings, Yale
1925 *Yale Univ.*
Fred Laprecht, Yale
1926 *Yale Univ.*
Fred Laprecht, Yale
1927 *Princeton Univ.*
Watts Gunn, Georgia Tech.
1928 *Princeton Univ.*
Maurice McCarthy, Georgetown
1929 *Princeton Univ.*
Tom Aycock, Yale
1930 *Princeton Univ.*
G.T. Dunlap Jr., Princeton
1931 *Yale Univ.*
G.T. Dunlap Jr., Princeton
1932 *Yale Univ.*
J.W. Fisher, Michigan
1933 *Yale Univ.*
Walter Emery, Oklahoma
1934 *Michigan Univ.*
Charles Yates, Georgia Tech
1935 *Michigan Univ.*
Ed White, Texas
1936 *Yale Univ.*
Charles Kocsis, Michigan
1937 *Princeton Univ.*
Fred Haas Jr., LSU

1938 *Stanford Univ.*
John Burke, Georgetown
1939 *Stanford Univ.*
Vincent D'Antoni, Tulane
1940 *Princeton Univ., LSU*
Dixon Brooke, Virginia
1941 *Stanford Univ.*
Earl Stewart, LSU
1942 *Stanford Univ., LSU*
Frank Tatum, Stanford
1943 *Yale Univ.*
Wallace Ulrich, Carleton
1944 *Notre Dame Univ.*
Louis Lick, Minnesota
1945 *Ohio State ' ' ìv.*
John Lorms, Ohio State
1946 *Stanford Univ.*
George Hamer, Georgia
1947 *Louisiana State Univ.*
Dave Barclay, Michigan
1948 *San Jose State Univ.*
Bob Harris, San Jose St.
1949 *North Texas State Univ.*
Harvie Ward, N. Carolina
1950 *North Texas State Univ.*
Fred Wampler, Purdue
1951 *North Texas State Univ.*
Tom Nieporte, Ohio State
1952 *North Texas State Univ.*
Jim Vickers, Oklahoma
1953 *Stanford Univ.*
Earl Moeller, Oklahoma St.
1954 *Southern Methodist Univ.*
Hillman Robbins, Memphis St.
1955 *Louisiana State Univ.*
Joe Campbell, Purdue
1956 *Univ. of Houston*
Rick Jones, Ohio State
1957 *Univ. of Houston*
Rex Baxter Jr., Houston
1958 *Univ. of Houston*
Phil Rodgers, Houston
1959 *Univ. of Houston*
Dick Crawford, Houston

1960 *Univ. of Houston*
Dick Crawford, Houston
1961 *Purdue Univ.*
Jack Nicklaus, Ohio State
1962 *Univ. of Houston*
Kermit Zarley, Houston
1963 *Oklahoma State Univ.*
R. H. Sikes, Arkansas
1964 *Univ. of Houston*
Terry Small, San Jose St.
1965 *Univ. of Houston*
Marty Fleckman, Houston
1966 *Univ. of Houston*
Bob Murphy, Florida
1967 *Univ. of Houston*
Hale Irwin, Colorado
1968 *Univ. of Florida*
Grier Jones, Oklahoma St.
1969 *Univ. of Houston*
Bob Clark, Los Angeles St.
1970 *Univ. of Houston*
John Mahaffey, Houston
1971 *Univ. of Texas*
Ben Crenshaw, Texas
Tom Kite, Texas
1972 *Univ. of Texas*
Ben Crenshaw, Texas
1973 *Univ. of Florida*
Ben Crenshaw, Texas
1974 *Wake Forest Univ.*
Curtis Strange, Wake Forest
1975 *Wake Forest Univ.*
Jay Haas, Wake Forest
1976 *Oklahoma State Univ.*
Scott Simpson, So. Cal.
1977 *Univ. of Houston*
Scott Simpson, So. Cal.
1978 *Oklahoma State Univ.*
David Edwards, Okla. St.
1979 *Ohio State Univ.*
Gary Hallberg, Wake Forest
1980 *Oklahoma State Univ.*
Jay Don Blake, Utah State
1981 *Brigham Young Univ.*
Ron Commans, So. Cal.

1982 *Univ. of Houston*
Billy Ray Brown, Houston
1983 *Oklahoma State Univ.*
Jim Carter, Arizona St.
1984 *Univ. of Houston*
John Inman, N. Carolina
1985 *Univ. of Houston*
Clark Burroughs, Ohio St.
1986 *Wake Forest Univ.*
Scott Verplank, Oklahoma St.
1987 *Oklahoma State Univ.*
Brian Watts, Oklahoma St.
1988 *UCLA*
E.J. Pfister, Oklahoma St.
1989 *Univ. of Oklahoma*
Phil Mickelson, Ariz St.
1990 *Arizona State Univ.*
Phil Mickelson, Ariz. St.
1991 *Oklahoma State Univ.*
Warren Schutte, Nevada-LV
1992 *Univ. of Arizona*
Phil Mickelson, Ariz. St.
1993 *Univ. of Florida*
Todd Demsey, Ariz. St.

NCAA Division II Men's Champions

1963 *Southwest Missouri State*
Gary Head, Middle Tenn. St.
1964 *Southern Illinois Univ.*
John Kurzynowski, Aquinas
1965 *Middle Tennessee State*
Larry Gilbert, Mid. Tenn. St.
1966 *Chico State Univ.*
Bob Smith, Sacramento St.
1967 *Lamar Univ.*
Larry Hinson, E. Tenn. St.
1968 *Lamar Univ.*
Mike Nugent, Lamar
1969 *Northridge State Univ.*
Mike Spang, Portland St.
Corky Bassler, Northridge St.
1970 *Rollins Univ.*
Gary McCord, Cal-Riverside

1971 *New Orleans Univ.*
  Stan Stopa, New Orleans
1972 *New Orleans Univ.*
  Jim Hilderbrand, Ashland
1973 *Northridge State Univ.*
  Paul Wise, Fullerton St.
1974 *Northride State Univ.*
  Matt Bloom, Cal-Riverside
1975 *California-Irvine*
  Jerry Wisz, Cal-Irvine
1976 *Troy State Univ.*
  Mike Nicolette, Rollins
1977 *Troy State Univ.*
  David Thornally, Ark.-L. Rock
1978 *Columbus*
  Thomas Brannen, Columbus
1979 *California-Davis*
  Tom Gleeton, Fla. South.
1980 *Columbus*
  Paul Perini, Troy State
1981 *Florida Southern Univ.*
  Tom Patri, Fla. Southern
1982 *Fla. Southern Univ.*
  Vic Wilk, Northridge State
1983 *S.W. Texas State Univ.*
  Greg Chapman, Stephen Austin
1984 *Troy State Univ.*
  Greg Cate, C. Connecticut
1985 *Florida Southern Univ.*
  Hugh Royer, Columbus
1986 *Florida Southern Univ.*
  Lee Janzen, Fla. South.
1987 *Univ. of Tampa*
  Jeff Leonard, Univ. of Tampa
1988 *Univ. of Tampa*
  Jeff Leonard, Univ. of Tampa
1989-1993 *Not available at press time*
1994 *Columbus*
  Briny Baird, Valdosta St.

NCAA Division III Men's Champions

1975 *Wooster College*
  Charles Baskervill, Hampden

1976 *Stanislaus State*
  Dan Lisle, Stanislaus St.
1977 *Stanislaus State*
  David Downing, S.E. Mass.
1978 *Stanislaus State*
  Jim Quinn, Oswego State
1979 *Stanislaus State*
  Mike Bender, Stanislaus St.
1980 *Stanislaus State*
  Mike Bender, Stanislaus St.
1981 *Stanislaus State*
  Ryan Fox, N.C.-Greensboro
1982 *Ramapo College*
  Cliff Smith, Stanislaus St.
1983 *Allegheny College*
  Matt Clarke, Allegheny St.
1984 *Stanislaus State*
  Bob Osborn, Redlands
1985 *Stanislaus State*
  Brian Goldsworthy, Central
1986 *Stanislaus State*
  Eric Meerbach, Worcester Poly
1987 *Stanislaus State*
  Pat Weishan, Cal-San Diego
1988 *Stanislaus State*
  Glenn Andrade, Stanislaus St.
1989-1993 *Not available at press time*
1994 *Methodist*
  Scott Scovil, CNC

NCAA Division I Women's Champions

1941 Eleanor Dudley, Alabama
1942 *No Meeting*
1943 *No Meeting*
1944 *No Meeting*
1945 *No Meeting*
1946 Phillis Otto, Northwestern
1947 Shirley Spork, Mich. St.
1948 Grace Lenczyk, Stetson
1949 Marilynn Smith, Kansas
1950 Betty Rowland, Rollins
1951 Barbara Bruning, Wellesley
1952 Mary Ann Villega, Ohio St.

1953 Patricia Lesser, Seattle
1954 Nancy Reed, Ga.-Peabody
1955 Jackie Yates, Redlands
1956 Marlene Stewart, Rollins
1957 Miriam Bailey, Northwestern
1958 Carole Pushing, Carleton
1959 Judy Eller, Miami-Fla.
1960 JoAnne Gunderson, Ariz. St.
1961 Judy Hoetmer, Washington
1962 Carol Sorenson, Ariz. St.
1963 Claudia Lindor, West. Wash.
1964 Patti Shook, Valparaiso
1965 Roberta Albers, Miami-Fla.
1966 Joyce Kazmierski, Mich. St.
1967 Martha Wilkinson, Cal-Fullerton
1968 Gail Sykes, Odessa
1969 Jane Bastanchury, Ariz. St.
1970 *Miami-Fla.*
    Cathy Gaughan, Ariz. St.
1971 *UCLA*
    Shelley Hamlin, Stanford
1972 *Miami-Fla.*
    Ann Laughlin, Miami-Fla.
1973 *N.C. State-Greensboro*
    Bonnie Lauer, Mich. St.
1974 *Rollins*
    Mary Budke, Oregon St.
1975 *Arizona State Univ.*
    Barbara Barrow, San Diego St.
1976 *Furman Univ.*
    Nancy Lopez, Tulsa
1977 *Miami-Fla.*
    Cathy Morse, Miami-Fla.

1978 *Miami-Fla.*
    Deborah Petrizzi, U. of Texas
1979 *Southern Methodist Univ.*
    Kyle O'Brien, SMU
1980 *Tulsa Univ.*
    Patty Sheehan, San Jose St.
1981 *Florida State Univ.*
    Terri Moody, Georgia
1982 *Tulsa Univ.*
    Kathy Baker, Tulsa
1983 *Tulsa Univ.*
    Penny Hammel, Miami-Fla.
1984 *Miami-Fla.*
    Cindy Schrayer, Georgia
1985 *Univ. of Florida*
    Danielle Ammacapane, Ariz. St.
1986 *Univ. of Florida*
    Page Dunlap, Univ. of Fla.
1987 *San Jose State Univ.*
    Caroline Keggi, U. New Mex.
1988 *Vacated*
    Vacated
1989 *San Jose State Univ.*
    Pat Hurst, San Jose St.
1990 *Arizona State Univ.*
    Susan Slaughter, Arizona
1991 *UCLA*
    Annika Sorenstam, Arizona
1992 *San Jose State Univ.*
    Vicki Goetze, Georgia
1993 *Arizona State Univ.*
    Charlotte Sorenstam, Texas

JUNIOR GOLF

OVERVIEW: *Winners and runners-up of all national junior amateur tournaments since inception, plus Junior amateur results for 1994 and Junior rankings since 1978. Winners for the American Junior Golf Association are through Oct. 31, 1994. Junior rankings are as reported by Golfweek magazine.*

U.S. Junior Boys' Amateur

1948 Dean Lind
1949 Gay Brewer
1950 Mason Rudolph
1951 K. Thomas Jacobs
1952 Donald Bisplinghoff
1953 Rex Baxter, Jr.
1954 Foster Bradley, Jr.
1955 Billy J. Dunn
1956 Harlan Stevenson
1957 Larry Beck
1958 Gordon Baker
1959 Larry J. Lee
1960 William J. Tindall
1961 Charles S. McDowell
1962 James L. Wiechers
1963 Gregg McHatton
1964 John Miller
1965 James Masserio
1966 Gary Sanders
1967 John T. Crooks
1968 Eddie Pearce
1969 Aly Trompas
1970 Gary Koch
1971 Mike Brannan
1972 Robert T. Byman
1973 Jack Renner
1974 David Nevatt
1975 Brett Mullin
1976 Madden Hatcher III
1977 Willie Wood
1978 Donald Hunter

1979 Jack Larkin
1980 Eric Johnson
1981 Scott Erickson
1982 Rick Marik
1983 Tim Straub
1984 Doug Martin
1985 Charles Rymer
1986 Brian Montgomery
1987 Brett Quigley
1988 Jason Widener
1989 David Duval
1990 Mathew Todd
1991 Eldrick (Tiger) Woods
1992 Eldrick (Tiger) Woods
1993 Eldrick (Tiger) Woods
1994 Terry Noe

U.S. Junior Girls' Amateur

1949 Marlene Bauer
1950 Patricia A. Lesser
1951 Arlene Brooks
1952 Mickey Wright
1953 Mildred Meyerson
1954 Margaret Smith
1955 Carole Jo Kabler
1956 JoAnne Gunderson
1957 Judy Eller
1958 Judy Eller
1959 Judy Rand
1960 Carol Sorenson
1961 Mary Lowell
1962 Mary Lou Daniel

1963 Janis Ferraris
1964 Peggy Conley
1965 Gail Sykes
1966 Claudia Mayhew
1967 Elizabeth Story
1968 Margaret Harmon
1969 Hollis Stacy
1970 Hollis Stacy
1971 Hollis Stacy
1972 Nancy Lopez
1973 Amy Alcott
1974 Nancy Lopez
1975 Dayna Benson
1976 Pilar Dorado
1977 Althea Tome
1978 Lori Castillo
1979 Penny Hammel
1980 Laurie Rinker
1981 Kay Cornelius
1982 Heather Farr
1983 Kim Saiki
1984 Cathy Mockett
1985 Dana Lofland
1986 Pat Hurst
1987 Michelle McGann
1988 Jamille Jose
1989 Brandie Burton
1990 Sandrine Mendiburu
1991 Emilee Klein
1992 Jaime Koisumi
1993 Kellee Booth
1994 Kelli Kuehne

American Junior Golf Association:
1994 winners: BOYS DIVISION

Taylor Made Pinelsle Jr. Classic	Ryuji Imada, Tampa, Fla.
Taylor Made Woodlands Jr. Classic	Landry Mahan, Richardson, Texas
Indigo Run Junior Classic	John Caddy, Wilmington, N.C.
Ping Phoenix Junior Championship	Charley Hoffman, Poway, Calif.
ClubCorp Junior Championship	Michael Boyd, Tulsa, Okla.
Freeport-McMoRan Junior Classic	Jeff Fahrenbruch, Plano, Texas
Bluegrass Junior Invitational	Ben Curtis, Ostrander, Ohio
Aspen Junior Classic	Kevin Muncrief, Ardmore, Okla.
Northern Telecom Jr. Team Challenge	Ryuji Imada, Tampa, Fla.
Ping Myrtle Beach Junior Classic	John Walker, Macon, Ga.
Mission Hills Desert Junior	Joel Kribel, Pleasanton, Calif.
Buick Junior Open	Matthew McDougall, Roch. Hills, Mich.
Texace San Antonio Shootout	Alberto Ochoa, Edinburg, Texas
Wilson Geneva Nat'l Junior Champ.	Alberto Ochoa, Edinburg, Texas
Las Vegas Founders' Legacy Junior	Darren Angel, Northridge, Calif.
Rolex Tournament of Champions	Robert Floyd, Miami Beach, Fla.
Todd Moore Memorial	Ty Cox, Amarillo, Texas
Marriott at Sawgrass First Coast Jr. Classic	G.W. Cable, Oakton, Va.
Oklahoma Junior Classic	Jeff Fahrenbruch, Plano, Texas
ClubCorp Junior Players Championship	Scott Volpitto, Augusta, Ca.
AJGA Boys Junior Championship	(17-18 Div.) Robert Floyd, Miami Beach, Fla.
Canon Cup	East Team
Kmart Greater Greensboro Junior	Jake Kransteuber, Greer, S.C.
Ray Floyd Tumberry Isle Junior	Steve Scott, Coral Springs, Fla.
Smith Corona Apawamis Junior	Ted Haley, Greenwich, Conn.
Southwestern Junior	Jay Osmon, Alamosa, Colo.
AJGA Cape Cod Junior	Brad Black, St. Catherines, Ontario
Robert Trent Jones Golf Trail Junior Classic	David Cossett, Germantown, Tenn.

1994 winners: BOYS 13-14 DIVISION

Taylor Made Pinelsle Jr. Classic	David Gossett, Germantown, Tenn.
Taylor Made Woodlands Jr. Classic	Jim Park, Fullerton, Calif.
Bluegrass Junior Invitational	Joe Redfearfi, Durham, N.C.
Aspen Junior Classic	Kevin Stadler, Englewood, Colo.
Ping Myrtle Beach Junior Classic	Alan Poole, Florence, S.C.
Mission Hills Desert Junior	John Ray Leary, Culver City, Calif.
Buick Junior Open	Jonathan Shelley, Sarasota, Fla.
Texace San Antonio Shootout	Matt Larson, Edmond, Okla.
Wilson Geneva Nat'l Junior Champ.	Trevor Imhielman, Somerset West, S. Africa
Las Vegas Founders' Legacy Junior	Ben Auten, Las Vegas, Nev.
Todd Moore Memorial	Nicholas Loar, Rockwall, Texas
Marriott at Sawgrass First Coast Jr. Classic	Lucas Glover, Greenville, S.C.
Oklahoma Junior Classic	Nicholas Loar, Rockwall, Texas
ClubCorp Junior Players Championship	Charles Chen, La Quinta, Calif.
AJGA Boys Junior Championship	(15-16 Div.) Robert Hooper, Coral Springs, Fla.
Kmart Greater Greensboro Junior	Lucas Glover, Greenville, S.C.
Ray Floyd Tumberry Isle Junior	Borja La Roche, Boca Raton, Fla.
Smith Corona Apawamis Junior	David Kwon, Dumont, N.J.
Southwestern Junior	Kevin Stadler, Englewood, Colo.
AJGA Cape Cod Junior	Ned Yetten, Andover, Mass.
Robert Trent Jones Golf Trail Junior Classic	Culley Barragan, Dallas, Texas

1994 winners: GIRLS DIVISION

Taylor Made Pinelsle Jr. Classic	Elizabeth Bauer, Brandon, Fla.
Taylor Made Woodlands Jr. Classic	Jenny Lee, Fullerton, Calif.
Indigo Run Junior Classic	Crisfie Kerr, Miami, Fla.
Ping Phoenix Junior Championship	Grace Park, Phoenix, Ariz.
Golf for Women Mag. Girls Championship	Jenny Lee, Fullerton, Calif.
Freeport-McMoRan Junior Classic	Grace Park, Phoenix, Ariz.
Bluegrass Junior Invitational	Ashley Winn, West Monroe, La.
Aspen Junior Classic	Heather Graff, Kennewick, Wash.
Ping Myrtle Beach Junior Classic	Shauna Estes, Orangeburg, S.C.
Mission Hills Desert Junior	Keree Booth, Coto de Caza, Calif.
Buick Junior Open	Jenny Chuasiripom, Timonium, Md.
Texace San Antonio Shootout	Jamie Hullett, Mesquite, Texas
Wilson Geneva Nat'l Junior Championship	Heather Graff, Kennewick, Wash.
Las Vegas Founders' Legacy Junior	Keree Booth, Coto de Caza, Calif.
Rolex Tournament of Champions	Elizabeth Bauer, Brandon, Fla.
Todd Moore Memorial	Stacy Rambin, Tulsa, Okla.
Marriott at Sawgrass First Coast Jr. Classic	Katy Loy, Ann Arbor, Mich.
McDonald's Betsy Rawls Girls Nat'l Champ.	Grace Park, Phoenix, Ariz.
Oklahoma Junior Classic	Kristen Register, Roswell, Calif.
Kmart Greater Greensboro Junior	Meredith Thomas, Murfreesboro, Tenn.
Ray Floyd Tumberry Isle Junior	Kristen Register, Roswell, Calif.
Smith Corona Apawamis Junior	Anne Cardea, Midlothian, Va.
Southwestern Junior	Kelli Kuehne, DaBas, Texas
AJGA Cape Cod Junior	Jenny Chuasiriporn, Timonium, Md.
Robert Trent Jones Golf Trail Junior Classic	Jenny Chuasiriporn, Timonium, Md.

U.S. Junior Boys' Amateur Rankings

1978
1. Willie Wood
2. Don Hurter
3. Larry Gosewehr
4. Monty Leong
5. Tracy Phillips

1979
1. Tracy Phillips
2. Jack Larkin
3. Rick Fehr
4. Andy Dilllard
5. Willie Wood

1980
1. Tommy Moore
2. Tracy Phillips
3. Eric Johnson
4. Adam Armagost
5. Bill Andrade

1981
1. Sam Randolph
2. Bill Andrade
3. Tommy Moore
4. Scott Erickson
5. Jerry Haas

1982
1. Stuart Hendley
2. Scott Verplank
3. Rich Marik
4. Bill Mayfair
5. Peter Jordan

1983
1. Michael Bradley
2. Brian Nelson
3. Tim Straub
4. Hank Pfister
5. Bill McDonald

1984
1. Doug Martin
2. Brian Watts
3. David Toms
4. Bob May
5. Blair Manasse

1985
1. Len Mattiace
2. Steve Termeer
3. Charles Rymer
4. Dudley Hart
5. Kevin Wentworth

1986
1. Brian Montgomery
2. Phil Mickelson
3. Chris Cain
4. Bryan Pemberton
5. Nicky Goetze

1987
1. Jeff Manson
2. Phil Mickelson
3. Brett Quigley
4. Jim Furyk
5. Brian Craig

1988
1. Jason Widener
2. Phil Mickelson
3. Nicky Goetze
4. Jason Brigman
5. Jean-Paul Hebert

1989
Not available

1990
1. Eldrick (Tiger) Woods
2. Notah Bogayr
3. Lee McEntee
4. Stewart Cink
5. Matthew Todd

1991
1. Eldrick (Tiger) Woods
2. Scott Johnson
3. Brad Zwelschke
4. Justin Roof
5. Marcus Jones

1992
1. Eldrick (Tiger) Woods
2. Justin Roof
3. Mark Wilson
4. Michael Jones
5. Todd Lynch

1993
1. Ted Oh
2. Michael Henderson
3. Robert Floyd
4. Jeff Fahrenbruch
5. Grady Girard

1994
1. Ryuji Imada
2. Joel Kribel
3. Landry Mahan
4. Ted Oh
5. Jeremy Anderson

U.S. Girls' Amateur Rankings

1979
1. Penny Hammel
2. Sharon Barrett
3. Amy Benz

4. Heather Farr
5. Viveca Vandergriff

1980
1. Laurie Rinker
2. Heather Farr
3. Kim Shipman
4. Jody Rosenthal
5. Joanne Pacillo

1981
1. Jenny Lidback
2. Cathy Johnston
3. Kay Cornelius
4. Flori Prono
5. Kathy Kostas

1982
1. Heather Farr
2. Tracy Kerdyk
3. Carey Ruffer
4. Robin Garnester
5. Melissa McNamara

1983
1. Kim Saiki
2. Page Dunlap
3. Melissa McNamara
4. Kris Tschetter
5. Tracy Kerdyk

1984
1. Susan Pager
2. Lisa Neodoba
3. Cheryl Morley
4. Cathy Mockett
5. Carey Ruffer

1985
1. Michiko Hattori
2. Dana Lofland
3. Pearl Sinn
4. Jean Zeditz
5. Kristen Parker

1986
1. Adele Moore
2. Pat Hurst
3. Michelle Lyford
4. Amy Fruhwith
5. Michelle McGann

1987
1. Michelle McGann
2. Adele Moore
3. Vicki Goetze
4. Christy Erb
5. Brandie Burton

1988
1. Vicki Goetze
2. Brandie Burton
3, Jamille Jose
4. Deborah Parks
5. Dana Arnold

1989
Not available

1990
1. Vicki Goetze
2. Emilee Kleinr
3. Maria Castelucci
4. Heather Bowie
5. Kellee Booth

1991
1. Emilee Klein
2. Kellee Booth
3. Heather Brown
4. Jeong Min Park
5. Kim Marshall

1992
1. Kellee Booth
2. Wendi Patterson
3. Betty Chen
4. Heather Bowie
5. Erika Hayashida

1993
1. Kellee Booth
2. Grace Ji-eun Park
3. Cristie Kerr
4. Kelli Kuehne
5. Betty Chen

1994
1. Grace Ji-eun Park
2. Cristie Kerr
3. Kelli Kuehne
4. Elizabeth Bauer
5. Jenny Lee

AWARDS

OVERVIEW: *Player, administrator, public and/or humanitarian service, and media awards from major organizations such as the PGA TOUR, LPGA Tour, National Golf Foundation, and the PGA of America.*

PGA TOUR Player of the Year
Awarded by:
PGA TOUR

1990	Wayne Levi
1991	Fred Couples
1992	Fred Couples
1993	Nick Price

Vardon Trophy
Awarded by:
PGA TOUR
Criteria:
Lowest stroke average, based on scaled PGA TOUR formula (minimum 60 rounds).

1937	Harry Cooper
1938	Sam Snead
1939	Byron Nelson
1940	Ben Hogan
1941	Ben Hogan
1942-46	No awards
1947	Jimmy Demaret
1948	Ben Hogan
1949	Sam Snead
1950	Sam Snead
1951	Lloyd Mangrum
1952	Jack Burke
1953	Lloyd Mangrum
1954	E.J. Harrison
1955	Sam Snead
1956	Cary Middlecoff
1957	Dow Finsterwald
1958	Bob Rosburg
1959	Art Wall
1960	Billy Casper
1961	Arnold Palmer
1962	Arnold Palmer
1963	Billy Casper
1964	Arnold Palmer
1965	Billy Casper
1966	Billy Casper
1967	Arnold Palmer
1968	Billy Casper
1969	Dave Hill
1970	Lee Trevino
1971	Lee Trevino
1972	Lee Trevino
1973	Bruce Crampton
1974	Lee Trevino
1975	Bruce Crampton
1976	Don January
1977	Tom Watson
1978	Tom Watson
1979	Tom Watson
1980	Lee Trevino
1981	Tom Kite
1982	Tom Kite
1983	Raymond Floyd
1984	Calvin Peete
1985	Don Pooley
1986	Scott Hoch
1987	Dan Pohl
1988	Chip Beck
1989	Greg Norman
1990	Greg Norman
1991	Fred Couples
1992	Fred Couples
1993	Nick Price
1994	Greg Norman

PGA Player of the Year
Awarded by:
PGA of America

1948	Ben Hogan
1949	Sam Snead
1950	Ben Hogan
1951	Ben Hogan
1952	Julius Boros
1953	Ben Hogan
1954	Ed Furgol
1955	Doug Ford
1956	Jack Burke
1957	Dick Mayer
1958	Dow Finsterwald
1959	Art Wall
1960	Arnold Palmer
1961	Jerry Barber
1962	Arnold Palmer
1963	Julius Boros
1964	Ken Venturi
1965	Dave Marr
1966	Billy Casper
1967	Jack Nicklaus
1968	Not Awarded
1969	Orville Moody
1970	Billy Casper
1971	Lee Trevino
1972	Jack Nicklaus
1973	Jack Nicklaus
1974	Johnny Miller
1975	Jack Nicklaus
1976	Jack Nicklaus
1977	Tom Watson
1978	Tom Watson
1979	Tom Watson
1980	Tom Watson
1981	Bill Rogers
1982	Tom Watson
1983	Hal Sutton
1984	Tom Watson
1985	Lanny Wadkins

1986	Bob Tway
1987	Paul Azinger
1988	Curtis Strange
1989	Tom Kite
1990	Nick Faldo
1991	Corey Pavin
1992	Fred Couples
1993	Nick Price

LPGA Player of the Year

Awarded by:
LPGA Tour

1966	Kathy Whitworth
1967	Kathy Whitworth
1968	Kathy Whitworth
1969	Kathy Whitworth
1970	Sandra Haynie
1971	Kathy Whitworth
1972	Kathy Whitworth
1973	Kathy Whitworth
1974	JoAnne Carner
1975	Sandra Palmer
1976	Judy Rankin
1977	Judy Rankin
1978	Nancy Lopez
1979	Nancy Lopez
1980	Beth Daniel
1981	JoAnne Carner
1982	JoAnne Carner
1983	Patty Sheehan
1984	Betsy King
1985	Nancy Lopez
1986	Pat Bradley
1987	Ayako Okamoto
1988	Nancy Lopez
1989	Betsy King
1990	Beth Daniel
1991	Pat Bradley
1992	Dottie Mochrie
1993	Betsy King

Vare Trophy

Awarded by:
LPGA Tour
Criteria:
Lowest stroke average (minimum 70 rounds).

1953	Patty Berg
1954	Babe Zaharias
1955	Patty Berg
1956	Patty Berg
1957	Louise Suggs
1958	Beverly Hanson
1959	Betsy Rawls
1960	Mickey Wright
1961	Mickey Wright
1962	Mickey Wright
1963	Mickey Wright
1964	Mickey Wright
1965	Kathy Whitworth
1966	Kathy Whitworth
1967	Kathy Whitworth
1968	Carol Mann
1969	Kathy Whitworth
1970	Kathy Whitworth
1971	Kathy Whitworth
1972	Kathy Whitworth
1973	Judy Rankin
1974	JoAnne Carner
1975	JoAnne Carner
1976	Judy Rankin
1977	Judy Rankin
1978	Nancy Lopez
1979	Nancy Lopez
1980	Amy Alcott
1981	JoAnne Carner
1982	JoAnne Carner
1983	JoAnne Carner
1984	Patty Sheehan
1985	Nancy Lopez
1986	Pat Bradley
1987	Betsy King
1988	Colleen Walker
1989	Beth Daniel
1990	Beth Daniel
1991	Pat Bradley
1992	Dottie Mochrie
1993	Betsy King

Richardson Award

Awarded by:
Golf Writers Association of America
Criteria:
Lifetime contribution to the game.

1948	Robert A. Hudson
1949	Scotty Fessenden
1950	Bing Crosby
1951	Richard Tufts
1952	Chick Evans
1953	Bob Hope
1954	Babe Zaharias
1955	Dwight Eisenhower
1956	George S. May
1957	Francis Ouimet
1958	Bob Jones
1959	Patty Berg
1960	Fred Corcoran
1961	Joseph C. Dey
1962	Walter Hagen
1963	Joe & Herb Graffis
1964	Cliff Roberts
1965	Gene Sarazen
1966	Robert E. Harlow
1967	Max Elbin
1968	Charles Bartlett
1969	Arnold Palmer
1970	Roberto De Vicenzo
1971	Lincoln Werden
1972	Leo Fraser
1973	Ben Hogan
1974	Byron Nelson
1975	Gary Player
1976	Herbert W. Wind
1977	Mark Cox
1978	Jack Nicklaus
1979	Jim Gaquin
1980	Jack Tuthill
1981	Robert Trent Jones
1982	Chi Chi Rodriguez
1983	William C. Campbell
1984	Sam Snead
1985	Lee Trevino
1986	Kathy Whitworth
1987	Frank Hannigan

1988	Roger Barry
1989	Ben Crenshaw
1990	P.J. Boatwright
1991	Tom Watson
1992	Deane R. Beman
1993	Harvey Penick
1994	Peggy Kirk Bell

Ben Hogan Award
Awarded by:
Golf Writers Association of America
Criteria:
Overcoming injury.

1954	Babe Zaharias
1955	Ed Furgol
1956	Dwight Eisenhower
1957	Clint Russell
1958	Dale Bourisseau
1959	Charlie Boswell
1960	Skip Alexander
1961	Horton Smith
1962	Jimmy Nichols
1963	Bobby Nichols
1964	Bob Morgan
1965	Ernest Jones
1966	Ken Venturi
1967	Warren Pease
1968	Shirley Englehorn
1969	Curtis Person
1970	Joe Lazaro
1971	Larry Hinson
1972	Ruth Jessen
1973	Gene Littler
1974	Gay Brewer
1975	Patty Berg
1976	Paul Hahn
1977	Des Sullivan
1978	Dennis Walters
1979	John Mahaffey
1980	Lee Trevino
1981	Kathy Linney
1982	Al Geiberger
1983	Calvin Peete
1984	Jay Sigel
1985	Rod Funseth
1986	Fuzzy Zoeller

1987	Charles Owens
1988	Pat Browne
1989	Sally Little
1990	Linda Craft
1991	Pat Bradley
1992	Jim Nelford
1993	Shelley Hamlin
1994	Jim Ferree

Charlie Bartlett Award
Awarded by:
Golf Writers Association of America
Criteria:
Unselfish contributions to the betterment of society.

1971	Billy Casper
1972	Lee Trevino
1973	Gary Player
1974	Chi Chi Rodriguez
1975	Gene Littler
1976	Arnold Palmer
1977	Lee Elder
1978	Bert Yancey
1979	No award
1980	No award
1981	No award
1982	Patty Berg
1983	No award
1984	Gene Sarazen
1985	No award
1986	No award
1987	No award
1988	Patty Sheehan
1989	Mary Bea Porter
1990	No award
1991	No award
1992	John Daly
1993	No award
1994	Betsy King

Joe Graffis Award
Awarded by:
National Golf Foundation
Criteria:
Contribution to education and junior golf.

1970	Ellen Griffin

1971	Barbara Rotvig
1972	Les Bolstad
1973	No award
1974	Opal Hill
1975	Patty Berg
1976	Shirley Spork
1977	Bill Strausbaugh
1978	Gary Wiren
1979	Conrad Rehling
1980	Bob Toski
1981	Peggy Kirk Bell
1982	Jim Flick
1983	Carol Johnson
1984	Paul Runyan
1985	No award
1986	DeDe Owens
1987	Edwin Cottrell
1988	Thomas Addis III
1989	Kathy Corbin
1990	Davis Love, Jr.
1991	Kerry Graham
1992	Robert F. MacNelly
1993	Chi Chi Rodriguez
1994	Dennis Walters

Herb Graffis Award
Awarded by:
National Golf Foundation
Criteria: *Contribution to golf as recreation, good fellowship, and as a happy pastime.*

1977	Joe Jemsek
1978	Arnold Palmer
1979	Carol McCue
1980	Bob Hope
1981	Patty Berg
1982	Jack Nicklaus
1983	Herb Graffis
1984	William Davis and Howard Gill
1985	Howard Clark
1986	Joe Dey
1987	Deane Beman
1988	John Laupheimer
1989	William Campbell
1990	Don Rossi
1991	P.J. Boatwright

NGF/Jack Nicklaus Golf Family of the Year Award

Awarded by:
National Golf Foundation
Criteria:
Families who have made significant contributions to the game.

1986	Jack Nicklaus Family
1987	Nancy Lopez/Ray Knight Family
1988	The Jim Cook Family
1989	The Pat Bradley Family
1990	The Jim Gallagher Family
1991	The Joe Jemsek Family
1992	The Renee Powell Family
1993	The Harold Eller Family
1994	The Karsten Solheim Family

PGA Golf Professional of the Year

Awarded by:
PGA of America
Criteria:
Distinguished service as a working club professional.

1955	Bill Gordon
1956	Harry Shepard
1957	Dugan Aycock
1958	Harry Pezzullo
1959	Eddie Duino
1960	Warren Orlick
1961	Don Padgett
1962	Tom LoPresti
1963	Bruce Herd
1964	Lyle Wherman
1965	Hubby Habjan
1966	Bill Strausbaugh
1967	Ernie Vossler
1968	Hardy Loudermilk
1969	Wally Mund and Hubert Smith
1970	Grady Shumate
1971	Ross Collins
1972	Howard Morrette
1973	Warren Smith
1974	Paul Harney
1975	Walker Inman
1976	Ron Letellier
1977	Don Soper
1978	Walter Lowell
1979	Gary Ellis
1980	Stan Thirsk
1981	John Gerring
1982	Bob Popp
1983	Ken Lindsay
1984	Jerry Mowlds
1985	Jerry Cozby
1986	David Ogilvie
1987	Bob Ford
1988	Hank Majewski
1989	Tom Addis III
1990	Jim Albus
1991	Joe Jemsek
1992	Martin Kavanaugh II
1993	Don Kotnik

PGA Club Pro of the Year

Awarded by:
PGA of America
Criteria:
Leading club pro player.

1984	Bill Schumaker
1985	Ed Dougherty
1986	Lonnie Lielsen
1987	Lonnie Nielsen
1988	Bob Ford
1989	Lonnie Nielsen
1990	Brett Upper
1991	Bruce Zabriski
1992	Tom Wargo
1993	Mike San Fillipo

Horton Smith Trophy

Awarded by:
PGA of America
Criteria:
Outstanding contribution by PGA Professionals to education.

1965	Emil Beck
1966	Gene C. Mason
1967	Donald Fischesser
1968	R. William Clarke
1969	Paul Hahn
1970	Joe Walser
1971	Irv Schloss
1972	John Budd
1973	George Aulbach
1974	Bill Hardy
1975	John Henrich
1976	Jim Bailey
1977	Paul Runyan
1978	Andy Nusbaum
1979	Howard Smith
1980	Dale Mead
1981	Tom Addis III
1982	Kent Cayce
1983	Bill Strausbaugh
1984	Don Essig
1985	Larry Startzel
1986	Mark Darnell
1987	Ken Lindsay
1988	Guy Wimberly
1989	Verne D. Perry
1990	Mike Hebron
1991	Joe Terry
1992	Conrad Rehling
1993	Rick Burton

Bob Jones Award

Awarded by:
United States Golf Association
Criteria:
Distinguished sportsmanship in golf.

1955	Francis Ouimet
1956	Bill Campbell
1957	Babe Zaharias
1958	Margaret Curtis
1959	Findley S. Douglas
1960	Charles Evans, Jr.
1961	Joe Carr
1962	Horton Smith
1963	Patty Berg
1964	Charles Coe
1965	Glenna Collett Vare
1966	Gary Player
1967	Richard S. Tufts
1968	Robert Dickson
1969	Gerald Micklem
1970	Roberto De Vicenzo
1971	Arnold Palmer
1972	Michael Bonallack
1973	Gene Littler

1974	Byron Nelson
1975	Jack Nicklaus
1976	Ben Hogan
1977	Joe Dey
1978	Bob Hope and Bing Crosby
1979	Tom Kite
1980	Charles R. Yates
1981	JoAnne Carner
1982	Billy Joe Patton
1983	Maureen Garrett
1984	Jay Sigel
1985	Fuzzy Zoeller
1986	Jess Sweetser
1987	Tom Watson
1988	Isaac Grainger
1989	Chi Chi Rodriguez
1990	Peggy Kirk Bell
1991	Ben Crenshaw
1992	Gene Sarazen
1993	P.J. Boatwright
1994	Lewis Oehmig

Card Walker Award

Awarded by:
PGA TOUR
Criteria:
Contribution to junior golf.

1981	Mrs. Lou Smith
1982	Fran Emmett
1983	Jack Nicklaus
1984	Sally Carroll
1985	Don Padgett, Sr.
1986	Chi Chi Rodriguez
1987	James S. Kemper
1988	William V. Powers
1989	Selina Johnson
1990	Tucson Conquistadores
1991	AJGA
1992	Bill Dickey
1993	Western Golf Assoc.
1994	Fred Engh

LPGA Teacher of the Year

Awarded by:
LPGA

1958	Helen Dettweiler
1959	Shirley Spork
1960	Barbara Rotvig
1961	Peggy Kirk Bell
1962	Ellen Griffin
1963	Vonnie Colby
1964	Sally Doyle
1965	Goldie Bateson
1966	Ann C. Johnstone
1967	Jackie Pung
1968	Gloria Fecht
1969	JoAnne Winter
1970	Gloria Armstrong
1971	Jeanette Rector
1972	Lee Spencer
1973	Penny Zavichas
1974	Mary Dagraedt
1975	Carol Johnson
1976	Marge Burns
1977	DeDe Owens
1978	Shirley Englehorn
1979	Bobbie Ripley
1980	Betty Dodd
1981	Jane Read
1982	Barbara Romack
1983	Rina Ritson
1984	Shirley Spork
1985	Annette Thompson
1986	B. Crawford-O'Brien
1987	Linda Craft
1988	Judy Whitehouse
1989	Sharon Miller
1990	Dana Rader
1991	Dr. Betsy Clark
1992	Lynn Marriott
1993	Dr. DeDe Owens

LPGA Golf Pro of the Year

Awarded by:
LPGA
Criteria:
Achievement by a woman managing a total golf program.

1980	Nancy Gammon
1981	Peggy Kirk Bell
1982	Nell Frewin
1983	Lorraine Klippel
1984	Mary Dagraedt
1985	Bobbie Stewart
1986	Margo Walden
1987	Becky Sauers
1988	Kathy Murphy
1989	Pat Lange
1990	Chris Burkhart
1991	Paula Wagasky
1992	Lorraine Kippel
1993	Sue Fiscoe

Patty Berg Award

Awarded by:
LPGA
Criteria: *Unselfish contribution to the game.*

1979	Marilynn Smith
1980	Betsy Rawls
1981	No award
1982	No award
1983	No award
1984	Ray Volpe
1985	Dinah Shore
1986	David Foster
1987	Kathy Whitworth
1988	No award
1989	John D. Laupheimer
1990	Patty Berg
1991	Karsten Solheim
1992	Judy Dickinson

Old Tom Morris Award

Awarded by:
GSCA of America.
Criteria:
Contribution to the game

1983	Arnold Palmer
1984	Bob Hope
1985	Gerald Ford
1986	Patty Berg
1987	Robert Trent Jones
1988	Gene Sarazen
1989	Chi Chi Rodriguez
1990	Sherwood Moore
1991	William C. Campbell
1992	Tom Watson
1993	Dinah Shore
1994	Byron Nelson

MEMORABLE DATES
IN GOLF HISTORY

OVERVIEW: *A selection of the major events in professional golf, the development of the rules, opening of prominent course and changes in their structure, plus the publishing of famous golf books, the passing of great players, and the sometimes harried world of golf legalities (from the banning of golf several times in its early history to the modern-day lawsuits between companies and the governing bodies of the game).*

1353
The first recorded reference to chole, the probable antecedent of golf. It is a derivative of hockey played in Flanders (Belgium).

1421
A Scottish regiment aiding the French against the English at the Siege of Bauge is introduced to the game of chole. Hugh Kennedy, Robert Stewart and John Smale, three of the identified players, are credited with introducing the game in Scotland.

1457
Golf, along with football, is banned by the Scots Parliament of James II because it has interfered with military training for the wars against the English.

1470
The ban on golf is reaffirmed by the Parliament of James III.

1491
The golf ban is affirmed again by Parliament, this time under King James IV.

1502
With the signing of the Treaty of Glasgow between England and Scotland, the ban on golf is lifted.

James IV makes the first recorded purchase of golf equipment, a set of clubs from a bow-maker in Perth, Scotland.

1513
Queen Catherine of England, in a letter to Cardinal Wolsey, refers to the growing popularity of golf in England.

1527
The first commoner recorded as a golfer is Sir Robert Maule, described as playing on Barry Links (near the modern-day Carnoustie).

1552
The first recorded evidence of golf at St. Andrews.

1553
The Archbishop of St. Andrews issues a decree giving the local populace the right to play golf on the links at St. Andrews.

1567
Mary, Queen of Scots, seen playing golf shortly after the death of her husband Lord Darnley, is the first known female golfer.

1589
Golf is banned in the Blackfriars Yard, Glasgow. This is the earliest reference to golf in the west of Scotland.

1592
The City of Edinburgh bans golfing at Leith on

1592 *(continued)*
Sunday "in tyme of sermonis."

1618
Invention of the feathery ball.

1618
King James VI and I confirms the right of the populace to play golf on Sundays.

1621
First recorded reference to golf on the links of Dornoch (later Royal Dornoch), in the far north of Scotland.

1641
Charles II is playing golf at Leith when he learns of the Irish rebellion, marking the beginning of the English Civil War. He finishes his round.

1642
John Dickson receives a license as ball-maker for Aberdeen, Scotland.

1659
Golf is banned from the streets of Albany, New York—the first reference to golf in America.

1682
In the first recorded international golf match, the Duke of York and John Paterstone of Scotland defeat two English noblemen in a match played on the links of Leith.

Andrew Dickson, carrying clubs for the Duke of York, is the first recorded caddy.

1687
A book by Thomas Kincaid, "Thoughts on Golve," contains the first references on how golf clubs are made.

1721
Earliest reference to golf at Glasgow Green, the first course played in the west of Scotland.

1724
"A solemn match of golf" between Alexander Elphinstone and Captain John Porteous becomes the first match reported in a newspaper. Elphinstone fights and wins a duel on the same ground in 1729.

1743
Thomas Mathison's epic The Goff is the first literary effort devoted to golf.

1744
The Honourable Company of Edinburgh Golfers is formed, playing at Leith links. It is the first golf club.

The City of Edinburgh pays for a Silver Cup to be awarded to the annual champion in an open competition played at Leith. John Rattray is the first champion.

1754
Golfers at St. Andrews purchase a Silver Cup for an open championship played on the Old Course. Bailie William Landale is the first champion.

The first codified Rules of Golf published by the St. Andrews Golfers (later the Royal &Ancient Golf Club).

1759
Earliest reference to stroke-play, at St. Andrews. Previously, all play was match.

1764
The competition for the Silver Club at Leith is restricted to members of the Honourable Company of Edinburgh Golfers.

The first four holes at St. Andrews are combined into two, reducing the round from twenty-two holes (11 out and in) to 18 (nine out and in). St. Andrews is the first 18-hole golf course, and sets the standard for future courses.

1766

The Blackheath Club becomes the first golf club formed outside of Scotland.

1767

The score of 94 returned by James Durham at St. Andrews in the Silver Cup competition sets a record unbroken for 86 years.

1768

The Golf House at Leith is erected. It is the first golf clubhouse.

1773

Competition at St. Andrews is restricted to members of the Leith and St. Andrews societies.

The Royal Burgess Golfing Society of Edinburgh is formed.

1774

Thomas McMillan offers a Silver Cup for competition at Musselburgh. He wins the first championship.

The first part-time golf course professional (at the time also the greenkeeper) is hired, by the Edinburgh Burgess Society.

1780

The Aberdeen Golf Club (later Royal Aberdeen) is formed.

1783

A Silver Club is offered for competition at Glasgow.

1786

The South Carolina Golf Club is formed in Charleston, the first golf club outside of the United Kingdom.

The Crail Golfing Society is formed.

1787

The Bruntsfield Club is formed.

1788

The Honourable Company of Edinburgh Golfers requires members to wear club uniform when playing on the links.

1797

The Burntisland Golf Club is formed.

The town of St. Andrews sells the land containing the Old Course (known then as Pilmor Links), to Thomas Erskine for £805. Erskine was required to preserve the course for golf.

1806

The St. Andrews Club chooses to elect its captains rather than award captaincy to the winner of the Silver Cup. Thus begins the tradition of the Captain "playing himself into office," by hitting a single shot before the start of the annual competition.

1810

Earliest recorded reference to a women's competition at Musselburgh.

1820

The Bangalore Club is formed, the first club outside of the British Isles.

1824

The Perth Golfing Society is formed, later Royal Perth (the first club so honored).

1826

Hickory imported from America is used to make golf shafts.

1829

The Calcutta Golf Club (later Royal Calcutta) is formed.

1832

The North Berwick Club is founded, the first to include women in its activities, although they are not permitted to play in competitions.

1833

King William IV confers the distinction of "Royal" on the Perth Golfing Society; as Royal Perth it is the first Club to hold the distinction. The St. Andrews Golfers ban the stymie, but rescind the ban one year later.

1834

William IV confers the title "Royal and Ancient" on the Golf Club at St. Andrews.

1836

The Honourable Company of Edinburgh Golfers abandons the deteriorating Leith Links, moving to Musselburgh.

The longest driver ever recorded with a feathery ball, 361 yards, is achieved by Samuel Messieux at Elysian Fields.

1842

The Bombay Golfing Society (later Royal Bombay) is founded.

1844

Blackheath follows Leith in expanding its course from five to seven holes. North Berwick also had seven holes at the time, although the trend toward a standard eighteen had begun.

1848

Invention of the "guttie," the gutta-percha ball. It flies farther than the feathery and is much less expensive. It contributes greatly to the expansion of the game.

1851

The Prestwick Golf Club is founded.

1856

The Royal Curragh Golf Club is founded at Kildare, the first golf club in Ireland.
Pau Golf Club is founded, the first on the Continent.

A rule change is enacted that, in match play, the ball must be played as it lies or the hole be conceded. It is the last recorded toughening of the rules structure.

1857

The Golfer's Manual, by "A Keen Hand" (H.B. Farnie), is published. It is the first book on golf instruction.

The Prestwick Club institutes the first Championship Meeting, a foursomes competition at St. Andrews attended by eleven golf clubs. George Glennie and J.C. Stewart win for Blackheath.

1858

The format of the Championship Meeting is changed to individual match play and is won by Robert Chambers of Bruntsfield.

Allan Robertson becomes the first golfer to break 80 at the Old Course, recording a 79.

1859

The first Amateur Championship is won by George Condie of Perth.

Death of Allan Robertson, the first great professional golfer.

1860

The Prestwick Club institutes a Professional Championship played at Prestwick—the first Championship Belt is won by Willie Park.

1861

The Professionals Championship is opened to amateurs, and the British Open is born. The first competition is won by Old Tom Morris.

1864

The North Devon Golf Club is founded at Westward Ho!

1867

The Ladies' Golf Club at St. Andrews is founded, the first golf club for women.

1869

The Liverpool Golf Club is founded at Hoylake, later Royal Liverpool.

Young Tom Morris, age 17, wins the first of four successive British Open championships. His streak would include an 11-stroke victory in 1869 and a 12-stroke victory in 1870 (in a 36-hole format). His 149 in the 1870 British Open over 36 holes is a stroke average that would not be equalled until the invention of the rubber-cored ball.

1870

Young Tom Morris wins his third consecutive British Open Championship, thus winning permanent possession of the Belt.

The Royal Adelaide Golf Club is founded, the first golf club in Australia.

1872

The British Open Championship is reinstituted when Prestwick, St. Andrews and the Honourable Company offer a new trophy, with the Open Championship to be hosted in rotation by the three clubs.

Young Tom Morris wins his fourth consecutive British Open Championship.

1873

The Royal Montreal Golf Club is formed, the first club in Canada.

The British Open is held for the first time at the Old Course.

1875

The Oxford and Cambridge University Golf Clubs are founded.

1878

The first University Match is played at Wimbledon, won by Oxford.

1880

Royal Belfast is founded.

The use of moulds is instituted to dimple the gutta-percha ball. Golfers had long noticed that the guttie worked in the air much better after it had been hit several times and scuffed up.

1883

Bob Ferguson of Musselburgh, losing the British Open in extra holes, comes one victory shy of equalling Young Tom Morris' record of four consecutive titles. Ferguson ends up later in life penniless, working out of the Musselburgh caddy-shack.

1884

The Oakhurst Golf Club is founded at White Sulphur Springs. The first hole at The Homestead survives from this course and is the oldest surviving golf hole in America.

1885

The Royal Cape Golf Club is founded at Wynberg, South Africa, the first club in Africa.

1886

A.J. Balfour is appointed Chief Secretary (Cabinet Minister) for Ireland—his rise to political and social prominence has an incalculable effect on the popularity of golf, as he is an indefatigable player and catalyzes great interest in the game through his writing and public speaking.

1887

The Art of Golf by Sir Walter Simpson is published.

1888

The St. Andrews Golf Club is founded in

1888 *(continued)*

Yonkers, N.Y., the oldest surviving golf club in America.

1890

John Ball, an English amateur, becomes the first non-Scotsman and first amateur to win the British Open.

Bogey is invented by Hugh Rotherham, as the score of the hypothetical golfer playing perfect golf at every hole. Rotherham calls this a "Ground Score," but Dr. Thomas Brown, honorary Secretary of the Great Yarmouth Club, christens this hypothetical man a "Bogey Man," after a popular song of the day, and christens his score a "Bogey." With the invention of the rubber-cored ball golfers are able to reach the greens in fewer strokes, and so bogey has come to represent one over the par score for the hole.

1891

Shinnecock Hills Golf Club is founded.

1892

Gate money is charged for the first time, at a match between Douglas Rollard and Jack White at Cambridge. The practice of paying for matches through private betting, rather than gate receipts and sponsorships, survives well into the 20th Century as a "Calcutta," but increasingly gate receipts are the source of legitimate prize-purses.

The Amateur Golf Championship of India and the East is instituted, the first international championship event.

1893

The [British] Ladies' Golf Union is founded and the first Open Championship won by Lady Margaret Scott, at St. Anne's.

1894

The Open is played on an English course for the first time and is won for the first time by an Englishman, J.H. Taylor.

The United States Golf Association is founded as the Amateur Golf Association of the United States. Charter members are the Chicago Golf Club, The Country Club, Newport Golf Club, St. Andrews Golf Club, and Shinnecock Hills Golf Club.

Tacoma Golf Club is founded, the first golf club on the Pacific Coast.

1895

The United States Open is instituted. Willie Anderson is the first winner.

Chicago Golf Club opens the United States' first 18-hole golf course.

The pool cue is banned as a putter by the USGA.

The U.S. Women's Amateur is instituted. Mrs. Charles S. Brown is the first winner.

1896

Harry Vardon wins his first British Open.

1897

The first NCAA championship is held. Louis Bayard Jr. is the champion.

Golf, America's first golfing magazine, is published for the first time.

1898

Freddie Tait, betting he could reach the Royal Cinque Ports G.C. clubhouse from the clubhouse at Royal St. George's—a three mile distance— in forty shots or less, puts his 32nd stroke through a window at the Cinque Ports club.

The Haskell ball is designed and patented by

1898 *(continued)*
Coburn Haskell. It is the first rubber-cored ball.
The term "birdie" is coined at Atlantic C.C.—
from "a bird of a hole."

1899
The Western Open is first played at Glenview
G.C.—the first tournament in what would
evolve into the PGA TOUR.

1900
Harry Vardon wins the U.S. Open, the first
golfer to win both the British and U.S. Opens.

Golf is placed on the Olympic calendar for the
2nd Games at Paris.

1901
Walter Travis becomes the first golfer, in the
U.S. Amateur, to win a major title with the
Haskell ball. When Sandy Herd wins the
British Open and Laurie Auchterlonie the U.S.
Open the next year with the Haskell, virtually
all competitors switch to the new ball.

Sunningdale, a course built amidst a cleared
forest, opens for play. It is the first course with
grass grown completely from seed. Previously,
golf courses were routed through meadows,
which frequently created drainage problems as
the meadows were typically atop clay soil.

The first course at the Carolina Hotel (later the
Pinehurst Resort & CC) in Pinehurst, N.C., is
completed by Donald Ross. Ross will go on to
design 600 courses in his storied career as a
golf course architect.

1902
England and Scotland inaugurate an Amateur
Team competition, with Scotland winning at
Hoylake.

The first grooved-faced irons are invented.

1903
Oakmont C.C. is founded in Oakmont,
Pennsylvania, designed by Henry Fownes. It is
widely regarded as one of the finest examples
of penal-style golf architecture.

1904
Walter J. Travis becomes the first American to
win the British Amateur.

1905
Women golfers from Great Britain and the
United States play an international match, with
the British winning 6 matches to 1.

The first dimple-pattern for golf balls is patented by William Taylor in England.

The Complete Golfer by Harry Vardon is published. It promotes and demonstrates the
Vardon or overlapping grip.

1906
Goodrich introduces a golf ball with a rubber
core filled with compressed air. The "Pneumatic" proves quite lively, but also prone to
explode in warm weather, often in a golfer's
pocket. The ball is eventually discontinued; at
this time the Haskell ball achieves a dominance
of the golf ball market.

1907
Arnaud Massey becomes the first golfer from
the Continent to win the British Open.

1908
Mrs. Gordon Robertson, at Princes Ladies GC,
becomes the first female professional.

The Mystery of Golf by Arnold Haultain is published.

1909
The USGA rules that caddies, caddymasters

1909 *(continued)*

and greenkeepers over the age of sixteen are professional golfers. The ruling is later modified and eventually reversed in 1963.

1910

The R&A bans the center-shafted putter while the USGA keeps it legal—marking the beginning of a 42-year period with two official versions of *The Rules of Golf*.

Steel shafts are patented by Arthur F. Knight.

1911

J.J. McDermott becomes the first native-born American to win the U.S. Open. At 17 years of age, he is also the youngest winner to date.

1912

John Ball wins his eighth British Amateur championship—a record not yet equalled.

1913

Francis Ouimet, age 20, becomes the first amateur to win the U.S. Open, defeating favorites Harry Vardon and Ted Ray in a play-off.

The first professional international match is played between France and the United States at La Boulie, France.

1914

Formation of The Tokyo Club at Komozawa kicks off the Japanese golf boom.

Harry Vardon wins his sixth British Open—a record to this day (Peter Thomson and Tom Watson have since won five Opens each).

1915

The British Open is discontinued for the duration of the First World War.

1916

The PGA of America is founded by 82 charter

members and the PGA Championship is inaugurated. James Barnes is the first champion.

The first miniature golf course opens in Pinehurst, North Carolina.

Francis Ouimet is banned from amateur play for his involvement with a sporting goods business. The ruling creates a stir of protest and is reversed in 1918.

1917

The PGA Championship and the U.S. Open are discontinued for the duration of the First World War.

1919

The R&A assumes control over the British Open and the British Amateur.

Pebble Beach Golf Links opens as the Del Monte G.L. in Pebble Beach, California.

1920

The USGA founds its famed Green Section to conduct research on turfgrass.

The first practice range is opened in Pinehurst, North Carolina.

The *Professional Golfer of America* is first published which, today known as PGA Magazine, is the oldest continually-published golf magazine in the United States.

1921

The R&A limits the size and weight of the ball.

1922

Walter Hagen becomes the first native American to win the British Open. He subsequently becomes the first professional golfer to open a golf equipment company under his own name.

The Walker Cup Matches are instituted. The

1922 *(continued)*
grandson of Walker Cup founder George Herbert Walker is George H.W. Bush, the 41st President of the United States.
The Prince of Wales is elected Captain of the R&A.

The Texas Open is inaugurated, the second-oldest surviving PGA TOUR event.

Pine Valley Golf Club opens.

1923
The West and East courses at Winged Foot Golf Club open for play, designed by A.W. Tillinghast.

1924
Joyce Wethered wins her record fifth consecutive English Ladies' Championship.
The Olympic Club in San Francisco opens for play.

The USGA legalizes steel shafted golf clubs. The R&A does not follow suit until 1929, widening the breach in *The Rules of Golf.*

1925
The first fairway irrigation system is developed in Dallas, Texas.

Deep-grooved irons are banned by both the USGA and the R&A.

1926
Jesse Sweetser becomes the first native-born American to win the British Amateur.

Bobby Jones wins the British Open.

Gate money is instituted at the British Open.

Walter Hagen defeats Bobby Jones 12 and 11 in a privately sponsored 72-hole match in Florida.

The Los Angeles Open is inaugurated, the third-oldest surviving PGA TOUR event. The L.A. Open is also the first tournament to offer a $10,000 purse.

1927
The inaugural Ryder Cup Matches are played between Britain and the United States.

Creeping bentgrass is developed for putting greens by the U.S. Department of Agriculture.

1928
Cypress Point Club opens, designed by Alister Mackenzie.

1929
Walter Hagen wins the British Open for the fourth time.

Seminole Golf Club opens in Palm Beach, Fla., from a design by Donald Ross.

1930
Bobby Jones completes the original Grand Slam, winning the U.S. and British Amateurs and the U.S. and British Opens in the same year. Since Jones is an amateur, however, the financial windfall belongs to professional Bobby Cruickshank, who bets on Jones to complete the Slam, at 120-1 odds, and pockets $60,000.

The Minehead Club makes Captaincy elective. They had been the last club to award the Captaincy to the winner of the annual competition.

The Duke of York (later King George VI) is elected Captain of the R&A.

Shinnecock Hill Golf Club opens its modern course on Long Island, NY.

Bob Harlow is hired as manager of the PGA's

1930 *(continued)*

Tournament Bureau, and he first proposes the idea of expanding "The Circuit," as the TOUR is then known, from a series of winter events leading up to the season ending North & South Open in spring, into a year-round TOUR.

1931

Billy Burke defeats George Von Elm in a 72-hole playoff at Inverness to win the 1931 U.S. Open, in the longest playoff ever played. They were tied at 292 after regulation play, and both scored 149 in the first 36-hole playoff. Burke is the first golfer to win a major championship using steel-shafted golf clubs.

The USGA increases the minimum size of the golf ball from 1.62 inches to 1.68 inches, and decreases the maximum weight from 1.62 ounces to 1.55. The R&A does not follow suit. The lighter, larger "balloon ball" is universally despised and eventually the USGA raises the weight back to 1.62 ounces.

1932

The first Curtis Cup Matches are held at Wentworth in England.

The concave-faced wedge is banned.

Gene Sarazen introduces the sand-wedge.

1933

The Prince of Wales reaches the final of the Parliamentary Handicap Tournament.

Augusta National Golf Club, designed by Alister Mackenzie with advice from Bobby Jones, opens for play.

Craig Wood hits a 430-yard drive at the Old Course's fifth hole in the British Open—this is still the longest drive in a major championship.

Hershey Chocolate Company, in sponsoring

the Hershey Open, becomes the first corporate title sponsor of a professional tournament.

1934

The first Masters is played. Horton Smith is the first champion. In this inaugural event, the present-day back and front nines were reversed.

1935

Glynna Collett Vare wins the U.S. Women's Amateur a record sixth time.

Pinehurst #2 is completed by Donald Ross, generally described as his masterpiece.

Gene Sarazen double-eagles the par-5 15th hole to catch the leaders at the Masters. His "Shot Heard Round the World" propels him to victory, and due to the coverage of his feat, propels both the game of golf and Augusta National to new heights of popularity.

1936

Henry Cotton wins his third consecutive British Open.

Johnny Fisher becomes the last golfer to win a major championship (the U.S. Amateur) with hickory-shafted clubs.

1937

The Bing Crosby Pro-Am is inaugurated in San Diego. A few years later it moves to the Monterey Peninsula.

1938

The British amateurs score their first victory over the United States in the Walker Cup Matches at the Old Course.

The Palm Beach Invitational becomes the first tournament to make a contribution to charity—$10,000.

The 14-club rule is instituted by the USGA.

1940

The British Open and Amateur are discontinued for the duration of the Second World War.

1942

The U.S. Open is discontinued for the duration of the war. A world-wide shortage of rubber, a vital military supply, creates a shortage and huge price increase in golf balls. Sam Snead manages to complete an entire four-day tournament playing one ball, but the professional circuit is severely curtailed.

The U.S. government halts the manufacture of golf equipment for the duration of the war.

1943

The PGA Championship is cancelled for the year, and the Masters is discontinued for the duration of the war.

1944

The PGA expands the TOUR to 22 events despite the absence of many of its star players due to military service.

1945

Byron Nelson wins 18 tournaments in a calendar year to set an all-time PGA TOUR record—including a record 11 in a row and a record 19 consecutive rounds under 70. His total prize earnings during his 11-win streak, $30,000, is less than last place money for the PGA TOURChampionship by 1992.

The Tam O'Shanter Open offers a then-record purse of $60,000.

1946

The U.S. Women's Open is instituted. Petty Berg is the first winner.

1947

Mildred "Babe" Zaharias becomes the first American to win the British Women's Open, at Gullane.

Golf is televised for the first time, in a local St. Louis telecast of the U.S. Open.

Golf World magazine is founded.

1948

Bobby Locke becomes the first South African to win the British Open.

Bobby Locke sets a PGA TOUR record with a 16-stroke winning margin in the Chicago Victory National Championship.

Herbert Warren Wind's authoritative *The Story of American Golf* is published.

The U.S. Junior Amateur is instituted. Ken Venturi loses to Dean Lind in the first final.

The *USGA Golf Journal* is founded.

1949

Louise Suggs wins the U.S. Women's Open by a record margin of 14 strokes.

Marie Roke of Wollaston, MA aces a 393-yard hole—the longest ace ever recorded by a woman.

1950

The LPGA is founded, replacing the ailing Women's Professional Golf Association.

Ben Hogan, only weeks after returning to the PGA TOUR following a near-fatal auto accident, wins the U.S. Open at Oakland Hills.

1951

Francis Ouimet becomes the first American Captain of the R&A.

The USGA and the R&A, in a conference, complete a newly revised *Rules of Golf*. Although

1951 *(continued)*

the R&A and the USGA continue to differ over the size of the golf ball, all other conflicts are resolved in this momentous conference. The center-shafted putter is legalized world-wide. The out-of-bounds penalty is standardized at stroke-and-distance, and the stymie is finally and forever abolished.

Golf Digest is founded, with Bill Davis as editor.

Al Brosch shoots 60 in the Texas Open to set an 18-hole PGA TOUR record.

1952

Marlene Hagge wins the Sarasote Open when she is 18 years 14 days old—an LPGA record.

Patty Berg shoots an LPGA-record of 64 for an 18-hole round.

The National Hole-in-One Clearing House is established by *Golf Digest*.

1953

Tommy Armour's *How to Play Your Best Golf All the Time* is published and becomes the first golf book ever to hit the best-seller lists.

Ben Hogan wins the first three legs of the modern "Grand Slam" (The Masters, U.S. Open, and British Open), but fails to win the final leg, the PGA Championship.

The Tam O'Shanter World Championship becomes the first tournament to be nationally televised. Lew Worsham holes a 104-yard wedge shot on the final hole for eagle and victory in one of the most dramatic finishes ever.

The Canada Cup is instituted, the first event that brings together teams from all over the world. After 1966 the tournament is known as the World Cup.

1954

Peter Thomson becomes the first Australian to win a major tournament with a victory in the British Open.

Architect Robert Trent Jones, upon receiving complaints that he has made the par-3 fourth hole at Baltusrol too hard for the upcoming U.S. Open, plays the hole to see for himself— and records a hole-in-one.

The U.S. Open is nationally televised for the first time.

The Tam O'Shanter World Championship offers the first $100,000 purse for a golf tournament.

"All-Star Golf," a filmed series of matches, debuts on network television.

Babe Zaharias returns to the LPGA Tour following cancer surgery and wins the U.S. Women's Open.

The first PGA Merchandise Show is held in a parking lot in Dunedin, Florida, outside the PGA National Golf Club. Salesmen work the show out of the trunks of their cars. The Show goes on to become one of the main events on the golfing calendar—by 1994 it grows to over 30,000 attendees, four days, and has become the single-largest tenant of the Orange County Convention Center in Orlando, spilling over 220,000 square feet of exhibit space.

1955

Mike Souchak shoots 60-68-64-65 for a PGA TOUR record 27-under-par 257 for 72 holes, at Brackenridge Park GC in the Texas Open. The record still stands today.

1956

The current yardage guides for par are adopted by the USGA.

1957
Great Britain wins the Ryder Cup matches at Lindrick—ending a drought that dates back to 1935.

E. Harvie Ward loses his amateur status for accepting expenses from sponsors for golf tournaments. The ruling is reversed in 1958.

Ben Hogan's *Five Lessons* is published.

1958
Arnold Palmer is allowed a controversial free drop to save par in the final round of the Masters, and he goes on to defeat Ken Venturi.

1959
Bill Wright, in winning the U.S. Amateur Public Links, becomes the first African-American to win a national championship.

Golf Magazine is founded, with Charles Price as the first editor.

1960
Arnold Palmer comes back from six shots down in the final round to win the US Open. With his victory, he completes the first two legs of the modern Grand Slam after winning the Masters in April, the first to do so since Ben Hogan in 1953. He finishes second to Kel Nagle in the British Open to end his bid. Palmer's entry in the British Open is credited with reviving world-wide interest in the championship. Palmer went on to win the British Open in both 1961 and 1962.

Lifting, cleaning, and repairing ballmarks is allowed on the putting green for the first time.

1961
Gary Player becomes the first foreign player to win the Masters.

Caucasians-only clause stricken from the PGA constitution, and at the Greater Greensboro Open Charlie Sifford becomes the first black golfer to play in a PGA co-sponsored tournament in the South.

1962
Dr. Joseph Boydstone records 11 aces in one calendar year. Three were recorded in one round, at Bakersfield C.C., Calif.

Jack Nicklaus wins his first professional tournament—the U.S. Open, the last player to win the U.S. Open as his first pro victory.

Painted lines are first utilized to mark water hazards at the U.S. Open.

1963
Arnold Palmer becomes the first professional to earn over $100,000 in official prize money in one calendar year.

Mickey Wright wins a record 13 events on the LPGA Tour in one year.

The casting method for irons is first employed.

1964
PGA National opens, in Palm Beach, Fla.

Mickey Wright sets the LPGA 18-hole record with a 62 at Hogan Park GC in the Tall City Open.

Norman Manley, an amateur from Long Beach, Calif., scores holes-in-one on two successive par-4s at Del Valley CC, Calif. It is the first and only time this feat has been accomplished.

1965
Sam Snead wins the Greater Greensboro Open—his 81st TOUR victory, a record. His victory is the eighth in the Greensboro event, also a record. Finally, he wins at the age of 52, also a PGA TOUR record to this day.

1965 *(continued)*
Jack Nicklaus sets a tournament record of 271 in winning the Masters.

Mrs. William Jenkins Sr. of Baltimore, Md., double-eagles the par-five 12th hole at Longview GC, the longest ever recorded by a woman.

PGA TOUR Qualifying School is inaugurated at PGA National, with 17 golfers of the 49 applicants winning their playing cards.

1966
Arnold Palmer blows a six-shot lead in the final round of the US Open, losing to a surging Billy Casper at Olympic.

1967
Charlie Sifford, by winning the Greater Hartford Open, becomes the first African-American to win a PGA TOUR event.

Catherine Lacoste becomes the first amateur to win the U.S. Women's Open.

The Canada Cup changes its name to the World Cup.

1968
Arnold Palmer passes the $1 million mark in career PGA earnings.

The PGA of America and the PGA TOUR officially split, with the professionals forming a breakaway group known as the Association of Professional Golfers. The breach is eventually healed, and a Tournament Players Division of the PGA is formed. Joe Dey is elected the next year as the first PGA TOUR commissioner.

Tommy Moore, age 6 years 1 month, 1 week, becomes the youngest player to score a hole-in-one. Moore also becomes, in 1975, the youngest player ever to score a double-eagle.

Roberto DeVicenzo ties Bob Goalby after regulation play in the Masters, but signs an incorrect scorecard and loses the event.

1969
Ollie Bowers of Gaffney, S.C. completes a record 542 rounds (9,756 holes) in one calendar year.

Jack Nicklaus concedes Tony Jacklin's final putt and England ties the U.S. in the Ryder Cup matches, after five consecutive defeats. The gesture is often hailed as "the greatest act of sportsmanship in history."

The trendsetting Harbour Town Golf Links opens on Hilton Head Island, S.C., designed by Pete Dye with assistance from Jack Nicklaus.

1970
Bill Burke, with a 57 at Normandie C.C., sets the all-time official record for low 18-hole score.

Thad Doker of Durham, N.C., records a record two-under par 70 in the World One Club Championship at Lochmere CC.

1971
Laura Baugh wins the US Amateur at 16 years 2 months of age.

Alan Shepard hits a six-iron at "Fra Mauro Country Club" on the moon.

1972
Carolyn Gidone wins the US Senior Women's Amateur for a record fifth consecutive time.

Dick Kimbrough completes 364 holes in 24 hours at the 6,068 North Platte CC in Nebraska.

Tom Doty records 10-under-par in four holes at Brookwood CC, Illinois. His streak includes a double-eagle, two holes-in-one, and an eagle. Spalding introduces the first two-piece ball, the Top-Flite.

1972 *(continued)*

Jack Nicklaus completes the first two legs of the modern Grand Slam winning the Masters and the US Open (at Pebble Beach), but like Arnold Palmer in 1960, falters in the British Open by finishing second (to Lee Trevino).

1973

Ben Crenshaw wins the NCAA title for a record 3rd consecutive time. Later in the year, after earning his PGA TOUR card, he wins the first event he plays as a PGA TOUR member, the San Antonio Open.

Johnny Miller fires a record 63 in the final round to win the US Open at Oakmont.

The graphite shaft is invented.

The classic golf book *Golf in the Kingdom*, by Michael Murphy, is published.

Jack Nicklaus wins the PGA Championship and breaks Bobby Jones' record for most major victories with his 14th.

1974

Deane Beman is elected as the second PGA TOUR commissioner.
Roberto DeVicenzo scores six birdies, an eagle, and three more birdies for a record 11-under par for ten holes, at Valla Allende GC, Argentina.

The World Golf Hall of Fame is opened in Pinehurst, North Carolina.

Mike Austin hits a 515-yard drive at the 1974 National Seniors Open in Las Vegas, Nev., the longest **drive** ever recorded in competition.

Jack Nicklaus' *Golf My Way* is published.
Tom Weiskopf strikes a 420-yard drive in the greenside bunker on the 10th hole at Augusta National—the longest drive in Masters history.

Muirfield Village Golf Club opens from a Desmond Muirhead/Jack Nicklaus design.

The Tournament Players Championship is inaugurated.

1975

Lee Elder becomes the first black golfer to play in the Masters.

Lee Trevino, Jerry Heard and Bobby Nichols are struck by lightning during the 1975 Western Open. The incident prompts new safety standards in weather preparedness at PGA events, but four spectators are killed when struck by lightning during the 1991 U.S. Open at Hazeltine National.

1976

Judy Rankin becomes the first LPGA professional to earn more than $100,000 in a season.

Richard Stanwood sets the record for fewest putts in one round—15— at Riverside GC in Pocatello, ID.

The USGA institutes the Overall Distance Standard—golf balls that fly more than 280 yards during a standard test are banned.

1977

Al Geiberger shoots 59 at Colonial CC in the second round of the Memphis Classic, to set a new PGA TOUR 18-hole record.

Bing Crosby dies after completing a round of golf in Spain. His Bing Crosby National Pro-Am continues for several years, but after relations sour between the PGA TOUR and the Crosby family, AT&T takes over sponsorship of the event.

The "sudden-death" playoff is used for the first time in a major championship, when Lanny Wadkins defeats Gene Littler for the PGA

1977 *(continued)*
Championship played at Pebble Beach G.L.

In what has been described as the most exciting tournament in history, Tom Watson defeats Jack Nicklaus by one stroke in the British Open, at Turnberry. They were tied after the second and third rounds, and were paired with each other during the final 36 holes.

1978
The Legends of Golf is inaugurated at Onion Creek C.C. in Austin, Texas. Its popularity leads to the formation of the Senior TOUR two years later.

1979
The Ryder Cup is reformatted to add European continent players to the British-Scottish-Irish side, making the event far more competitive.

Taylor Made introduces the first metal woods.

1980
Tom Watson is the first golfer to earn $500,000 in prize money in a single season.

The PGA Senior TOUR is born, with four official events.

The U.S. Senior Open is instituted. Roberto De Vicenzo is the first winner.

Jack Nicklaus sets a record of 272 in the U.S. Open at Baltusrol. His mark is equalled in the 1993 U.S. Open by Lee Janzen, also at Baltusrol.

The USGA introduces the Symmetry Standard, banning balls such as the Polaris which correct themselves in flight.

Gary Wright completes 18 holes in a record 28 minutes 9 seconds at Twantin Noosa GC, Australia (6,039 yards).

1981
The Tournament Players Club at Sawgrass opens, with its controversial island green 17th hole, and immediately becomes the permanent host of the Tournament Players Championship. The TPC at Sawgrass becomes the prototype for a dozen "stadium" TPC courses around the United States, built specifically to host PGA TOUR co-sponsored events and affording better viewing for spectators.

The USGA institutes the Mid-Amateur.

Kathy Whitworth becomes the first woman to earn $1 million in career prize money.

1982
Kevin Murray double-eagles the 647-yard second hole at the Guam Navy GC, the longest double-eagle ever recorded.

1983
The PGA TOUR introduces the all-exempt Tour, with the top 125 players exempt from qualifying tournaments.

1984
Desert Highlands opens in Phoenix from a design by Jack Nicklaus utilizing only 80 irrigated acres for 18 holes, instead of the typical 100-150 for a major course. The success of Nicklaus' concept of "target golf" ushers in the era of environmentally-sensitive desert design.

1985
Nancy Lopez sets the LPGA 72-hole record with 268 in the Henredon Classic.

The United States loses the Ryder Cup matches for the first time since 1957, to the expanded European team.

The USGA introduces the Slope System to allow golfers to adjust their handicaps to allow

1985 *(continued)*

for the relative difficulty of a golf course compared to players of their own ability.

1986

Bob Tway sinks a miracle bunker shot to beat a stunned Greg Norman in the PGA Championship. Norman had held the lead on Sunday morning in each of the four major championships of 1986, but was able to win only in the British Open. Only Bobby Jones had previously held the Sunday morning lead in each Grand Slam event. Tway's stroke inaugurated a celebrated series of miracle shots holed by various golfers to defeat Norman.

The Pete Dye-designed PGA West opens amid great controversy concerning the difficulty of the course.

The Panasonic Las Vegas Invitational offers the first $1 million purse.

The PGA TOUR Team Charity Competition debuts. By 1987, TOUR-related contributions to charity exceed $100,000,000, and by 1992 they reach a total of $200,000,000.

1987

The Links at Spanish Bay opens, the first true links course in the Western United States. It is a co-design by Robert Trent Jones, Jr., Tom Watson, and former USGA President Frank "Sandy" Tatum.

Judy Bell becomes the first woman elected to the USGA Executive Committee.
The Nabisco Championships (later the TOUR Championship) debuts as a season-ending event for the top 30 money winners. The first winner is Tom Watson, breaking a three year victory drought.

Walter Dietz, a blind golfer, aces the 155-yard seventh hole at Manakiki G.C., California.

1988

Links Magazine is founded (originally *Southern Links*), with Mark Brown as editor-in-chief.

Lori Garbacz orders a pizza between holes at the U.S. Women's Open to protest slow play.

Square-grooved clubs such as the PING Eye2 irons are banned by the USGA, which claims that tests show the clubs give an unfair competitive advantage to PING customers. The PGA TOUR also bans the clubs in 1989. Karsten Manufacturing, maker of the clubs, fights a costly two-year battle with both the USGA and the PGA TOUR to have the ban rescinded after winning a temporary injunction. Eventually both organizations drop the ban, while Karsten acknowledges the right of the organizations to regulate equipment and pledges to make modifications to future designs.

Curtis Strange wins the season-ending Nabisco Championships at Pebble Beach, and his $360,000 paycheck lifts his official 1988 TOUR earnings to $1,147,644—and thus he becomes the first player to win over $1,000,000 in a single season.

1989

Four golfers, Doug Weaver, Mark Wiebe, Jerry Pate and Nick Price, hit aces on the par-three sixth hole on the same day in the U.S. Open at Oak Hill.

Nick Faldo sinks a 100-foot birdie putt on the second hole at Augusta National in the Masters—the longest putt holed to date in a major tournament. Faldo goes on to win the Masters.

1990

Hall Thompson of Shoal Creek GC, on the eve of the PGA Championship at Shoal Creek, defends his club's policy of not admitting black members. Amidst a public outcry, Shoal Creek

1990 *(continued)*

is forced to change its policy and the PGA TOUR and the USGA insist that in future all clubs submit to a standard set of guidelines on membership policies. Cypress Point Club and Aronimink, among others, decide they are unable to comply and withdraw from the professional tournament arena.

Bill Blue resigns after a short reign as LPGA Commissioner. Charles Mecham is selected as his successor.

Construction begins on Shadow Creek Golf Club, the most expensive golf course ever built, with cost estimates ranging from $35 to $60 million as Tom Fazio creates an oasis in the Las Vegas desert . The club in 1994 vaults into eighth place on the Golf Digest top-100 course rankings, sparking controversy.

The R&A, after 38 years, adopts the 1.68 inch diameter ball, and for the first time since 1910 *The Rules of Golf* are standardized throughout the world.

The initial Solheim Cup is played at Lake Nona G.C., Orlando, commencing a biennial USA vs. Europe competition for women, a recognition of the growing strength of women's golf on both sides of the Atlantic.

The Ben Hogan Tour is launched as a minor league for the PGA TOUR, following the increased success of mini-tours such as the U.S. Golf Tour in 1989.

1991

The Ocean Course at Kiawah Island, S.C., the first course to be awarded the Ryder Cup Matches before the course has been completed, is the scene of the United States' first victory in

the event since 1983. The competition comes down to a twisting seven-footer on the 18th hole missed by Bernhard Langer in the final match (against Hale Irwin).

John Daly wins the PGA Championship at Crooked Stick when, as ninth alternate, a slot in the tournament opens up for him on the night before the Championship began. The golfer who withdrew and gave Daly his place, Nick Price, wins the PGA Championship in 1992 at Bellerive.

Phil Mickelson, an amateur, wins the PGA TOUR's Northern Telecom Open.

Oversized metal woods are introduced, with Callaway Golf's Big Bertha quickly establishing itself as the dominant brand—the Big Bertha driver becomes one of the biggest-selling clubs of all time.

Harvey Penick's Little Red Book becomes the all-time best selling golf book.

1992

Simon Clough and Boris Janic complete 18-hole rounds in five countries in one day, walking each course. They played rounds in France, Luxembourg, Belgium, Holland, and Germany, and completed their journey in 16 hours, 35 minutes.

Brittany Andres, age 6 years 19 days, scores an ace at the 85-yard second hole at the Jimmy Clay G.C. in Austin, Texas.

1993

An ownership group led by Joe Gibbs and Arnold Palmer announce plans for The Golf Channel, a 24-hour, 365-day cable service. The channel will launch in 1995.

GOLF, BY NATION

OVERVIEW: *Key statistics, history, prominent players, tournaments, and courses, plus a census of golfers.*

ANTIGUA and BARBUDA

No. of Players (Rank): 100 (74)
No. of Courses (Rank): 1 (69)
Players/Course (Rank): 100 (6)
World Cup results 1993: Did not compete.

History: Golf has had limited exposure in Antigua and Barbuda, two of the former British West Indies which have only 32 square miles of arable land for its 64,000 inhabitants. Nevertheless, Antigua has the Cedar Valley C.C. to service the small number of local golfers, and tourists who swing through the islands on cruise ship packages. The islands have yet to produce a golfer of world-class ability.

ARGENTINA

No. of Players (Rank): 30,000 (21)
No. of Courses (Rank): 160 (13)
Players/Course (Rank): 188 (24)
National Open Champion: Mark Calcavecchia
World Cup results 1993: 19th
Prominent Players: Ruben Alvarez, Roberto de Vicenzo, Miguel Guzman, Fabian Montovia, Antonio Ortiz, Eduardo Romero, Adan Sowa.
Prominent courses: Jockey Club.
Golf Professionals: 350
Prominent publications: Golf en la Argentina, Golf Digest Argentina, Notigolf, and Green Fields.
National Golf Association: Asociacion Argentina de Golf, Calle Corientes 538 -piso 11, 1043 Buenos Aires, Tel. 54-1-325-7498

History: In 1885, a group of British subjects brought golf to Argentina. The first golf club was founded in 1890, and the Association of Golf Clubs of the River Plate was founded in 1897. The Argentine Golf Association was founded in 1926, but it wasn't until the 1950s that Argentina first played a role on the world golfing stage, when the emergence of the great Roberto de Vicenzo led to Argentina's victory in the inaugural Canada Cup in 1953. The Canada Cup was subsequently hosted by the Jockey Club in Buenos Aires in 1962 and again in 1970. Roberto de Vicenzo was the victim in the famed scorecard controversy in the 1968 Masters, when he was excluded from a play-off because he had signed an incorrect scorecard (de Vicenzo did win one major in his career, the 1967 British Open in which he bested Jack Nicklaus by two strokes at Hoylake.)

In recent years Eduardo Romero has emerged as a prominent international player, winning both the Spanish and French Opens in 1991 after dominating the South American circuit early in his career. After the initial success in the Canada Cup (now the World Cup), Argentina was the runner-up in 1954, 1962, 1964, and 1970.

AUSTRALIA

No. of Players (Rank): 1,750,000 (4)
No. of Courses (Rank): 1,495 (4)
Players/Course (Rank): 1,171 (68)
National Open Champion: Brad Faxon.
World Cup results 1993: 4th. Robert Allenby placed 6th in the individual competition.
Prominent Players: Greg Norman, Jack Newton, Ian Baker-Finch, Peter Thomson, Craig Parry, Brett Ogle, Kel Nagle, Graham Marsh, Mike Harwood, Peter Senior, Wayne Grady, Steve Elkington.
Prominent Courses: Royal Melbourne, Royal Sydney, Royal Adelaide, The Australian National GC.
Golf Professionals: 1,400.
Prominent Publications: Australian Golf Digest, Golf Australia.
Collegiate Golf Programs: Australian Institute of Sport.
Golf Schools: Kooralbyn International School.
National Golf Association: Australian Golf Union, 153-155 Cecil Street, South Melbourne, Victoria 3205.

History: Golf was first recorded in the colony of Victoria, in Melbourne, in 1847. By 1851 golf had been introduced to Sydney by a Scottish-born enthusiast named John Dunsmore. Royal Adelaide was the first permanent club (although it was in hiatus for sixteen years from 1876-1892). The Australian Golf Club and Royal Brisbane followed in the 1880s but it wasnot until 1891 and the founding of Royal Melbourne that a club was founded that has survived without interruption until today. In the 20th century golfers such as Norman Von Nida and Peter Thomson brought Australian professional golf into the international spotlight with Thomson winning the British Open in 1951 for the first major victory by an Australian.

During the 1950's golf in Australia bloomed (albeit with an image as an elitist sport) with Australia winning the Canada Cup in 1954 and 1959, and the World Cup in 1970 and 1989, and Brett Ogle in 1992 and Peter Fowler in 1989 taking the individual medal in the event. Peter Thomson won the British Open five times between 1953 and 1965, while Kel Nagle edged out Arnold Palmer at St. Andrews. Graham Marsh and Jack Newton kept Australia in the international spotlight through the 1970s.

Golf boomed in the 1980s in Australia, with the emergence of international stars such as Wayne Grady (U.S. PGA champion in 1990), Ian Baker-Finch (British Open victor in 1992), and the hugely popular Greg Norman, winner of the 1986 and 1993 British Opens as well as over sixty tournaments world-wide. Economic downturns forced a reduction in the tour in the early 1990s, resulting in an exodus of the nation's most prominent players for the European and American circuits, with Brett Ogle and Robert Allenby showing the most promise. But Australia remains both in public enthusiasm and international success at the forefront of international golf.

AUSTRIA

No. of Players (Rank): 24,735 (22)
No. of Courses (Rank): 73 (20)
Players/Course (Rank): 339 (40)
National Open Champion: No national open currently played.
World Cup results 1993: Did not compete.
Prominent courses: G.C. of Vienna, Murhof.
Prominent Players: Marcus Burger, Oswald Gartenmaier, Rudolph Hauser, Franz Laimer, Johannes Lamberg, Klaus Nierlich.
Golf Publications: Golf-Revue.
Golf Professionals: 80
National Golf Association: Orreicher Golf-Verband, Eugen-Strasse 12, Vienna

History: Golf has been a minor sport until recently in Austria, but the Golf Club of Vienna dates back to 1901. The Golf Association was founded in 1931, but the game was abandoned during the Second World

War, and the GC of Vienna was not refounded until 1947.

Oswald Gartenmaier and Rudolph Hauser became a well-known pairing in the World Cup and, although in eleven consecutive appearances together they finished no higher than a tie for 17th in 1974, both Gartenmaier (T11th, 1978) and Hauser (T16th, 1974) found individual success in the event. Gartenmaier made 21 appearances in the World Cup between 1965 and 1991.

The golf boom reached Austria in the late 1980s and, after playing host to the European Amateur Team Championship in 1987, by 1990 an Austrian Open was held as a stop on the European PGA Tour, the last in 1992 at the Gut Altenann G. & C.C. in Salzburg.

THE BAHAMAS

No. of Players (Rank): (est.) 1,100 (54)
No. of Courses (Rank): (est.) 26 (36)
Players/Course (Rank): 42 (1)
World Cup results 1993: Did not compete
Prominent Courses: Cotton Bay Club, Paradise Island G.C., Lucaya G. & C.C., Divi Bahamas C.C., Bahama Princess Resort.
National Golf Association: Bahamas Golf Federation, P.O. Box N 4568, Nassau, The Bahamas

History: Golf in the Bahamas dates back to the late 18th century, but an early course laid out by Alexander Campbell did not survive. The first modern course dates from the 1920s, and while The Bahamas have yet to compete successfully on an international basis since earning independence from Great Britain in 1973, they have certainly provided some of golf's most stunning Caribbean-style courses. With the plentiful supply of resort courses, in fact, The Bahamas have the lowest ratio of golfers-to-courses in the world.

The Duke of Windsor (an enthusiastic golfer and former captain of the R&A) served as Governor here during the Second World War, and construction of The Bahamas' legendary courses began shortly afterwards with the completion of Cotton Bay (designed by Robert Trent Jones) in the late 1950s. Jones' design rival Dick Wilson was also active as a designer in these parts during the early 1960s. In recent years new courses by Joe Lee have added to the allure of the islands.

BARBADOS

No. of Players (Rank): 120 (73)
No. of Courses (Rank): 2 (66)
Players/Course (Rank): 60 (2)
World Cup results 1993: Did not compete

Prominent Courses: Sandy Lane G.C.
National Golf Association: None.

History: As with many of the Caribbean island-nations, Barbados has lacked the large base of active golfers necessary to compete internationally, and is best known as the home of the outstanding Sandy Lane course.

BELGIUM

No. of Players (Rank): 15,000 (25)
No. of Courses (Rank): 40 (27)
Players/Course (Rank): 375 (44)
National Open Champion: N/A
World Cup results 1993: Did not compete
Prominent Players: King Leopold of the Belgians, Arthur de Vulder, Donald Swaelens, Phillippe Toussaint, Flory Van Donck.
Prominent Courses: Royal Zoute.
National Golf Association: Federation Royale Belge de Golf Chemin de Baudemont, 23B-1400 Nivelles Belgium 32-67-220440

History: Belgium has an association with golf that, in its probable early form of chole, precedes even that of the Scots. Chole was a game that combined elements of hockey and modern golf, and was played in the fields of Flanders as early as 1353. The game, which survives in Belgium, is thought to have been imported by Scots mercenaries and modified for play in the linksland surrounding Scottish port-towns. The modern game of golf was introduced to continental Europe in the late-19th century, with the oldest course—Royal Antwerp— founded in 1888. The Belgians' interest in it was sparked primarily by that zeal and success of Leopold, King of the Belgians (a cousin to the English royal family) who played very successfully in a limited number of amateur events in the 1940s, including advancing to the final eight in the 1949 French Amateur.

In the 1950s Flory Van Donck became one of the leading golfers in the world, tying for individual medalist in the 1954 Canada Cup and taking the Individual title in 1960 at Portmarnock. He also finished runner-up in the British Open in 1956 (to Peter Thomson) and 1959 (to a young Gary Player) Van Donck and Donald Swaelens were formidable in team play..

In recent years Royal Zoute has been the site of the Belgian Open, an annual stop on the European PGA Tour, but no Belgians have recorded any major successes on the Tour itself. Phillippe Toussaint and Andre Van Damme have been the most prominent golfers in the past decade. Belgium has also hosted two European Ladies Amateur Championships and the 1961 European Amateur Team Championship.

BERMUDA

No. of Players (Rank): 3,000 (44)
No. of Courses (Rank): 8 (49)
Players/Course (Rank): 375 (44)
National Open Champion: Jeff Lewis.
World Cup results 1993: 25th. Kim Swan placed 49th in the individual competition.
Prominent Players: Dwayne Pearman, Keith Smith, Kim Swan.
Prominent Courses: Castle Harbour G.C., Mid-Ocean C., Port Royal G.C., St. George's G.C..
National Golf Association: Bermuda Golf Association, Box HM BX-433, Hamilton

History: Golf first organized on Bermuda in 1950 with the formation of the Bermuda Golf Association and, since 1953, Bermuda has been the site of the club-oriented Bermuda Goodwill Tournament which attracts teams from the United States and Europe.

One of the chief attractions of Bermudan golf is the Mid-Ocean Club, revered as one of the finest tests of golf in the world since its opening in 1925. But Bermuda has an excellent assortment of public courses and has become a highly-regarded tourism destination for golf.

In the 1980s Bermuda began competing in the World Cup; the team's best finish was 25th in 1993.

BOTSWANA

No. of Players (Rank): 1,100 (57)
No. of Courses (Rank): 6 (54)
Players/Course (Rank): 142 (21)
World Cup results 1993: Did not compete

History: Botswana is better known as the home of the Kalahari Desert than as a golfing nation, but several courses have been built as a result of the British colonial influence dating back to the late 1880s. The proximity of Southern Botswana to the South African metropolis of Johannesburg and the fabulous resort complex at Sun City may mean that more courses may be erected in the interesting mountain terrain to the south, but for the present Botswana has yet to make a mark in the international arena.

BRAZIL

No. of Players (Rank): 8,000 (34)
No. of Courses (Rank): 42 (28)
Players/Course (Rank): 190 (30)
National Open Champion: Pedro Martinez
World Cup results 1993: 17th. Antonio

Barcellos finished 21st in the individual competition.

Prominent Players: Antonio Barcellos, Joao Corteiz, Jaime Gonzalez, Jose Gonzalez, Merio Gonzalez, Rafael Navarro.

Prominent Courses: PL Golf Club.

Prominent Publications: Golf Sport.

Golf Professionals: 50.

National Golf Association: Confederacao Braseleira de Golf, Rua 7 de Abril, 282-s/83 01044 Sao Paolo

History: Golf was introduced to Brazil by the English and Scots, and the first club founded was Sao Paolo G.C. in 1903. The second course to open was the Gavea Golf & Country Club in Rio de Janeiro, in 1924. The first competition was the Trophy Boies Harte, which featured two eight-man teams.

The first amateur championship was played in 1934 at Gavea, won by a Mr. Bill Wooley. Martin Pose of Argentina subsequently became the first winner of the Brazil Open.

Golf has become relatively well-established in Brazil despite the overwhelming popularity of football and the prohibitive cost of course construction. Brazil has competed successfully internationally since the 1950s. The high point in Brazilian golf to date has been the 4th place finish of the national team at the 1979 World Cup played in Athens, where Jaime Gonzalez also finished fourth in the individual competition after being tied for the lead through the third round.

CANADA

No. of Players (Rank): 2,200,000 (3)
No. of Courses (Rank): 1,796 (2)
Players/Course (Rank): 1,225 (71)
National Open Champion: Nick Price
World Cup results 1993: T11th. Dave Barr finished
Prominent Players: Dave Barr, Al Balding, Dan Halldorson, George Knudson, Stan Leonard, Jim Nelford, Moe Norman, Richard Zokol.
Prominent Courses: Banff Springs G.C., Capilano G. & C.C., Glen Abbey G.C., The Hamilton G. & C.C., The National G.C., The Royal Montreal G.C., St. George's G.C.
Prominent publications: Score Magazine.
National Golf Association: Canadian Golf Foundation, 1333 Dorval Drive Oakville Ontario L6J 4Z3, Canada (905) 849-9700

History: There is evidence of golf arriving in Canada as early as 1824, but the game began to flourish in Canada after the organization of Royal Montreal in 1873, only a few years after Confederation and well before the game took root in the United States. A club was subsequently founded in Quebec in 1875 by a daughter of Old Tom Morris. The first inter-club match in the Americas was staged between the clubs in 1876 and, with the founding of the Toronto Club in 1976, the oldest trio of North American courses was complete. One of the great curiosities of the development of the modern game is that no Canadian golfers emerged early on to further the popularity of the game in the manner of Hagen, Jones, et al in the United States. So, although the Canadian Open has been played continuously throughout this century and still forms a cornerstone of the PGA TOUR, Canadian golf has continued to be quite popular among the Canadians but very much a step-child of the American game in terms of mass appeal and international success.

Nevertheless, Canada has produced some excellent golfers and from time to time golfers such as George Knudson and Dave Barr have been prominent on the PGA TOUR. The World Cup originated at Royal Montreal in 1953 as the Canada Cup and was known as such through 1966. The Canadians themselves have won the Cup three times (in 1968, 1980, and 1985), while Canadians have taken the individual competition five times (Stan Leonard in 1954 and 1959, George Knudson in 1966, Al Balding in 1968, and Dave Barr in 1983. Canada also won the Eisenhower Trophy (World Amateur Team Championship) in 1986 at Caracas.

In recent years a Canadian Tour has sprung up involving a dozen or so tournaments, but the Canadian Open is still considered an official PGA TOUR event and the Canadian circuit only occasionally is able to attract the top players.

Canada pulled a major upset in late 1994 in winning the Alfred Dunhill Cup with a 2-1 victory over the United States in the final. The victory was Canada's most significant to date in proving the quality of Canadian golf.

CAYMAN ISLANDS

No. of Players (Rank): 100 (74)
No. of Courses (Rank): 1 (69)
Players/Course (Rank): 100 (6)
World Cup results 1993: Did not compete
Prominent Courses: Cayman G.C.

History: The Cayman Islands, one of the last vestiges of British colonial power in the West Indies, has had a rather interesting impact on the history of golf because of the (failed) Cayman course experiment carried out in constructing a course on Grand Cayman. The land was too small for a regulation course, so rather than put in a precision-length course the developers hired Jack Nicklaus and developed the Cayman ball, which travels a much shorter distance than the standard ball. The intention was to build a series of Cayman courses where land prices or availability stifled golf course development, but the concept did not prove a hit with golfers and the original Cayman course is now something of a curiosity.

CHILE

No. of Players (Rank): 4,000 (38)
No. of Courses (Rank): 36 (29)
Players/Course (Rank): 111 (11)
National Open Champion: Francisco Cerda.
World Cup results 1993: DNF (Roy Mackenzie withdrew due to injury). Guillermo Encina finished 40th in the individual competition.
Prominent Players: Francisco Cerda, Guillermo Encina, Roy Mackenzie, Enrique Orellana, Luis Alberto Salas.
Prominent Courses: Granadilla C.C., Prince of Wales G.C.
Prominent Golf Publications: Golf Digest Argentina; Golf Chilean Magazine.
Number of Golf Professionals: 58
National Golf Association: Federacion Chilena de Golf, California #1945 Dpto. F, 49-Correo 29, Casilla, Santiago

History: Golf arrived in Chile during the late 19th century, with the formation of the Valparaiso Golf Club in 1897 (the club and course still exist today, as Granadilla).

The Federation was founded in 1932 and beginning in 1954 Chile has made regular appearances in the World Cup, with the 1992 entry (finishing in a tie for 11th place) being the most successful to date. Chileans have not been able to crack the Sony World rankings for individual play, but Francisco Cerda in the 1970s put in quite credible showings at the World Cup, his high point in 1974 at Lagunita in Caracas when he finished in a tie for 11th place.

In recent years the Prince of Wales Open has been considered part of the fledgling South American PGA circuit, and the Chile Open has been a regular stop for the top South Americans, with Eduardo Romero winning in 1984 and 1986.

CHINA

No. of Players (Rank): 500 (64)
No. of Courses (Rank): 2 (66)
Players/Course (Rank): 250 (36)
World Cup results 1993: Did not compete

History: A shortage of suitable land and a capitalistic image have prevented golf from establishing more

than a toehold on the mainland of China. The mainland had several courses built during the last years of the Manchu dynasty and the Nationalist period, but were abandoned after the Communist Party acceded to power in 1949. The Chinese have a limited number of golfers and only two courses to date in the fourth largest nation on earth. The construction of an Arnold Palmer course in Guandong province by Arnold Palmer and Ed Seay, however, has been seen by many as the harbinger of change. To date, China has entered few regional and no international competitions, professional or amateur, of any consequence, although the Asian Games of 1990 played in Beijing included golf as a competitive sport. In a recent development, China has been selected to host the 1995 World Cup, which should bring international attention to the attractions of Chinese golf.

COLOMBIA

No. of Players (Rank): 8300 (34)
No. of Courses (Rank): 35 (30)
Players/Course (Rank): 237 (33)
National Open Champion: N/A
World Cup results 1993: Did not compete
Prominent Players: Alfonso Bohorquez, Eduardo Herrera, Juan Pizon, Paul Posse, Alberto Rivadeneira, Miguel Sala.
Prominent Courses: El Rincon.
National Golf Association: Federacion Colombiana de GolfCarrera 7a N. 72-64, Of. Int. 26Apartado Aereo 90985 Bogota, D.E. Columbia

History: Although golf in Columbia dates back to the establishment of the C.C. of Bogota in the 1910s, the game began to flourish in Colombia in the 1950s, when golfers such as Paul Posse and Pablo Molina found success in the Canada Cup (placing 10th in 1955 and 1958). Late in the 1950s Miguel Sala (who finished 4th in the individual competition in the 1958 Canada Cup) established himself as perhaps the greatest South American golfer after Roberto de Vicenzo. Sala continued to play a leading role in Colombian golf through the late 1960s.

In addition to international success, Colombia is home to one of the finest courses in the world in Bogota's El Rincon, which hosted the 1980 World Cup.

Since the 1970s Colombia has enjoyed less conspicuous success in international competition, but Alberto Rivadeneira placed fifth in the 1980 World Cup.

COSTA RICA

No. of Players (Rank): 400 (64)

No. of Courses (Rank): 4 (58)
Players/Course (Rank): 100 (6)
Prominent Players: Jose Chavez, Manfred Hachner, Mario Herrera, Francisco Jimenez, Hector Jimenez.
Golf Professionals: 8.
World Cup results 1993: Did not compete
National Golf Association: Associacion Nacional de Golf, Apartdao 10969, 1000 San Jose

History: Golf has had a foothold in Costa Rica since the Second World War, but the relative prosperity of this Central American nation has not yet translated into significant golf development. Costa Rica did field teams in the World Cup during the 1970s and early 1980s, finishing no higher than 36th. In recent years Costa Ricans have won the Central America and Panama Opens, and golf is experiencing a modest boom with the construction of several courses in the past decade, with a new layout on the Pacific Coast by Robert Trent Jones eagerly awaited.

CZECH REPUBLIC

No. of Players (Rank): 1371 (53)
No. of Courses (Rank): 7 (52)
Players/Course (Rank): 196 (25)
National Amateur Champion: N/A
World Cup results 1993: Did not compete
Prominent Players: Jari Dvorak, J. Janda, Jan Kunstra, Miroslav Plodek.
National Golf Association: Czech Golf Federation, Na Porici 12, CS-11530 Praha 1 Czech Republic 42(2) 2350065-84

History: Golf was played in the old Austria-Hungarian empire—with the first course, at Carlsbad, dating from 1904—but golf has developed slowly in the Czech Republic largely due to the effects of the Cold War.

Beginning in 1965 Czech teams were permitted to compete in the World Cup: amateurs Jari Dvorak and Jan Kunstra played together in five consecutive events without much success, their best finish being 36th place in 1966.

Since 1971, Czechs have rarely competed internationally but have maintained a lively amateur championship for men and women. The Czech Republic has been mentioned frequently as a country well-suited to a rapid expansion of the game.

DENMARK

No. of Players (Rank): 34,000 (20)
No. of Courses (Rank): 55 (23)
Players/Course (Rank): 618 (58)
National Amateur Champion: N/A

World Cup results 1993: Did not compete
Prominent Players: Per Greve, Herluf Hansen, Jorgen Korfitzen, Henning Kistensen, Hans Hendrik Larsen, Henrik Lund, Carl Poulsen, Jacob Rasmussen, Anders Sorenson, Steen Tinning.
National Golf Association: Danish Golf Union, Golfsvingt 22625 Vallensbaek Denmark 45-4-264-0666

History: Danish golf began early in this century, but reached a new level of success when Carl Poulsen played on an all-Scandinavian team in the 1954 and 1955 Canada Cup competitions, placing 25th individually in 1955. From 1956 Denmark has fielded its own team, with Poulsen making eight more appearances along with players such as Henning Kristensen and Jorgen Korfitzen.

Denmark reached a new level of success in world competition in the 1980s when 25-year-old Anders Sorenson and Steen Tinning joined together in 1987 and finished in 12th place. Both Tinning and Sorenson have gone on to distinguished careers on the European Tour. Sorenson has distinguished himself as Denmark's greatest golfer, winning the Nescafe Cup and the Volva Albatross Open on the European Tour as well as finishing second in the 1989-90 World Cups in individual competition.

DOMINICAN REPUBLIC

No. of Players (Rank): 700 (59)
No. of Courses (Rank): 5 (55)
Players/Course (Rank): 140 (20)
World Cup results 1993: Did not compete
Prominent Players: Edwin Corrie, Jack Corrie, Guillermo Gomez, Ricardo Orellana, Arturo Pellermo, Carlos Puebla
Prominent Courses: Casa de Campo (Teeth of the Dog)
National Golf Association: Dominican Golf Association, P.O. Box 641, Santo Domingo, Dominican Republic

History: The Dominican Republic is best known in the world of golf for Teeth of the Dog, the astonishing course built by Pete Dye which has been at the pinnacle of the world course rankings since it opened twenty years ago.

However, the tiny republic does have a small contingent of golfers and fielded several teams in the World Cup during the 1970s, although without conspicuous success. Carlos Puebla was selected three times, as was Edwin Corrie. The team's best finish was 31st in 1971.

Robert Trent Jones is now completing a course called Palaya Garnde which, situated on the northern shores of the island, is said to be a classic in the making, and it may prove a catalyst for a golf renaissance.

EGYPT

No. of Players (Rank): 1,100 (59)
No. of Courses (Rank): 5 (55)
Players/Course (Rank): 220 (31)
World Cup results 1993: Did not compete
Prominent Players: Naaman Aly, Farouk Badr, Mohamed Abdel Hanfi, Abdel Halim, Mohamed Said Moussa, Cherif Said.
National Golf Association: The Egyptian Golf Federation, Gezira Sporting Club, Gezira Cairo, Egypt

History: Golf in Egypt dates back to the First World War when a course was laid out by the Gezira Sporting Club, and golf proved quite popular in the country. The country competed quite successfully on an international level in the years following the Second World War. The Egyptian Open and the Egyptian Match Play became prominent tournaments during the reign of King Farouk in the 1950s. Following the coup by Nasser, golf continued but its growth was minimal. The Egyptian national team during this period was led by Mohamed Said Moussa, who represented Egypt no less than 22 times between 1957 and 1980, finishing as high as 18th in the individual competition. Egypt managed to place 10th in 1977, but shortly after that the tightening of the field left the nation out, and Egypt hasn't returned since1980.

ENGLAND

No. of Players (Rank): 596,000 (5)
No. of Courses (Rank): 1,300 (5)
Players/Course (Rank): 458 (48)
National Open Champion: Nick Price
World Cup results 1993: T11. David Gilford tied for 19th place in the individual competition.
Prominent Players: Peter Alliss, John Ball, Howard Clark, Sir Henry Cotton, Nick Faldo, David Gilford, Harold H. Hilton, Bernard Hunt, Tony Jacklin, Mark James, Barry Lane, Ted Ray, Steven Richardson, John H. Taylor, Harry Vardon, Brian Waites, Harry Weetman
Prominent Courses: Alwoodley, The Belfry, Berkshire, Formby, Ganton, Hillside, Lindrick, Little Aston, Notts, Royal Birkdale, Royal Cinque Ports (Deal), Royal Liverpool (Hoylake), Royal Lytham & St. Anne's, Royal North Devon (Westward Ho!), Royal St. George's, Sunningdale, Swinley Forest, Walton Heath, Wentworth, Woodhall Spa.

National Golf Association: The English Golf Union, 1-3 Upper King Street, Leicester LE1 6XF

History: The first reference we have for golf in England is a letter written in 1513 by Queen Catherine to Cardinal Wolsey referring to the growing popularity of the game. The first evidence of a golf course in England was the formation of The Blackheath Club in 1766; the Old Manchester Club was founded in 1818 and shortly after the invention of the gutta-percha ball in 1848 the (now Royal) North Devon Golf Club was formed and golf was well underway in England.

The cause of English golf was aided socially by the prominent backing and enthusiasm of Arthur Balfour, a darling of the social and aesthetic sets who went on to Parliament and eventually became Prime Minister. The game was advanced materially by the success of John Ball who, in 1890, became the first Englishman to win the British Open, and at the same time became the first to win the Amateur and the Open in the same year. Shortly afterwards Harry Vardon and John H. Taylor became two, along with Scotsman James Braid, of "The Great Triumvirate" which dominated open golfing competition for twenty years.

After the War the English began to pick up where they left off with Ted Ray coming to the fore and winning the Open in 1922, but a period of decline set in and the English became perpetual bridesmaids in the Ryder Cup matches with America and in their own British Open. The success of Sir Henry Cotton in the 1930s was one of the few bright lights.

Following the Second World War, economic exhaustion prostrated many golf clubs and English golf ceased to produce champions almost entirely. Only the fantastic upset victory at Lindrick in the 1957 Ryder Cup and a second place finish in the 1960 World Cup gave much encouragement to the English, who now faced international competition from Australians, South Africans, Canadians and Americans. The rise of Peter Alliss and Bernard Hunt in the late 1950s and early 1960s was encouraging, but they could do little to stop the foreign onslaught on the British Open crown by the likes of Palmer, Nicklaus, Trevino, and Player.

In 1969 young Tony Jacklin won the British Open and was a key player in the British halve with America in the Ryder Cup. Later on his captaincy of the European side was to prove a decisive factor in swinging the balance of power back toward the Continent. In the 1970s players like Howard Clark, Mark James, Nick Faldo and Mark Roe began to achieve international prominence on the European and American tours and in international competitions. Howard Clark won the individual competition at the 1985 World Cup (in which the English team finished second); Nick Faldo was runner-up in the 1983 World Match Play Championship and won in 1987; England emerged victorious in the 1987 Alfred Dunhill Cup competition; Nick Faldo won the 1987, 1990 and 1992 British Opens and the 1989 and 1990 Masters. In short, England had regained a position in world golf by the late 1980s that it had not held since the late 1920s. Currently younger players such as Steven Richardson and Peter Baker are thought to be the best hopes for England in continuing their conspicuous success throughout the 1990s.

FIJI

No. of Players (Rank): 700 (59)
No. of Courses (Rank): 9 (48)
Players/Course (Rank): 78 (5)
World Cup results 1993: 27th. Dharam Prakash finished 55th in the individual competition.
Prominent Players: Arun Kumar, Bose Lutunatabua, Vilikese Kalou, Dharam Prakesh, Mamoa Rsigatale, Vijay Singh.
National Golf Association: Fiji Golf Association, P.O. Box 177, Suva, Fiji

History: Golf in Fiji has been in part based on the resort traffic, which boomed in the 1970s as jets travelling between Australia and America stopped in Fiji for refueling. A small but active band of Fiji golfers thus have one of the lowest golfer/course ratios in the world.

Fiji stepped into the international competitive arena in the mid-1970s, entering the World Cup competition. Six subsequent appearances have yielded little success, with the best finish to date a 26th place result in 1980. Fiji also hosted the 1978 Eisenhower Trophy matches won by the United States.

In recent years the most exciting Fijian development has been the rise of Vijay Singh, easily the greatest Fijian golfer of all time, who has made strong showings on both the American and European tours in the 1990s, even leading by four strokes after the second round of the 1992 PGA Championship (he finished fourth).

FINLAND

No. of Players (Rank): 12,200 (29)
No. of Courses (Rank): 33 (32)
Players/Course (Rank): 370 (42)
World Cup results 1993: Did not compete
Prominent Players: Juhani Hamalainen, Anssi Kankkonnen, Markku Louhid, Sigurd Nystrom, Mikael Piltz, Timo Sipponen.
Prominent Publications: Suomen Golf.
National Golf Association: Finlands Golfforbund, Radiokatu 12, SF-00240, Helsinki, Finland

History: Of all the Scandinavian states Finland has had the slowest golf development, no doubt a product of its relative remoteness and harsh climate. The game was not introduced to Finland until 1930 and the Helsinki Golf Club, the first formal club, not opened until 1932. Golf remains an acquired taste here but golfers have a good selection of courses to choose from and have fielded four teams in the World Cup with increasing success, the best to date being the 22nd place finish in 1988.

FRANCE

No. of Players (Rank): 220,000 (22)
No. of Courses (Rank): 480 (14)
Players/Course (Rank): 458 (48)
National Open Champion: Mark Roe
World Cup results 1993: Tied for 13th. Jean Van de Velde finished fifth in the individual competition.
Prominent Players: Michel Besanceney, Patrick Cotton, Emmanuel Dussart, Marc Farry, Jean Garaiade, Jean Harismendy, Arnaud Massy, Bernard Pascassio, Francis Saubaber, Jean van de Velde, Gery Watine.
Prominent Courses: Chantilly, Golf de St-Nom-la-Breteche Le Tocquet, Morfontaine, Seignosse.
Federation Francaise de Golf, 69 Victor Hugo, F-75783, Paris Cedex 16, France
Tel. 33-1-4-4176300   Fax 33-1-4-4176363

History: Pau was founded in 1856 as a nine-hole course with a clubhouse in a room in a wayside inn, and it specialized for years as a French resort geared to the needs of the British tourist who required golf. It wasn't until 1907 when French professional Arnaud Massy won the British Open that golf much exceeded this humble role in France. British professionals flocked to France to avenge the defeat, but this time they were held off by Massy and Jean Gassiat. Golf thus achieved a certain status and courses began to be established in the Riviera and around Biarritz to accommodate English tourists and the small legion of French enthusiasts.

By the 1920s French players were routinely competing at the championship level in golf. French women Maette le Blan and Simone Thion de la Chaume won the 1928-9 Ladies' Championship in Britain. Their success dwindled after the Second World War in the face of American competition, but Jean Garaiade led the national team to success in the World Cup during the 1950s. Garaiade finished ninth in the individual competition in 1954 and 1963 and improved to sixth in 1970. The French team placed 5th in 1962 behind the combined efforts of Garaiade and Roger Cotton, and in 1963 France hosted the

World Cup. 1969 was a high point for France in these years when France won both the European Ladies Amateur Team Championship in Sweden, and hosted the Vagilano Trophy at Chantilly where Europe defeated the British Isles.

French golf fell into the second tier during the 1970s for the male professionals (although the women amateurs won the European Ladies' Amateur in 1975 and were runners-up in 1969, 1971 and 1973), but in the 80s one of the most astonishing revivals took place at the amateur level. France hosted the European Amateur Team Championship in 1983 at Chantilly, while in the 80s the number of courses doubled and France produced Jean van de Velde, who placed fifth in the individual competition in 1993.

French courses have also had increasing exposure as golfing tourism to the South of France has long ago exceeded just the number of British visitors. Cannes Mougins hosts the annual Cannes Open, while Monte Carlo hosts the Monte Carlo Open at Mont Agel. The Lancome Trophy and Peugeot French Open are still highly prized victories on the PGA European Tour, as well.

GERMANY

No. of Players (Rank): 95,863 (15)
No. of Courses (Rank): 239 (11)
Players/Course (Rank): 401 (47)
World Cup results 1993: 8th. Bernhard Langer finished in first place in the individual competition.
Prominent Players: Georg Bessner, Oliver Ekstein, Torsten Giedeon, Jurgen Harder, Tony Kugelmueller, Bernhard Langer, Friedal Schmaderer, Heinz-Peter Thuel.
Prominent Courses: Club Zur Vahr, Hamburger.
National Golf Association: Deutscher Golf Verband, eV. Postfach 2106,Wiesbaden D-6200 Germany 49 (6121) 526-041

History: A The enthusiastic golfers of England's Royal family were closely related to the German aristocracy, and close ties between the two countries that resulted led to golf arriving in the country as early as 1895 with the building of a course in Berlin. A German Open was played as early as 1912—but golf did not truly flower until after the Second World War, when the team of Georg Bessner and Hans Goermert represented Germany in the first Canada Cup. After some early success in international golf (a sixth-place finish in 1953 and 1955), the German national teams had little or no success in the international arena until the late 1970s and the emergence of the country's greatest golfer, Bernhard Langer.

Langer was successful on the European PGA TOUR since the mid-1970s, but two back-to-back second-place finishes in the 1979-80 World Cup matches and a spot on the 1981 Ryder Cup team sealed his place in the top-rank of European players. Germany's subsequent success in international team competition has largely rested on their success in finding a suitable partner for Langer.

In the 1980s a great wave of interest in golf was sparked by Langer's victory in the 1985 Masters, and the reunification of Germany made more land available for courses. By 1990 a new generation of German professionals were more competitive on the European PGA Tour and Germany won the 1990 World Cup when Langer and Torsten Giedeon tied for fifth in the individual competition. Golfers such as Heinz-Peter Thuel and Sven Struver have also recently found success on the European PGA Tour and the European Challenge Tour. Meanwhile golf continues to expand in Germany with the enthusiastic backing of German corporations such as BMW and Mercedes-Benz which have developed a close association with the game in the United States and other areas of operation. A new three-course complex outside of Berlin with courses by Langer, Nick Faldo, and Arnold Palmer/Ed Seay is scheduled to open next year as the largest golf facility yet constructed in the country.

GREECE

No. of Players (Rank): 2,500 (47)
No. of Courses (Rank): 4 (58)
Players/Course (Rank): 625 (59)
National Open Champion: No national open championship. Top ranked professional is G. Nikitaidis.
World Cup results 1993: 23rd. George Nikitaidis finished 43rd in the individual competition.
Prominent Players: Basilli Anastassiou, Basilli Karatzias, Vassilios Karatzias, George Nikitaidis, Craigen Pappas, John Sotiropoulos, Stefano Vafiadis
Prominent Courses: Glyfada G.C.
Prominent Publications: Golf News.
Number of golf professionals: 8
National Golf Association: Hellenic Golf Federation, P.O. Box 70003, GR 166 10 Athens
History: Golf was played on a nine-hole course in Athens until that with 1962, when the 18-hole Glyfada G.C. was founded. Greece fielded its first international team in 1968 in the World Cup, finishing 41st. John Sotiropoulos was selected ten times to represent Greece in World Cup competition, but the best Greece could manage was a 20th place finish in 1976

behind George Vafiadis' 29th place finish in the individual competition.

In 1979 Greek golf took a major step forward when Glyfada played host to the World Cup, and in 1981 the Hellenic Golf Federation was founded. Greece has not yet had a high finish in international competition, but there are now additional courses in Corfu, on Rhodes, and in Khalkadiki near Thessalonica.

GUADALOUPE

No. of Players (Rank): 200 (71)
No. of Courses (Rank): 1 (69)
Players/Course (Rank): 200 (26)
World Cup results 1993: Did not compete

HONG KONG

No. of Players (Rank): 20,000 (25)
No. of Courses (Rank): 7 (52)
Players/Course (Rank): 2,667 (71)
National Open Champion: David Frost
World Cup results 1993: Did not compete
Prominent Players: Dominique Boulet, Joe Hardwick, Richard Kan, Lai Wau Che, Lee Parker, Alex Tang, Peter Tang, Yau Sui Ming, Yau Wah Tah
Prominent Courses: The Royal Hong Kong G.C., Iris G.C.
National Golf Association: The Hong Kong Golf Association, Ltd., 1420 Prince's Building, 10 Charter Road, Central Hong Kong

History: Hong Kong was the original home of Far East Asian golf, for The Royal Hong Kong Golf Club's history dates all the way back to 1889. The mountainous terrain and the need to build housing on every available space has greatly slowed golf's growth, but Iris has 63 holes. Green fees and memberships are among the highest in the world.

Hong Kong has distinguished itself, though, in the international arena with fourteen appearances in the World Cup between 1973 and 1993, with a 23rd place finish in 1985 behind Yau Sui Ming's 32nd place finish in the individual competition. Hong Kong was also in the news recently because Tom Watson, in winning the 1992 Hong Kong Open, broke his five-year winless streak. Hong Kong stages an annual PGA championship in addition to the Open, and has competed in the Eisenhower (World Amateur) Cup. The Hong Kong team managed a 20th place finish in the 1993 World Cup, its best-ever finish, with rookie Richard Kan placing 39th in the individual competition.

With the return of Hong Kong to Chinese control in 1997, many have specualted that Hong Kong's golfing future may be bright indeed, given the recent Chinese interest in the game.

ICELAND

No. of Players (Rank): 3,500 (43)
No. of Courses (Rank): 29 (33)
Players/Course (Rank): 121 (14)
World Cup results 1993: Did not compete
Prominent Players: Ragnar Olasson, Sigurdur Petursson, Bjorgvin Thorsbeinsson.
National Golf Association: Golfsamband Islands P.O. Box 1076, Reykjavik IS-101 Iceland 354-168-6686

History: Golf arrived in the island kingdom in 1934, and Iceland emerged from relative obscurity to place two teams of amateurs in the World Cup in the late 1970s, with a best finish of 43rd in 1977. Another appearance with a 29th place finish in 1984 marked the high point in Icelandic golf to date.

INDIA

No. of Players (Rank): 15,000 (25)
No. of Courses (Rank): 150 (15)
Players/Course (Rank): 100 (6)
World Cup results 1993: Did not compete
Prominent Players: Basad Ali, Brandon de Souza, Shadi Lal, Rohta Singh, Ruda Valjii.
Prominent Courses: Royal Calcutta, Royal Bombay, Tollyguge, Bangalore
National Golf Association: The Indian Golf Union, Tta Centre, 3rd. Floor, 43 Chowringhee Road, Calcutta 700-071 India

History: The Calcutta Golf Club was founded in 1829 and is the oldest surviving golf club outside of the British Isles (it became Royal Calcutta in 1912). Royal Bombay was founded in 1842—thus in the mid-19th century there were as many golf clubs in India as in England. Bangalore was founded in 1870.

The Amateur Championship was founded in 1892, open to club members from India, Burma, Ceylon, and the Straits Settlements. Prominent courses of the era were all nine-holes, and the first eighteen-hole course was the Tollygune Club's course which was completed in 1906. Golf in this era was exclusively for British colonists and a select band of the Indian elite.

With the arrival of the Second World War and the subsequent independence of India from Britain granted in 1947, the growth of golf slowed to a crawl through the 1950s and 1960s. Consequently India has one course today for every 100 golfers, an astonishingly good supply.

In the 1970s and 80s, India fielded a few teams in international tournaments with limited success. Their 24th place finish, however, in their last World Cup appearance in 1988 was the best yet, with Rohtas

Singh finishing 41st in the individual competition.

As a golfing destination, the primary drawing card for India is still the India Open Championship, which has attracted some top-ranked international players over the years, and was won by Payne Stewart in 1981.

INDONESIA

No. of Players (Rank): 11,600 (31)
No. of Courses (Rank): 70 (21)
Players/Course (Rank): 166 (22)
World Cup results 1993: Did not compete
Prominent Players: Salam Denin, Mamatkajal, Aziz Narwi, Sumarno, Suparman.
Prominent Courses: Gunung Geulis, Jagorawl, Pondok Indah
National Golf Association: Indonesian Golf Association J1. Rawamangun Muka Taya , Jakarta 13220, Indonesia

History: There are two distinct phases of golf in Indonesia, the first beginning with the founding of Royal Batavia Golf Club in 1872 and the construction of a nine-hole course—the first in Asia outside of India and twenty years before the building of the first course in Holland, whence the colonists came. The game never caught on strongly, perhaps due to climate, and with independence from the Netherlands the Indonesians did not encourage growth of the game.

Nevertheless, Indonesia fielded teams with success in the World Cup in late 1970s and in 1980 had its best season, with a 20th place finish in the World Cup which was played at Pondok Indah at home. Subsequently the Indonesians have been quiet in the arena of international golf, but course development has begun to take off in the 1990s.

IRELAND

No. of Players (Rank): 160,000 (12)
No. of Courses (Rank): 253 (10)
Players/Course (Rank): 632 (60)
National Open Champion: Bernhard Langer.
Golf Professionals: 140
World Cup results 1993: 9th. Ronan Rafferty finished 12th in the individual competition.
Prominent Players: Hugh Boyle, Harry Bradshaw, Fred Daly, Eamonn Darcy, Norman Drew, David Feherty, Christy Greene, Hugh Jackson, Ernie Jones, Jimmy Kinsella, Jimmy Martin, Christy O'Connor, Sr., Christy O'Connor, Jr., John O'Leary, Eddie Pollard, Ronan Rafferty, Des Smyth.
Prominent Courses: Ballybunion, County Louth, County Sligo, Lahinch, Portmarnock,

Royal County Down, Royal Portrush.
Prominent Golf Publications: Golfer's Companion, Golf Link Magazine.
National Golf Association: Golfing Union of Ireland, Glancar House 81, Elginton Road, Donnybrook Dublin 4

History: The roots of Irish golf go back as far as the 17th century, when Viscount Montgomery of the Ards made a gift of land for a school that included grounds for golf. But the story of Irish golf properly picks up in the 1850s with the Scots regiments quartered at Curragh who played golf there and laid the grounds for the Royal Curragh Club. The formal history opens with the founding of Royal Belfast Golf Club by George Baillie in 1881. The game expanded to Dublin by 1884 with a few short holes laid out in Phoenix Park. The Irish Secretary of the time was England's most socially prominent golfer, Arthur Balfour, whose enthusiasm for the game at Phoenix Park led to its destruction by Irish separatists. Subsequently Royal Dublin Golf Club was founded in 1887.

By 1899 Ireland had its first champions in May Hezlet and Rhona Adair who won the Ladies' Championship five times between 1899 and 1907, with the Championship taking place in Ireland in 1899.

Despite the excellent and plentiful supply of courses, Irish golf went into a coma during the mid-war years, but after the Second World War Irish golf came to the forefront with the victories of James Bruen in 1946, Max McCready in 1949 (at Portmarnock) and Joe Carr in 1953 in the Amateur. In addition, Fred Daly won the 1947 British Open, and was selected to the Ryder Cup team in 1947.

Highlights of Irish golf in the 1950s included a victory in the 1956 World Cup when Harry Bradshaw finished second and Christy O'Connor tenth, and the emergence of Christy O'Connor as a top-ranked international player. O'Connor was selected to four World Cup teams and three Ryder Cups in the 1950s, including a resounding 7&6 defeat of Dow Finsterwald in the 1957 Ryder Cup matches at Lindrick that marked the first American defeat since 1933.

The 1960s opened with the hosting of the World Cup at Portmarnock (the Irish team finishing fourth), and O'Connor continued to be a force in world golf, winning spots on all five Ryder Cup teams in the 60s as well as finishing third in the 1961 World Cup individual standings, but other Irish successes were primarily on the amateur side. The Great Britain & Ireland team won the Eisenhower Trophy (World Amateur Championship) in 1968, and Ireland took home the European Amateur Team Championship in 1965 and '67.

In the 1970s Irish golf expanded with the growth of the European PGA Tour, and the Carrolls Irish Open has proved to be a successful venue at Royal Dublin and Portmarnock.

In the 1980s, Irish golf became stronger with the emergence of players such as Ronan Rafferty and David Feherty. Ronan Rafferty in particular has enjoyed great success, winning over fourteen tournaments and winning a spot on the victorious 1989 Ryder Cup. Ireland was victorious in the 1988 Alfred Dunhill Cup tournament.

By the early 1990s the late-80s golf boom had faded, but new courses such as The European Club were opening, and players such as Rafferty, Feherty, and Eamonn Darcy were finding regular success on the European Tour. The Irish team placed 2nd in the 1990 World Cup behind David Feherty's strong 3rd place finish.

ISRAEL

No. of Players (Rank): 600 (62)
No. of Courses (Rank): 1 (69)
Players/Course (Rank): 600 (57)
Number of golf professionals: 5
National Open Champion: No national open.
World Cup results 1993: 29th. Rami Assyag finished 58th in the individual competition.
Prominent Players: Rami Assyag, Jacob Avnaim, Lauie Been, Brian Cooper, Barry Mandel, Neil Shochet.
Prominent Courses: Caesarea GC
National Golf Association: Israel Golf Federation, P.O. Box 1010, Caesarea
History: Golf began in Israel in 1961 when the Rothschild family founded the nation's first and only (to date) golf course amongst the ruins of the ancient city of Caesarea, where Roman relics are an integral part of the course. Israel began competing internationally in 1974 with a team in the World Cup which placed 44th. Subsequently the Israelis competed four more times in the World Cup during the 1970s with only limited success, their highest finish being 42nd place in 1979.

During the 1980s Israel had only a limited international golfing exposure, and development of the game was limited due to having only one course in the country. But an Israeli team qualified for the 1993 World Cup and finished 29th.

ITALY

No. of Players (Rank): 24,000 (23)
No. of Courses (Rank): 82 (19)
Players/Course (Rank): 293 (37)
World Cup results 1993: 9th. Constantino Rocca finished in 11th place in the individual competition.
Prominent Players: Alfonso Angelini, Roberto Bernardini, Alberto Binaghi, Olivio Bolognesi, Giuseppe Cali, Renato Campagnoli, Baldovino Dassu, Gerolamo Dellfino, Ettore Della Torre, Silvio Grappasonni, Ugo Grappasonni, Silvio Locatelli, Delio Lovato, Massimo Mannelli, Constantino Rocca
Prominent Courses: Castelgondolfo, Circolo Golf Olgiata, Le Querce, Monticello, Milano, Pevero
National Golf Association: Federazione Italiana Golf, Via Flaminia 388, Roma 1-00196 Italy 39(6) 394641

History: The archival record indicates that golf's Italian history dates from the life in exile spent here by James III and VIII and his son Charles III (Bonnie Prince Charlie) in the 17th century. Italy has had a prominent place in world golf since the Second World War, although the absence of top-ranked international players has kept Italian golf a secret internationally.

In the 1950s the Italian team first competed in the Canada Cup, finishing in a strong 9th place in 1955. Alfonso Angelini was a consistently strong international player throughout this decade, with a 12 place individual finish in the 1956 Canada Cup.

In the 1960s Italy began to host major international tournaments, with the 1968 World Cup played in Rome, the 1964 Eisenhower (World Amateur) Trophy also played at Olgiata in Rome, and the 1967 European Amateur Team Championship played in Turin. The Italian team placed 3rd in the 1968 World Cup, with Roberto Bernardini placing second in the individual competition. Bernardini, Angelini, and Olivio Bolognesi were the best players during this time.

In the 1970s Italy continued to have success in the World Cup but not as consistently, with a 5th place finish in 1970 their best. Roberto Bernardini, who placed 7th individually in the 1970 World Cup, continued to be Italy's best player, although Baldovino Dassu had replaced him by the end of the decade. The 1975 European Amateur Championship team finished second at Killarney.

The 1980s marked a resurgence of Italian golf, with the 1984 World Cup returning to Rome and the women amateurs finishing runners-up in the 1985 European Ladies Amateur Team Championship. Italy placed third in the 1982 World Cup and seventh in 1984. Baldovino Dassa, who finished fourth individually at the 1982 World Cup, began the decade as Italy's best player, but by the end of the decade Constantino Rocca had emerged from the pack. With the surge in interest in the European PGA Tour, the Italian Open was attracting a strong international field throughout the 1980s with winners including Bernhard Langer, Sandy Lyle and Greg Norman.

Golf in Italy has continued to grow in the 1990s with the Roma Masters and the Italian Open drawing strong fields to Milano and Rome. Rome also hosted the 1991 World Cup, in which the Italian team finished 15th. Perhaps the highlight of the decade, though, came in 1993 when the Italian team finished ninth in the World Cup and its top player Constantino Rocca became the first Italian to qualify for the Ryder Cup team.

JAMAICA

No. of Players (Rank): 1,600 (52)
No. of Courses (Rank): 12 (44)
Players/Course (Rank): 133 (18)
World Cup results 1993: 28th place. Seymour Rose finished 54th in the individual competition.
Prominent Players: Christian Bernard, Basil Campbell, Alvin Cunningham, Jasper Markland, Norman Marsh, Peter Millhouse, Seymour Rose, Wesley Scott.
Prominent Courses: Half Moon Club, Tryall.
National Golf Association: Jamaica Golf Association, P.O. Box 743 Kingston 8, Jamaica

History: Golf on Jamaica dates back to the mid-19th century, with the Manchester Club founded in 1868, but golf has generally played a minor role on Jamaica, with the island generally having more of a reputation as home to great golf courses more than great golfers, but the Jamaicans have had some success at the international level, too.

Big time golf first beckoned in 1961 when Robert Trent Jones completed his course at Half Moon Club. Tryall followed afterwards, from a design by Ralph Plummer. The Jamaican national team first broke through into the World Cup field later in the decade, in 1967, when they placed 33rd at Mexico City. Seymour Rose, now 54, has managed to win a slot on each one of the eleven teams fielded by Jamaica in the Cup, a remarkable feat of longevity. It's only in recent years that he has been able to find a partner up to his caliber, and thus Jamaica has struggled in the World Cup, recording a best of 28th place in 1974, and in 1993 at Orlando.

Jamaica has perhaps become best known as the host of the Johnnie Walker World Championship at Tryall, played at the end of the golf season and generating solid television ratings.

JAPAN

No. of Players (Rank): 11,300,000 (2)
No. of Courses (Rank): 1558 (3)
Players/Course (Rank): 7,253 (72)
World Cup results 1993: 18th. Katsuyoshi Tomori finished 31st in the individual competition.
Prominent Players: Isao Aoki, Michio Ishii, Tomoo Ishii, Tadashi Kitta, Misutaka Kono, Takaaki Kono, Takashi Murakami, Tommy Nakajima, Torokichi Nakamura, Koichi Ono, Mashashi Ozaki, Naomichi Ozaki, Tateo zaki, Kosaku Shimada, Hideyo Sugimoto, Norio Suzuki, Namio Takasu, Harou Yasuda.
Prominent Courses: Hirono, Kasumigaseki, Kawana, Tokyo , Yomiuri
National Golf Association: National Golf Foundation Japan, 3-3-4 Sebdagaya Shibuya-ku, Tokyo, Japan 81 (03) 478-4355

History: The story of Japanese golf began with the construction of a course by Arthur Groom, and the founding of a four-holer at Mt. Rokko, near Kobe, in 1903. The course was subsequently expanded to eighteen holes, but the golf boom in Japan truly dates from the opening of the Tokyo Klub in 1914.

Prior to the Second World War Japanese golfers appeared in European and American competitions; but the game became even more firmly established in Japan after the Second World War.

Japan quickly became one of the leading international teams in the early Canada Cup competitions of the 1950s, finishing fourth in 1956 and winning in 1957 at Kasumagaseki in Tokyo. Torakichi Nakamura took an incredible nine-stroke lead into the final round and emerged with a seven shot victory in the individual competition.

In the 1960s success was not as conspicuous, but Japan secured six top-10 finishes in the World Cup in the decade including second place in 1969, while in 1966 at Yomiuri, Japan, Hideyo Sugimoto lost the individual medal in a play-off. In the amateur arena Japan hosted the 1962 Eisenhower (World Amateur) Trophy.

The golf boom accelerated in Japan throughout the 1970s as prosperity increased rapidly, and many more courses were constructed, including many by celebrated international players such as Arnold Palmer, putting pressure on land availability. Japanese international success in golf also increased with players such as Takaaki Kono, Mashaski Ozaki, Seiichi Kanai and most importantly Isao Aoki emerging as first-class golfers. Aoki not only enjoyed success in Japan and in the World Cup, but was victorious in the 1978 World Match Play Championships at Wentworth, England in 1978 (and runner-up in 1979), as well as proving a tough competitor in US and European PGA Tour events. Japanese amateurs finished runners-up in the Eisenhower Trophy in both 1976 and 1978.

By the 1980s the quality of play in Japan was strong enough that the Nissan Cup was born, pitting touring pros from each of the four "major" tour circuits (US, European, Australian, and Japanese). Japan finished runner-ups, also, in the 1986 Dunhill Cup as well as winning in the 1986 Nissan Cup. Isao Aoki, in his defeat by Jack Nicklaus at Baltusrol in the 1980 U.S. Open, came the closest of any Japanese golfer to winning a major. Prominent new stars of the decade included Takaaki Ono and Koichi Suzuki.

Japanese expansion in golf, by the 1990s, included strategic properties in the United States, and by 1994 Japanese investors either held major positions in or owned outright such top-ranked American gems as Pebble Beach, Riviera, the GC of Georgia, and World Woods. Japanese equipment manufacturers also continued to expand international operations, with such companies as Yonex, Yamaha, Mizuno, Bridgestone and Maruman active throughout the world.

In competition, Japan has fared less successfully in the 1990s, with only Satoshi Higashi cracking the top-10 at the World Cup in the decade.

KENYA

No. of Players (Rank): 3,000 (45)
No. of Courses (Rank): 29 (33)
Players/Course (Rank): 103 (10)
National Open Champion: Craig Maltman
World Cup results 1993: Did not compete
Prominent Course: Muthaiga G.C.

History: Kenya has been a home to golf since the British colonial period, with seniority belonging to the Nairobi (now Royal Nairobi) Golf Club founded in 1906. The Kenya Open has been played for may years and has attracted a number of prominent international players, including past winners such as Jose Canizares, Ian Woosnam and Christy O'Connor, Jr. The Kenya Open is now a stop on the small but fertile African Tour and is played annually at Muthaiga in Nairobi. Kenya has yet to produce a player of world-class calibre.

KOREA

No. of Players (Rank): 260,000 (6)
No. of Courses (Rank): 30 (26)
Players/Course (Rank): 11,628 (73)
National Open Champion: Nam Sin Park
World Cup results 1993: Disqualified
Prominent Players: Yoo Soo Choi, Sang Ho Choi, Chang Sang Hahn, Seung Hak Kim, Kang-Sun Lee, Nam-Sin Park
Prominent Course: Nam Seoul, New Korea.
National Golf Association: Korea Golf Association, Room 18 - 13 Floor Manhattan Building, 36-2 Yeo Eui Do-Dong, Yeong Deung Po-Ku, Seoul, Korea 82 (02)783-4748

History: Korea is making up for its short golf history

with one of the most vigorous golf booms in the world, producing tremendous pressure on the limited number of courses in the country.

The first course, Seoul Country Club, dates to 1931, but it wasn't until the 1950s that the Republic of Korea teams first participated in world golf via the Canada Cup matches, with Hak Young Kim finishing 40th in the individual competition in 1959. After an absence of several years, the ROK team, featuring star player Chang Sang Hahn, became a strong contender in the Canada and World Cup event, finishing as high as 5th in 1971 at PGA National, with Hahn placing 13th.

Although Korean players have not played on the high-profile American and European tours, throughout the 1970s players such as Jung Ung Park, Chang, and Il Ahn Lee played world-class golf that kept Korea in the top ten at the World Cup in 1971, 1972, 1975, 1977 and 1978. By the 1980s new players such as Sang Ho Choi and Nam Sin Park were figuring prominently, each winning the Korea Open and appearing on several World Cup teams.

Golf course construction is at an all-time high in Korea at present, and the locals have continued to hold their own in the Korea Open despite the increasing presence of PGA TOUR veterans such as Guy Boros, Ray Stewart, and former U.S. Amateur Champion Eric Meeks.

MALAWI

No. of Players (Rank): 600 (62)
No. of Courses (Rank): 10 (46)
Players/Course (Rank): 60 (2)
World Cup results 1993: Did not compete

History: Golf here dates back to the establishment of Blantyre in 1911.

MALAYSIA

No. of Players (Rank): 120,000 (14)
No. of Courses (Rank): 150 (15)
Players/Course (Rank): 800 (63)
National Open Champion: Joakim Haeggman
World Cup results 1993: Did not compete.
Prominent Players: Zainal Abadin, Eshak Buluah, Jalal Deran, Lim Voot Fung, Marmuthe Ramayah, Nazaruddin Yusoff.
Prominent Courses: Bukit Jumbul, Kelab Rahman Putra G.C., Royal Selangor G.C.
Number of golf professionals: 98
Prominent golf publications: FORE, Golf Malaysia.
National Golf Association: Malaysian Golf

Association, No. 12-A Persiaran Ampang, 55000 Kuala Lumpur

History: Malaysia has only recently entered into the international golf arena but golf dates back to 1890 with the founding of the New Taiping Club. The Malaysian Golf Association was founded in 1894 with a mission to organize the Malaysian Amateur and other amateur golf matters. Following the withdrawal of British colonial forces in the 1960s, Malaysians have been able to take advantage of courses built by the British colonists, and a relatively strong golf boom has been underway since then.

Malaysia has been fielding international golf teams since the late 1960s without notable success, although the team of Ramayah and Yusoff placed 11th in the 1979 World Cup at Athens. The Malysian Open has been a regular stop on the Asian Tour for many years and has attracted many prominent pros (including past winners Stewart Ginn, Glen Day and Jeff Maggert), while a Women's Open has been staged annually since 1987 and is now part of the Asian Women's Tour. The Malaysian Open continues to be one of the more lucrative stops on the Asian PGA Tour, and Vijay Singh has been particularly strong here.

MEXICO

No. of Players (Rank): 14,670 (27)
No. of Courses (Rank): 124 (17)
Players/Course (Rank): 118 (12)
National Open Champion: Fred Funk (1993)
World Cup results 1993: T20. Rodolfo Cazaubon finished T40 in the individual competition.
Prominent Players: Ernesto Acosta, Rafael Alarcon, Antonio Cerda, Ramon Cruz, Carlos Espinoza, Jose Gonzalez, Augustin Martinez, Margaroto Martinez, Juan Neri, Victor Regaldo, Enrique Serna.
Prominent Courses: Cabo del Sol, Club de Golf, La Hacienda, Palmilla, Pierre Margues.
National Golf Association: Federacion Mexicana de Golf, Cincinati No 40-104 Col Napoles, 03710, Mexico (5) 563-9194

History: Mexico has been overshadowed by Canada and the United States, but has achieved a measure of success in developing its own golf story. "South of the Border" development began in the 1890s with the establishment of Puebla in Mexico City in 1897. Mexico did not produce a world-class player until the team of Al Escalante and Juan Neri began competing in the Canada Cup in the 1950s (along with several "guest" appearances by Roberto de Vicenzo and

Antonio Cerda). In 1958 Mexico cemented its place in world golf by successfully hosting the 1958 Canada Cup, the first Hispanic country so honored.

By the mid 1960s, Mexico had put a team as high as third in the World Cup (in 1967, when the competition returned to Club de Golf in Mexico City), and begun to establish the Mexican Open as an increasingly lucrative and challenging stop on the golf calendar.

In the 1970s Ernesto Acosta became the first Mexican player to take first place in the World Cup competition, and Mexico continued to place highly in the event throughout the late 1970s and 1980s. By the late 1980s Rafael Alarcon had replaced Acosta as Mexico's leading player, and led a spirited run at the 1993 Dunhill Cup in which the Mexicans nearly pulled off an upset over England and defeated South Africa in bitter cold at St. Andrews.

MOROCCO

No. of Players (Rank): 2,000 (50)
No. of Courses (Rank): 4 (58)
Players/Course (Rank): 500 (49)
National Open Champion: David Gilford
World Cup results 1993: Did not compete.
Prominent Courses: Golf Royal de Agadir, Royal Golf Dar-es-Salaam
National Golf Association: Federation Royale Marociane de Golf, Royal Golf Rabat dar es Salam, Route des Zaers, Rabat, Morocco

History: Golf has had the steady support of the royal family of Morocco for many years (hence the proliferation of "Royal" courses), and provides the arena for events on both the European PGA Tour (the Moroccan Open), and the African Tour (the Hassan II Trophy). Despite the enthusiasm of Morrocco's royals, the game has not acquired massive popularity in the small northern African country and thus the country is yet to produce its first world-class player. After a fifteen-year hiatus, Morocco fielded an entry for the 1993 World Cup, but the lack of international experience showed and the team finished a disappointing 32nd.

NETHERLANDS

No. of Players (Rank): 23,975 (24)
No. of Courses (Rank): 44 (25)
Players/Course (Rank): 545 (54)
National Open Champion: Colin Montgomerie (1993)
World Cup results 1993: 22nd. Chris Van de Velde placed 44T in the individual competition.
Prominent Players: Kees Borst, Ruud Bos,

Kees Cramer, Jan Dorrestein, Gerry de Wit, Martin Roesink, Chris van der Velde, Bertus van Mook, Constant Smits van Waesberghe, Piet Witte.
Prominent Courses: Eindhovensche, Haagsche, Hattemse, Kennemer, Noordwik, Oosterhout, Utrechtse.
National Golf Association: Nederlandse Golf Federatie P.O. Box 2213454 PV De Meern Netherlands (31) 34-06-21888

History: The Netherlands has a connection with golf that stretches back to the turn of the century...or back into the 15th century, depending on which history of golf one consults. The Dutch game of kolven dates back in the records to the mid-1400s, and several pictures of Dutch town life include portraits of the people playing their game of kolven, with clubs called kolf, across the ice or in courtyards attached to inns. The Kolf or club looks something like a crude one-iron made with a brass head and the ball is the size of a baseball. Kolven is still played in Northern Holland, but efforts to link the game with the evolution of golf have lost favor in recent years. The most plausible connection may well be that, since there was active trading between Scotland and the Low Countries in the 14th and 15th centuries, and since Scotland did not have any organized metalworks in these years, that The Netherlands may well have been the source of the early equipment, if not the game itself—and like the equally popular game of football the game eventually acquired the name of the equipment—hence golf.

Modern golf history in The Netherlands dates back to the last years of the 19th century—several courses, namely Haagsche (1893), Utrechtse (1894), and Rosendaelsche (1895) date from before the turn of the century. Fourteen of the present-day courses were established prior to the Second World War, making The Netherlands one of the earliest European countries to embrace modern golf.

After the war, teams from The Netherlands began competing in world competition, but the country has produced few golfers who have made a mark on the international scene, and only Gerry de Wit (in 1960) and Martin Roesink (in 1969) managed a top ten finish in the individual competition at the World Cup.

In the 1990s Chris van der Velde has been the most consistent Dutch player—playing the European Tour with some success. In addition, The Netherlands play host to the Dutch Open which attracts a top field of European PGA players, and the Leiden Open on the fledgling Women's European Tour.

NEW ZEALAND

No. of Players (Rank): 350,000 (8)
No. of Courses (Rank): 412 (9)
Players/Course (Rank): 850 (65)
National Open Champion: Craig Jones.
World Cup results 1993: 6th-tie. Frank Nobilo finished 11th-tie in the individual competition.
Prominent Players: Frank Buckler, Bob Charles, John Lister, Frank Nobilo, Peter Oosterhuis, Simon Owen, Ernie Southerden, Greg Turner.
Prominent Courses: The Grange, Paraparaumu, Rotorua.
National Golf Association: New Zealand Golf Association, Dominion Sports House, Mercer Street, P.O. Box 11842, Wellington, New Zealand

History: Formal golf history began in New Zealand with the founding the Christchurch Golf Club in 1873, one of the first golf clubs formed within the Commonwealth of Nations and outside of the immediate British Isles (only Royal Adelaide, Bangalore, Royal Calcutta and Royal Bombay have seniority). New Zealand is possessed of a climate and geology perfect for golf, and the strong Scottish immigrant element ensured the success of the game, so much so that New Zealand today has one of the highest per-capita participation rates in the world. Limited population, however, has prevented New Zealand from a place in the first rank of golfing nations until recent years.

The first great New Zealand golfer was left-handed Bob Charles, who emerged in the early 1960s as a first-class player and scored well at both the Canada Cup and in winning the British Open in 1963. Charles also won the World Match Play title in 1969. Indeed, Charles led New Zealand to a second place finish at the World Cup in 1967.

In the 1970s John Lister and Simon Owen were New Zealand's dominant players, with Frank Nobilo and Greg Turner succeeding them in the 1980s. Bob Charles, meanwhile, has become one of the leading all-time greats of the PGA Senior Tour.

In addition to the individual play of great golfers, New Zealand has become a key stop on the Australian PGA Tour, with the Air New Zealand and the New Zealand Opens. In addition to regular World Cup appearances, New Zealand has had success in the Alfred Dunhill Cup with a third place finish in 1990.

In amateur golf New Zealand has fared well, with Marnie McGuire winning the 1986 British Amateur, while the New Zealand men finished runners up in the 1970 Eisenhower Trophy at Madrid, and again in 1990 when Christchurch was the venue. In 1992 the

Kiwis finally brought home the Eisenhower Trophy, representing the pinnacle of world amateur golf.

NORWAY

No. of Players (Rank): 10,000 (33)
No. of Courses (Rank): 12 (49)
Players/Course (Rank): 833 (70)
World Cup results 1993: Did not compete
Prominent Players: Per Haugsrud, Johan Horn, Gard Midtvage, Tore Sviland, Arne Werkel.
Prominent Courses: Onsoy, Oslo, Oustoen, Stavanger.
National Golf Association: Norwegian Golf Association, Hauger Skolevie 11351 Rud Oslo Norway   47 (2) 518800

History: Norway is a relatively late entrant to the world golf scene, although the first courses were built well before the Second World War at Oslo (1924) and Borregaard (1927). The dozen courses and short golfing season have yet to produce an international champion, but Norwegian teams have competed internationally since 1954 with some success, with a 16th place finish at the 1991 World Cup.

PAKISTAN

No. of Players (Rank): 10,000 (33)
No. of Courses (Rank): 8 (49)
Players/Course (Rank): 1,125 (63)
World Cup results 1993: Did not compete
Prominent Players: Muhammed Ejaz, Tamiur Hassan, Ghulam Nabi, Muhammed Shafique.
National Golf Association: Pakistan Golf Federation, P.O. Box No. 1295, Rawalpindi, Pakistan

History: Pakistan has had only a limited impact on world golf, but the British colonial influence has left Pakistan with a rich legacy of golf courses and an active amateur group.

In the 1970s Pakistan began to field teams in the World Cup with some success, placing 29th in their initial outing in 1975 and, by their final appearance in 1982, improving to a 24th place finish behind the play of Mohammed Shafique and Ghulam Nabi. Pakistan does not yet host a tournament on the Asian Tour, but the Pakistan Open, Amateur, and Ladies Amateur are fixtures on the local calendar. Nabi is a four-time winner of the Pakistan Open.

PANAMA

No. of Players (Rank): 3,000 (45)
No. of Courses (Rank): 8 (49)
Players/Course (Rank): 375 (43)
World Cup results 1993: Did not compete.
Prominent Players: Leo Dehlinger, Anaibel Galindo, Alberto Gonzalez, Ricardo Jurado, Juan Rivera.
National Golf Association: Panama Golf Association, P.O. Box 8613, Panama 5, Panama

History: Panama has a small but dedicated band of golfers who have managed some excellent results in international golf considering the small base of golfers.

Although the Panama Open and the first courses date back to the 1930s, Panama's first world-class player was Ricardo Jurado, who managed a 20th place finish in the 1962 Canada Cup. Panama has made five additional appearances in Canada/World Cup competition, with three 30th place finishes (in '62, '71, and '74) their best results to date.

The military regime in Panama did not favor golf and the Panama Open, won in the past by luminaries such as Curtis Strange, Sam Snead, Roberto De Vicenzo, Art Wall, Arnold Palmer and Chi Chi Rodriguez will be revived in 1995. A senior tournament was inaugurated recently won by Orville Moody over Billy Casper.

PARAGUAY

No. of Players (Rank): 400 (69)
No. of Courses (Rank): 3 (65)
Players/Course (Rank): 133 (18)
National Open Champion: Raul Fretes (1993)
World Cup results 1993: 15th. Pedro Rodolfo Martinez finished 22nd-tie in the individual competition.
Prominent Players: Luis Boschian, Genaro Espinola, Angel Franco, Eladio Franco, Ramon Franco, Sebastian Franco, Raul Fretes, Angel Gimenez.
Prominent Courses: Yacht y Golf Club.
National Golf Association: Asociacion Paraguaya de Golf   Casilla de Correo 1795 Asuncion, Paraguay
History: Paraguay is not known as a great golfing nation but in recent years the country has produced some outstanding golf teams.

Paraguay's first appearances in international golf, in the Canada Cup competitions in the early 1960s, were not successful, with a best finish of 32nd in 1961. The teams did not break into the top thirty until the early 1980s, but in 1992 two rookies, Raul Fretes and Carlos Franco, managed to place 13th (with Fretes placing 14th in the individual competition). Two new players, Ramon Franco and Pedro Martinez, took the field in the 1993 World Cup and finished 15th.

In addition, Paraguay scored huge upsets over Scotland and Wales in the 1993 Alfred Dunhill Cup behind Fretes and Carlos Franco's efforts, and narrowly missed the semi-finals. Paraguayans have dominated the South American Tour in recent years, winning four tournaments in 1993 alone with two runner-up finishes.

PERU

No. of Players (Rank): 2, 500 (47)
No. of Courses (Rank): 13 (43)
Players/Course (Rank): 192 (14)
World Cup results 1993: Did not compete
Prominent Players: Eugenio Dunezat, Benarbe Fajardo, Hugo Nari, Sabino Quispe, Alex Tibbles, Wilfredo Uculmana.
Prominent Courses: Lima, Los Inkas
Prominent Publications: Golf Madera 3
Golf Professionals: 30.
National Golf Association: Federacion Peruana de Golf, Estadio Nacional Puerto 4, Piso 4, Casilla 5637, Lima

History: The English introduced golf to Peru around the turn of the century, utilizing land near Callao for practice-fields. They moved to Santa Beatriz, a racetrack, by 1915. The first golf course, Lima Golf Club, was built in 1926.

Today, Lima and Los Inkas are the two best-known Peruvian courses: golf is established in most regions of the country, but the two most important events on the golf calendar, International de Nobles and the Peru Open, are played at Lima and Los Inkas. The Peru Open is now a part of the South American circuit and is played by all the leading South American pros.

THE PHILIPPINES

No. of Players (Rank): 40,000 (17)
No. of Courses (Rank): 46 (24)
Players/Course (Rank): 870 (66)
National Open Champion: Wang Ter Chang
World Cup results 1993: Did not compete.
Prominent Players: Ben Arda, Antolin Fernando, Rudy Lavares, Ireneo Legaspi, Frankia Minoza, Eleuterio Nival, Robert Pactolerin, Mario Siodina, Celestino Tugot.
Prominent Courses: Manila Southwoods, Puerto Azul, Wack Wack.
National Golf Association: Republic of the Philippines Golf Association, Rm. 209 Administration Building, Rizal Memorial Sports Complex, Vito Cruz, Manila, The Philippines

History: Golf arrived in The Philippines during the 1900s, in the first years of American occupation. Among Asian nations, The Philippines were the first to compete successfully in world golfing competition after the Japanese, playing annually in the Canada Cup from the mid-1950s with conspicuous success. Celestine Tugot was the first great Philippine player, finishing 10th in the 1955 Canada Cup and anchoring the strong Philippine team throughout the 1960s. In the mid-1960s Ben Arda became the leading player, and with Eleuterio Nival formed a contending pair at the World Cup, with sixth place finishes in 1969, 1971 and 1975, with Arda finishing second to Johnny Miller in 1975 at Bangkok.

The World Cup came to The Philippines in 1977, at Wack Wack, and the team had its best ever finish, second place behind Spain, with Rudy Lavares' individual second place finish providing the impetus.

Since 1977, Philippine golfers have been hard pressed to duplicate this high level of achievement, and they have not managed a top-ten finish in the World Cup since 1978. The Philippine Open is one of the regular events on the Asian Tour, and continues to attract a top field.

PORTUGAL

No. of Players (Rank): 4,000 (38)
No. of Courses (Rank): 20 (39)
Players/Course (Rank): 200 (26)
National Open Champion: David Gilford (1993)
World Cup results 1993: Did not compete
Prominent Players: Henrique Paulino, Hernando Pina, Manuale Ribeiro, Joaquim Rodrigues, Daniel Silva, David Sulva, Fernando Silva, Rogerio Valente
Prominent Courses: Lisbon Sports Club, Quinta Do Lago, San Lorenzo, Vale Do Lobo, Vilamoura, Vila-Sol.
National Golf Association: Federacao Portuguesa de Golf Rua Almeida Brandao, 39P-1200 Lisboa, Portugal   351 (1) 661121

History: Portugal has not yet become the prominent golfing nation that Spain is, but the nation is home to some of Europe's most spectacular courses so hopes are high for a golf boom.

Golf in Portugal dates back to the founding of Oporto in 1890, making Portugal one of the oldest non-English speaking golf nations. After the founding of the Lisbon Sports Club in 1922, a few more courses were built before the war including the prestigious Estoril in 1929, but subsequently golf course construction halted.

Portugal began competing in the Canada Cup in the mid-1950s but has never enjoyed conspicuous success, with a best finish of 21st in 1966. Portugal has been host to an annual Open Championship which attracts a good field, and Portugal also hosted the 1976 Eisenhower Trophy (symbolic of the pinnacle of amateur golf achievement).

In the late 1960s and early 1970s, the opening of courses such as Quinta do Lago and Vilamoura signalled a new commitment to course quality, and since then Portugal has been promoted as a golf destination.

PUERTO RICO

No. of Players (Rank): 2,500 (47)
No. of Courses (Rank): 11 (39)
Players/Course (Rank): 227 (32)
National Open Champion (USA): Ernie Els
World Cup results 1993: 26th. Rafael Castrillo tied for 52nd in the individual competition.
Prominent Players: Rafael Castrillo, Juan Gonzalez, David Jimenez, Chi Chi Rodriguez, Jesus Rodriguez.
Prominent Courses: Dorado Beach, Palmas del Mar.
Number of Golf Professionals: 21
Prominent golf publications: Golf y Leisure, Puerto Rico Golf Magazine.
National Golf Association: Puerto Rico Golf Association, GPO Box 3862, San Juan, PR 00936

History: Golf was introduced to Puerto Rico in early 1920, through the military presence of the United States and through the growth of the large sugar plantations on the islands. Golf expanded after the Second World War and the Puerto Rico Golf Association was organized in 1954. About this time the first major resorts were built on the island, the best known of them the complex at Dorado Beach, including the famed Trent Jones-designed Dorado Beach G.C., which brought international exposure to the island.

The first world-class Puerto Rican golfer was Juan "Chi Chi" Rodriguez, who rose to prominence in the early 1960s and eventually became a multiple winner on the PGA TOUR. The 1961 World Cup was staged at Dorado, and Chi Chi Rodriguez teamed with his mentor Pete Cooper to finish in seventh place. The Puerto Rican team, usually featuring Chi Chi and David Jimenez, placed several times in the top ten during the 1960s in Canada/World Cup competition, although the team's fortunes faded in the 1970s.

In the 1980s Puerto Rico has become known mostly as a resort haven, with development of Palmas Del Mar complimenting the Dorado complex. The Johnnie Walker World Championship has been played here, as well as several Senior events. In addition to high-profile tournaments, the 1980s brought Chi Chi back

to prominence, this time on the PGA Senior TOUR where he won many tournaments and lost in a heart-breaking playoff to Jack Nicklaus in the 1991 Senior Open.

After an absence of several years, the Puerto Rican team reappeared in the World Cup in 1992-93, managing a 26th place finish in '93.

ST. MAARTEN

No. of Players (Rank): 200 (71)
No. of Courses (Rank): 1 (69)
Players/Course (Rank): 200 (26)

History: St Maarten has a modest place in golf lore, but Joe Lee has designed the very playable Mullet Bay course which has attracted a certain following amongst aficionados of Caribbean golf.

SCOTLAND

No. of Players (Rank): 143,000 (13)
No. of Courses (Rank): 485 (6)
Players/Course (Rank): 295 (39)
National Open Champion: Peter O'Malley (1993)
World Cup results 1993: 3rd. Sam Torrance finished 7th-tie in the individual competition.
Prominent Players: Laurie Auchterlonie, James Braid, Gordon Brand Jr., Eric Brown, Ken Brown, Bob Ferguson, Willie Fernie, Bernard Gallagher, Thomas Haliburton, Sandy Lyle, Colin Montgomerie, Old Tom Morris, Young Tom Morris, John Panton, Willie Park Jr., Willie Park Sr., Allan Robertson, Sam Torrance.
Prominent Courses: Blair Atholl, Blairgowrie, Bruntsfield, Burntisland, Carnoustie, Crail, Cruden Bay, Dumfries, Gleneagles, Gullane, Kilmarnock, Muirfield, Musselburgh, Nairn, North Berwick, North Inch, Prestwick, Royal Aberdeen, Royal Burgess Golfing Society of Edinburgh, Royal Dornoch, Royal Montrose, Royal Troon, St. Andrews, Turnberry, Wick.
National Golf Association: Scottish Golf Union, The Cottage 181A Whitehouse Road, Barnton, Edinburgh EH4 6BY Scotland 44(31) 339-7546

History: Although the dispute about the actual origin of golf will likely never be solved to everyone's satisfaction, the plain truth is that, wherever golf was first played, it achieved its world-wide popularity due to its adoption by the Scottish people and by Scots royalty in particular (after 1503).

Golf almost certainly is a descendent of a rudimentary form of hockey, and the antiquity of the word

Goff in the Scots dialect of English (which is in turn descended from the Northumbrian dialect of Anglo-Saxon), seems to suggest that golf was well-established in Scotland before it first appeared in written records in the mid-15th century. The term links is also derived from the Anglo-Saxon tongues. All the evidence thus points to golf developing from a form of hockey played by the English-speaking Lowland Scots. Its connection to the aristocracy and military training grounds (such as St. Andrews) also strongly suggests that it was particularly popular among feudal knights and the small private armies of Scottish nobles.

The Scottish economy was enjoying a particular boom in the early years of the 15th century and while it is ultimately unclear exactly what the connection between golf and the European games of *chole* and *kolven* (the most plausible connection is that the Scottish game of golf was improved by the adaptation of some of the ideas of chole and the equipment of kolven)—golf certainly acquired relatively massive popularity by 1457. In that year King James IV banned golf because its popularity had superceded archery and thus interfered with Scottish military preparations in the ongoing struggle with the English.

The ban on golf was renewed several times in the late 15th century, suggesting that its popularity continued to grow. But in 1502 a lasting peace between Scotland and England was announced, and the daughter of Henry VII was married to the heir to the Scottish throne. The ban on golf was rescinded and James IV himself took up the game. Golf thus has always been one of the key symbols of the peace (and eventual union) of Scotland and England. By 1513 we have evidence that the game had spread to England.

The first grounds for which we have evidence of golf in Scotland are Barrie Links (near what is now Carnoustie) in 1527—St. Andrews figures in the historical records from 1552 and Leith Links from 1592. Royal Dornoch is the fourth course we know of, dating back to at least 1621. Golf, due to the expense of equipment, was a wealthy man's game and particularly at this stage a royal one. Eight consecutive Stuart monarchs from James IV through Charles II were active golfers.

Although the game had spread to England by the early 16th century, golf was primarily a Lowland game in Scotland and is not known to have been played in the west of Scotland before 1721. By 1744 the first golf club was formed (the Honourable Company of Edinburgh Golfers, at Leith), and the St. Andrews golfers formed a club (which became the R&A) in 1754.

The Scots began to standardize the game in the mid-18th century, with the publication of an official rulebook and the standardization of courses at eigh-

teen holes. Also in the late 18th century the first clubhouses were built and (in 1774) the first full-time greenkeeper and professional was hired. Golf continued to grow in popularity and clubs such as Burntisland, Aberdeen, Crail, and Bruntsfield were formed.

The early 19th century was a time of further expansion in Scotland, with Perth and Prestwick opening—professionals were in place at most clubs, and Allan Robertson was considered the greatest professional of his day. The expansion in the number of clubs (and in the professional ranks) led to calls for a national championship, and the Open Championship was established in 1861 (The Amateur dates back to 1859).

The popularity of golf began to soar in the second half of the 19th century as the introduction of the gutta-percha ball made the game much more affordable. At the same time the growth of modern mass-circulation newspapers (which emphasized sports coverage) and a drive for more open space and a more active lifestyle by English aristocrats led many to take up golf and bring a new popularity to the game. By 1872 the Open was no longer played exclusively at Prestwick but included a rotation of the courses (St. Andrews, Musselburgh, and Prestwick) in the Scottish Lowlands.

By the late 1890s the popularity of the game had increased so much that Scotland, with its smaller population, was superceded by England as the epicenter of golf. For the first time professionals such as J.H. Taylor (from England), Harry Vardon (from the Channel Isles), as well as amateurs such as John Ball were considered the leading players. In 1894 the Open Championship course rotation was expanded to include Hoylake and Royal St. George in England.

In the early 1900s Scottish professional James Braid emerged as the leading Scottish player, and with Taylor and Vardon was part of the Great Triumvirate of leading players that dominated golf until the First World War. With the introduction of the Haskell (rubber-core) ball, golf found new popularity around the globe and Scotland lost its dominant position in the game, although its courses are still considered the traditional home of golf.

Muirfield was added to the Open rotation in 1892 (replacing Musselburgh), Troon in 1923, Carnoustie in 1931, and Turnberry in 1977 as championship golf was extended to the West of Scotland. The Royal & Ancient assumed direction of the Open in the early 1900s, ensuring that Scotland and Scottish golfers remained at the helm of championship golf even as the Open rotation of courses expanded to include English courses such as Birkdale, Deal and even Portrush in Ireland.

After a drought of great players between the 1920s and 1940s, Scotland's Eric Brown and John Panton combined in the 1950s and 1960s to restore a certain glamour to Scottish golf with several top-five finishes in the Canada Cup. In the late 1960s a new generation of Scottish players such as Bernard Gallacher, Brian Barnes and Sandy Lyle emerged to lead Scotland to four top-five finishes in five years in the 1975-79 World Cups.

With the founding of the Alfred Dunhill Cup matches at St. Andrews, a return to traditional principles of golf course design, and the ascendancy of Sandy Lyle in the late 1980s, Scotland achieved a prominence in modern golf that it had hitherto lacked. American golfers in particular have made pilgrimages to the great Scottish courses in large numbers, and such revered golf books such as *Golf in the Kingdom* have celebrated Scotland and golf. In 1985 Sandy Lyle became the first Scotsman to win the Open in generations (ironically, he won in England, at Royal St. George), a triumph he followed up with a victory in the 1988 Masters (previously the only major championship never won by a Scotsman). Scotland reached the finals of the 1987 and 1992 Dunhill Cups, losing each time to England.

In the late 1980s and early 1990s Scotland provided a number of key players to the European Ryder Cup teams, notably Sam Torrance and Colin Montgomerie. In addition, the amateur game continues to flourish with Scotland maintaining one of the highest per-capita participation rates in the world in addition to winning the European Amateur Team Championship in 1975, 1977 and 1985. Scotland also continues to host a large percentage of international golf championships over its classic links courses, and is revered internationally as the ancestral home of the game and, through the offices of the Royal & Ancient Golf Club, as its primary international authority.

SINGAPORE

No. of Players (Rank): 12,000 (30)
No. of Courses (Rank): 16 (42)
Players/Course (Rank): 750 (62)
World Cup results 1993: Did not compete
Prominent Players: Phua Thiu Kiay, Kim Swee Chew, Samson Grimson, Bill Fung Hee Kwan, Alvin Liau, Lim Kian Kee, Lim Kian Tiong, Lim See Wah.
Prominent Courses: Singapore Island, Tanah-Marah.
National Golf Association: Singapore Golf Association, c/o C.L. Loong & Company, 4 Battery Road, #12000 Bank of China Building Singapore 0104, Singapore

History: Golf in Singapore dates back to 1891 when a nine-hole course, Singapore Golf Club, was built in the British fortress city. For most of its history Singapore was considered part of Malaysia, and so the city-state did not begin to field its own teams in international events until after independence in 1965. In the late 1960s Singapore entered teams in the World Cup without significant success, but the city played host to the 1969 World Cup and the team of Phua Thiu Kiay and Alvin Liau finished in 25th place.

In the 1970s Singapore continued to compete in the World Cup, with a best finish of 23rd in 1975. However, in the 1980s Singapore improved considerably, finishing 17th in 1984 and tied for tenth in 1984 with Lim See Wah finishing seventh in the individual competition.

The Singapore Open is, interestingly, not a part of the Asian Tour but rather the Australasian Tour, and thus attracts perhaps a stronger field at the present time than other tournaments in the region—but at present Singapore does not have any native-born players in the Sony 200 rankings.

SLOVENIA

No. of Players (Rank): 980 (56)
No. of Courses (Rank): 4 (58)
Players/Course (Rank): 245 (35)
World Cup results 1993: Did not compete
National Open Champion: Urban Lega.
Prominent Players: Rafael Jerma, Slavko Vodnjov, Marko Vovk.
Prominent Courses: Bled, Golf Lupica
Number of golf professionals: 11
National Golf Association: Golf Association of Slovenia c/o Golf Club Bled Svbode 1364260 Bled, Slovenia 38 (64) 78282

History: Slovenia formed the heart of what used to be the Yugoslavian golf scene, with four courses—the oldest of which, Bled Golf Club, is considered first-rate and which dates back to 1938.

The former country of Yugoslavia entered several teams in World Cup competition during the mid-to-late 1970s without notable success. Today, Slovenia is the home of the Slovenian Open which attracts an international field and which this year was won by a native Slovenian, Urban Lega.

SOUTH AFRICA

No. of Players (Rank): 250,000 (9)
No. of Courses (Rank): 441 (8)
Players/Course (Rank): 567 (56)
National Open Champion: Tony Johnstone (1993)
World Cup results 1993: 6th-tie. Ernie Els finished 3rd-tie in the individual competition.

Prominent Players: Bobby Cole, Ernie Els, Retief Goosen, Dale Hayes, Harold Henning, Bobby Locke, Gary Player.

Prominent Courses: Durban, Glendower, Kempton Park, Mobray, Roodeport, Royal Johannesburg, Sun City, Wanderers, Wingate Park, Zwartkop.

National Golf Association: South Africa Golf Union, P.O. Box 1537, Cape Town 8000, South Africa

History: South Africa has a long and successful association with golf, but there is some confusion over whether seniority belongs to the Cape Golf Club founded at Wynberg in 1885, or Maritzberg Golf Club in Natal Province, which was either founded in 1886 or 1884. Certainly they were the first two clubs, with Harrismith founded shortly thereafter.

The 1890s were a time of great expansion due to the increasing commercial viability of the Cape Colony, and because of the increasing numbers of British troops stationed in South Africa due to tensions with the Boers. The game was primarily played by British regimental officers quartered in the Cape Colony and other provinces. Bleomfontein had a six-hole course as early as 1888. Klerksdorpf dates to 1889, while Port Elizabeth, Mermiston, Uitenhage, Johannesburg and Maseru date back to the 1890s.

Following the independence of South Africa in 1911, golf languished somewhat due to the difficulty of maintaining turf in the sun-baked conditions that the nation expanded into. The first great South African golfers were active after the Second World War, beginning with Bobby Locke's runner-up finish to Sam Snead in the 1946 British Open. Locke won many tournaments in the late 1940s and early 1950s in an astonishing array of countries, including Britain, South Africa and the United States, culminating in three great British Open victories in 1949, 1950 and 1952. Locke's career provided a prototype for modern "world tour" golfers such as Gary Player in the 1960s and 1970s and Greg Norman today.

Gary Player emerged as Locke's successor in South Africa during the mid-1950s, pairing with Locke to finish second in the 1955 Canada Cup. Player was the first in a long line of first-class players out of South Africa in the 1960s, the most prominent of which were Bobby Cole, Harold Henning, and Retief Waltman. Player was by far the most successful, winning nine major championships over a span of 21 seasons, beginning with the 1959 British Open. In the 1960s Player was one of golf's Big Three along with Jack Nicklaus and Arnold Palmer and he became only the second player to win each of golf's four major championships. In addition to his personal achievements, Player was a regular in the Canada and World Cups in the 1960s and led South Africa to many top-three

finishes and a victory in 1965. He also was a multiple winner of the World Match Play title. But his services were not indispensable, as seen when in 1974 the team of Dale Hayes and Bobby Cole won South Africa's second World Cup.

In the late 1970s and early 1980s the world of golf became increasingly closed to South Africa and South Africans as the protests against South African apartheid policies intensified and led to the breaking of sporting ties. Golf had been exempted for many years because it is largely an individual sport, but South Africa's final World Cup appearance came in 1980, and their final major amateur challenge (a runner-up finish in the Eisenhower Trophy) came that same year. During the 1980s South Africa was virtually cut-off from world golf, although spectacular purses and the spectacular golf complex at Sun City lured many foreign pros to the South African Open. Gary Player and Harold Henning both found success in this decade on the PGA Senior TOUR.

Since the modification of apartheid policies (and their eventual elimination) South Africa has undergone a transformation in golf, making strong runs at the World Cup, Dunhill Cup, and in major championship golf. Exciting new players such as David Frost and Ernie Els (who became the second South African to win the United States Open, in 1994) have emerged along with promising players such as Retief Goosen. Currently first-rank South African golfers are relocating full-time to the European and American Tours, but South Africa is also the home to most of the African Tour, and many exciting players such as Tony Johnstone play here in the South African summer and switch at mid-year to the Northern Hemisphere tours.

SPAIN

No. of Players (Rank): 85,000 (16)
No. of Courses (Rank): 160 (13)
Players/Course (Rank): 531 (52)
National Open Champion: Craig Parry
World Cup results 1993: 5th. Miguel Angel Jimenez finished 9th-tie in the individual competition.
Prominent Players: Seve Ballesteros, Jose-Maria Canizares, Antonio Garrido, Angel Miguel, Sebastian Miguel, Jose-Maria Olazabal, Jose Rivero, Ramon Sota.
Prominent Courses: Club de Campo, El Prat, El Saler, Las Brisas, Puerto de Hierro Sotogrande (old), Valderrama
National Golf Association: Real Federacion Espanola De Golf, Capitan Haya, 9-5E-28020 Madrid, Spain, 34 (1) 555-2757

History: The story of Spanish golf begins in the Canary Islands, where the Real Golf de Las Palmas was founded in 1891 by a group of British expatriates. Golf arrived on the mainland in 1904 with the building of Puerta de Hierro in 1904 in the Madrid vicinity. But the real expansion of Spanish golf happened on the north coast, where several courses were built near the French-Spanish border near the French resort town of Biarritz, favored by the European aristocracy (especially England's King Edward VII) in the years prior to the First World War. In the 1920s a few courses were built in the Barcelona vicinity.

Following the Second World War course construction was sluggish, but Spain entered teams in the early Canada Cups and did surprisingly well, finishing as runner-up in 1958, 1963 and 1965 with key players such as Angel Miguel, Sebastian Miguel, and Ramon Sota. Classic golf courses were laid out during this era in golf, including El Prat near Barcelona in 1956 and Sotogrande, the prototypical Costa del Sol course opening near Gibraltar in 1964.

With the 1970s came a significant boom in Spanish golf—courses were built in relatively large numbers, and at the same time Spanish golfers began achieving world class tournament victories and results. Jose-Maria Canizares, Manuel Pinero and Seve Ballesteros formed the nucleus of the Spanish renaissance. Spanish teams won the 1976, 1977, 1982 and 1984 World Cups, and individual players began to win frequently on the European and American tours, culminating in Seve Ballesteros' extraordinary 1979 Open victory at Royal Lytham, the first major ever won by a Spaniard. In fact it was primarily the success of Spanish golfers that led to the expansion of the Ryder Cup format to include a European rather than a Great Britain & Ireland team—and the Spaniards responded with tremendous success, particularly in the 1985 matches.

The 1980s were an auspicious time for Spanish golf—excellent courses continued to be developed, and Ballesteros matured into the world's leading player with two victories at Augusta and two more in the British Open.

The 1990s have been witness to the rise of a new Spanish star, Jose-Maria Olazabal, who experienced great success in Europe while also playing a limited schedule in the United States. Olazabal crowned his as-yet-young career by winning the Masters in 1994. Spain continues to contribute key players to the Ryder Cup team, and will host the Ryder Cup matches in 1997. In addition Spain is host to several key events on the European PGA Tour, and fields a formidable amateur team which finished runner-up in the 1983 European Amateur Team Championship. The women's amateur teams are also quite successful, finishing runner-up in the 1975 and 1977 European Team championships as well as winning the Women's World Amateur Team Championship in Caracas in 1986.

SRI LANKA

No. of Players (Rank): 700 (59)
No. of Courses (Rank): 66 (2)
Players/Course (Rank): 350 (41)
World Cup results 1993: Did not compete
Prominent Players: H.L. Premedasa, W.P. Fernando.
National Golf Association: Ceylon Golf Union, P.O. Box 309, Model Farm Road, Colombo 8, Sri Lanka

History: The history of golf in Sri Lanka dates back far indeed, back to the founding of the Colombo Club in 1881. Lacking a large population however, Sri Lanka has not made a great impact on the international game. Sri Lanka did field a team in the 1975 World Cup played in Bangkok—the team of Premedasa and Fernando finished 36th.

SWEDEN

No. of Players (Rank): 360,000 (11)
No. of Courses (Rank): 365 (12)
Players/Course (Rank): 952 (67)
National Open Champion: Eric Carlberg
World Cup results 1993: 13th-tie. Anders Forsbrand finished 9th-tie in the individual competition.
Prominent Players: Ake Berquist, Anders Forsbrand, Joakim Haeggman, Per-Ulrik Johansson, Harry Karlson, Matts Lanner, Gunnar Malmar, Magnus Persson, Ove Sellberg, Jan Sonnevi, Sven Tumba, Arne Werkell.
Prominent Courses: Barsebacks, Falsterbo, Forsgardens, Haninge.
Number of golf professionals: 800.
Number of golf schools: 2.
Major golf magazines: Svensk 205,000; Golf Digest 20,000.
National Golf Association: Svenska Golfforbundet, Box 84 (Kevingestrand) S182 11 Danderyd

History: Sweden has had a long association with golf, dating back to a six-hole course built in 1888 at Ryfors. The members of Gothenburg Golf Club, however, were primarily responsible for the development of Swedish golf after the club's establishment in 1891. Several clubs were built before the First World War, notably Stockholm Golf Club in 1904, Falsterbo in 1909, and by the end of the Second World War Sweden had one of the most extensive array of courses in Europe outside of Great Britain.

The Swedish Golf Federation was organized in 1904, and the country has long been active in world amateur competition and in the Canada Cup throughout the 1950s and 1960s, but the best the Swedes could manage was an 18th place finish in 1956. It wasn't until the 1970s when Gunnar Mueller finished fifth in the 1978 World Cup, that Sweden posed a credible threat in first-class competition, although the amateurs managed to finish runners-up in the 1963 European Amateur Team Championship played at Falsterbo.

With the 1980s Swedish golf hit new heights with high achievement in practically every competitive level. The Women's Amateurs managed victories in the 1981 and 1987 European Amateur Team championships, while the Amateur men finished runner-up in 1985 in the same European Team championships at Halmstad, before winning the Eisenhower Trophy in 1990 at Christchurch.

The professional women's outlook also brightened considerably in the 1980s with the rise of international star Liselotte Neumann, who won the 1988 U.S. Women's Open in addition to several other titles internationally. Teamed with rising star Helen Alfredsson, she took home the Sunrise Cup (the women's equivalent to the World Cup) in 1992. Alfredsson won her own first major in 1993 with a victory in the Dinah Shore.

The Swedish men have yet to win a major championship, but players such as Anders Forsbrand, Mats Lanner, Magnus Persson and Per-Ulrik Johannsen, in addition to newcomers Joakim Haeggman and Jesper Parnevik make up one of the strongest international contingents. The Swedes scored a victory in the 1991 World Cup at Rome with the team of Forsbrand and Johannsen, and reached the semi-finals of the Alfred Dunhill Cup in 1993.

In the 1990s Sweden continues to move from strength to strength, with Joakim Haeggman becoming the first Swede selected to the Ryder Cup team (in 1993), while Jesper Parnevik made a bold run at the British Open before faltering on the final hole. The Swedish women form a dependable part of the surprisingly strong European team in the Solheim Cup. The Swedes host annual events on the European PGA Tour, the European Senior Tour, and the European Women's Tour, and participation in golf continues to build strongly in part due to the continuing success at the professional level.

SWITZERLAND

No. of Players (Rank): 23,000 (28)
No. of Courses (Rank): 47 (30)
Players/Course (Rank): 489 (46)
National Open Champion: Barry Lane (1993)
World Cup results 1993: Did not compete.
Prominent Players: Patrick Bagnoud, Jacky Bonvin, Andre Bossert, Bernard Codonier, Robert Lanz, Paolo Quirici, Franco Salmina, Otto Schoepfer, Ronald Tingley
Prominent Courses: Crans-sur-Sierre, Geneva, Lausanne, Montreux
National Golf Association: Association suisse de golf, En Ballque, Case Postale, 1066 Epalinges

History: Switzerland had its first course as far back as 1893, a course built on the initiative of the Hotel Kulm at St. Moritz. Montreux dates back to 1900, and the Association suisse de golf to 1902. Switzerland maintained one of the most complete golfing calendars in the pre-Second World War era, with the annual match-play national championship dating back to 1907.

Switzerland has placed teams regularly in Canada and World Cups since 1954, but without particular success since the stunning fourth place finish of Andre Bossert in 1991 at Rome elevated the Swiss to an 11th place finish. Switzerland continues to host many Tour events and international tournaments, the most prominent of which are the Senior Zurich Pro-Am and the Canon European Masters.

TAIWAN

No. of Players (Rank): 400,000 (7)
No. of Courses (Rank): 29 (33)
Players/Course (Rank): 13,793 (74)
National Open Champion: N/A
World Cup results 1993: 26th. Hsieh Yu-Shu finished 47th-tie in the individual competition.
Prominent Players: Chen Ching Po, Hsieh Yung Yo, Kuo Chie Hsiung, Li Wen-Shen, Lin Wen Li, Lu Hsi Chuen, Lu Ling Huan, Mei Yun Wang.
Prominent Courses: Chang Gung, Sunrise, Taiwan.
National Golf Association: Golf Association of the Republic of China 71, Lane 369 Tunhua South Road, Taipei, Taiwan (106)

History: Taiwan has an extremely successful golfing record, second only to Japan, among Asian nations, and the record is particularly strong when the small number of available courses is considered. The Shanghai Club, founded in 1896, was the first Chinese golf club, and after the Chinese Nationalists fled to Taiwan in 1949, golf followed and met up with the course established by American occupying forces. Shortly afterwards Taiwan (sometimes referred to as the Republic of China, or Chinese Taipei) established itself as one of the major forces in international golf.

From the late 1950s Taiwan has had particular success in the World Cup, rarely finishing out of the top ten and scoring a victory in 1972 when Hsieh Mon Nam took the individual trophy and Lu Liang Huan finished fourth to defeat the Japanese and South Africans at Royal Melbourne. Lu had made a huge impression on the golfing world a year earlier when he finished second in the British Open to Lee Trevino at Royal Birkdale.

Throughout the remainder of the 1970s Taiwan remained a perennial threat in the World Cup, with six more top-five finishes and a second-place finish in the 1976 individual competition from Kuo Chie-Hsiung.

In the 1980s the Taiwan team disappeared from international competition for political reasons, and since returning in 1987 the team has been less of a threat although still typically finishing in the top ten. Taiwan currently hosts several Tour events on a variety of tours, and players such as Chen Tze Chung are perennial title favorites, with Chen holding the lone Sony Top 100 ranking among Taiwan professionals.

TANZANIA

No. of Players (Rank): 350 (70)
No. of Courses (Rank): 5 (55)
Players/Course (Rank): 70 (4)
World Cup results 1993: Did not compete

THAILAND

No. of Players (Rank): 10,300 (32)
No. of Courses (Rank): 19 (41)
Players/Course (Rank): 542 (53)
National Open Champion: Craig Mann (1993)
World Cup results 1993: Did not compete
Prominent Players: Uthai Dabphavibul, Suthep Messawud, Sukree Oncham, Sareh Sangsui, Samsadi Srinagar.
Prominent Courses: Panya Resort, The Royal Gems, Royal Thai Army
National Golf Association: Thailand Golf Association Railway Training, Centre Vibhavadee Rangsit Road, Bangkok Thailand

History: Golf in Thailand stretches back to 1890, with the founding of the Royal Bangkok Club which had a temple for its clubhouse. Since Siam maintained its independence throughout the 19th-20th centuries, the earliest courses were built by British engineers working in Siam rather than the British military occupying the country.

Thailand has competed quite successfully in the Canada and World Cups since 1957, with solid performances occasionally broken by flashes of brilliance such as the fourth place finish in 1969 at Singapore, when Suchee Onchum finished 3rd in the individual

competition. Navantnee, in Bangkok, played host to the 1975 World Cup and the Thai team finished a quite credible seventh. Since then, however, the team has finished no better than 19th, although a Thai team competed in the final sixteen of the Alfred Dunhill Cup in 1992.

Today Thailand plays host to international tournaments on the Women's Asian Tour and the Asian PGA Tour, as well as hosting the Johnnie Walker Asian Classic in 1992 at Pinehurst, an official event on the PGA European Tour.

TRINIDAD & TOBAGO

No. of Players (Rank): 3,100 (44)
No. of Courses (Rank): 10 (46)
Players/Course (Rank): 310 (40)
World Cup results 1993: Did not compete.
Prominent Players: Peter Singh, Lennox Yearwood.
National Golf Association: Trinidad & Tobago Golf Association, 7A Warner Street, New Town Port of Spain,Trinidad
History: Trinidad's lone foray into major world competition was the 1974 World Cup, in which the team finished a respectable 20th place. Since then, Trinidad has been principally known in golf as a winter destination, with the Mount Irvine Bay course on Trinidad the most popular.

UNITED STATES

No. of Players (Rank): 24,563,000 (1)
No. of Courses (Rank): 14,000 (1)
Players/Course (Rank): 1,754 (71)
National Open Champion: Ernie Els.
World Cup results 1993: 1st. Fred Couples finished 2nd in the individual competition; Davis Love III finished 7th-tie.
Prominent Players: Amy Alcott, Paul Azinger, Jim Barnes, Patty Berg, Jane Blalock, Julius Boros, Pat Bradley, Jack Burke, Jr., Donna Caponi, JoAnne Carner, John Cook, Fred Couples, Ben Crenshaw, Beth Daniel, Jimmy Demaret, Judy Dickinson, Leo Diegel, Olin Dutra, Chick Evans, Doug Ford, Ed Furgol, Hubert Green, Ralph Guldahl, Walter Hagen, Chick Harbert, Dutch Harrison, Sandra Haynie, Ben Hogan, Jock Hutchinson, Juli Inkster, Hale Irwin, Bobby Jones, Betsy King, Tom Kite, Lawson Little, Gene Littler, Nancy Lopez, Davis Love III, John McDermott, Charles Blair Macdonald, Meg Mallon, Lloyd Mangrum, Carol Mann, Laurie Merten, Cary Middlecoff, Johnny Miller, Dottie Mochrie, Orville Moody, Byron Nelson, Jack Nicklaus,

Andy North, Francis Ouimet, Arnold Palmer, Henry Picard, Jerry Pate, Judy Rankin, Betsy Rawls, Paul Runyan, Gene Sarazen, Patty Sheehan, Denny Shute, Horton Smith, Sam Snead, Hollis Stacy, Payne Stewart, Dave Stockton, Louise Suggs, Jerome Travers, Lee Trevino, Sherry Turner, Lanny Wadkins, Tom Watson, Tom Weiskopf, Kathy Whitworth, Craig Wood, Mickey Wright, Babe Zaharias.

Prominent Courses: Aronimink, Atlanta Athletic Club, Augusta National, Baltimore, Baltusrol, Barton Creek, Bay Hill, Bellerive, Bethpage, Black Diamond, Blackwolf Run, Brooklawn, Butler National, C.C. of Detroit, C.C. of Indianapolis, Camargo, Canterbury, Cascades, Castle Pines, Cedar Ridge, Champions, Charlotte, Cherry Hills, Chicago, Cog Hill, Colonial, Congressional, C.C. of North Carolina, The Country Club (Mass.), The Country Club (Ohio), Crooked Stick, Crystal Downs, Cypress Point, Del Paso, Desert Forest, Desert Highlands, Desert Mountain, Doral, Double Eagle, Dunes Club, Eugene, Firestone, Firethorn, Fishers Island, Forest Highlands, Garden City, The Golf Club, G. C. of Georgia, Grandfather, Greenville, Haig Point, Harbour Town, Hazeltine National, High Pointe, The Honors Course, Indianwood, Interlachen, Inverness, Jupiter Hills, Kahkwa Club, Kauai Lagoons, Kiawah, Kittansett Club, La Grange, Lake Nona, La Quinta, Laurel Valley, The Links at Spanish Bay, Long Cove, Los Angeles, Maidstone, Mauna Kea, Meadow Brook, Medinah, Merion, Milwaukee, Montclair, Muirfield Village, Muskogee, NCR, National Golf Links of America, North Shore, Northwood, Oak Hill, Oakland Hills, Oakmont, Oak Tree, Ohio State, Old Marsh, Old Tabby, Old Warson, Olympia Fields, Olympic, PGA National, PGA West, Pasatiempo, Peachtree, Pebble Beach, Pinehurst, Pine Tree, Pine Valley, Plainfield, Point O'Woods, Prairie Dunes, Princeville, Pumpkin Ridge, Quaker Ridge, Richland, Ridgewood, Riviera, Rolling Green, Sahalee, St. Louis, Salem, San Francisco, Saucon Valley, Scioto, Shadow Creek, Sherwood, Shinnecock Hills, Shoal Creek, Shoreacres, Skokie, Somerset Hills, Southern Hills, Spyglass Hill, Stanford University, Stanwich Club, Sycamore Hills, TPC at Sawgrass, Tanglewood, Troon, Troon North, Valhalla, Valley Club of Montecito, Wade Hampton, Wannamoisett, Waverly, Wild Dunes, Wilmington, Winged Foot, World Woods, Wynstone

National Golf Association: United States Golf Association, Golf House, Far Hills, NJ 07931, (708) 234-2300.

History: Aside from Scotland and England, no country has had a greater impact on the history of golf than the United States: its effect on the modern game, its popularity and rules is simply incalculable.

Golf had a rather humble origin in the United States, for like Scotland the first appearance of golf in the public records is by way of banning it, in this case a ban applying to the streets of Albany, New York issued in 1659.

Golf disappeared for over a century until the formation of the South Carolina Golf Club in 1786 in Charleston, which was the first golf club formed outside of the United Kingdom. Golf flourished in South Carolina for a short period of time, but then again died out—the primary connection of the USA to golf throughout the 19th century was the hickory exported from America to construct good club shafts.

Golf was permanently established in 1884 in Virginia, with the first surviving course constructed for the St. Andrews Club (New York) which was founded in 1888. In the 1890s the popularity of golf increased rapidly, helped by the efforts of Charles Blair Macdonald, a former pupil of Old Tom Morris who was instrumental in the foundation of the Chicago Golf Club and, in 1895, the United States Golf Association. The USGA immediately established both Amateur and Open Championships; the Open was in particular dominated by foreign-born players for two decades. In addition the Western Golf Association was founded and staged the annual Western Open which in its first decades had quasi-major status and was, as a PGA TOUR event today, the first tournament with ties to the present TOUR.

The early 1900s were a time of great expansion of the game to the Southeast and Western States. The era of the great amateur course architects was in early flower, yielding courses such as Oakmont and the National Golf Links. English stars such as Harry Vardon made their first visits to the United States, and Donald Ross began his pivotal tenure at Pinehurst.

The 1910s proved to be a time of even greater expansion, with courses such as Pebble Beach, Merion, Oakland Hills, San Francisco Golf Club, Scioto, and Inverness opening for play. John J. McDermott became the first American-born player to win the U.S. Open, and in 1913 Francis Ouimet defeated heavy favorites Harry Vardon and Ted Ray to win the Open in the championship that first brought large-scale national attention to the game. During the decade the careers of Walter Hagen and Bobby Jones first got underway, and in 1910 the USGA took the momentous decision to issue Rules of Golf separately from the Royal & Ancient Golf Club, beginning a period of eighty years in which two different rules systems were in force. The Professional Golfers

Association of America was founded and began staging the PGA Championship in 1916.

The 1920s are known as the Golden Era of American golf, for the massive national popularity of champions such as Jones, Hagen and Gene Sarazen and the abundance of outstanding courses opened, including Pine Valley, Cypress Point, Winged Foot, Olympic, Seminole, Medinah, Oak Hill, Los Angeles, and Quaker Ridge. Jones in particular reached heights of popularity unmatched by golfers until the 1960s, and thousands of new golfers flocked to the game nationwide. During this decade tournaments such as the Texas Open, the North & South, the Western Open, and several winter tournaments in Florida provided the beginnings of a men's professional circuit. The Ryder Cup and Walker Cups also date back to this decade, which marked the first real beginnings of worldwide golf with the leading players regularly crossing the Atlantic to play in the major championships and Cup matches.

The Great Depression ended the golf boom and the 1930s were a time of retrenchment for the game, but the work of enterprising individuals ensured that the popularity of the game continued to increase even if the capital to bankroll flocks of new courses and tournaments was lacking. Augusta National, Shinnecock Hills, Pinehurst No. 2, Southern Hills and Prairie Dunes were the great new courses of the era, which also saw the rise of the professional golf architect in Robert Trent Jones. The increasing number of professional tournaments led to the formation of a PGA Circuit in 1933 and The Masters also dates to that year. Only a few players could (or were willing to) support themselves via the professional tournament Circuit, but in the mid-1930s Lawson Little became the first prominent amateur to switch over the the touring pro side, a milestone in the growth of the TOUR. Another TOUR tradition, the pro-am, found its beginnings in the 1930s at the Bing Crosby National Pro-Am. The late 1930s also marked the emergence of Byron Nelson, Sam Snead and Ben Hogan, who would become golf's second generation of dominating players.

Golf went into a state of hibernation during the early 1940s due to World War Two, with the fledgling PGA TOUR reduced to a few dates which paid prize money in War Bonds, and the major championships and international matches sharply curtailed. However, the TOUR came back to life in 1945 with Byron Nelson winning eleven consecutive tournaments and 17 for the year to become the Associated Press' Athlete of the Year (the first golfer to win the honor since Bobby Jones). The TOUR reached new heights of popularity in the post-war years and in 1947 golf was first televised with a local St. Louis station providing limited coverage of the U.S. Open. The LPGA dates to the late 1940s due to the efforts of a forceful group of women golfers led by Babe Zaharias.

Golf boomed anew in the 1950s in part due to its popularity with leading entertainers such as Bing Crosby and Bob Hope as well as President Dwight Eisenhower who joined Augusta National and was popularly associated with the game. Ben Hogan won three legs of the modern Grand Slam in 1953 and become the decade's leading player, while the PGA TOUR as a whole was able to expand to a nearly full annual schedule of events, one of which (the World Championship of Golf) offered the first $100,000 purse. Aggressive course-building resumed in the 1950s and it was the era of Robert Trent Jones and Dick Wilson, with courses such as Point O'Woods, Bellerive, Firestone, and Meadow Brook opening during the decade.

During the 1960s golf experienced its greatest boom to date, as the growth of television and televised sports coincided with the emergence of Arnold Palmer, Jack Nicklaus, and Gary Player as golf's Big Three. Palmer in particular captured the public's fancy in a way no golfer has before or since, and millions of Americans took up the game at courses built around the new suburban communities that were being developed. PGA TOUR purses skyrocketed during the decade and golfers such as Palmer had an international schedule of endorsements, exhibitions, and tournaments that catapulted them to the top-rank of American sportsmen. Their success led them to break away from the PGA of America and form the PGA TOUR as an independent organization with Joe Dey as the first Tour commissioner. The LPGA also expanded significantly in this decade with the dominating play of Mickey Wright and Kathy Whitworth. Architects such as Pete Dye, Ed Seay, Tom Fazio and Ted Robinson did their early work in this decade, with courses such as Harbour Town, Spyglass Hill, Mauna Kea, The Golf Club and Doral showing new design ideas to golfers.

In the 1970s the career of Jack Nicklaus, Lee Trevino, Johnny Miller, and Tom Watson ensured even greater popularity for professional golf, which now had become a big business under the direction of administrators such as Deane Beman and super-agents like Mark McCormack. The LPGA likewise flourished with popular new players such as Jane Blalock, Judy Rankin, JoAnne Carner and Nancy Lopez, and in the late 1970s the establishment of the Legends of Golf tournament presaged the launch of the PGA Senior TOUR. Courses such as Jupiter Hills and Muirfield Village were the highlights of a decade of decline in the opening of new courses.

Prosperity and the emergence of new stars and the Senior TOUR made the 1980s a decade of huge growth for the game both at the professional and amateur level. The PGA TOUR went to an all-exempt list of 125 players in 1981 and also launched the

Tournament Players Clubs, an ambitious plan for a network of "stadium" design courses that would host PGA Tournaments across the country, beginning with The Players Championship at the TPC at Sawgrass. Television also became a backbone of TOUR revenues as virtually every date on the TOUR calendar was televised, and several made-for-television events such as the Skins Game debuted. The LPGA and the PGA Senior TOUR flourished, although the LPGA to a lesser degree due to the lack of good television and print exposure. The emergence of top-flight foreign players such as Greg Norman, Seve Ballesteros, Bernhard Langer and Nick Faldo ensured a greater rivalry in the Ryder Cup matches and major championships, thus further stimulating interest in the game and in a world tour. While the business of golf was booming in the sales of equipment, real estate, apparel, and resort vacations, late in the decade several conflicts over the legality of high-tech equipment prompted several lawsuits between companies and the governing bodies in the game. With players flocking to the game, courses were opened at a record pace in the 1980s, including classics such as Black Diamond, Haig Point, Desert Highlands, Lake Nona, PGA West and the TPC at Sawgrass, although some designs were considered overly radical and often overly penal.

In the 1990s a new generation of leading professionals led by Fred Couples, Paul Azinger and Davis Love III has emerged, and interest in the game (stimulated also by the rivalries created by the rise of golf stars in other nations) has heightened interest in golf as never before. The LPGA has also experienced rapid growth, as well as mini-tours such as the NIKE TOUR launched in 1990 by the PGA TOUR and the Ben Hogan Company. A new level of variety and creativity is evident in course design with new courses such as the World Woods, Old Tabby, The Ocean Course, Sandhills, Shadow Creek and Pumpkin Ridge.

URUGUAY

No. of Players (Rank): 500 (64)
No. of Courses (Rank): 4 (58)
Players/Course (Rank): 125 (15)
National Open Champion: Carlos Franco (1993)
World Cup results 1993: Did not compete
Prominent Players: Juan Dapiaggi, Juan Esmoris, Enrique Fernandez, Clever Menendez, Juan Sereda, Pascual Viola
Prominent Courses: Club de Golf del Uruguay

History: Uruguay first appeared on the international

golf scene in 1961, fielding a team which finished 25th in the Canada Cup. Juan Sereda and Jose Esmoris went on to finish 13th in the 1962 event, which remains the high point in Uruguay's competitive record, but the Uruguayans continued to field teams throughout the 1960s and early 1970s with some success. The Uruguayan Open played at Club de Golf del Uruguay in Montevideo is a regular stop on the South American tour and continues to attract a strong regional field.

VENEZUELA

No. of Players (Rank): 4,000 (38)
No. of Courses (Rank): 23 (37)
Players/Course (Rank): 174 (23)
World Cup results 1993: Did not compete
Prominent Players: Manuelo Bernardez, Francisco Gonzalez, Ramon Munoz, Teobaldo Perez, Angel Sanchez.
Prominent Courses: Lagunita.
National Golf Association: Federacion Venezolana de Golf Unidad Comercial "La Florida," Local 5, Avenida Avila La Florida Caracas 1050 Venezuela

History: Venezuela was the second South American country, after Argentina, to prove to be a force in international golf, fielding Canada Cup teams since 1958 and finishing in the top ten on two occasions (1958 and 1974), while playing host to the World Cup at Lagunita in 1974. Lagunita also was the site of a South American tour stop, and hosted the Eisenhower Trophy competition in 1986.

VIRGIN ISLANDS

No. of Players (Rank): 500 (64)
No. of Courses (Rank): 4 (58)
Players/Course (Rank): 125 (15)
National Open Champion: Ernie Els (US Open)
World Cup results 1993: Did not compete
Prominent Courses: Carambola, Mahogany Run.
National Golf Association: United States Golf Association, Golf House, Far Hill, NJ 07931

History: The Virgin Islands have been known largely as a popular golfing destination more than as a source of international golfers, due to the small population base and generally spotty economic progress. Carambola and Mahogany Run are the best known of the resort courses (Carambola on St. Croix, and Mahogany Run on St. Thomas).

WALES

No. of Players (Rank): 35,000 (18)
No. of Courses (Rank): 119 (18)
Players/Course (Rank): 294 (38)
World Cup results 1993: 16th. Mark Mouland finished 18th-tie in the individual competition.
Prominent Players: Craig Defoy, Harold Gould, Brian Huggett, David Llewellyn, Sid Mouland, Mark Mouland, Philip Parkin, Dai Rees, Dennis Smalldon, Dave Thomas, David Vaughan, Ian Woosnam.
Prominent Courses: Royal Porthcawl.
National Golf Association: Welsh Golfing Union Powys House, Cwmbran Gwent, NP44 1PB Wales 44(633) 870261

History: Golf arrived comparatively late in Wales with the oldest club, Pontnewydd, dating back to 1875. Development was rapid, with many clubs dating back before the turn of the century, most notably Royal Porthcawl which is the only Welsh club given the "royal" honorific.

The Welsh national team has yet to succeed in the home internationals against Ireland, Scotland, and England, but the Welsh team has fared extremely well in Canada Cup and World Cup team competitions with eighteen top-ten finishes since 1954, including eight consecutive top-eight finishes between 1956 and 1963 when Dai Rees and Dave Thomas were at the height of their careers. Rees also served as Captain of the British Ryder Cup squad.

Leading players emerging in the 1960s were Brian Huggett and Sid Mouland, and Wales managed a fifth-place finish in the 1970 World Cup. During the 1970s Wales produced David Vaughan, David Llewellyn and Craig Defoy, but struggled to reproduce the results of the past until 1979, when the Welsh team placed second in the European Amateur Team Championship.

In the 1980s Ian Woosnam, David Llewellyn and Mark Mouland raised the profile of Welsh golf to its highest-ever level, Llewellyn and Woosnam combining for a victory in the World Cup and Woosnam and Mouland subsequently teaming for several top-five finishes. Woosnam became the first Welshman to win a major championship in 1992 with a victory in The Masters, and he remains Wales' number-one golfer although he has slipped far from the number-one world ranking he held briefly in 1991.

ZAMBIA

No. of Players (Rank): 4,000 (38)
No. of Courses (Rank): 20 (39)

Players/Course (Rank): 200 (26)
National Open Champion: Peter Harrison (1993)
World Cup results 1993: Did not compete
Prominent Courses: Lusaka.

History: Zambia has yet to be considered one of the major players in the international arena—however, 1994 U.S. Senior Open champ Simon Hobday is a veteran of the Zambian national amateur team from the 1960s. In addition, the country hosts the annual Zambian Open at Lusaka Golf Club in the capital city, which has attracted an international field including past winners Ian Woosnam, David Llewellyn and Gordon Brand. Golf in Zambia dates back to 1908 and the founding of Livingstone by the British colonists.

ZIMBABWE

No. of Players (Rank): 35,000 (18)
No. of Courses (Rank): 62 (22)
Players/Course (Rank): 565 (55)
National Open Champion: Tony Johnstone (1993)
World Cup results 1993: 2nd. Nick Price finished 3rd-tie in the individual competition; Mark McNulty finished 10th-tie.
Prominent Players: Antony Edwards, Leon Evans, Donald Gammon, William Koen, Mark McNulty, Nick Price, Tim Price.
Prominent Courses: Chapman, Royal Harare.
National Golf Association: Zimbabwe Golf Association, P.O. Box 3327, Harare, Zimbabwe

History: Golf arrived in Zimbabwe (then known as Rhodesia) in 1895 with the founding of Bulawayo. Royal Salisbury (now Royal Harare), the most prestigious course in the country, dates from 1899. Zimbabwe arrived late as a leading golfing nation, but has hosted a regular stop on the African Tour for years in the Zimbabwe Open, which is usually staged at Royal Harare.

As Rhodesia, Zimbabwe competed in the 1971 World Cup with a respectable 21st place finish behind the outstanding play of Donald Gammon, but has emerged as a leading golf nation only in the late 1980s with the emergence of Nick Price and Mark McNulty as world-class golfers. Price and McNulty both cracked the top-twenty in the Sony Rankings during 1992 with Price reaching eighth. Both improved in 1993 with Price reaching fourth before scaling to number-one in 1994. The two combined in the 1993 World Cup to finish second behind the United States.

GOLF, BY U.S. STATE

OVERVIEW: *Key statistics, history, prominent players, tournaments, and courses, plus a census of golfers.*

ALABAMA

No. of Players (Rank): 203,000 (32)
No. of Rounds played (Rank): 4,892,300 (29)
Percentage of Female Players (Rank): 12.9 (47)
Percentage of Senior Golfers (Rank): 23.5 (15)
Prominent Golfers: Glen Day, Gardner Dickinson, Buddy Gardner, Hubert Green, Steve Lowery, Larry Nelson, Dicky Pride, Nancy Ramsbottom, Mike Smith.
Major Golf Companies: Burton.
Prominent Courses: Shoal Creek, Grand National, Birmingham C.C.
State Golf Association: Alabama Golf Association, P.O. Box 20149, Birmingham, AL 35216—(205) 979-1234.

Highlights: Alabama has been in the news in recent years primarily for the controversy at Shoal Creek Golf Club, the highly-ranked Jack Nicklaus-designed private club that was accused of race discrimination just prior to hosting the 1990 PGA Championship. In 1992 the State embarked on the remarkable development of the Robert Trent Jones Golf Trail, seven 36- and 54-hole golf centers situated throughout the state combining low fees and quality courses from Robert Trent Jones, Inc.

Prior to the 1980s, Alabama had hosted the Montgomery and Mobile Opens on the PGA TOUR as early as 1946, but the tournaments did not last. The 1974 and 1986 Senior Women's Amateurs were staged in Point Clear.

ALASKA

No. of Players (Rank): N/A
No. of Rounds played (Rank): 14,000,000 (6)
Percentage of Female Players (Rank): N/A
Percentage of Senior Golfers (Rank): N/A
Prominent Golfers: Danny Edwards.
Prominent Courses: Eagle Glen.
State Golf Association: Anchorage Golf Association, P.O. Box 112210, Anchorage, AK 99511—(907) 349-4653.

Highlights: Alaska has yet to host a prominent tournament, but has the advantage of offering over 18 hours of sunshine during the peak summer months. Several courses, such as Eagle Glen at Elmendorf Air Force Base, come highly recommended.

ARIZONA

No. of Players (Rank): 465,000 (18)
No. of Rounds played (Rank): 11,020,500 (14)
Percentage of Female Players (Rank): 21.6 (22)
Percentage of Senior Golfers (Rank): 30.2 (4)
Prominent Golfers: Todd Barranger, Amy Fruhwirth, Robert Gaona, Dick Lotz, Billy Mayfair, Deborah Parks, Don Pooley, Howard Twitty.
Major Golf Companies: Antigua Sportswear, Arizona Manufacturing, Karsten Manufacturing, Royal Grip.
Prominent Courses: Desert Forest, Desert Highlands, Desert Mountain-Cochise, Desert Mountain-Renegade, Forest Highlands, La Paloma, Troon, Troon North, Ventana Canyon-Canyon.
State Golf Association: Arizona Golf Association, 11801 North Tatum Blvd., Suite 247, Phoenix, AZ 85028—(602) 953-5990

Highlights: Arizona is far too hot to host USGA Championships, but the state has played host to both the Phoenix Open and the Tucson Open since the close of the Second World War, as well as the Skins Game in recent years. But it is more as a golfing destination for amateur players and retirees that Arizona has made its mark, with its sparkling array of desert courses. It was the tight restrictions on water usage and irrigation (usually limiting new golf courses to 80 acres of grass) that led architects to develop the "target golf" design approach in the early 1980s where grassed tee-to-green areas are replaced by small, pocketed landing areas. This type of design has become associated with Arizona and in particular the designs of Jack Nicklaus.

ARKANSAS

No. of Players (Rank): 121,000 (39)
No. of Rounds played (Rank): 3,832,000 (32)
Percentage of Female Players (Rank): 19.7 (29)
Percentage of Senior Golfers (Rank): 30.6 (2)
Prominent Golfers: Bill Hall, Paul Runyan, John Daly.
Prominent Courses: Texarkana, Hardscrabble.
State Golf Association: Arkansas State Golf Association, 2311 Biscayne Drive, Suite 308, Little Rock, AR 72207—(501) 227-8555

Highlights: Arkansas is known as the home of John Daly, as well as the home of several outstanding courses. The state was home to the Ozark Open, which briefly graced the PGA TOUR in the late 1940s, but since then the state has seen little of major golf tournaments until the 1990s, when the Texarkana Open became a regular stop on the Hogan and later NIKE TOUR. Chenal Country Club in Little Rock was recently named the third best new private golf course by Golf Digest, while several retirement communities such as Hot Springs Village, Bellas Vista and Cherokee Village have proved popular for year-round golfers.

CALIFORNIA

No. of Players (Rank): 2,758,000 (1)
No. of Rounds played (Rank): 54,884,200 (1)
Percentage of Female Players (Rank): 20.3 (25)
Percentage of Senior Golfers (Rank): 25.9 (10)
Prominent Golfers: Amy Alcott, George Archer, Brandie Burton, Billy Casper, John Daly, Al Geiberger, Juli Inkster, Gene Littler, Nancy Lopez, Gary McCord, Phil Mickelson, Johnny Miller, Corey Pavin, Loren Roberts, Bob Rosburg, Scott Simpson, Craig Stadler, Dave Stockton, Ken Venturi, Mickey Wright.
Major Golf Companies: Aldila, Ashworth, Belding Sports, Callaway, Cleveland, Cobra, Ray Cook, Cubic Balance, Daiwa, Fila, Founders Club, Garfalloy, Kunnan, Langert, Lyle & Scott, Lynx, Mitsushiba, Odyssey, Plop Putter, Rawlings, Slotline, Stan Thompson, Taylor Made, Tiger Shark, Yamaha, Yonex.
Prominent Courses: Carmel Valley Ranch, Cypress Point, Del Paso, Haggin Oaks, Half Moon Bay, La Quinta-Mountain, Links at Monarch Beach, Links at Spanish Bay, Los Angeles (North), PGA West (Nicklaus Private), PGA West (Stadium), Pasatiempo, Pebble Beach, Riviera, San Francisco, Sherwood, Silverado, Spyglass Hill, Stanford University, Valley Cub of Montecito.

State Golf Association: (Northern) California Golf Association, P.O. Box NCGA, Pebble Beach, CA 93953—(408) 625-4653

Highlights: While California was not the first Pacific Coast state in which golf was played, Californians have taken to the game with great zeal over the past 70 years, and since 1919 California has been home to Pebble Beach, universally recognized as one of the five greatest courses in the world. Cypress Point, also considered in that group, dates from 1929.

From the early 1920s California anchored the first weeks on the PGA tournament circuit, with the Los Angeles Open and later the Bing Crosby National Pro-Am on the Monterey Peninsula offering excellent courses, top fields, and good purses. California, in fact, is the birthplace of the pro-am—an idea which grew out of the Crosby.

There are several regular major tour tournament stops today in California including the Mercedes Championships (La Costa), the AT&T National Pro-Am (Pebble Beach et al), the Bob Hope Chrysler Classic (several Palm Springs area courses), the Buick Invitational of California (Torrey Pines), the Nissan Los Angeles Open (Riviera), the Shark Shootout (Sherwood Oaks), the Skins Game (Bighorn), Inamori Classic (StoneRidge), The Transamerica (Silverado), Ralph's Senior Classic (Rancho Park), and the Raley's Senior Gold Rush (Rancho Murieta).

The PGA Championship was held at Pebble Beach in 1929, and since then California has hosted many major championships of golf, including acting as the permanent home of the Dinah Shore, a major championship on the LPGA Tour.

California is home to many famed golf resorts, including PGA West, La Quinta, Silverado, La Costa, Rancho Bernardo, and the famed complex at Pebble Beach comprising Pebble Beach, Spyglass Hill, and the Links at Spanish Bay. In addition, California is home to many golf-oriented residential and retirement communities of the first rank.

The state is headquarters for many of golf's best known manufacturing concerns, and has played host to the National Golf Foundation's Golf Summit.

COLORADO

No. of Players (Rank): 355,000 (23)
No. of Rounds played (Rank): 6,461,000 (26)
Percentage of Female Players (Rank): 23.8 (14)
Percentage of Senior Golfers (Rank): 22.8 (22)
Prominent Golfers: Tommy Armour III, Lori West.
Major Golf Companies: Descente.
Prominent Courses: Bear Creek, Broadmoor-

East, Castle Pines, Cherry Hills, C.C. of the Rockies, Keystone Ranch, Telluride.
State Golf Association: The Colorado Golf Association, Suite 101, 5655 South Yosemite, Englewood, CO 80111—(303) 779-4653

Highlights: Colorado offers 300 days of sunshine, breathtaking mountain vista, and thin air that allows the ball to travel 8-15 percent farther than at sea level. With over 175 courses, Colorado is home to one of the most extensive collections of courses in the nation. Cherry Hills and Castle Pines are perennials in the top-100 rankings, while courses such as Arrowhead, Hyland Hills, Pole Creek, and Riverdale Dunes grace the public course rankings and Keystone, Singletree, Broadmoor and Tamarron are always present in golf resort rankings. Colorado has been known as a skiing mecca but increasingly attracts out-of-state golfers.

Colorado was the first western state to host a United States Open (1938—Cherry Hills) and the state hosted the Denver Open in the early days of the PGA TOUR. Recently Colorado has been home to The International at Castle Pines, the only TOUR event employing a modified Stableford system.

Colorado leapt into golf history in 1960 with the electrifying final round of the U.S. Open at Cherry Hills, when Arnold Palmer swept the field with a final round 65. The 1960 Open is generally regarded as the beginning of the Palmer era in golf—although it also featured the last final round challenge from Ben Hogan, as well as the first challenge from Jack Nicklaus. Colorado continues to host major championships in addition to TOUR Events—the 1978 U.S. Open won by Andy North, the 1993 U.S. Senior Open at Cherry Hills in addition to the U.S. Amateur and Women's Amateur.

In 1982 the Colorado Golf Association became the first state to rate courses for the USGA Slope system, and the state's successful experience prompted the USGA to extend the concept nationwide.

CONNECTICUT

No. of Players (Rank): 398,000 (21)
No. of Rounds played (Rank): 8,039,600 (20)
Percentage of Female Players (Rank): 17.1 (39)
Percentage of Senior Golfers (Rank): 22.2 (19)
Prominent Golfers: Julius Boros, Doug Ford, Ken Green, Joan Joyce, Glenna Collett Vare.
Major Golf Companies: BJ Designs.
Prominent Courses: Brooklawn, Stanwich, Yale University.
State Golf Association: Connecticut State Golf Association, 35 Cold Spring Road, Suite 212,

Rocky Hill, CT 06067—(203) 257-4171.

Highlights: Connecticut has a long association with the game, with the state golf association dating back to 1899. Connecticut's most prominent tournament is the Canon Greater Hartford Open, which is one of the steadiest dates on the PGA TOUR calendar with a continuous history stretching back to 1952. Sammy Davis was for many years associated with the event. In 1979 Brooklawn became the first Connecticut course to host a major championship by staging the U.S. Women's Open. Subsequently Brooklawn also hosted the 1987 U.S. Senior Open won by Gary Player. The outstanding Yale University course is home to the annual Connecticut Open on the NIKE TOUR.

DELAWARE

No. of Players (Rank): 57,000 (46)
No. of Rounds played (Rank): 1,214,100 (46)
Percentage of Female Players (Rank): 10.6 (49)
Percentage of Senior Golfers (Rank): 23.5 (15)
Prominent Golfers: Jim Woodward.
Prominent Courses: Biderman, Wilmington-North, Wilmington-South.
State Golf Association: Delaware State Golf Association, 100 Greenhills Avenue, Suite D, Wilmington DE 19805

Highlights: The tiny state is home to only 22 golf clubs and public courses, but among them are Wilmington and the Dupont Country Club, two of the best courses in the country. Wilmington was the site of the 1971 U.S. Amateur won by Gary Cowan over Eddie Pearce.

DISTRICT OF COLUMBIA

No. of Players (Rank): 23,000 (49)
No. of Rounds played (Rank): N/A
Percentage of Female Players (Rank): N/A
Percentage of Senior Golfers (Rank): N/A
Prominent Golfers: Michell Mackall.
State Golf Association: Washington Metropolitan Golf Association, 8012 Colorado Springs Dr., Springfield, VA 22153

Highlights: Washington, DC, and the District of Columbia proper are home to just four golf courses—the District is closely associated in the public's mind with the Congressional, which hosted the famed 1964 U.S. Open won by Ken Venturi in record heat, and the 1976 PGA Championship. East Potomac Park hosted the Publinx in 1923, and Columbia Golf Club was the site of the 1955 Canada Cup (now the World Cup).

FLORIDA

No. of Players (Rank): 1,161,000 (7)
No. of Rounds played (Rank): 41,099,400 (2)
Percentage of Female Players (Rank): 23.9 (15)
Percentage of Senior Golfers (Rank): 42.3 (1)
Prominent Golfers: Laura Baugh, Guy Boros, Michael Bradley, Tom Garner, Scott Gump, Mark McCumber, Shaun Michael, Charles Raulerson, Larry Rinker, Colleen Walker.
Major Golf Companies: Boast, Golden Bear, LPGA, National Golf Foundation, Nicklaus Equipment, PGA of America, PGA Tour, Palmer Course Design Company, Tail, Toney Penna.
Prominent Courses: Bay Hill, Black Diamond-Quarry, Bonita Bay, Doral-Blue, Fiddlesticks, Foxfire, Hammock Dunes, Innisbrook-Copperhead, JDM, Jupiter Hills, Lake Nona, Long Point, Loxahatchee, Mayacoo Lakes, Old Marsh, PGA National Champions, Pine Tree, Sawgrass, Southern Dunes, TPC at Sawgrass, Walt Disney World-Osprey Ridge, World Woods-Pine Barrens.
State Golf Association: Florida State Golf Association, 5710 Draw Lane, Sarasota, FL 34238—(813) 921-5695.

Highlights: Florida was far from the first home of American golf, but since the introduction of the game in the early 20th century golf has sunk deep roots, and today there are over 1,000 courses in the Sunshine State. The Florida land boom of the mid-1920s and the winter holiday opportunities led to the staging of many winter golf tournaments in Florida from the 1920s onward, from *mano-a-mano* matches, such as the famed Bobby Jones/Walter Hagen 72-hole match in 1926 won by Hagen 12 and 11, to standard stroke play events. By the 1940s Florida was the home of several annual stops on the PGA Tour and in the 1950s the fledgling LPGA also had a Florida-heavy schedule. Both Robert Trent Jones and Dick Wilson constructed a number of their best-known courses in Florida during the 1950s and 1960s as Miami and the east coast became established as the leading winter vacation destination.

By the 1970s large numbers of touring pros made Florida their home base, as did the PGA of America and the PGA Tour, the National Golf Foundation, the famed PGA Merchandise Show—and thus Florida has been able to claim truthfully that it is the home base of American golf. Due to summer weather conditions the state has rarely hosted major national championships; nevertheless the 1969 U.S. Women's Open and the 1971 and 1987 PGA Championships were staged in the state. In the amateur ranks the 1987 U.S. Amateur (at Jupiter Hills) was played at Jupiter Hills, while in team events Florida has hosted the 1990 Solheim Cup, the 1990 and 1993 World Cups, and the 1983 Ryder Cup matches. With the relocation of the LPGA to Florida, the World Golf Hall of Fame and Museum is scheduled to open in 1995, which combined with the launch of The Golf Channel from Orlando again affirms Florida as a capital of American golf.

GEORGIA

No. of Players (Rank): 458,000 (19)
No. of Rounds played (Rank): 9,022,600 (17)
Percentage of Female Players (Rank): 12.7 (48)
Percentage of Senior Golfers (Rank): 23.0 (20)
Prominent Golfers: Tommy Aaron, Andy Bean, Jim Dent, Bobby Jones, Kenny Knox, Steve Melnyk, Larry Mize, Jerry Pate, Doug Sanders, Gene Sauers, Cindy Schreyer, Hollis Stacy, Louise Suggs.
Major Golf Companies: Bridgestone, Cayman Golf, Club Car, Divots, E-Z-Go, Kasco, Macgregor, Merit, Mizuno, Sporthompson
Prominent Courses: Atlanta A.C., Atlanta C.C., Augusta National, Callaway Gardens (Mountain View), G.C. of Georgia, Peachtree, Reynolds Plantation.
State Golf Association: Georgia State Golf Association, Building 9, Suite 100, 42200 Northside Parkway, Atlanta, GA 30327—(404) 233-4742

Highlights: Georgia has played a central role in American golf since the era of Bobby Jones. Jones' association with Augusta National Golf Club and The Masters also affirmed Georgia's position as a leading golf state—a position solidified through the construction of other top clubs such as Peachtree and Atlanta Athletic Club as well as resorts such as Reynolds Plantation. In addition to the Masters, Georgia has hosted the U.S. Open (1976), the PGA Championship (1981), the U.S. Women's Open (1951 and 1990), and the 1950 and 1971 Women's Amateur. In addition the 1963 Ryder Cup matches were staged at East Lake. In addition to staging major tournaments, Georgia has become known as a home of golf manufacturing concerns, with a number of key manufacturers based in-state. In 1994, Georgia played host to the 1994 Senior Women's Amateur at Sea Island G.C., as well as a large number of TOUR, Senior TOUR, LPGA and NIKE TOUR events.

HAWAII

No. of Players (Rank): N/A
No. of Rounds played (Rank): N/A
Percentage of Female Players (Rank): N/A
Percentage of Senior Golfers (Rank): N/A
Prominent Golfers: David Ishii, Ted Makalena.
Major Golf Companies: Tall-Sax.
Prominent Courses: The Experience at Koele, Kapalua-Plantation, Kauai Lagoons (Kiele), Ko Olina, Mauna Kea (Jones), Mauna Lani (South), Princeville-Prince, Royal Kaanapali (South), Turtle Bay.
State Golf Association: Hawaii State Golf Association, 3221 Waialae Avenue, Suite 305, Honolulu, HI 96816—(808) 732-9785.

Highlights: Hawaii first began to boom as a golfing state in the late 1940s, when postwar travel to the islands grew and led to the staging of the first PGA TOUR events in the islands, the 1947-48 Hawaiian Opens. But Hawaii became firmly established as a golf mecca beginning in the 1950s, when commercial airlines were first able to offer non-stop jet service to the islands. With the addition of the Hawaiian Open to the PGA TOUR calendar in the early 1960s, the allure of Hawaii and courses such as Kaanapali and Mauna Kea beckoned in annual telecasts. Due to the travel distance (not to mention time-zone difference) Hawaii has to date staged only the 1960, 1975 and 1985 Publinx and the 1983 Women's Publinx in the USGA rota, but Hawaii has hosted the World Cup on three occasions (1964, 1978 and 1987), as well as annual events on all of the major tours. Interestingly, Hawaii was allowed to field its own team (separate from the regular American contingent) in the Canada Cup during the 1960s! Today, Hawaii is better recognized as a part of the United States and has a reputation as one of its prime golfing meccas, with many national-ranked resort courses and good year-round golfing weather.

IDAHO

No. of Players (Rank): 122,000 (38)
No. of Rounds played (Rank): 2,037,400 (40)
Percentage of Female Players (Rank): 33.1 (5)
Percentage of Senior Golfers (Rank): 20.1 (36)
Prominent Golfers: Don Bies.
Major Golf Companies: Henry-Griffits.
Prominent Courses: Coeur D'Alene, Elkhorn, Sun Valley.
State Golf Association: Idaho Golf Association, P.O. Box 3025, Boise, ID 83703.

Highlights: Idaho has enhanced its golfing profile in recent years with the opening of the Coeur D'Alene resort and the annual staging of the NIKE Boise Open. Prior to the 1990s, Idaho had an LPGA event briefly in the 1960s but overall was not a major player on the national golf map, despite a high participation rate in the amateur ranks. The Sun Valley resort area has grown considerably in popularity as a summer golfing destination in recent years.

ILLINOIS

No. of Players (Rank): 1,526,000 (3)
No. of Rounds played (Rank): 22,127,000 (7)
Percentage of Female Players (Rank): 25.2 (12)
Percentage of Senior Golfers (Rank): 23.0 (20)
Prominent Golfers: Butch Baird, Jerry Barber, Jill Briles-Hinton, Bob Goalby, Gary Hallberg, John Huston, Pete Jordan, David Ogrin, Nancy Scranton, D.A. Weibring.
Major Golf Companies: Tommy Armour, Hyatt Golf Resorts, Northwestern, Pro-Select, Ram, Wilson.
Prominent Courses: Bob O'Link, Butler National, Chicago, Cog Hill (No. 4), Kemper Lakes, Knollwood, La Grange, Medinah (No. 3), North Shore, Olympia Fields, Pine Meadow, Shoreacres, Skokie, Wynstone.

Highlights: Illinois has been central to the American golf story since its earliest years, since Charles Balir Macdonald was a founding father of the Chicago Golf Club and it was at his instigation that the United States Golf Association was founded. In fact Illinois has hosted 45 national championships to date through the USGA including 12 U.S. Opens, the latest the heart-stopping victory of Hale Irwin over Mike Donald in 1990 at Medinah. Illinois has also been the site of four PGA Championships, the latest in 1989 at Kemper Lakes, as well as four PGA Grand Slam of Golf events from 1986-89.

In addition to national championships, Chicago was from the start the capital of Western golf, as suggested by the establishment of the Western Golf Association at Chicago in 1899, which led directly to the institution of the Western Open, a tournament which in its heyday had quasi-major status and today (known as the Motorola Open) remains a key event on the PGA TOUR. The Western Open was staged throughout the Western U.S. in its early years but now is a Chicago event.

Illinois had perhaps its greatest impact on American golf in the 1940s and 1950s, when events such as the All-America Open, the Tam O'Shanter, and the World Championship took PGA TOUR purses to new heights and did much to establish a foundation for the explosive growth of golf in the 1960s. In 1954, for instance, the winner of the World Championship banked $50,000, while the next most lucrative tournament (the Tournament of Champions) paid $10,000 to the winner.

In addition to its many tournaments, Illinois is home to several of the most prestigious clubs in the country and also several major golf manufacturing concerns, notably Wilson Sporting Goods.

INDIANA

No. of Players (Rank): 614,000 (13)
No. of Rounds played (Rank): 11,052,000 (13)
Percentage of Female Players (Rank): 20.2 (25)
Percentage of Senior Golfers (Rank): 27.5 (8)
Prominent Golfers: Chick Evans, Jackie Gallagher-Smith, Lori Garbacz, Cathy Gerring, Herb Graffis, Sandra Spuzich, Mike Sullivan, Fuzzy Zoeller.
Major Golf Companies: Sansabelt.
Prominent Courses: C.C. of Indianapolis, Crooked Stick, Meridian Hills, Sycamore Hills.
State Golf Association: Indiana Golf Association, 111 East Main Street, Carmel, IN 46032—(317) 844-7271.

Highlights: By hosting the 1991 PGA Championship and the 1993 U.S. Women's Open, Indiana emerged from under the shadow of several more traditionally prominent golfing states of the Midwest—and with the launching of tournaments such as the Brickyard Crossing, it looks as if Indiana plans to stay on centerstage for a few years.

Crooked Stick was, of course, the host of the famed 1991 PGA Championship in which John Daly, gaining entrance to the tournament as the ninth alternate with less than 24 hours' notice, went on to win the tournament. Crooked Stick is also known for a top-100 ranking from several golf magazines, the hosting of the 1989 Mid-Amateur and as one of the earliest courses designed by Pete Dye. But other courses in the state have hosted PGA TOUR, LPGA, Senior PGA TOUR and NIKE TOUR events as well as the Girls' Junior Amateur, the Publinx, and the PGA Championship.

For all these recent developments, prominent golf tournaments have been staged in Indiana for many years, beginning in 1926 when the Western Open visited the state. Ft. Wayne was the site of a PGA TOUR event as early as 1951, while three of the first six LPGA Championships were played here in 1955 and 1958-59.

IOWA

No. of Players (Rank): 407,000 (20)
No. of Rounds played (Rank): 7,000,400 (24)
Percentage of Female Players (Rank): 30.3 (5)
Percentage of Senior Golfers (Rank): 17.8 (44)
Prominent Golfers: Jack Fleck, Sean Murphy, Tom Purtzer, Dave Rummells, Clifford Roberts, Barb Thomas.
Major Golf Companies: AER, Inc.
Prominent Courses: Wakonda, Des Moines (Red).
State Golf Association: Iowa Golf Association, 1930 St. Andrews Court NE, Cedar Rapids, IA 52402—(319) 378-9142

Highlights: Although Iowa does not command a high profile on the national golfing scene, Iowans such as Jack Fleck and Cliff Roberts have played a major role in the development and popularization of the game—and Iowa has hosted several tournaments of national import since it first hosted the Western Open in 1936 and an annual PGA TOUR event, the Cedar Rapids Open, first staged in 1949. The Waterloo Open was a fixture on the LPGA TOUR in the late 1950s and early 1960s, while Wakonda Club hosted the 1963 Amateur won by Deane Beman. Today, Iowa is home to the Nike Hawkeye Open played in Iowa City.

KANSAS

No. of Players (Rank): 279,000 (28)
No. of Rounds played (Rank): 5,552,100 (28)
Percentage of Female Players (Rank): 18.0 (34)
Percentage of Senior Golfers (Rank): 21.0 (33)
Prominent Golfers: Dick Goetz, Steve Gotsche, Bruce Lietzke, Tom Shaw, Tom Watson.
Major Golf Companies: Excelerator, Gear for Sports.
Prominent Courses: Prairie Dunes, Wolf Creek.
State Golf Association: Kansas Golf Association, 3301 Clinton Parkway Court, Suite 4, Lawrence, KS 66047—(913) 842-4833

Highlights: Golf in Kansas dates back to the first decade of the century, with the Kansas Golf Association being formed in 1908. The construction of Prairie Dunes in 1937 gave Kansas a focus of state golfing pride and the course continues to be regarded as one of the all-time great national courses, and indeed has hosted several major national and international tournaments, notably the Women's Amateur, the Mid-Amateur and the Curtis Cup. Kansas has also hosted the U.S. Women's Open (1955), the Senior Amateur, the Women's Publinx, and both the Girls' Junior and the Junior Amateur. The Kansas City Open, first staged in 1949, also gave Kansas exposure on the PGA TOUR. Today, Kansas is home to the Wichita Charity Classic on the NIKE TOUR.

KENTUCKY

No. of Players (Rank): 315,000 (26)
No. of Rounds played (Rank): 9,292,500 (16)
Percentage of Female Players (Rank): 20.5 (24)
Percentage of Senior Golfers (Rank): 20.5 (35)
Prominent Golfers: Russ Cochrane, Brad Febal, Larry Gilbert, Jodie Mudd, Bobby Nichols, Kenny Perry, Joey Sindelar, Ted Schulz, DeWitt Weaver, Bob Wynn.
Major Golf Companies: H&B/Powerbilt.
Prominent Courses: Idle Hour, Louisville, Persimmon Ridge, Valhalla.
State Golf Association: Kentucky Golf Association, P.O. Box 20146, Louisville, KY 40250—(502) 499-7255

Highlights: Kentucky first hosted a national championship when Shawnee G.C. was the site of the 1932 Publinx—the Publinx returned in 1950 and the PGA Championship was played in Louisville in 1952, firmly establishing Kentucky as a championship golf state. While the Kentucky Derby Open faltered after a few years on the PGA TOUR calendar in the late 1950s, the Bluegrass Invitational was a fixture for years on the LPGA from the 1960s into the 1970s. Recently, Valhalla Golf Club reached the top-100 rankings, raising the possibility that high profile tournaments might be staged in Kentucky once again. At present, though, Kentucky's leading tournament is a date on the T.C. Jordan-Hooter's Tour.

LOUISIANA

No. of Players (Rank): 168,000 (33)
No. of Rounds played (Rank): 4,687,200 (30)
Percentage of Female Players (Rank): 15.8 (43)
Percentage of Senior Golfers (Rank): 21.3 (30)
Prominent Golfers: Miller Barber, Kelly Gibson, Jay Hebert, Lionel Hebert, Mike Heinen, Gary Koch, Tommy Moore, Deb Richard, Hal Sutton, Doug Tewell, Rocky Thompson, David Toms.
Major Golf Companies: River City Trading Co.
Prominent Courses: C.C. of Louisiana, English Turn, Oakbourne.
State Golf Association: Louisiana State Golf Association, 1305 Emerson Street, Monroe, LA 71201—(318) 342-1967.

Highlights: Louisiana has maintained a consistent presence on the PGA TOUR since the 1938 campaign via the Greater New Orleans Open (now known as the Freeport McMoRan Open). The tournament has always been well regarded but is especially so since moving to the Jack Nicklaus designed English Turn course, one of the most difficult on the TOUR, in addition to landing the coveted slot a week prior to the Masters, a date which ensures a quality field.

In addition to the annual PGA tournament, Louisiana has had LPGA tournaments (most prominently the Baton Rouge Ladies' Invitational in the mid-1960s) and the 1966 Senior Women's Amateur.

MAINE

No. of Players (Rank): 92,000 (45)
No. of Rounds played (Rank): 1,913,600 (42)
Percentage of Female Players (Rank): 22.6 (17)
Percentage of Senior Golfers (Rank): 29.7 (5)
Prominent Golfers: Laura Kean, David Peoples.
Prominent Courses: Sugarloaf, Portland.
State Golf Association: Maine State Golf Association, 40 Pierce Street, Gardiner, ME 04345—(207) 582-7130

Highlights: With a short summer golf season, Maine has had limited opportunities to stage tournaments and build resorts that bring national golfing attention to the state—nevertheless the 1978 Publinx was staged in Bangor at Bangor Municipal G.C.

MARYLAND

No. of Players (Rank): 370,000 (22)
No. of Rounds played (Rank): 7,696,000 (22)
Percentage of Female Players (Rank): 18.0 (34)
Percentage of Senior Golfers (Rank): 23.5 (15)
Prominent Golfers: Tina Barrett, Mark Carnevale, Fred Funk, Donnie Hammond, Katie Peterson-Parker, Mike Reid, Tina Barrett.
Major Golf Companies: Head Golf Co.
Prominent Courses: Baltimore - Five Farms, Congressional-Composite, Columbia, Burning Tree.
State Golf Association: Maryland State Golf Association, P.O. Box 16289, Baltimore, MD 21210.

Highlights: The Maryland State Golf Association was formed in 1921 and since then Maryland has hosted many national championships and tournaments, foremost among them the 1964 U.S. Open and 1976 PGA Championship at Congressional. Five Farms has been the site of both the Walker Cup and the 1988 U.S. Women's Open, while courses such as Burning Tree have some of the most exclusive membership lists in the country. In recent years both the Kemper Open and the LPGA Championship have been located in Maryland, and the Senior Open is scheduled to come to Congressional in 1995.

MASSACHUSETTS

No. of Players (Rank): 593,000 (14)
No. of Rounds played (Rank): 11,089,100 (12)
Percentage of Female Players (Rank): 15.7 (45)
Percentage of Senior Golfers (Rank): 24.8 (13)
Prominent Golfers: Billy Andrade, Paul Azinger, Michelle Bell, Pat Bradley, Fred Corcoran, Paul Harney, Meg Mallon, Francis Ouimet, Bob Toski, Richard Tufts.
Major Golf Companies: Acushnet, Dexter, Etonic, Reebok, Spalding, Textron.
Prominent Courses: Brae Burn, The Country Club, Kittansett, Myopia Hunt Club, Pleasant Valley, Salem.
State Golf Association: Massachusetts Golf Association, Golf House, 190 Park Road, Weston, MA 02193—(617) 891-4300

Highlights: Massachusetts played a critical role in the development of the game in the United States—with The Country Club in Brookline becoming a charter member of the United States Golf Association. Massachusetts clubs have subsequently hosted 41 national championships through the USGA, as well as numerous Tour events, PGA Championships, and the initial Ryder Cup match in 1927.

Massachusetts has hosted nine U.S. Opens beginning with the 1898 Open at Myopia Hunt Club. Perhaps the best-known of these was the 1913 Open where Francis Ouimet scored his historic upset over Harry Vardon and Ted Ray. Walter Hagen won the 1919 Open here and Bobby Jones the 1928 Amateur at Brae Burn.

Three Walker Cups and three Curtis Cups have been held in Massachusetts as well as nine Women's Amateurs. In addition the 1956 PGA Championship was held at Blue Hill in Canton.

The PGA TOUR has been represented in the state by the New England Classic, Kemper Open, and the Carling Open. Women's professional golf has maintained an even more consistent presence in the state—two U.S. Women's Opens (1954 and 1984) and seven LPGA Championships (1967-68, 1970-74), as well as regular tour events such as the Lady Carline, the Boston Five Classic, and the World Championship of Women's Golf.

In addition to tournament play, Massachusetts is notable in golf for the large concentration of major golf manufacturers in the state, notably Spalding and Acushnet.

MICHIGAN

No. of Players (Rank): 1,297,000 (6)
No. of Rounds played (Rank): 25,810,300 (6)
Percentage of Female Players (Rank): 27.9 (8)
Percentage of Senior Golfers (Rank): 23.4 (18)
Prominent Golfers: Mike Donald, Nolan Henke, Dave Hill, Mike Hill, Lon Hinkle, Ed Humenik, Debbie Massey, Calvin Peete, Dan Pohl, Chris Tschetter, Tom Wargo.
Major Golf Companies: Ball-o-Matic.
Prominent Courses: The Bear, Boyne Highlands-Composite, C.C. of Detroit, Crystal Downs, Grand Traverse, High Pointe, Indianwood, Oakland Hills (South), Point O'Woods, Shanty Creek, Treetops, Warwick Hills.
State Golf Association: Golf Association of Michigan, 37935 Twelve Mile Road, Suite 200, Farmington Hills, MI 48331—(313) 553-4200

Highlights: Despite its northern location, Michigan has the third highest number of golf courses of any state in the U.S., and has been a mainstay of both the professional tours and national championships since early in the century. The state has hosted 23 national championships since the Country Club of Detroit first hosted the Amateur in 1915, and five U.S. Opens and two U.S. Women's Opens have been played here to date between 1924 and 1989, as well as five PGA Championships and the 1956 LPGA Championship.

Oakland Hills, designed by Donald Ross, is considered the leading championship course, but fifteen other courses have hosted national championships to date. In addition, Michigan has hosted many PGA TOUR events dating back to the Western Open which was staged in Grand Rapids in 1904. The best known professional tournament today is the Buick Open, which dates back on the PGA TOUR to 1958, although the Motor City Open was a PGA TOUR event in the late 40s and early 50s. The LPGA arrived in Michigan with the Wolverine Open in 1955, and today stages the Oldsmobile Classic in Detroit. The Senior PGA TOUR also stops in Michigan, giving the state an unusually strong tournament line-up.

In recent years Michigan has grown significantly in stature as a golfing destination with the continuation of development of public and resort courses in the Boyne area in the north of the state. Complexes such as Grand Traverse have vaulted Michigan into the top five among golf vacation states, despite the short golfing season.

MINNESOTA

No. of Players (Rank): 711,000 (10)
No. of Rounds played (Rank): 9,740,700 (14)
Percentage of Female Players (Rank): 27.4 (9)
Percentage of Senior Golfers (Rank): 21.1 (32)

Prominent Golfers: Patty Berg, Jerilyn Britz, Lee Janzen, Howie Johnson, Tom Lehman, Mac O'Grady, Becky Pearson, Cindy Rarick, Karen Weiss.
Major Golf Companies: Munsingwear.
Prominent Courses: Hazeltine, Interlachen, Minikahda, Minneapolis, Rochester.
State Golf Association: Minnesota Golf Association, 6550 York Avenue South, Suite 405, Edina, MN 55435-2383—(612) 927-4643

Highlights: Enthusiasm for golf has been strong and consistent through the years since the first course—Town & Country Club—opened for play in 1888 as the first golf course west of the Mississippi. Today Minnesota has over 400 courses and the highest number of golfers per capita of any state in the Union.

The state has hosted 27 national championships to date, the eighth largest number among all the states. Four U.S. Opens have been staged here, including the 1930 Open that was the first leg of Bobby Jones' Grand Slam, as well as two U.S. Women's Opens and two Walker Cups. The first national championship staged in the state was the 1916 Open and the most recent was the 1993 Walker Cup and the 1993 Women's Mid-Amateur. Minnesota has also played host to three PGA Championships, the most recent in 1959.

The professional tours have frequently staged tournaments in Minnesota, dating back to the 1914 Western Open at Interlachen, although there has not been a regular PGA TOUR stop in Minnesota since the demise of the Minnesota Classic after the 1969 season. The LPGA arrived with the American Women's Open in 1958 and continues today with the Minnesota LPGA Classic.

Minnesota is not a major player in the golf manufacturing economy, but the revenues generated by the daily fee golfers and private clubs, as well as by the small but vibrant group of in-state resorts, makes Minnesota a key state in the national golf economy.

MISSISSIPPI

No. of Players (Rank): 127,000 (37)
No. of Rounds played (Rank): 2,565,400 (38)
Percentage of Female Players (Rank): 17.0 (41)
Percentage of Senior Golfers (Rank): 22.8 (22)
Prominent Golfers: J.R. Richardson.
Prominent Courses: Annandale, Laurel, Hattiesburg, Old Waverly.
State Golf Association: Mississippi Golf Association, P.O. Box 684, 515 Central Avenue, Laurel, MS 39441—(601) 649-0570

Highlights: Mississippi golf dates back to the early part of the century with the construction of the Laurel Country Club in 1917 from a design by Seymour Dunn. The Mississippi Golf Association was formed in 1925 and in the early days of the PGA Circuit Mississippi played a somewhat prominent role due to the warm winters providing good weather for winter tournaments. The Gulfport Open was staged on the TOUR as early as 1946. During the late 1960s the PGA TOUR experimented with satellite events—non-official tournaments that would be staged the same week as limited-field events such as the Tournament of Champions and the Masters, and Mississippi's Magnolia State Classic was born. After years of non-official status, it became an official PGA TOUR event in 1994. The USGA staged the Mid-Amateur at the same course, Annandale, in 1986, which to date has been Mississippi's lone national championship.

With the expansion of gambling and resort development in the Gulfport and Biloxi areas on the coastline, Mississippi seems poised for considerable golf expansion in the late 1990s.

MISSOURI

No. of Players (Rank): 545,000 (15)
No. of Rounds played (Rank): 9,537,500 (15)
Percentage of Female Players (Rank): 20.5 (24)
Percentage of Senior Golfers (Rank): 19.3 (38)
Prominent Golfers: Jay Delsing, David Edwards, Robin Freeman, Jay Haas, Hale Irwin, Jeff Maggert, Judy Rankin, Horton Smith, Payne Stewart, Tom Watson, Larry Ziegler.
Major Golf Companies: Intec Laboratories.
Prominent Courses: Bellerive, Old Warson, St. Joseph, St. Louis.
State Golf Association: Missouri Golf Association, P.O. Box 104164, Jefferson City, MO 65110—(314) 636-4225

Highlights: Missouri was one of the first states west of the Appalachians to embrace golf, with the 1904 Olympic Games in St. Louis featuring golf on the program, and the 1908 Western Open played in St. Louis as well. The first national championship staged in the state was the 1921 Amateur, followed by the 1925 Women's Amateur. The St. Louis Country Club hosted the 1947 U.S. Open, which was the first ever televised, and the Open returned to the state in 1965 where Gary Player completed his career Grand Slam. In addition the 1948 and 1992 PGA Championships were played here, and the 1971 Ryder Cup matches were played at Old Warson.

After hosting the 1938 Western Open, St. Louis acquired a PGA TOUR stop of its own in 1950, but today Missouri is host to the Southwestern Bell Classic in Kansas City and a NIKE TOUR event, the Greater Ozarks Open.

MONTANA

No. of Players (Rank): 98,000 (42)
No. of Rounds played (Rank): 1,617,000 (45)
Percentage of Female Players (Rank): 38.5 (1)
Percentage of Senior Golfers (Rank): 16.1 (46)
Prominent Golfers: Bob Betley, Alice Ritzman.
Major Golf Companies: Sun Mountain Sports.
Prominent Courses: Briarwood, Buffalo Hill, Eagle Bend.
State Golf Association: Montana State Golf Association, P.O. Box 3389, Butte, MT 59701—(406) 782-9208.

Highlights: Due to a short golfing season and a small resident population, Montana has lacked the essentials for a vibrant national golfing presence, but in recent years there have been some very good courses built, such as Eagle Bend, which in 1994 hosted Montana's first-ever national championship, the Publinx. Montana combines low green fees and spectacular scenery around its courses, and the state has thus one of the highest per-capita participation rates for golf in the country, despite the short golf season.

NEBRASKA

No. of Players (Rank): 228,000 (31)
No. of Rounds played (Rank): 4,240,800 (31)
Percentage of Female Players (Rank): 16 (6)
Percentage of Senior Golfers (Rank): 29 (29)
Prominent Golfers: Mark Calcavecchia, Tom Sieckmann, Val Skinner.
Prominent Courses: Firethorn, Happy Hollow, Highland, Sandhills.
State Golf Association: Nebraska Golf Association, 6001 South 72nd Street, Lincoln, NE 68516—(402) 486-1440

Highlights: Recent golf course openings such as Firethorn and the much-awaited opening of Crenshaw and Coore's Sandhills complex have considerably raised Nebraska's profile in golfdom. Prior to the 1990s, Nebraska has hosted the occasional tournament, such as the 1941 U.S. Amateur at Omaha Field Club, but the professional tours and the major championships have eluded the state.

NEVADA

No. of Players (Rank): 150,000 (35)
No. of Rounds played (Rank): 2,970,000 (34)
Percentage of Female Players (Rank): 22.0 (20)

Percentage of Senior Golfers (Rank): 28.8 (6)
Prominent Golfers: Robert Gamez, Deborah McHaffie.
Major Golf Companies: Carsonite International.
Prominent Courses: Desert Inn, Edgewood Tahoe, Las Vegas, Shadow Creek.
State Golf Association: Nevada State Golf Association, P.O. Box 5630, Sparks, NV 89432—(702) 673-4653

Highlights: Nevada's intimate involvement with golf stems from the Tournament of Champions which was first staged as a PGA TOUR event in 1953 and offered at the time the second-highest purse on the Tour. The tournament stayed in Las Vegas at the Desert Inn through 1966, decamped for two years to the Stardust Country Club, and subsequently moved to California.

By the 1980s, however, Nevada's profile as a golf state had increased considerably, as the result of population growth, the construction of top-ranked courses such as the Edgewood Tahoe in the north and the TPC at Summerlin near Las Vegas, plus the addition of Senior PGA TOUR and LPGA events to the golf calendar. Nevada hosted the 1980 Publinx at the Edgewood Tahoe and in 1985 hosted the U.S. Senior Open.

Nevada was in the news during the 1990s when Chip Beck tied the all-time 18-hole record with a 59 in the 1991 Las Vegas Invitational—and also for the awarding of a top-10 ranking to the brand-new Tom Fazio course at Shadow Creek.

NEW HAMPSHIRE

No. of Players (Rank): 110,000 (40)
No. of Rounds played (Rank): 1,727,000 (43)
Percentage of Female Players (Rank): 29.1 (6)
Percentage of Senior Golfers (Rank): 18.4 (41)
Prominent Golfers: Jane Blalock.
Prominent Courses: Manchester, Portsmouth.
State Golf Association: New Hampshire Golf Association, 45 Kearney Street, Manchester, NH 03104—(603) 623-0396

Highlights: A short playing season and a limited base of golfers has prevented New Hampshire from achieving status as a major golf state, but nevertheless there are several very scenic courses, such as the Balsams Grand Hotel and the Mount Washington Hotel, which draw a number of visitors northward.

NEW JERSEY

No. of Players (Rank): 657,000 (11)
No. of Rounds played (Rank): 12,088,800 (10)

Percentage of Female Players (Rank): 17.4 (38)
Percentage of Senior Golfers (Rank): 25.7 (11)
Prominent Golfers: Jim Colbert, Brad Faxon, Jim McGovern, Karen Noble, Walt Zembriski.
Major Golf Companies: Le Coq Sportif, United States Golf Association.
Prominent Courses: Baltusrol-Lower, Baltusrol-Upper, Pine Valley, Plainview, Ridgewood (East & West), Somerset Hills.
State Golf Association: New Jersey State Golf Association, 1000 Broad Street, Bloomfield, NJ 07003—(201) 338-8334

Highlights: New Jersey has played an integral role in American golf since before the turn of the century, hosting the Women's Amateur in 1896, the Amateur in 1898, and staging its first U.S. Open at Baltusrol in 1903. The state is tiny in area but large in the number of courses—over 250—and 16 of those courses have hosted 45 national championships to date including eight U.S. Opens. Seven of those Opens were held at Baltusrol, the latest in 1993 won by Lee Janzen.

In addition, New Jersey played host to the 1942 PGA Championship and the 1935 Ryder Cup matches at Ridgewood Country Club.

Despite Baltusrol's seven U.S. Opens, the most revered course in the state is in fact Pine Valley, in Clementon, widely regarded as the finest golf course ever built. The course has never hosted a major tournament except for the Walker Cup (in 1936 and 1985), but it is consistently ranked number one by the leading golf publications.

New Jersey has hosted professional tournaments since the early days of the PGA Circuit, from the Atlantic City Open of the 1940s to the Shoprite LPGA Classic today. New Jersey is also home to a first-class golf resort in the Marriott Seaview. Golfers in the Garden State also take advantage of the United States Golf Association's Golf Museum, featuring regular and special exhibits.

NEW MEXICO

No. of Players (Rank): 154,000 (34)
No. of Rounds played (Rank): 2,802,800 (36)
Percentage of Female Players (Rank): 18.6 (31)
Percentage of Senior Golfers (Rank): 27.4 (9)
Prominent Golfers: Ronnie Black, Steve Jones.
Major Golf Companies: New Mexico State University golf management program, Resortowels.
Prominent Courses: Inn of the Mountain Gods, Picacho Hills.
State Golf Association: Sun Country Amateur Golf Association, 10035 Country Club Lane NW, Suite 5, Albuquerque, NM 87114—(505)

897-0864

Highlights: New Mexico is home to only 88 golf courses and has yet to host a national championship event, but it is home to several very testing courses including the Inn of the Mountain Gods resort. Albuquerque briefly had a PGA TOUR stop in the late 1940s, and had an LPGA event in the early 1960s known as Bill Brannin's Swing Parade, the Albuquerque Swing Parade, and finally as the Albuquerque Professional Amateur. In recent years noted designers such as Jack Nicklaus have been active in the state, raising the possibility that the professional tours will return.

NEW YORK

No. of Players (Rank): 1,703,200 (2)
No. of Rounds played (Rank): 29,802,500 (5)
Percentage of Female Players (Rank): 22.7 (16)
Percentage of Senior Golfers (Rank): 25.7 (11)
Prominent Golfers: Jim Albus, Danielle Ammaccapane, George Burns, Jane Geddes, Dudley Hart, Walter Hagen, Mike Hulbert, Brian Kamm, Larry Laoretti, Wayne Levi, Dottie Mochrie, Bob Murphy, Gene Sarazen, Jeff Sluman, Jerome Travers.
Major Golf Companies: Adrienne Vittadini, Bobby Jones, Quantum, Titleist by Corbin.
Prominent Courses: Bethpage (Black), Concord Hotel, Fishers Island, Garden City, Maidstone, National Golf Links of America, Oak Hill, Quaker Ridge, Shinnecock Hills, Westchester (West), Winged Foot (East), Winged Foot (West).
State Golf Association: New York State Golf Association, P.O. Box 3459, Elmira, NY 14905—(607) 733-0007

Highlights: New York was the site of the first 18-hole golf course, St. Andrews, and provided the bulk of the founding membership of the United States Golf Association; therefore, it would be fair to dub the state "The Cradle of American Golf." New York has been home to 54 national championships to date plus nine PGA Championships and, in 1995, its first Ryder Cup (at Oak Hill). Oak Hill, Winged Foot, and Shinnecock Hills are considered a firm part of the Open rota and a total of 13 U.S. Opens have been staged here beginning in 1896 and continuing through 1989 (again at Oak Hill).

Many PGA, LPGA and Senior PGA events have been held in New York over the years, of which perhaps the Buick Classic (formerly the Westchester Classic) is the best known. New York's connection with the PGA TOUR goes back before the Second

World War, to the Rochester Times-Union Open. The LPGA had a New York date on the calendar in its first season and continues today with the JAL/Big Apple Classic.

New York is home to some of the most revered public and resort courses in the country, principally Bethpage on Long Island and En-Joie and the Concord Hotel in the Catskills. But it is the private clubs such as Shinnecock, National Golf Links, and Garden City on Long Island, plus Winged Foot and Quaker Ridge in Westchester and Oak Hill in Rochester that have secured New York its place in history. Laurie Auchterlonie, Bobby Jones, and Gene Sarazen are among the winners of U.S. Opens in New York, along with Walter Hagen, Tommy Armour, and Jack Nicklaus in the PGA Championship.

NORTH CAROLINA

No. of Players (Rank): 625,000 (12)
No. of Rounds played (Rank): 16,187,500 (9)
Percentage of Female Players (Rank): 15.8 (43)
Percentage of Senior Golfers (Rank): 22.7 (24)
Prominent Golfers: Chip Beck, Lennie Clements, Jim Ferree, Raymond Floyd, Scott Hoch, John Inman, Neal Lancaster, Davis Love III, Mark O'Meara, Charlie Sifford, Leonard Thompson, Jim Thorpe.
Major Golf Companies: Cross Creek, Golf Pride, Kangaroo Motorcaddies.
Prominent Courses: Cape Fear, Champion Hills, Charlotte, C.C. of North Carolina, Elk River, Grandfather Mountain, Linville Ridge, Mid Pines, Mt. Mitchell, Nags Head, Oyster Bay, Pinehurst (No. 2), Pinehurst (No. 5), Pinehurst (No. 6), Pinehurst (No. 7), Pine Needles, The Pit, Tanglewood, Wade Hampton.
State Golf Association: Carolinas Golf Association, P.O. Box 428, West End, NC 27376—(919) 673-1000

Highlights: North Carolina is central to the American golf story because of the village known as Pinehurst, the American alternative to St. Andrews, and the impact that the Pinehurst development and its employees and owners have had on American golf.

Pinehurst was founded as a health resort, but added golf in 1900 and hired Donald Ross as greenkeeper and professional. Ross' design work included five courses at Pinehurst, including the famed No. 2 course, and he took on additional work originally in the Pinehurst area but eventually across the entire United States, contributing greatly to the Golden Age of course architecture of the 1920s and 1930s. Pinehurst has hosted the Ryder Cup, the Amateur, the

Women's Amateur, the Eisenhower Trophy, the Women's World Amateur, the World Senior Amateur, the PGA Championship, the TOUR Championship, and in 1999 will host the United States Open for the first time, making it perhaps the most widely employed course in the United States for championship golf. In addition to national championships, Pinehurst was the host of the North and South Open, one of the earliest annual professional tournaments and one which provided the season finale in the earliest days of the PGA Circuit. The North and South Amateur is still played today and is one of the most prestigious amateur events.

The success of Pinehurst spawned a tremendous amount of quality golf development in North Carolina over the years, and five other courses to date have hosted national championships beginning with the 1955 Women's Amateur at Myers Park and continuing through the 1995 U.S. Women's Open at Pine Needles.

In addition to a host of national and world events, North Carolina has been home to a great number of touring professional events owing to the state's mild winters and convenience to both northern and southern states. The K-Mart Greater Greensboro Open, for instance, dates back to 1938, and at one point in the early 1940s North Carolina hosted four PGA TOUR tournaments. The LPGA had its first tournament in state in 1957 and the Senior PGA TOUR is playing annually at Piper Glen.

In addition to coastal communities and the Pinehurst-Raleigh-Durham triangle, North Carolina features a number of private and resort courses in the Great Smoky Mountains near Asheville that are hugely popular with both southerners and northerners—chief among these are Grandfather Mountain and Wade Hampton Golf Club.

NORTH DAKOTA

No. of Players (Rank): 97,000 (43)
No. of Rounds played (Rank): 1,649,000 (44)
Percentage of Female Players (Rank): 30.8 (4)
Percentage of Senior Golfers (Rank): 27.9 (7)
Prominent Golfers: Pat McGowan.
Prominent Courses: Fargo, Minot.
State Golf Association: North Dakota Golf Association, P.O. Box 452, Bismark, ND 58502—(701) 255-0242.
Highlights: North Dakota ranks third in the nation in golfers per capita population—rates are low and land is plentiful. But North Dakota has been hampered by a tiny population base and major championship or touring professional golf has eluded the state entirely.

OHIO

No. of Players (Rank): 1,367,000 (5)
No. of Rounds played (Rank): 26,793,200 (5)
Percentage of Female Players (Rank): 22.6 (17)
Percentage of Senior Golfers (Rank): 20.1 (36)
Prominent Golfers: Gay Brewer, John Cook, Marty Dickerson, Judy Dickinson, Dow Finsterwald, Robert Lohr, Dick Mast, Jack Nicklaus, Muffin Spencer-Devlin, Tom Weiskopf.
Major Golf Companies: The Golfworks, Medicus, Ryobi-Toski.
Prominent Courses: Camargo, Canterbury, Coldstream, The Country Club, Double Eagle, Firestone-South, Firestone-North, The Golf Club, Inverness, Muirfield Village, NCR-South, Ohio State Univ. (Scarlet), Scioto, Shaker Run.
State Golf Association: Northern Ohio Golf Association, 17800 Chillicothe Road, Suite 210, Chagrin Falls, OH—(216) 543-6320; Toledo District Golf Association, P.O. Box 6313, Toledo, OH 43614—(419) 866-4771; The Greater Cincinatti Golf Association, P.O. Box 317825, Cincinatti, OH 45231—(513) 522-5780; Columbus District Golf Association, 437 Pamlico, Columbus, OH 43228—(614) 274-5441

Highlights: Ohio first leapt into national prominence as early as 1902 when the Euclid Club hosted the Western Open (the U.S. Amateur followed five years later), but the state's reputation was significantly bolstered after the First World War, when courses such as Inverness and Scioto hosted U.S. Opens and the Western Open made several stops in the state. The addition of Canterbury to the Open rota in the 1940s added considerably to the state's luster, but it was the building of the golf complexes at Firestone and Muirfield Village in the 1950s and 1970s that firmly established Ohio as one of the handful of leading golf states.

29 national championships to date have been played in Ohio as well as nine PGA Championships and the 1931 and 1987 Ryder Cup matches. In addition, quasi-majors The Memorial and the World Series of Golf are annual PGA TOUR stops, and the LPGA Championship was held four consecutive years in Ohio in the mid 1980s.

Ohio native Jack Nicklaus is still closely associated with the state through Muirfield Village and the Jack Nicklaus golf complex at Kings Island. Pete Dye's work was also seen here quite early in his career, as was Donald Ross'—and thus Ohio is also quite a showcase for golf course architecture.

In addition to the World Series and the Memorial,

Ohio is also home to annual events on the Senior PGA TOUR and the LPGA Tour, as well as the NIKE TOUR.

OKLAHOMA

No. of Players (Rank): 276,000 (29)
No. of Rounds played (Rank): 6,624,000 (25)
Percentage of Female Players (Rank): 21.8 (21)
Percentage of Senior Golfers (Rank): 20.6 (34)
Prominent Golfers: John Adams, Tommy Bolt, Bob Dickson, Dale Douglass, Bill Glasson, Mark Hayes, Gil Morgan, Orville Moody, Ron Streck, Bob Tway.
Major Golf Companies: Swingtrac.
Prominent Courses: Cedar Ridge, Muskogee, Oak Tree, G.C. of Oklahoma, Southern Hills, Twin Hills.
State Golf Association: Oklahoma Golf Association, P.O. Box 449, Enid, OK 73083—(405) 340-6333.

Highlights: Oklahoma is rarely on the short list of great golfing states, but in fact the state has hosted 15 national championships including three U.S. Opens, four PGA Championships, has several top-ranked courses and a long list of native Oklahomans who have gone on to great success in the professional ranks.

Perry Maxwell is the architect most closely associated with the state, beginning with Dornick Hills in 1919 and going on to design both Twin Hills and Southern Hills. Twin Hills hosted the state's first PGA Championship in 1935.

After the Second World War Southern Hills became the best-known course in the state and it was the site of the 1958 Open, the 1970 PGA Championship, the 1977 Open, and the PGA Championship again in 1982 and 1994. Oak Tree, a Pete Dye design, has also hosted the 1984 Amateur and the 1988 PGA Championship. The PGA TOUR stopped in Tulsa as early as 1945, but has been absent most years with the major exception being the Oklahoma City Open played in the early 1960s.

OREGON

No. of Players (Rank): 321,000 (25)
No. of Rounds played (Rank): 5,778,000 (27)
Percentage of Female Players (Rank): 26.4 (11)
Percentage of Senior Golfers (Rank): 22.5 (25)
Prominent Golfers: Bob Gilder, Fred Haas, Peter Jacobsen, Susan Sanders, Mark Wiebe.
Major Golf Companies: Nike.
Prominent Courses: Columbia-Edgewater, Eugene, Pumpkin Ridge, Salishan, Sunriver, Waverly.

State Golf Association: 8364 S.W. Nimbus Avenue, Beaverton, OR 97005—(503) 643-2610.

Highlights: Oregon had a limited exposure as a golfing state prior to the Second World War because of the time involved in traveling to the state. Nevertheless the 1933 Publinx and the 1937 Amateur were held in Oregon.

The war years were crucial to Oregon golf because the key role played in the war by the West Coast port cities put Portland in a position to stage golf tournaments like never before. In 1944 Portland had its first PGA TOUR event; in 1946 the city hosted the PGA Championship; in 1947 Oregonians made perhaps their most important contribution to golf by rescuing the Ryder Cup from its WWII hiatus, staging the matches in Portland and going considerable lengths to aid the British team in making the voyage to the West Coast. But by the late 1950s Oregon had slid back into the second rank of golfing states.

In recent years, however, Oregon has been undergoing a renaissance based on the development of new resorts areas such as Sunriver, and building new metropolitan golf clubs of the first rank such as the Oregon Golf Club and Pumpkin Ridge. Interest in Oregon has been renewed, with the Mid-Amateur and the Junior Amateur both staged in the state in 1993, and with Pumpkin Ridge considered to have an inside track to hosting the PGA Championship and the U.S. Open in the future.

PENNSYLVANIA

No. of Players (Rank): 1,122,000 (8)
No. of Rounds played (Rank): 21,430,200 (8)
Percentage of Female Players (Rank): 17.6 (37)
Percentage of Senior Golfers (Rank): 21.2 (31)
Prominent Golfers: Missie Bertiotti, Jim Furyk, Jim Gallagher Jr., Betsy King, Rocco Mediate, Arnold Palmer, Jay Sigel, Mike Souchak, Ted Tryba, Art Wall Jr.
Major Golf Companies: Adidas, Izod, Aureus/Aurea.
Prominent Courses: Aronimink, Hershey, Kahkwa, Laurel Valley, Merion-East, Moselem Springs, Oakmont, Philadelphia, Philadelphia Cricket Club, Rolling Green, Saucon Valley-Grace.
State Golf Association: Pennsylvania Golf Association, 700 Croton Road, Wayne, PA 19087—(215) 687-2340

Highlights: Pennsylvania, along with Massachusetts, Illinois, New Jersey and New York, was the site of some of the earliest organized golf in the Union, with a rich golf history stretching back into the 19th century and 63 national championships completed here beginning in 1904.

Some of the earliest of the great American golf courses were built in the state with the help of amateur golf architects—including Oakmont, Merion and Philadelphia Cricket Club. The U.S. Open was first staged in Pennsylvania in 1907, and a total of 14 Opens and nine PGA Championships have been played here in total, including seven Opens at Oakmont alone. The first PGA Championship was played at Oakmont in 1922. Bobby Jones, incidentally, completed his Grand Slam in the U.S. Amateur at Merion in 1930.

In addition to USGA-conducted national events, Pennsylvania has hosted a number of international events including the 1960 Eisenhower Trophy and 1954 Curtis Cup at Merion, and the 1975 Ryder Cup matches at Laurel Valley.

In professional tour events, the Hershey Open was the first PGA TOUR event sponsored by a corporation, and Pennsylvania has hosted at least one tournament annually from the late 1930s until the early 1980s. The state is not currently home to a PGA TOUR event but hosts several Senior PGA TOUR and LPGA events.

Today, Pennsylvania is home to over 600 courses and remains one of the largest bases for American golf, both at the public-golf level and at the championship level with five of Golf Digest's top-100 ranked courses within state borders.

RHODE ISLAND
and Providence Plantations

No. of Players (Rank): 106,000 (41)
No. of Rounds played (Rank): 2,618,200 (37)
Percentage of Female Players (Rank): 19.2 (30)
Percentage of Senior Golfers (Rank): 21.6 (29)
Prominent Golfers: Bob Eastwood, P.H. Horgan III, Ed Kirby, Lawson Little.
Prominent Courses: Newport, Rhode Island, Wannamoisett.
State Golf Association: Rhode Island Golf Association, 10 Orms Street, Suite 326, Providence, Rhode Island 02904—(401) 272-1350

Highlights: The tiny state of Rhode Island has a small base of golfers and golf courses—just 40 in all—but a history closely intertwined with golf ever since the first U.S. Open was played at Newport Country Club in 1895. The Amateur was also played at Newport that year and Newport will host the Amateur in 1995 to celebrate the centennial of the event and the USGA.

A large percentage of Rhode Island's courses were designed by famed architect Donald Ross, owing to the fact that Ross had his summer house in Rhode Island—the Women's Amateur has been played three times at his Rhode Island Country Club, and his Wannamoisett hosts a prestigious amateur event, the Northeast Amateur Invitational as well as the 1931 PGA Championship.

Rhode Island has hosted several tour events over the years dating back to the Providence Open in 1948. Most recently the state hosted the PGA Senior TOUR's Newport Cup through the 1992 season.

SOUTH CAROLINA

No. of Players (Rank): 329,000 (24)
No. of Rounds played (Rank): 8,586,900 (18)
Percentage of Female Players (Rank): 20.2 (25)
Percentage of Senior Golfers (Rank): 30.4 (3)
Prominent Golfers: Beth Daniel, Dillard Pruitt, Betsy Rawls.
Major Golf Companies: Maxfli, Slazenger, Zett Golf.
Prominent Courses: Callawassie, Colleton River, Dataw Island, Dunes, Greenville, Haig Point, Harbour Town, Kiawah-Ocean, Kiawah (Turtle Point), The Legends-Moorland, Long Bay, Long Cove, Old Tabby, Tidewater, Wild Dunes.
State Golf Association: South Carolina Golf Association, 145 Birdsong Trail, Chapin, SC 29036—(803) 781-6992

Highlights: South Carolina was home to the first chartered golf club in the Western Hemisphere, the South Carolina Golf Club at Harleston Green which was organized in the late 18th century and continued for several years.

Golf was reinstituted in the state at the turn of the century, but golf did not achieve its present prominence until after the Second World War and the expansion of major resorts such as Myrtle Beach and Hilton Head Island. Florence Country Club hosted the Girls Junior Amateur in 1955 and the LPGA's Peach Blossom Invitational was held in the western part of the state during the early 1960s, but it was the PGA TOUR's Heritage Tournament on Hilton Head Island, and the golf explosion at Myrtle Beach that put South Carolina on the national map. Hilton Head hosted the Senior Amateur in 1974 and Myrtle Beach the U.S. Women's Open in 1962 and the LPGA Championship in 1977. Subsequently Harbour Town has hosted the Nabisco Championships (now the TOUR Championship), while Kiawah Island hosted the famous 1991 "War by the Shore" in the Ryder Cup matches that year. Various PGA TOUR, Senior PGA TOUR and LPGA events have been played in the state during the 1980s and 1990s, notably the Heritage, the Wendy's

Three Tour Challenge, and the Hilton Head Seniors International. The Dunes Club in Myrtle Beach is scheduled to host the Senior TOUR Championship for several years beginning in 1994.

In addition to the various championship events, South Carolina is now considered one of the leading golf destination states in the country, with extensive golf offerings in the Charleston, Hilton Head Island, and Myrtle Beach areas. In addition, the state has become a major center for golf-oriented planned communities.

SOUTH DAKOTA

No. of Players (Rank): 93,000 (44)
No. of Rounds played (Rank): 1,980,900 (41)
Percentage of Female Players (Rank): 33.4 (2)
Percentage of Senior Golfers (Rank): 12.4 (48)
Prominent Golfers: Curt Byrum, Tom Byrum, Marlene Hagge.
Prominent Courses: Dakota Dunes, Meadowbrook, Minnehaha.
State Golf Association: South Dakota Golf Association, 509 South Holt, Sioux Falls, SD 57103—(605) 338-7499

Highlights: South Dakota hosted its first national championship in 1984 when Meadowbrook in Rapid City played host to the Women's Publinx. Subsequently South Dakota has become home to a NIKE TOUR event, the Dakota Dunes Open, and the future looks promising for the state after many years without major golf events on the calendar.

TENNESSEE

No. of Players (Rank): 299,000 (27)
No. of Rounds played (Rank): 8,043,100 (19)
Percentage of Female Players (Rank): 12.9 (47)
Percentage of Senior Golfers (Rank): 23.1 (19)
Prominent Golfers: Bruce Fleisher, Gibby Gilbert, Lou Graham, Cary Middlecoff.
Major Golf Companies: Johnston & Murphy.
Prominent Courses: Belle Meade, The Honors Course, Memphis, Richland.
State Golf Association: Tennessee G.A., 4711 Trousdale Drive, Nashville, TN 37220—(615) 833-9689
Highlights: Tennessee first reached the mainstream as a golfing state in the late 1930s when Memphis Country Club hosted the Women's Amateur in 1937. Subsequently the state hosted the PGA TOUR in several stops in the early years of the TOUR, beginning with the Knoxville War Bond and the Nashville Open as early as 1944, and including the Memphis Invitational and the Memphis Open along the way.

The LPGA followed suit in the late 1950s with a Memphis Open of its own. National Championships continued to return with the Amateur in 1948, the Senior Amateur in 1955 and 1959, the Women's Amateur in 1979 and the U.S. Women's Open at Richland Country Club in 1980. In the past decade, the LPGA's Sara Lee Classic has been played in the state, along with the FedEx-St. Jude Classic on the PGA TOUR. Tennessee has become the home of one of the most highly-regarded courses in the country with the construction of The Honors Course in the early 1980s, from a Pete Dye design, and the course hosted the Amateur in 1991; recently the PGA TOUR-developed TPC at Southwind was constructed in Memphis.

TEXAS

No. of Players (Rank): 1,402,000 (4)
No. of Rounds played (Rank): 31,965,600 (3)
Percentage of Female Players (Rank): 18.3 (33)
Percentage of Senior Golfers (Rank): 18.8 (39)
Prominent Golfers: Frank Beard, Homero Blancas, Ben Crenshaw, Charles Coody, Jimmy Demaret, Lee Elder, Ralph Guldahl, Sandra Haynie, Ben Hogan, Don January, Tom Kite, John Mahaffey, Byron Nelson, Sandra Palmer, Lee Trevino, Scott Verplank, Kathy Whitworth, Babe Zaharias.
Major Golf Companies: American Ball Manufacturing Corp., Hogan, Nitro, Pro-Gear, Sahara, Tempo, Texace, Wood Brothers.
Prominent Courses: Austin, Barton Creek, Champions (Cypress Creek), Colonial, Homestead Bay, TPC at Las Colinas, TPC at The Woodlands.
State Golf Association: Dallas District Golf Association, 4321 Live Oak, Dallas, TX 75204—(214) 823-6004; Houston Golf Association, 1830 South Millbend Drive, The Woodlands, TX 77830—(713) 367-7999; San Antonio Golf Association, 70 N.E. Loop 410, Suite 370, San Antonio, TX 78216—(512) 341-0823

Highlights: Texas, along with California and Florida, was one of the hotbeds of professional golf, and from the late 1910s has been one of the major centers of the game. The Texas Open is, next to the Western Open, the oldest PGA TOUR event with a history that stretches back into the Golden Age of golf in the 1920s, with winners such as Walter Hagen and Mac Smith on the victory roll. The PGA Championship arrived as early as 1927, when Hagen recorded his fourth consecutive win, and the U.S. Open was played at the brand-new Colonial C.C. in 1941. Colonial subsequently became the host site of the prestigious Colonial Invitational on the PGA TOUR, while Texas continued to add tournaments until today eight PGA, LPGA, and Senior PGA TOUR events are played in the Lone Star State.

National championships were plentiful in Texas during the 1960s, with two PGA Championships and the 1969 U.S. Open. Weather conditions have subsequently hampered efforts to bring the majors to Texas. But in the last decade the 1991 U.S. Women's Open was played at Colonial and the 1993 Amateur at Champions. In addition, Texas hosted the 1967 Ryder Cup matches, the 1975 TPC, and the 1986-87 TOUR Championship (then known as the Nabisco Championships).

In addition to hosting numerous distinguished tournaments, Texas is known as a state that has for several generations produced many of golf's greatest players on the extensive collection of municipal courses, as well as several of the best-known golf writers and broadcasters. The state is also known increasingly as a golf resort destination since the construction of the Las Colinas complex, as well as The Woodlands and Barton Creek.

UTAH

No. of Players (Rank): 243,000 (30)
No. of Rounds played (Rank): 3,353,400 (33)
Percentage of Female Players (Rank): 22.2 (19)
Percentage of Senior Golfers (Rank): 18.3 (42)
Prominent Golfers: Jay Don Blake.
Major Golf Companies: Carbon Fiber.
Prominent Courses: Park Meadows, The Country Club.
State Golf Association: Utah Golf Association, 1512 South 1100 East, Salt Lake City, UT 84105—(801) 299-8421

Highlights: Utah has not promoted itself as a leading golf state—nevertheless there are several outstanding courses and resorts and not a little golf history. There have been no national championships staged in the state, but Utah did have a PGA TOUR event as early as the 1948 Utah Open, which did not survive but was briefly revived in the late 1950s and early 1960s. The Salt Lake City Open was also briefly played on the LPGA Tour in the early 1960s. In recent years Utah has been known more for a Senior PGA TOUR event played at the Park Meadows complex, and a NIKE TOUR event.

VERMONT

No. of Players (Rank): 42,000 (48)
No. of Rounds played (Rank): 978,600 (47)
Percentage of Female Players (Rank): 16.2 (42)
Percentage of Senior Golfers (Rank): 23.7 (14)

Prominent Golfers: Patty Sheehan.
Major Golf Companies: Bogner of America.
Prominent Courses: Ekwanok, Rutland.
State Golf Association: Vermont Golf Association, P.O. Box 1612, Station A, Rutland, VT 05701—(802) 773-7180

Highlights: Vermont's involvement with golf on a national scale dates back to the 1914 Amateur which was played at Ekwanok, and which provided Francis Ouimet with a worthy follow-up to his triumph in the 1913 U.S. Open. Subsequently, Vermont has not been able to maintain a high profile due to the short summer golf season and the small number of local golfers, but the state has an excellent resort at Stratton Mountain which is the host of an LPGA event, the McCall's LPGA Classic.

VIRGINIA

No. of Players (Rank): 520,000 (17)
No. of Rounds played (Rank): 11,284,000 (11)
Percentage of Female Players (Rank): 17.1 (39)
Percentage of Senior Golfers (Rank): 22.1 (27)
Prominent Golfers: Donna Andrews, Joe Dey, Page Dunlap, Vinny Giles, Bill Kratzert, Kathy Postlewait, J.C. Snead, Sam Snead, Ed Snead, Curtis Strange, Bobby Wadkins, Lanny Wadkins, Robert Wrenn.
Major Golf Companies: Hi Tech Golf.
Prominent Courses: C.C. of Virginia, Cascades, Golden Horseshoe-Gold, The Homestead, Kingsmill, Lower Cascades, Robert Trent Jones.
State Golf Association: Virginia State Golf Association, 830 Southlake Boulevard, Suite A, Richmond, VA 23236—(804) 378-2300

Highlights: The Oakhurst Golf Club, built in 1884, represented the first identifiable golf course built in the United States. The course is currently undergoing restoration, but the next instances of golf occur in the western part of the state where the Virginia Hot Springs G.C. was built—the first tee there, built in the early 1890s, remains open today and is the oldest tee in continuous use in the Union.

Despite these early golfing roots, Virginia found itself outside the mainstream of golf development—both the Amateur game which was centered on the Northeast and Midwest, and the professional game which centered on Florida, Texas, and California. The state did not host its first national championship until 1928 when the Virginia Hot Springs course hosted the Women's Amateur. The center of Virginia moved eastward in the 1940s as Richmond was the site of a PGA TOUR event in the mid-1940s and hosted the

PGA Championship at the Hermitage in 1949. Richmond also hosted an LPGA event, the Richmond Open, in the mid-1950s, as well as the 1955 Amateur, while Virginia Beach briefly became home to another PGA TOUR event. In the 1960s the western part of the state saw the Hot Springs Open and two major women's events, the 1966 Curtis Cup and the 1967 U.S. Women's Open. Amateur golf was also fiercely contested in the 1960s and early 1970s with amateurs such as Vinny Giles, Lanny and Bobby Wadkins, and Curtis Strange.

In the 1980s the PGA TOUR returned to Virginia with the Anheuser-Busch Classic in Williamsburg, sparking off a tremendous rush of golf development in the Williamsburg area that continues today in private and public course development. The LPGA staged its Crestar Classic in Virginia from the mid-1980s through 1992, while the 1991 Publinx and the 1993 Senior Amateur were held in the Charlottesville area and the 1988 Amateur at Virginia Hot Springs.

WASHINGTON

No. of Players (Rank): 543,000 (16)
No. of Rounds played (Rank): 7,221,900 (23)
Percentage of Female Players (Rank): 21.4 (23)
Percentage of Senior Golfers (Rank): 17.8 (44)
Prominent Golfers: Rick Acton, JoAnne Gunderson Carner, Fred Couples, Bing Crosby, Rick Fehr, Mary Bea Porter-King, Anne Sander, Bill Sander, Ken Still, Kirk Triplett, Audrey Wooding, Mark Wurtz, Kermit Zarley.
Major Golf Companies: G. Loomis.
Prominent Courses: Canterwood, Harbour Pointe, Indian Canyon, Port Ludlow, Seattle, Semi-ah-moo.
State Golf Association: Washington State Golf Association, Northgate Executive Center #1, 155 NE 100th Street #302, Seattle, WA 98125—(206) 526-1238

Highlights: While the Tacoma Golf Club, founded in 1904, was the first golf club formed in any of the Pacific Coast states, Washington has lagged behind other Pacific states in golf development over the years—due in part to the short golfing season and often-inclement weather. Clubs such as Seattle G.C. were the site of a significant number of exhibitions in the 1920s and 1930s, and Washington produced a number of fine amateurs in the pre-Second World War era. But during and after the war golf boomed significantly—Spokane hosted the 1941 Publinx and the 1944 PGA Championship, while in 1945 alone two PGA TOUR events were played in the Puget Sound area. Tacoma subsequently hosted the occasional

PGA TOUR event in the 1950s while Seattle played host to the 1952 Amateur and the 1953 Publinx.

In the 1960s Washington's economy boomed with the growth of the aerospace industry, and both eastern Washington (hosting an LPGA TOUR event) and in particular Western Washington (hosting the Seattle Open and the 1961 Walker Cup, and the 1961 Women's Amateur) were experiencing dramatic surges in golf interest. Seattle's first top-100 ranked course, Sahalee, also dates from the 1960s.

In the 1970s golf did not experience the excitement of the 1960s, with Washington hosting only the 1974 Women's Amateur, but the 1980s brought a revival with the Senior PGA TOUR and the LPGA hosting events, and the Senior Amateur, Women's Amateur and the Publinx coming to the state. Resort development also began to grow in Washington state in the 1980s such as the Resort Semiahmoo, taking advantage of the excellent turf-growing conditions. The trend continues into the 1990s.

WEST VIRGINIA

No. of Players (Rank): 131,000 (36)
No. of Rounds played (Rank): 2,358,000 (39)
Percentage of Female Players (Rank): 18.6 (31)
Percentage of Senior Golfers (Rank): 18.0 (43)
Prominent Courses: Greenbrier-Greenbrier, Greenbrier (Old White), Pete Dye, Sheraton Lakeview.
State Golf Association: West Virginia Golf Association, P.O. Box 8133, Huntington, WV 25705-0133—(304) 525-0000

Highlights: West Virginia golf has until recently largely revolved around the golf at The Greenbrier, site of the 1922 Women's Amateur and a brief PGA TOUR event in the late 1950s. The Greenbrier also hosted the 1979 Ryder Cup Matches in which the combined European team played for the first time. Also in the 1970s Guyan Golf and Country Club hosted the 1977 Girls' Junior Amateur. The LPGA staged the West Virginia LPGA Classic in Wheeling during the early 1980s. The Solheim Cup was staged at The Greenbrier in 1994, marking the return of championship golf to the area—while quality golf development is growing as indicated by the construction of the Pete Dye Golf Club in the state.

WISCONSIN

No. of Players (Rank): 788,000 (9)
No. of Rounds played (Rank): 12,135,200 (9)

Percentage of Female Players (Rank): 28.7 (7)
Percentage of Senior Golfers (Rank): 22.1 (27)
Prominent Golfers: Bob Brue, Stephanie Farwig, Dan Forsman, Skip Kendall, Laurie Merten, Martha Nause, Andy North, Sherri Steinhausen, Steve Stricker.
Major Golf Companies: Hornung.
Prominent Courses: Americana Lake Geneva, Blackwolf Run, Geneva National., Milwaukee, SentryWorld.
State Golf Association: Wisconsin State Golf Association, P.O. Box 35, Elm Grove, WI 53122—(414) 786-4301

Highlights: Championship golf arrived in Wisconsin as early as 1933 when Gene Sarazen won the PGA championship at Blue Mound in Milwaukee. Subsequently the LPGA staged the Milwaukee Jaycee Classic in the state during the 1960s, while the Milwaukee Country Club hosted the 1969 Walker Cup. The event that the state is best known for, the Greater Milwaukee Open, debuted in 1968 on the PGA TOUR. Among national championships both the Publinx and Women's Publinx were held in the state in 1977, while the Women's Publinx returned in 1986. The Senior Amateur was also staged in Wisconsin in 1986. Wisconsin has been long noted for having one of the most enthusiastic golfing populations in the country, with a high per-capita participation rate and a surprisingly strong number of out-of-state visitors.

WYOMING

No. of Players (Rank): 56,000 (47)
No. of Rounds played (Rank): 834,400 (48)
Percentage of Female Players (Rank): 24.3 (13)
Percentage of Senior Golfers (Rank): 14.3 (47)
Prominent Golfers: Jim Benepe.
Prominent Courses: Jackson Hole, Old Baldy.
State Golf Association: Wyoming Golf Association, 1808 Kit Carson, Casper, WY 82604—(307) 265-3216

Highlights: Wyoming has an enthusiastic golf population, but only a small number of courses. A short golf season hinders golf development in most parts of the state. Nevertheless the state has a top-100 ranked course in Old Baldy, an outstanding resort at Jackson Hole in the western part of the state, and a small number of national championships to its credit in recent years. The first national played in Wyoming was the 1988 Publinx, played at Jackson Hole—the Women's Publinx was also played there in 1993.

THE TOP 250 COURSES

OVERVIEW: *Courses included are those which met any of the following criteria: Listed in the 1993 Golf Digest ranking of the top 100 courses in the United States; listed in the 1991 or 1993 Golf Magazine Top 100 Courses in the United States and the World, or Hidden Gems, 1993; host courses for the United States Open and the British Open since 1945; host courses for the PGA Championship, United States Amateur, or United States Women's Open since 1970; listed in the Golf World (U.K.) ranking of the Top 40 courses in the United Kingdom and Ireland; listed in the Golf World (U.K.) Top 20 Courses in Continental Europe; listed in Golf Digest's Top 20 Courses in Canada.*

Two newer courses not otherwise qualified for consideration on these lists, Old Tabby (South Carolina, U.S.) and Grand National (Alabama, U.S.), were added to the 248 qualifying courses. In total, 150 courses were selected from the United States, and 100 from the rest of the world.

No ranking of courses should be considered as authoritative; rather, they represent the attempt of the rating boards to balance the aesthetic, strategic, and historical appeal of a small percentage of the world's golf courses. There is room for disagreement.

Tom Fazio recently made the apt observation that with modern rankings it is not a question of which courses should "get in," but which will have to be left out to make room. Thus, readers will note that courses such as Prestwick, Musselburgh, Royal Cinque Ports (Deal), Royal North Devon (Westward Ho!), Royal Calcutta, and Lagunita are among the established clubs which, having made immeasurable contributions to golf's storied past, are overlooked; while newer courses such as Palmilla, Devil's Pulpit, Colleton River, Tidewater, World Woods and Kuilima likewise were omitted.

Each course, however, is able to qualify for this list through the hosting of championships or the voting of experienced critics. If the results are sometimes controversial, the process is one that is fair and for the vast majority of courses provides well-deserved recognition.

UNITED STATES

ARONIMINK
LOCATION: Newtown Square, Penn.
FOUNDED: 1928 **PAR:** 70 **YARDAGE:** 6974
SELECTION CRITERIA: Golf Digest #77 (1993)
NOTES: Donald Ross's great Philadelphia course; hosted the 1977 U.S. Amateur where John Fought recorded the most lopsided victory (9&8 over Doug Fischesser) since 1949. Also the site of Gary Player's 1962 PGA Championship.

ATLANTA ATHLETIC CLUB (HIGHLANDS)
LOCATION: Atlanta, Ga.
FOUNDED: 1967 **PAR:** 72 **YARDAGE:** 6976
CRITERIA: Host, 1976 U.S. Open.

NOTES: Hosted 1976 U.S. Open, a rare foray into the South by the USGA and a championship won with a rare birdie on the final hole by Jerry Pate. Atlanta A.C. recently tumbled out of the Golf Digest top-100 rankings but continues to be part of the USGA rotation, hosting the 1990 U.S. Women's Open.

AUGUSTA NATIONAL
LOCATION: Augusta, Ga.
FOUNDED: 1933 **PAR:** 72 **YARDAGE:** 6905
CRITERIA: Golf Digest #3, 1993
NOTES: Hosted The Masters each April since 1934; Alister Mackenzie designed with advice from Bobby Jones, with Perry Maxwell, Robert Trent Jones, George Cobb, Jack Nicklaus, and Tom Fazio credited with remodeling over the years; ranked #4 in the world by Golf Magazine, 1993.

BALTIMORE (FIVE FARMS)
LOCATION: Timonium, Md.
FOUNDED: 1926 PAR: 70 YARDAGE: 6662
CRITERIA: Golf Digest #62, 1993.
NOTES AND AWARDS: Hosted the 1899 U.S. Open; 1932 Amateur; 1965 Walker Cup; and site of Liselotte Neumann's record 277 in the 1988 U.S. Women's Open.

BALTUSROL G.C. (LOWER)
LOCATION: Springfield, N.J.
FOUNDED: 1922 PAR: 72 YARDAGE: 7138
CRITERIA: Golf Digest #20, 1993.
NOTES: Site of 14 different USGA Championships, including seven U.S. Opens; Lee Janzen and Jack Nicklaus' low U.S. Open scores set here in 1993. Ranked #30 in the world by Golf Magazine.

BALTUSROL (UPPER)
LOCATION: Philadelphia, PA.
FOUNDED: 1916 PAR: 72 YARDAGE: 6807
CRITERIA: Golf Magazine #99, 1993.
NOTES: Snuck onto the tail-end of the rankings; Baltusrol joins Winged Foot and Sunningdale (England) among the few clubs with two ranked courses.

BARTON CREEK C.C. (FAZIO)
LOCATION: Austin, Tex.
FOUNDED: 1986 PAR: 72 YARDAGE: 6956
CRITERIA: Golf Digest #60, 1993.
NOTES: Acclaimed Tom Fazio design from his "golden" period in the mid-80s once overshadowed by Lake Nona, Wade Hampton, and Black Diamond; now recognized as one of his best.

BAY HILL CLUB
LOCATION: Orlando, Fla.
FOUNDED: 1961 PAR: 72 YARDAGE: 7114
CRITERIA: Golf Digest #80, 1993.
NOTES: Site of the Nestle Classic; hosted the 1991 Junior Amateur where winner Tiger Woods, age 15, first leapt into the public eye. Course redesigned by and once the Florida base for Arnold Palmer.

BELLERIVE C.C.
LOCATION: St. Louis, Mo.
FOUNDED: 1960 PAR: 71 YARDAGE: 7,302
CRITERIA: Golf Digest # 56, 1993.
NOTES: Site of several national championships

including Nick Price's 1992 PGA Championship, and Gary Player's completion of the career Grand Slam in the 1965 U.S. Open. One of the longest courses in the country when it first opened from a design by Robert Trent Jones, curiously it has favored the shorter hitters.

BETHPAGE (BLACK)
LOCATION: Farmingdale, N.Y.
FOUNDED: 1936 PAR: 71 YARDAGE: 7065
CRITERIA: Golf Magazine #92, 1993.
NOTES: A late design by A.W. Tillinghast (of Winged Foot fame, &c.), this course has become increasingly popular as a Hidden Gem. One of the few ranked U.S. courses open to the public; hosted the Publinx in its first year and virtually nothing since.

BLACK DIAMOND (QUARRY)
LOCATION: Lecanto, Fla.
FOUNDED: 1988 PAR: 72 YARDAGE: 7159
CRITERIA: Golf Digest #51, 1993.
NOTES: Tom Fazio's masterpiece? The quarry holes are perhaps his most-admired work. Black Diamond has yet to host a significant tournament due to its tender years and middle-of-nowhere location. But a classic, nonetheless.

BLACKWOLF RUN (RIVER)
LOCATION: Kohler, Wisc.
FOUNDED: 1989 PAR: 72 YARDAGE: 6991
CRITERIA: Golf Digest #31, 1993.
NOTES: Only Fazio's Shadow Creek is younger and higher in the Golf Digest rankings; curiously unranked by Golf Magazine.

BROOKLAWN
LOCATION: Fairfield, Conn.
FOUNDED: N/A PAR: 71 YARDAGE: 6599
CRITERIA: 1979 U.S. Women's Open host.
NOTES: A short course, Brooklawn was the site of Gary Player's 1987 Senior Open victory (his record 14-under par score is still the Senior Open record); however, even par won for Jerilyn Britz in the 1979 U.S. Women's Open.

BUTLER NATIONAL
LOCATION: Oak Brook, Ill.
FOUNDED: 1974 PAR: 72 YARDAGE: 7309

CRITERIA: Golf Digest #45, 1993.
NOTES: Longtime host of the Western Open, the members opted out of the PGA TOUR after the Shoal Creek-inspired focus on minority membership policies.

CAMARGO
LOCATION: Indian Hill, Ohio
FOUNDED: 1921 PAR: 70 YARDAGE: 6559
CRITERIA: Golf Digest #71, 1993.
NOTES: Never the site of a major championship of golf, nevertheless this Seth Raynor design has ridden the crest of Raynor's increasing reputation.

CANTERBURY
LOCATION: Shaker Heights, Ohio
FOUNDED: 1922 PAR: 72 YARDAGE: 6911
CRITERIA: Golf Digest #89.
NOTES: Considered just a notch or two behind the likes of Scioto, Inverness, and Muirfield Village as one of Ohio's premier courses, Canterbury has hosted the 1940 and 1948 U.S. Opens, the 1946 Open featuring a three-way, 36-hole playoff resulting in Lloyd Mangrum's one-stroke victory.

CASCADES
LOCATION: Hot Springs, Va.
FOUNDED: 1923 PAR: 70 YARDAGE: 6566
CRITERIA: Golf Digest #95, 1993.
NOTES: Long-renowned as one of the finest mountain courses, Cascades has hosted five national championships, including Glenna Collett Vare's record 13 & 12 win in the U.S. Amateur files.

CASTLE PINES
LOCATION: Castle Rock, Colo.
FOUNDED: 1981 PAR: 72 YARDAGE: 7559
CRITERIA: Golf Digest #42, 1993.
NOTES: Host of popular PGA TOUR tournament The International, featuring a modified Stableford scoring system which makes the reachable par-fives the key holes. Designed by Jack Nicklaus.

CEDAR RIDGE
LOCATION: Broken Arrow, Okla.
PAR: 71 YARDAGE: 7230
CRITERIA: Host, 1983 U.S. Women's Open.
NOTES: Overshadowed in Tulsa by Southern Hills, this course became part of the golfing

map with Pat Bradley's front nine 31 in 1983, tying a 19-year old Open record.

CHAMPIONS (CYPRESS CREEK)
LOCATION: Houston, Tex.
FOUNDED: 1959 PAR: 71 YARDAGE: 7147
CRITERIA: #83, Golf Magazine, 1993.
NOTES: Hosted 1969 U.S. Open (won by Orville Moody), and the 1967 Ryder Cup matches; also was the stage of the 1990 Nabisco Championships (now the TOUR Championship) won by Jodie Mudd. Designed by Ralph Plummer.

CHARLOTTE
LOCATION: Charlotte, N.C.
PAR: 71 YARDAGE: 6726
CRITERIA: Host, 1972 U.S. Amateur.
NOTES: Highly regarded in North Carolina, its reputation has faded in recent years; hosted the U.S. Amateur where Marvin "Vinny" Giles III recorded his sole Amateur title after four second-place finishes.

CHERRY HILLS
LOCATION: Englewood, Colo.
FOUNDED: 1923 PAR: 72 YARDAGE: 7160
CRITERIA: #32, Golf Digest, 1993.
NOTES: Immortalized as the site of Arnold Palmer's famous charge to victory in the 1960 U.S. Open; also hosted the 1978 Open won by unknown Andy North; designed by William Flynn and remodeled by Arnold Palmer and Ed Seay in 1978, and by Geoffrey Cornish in 1992.

CHICAGO
LOCATION: Wheaton, Ill.
FOUNDED: 1894 PAR: 70 YARDAGE: 6574
CRITERIA: #33 Golf Digest, 1993.
NOTES: The oldest ranked American course, a classic designed by U.S. golf pioneer Charles Blair Macdonald and remodeled in 1923 by Seth Raynor; ranked #45 in the world by Golf Magazine (1993). Bobby Jones still holds the course record of 66.

COG HILL (NO. 4)
LOCATION: Lemont, Ill.
FOUNDED: 1964 PAR: 72 YARDAGE: 6992
CRITERIA: #68, Golf Digest, 1993.
NOTES: No. 4, also known as Dubsdread, has hosted the Western Open since 1991. One of

the most highly regarded public courses in the country, the design is by Dick Wilson and Joe Lee.

COLONIAL

LOCATION: Fort Worth, Tex.
FOUNDED: 1935 PAR: 70 YARDAGE: 7010
CRITERIA: #47, Golf Digest, 1993.
NOTES: The best-known Texan course and host to the Colonial Invitational, in addition to the 1941 U.S. Open and the 1975 Players Championship won by Al Geiberger (back when that tournament rotated between great courses).

CONGRESSIONAL (BLUE)

LOCATION: Bethesda, Md.
FOUNDED: 1961 PAR: 72 YARDAGE: 7270
CRITERIA: #73, Golf Digest, 1993.
NOTES: Hosted the 1964 U.S. Open famed for extremely high temperatures and the heroic persistence of winner Ken Venturi. Designed by Robert Trent Jones and later remodeled by Rees Jones.

C.C. OF DETROIT

LOCATION: Grosse Pointe Farms, Mich.
FOUNDED: 1914 PAR: 72 YARDAGE: 6800
CRITERIA: #86, Golf Magazine, 1993.
NOTES: Hosted the 1915 and 1954 Amateurs, the latter won by a young Arnold Palmer in his first major victory. Designed by Colt & Alison, later remodeled by Robert Trent Jones.

C.C. OF INDIANAPOLIS

LOCATION: Indianapolis, Ind.
PAR: 71 YARDAGE: 6544
CRITERIA: Host, 1983 U.S. Women's Open.
NOTES: Host of the 1978 U.S. Women's Open where Hollis Stacy won her second consecutive title and became the youngest golfer to successfuly defend an Open title.

C.C. OF NORTH CAROLINA (DOGWOOD)

LOCATION: Pinehurst, N.C.
FOUNDED: 1963 PAR: 72 YARDAGE: 7154
CRITERIA: #98, Golf Digest, 1993.
NOTES: Host of 1980 Amateur won by Hal Sutton in a stunning 9&8 victory. Designed by Willard Byrd and Ellis Maples in the early 1960s, it has remained a prestigious course even among Pinehurst's riches.

THE COUNTRY CLUB

LOCATION: Brookline, Mass.
FOUNDED: 1895 PAR: 71 YARDAGE: 7010
CRITERIA: #17, Golf Digest, 1993.
NOTES: Host of three U.S. Opens, the latest in 1988, won by Curtis Strange after a widely praised remodeling by Rees Jones; also the site of the famed 1913 U.S. Open won by underdog Francis Ouimet over heavy favorites Harry Vardon and Ted Ray. Hosted five U.S. Amateurs; one of the oldest courses in the United States; ranked #34 in the world by Golf Magazine.

THE COUNTRY CLUB

LOCATION: Pepper Pike, Ohio
FOUNDED: 1931
CRITERIA: #56, Golf Magazine, 1993.
NOTES: Hosted 1935 U.S. Amateur won by Lawson Little; ranked #93 in the world by Golf Magazine.

CROOKED STICK

LOCATION: Carmel, Ind.
FOUNDED: 1964 PAR: 72 YARDAGE: 7516
CRITERIA: #76, Golf Digest, 1993.
NOTES: The course which put Pete Dye on the golfing map, it also was the site of John Daly's miraculous win in the 1991 PGA Championship after receiving the final spot in the field. Also hosted the 1993 U.S. Women's Open won by Laurie Merten.

CRYSTAL DOWNS

LOCATION: Frankfort, Mich.
FOUNDED: 1931 PAR: 70 YARDAGE: 6518
CRITERIA: #14, Golf Digest, 1993.
NOTES: Perhaps the definitive "hidden gem," Crystal Downs had never hosted a national tournament until the 1991 U.S. Senior Amateur; designed by Alister Mackenzie and Perry Maxwell; ranked #15 in the world by Golf Magazine, 1993.

CYPRESS POINT

LOCATION: Pebble Beach, Calif.
FOUNDED: 1928 PAR: 72 YARDAGE: 6536
CRITERIA: #4, Golf Digest, 1993.
NOTES: Long-time host of the Crosby (later the AT&T National Pro-Am); also hosted the 1981 Walker Cup Matches. Designed by Alister

Mackenzie; ranked #2 in the world by Golf Magazine; frequently cited as the greatest 17-hole course in the world, due to its weak 18th.

DEL PASO
LOCATION: Sacramento, Calif.
FOUNDED: 1982 PAR: 72 YARDAGE: 6300
CRITERIA: Host, 1982 U.S. Women's Open.
NOTES: In addition to Janet Alex's six-stroke victory in the 1982 Women's Open, Del Paso has hosted two U.S. Women's Amateurs (1957, 1976) and the 1964 Senior Women's Amateur.

DESERT FOREST
LOCATION: Carefree, Ariz.
FOUNDED: 1962 PAR: 72 YARDAGE: 6981
CRITERIA: #94, Golf Digest, 1993.
NOTES: The first Arizona course to crack the rankings, the Red Lawrence design is still one of the top-ranked Southwestern tracks, hosting the 1990 Senior Amateur. Ranked #91 by Golf Magazine, 1993.

DESERT HIGHLANDS
LOCATION: Scottsdale, Ariz.
FOUNDED: 1984 PAR: 72 YARDAGE: 7099
CRITERIA: #67, Golf Digest, 1993.
NOTES: Host of 1983-1984 Skins Game. One of the few genuine trendsetters in golf course design, Jack Nicklaus' revolutionary "target golf" concept, with only 80 acres of grass surrounded by virgin desert, has led to a host of imitators in the American Southwest.

DESERT MOUNTAIN (RENEGADE)
LOCATION: Scottsdale, Ariz.
FOUNDED: 1986 PAR: 72 YARDAGE: 7515
CRITERIA: #53, Golf Digest, 1993.
NOTES: Host of The Tradition since 1989; designed by Jack Nicklaus.

DESERT MOUNTAIN (COCHISE)
LOCATION: Scottsdale, Ariz.
FOUNDED: 1987 PAR: 72 YARDAGE: 7045
CRITERIA: #87, Golf Digest, 1993.
NOTES: Host of The Tradition since 1989; designed by Jack Nicklaus; Winged Foot, PGA West, and Sunningdale are the only other clubs to have two ranked courses.

DORAL (BLUE MONSTER)
LOCATION: Miami, Fla.
FOUNDED: 1916 PAR: 72 YARDAGE: 6939

CRITERIA: #71, Golf Magazine, 1993.
NOTES: Host of Doral Ryder Open since 1962; designed by Dick Wilson and Joe Lee.

DOUBLE EAGLE
LOCATION: Galena, Ohio
FOUNDED: 1991
CRITERIA: #62, Golf Magazine, 1993.
NOTES: One of the first 1990s designs to make it into the rankings; designed by Jay Morrish and Tom Weiskopf; just missed Golf Magazine's top-100 courses in the world.

DUNES CLUB
LOCATION: Myrtle Beach, S.C.
FOUNDED: 1949 PAR: 72 YARDAGE: 7165
CRITERIA: #93, Golf Magazine, 1993.
NOTES: Will host the Senior TOUR Championship several times in the 1990s; hosted the 1962 U.S. Women's Open won by Murle Lindstrom; one of the definitive heroic designs of Robert Trent Jones.

EUGENE
LOCATION: Eugene, Ore.
FOUNDED: 1967 PAR: 72 YARDAGE: 6847
CRITERIA: #82, Golf Digest, 1993.
NOTES: Hosted the 1993 Mid-Amateur; designed by Robert Trent Jones. Ranked #78 by Golf Magazine.

FIRESTONE (SOUTH)
LOCATION: Akron, Ohio
FOUNDED: 1960 PAR: 70 YARDAGE: 7139
CRITERIA: #47, Golf Magazine, 1993.
NOTES: Longtime host of the NEC World Series of Golf; 3-time host of the PGA Championship (1960, 1966 and 1975); designed by Robert Trent Jones; ranked #79 in the world by Golf Magazine.

FIRETHORN
LOCATION: Lincoln, Neb.
FOUNDED: 1985 PAR: 71 YARDAGE: 6762
CRITERIA: Hidden Gem, Golf Magazine, 1993.
NOTES: A recent Pete Dye design that is not widely known but highly regarded by those who have seen it.

FISHERS ISLAND
LOCATION: Fishers Island, N.Y.
FOUNDED: 1917 PAR: 72 YARDAGE: 6544

CRITERIA: #25, Golf Magazine, 1993.
NOTES: A hidden gem designed by cult-figure Seth Raynor; ranked #47 in the world by Golf Magazine; ultra-private, bordering on reclusive.

FOREST HIGHLANDS
LOCATION: Scottsdale, Ariz.
FOUNDED: 1988 PAR: 71 YARDAGE: 7051
CRITERIA: #38, Golf Digest, 1993.
NOTES: One of several Morrish/Weiskopf courses leaping into the rankings in the 1990s.

GARDEN CITY
LOCATION: Garden City, N.Y.
FOUNDED: 1899 PAR: 72 YARDAGE: 7064
CRITERIA: #28, Golf Digest, 1993.
NOTES: Hosted the 1902 U.S. Open, four U.S. Amateurs, and the 1924 Walker Cup matches; designed by Devereux Emmet and remodeled by Walter Travis in 1926; ranked #58 in the world by Golf Magazine, 1993.

THE GOLF CLUB
LOCATION: New Albany, Ohio
FOUNDED: 1967 PAR: 72 YARDAGE: 7268
CRITERIA: #34, Golf Digest, 1993.
NOTES: An early milestone for designer Pete Dye; forbids tournaments not open to the membership; ranked #32 in the world by Golf Magazine, 1993.

THE GOLF CLUB OF GEORGIA
LOCATION: Alpharetta, Ga.
FOUNDED: 1991 PAR: 72 YARDAGE: 7020
NOTES: One of the first 1990s courses to reach the rankings; designed by Arthur Hills.

GRANDFATHER
LOCATION: Linville, N.C.
FOUNDED: 1968 PAR: 72 YARDAGE: 7010
CRITERIA: #92, Golf Digest, 1993.
NOTES: A hidden gem from Ellis Maples that snuck into the rankings this year.

GRAND NATIONAL (LINKS)
LOCATION: Opelika, Ala.
FOUNDED: 1993 PAR: 72 YARDAGE: 7089
CRITERIA: Complete Golfer's Almanac selection.
NOTES: Designed by Robert Trent Jones; star attraction on the seven-site Robert Trent Jones Golf Trail in Alabama.

GREENVILLE (CHANTICLEER)
LOCATION: Greenville, S.C.
FOUNDED: 1966 PAR: 72 YARDAGE: 6668
CRITERIA: #66, Golf Digest, 1993.
NOTES: Shorter design from Robert Trent Jones that rarely hosts national tournaments.

HAIG POINT (CALIBOGUE)
LOCATION: Daufuskie Island, S.C.
FOUNDED: 1986 PAR: 72 YARDAGE: 7114
NOTES: A hard-to-find Rees Jones design tucked on a South Carolina barrier island; not accessible for national tournaments; ranked #87 by Golf Magazine, 1993.

HARBOUR TOWN
LOCATION: Hilton Head Island, S.C.
FOUNDED: 1969 PAR: 71 YARDAGE: 6912
CRITERIA: #70, Golf Digest, 1993.
NOTES: The prototypical Southern coastal course designed by Pete Dye with Jack Nicklaus; hosted the Nabisco Championships (now the TOUR Championship) in 1989; hosted the 1974 Senior Amateur; site of the MCI Heritage Classic; ranked #42 in the world by Golf Magazine.

HAZELTINE NATIONAL
LOCATION: Chaska, Minn.
FOUNDED: 1962 PAR: 72 YARDAGE: 7237
CRITERIA: #57, Golf Digest, 1993.
NOTES: Hosted the 1970 and 1991 U.S. Opens, the 1966 and 1977 U.S. Women's Opens, and the 1983 Senior Open; designed by Robert Trent Jones and remodeled in 1990 by son Rees; ranked #72 by Golf Magazine.

HIGH POINTE
LOCATION: Williamsburg, Mich.
FOUNDED: 1989 PAR: 71 YARDAGE: 6819
CRITERIA: #97, Golf Magazine, 1993.
NOTES: Acclaimed new design by Tom Doak, Golf Magazine's achitectural critic.

THE HONORS COURSE
LOCATION: Chattanooga, Tenn.
FOUNDED: 1983 PAR: 72 YARDAGE: 7064
CRITERIA: #29, Golf Digest, 1993.
NOTES: Host of the 1991 U.S. Amateur; regarded by many experts as Pete Dye's finest creation in the U.S. (Pete was aided by son P.B. in the design); ranked #60 in the world by Golf Magazine, 1993.

INDIANWOOD (OLD)
LOCATION: Lake Orion, Mich.
FOUNDED: 1928 PAR: 71 YARDAGE: 6814
CRITERIA: #74, Golf Magazine, 1993.
NOTES: Hosted the 1989 U.S. Women's Open won by Betsy King, as well as last year's 1994 U.S. Women's Open won by Patty Sheehan.

INTERLACHEN
LOCATION: Edina, Minn.
FOUNDED: 1911 PAR: 73 YARDAGE: 6733
CRITERIA: #72, Golf Digest, 1993.
NOTES: Hosted the 1930 U.S. Open where Bobby Jones won the first leg of the Grand Slam; hosted the 1993 Walker Cup matches; designed by Willie Watson and remodeled by Donald Ross in 1919.

INVERNESS
LOCATION: Toledo, Ohio
FOUNDED: 1919 PAR: 71 YARDAGE: 6952
CRITERIA: #48, Golf Digest, 1993.
NOTES: Host of four U.S. Opens (the last in 1979) and the 1973 U.S. Amateur; the first major club to allow professionals into the clubhouse; designed by Donald Ross, remodeled by Tom Fazio in 1977; rated #51 in the world by Golf Magazine.

JUPITER HILLS CLUB (HILLS)
LOCATION: Tequesta, Fla.
FOUNDED: 1970 PAR: 72 YARDAGE: 6911
CRITERIA: #96, Golf Digest, 1993.
NOTES: Host of the 1987 U.S. Amateur; ranked #91 in the world by Golf Magazine.

KAHKWA CLUB
LOCATION: Erie, Penn.
PAR: 72 YARDAGE: 6488
CRITERIA: Host, 1971 U.S. Women's Open.
NOTES: Site of JoAnne Carner's seven-stroke victory in the 1971 U.S. Women's Open.

KAUAI LAGOONS (KIELE)
LOCATION: Lihue, Ha.
FOUNDED: 1989 PAR: 72 YARDAGE: 7070
CRITERIA: #88, Golf Digest, 1993.
NOTES: Designed by Jack Nicklaus.

KIAWAH (OCEAN)
LOCATION: Kiawah Island, S.C.
FOUNDED: 1991 PAR: 72 YARDAGE: 7371
CRITERIA: #77, Golf Magazine, 1993.

NOTES: Host of the 1991 Ryder Cup Matches won by the United States.

KITTANSETT CLUB
LOCATION: Marion, Mass.
FOUNDED: 1922 PAR: 71 YARDAGE: 6640
CRITERIA: #75, Golf Digest, 1993.
NOTES: Hosted the 1953 Walker Cup matches; designed by Frederic Hood.

LA GRANGE
LOCATION: LaGrange, Ill.
PAR: 72 YARDAGE: 6685
CRITERIA: Host, 1974 U.S. Women's Open.
NOTES: Hosted 1974 U.S. Women's Open won by Sandra Haynie.

LAKE NONA
LOCATION: Orlando, Fla.
FOUNDED: 1986 PAR: 72 YARDAGE: 7011
CRITERIA: #44, Golf Magazine, 1993.
NOTES: Hosted 1990 Solheim Cup matches and 1993 World Cup; designed by Tom Fazio; ranked #71 in the world by Golf Magazine.

LA QUINTA (MOUNTAIN)
LOCATION: La Quinta, Calif.
FOUNDED: 1981 PAR: 72 YARDAGE: 6402
CRITERIA: #98, Golf Magazine, 1993.
NOTES: Designed by Pete and Alice Dye.

LAUREL VALLEY
LOCATION: Ligonier, Penn.
FOUNDED: 1960 PAR: 72 YARDAGE: 7060
CRITERIA: #41, Golf Digest, 1993.
NOTES: Hosted the 1989 U.S. Senior Open (won by Orville Moody), the 1975 Ryder Cup matches, and the 1965 PGA Championship (won by Dave Marr); designed by Dick Wilson, remodeled by Arnold Palmer and Ed Seay in 1988.

THE LINKS AT SPANISH BAY
LOCATION: Pebble Beach, Calif.
FOUNDED: 1987 PAR: 72 YARDAGE: 6820
CRITERIA: Golf Magazine top-100 ranking, 1991.
NOTES: designed by Robert Trent Jones, Jr, Sandy Tatum, and Tom Watson; the ecosystem is too fragile to host national tournaments.

LONG COVE
LOCATION: Hilton Head Island, S.C.

FOUNDED: 1981 PAR: 71 YARDAGE: 6900
CRITERIA: #44, Golf Digest, 1993.
NOTES: Hosted the 1991 U.S. Men's Mid-
Amateur; designed by Pete Dye; ranked #63
in the world by Golf Magazine, 1993.

LOS ANGELES (NORTH)
LOCATION: Los Angeles, Calif.
FOUNDED: 1921 PAR: 71 YARDAGE: 6895
CRITERIA: #37, Golf Digest, 1993.
NOTES: Hosted the 1930 U.S. Women's
Amateur and the 1954 Junior Amateur;
designed by George Thomas, Jr.; ranked #49
in the world by Golf Magazine, 1993.

MAIDSTONE
LOCATION: East Hampton, N.Y.
FOUNDED: 1899 PAR: 72 YARDAGE: 6390
CRITERIA: #46, Golf Digest, 1993.
NOTES: Designed by W.H. Tucker, remodeled
by Willie Park, Jr. in 1925.

MAUNA KEA
LOCATION: Kohala Coast, Ha.
FOUNDED: 1965 PAR: 72 YARDAGE: 7114
CRITERIA: #69, Golf Digest, 1993.
NOTES: Designed by Robert Trent Jones; a
landmark Hawaiian design, as it was the first
built on a bed of lava rock.

MEADOW BROOK
LOCATION: Westbury, N.Y.
FOUNDED: N/A PAR: 72 YARDAGE: 7101
CRITERIA: Golf Magazine top-100, 1991.
NOTES: Designed by Dick Wilson.

MEDINAH C.C. (NO. 3)
LOCATION: Medinah, Ill.
FOUNDED: 1928 PAR: 72 YARDAGE: 7366
CRITERIA: #13, Golf Digest, 1993.
NOTES: Hosted three U.S. Opens, the latest in
1990 (won by Hale Irwin), and the 1988 U.S.
Senior Open; designed by Tom Bendelow,
remodeled in 1986 by Roger Packard; ranked
#47 in the world by Golf Magazine.

MERION (EAST)
LOCATION: Ardmore, PA.
FOUNDED: 1912 PAR: 70 YARDAGE: 6482
CRITERIA: #10, Golf Digest, 1993.
NOTES: Hosted four U.S. Opens, the latest in
1981 (won by David Graham of Australia),
and five U.S. Amateurs; designed by Hugh

Wilson, remodeled in 1925 by William Flynn;
ranked #10 in the world by Golf Magazine.

MILWAUKEE
LOCATION: Milwaukee, Wisc.
FOUNDED: 1929 PAR: 72 YARDAGE: 6868
CRITERIA: #81, Golf Digest, 1993.
NOTES: Hosted the 1969 Walker Cup matches,
and the 1988 Men's Senior Amateur; designed
by Colt and Alison.

MONTCLAIR
LOCATION: West Orange, N.J.
PAR: 70 YARDAGE: 6567
CRITERIA: Hosted U.S. Amateur, 1985.
NOTES: Hosted the 1973 Women's Amateur,
and the 1985 Amateur.

MUIRFIELD VILLAGE
LOCATION: Dublin, Ohio
FOUNDED: 1974 PAR: 72 YARDAGE: 7104
CRITERIA: #9, Golf Digest, 1993.
NOTES: Annual site of The Memorial; hosted
the 1987 Ryder Cup matches and the 1992
Amateur; designed by Jack Nicklaus and
Desmond Muirhead; ranked #24 in the world
by Golf Magazine.

MUSKOGEE
LOCATION: Muskogee, Okla.
PAR: 71 YARDAGE: 6740
CRITERIA: Host, 1970 U.S. Women's Open.
NOTES: Hosted 1970 U.S. Women's Open won
by Donna Caponi.

NCR (SOUTH)
LOCATION: Kettering, Ohio
FOUNDED: 1954 PAR: 71 YARDAGE: 6824
CRITERIA: #91, Golf Digest, 1993.
NOTES: Hosted the 1986 U.S. Women's Open
(won by Jane Geddes), and the 1969 PGA
Championship (won by Ray Floyd); designed
by Dick Wilson.

NATIONAL GOLF LINKS OF AMERICA
LOCATION: Southampton, N.Y.
FOUNDED: 1911 PAR: 73 YARDAGE: 6779
CRITERIA: #22, Golf Digest, 1993.
NOTES: Hosted the 1922 Walker Cup matches;
designed by Charles Blair Macdonald; ranked
#44 in the world by Golf Magazine.

NORTH SHORE

LOCATION: Glenview, Ill.
FOUNDED: N/A PAR: 72   YARDAGE: 7031
CRITERIA: Host, 1983 U.S. Amateur.
NOTES: Hosted 1933 U.S. Open, plus 1939 and 1983 US. Amateurs.

NORTHWOOD CLUB

LOCATION: Dallas, Tex.
FOUNDED: N/A PAR: 71   YARDAGE: 6835
CRITERIA: Host, 1952 U.S. Open.
NOTES: The site of Julius Boros' first Open crown in 1952.

OAK HILL (EAST)

LOCATION: Rochester, N.Y.
FOUNDED: 1925 PAR: 71   YARDAGE: 6902
CRITERIA: #15, Golf Digest, 1993.
NOTES: Hosted three U.S. Opens (the latest in 1989, won by Curtis Strange), plus the 1980 PGA Championship, the 1949 U.S. Amateur, and the 1984 Senior Open; will host the 1995 Ryder Cup matches; designed by Donald Ross, remodeled by Tom Fazio in 1979; ranked #37 in the world by Golf Magazine.

OAKLAND HILLS (SOUTH)

LOCATION: Bloomfield Hills, Mich.
FOUNDED: 1918 PAR: 72   YARDAGE: 7105
CRITERIA: #16, Golf Digest, 1993.
NOTES: Hosted five U.S. Opens, the latest in 1985 (won by Andy North), the 1972 and 1979 PGA Championships , the 1981 and 1991 U.S. Senior Opens (the latest won by Jack Nicklaus in a playoff), and the 1929 U.S. Women's Amateur; designed by Donald Ross, remodeled by Robert Trent Jones in 1950; ranked #22 in the world by Golf Magazine.

OAKMONT

LOCATION: Oakmont, Penna.
FOUNDED: 1903 PAR: 71   YARDAGE: 7018
CRITERIA: #6, Golf Digest, 1993.
NOTES: Hosted seven U.S. Opens (the latest in 1994, won by South African Ernie Els), four U.S. Amateurs, the 1992 U.S. Women's Open, and the 1922 and 1951 PGA Championships; designed by Henry Fownes; ranked #14 in the world by Golf Magazine.

OAK TREE

LOCATION: Edmond, Okla.
FOUNDED: 1976 PAR: 71   YARDAGE: 7015

CRITERIA: #52, Golf Digest, 1993.
NOTES: Hosted the 1988 U.S. Amateur (won by Jeff Sluman) and the 1984 U.S. Amateur; designed by Pete Dye; ranked #92 in the world by Golf Magazine.

OHIO STATE (SCARLET)

LOCATION: Columbus, Ohio
FOUNDED: N/A PAR: 72   YARDAGE: 7140
CRITERIA: #94, Golf Magazine, 1993.
NOTES: Hosted the 1977 Junior Amateur; designed by Alister Mackenzie and Perry Maxwell.

OLD MARSH

LOCATION: Palm Beach Gardens, Fla.
FOUNDED: 1987 PAR: 72   YARDAGE: 6914
CRITERIA: #78, Golf Digest, 1993.
NOTES: Hosted the 1992 Women's Mid-Amateur; designed by Pete Dye.

OLD TABBY

LOCATION: Spring Island, S.C.
FOUNDED: 1993 PAR: 72   YARDAGE: 7180
CRITERIA: Complete Golfer's Almanac selection.
NOTES: Designed by Arnold Palmer and Ed Seay; situated on a remote private island, it is unlikely to host national tournaments due to limited access.

OLD WARSON

LOCATION: Ladue, Mo.
FOUNDED: 1955 PAR: 71   YARDAGE: 6926
CRITERIA: Golf Magazine top-100 ranking, 1991.
NOTES: Host of 1971 Ryder Cup matches; designed by Robert Trent Jones.

OLYMPIA FIELDS (NORTH)

LOCATION: Olympia Fields, Ill.
FOUNDED: 1922 PAR: 70   YARDAGE: 6857
CRITERIA: #84, Golf Digest, 1993.
NOTES: Host of 1928 U.S. Open (won by Johnny Farrell); designed by Willie Park, Jr.; ranked #96 by Golf Magazine.

PGA NATIONAL (GENERAL)

LOCATION: Palm Beach Gardens, Fla.
FOUNDED: 1983 PAR: 72   YARDAGE: 6768
CRITERIA: Host, 1971 PGA Championship.
NOTES: Hosted the 1983 Ryder Cup matches as well as the 1971 PGA Championship; site of

the PGA Seniors' Championship; designed by Tom Fazio.

PGA WEST (NICKLAUS PRIVATE)
LOCATION: La Quinta, Calif.
FOUNDED: 1990 PAR: 72 YARDAGE: 6807
NOTES: Designed by Jack Nicklaus.

PGA WEST (STADIUM)
LOCATION: La Quinta
FOUNDED: 1986 PAR: 72 YARDAGE: 7261
CRITERIA: #93, Golf Digest, 1993.
NOTES: Host of Skins Game, 1986-91; designed by Pete and Alice Dye; ranked #75 by Golf Magazine.

PASATIEMPO
LOCATION: Santa Cruz, Calif.
FOUNDED: 1929 PAR: 71 YARDAGE: 6483
CRITERIA: #83, Golf Digest, 1993.
NOTES: Host of 1986 Women's Amateur; designed by Alister Mackenzie, one of his few public courses; ranked #100 in the world by Golf Magazine.

PEACHTREE
LOCATION: Atlanta, Ga.
FOUNDED: 1947 PAR: 72 YARDAGE: 7043
CRITERIA: #30, Golf Digest, 1993.
NOTES: Host of 1989 Walker Cup matches; designed by Robert Trent Jones with Bobby Jones; ranked #87 in the world by Golf Magazine, 1993.

PEBBLE BEACH
LOCATION: Pebble Beach, Calif.
FOUNDED: 1919 PAR: 72 YARDAGE: 6799
CRITERIA: #2, Golf Digest, 1993.
NOTES: Host of three U.S. Opens, the latest in 1992 (won by Tom Kite), three U.S. Amateurs, two U.S. Women's Amateurs, the 1988 Nabisco Championships (now the TOUR Championship); annual site of the AT&T National Pro-Am; designed by Jack Neville and Douglas Grant; ranked #3 in the world by Golf Magazine, 1993.

PINEHURST (NO. 2)
LOCATION: Pinehurst, N.C.
FOUNDED: 1935 PAR: 72 YARDAGE: 7020
CRITERIA: #11, Golf Digest, 1993.
NOTES: Host of the 1994 U.S. Senior Open, the 1962 U.S. Amateur, the 1989 U.S. Women's

Amateur, the 1992-93 TOUR Championships, the 1936 PGA Championship, and the 1951 Ryder Cup Matches; the masterpiece of architect Donald Ross; ranked #11 in the world by Golf Magazine, 1993.

PINE TREE
LOCATION: Boynton Beach, Fla.
FOUNDED: 1962 PAR: 72 YARDAGE: 7201
CRITERIA: #63, Golf Magazine, 1993.
NOTES: Host of the 1978 Senior Amateur; designed by Dick Wilson; just missed the top-100 world rankings by Golf Magazine for 1993.

PINE VALLEY
LOCATION: Pine Valley, N.J.
FOUNDED: 1922 PAR: 70 YARDAGE: 6667
CRITERIA: #1, Golf Digest, 1993.
NOTES: Hosted the 1936 and 1985 Walker Cup matches; designed by George Crump and H.S. Colt; ranked #1 in the world by Golf Magazine, 1993.

PLAINFIELD
LOCATION: Plainfield, N.J.
FOUNDED: 1920 PAR: 72 YARDAGE: 6865
CRITERIA: #49, Golf Digest, 1993.
NOTES: Hosted the 1987 U.S. Women's Open (won by Laura Davies) and the 1978 U.S. Amateur; designed by Donald Ross; ranked #97 in the world by Golf Magazine, 1993.

POINT O'WOODS
LOCATION: Benton Harbor, Mich.
FOUNDED: 1958 PAR: 72 YARDAGE: 7050
CRITERIA: #61, Golf Digest, 1993.
NOTES: Designed by Robert Trent Jones.

PRAIRIE DUNES
LOCATION: Hutchinson, Kan.
FOUNDED: 1937 PAR: 70 YARDAGE: 6593
CRITERIA: #25, Golf Digest, 1993.
NOTES: Host of three U.S. Women's Amateurs, the 1986 Cutis Cup matches, and the 1988 U.S. Mid-Amateur; designed by Perry Maxwell, remodeled by Press Maxwell in 1957; ranked #20 in the world by Golf Magazine.

PRINCEVILLE (THE PRINCE)
LOCATION: Princeville, Ha.
FOUNDED: 1990 PAR: 72 YARDAGE: 7309
CRITERIA: #43, Golf Digest, 1993.

NOTES: One of the first 1990s designs to be ranked; designed by Robert Trent Jones, Jr.

PUMPKIN RIDGE (WITCH HOLLOW)
LOCATION: Cornelius, Ore.
FOUNDED: 1991 PAR: 72 YARDAGE: 7014
CRITERIA: Golf Magazine Hidden Gem, 1993.
NOTES: Designed by Bob Cupp and John Fought; hosted the 1993-94 NIKE TOUR Championships.

QUAKER RIDGE
LOCATION: Scarsdale, N.Y.
FOUNDED: 1926 PAR: 70 YARDAGE: 6819
CRITERIA: #21, Golf Digest, 1993.
NOTES: Designed by A.W. Tillinghast, remodeled by Robert Trent Jones in 1960; ranked #41 in the world by Golf Magazine.

RICHLAND
LOCATION: Nashville, Tenn.
PAR: 71 YARDAGE: 6825
CRITERIA: Host, 1980 U.S. Women's Open.
NOTES: Host of 1975 Junior Amateur and 1980 U.S. Women's Open.

RIDGEWOOD (EAST-WEST)
LOCATION: Paramus, N.J.
FOUNDED: 1927 PAR: 71 YARDAGE: 6938
CRITERIA: #99, Golf Digest, 1993.
NOTES: Host of 1990 U.S. Senior Open, 1974 U.S. Amateur, the 1957 U.S. Senior Amateur, and the 1935 Ryder Cup matches; designed by A.W. Tillinghast.

RIVIERA
LOCATION: Pacific Palisades, Calif.
FOUNDED: 1926 PAR: 72 YARDAGE: 7016
CRITERIA: #39, Golf Digest, 1993.
NOTES: Host of 1983 PGA Championship and 1948 U.S. Open; designed by George Thomas, Jr.; ranked #49 in the world by Golf Magazine.

ROLLING GREEN
LOCATION: Springfield, Penn.
FOUNDED: 1926 PAR: 71
CRITERIA: Golf Magazine Hidden Gem, 1993.
NOTES: Host of 1976 U.S. Women's Open (won by JoAnne Carner).

SAHALEE (SOUTH/NORTH)
LOCATION: Redmond, Wash.
FOUNDED: 1969 PAR: 72 YARDAGE: 6955

CRITERIA: #74, Golf Digest, 1993.
NOTES: Designed by Ted Robinson.

ST. LOUIS
LOCATION: St. Louis, Mo.
PAR: 71 YARDAGE: 6494
CRITERIA: Host, 1947 U.S. Open.
NOTES: Host of 1921 and 1960 U.S. Amateurs, 1925 and 1972 U.S. Women's Amateur, and the 1947 U.S. Open.

SALEM
LOCATION: Peabody, Mass.
FOUNDED: 1963 PAR: 72 YARDAGE: 6807
CRITERIA: #62, Golf Digest, 1993.
NOTES: Host of the 1954 and 1984 U.S. Women's Open, the 1932 U.S. Women's Amateur; and the 1977 U.S. Senior Amateur; designed by Donald Ross.

SAN FRANCISCO
LOCATION: San Francisco, Calif.
FOUNDED: 1914 PAR: 71 YARDAGE: 6627
CRITERIA: #27, Golf Digest, 1993.
NOTES: Designed by A.W. Tillinghast and one of his earliest courses; in contrast to Olympic Club, San Francisco G.C. generally frowns on big tournaments, although it hosted the 1974 Curtis Cup.

SAUCON VALLEY (GRACE)
LOCATION: Philadelphia, PA.
FOUNDED: 1957 PAR: 72 YARDAGE: 7051
CRITERIA: #90, Golf Digest, 1993.
NOTES: Designed by William and David Gordon, the Grace course is more highly rated than Saucon Valley's Old Course despite hosting fewer national championships.

SCIOTO
LOCATION: Columbus, Ohio
FOUNDED: 1916 PAR: 71 YARDAGE: 6901
CRITERIA: #35, Golf Digest, 1993.
NOTES: Host of 1926 U.S. Open (won by Bobby Jones), the 1986 U.S. Senior Open (won by Dale Douglass), and the 1968 U.S. Amateur; designed by Donald Ross, remodeled by Dick Wilson in 1963; ranked 52nd in the world by Golf Magazine.

SHADOW CREEK
LOCATION: Las Vegas, Nev.
FOUNDED: 1990 PAR: 72 YARDAGE: 7194

CRITERIA: #8, Golf Digest, 1993.
NOTES: One of the fastest appearances in Golf Digest's top-10 rankings ever; designed by Tom Fazio; ultra-private; ranked #70 in the world by Golf Magazine.

SHERWOOD
LOCATION: Thousand Oaks, Calif.
FOUNDED: 1989 PAR: 72 YARDAGE: 7025
CRITERIA: #79, Golf Digest, 1993.
NOTES: Hosts annual Shark Shootout; designed by Jack Nicklaus.

SHINNECOCK HILLS
LOCATION: Southampton, N.Y.
FOUNDED: 1931 PAR: 70 YARDAGE: 6813
CRITERIA: #5, Golf Digest, 1993.
NOTES: Host of 1986 and 1995 U.S. Opens, 1967 Senior Amateur, and the 1977 Walker Cup matches; original course hosted 1896 U.S. Open and Amateur, and 1900 U.S. Women's Amateur; designed by William Flynn; ranked #9 in the world by Golf Magazine.

SHOAL CREEK
LOCATION: Shoal Creek, Ala.
FOUNDED: 1977 PAR: 72 YARDAGE: 7145
CRITERIA: #50, Golf Digest, 1993.
NOTES: Hosted 1984 and 1990 PGA Championships; designed by Jack Nicklaus; ranked #57 in the world by Golf Magazine.

SHOREACRES
LOCATION: Lake Bluff, Ill.
FOUNDED: 1919 PAR: N/A YARDAGE: N/A
CRITERIA: Golf Magazine Hidden Gem, 1993.
NOTES: Designed by Seth Raynor.

SKOKIE
LOCATION: Glencoe, Ill.
FOUNDED: 1915 PAR: 72 YARDAGE: 6913
CRITERIA: #97, Golf Digest, 1993.
NOTES: Hosted 1922 U.S. Open (won by Gene Sarazen); designed by Donald Ross, remodeled by W.B. Langford in 1938.

SOMERSET HILLS
LOCATION: Bernardsville, N.J.
FOUNDED: 1917 PAR: 71 YARDAGE: 6512

CRITERIA: #64, Golf Digest, 1993.
NOTES: Hosted 1990 Curtis Cup matches, 1973 and 1983 U.S. Girls' Junior Amateur; designed by A.W. Tillinghast; ranked #84 in the world by Golf Magazine, 1993.

SOUTHERN HILLS
LOCATION: Tulsa, Okla.
FOUNDED: 1936 PAR: 71 YARDAGE: 6931
CRITERIA: #23, Golf Digest, 1993.
NOTES: Host of two U.S. Opens (the latest in 1977 won by Hubert Green), the 1965 U.S. Amateur, the 1946 U.S. Women's Amateur, and the 1982 PGA Championship (won by Ray Floyd); designed by Perry Maxwell; ranked #38 in the world by Golf Magazine.

SPYGLASS HILL
LOCATION: Pebble Beach, Calif.
FOUNDED: 1966 PAR: 71 YARDAGE: 6627
CRITERIA: #26, Golf Digest, 1993.
NOTES: Annual host of AT&T National Pro-Am; designed by Robert Trent Jones; ranked #68 by Golf Magazine, 1993.

STANFORD UNIVERSITY
LOCATION: Palo Alto, Calif.
FOUNDED: N/A PAR: 71 YARDAGE: 6770
CRITERIA: Golf Magazine Top 100, 1991.
NOTES: Hosted 1959 U.S. Junior Amateur.

STANWICH CLUB
LOCATION: Greenwich, Conn.
FOUNDED: 1964 PAR: 72 YARDAGE: 7133
CRITERIA: #86, Golf Digest, 1993.
NOTES: Designed by William and David Gordon.

SYCAMORE HILLS
LOCATION: Fort Wayne, Ind.
FOUNDED: 1989 PAR: 72 YARDAGE: 7240
CRITERIA: #40, Golf Digest, 1993.
NOTES: Designed by Jack Nicklaus.

TPC AT SAWGRASS
LOCATION: Ponte Vedra, Fla.
FOUNDED: 1981 PAR: 72 YARDAGE: 6857
CRITERIA: #59, Golf Digest, 1993.
NOTES: Annual site of The Player's Championship; hosted the 1994 U.S. Amateur; designed by Pete Dye; ranked #74 in the world by Golf Magazine.

TANGLEWOOD
LOCATION: Clemmons, N.C.
PAR: 72 YARDAGE: 6469

CRITERIA: Hosted 1974 PGA Championship.
NOTES: Hosted 1986 Publinx and 1974 PGA
Championship (won by Lee Trevino).

TROON

LOCATION: Scottsdale, Ariz.
FOUNDED: 1985 PAR: 72 YARDAGE: 7041
CRITERIA: #55, Golf Digest, 1993.
NOTES: Hosted the 1990 Men's Mid-Amateur;
designed by Jay Morrish and Tom Weiskopf;
ranked #81 in the world by Golf Magazine,
1993.

TROON NORTH

LOCATION: Scottsdale, Ariz.
FOUNDED: 1990 PAR: 72 YARDAGE: 7008
CRITERIA: #65, Golf Digest, 1993.
NOTES: One of the few courses to have two
ranked courses; designed by Jay Morrish and
Tom Weiskopf; ranked #70 by Golf Magazine,
1993.

VALHALLA

LOCATION: Louisville, Ky.
FOUNDED: 1986 PAR: 72 YARDAGE: 7115
CRITERIA: #36, Golf Digest, 1993.
NOTES: Designed by Jack Nicklaus.

VALLEY CLUB OF MONTECITO

LOCATION: Santa Barbara, Calif.
FOUNDED: 1926 PAR: 72 YARDAGE: 6623
CRITERIA: #64, Golf Magazine, 1993.
NOTES: Designed by Alister Mackenzie.

WADE HAMPTON

LOCATION: Cashiers, N.C.
FOUNDED: 1987 PAR: 72 YARDAGE: 7154
CRITERIA: #18, Golf Digest, 1993.
NOTES: Designed by Tom Fazio; ranked #66 in
the world by Golf Magazine, 1993.

WANNAMOISETT

LOCATION: Rumford, R.I.
FOUNDED: 1916 PAR: 69 YARDAGE: 6631
CRITERIA: #54, Golf Digest, 1993.
NOTES: Hosted the 1931 PGA Championship
(won by Tom Creavy); designed by Donald
Ross; ranked #65 by Golf Magazine, 1993.

WAVERLY

LOCATION: Portland, Ore.
FOUNDED: N/A PAR: 72 YARDAGE: 6553
CRITERIA: Hosted 1970 U.S. Amateur.

NOTES: Hosted 1952, 1981 U.S. Women's
Amateurs and 1970 U.S. Amateur (won by
Lanny Wadkins); hosted 1993 U.S. Junior
Amateur.

WILD DUNES (LINKS)

LOCATION: Isle of Palms, S.C.
FOUNDED: 1980 PAR: 72 YARDAGE: 6722
CRITERIA: #100, Golf Digest, 1993.
NOTES: Hosted the 1985 U.S. Senior Amateur;
designed by Tom Fazio.

WILMINGTON

LOCATION: Wilmington, Del.
CRITERIA: Hosted 1971 U.S. Amateur.
NOTES: Hosted 1913 U.S. Women's Amateur,
1971 U.S. Amateur, 1965, 1978 U.S. Junior
Amateur, and the 1978 U.S. Girls' Junior
Amateur.

WINGED FOOT (EAST)

LOCATION: Mamaroneck, N.Y.
FOUNDED: 1923 PAR: 72 YARDAGE: 6664
CRITERIA: #24, Golf Digest, 1993.
NOTES: One of the few clubs to have two
ranked courses; designed by A.W. Tillinghast;
ranked #83 in the world by Golf Magazine,
1993.

WINGED FOOT (WEST)

LOCATION: Mamaroneck, N.Y.
FOUNDED: 1923 PAR: 72 YARDAGE: 6956
CRITERIA: #7, Golf Digest, 1993.
NOTES: Hosted four U.S. Opens (the latest in
1984 won by Fuzzy Zoeller), two U.S.
Women's Opens (the latest in 1972 won by
Susie Berning), the 1940 U.S. Amateur, the
1980 U.S. Senior Open, and the 1949 Walker
Cup matches; designed by A.W. Tillinghast;
ranked #17 in the world by Golf Magaizne,
1993.

WYNSTONE

LOCATION: North Barrington, Ill.
FOUNDED: 1989 PAR: 72 YARDAGE: 7003
CRITERIA: #85, Golf Digest, 1993.
NOTES: Designed by Jack Nicklaus.

AUSTRALIA

THE AUSTRALIAN

LOCATION: Sydney, New South Wales

FOUNDED: 1978 PAR: 72 YARDAGE: 7148
CRITERIA: Golf Magazine Top 100 ranking,
1991.
NOTES: Occasional site of the Australian
Open; designed by Jack Nicklaus.

COMMONWEALTH
LOCATION: South Oakleigh, Victoria
FOUNDED: 1919 PAR: 73 YARDAGE: 6777
CRITERIA: #88 (World), Golf Magazine, 1993.
NOTES: Designed by S. Bennett, Charles Lane
and Sloan Morpeth.

KINGSTON HEATH
LOCATION: Cheltenham, Victoria
FOUNDED: 1925 PAR: 72 YARDAGE: 6814
CRITERIA: #35 (World), Golf Magazine, 1993.
NOTES: Hosts the annual Mercedes-Benz
Australian Match Play Championship.
Remodeled in 1928 by Alister Mackenzie.

NEW SOUTH WALES
LOCATION: La Perouse, New South Wales
FOUNDED: 1928 PAR: 72 YARDAGE: 6768
CRITERIA: #59 (World), Golf Magazine, 1993.
NOTES: Designed by Alister Mackenzie.

ROYAL ADELAIDE
LOCATION: Seaton, South Australia
FOUNDED: 1904 PAR: 73 YARDAGE: 7000
CRITERIA: #53 (World), Golf Magazine, 1993.
NOTES: Hosts the annual South Australian
Open, and is in the Australian Open rotation;
remodeled by Alister Mackenzie, 1926.

ROYAL MELBOURNE (COMPOSITE)
LOCATION: Black Rock, Victoria
FOUNDED: 1926 PAR: 72 YARDAGE: 6586
CRITERIA: #5 (World), Golf Magazine, 1993.
NOTES: Is in the Australian Open rotation;
designed by Alister Mackenzie. Generally
regarded as the finest course outside of the
United States and the British Isles.

VICTORIA
LOCATION: Cheltenham
FOUNDED: 1927 PAR: 72 YARDAGE: 6801
CRITERIA: #77 (World), Golf Magazine, 1993.
NOTES: In the Australian Open and Australian
Masters rotations; designed by Alister
Mackenzie.

CANADA

ASHBURN G.C.
LOCATION: Kinsac Lake, Nova Scotia
FOUNDED: N/A PAR: 72 YARDAGE: 7121
CRITERIA: Canadian Top 25, Golf Digest, 1982.

BANFF SPRINGS G.C.
LOCATION: Banff, Alberta
FOUNDED: 1911 PAR: 71 YARDAGE: 6729
CRITERIA: Canadian Top 25, Golf Digest, 1982.
NOTES: Designed by Stanley Thompson

BRANTFORD G. & C.C.
LOCATION: Brantford, Ontario
FOUNDED: N/A PAR: 72 YARDAGE: 6612
CRITERIA: Canadian Top 25, Golf Digest, 1982.

CAPILANO
LOCATION: Vancouver, British Columbia
FOUNDED: 1937 PAR: 72 YARDAGE: 6562
CRITERIA: Canadian Top 25, Golf Digest, 1982.
NOTES: Designed by Stanley Thompson.

CHERRY HILL
LOCATION: Ridgeway, Ontario
FOUNDED: N/A PAR: 72 YARDAGE: 6755
CRITERIA: Canadian Top 25, Golf Digest, 1982.

GLEN ABBEY
LOCATION: Oakville, Ontario
FOUNDED: 1976 PAR: 72 YARDAGE: 7133
CRITERIA: Canadian Top 25, Golf Digest, 1982.
NOTES: Annual host of the Canadian Open;
designed by Jack Nicklaus.

THE HAMILTON
LOCATION: Ancaster, Ontario
FOUNDED: N/A PAR: 70 YARDAGE: 6750
CRITERIA: Canadian Top 25, Golf Digest, 1982.

LONDON HUNT
LOCATION: London, Ontario
FOUNDED: N/A PAR: 72 YARDAGE: 7168
CRITERIA: Canadian Top 25, Golf Digest, 1982.

MAYFAIR
LOCATION: Edmonton, Alberta
FOUNDED: N/A PAR: 70 YARDAGE: 6632
CRITERIA: Canadian Top 25, Golf Digest, 1982.

MISSISSAUGUA
LOCATION: Mississaugua, Ontario
FOUNDED: N/A   PAR: 72   YARDAGE: 6860
CRITERIA: Canadian Top 25, Golf Digest, 1982.

THE NATIONAL
LOCATION: Woodbridge, Ontario
FOUNDED: 1974   PAR: 71   YARDAGE: 6975
CRITERIA: Canadian Top 25, Golf Digest, 1982.
NOTES: Designed by George and Tom Fazio;
rated #1 in Canada by SCORE Magazine.

THE ROYAL COLWOOD
LOCATION: Victoria, British Columbia
FOUNDED: N/A   PAR: 70   YARDAGE: 6425
CRITERIA: Canadian Top 25, Golf Digest, 1982.

THE ROYAL MONTREAL (BLUE)
LOCATION: Ile Bizard, Quebec
FOUNDED: 1873   PAR: 70   YARDAGE: 6433
CRITERIA: Canadian Top 25, Golf Digest, 1982.
NOTES: Hosted the 1975 and 1980 Canadian
Opens; present facility designed by Dick
Wilson in 1959.

ST. GEORGE'S
LOCATION: Islington, Ontario
FOUNDED: N/A   PAR: 71   YARDAGE: 6797
CRITERIA: Canadian Top 25, Golf Digest, 1982.

COLOMBIA

EL RINCON
LOCATION: Bogota
FOUNDED: 1960   PAR: 72   YARDAGE: 7516
CRITERIA: Golf Magazine Top 100 (World),
1991.
NOTES: Along with Lagunita, considered the
finest of the South American courses;
designed by Robert Trent Jones.

DOMINICAN REPUBLIC

CASA DE CAMPO
LOCATION: La Romana
FOUNDED: 1972   PAR: 72   YARDAGE: 6888
CRITERIA: #29 Golf Magazine (World), 1993.
NOTES: The course is known as Teeth of the
Dog. One of the earliest gems from the design
portfolio of Pete Dye. Considered the finest
Caribbean course.

ENGLAND

ALWOODLEY
LOCATION: Leeds, Yorkshire
FOUNDED: 1908   PAR: 70   YARDAGE: 6686
CRITERIA: #33 Golf World (U.K.), 1988.
NOTES: Designed by Colt and Alison.

THE BELFRY (BRABAZON)
LOCATION: Sutton Coldfield, West Midlands
FOUNDED: 1977   PAR: 73   YARDAGE: 6975
CRITERIA: #35 Golf World (U.K.), 1988.
NOTES: Hosted the 1985, 1987, and 1993 Ryder
Cup matches; designed by Peter Alliss.

BERKSHIRE (RED)
LOCATION: Ascot, Berkshire
FOUNDED: 1928   PAR: 72   YARDAGE: 6356
CRITERIA: #20 Golf World (U.K.), 1988.
NOTES: Designed by Herbert Fowler, H.S. Colt
and Tom Simpson.

FORMBY
LOCATION: Formby, Merseyside
FOUNDED: 1884   PAR: 72   YARDAGE: 6781
CRITERIA: #23 Golf World (U.K.), 1988.

GANTON
LOCATION: Ganton, Yorkshire
FOUNDED: 1891   PAR: 72   YARDAGE: 6693
CRITERIA: #14 Golf World (U.K.), 1988.
NOTES: Hosted the 1949 Ryder Cup; ranked
#68 in the world by Golf Magazine, 1993;
designed by Tom Dunn and Harry Vardon.

HILLSIDE
LOCATION: Southport, Merseyside
FOUNDED: 1909   PAR: 72   YARDAGE: 6850
CRITERIA: #19 Golf World (U.K.), 1988.
NOTES: Designed by Fred Hawtree.

LINDRICK
LOCATION: Worksop, Yorkshire
FOUNDED: 1891   PAR: 71   YARDAGE: 6615
CRITERIA: #31 Golf World (U.K.), 1988.
NOTES: Hosted 1957 Ryder Cup matches;
designed by Tom Dunn.

LITTLE ASTON
LOCATION: Streetly, West Midlands
FOUNDED: 1908   PAR: 72   YARDAGE: 6724
CRITERIA: #27 Golf World (U.K.), 1988.
NOTES: Designed by Harry Vardon.

NOTTS

LOCATION: Hollinwell, Nottinghamshire
FOUNDED: 1887 PAR: 72 YARDAGE: 7020
CRITERIA: #24 Golf World (U.K.), 1988.
NOTES: Designed by Willie Park, Jr.

ROYAL BIRKDALE

LOCATION: Southport, Merseyside
FOUNDED: 1889 PAR: 71 YARDAGE: 6968
CRITERIA: #2 Golf World (U.K.), 1988.
NOTES: Hosted six British Opens (the latest in 1991 won by Ian Baker-Finch), and the 1965 and 1969 Ryder Cup matches; designed by George Lowe, remodeled in 1931 by Fred Hawtree; ranked #21 in the world by Golf Magazine, 1993.

ROYAL LIVERPOOL (HOYLAKE)

LOCATION: Hoylake, Merseyside
FOUNDED: 1869 PAR: 72 YARDAGE: 7110
CRITERIA: #26 Golf World (U.K.), 1988.
NOTES: Hosted ten British Opens (the latest in 1967, won by Roberto De Vicenzo); designed by R. Chambers, G. Morris, and John Braid; ranked #78 in the world by Golf Magazine, 1993.

ROYAL LYTHAM & ST. ANNE'S

LOCATION: Lytham St. Anne's, Lancashire
FOUNDED: 1886 PAR: 71 YARDAGE: 6673
CRITERIA: #13 Golf World (U.K.), 1988.
NOTES: Hosted eight British Opens (the latest, in 1988, won by Seve Ballesteros), plus the 1961 and 1977 Ryder Cup matches; designed by George Lowe; ranked #67 in the world by Golf Magazine, 1993.

ROYAL ST. GEORGE'S

LOCATION: Sandwich, Kent
FOUNDED: 1887 PAR: 70 YARDAGE: 6891
CRITERIA: #18 Golf World (U.K.), 1988.
NOTES: Hosted twelve British Opens (the latest in 1993 won by Greg Norman); designed by Laidlaw Purves; ranked #26 in the world by Golf Magazine, 1993.

ROYAL WEST NORFOLK

LOCATION: Brancaster, Norfolk
FOUNDED: 1892 PAR: 71 YARDAGE: 6428
CRITERIA: #39 Golf World (U.K.), 1988.
NOTES: Designed by Horace Hutchinson.

SAUNTON (EAST)

LOCATION: Braunton, Devon
FOUNDED: 1897 PAR: 71 YARDAGE: 6703
CRITERIA: #29 Golf World (U.K.), 1988.
NOTES: Designed by Herbert Fowler.

SUNNINGDALE (NEW)

LOCATION: Sunningdale, Surrey
FOUNDED: N/A PAR: 70 YARDAGE: 6676
CRITERIA: #25 Golf World (U.K.), 1988.
NOTES: One of the few clubs to have two ranked courses; designed by Harry Colt.

SUNNINGDALE (OLD)

LOCATION: Sunningdale, Surrey
FOUNDED: 1901 PAR: 70 YARDAGE: 6580
CRITERIA: #8 Golf World (U.K.), 1988.
NOTES: designed by Willie Park, Jr.; ranked #40 in the world by Golf Magazine, 1993. Hosted 1903 British Match Play and remains on the European Tour rotation.

SWINLEY FOREST

LOCATION: Ascot, Berkshire
FOUNDED: 1909 PAR: 68 YARDAGE: 6001
CRITERIA: #36 Golf World (U.K.), 1988.
NOTES: designed by Harry Colt.

WALTON HEATH (OLD)

LOCATION: Tadworth, Surrey
FOUNDED: 1904 PAR: 73 YARDAGE: 6813
NOTES: Hosted 1981 Ryder Cup matches, and two European Opens; designed by Herbert Fowler; ranked #76 in the world by Golf Magazine, 1993.

WENTWORTH (WEST)

LOCATION: Virginia Water, Surrey
FOUNDED: 1924 PAR: 72 YARDAGE: 6945
CRITERIA: #12 Golf World (U.K.), 1988.
NOTES: Hosted the 1953 Ryder Cup; designed by Colt, Alison, and Morrison; ranked #61 in the world by Golf Magazine, 1993.

WOODHALL SPA

LOCATION: Woodhall Spa, Lincolnshire
FOUNDED: 1905 PAR: 73 YARDAGE: 6866
CRITERIA: #10 Golf World (U.K.), 1988.
NOTES: Designed by S.V. Hotchkin and Harry Vardon; ranked #27 in the world by Golf Magazine, 1993.

FRANCE

CHANTILLY (OLD)
LOCATION: Chantilly
FOUNDED: N/A PAR: 71 YARDAGE: 7214
CRITERIA: European Top 20 Courses, Golf World (U.K.), 1988.
NOTES: Hosted many French Opens, beginning in 1913; designed by Tom Simpson.

LE TOQUET (MER)
LOCATION: Le Toquet
FOUNDED: 1916 PAR: 72 YARDAGE: 6807
CRITERIA: European Top 20 Courses, Golf World (U.K.), 1988.
NOTES: Designed by Harry Holt.

MORFONTAINE
LOCATION: Senlis
FOUNDED: 1927 PAR: 70 YARDAGE: 6630
CRITERIA: European Top 20 Courses, Golf World (U.K.), 1988.
NOTES: designed by Tom Simpson; ranked #85 in the world by Golf Magazine, 1993.

SEIGNOSSE
LOCATION: Seignosse
FOUNDED: 1990 PAR: N/A YARDAGE: N/A
CRITERIA: Golf Magazine Hidden Gem, 1993.
NOTES: Designed by Robert von Hagge.

GERMANY

CLUB ZUR VAHR
LOCATION: Bremen
FOUNDED: N/A PAR: 74 YARDAGE: 7037
CRITERIA: European Top 20 Courses, Golf World (U.K.), 1988.
NOTES: Designed by Bernard von Limburger.

HAMBURGER (FALKENSTEIN)
LOCATION: Hamburg
FOUNDED: N/A PAR: 71 YARDAGE: 6480
CRITERIA: European Top 20 Courses, Golf World (U.K.), 1988.
NOTES: Designed by Colt, Alison, and Morrison.

HOLLAND

KENNEMER
LOCATION: Kennemerweg, Zandvoort
FOUNDED: N/A PAR: 72 YARDAGE: 6408
CRITERIA: European Top 20 Courses, Golf World (U.K.), 1988.
NOTES: Designed by Colt and Morrison.

NOORDWIJK
LOCATION: Noordwijk
FOUNDED: N/A PAR: 72 YARDAGE: 6463
NOTES: Designed by Frank Pennink.

INDONESIA

JAGORAWL
FOUNDED: 1978 PAR: N/A YARDAGE: N/A
CRITERIA: Golf Magazine Hidden Gem, 1993.
NOTES: A magnet for national and Asian tournaments.

IRELAND

BALLYBUNION (NEW)
LOCATION: Ballybunion, Kerry
FOUNDED: N/A PAR: 72 YARDAGE: 6477
CRITERIA: #28 Golf World (U.K.), 1988.
NOTES: One of the few clubs to have two ranked courses; designed by Robert Trent Jones.

BALLYBUNION (OLD)
LOCATION: Ballybunion, Kerry
FOUNDED: 1896 PAR: 71 YARDAGE: 6542
CRITERIA: #3 Golf World (U.K.), 1988.
NOTES: Designed by P. Murphy and M. Smyth; ranked #12 in the world by Golf Magazine, 1993.

COUNTY LOUTH
LOCATION: Baltray, Drogoheda, Louth
FOUNDED: 1892 PAR: 73 YARDAGE: 6978
CRITERIA: #37 Golf World (U.K.), 1988.
NOTES: Designed by Tom Simpson.

COUNTY SLIGO
LOCATION: Rosses Point, Sligo
FOUNDED: 1894 PAR: 72 YARDAGE: 6600
CRITERIA: #34 Golf World (U.K.), 1988.
NOTES: Designed by Colt & Alison.

LAHINCH
LOCATION: Lahinch, Clare
FOUNDED: 1892 PAR: 72 YARDAGE: 6699
CRITERIA: #30, Golf World (U.K.), 1988.
NOTES: Designed by Old Tom Morris; ranked #89 in the world by Golf Magazine, 1993.

PORTMARNOCK
LOCATION: Portmarnock, Dublin
FOUNDED: 1894 PAR: 72 YARDAGE: 7097
CRITERIA: #6 Golf World (U.K.), 1988.
NOTES: Designed by G. Ross and W.L. Pickeman; ranked #31 in the world by Golf Magazine, 1993.

ROYAL COUNTY DOWN
LOCATION: Newcaster, Down
FOUNDED: 1889 PAR: 71 YARDAGE: 6968
CRITERIA: #9 Golf World (U.K.), 1988.
NOTES: designed by Old Tom Morris; ranked #7 in the world by Golf Magazine, 1993.

ROYAL PORTRUSH (DUNLUCE)
LOCATION: Portrush, Antrim
FOUNDED: 1888 PAR: 72 YARDAGE: 6772
CRITERIA: #15 Golf World (U.K.), 1988.
NOTES: Hosted 1951 British Open (the only course outside of England and Scotland to have the honor) and 1993 British Amateur; designed by Harry Colt; ranked #18 in the world by Golf Magazine, 1993.

ITALY

MILANO
LOCATION: Monza
FOUNDED: N/A PAR: 72 YARDAGE: 6799
CRITERIA: European Top 20 Courses, Golf World (U.K.), 1988.
NOTES: Designed by John Blenford.

PEVERO
LOCATION: Porto Cervo, Sardinia
FOUNDED: N/A PAR: 72 YARDAGE: 6386
CRITERIA: European Top 20 Courses, Golf World (U.K.), 1988.
NOTES: Designed by Robert Trent Jones.

JAPAN

HIRONO
LOCATION: Kobe
FOUNDED: 1932 PAR: 72 YARDAGE: 6950
CRITERIA: #40 (World), Golf Magazine, 1993.
NOTES: Designed by Charles Alison; ultra-private membership, no major tournaments.

KASUMIGASEKI (EAST)
LOCATION: Kawagoe
FOUNDED: 1929 PAR: N/A YARDAGE: N/A
CRITERIA: #54 (World) Golf Magazine, 1993.
NOTES: Hosted the 1957 Canada Cup; designed by Kinya Fujita, remodeled by Charles Alison in 1931

KAWANA (FUJI)
LOCATION: Shizuoka
FOUNDED: 1936 PAR: 70 YARDAGE: 6970
CRITERIA: #50 (World) Golf Magazine, 1993.
NOTES: Designed by Alison and Fuijita.

TOKYO
LOCATION: Tokyo
FOUNDED: 1940 PAR: N/A YARDAGE: N/A
CRITERIA: Golf Magazine Hidden Gem, 1993.
NOTES: Designed by Komei Ohtani.

MOROCCO

ROYAL DAR-ES-SALAAM
LOCATION: Rabat
FOUNDED: 1971 PAR: 73 YARDAGE: 7329
CRITERIA: #99 (World) Golf Magazine, 1993.
NOTES: Annual host of Morocco Open; designed by Robert Trent Jones.

NEW ZEALAND

PARAPARAUMU BEACH
LOCATION: Paraparaumu Beach
FOUNDED: 1949 PAR: 71 YARDAGE: 6510
CRITERIA: #72 (World) Golf Magazine, 1993.
NOTES: Designed by Alex Russell and Douglas Whyte.

PORTUGAL

QUINTO DO LAGO (B&C)
LOCATION: Quinto do Lago
FOUNDED: N/A PAR: 72 YARDAGE: 7032

CRITERIA: European Top 20 Courses, Golf World (U.K.), 1988.
NOTES: Designed by William Mitchell.

SAN LORENZO

LOCATION: Quinto do Lago
FOUNDED: 1987 PAR: N/A YARDAGE: N/A
CRITERIA: Golf Magazine Hidden Gem, 1993.
NOTES: Designed by Joe Lee.

VILAMOURA (NO. 1)

LOCATION: Quarteria, Algarve
FOUNDED: 1969 PAR: 73 YARDAGE: 6924
CRITERIA: European Top 20 Courses, Golf World (U.K.), 1988.
NOTES: Designed by Frank Pennick.

SCOTLAND

BLAIRGOWRIE (ROSEMOUNT)

LOCATION: Blairgowrie, Perthshire
FOUNDED: 1889 PAR: 72 YARDAGE: 6588
CRITERIA: #38 Golf World (U.K.), 1988.
NOTES: Designed by James Braid.

CARNOUSTIE (CHAMPIONSHIP)

LOCATION: Carnoustie, Angus
FOUNDED: 1842 PAR: 72 YARDAGE: 6931
CRITERIA: #7 Golf World (U.K.), 1988.
NOTES: Hosted five British Opens (the latest, in 1975, won by Tom Watson); designed by Allan Robertson, Tom Morris, and Willie Park, Jr.; ranked #25 in the world by Golf Magazine, 1993.

CRUDEN BAY

LOCATION: Cruden Bay, Aberdeenshire
FOUNDED: 1791 PAR: 70 YARDAGE: 6370
CRITERIA: #40 Golf World (U.K.), 1988.
NOTES: Designed by Herbert Fowler and Tom Simpson.

GLENEAGLES (KINGS)

LOCATION: Auchterarder, Perthshire
FOUNDED: 1919 PAR: 72 YARDAGE: 6826
CRITERIA: #22 Golf World (U.K.), 1988.
NOTES: Designed by James Braid; has played host to the Scottish Open.

MUIRFIELD

LOCATION: Gullane, East Lothian
FOUNDED: 1891 PAR: 71 YARDAGE: 6963
CRITERIA: #1 Golf World (U.K.), 1988.
NOTES: Hosted fourteen British Opens (the latest, in 1992, won by Nick Faldo), and the 1973 Ryder Cup matches; designed by Old Tom Morris; home club of the Honourable Company of Edinburgh Golfers, the oldest golf club in existence; ranked #6 in the world by Golf Magazine, 1993.

ROYAL DORNOCH

LOCATION: Dornoch, Sutherland
FOUNDED: Unknown PAR: 70 YARDAGE: 6751
CRITERIA: #11 Golf World (U.K.), 1988.
NOTES: Designed by Old Tom Morris; ranked #13 in the world by Golf Magazine, 1993; the third oldest golf course, and the second oldest still surviving (after the Old Course).

ROYAL TROON (OLD)

LOCATION: Troon, Ayrshire
FOUNDED: 1878 PAR: 72 YARDAGE: 7067
CRITERIA: #16 Golf World (U.K.), 1988.
NOTES: Hosted six British Opens (the latest, in 1989, won by Mark Calcavecchia); designed by C. Hunter and Willie Fernie; the last course to date to receive the honorific "Royal" (1978); ranked #28 in the world by Golf Magazine, 1993.

ST. ANDREWS (OLD)

LOCATION: St. Andrews, Fife
FOUNDED: Unknown PAR: 72 YARDAGE: 6933
CRITERIA: #5 Golf World (U.K.), 1988.
NOTES: Host of 24 British Opens (the latest, in 1990, won by Nick Faldo), and the annual Alfred Dunhill Cup matches; the home of golf; the home of the Royal & Ancient Golf Club of St. Andrews, golf's original governing body; ranked #8 in the world by Golf Magazine, 1993.

TURNBERRY (AILSA)

LOCATION: Turnberry, Ayrshire
FOUNDED: 1909 PAR: 70 YARDAGE: 6950
CRITERIA: #4 Golf World (U.K.), 1988.
NOTES: Host of four British Opens (the latest, in 1994, won by Nick Price); course reconstructed in 1947 by C.K. Hutchinson and P. Mackenzie Ross; ranked #16 in the world by Golf Magazine, 1993.

SOUTH AFRICA

DURBAN
LOCATION: Durban
FOUNDED: 1922 PAR: 72 YARDAGE: 6576
CRITERIA: #6 Golf Magazine (World), 1993.
NOTES: Designed by Waters & Waterman, remodeled by Hotchkin, 1928; ranked #56 in the world, Golf Magazine, 1993; hosted many South African Opens, beginning in 1924.

SPAIN

CLUB DE CAMPO
LOCATION: Carretera Castilla, Madrid
FOUNDED: N/A PAR: 72 YARDAGE: 6691
CRITERIA: European Top 20, Golf World (U.K.), 1988.
NOTES: Designed by Javier Arana.

EL PRAT
LOCATION: Prat de Llobregat, Barcelona
FOUNDED: N/A PAR: 72 YARDAGE: 6452
CRITERIA: European Top 20, Golf World (U.K.), 1988.
NOTES: Designed by Javier Arana.

EL SALER
LOCATION: Valencia
FOUNDED: 1967 PAR: 72 YARDAGE: 7092
CRITERIA: European Top 20, Golf World (U.K.), 1988.
NOTES: Designed by Javier Arana; ranked #55 in the world by Golf Magazine, 1993.

LAS BRISAS
LOCATION: Nueva Andalusia, Costa del Sol
FOUNDED: N/A PAR: 72 YARDAGE: 6778
CRITERIA: European Top 20, Golf World (U.K.), 1988.
NOTES: Designed by Robert Trent Jones.

PUERTO DE HIERRO
LOCATION: Madrid
FOUNDED: N/A PAR: 72 YARDAGE: 6941
CRITERIA: European Top 20, Golf World (U.K.), 1988.
NOTES: Designed by Colt and Alison.

SOTOGRANDE (OLD)
LOCATION: Sotogrande, Costa del Sol
FOUNDED: 1965 PAR: 72 YARDAGE: 6849
CRITERIA: European Top 20, Golf World (U.K.), 1988.
NOTES: Designed by Robert Trent Jones; ranked #98 in the world by Golf Magazine, 1993; will host the 1997 Ryder Cup matches.

VALDERRAMA
LOCATION: Sotogrande, Cadiz
FOUNDED: 1975 PAR: 72 YARDAGE: 6691
CRITERIA: #86 (World) Golf Magazine, 1993.
NOTES: Designed by Robert Trent Jones and Cabell Robinson.

SWEDEN

FALSTERBO
LOCATION: Falsterbo
FOUNDED: N/A PAR: 71 YARDAGE: 6671
CRITERIA: European Top 20, Golf World (U.K.), 1988.
NOTES: Designed by Gunnar Bauer.

HALMSTAD
LOCATION: Halmstad
FOUNDED: N/A PAR: 72 YARDAGE: 6540
CRITERIA: European Top 20, Golf World (U.K.), 1988.
NOTES: Designed by Frank Pennick.

SWITZERLAND

LAUSANNE
LOCATION: Lausanne
FOUNDED: N/A PAR: 72 YARDAGE: 6742
CRITERIA: European Top 20, Golf World (U.K.), 1988.
NOTES: Designed by Oscar Dollfus.

WALES

ROYAL PORTHCAWL
LOCATION: Porthcawl, Mid Glamorgan
FOUNDED: 1891 PAR: 72 YARDAGE: 6643
CRITERIA: #21 Golf World (U.K.), 1988.
NOTES: Designed by Charles Gibson, with James Braid, Harry Colt, John H. Taylor, Fred Hawtree, Tom Simpson, and C.K. Cotton credited in remodeling; the only course in Wales given the honorific "Royal."

GOLF SCHOOLS

OVERVIEW: *Locations, rates, teacher/student ratios, and head instructors at every major golf school in the United States. Brief descriptions are included which discuss the program, and the staff in detail, including the names of prominent students and national awards and recognition. The Almanac does not endorse any particular instruction methodology or instruction school.*

THE ACADEMY OF GOLF AT PGA NATIONAL

Locations: Palm Beach Gardens, Fla.
Head Instructor: Mike Adams.
Student/Teacher Ratios: 3/1.
Rates: From $895 for the three-day program.
Description: If there's a "hot seat" in golf instruction, the head instructor at PGA National, the home of the PGA of America, has to be the one sitting on it. The fact that Mike Adams at PGA National has earned nothing but respect from his 14,000 colleagues is a real testament to the program he has created that was voted the best in the country by The Robb Report. Biomechanical computer analysis, high-speed split screen video analysis, l;laser analysis for putting, and a staff psychologist and physiologist are just a few of the touches the PGA has chosen to showcase at their premier facility. Each student is treated] individually and videotaped daily to monitor progress. Personal fitness and mental toughness training are also emphasized.

ACADEMY OF GOLF DYNAMICS

Locations: Lake Travis, Texas and Colorado Springs, Colorado.
Head Instructor: Bill Moretti
Student/Teacher Ratios: 3:1
Rates: All 3-day sessions from $600-995/person.
Description: Named among the nation's top golf schools, teachers Bill Moretti (contributor to *Golf Magazine*) and Jay Bowden provide individualized instruction in all areas of the game. The school offers low student teacher ratios, video swing analysis, and a learning center designed by Jack Nicklaus.

AMELIA ISLAND PLANTATION GOLF SCHOOL

Locations: Amelia Island, Fla. (800) 874-6878.
Head Instructor: Ron Philo.
Student/Teacher Ratios: 5/1.
Rates: From $195 for a mini-school; full three- and four-day sessions offered.
Description: Ron Philo combines video analysis, numerous visual aids, and an outstanding resort location into an impressive golf school offering. Philo concentrates on "Big Muscle Leadership" and "The Inside Moves The Outside" in guiding his students through classes limited to a maximum of 20 participants.

AMERICA'S FAVORITE GOLF SCHOOLS

Locations: Headquarters in Ft. Pierce, Fla; 20 locations nationwide including California, Nevada, Colorado, Arizona, Oklahoma, Illinois, Ontario, Connecticut, Pennsylvania, South Carolina, Florida, and The Bahamas.
Head Instructor: Sixteen instructors.
Student/Teacher Ratios: 4/1.
Rates: From $585 for a three-day school; five-day programs available.
Description: America's Favorite Golf Schools are situated in key scenic and historic destination areas of the country and are among the most reasonable priced nationwide. The typical day at a school includes five hours of lessons utilizing championship courses and practice areas, video analysis, classroom theory sessions and on-course play with the professional. The schools emphasize a relaxed teaching style and group players by ability level.

ARNOLD PALMER GOLF ACADEMY

Locations: Bay Hill Club, Orlando, FL; Saddlebrook Resort, Tampa, FL.
Head Instructor: Brad Brewer.
Student/Teacher Ratios: 5/1.
Rates: Three-day "commuter rate" is $750.
Description: The Palmer philosophy is to work with the

individual's skills rather than forcing a new technique. Director Brad Brewer currently instructs PGA TOUR pros Steve Lowery, Tom Garner, Todd Barringer, and Arnold Palmer. Dick Tiddy, who heads instruction at the Bay Hill site, was voted North Florida PGA Professional of the Year in 1993. APGA operates the only accredited boarding school for junior golfers (ages 12-18), at Saddlebrook. Video analysis is available; corporate seminars, junior instruction, hourly to 5-day instruction programs available.

BARTON CREEK GOLF ADVANTAGE SCHOOL

Locations: Barton Creek Country Club, Austin, TX
Head Instructor: Joe Beck
Student/Teacher Ratios: 4/1.
Rates: 2 1/2 days Fri., Sat., & Sun. $1465
Description: Founded by former British Ryder Cup captain and legendary instructor John Jacobs, the schools have grown into the nation's largest golf school concern by centering its activities around practical instruction, low teacher/student ratios, and attractive packages including accommodations at some of the nation's finer resorts. Shelby Futch, a renowned instructor in his own right, has been the day-to-day head of the schools for some time. John Jacobs' also has a course ownership and travel agency wing, which allows for complete control of the packaging process. A proven value.

BERTHOLY-METHOD GOLF SCHOOLS

Locations: Jackson Springs, NC.
Head Instructor: Paul Bertholy.
Student/Teacher Ratios: 1/2 private lessons; 4/1 group.
Rates: From $500 for a three-day school.
Description: The irrepressible Paul Bertholy, once described as "the best [instructor] in golf history" holds court adjacent to Foxfire G.C. in Jackson Springs, in the Pinehurst area. It's one of the most interesting programs around, where instructors will sometimes outnumber the students, and where students will experience the Bertholy-Method Isotonic Swing Trainer, one of the earliest swing trainers developed and still one of the best. Bertholy offers his own indoor/outdoor facilities and, if in the area, he's worth a call. Bob Toski, who knows a bit about the game, calls Bertholy "unquestionable the finest teacher of the golf swing that I have encountered."

BEN SUTTON GOLF SCHOOLS

Location: Tampa, Fla. (800) 225-6923
Head Instructor: Dick Sutton
Student/Teacher Ratios: N/A.
Rates: Three-, five-, and eight-day programs available.

Description: On e of the first golf schools to successfully expand into a national concern, Sutton is all over the country and perhaps is rivaled only by Golf Digest and John Jacobs for sheer volume of instruction.

BILL SKELLEY GOLF SCHOOLS

Location: N/A.
Head Instructor: Bill Skelley.
Student/Teacher Ratios: N/A.
Rates: N/A.
Description: The Skelley schools are one of the largest golf-school companies in the country, offering schools at several sites throughout the year.

BOB TOSKI GOLF SCHOOL

Location: N/A.
Head Instructor: Bob Toski.
Student/Teacher Ratios: N/A.
Rates: N/A.
Description: Toski was, with perhaps Gardner Dickinson, the first of the celebrity instructors—a successful touring pro who found continued success in the arena of instruction. Toski offers his own golf clubs, his own instruction system, and has remained one of the most influential teachers of all time. His book with Jim Flick, "How to become a Complete Golfer," is still on the short list of all-time great instruction books.

THE CONCORD GOLF SCHOOL

Location: Kiamesha Lake, N.Y. (800) 431-3850.
Head Instructor: Bill Burke.
Student/Teacher Ratios: 5/1.
Rates: From $715 for a weekend school; four-day sessions available.
Description: Veteran Director of Golf Bill Burke emphasizes simplicity of technique and a "learn-as-you-play" teaching style in a quintessential resort program designed to enhance your skills without distracting you too much from the resort's chief golf attraction, the Concord's Monster Course, the longest and perhaps toughest resort course in the country. Video analysis, range work, physical and game/course management are all offered during the four-day school.

CRAFT-ZAVICHAS GOLF SCHOOL

Locations: Several locations throughout the Southeast, West, and Midwest; headquarters are in Pueblo, Colo. (800) 858-9633.
Head Instructor: Penny Zavichas.
Student/Teacher Ratios: Maximum of 4/1.
Rates: From $535 for a three-day school. Four- and five-day schools also offered.
Description: A pioneer among golf schools, operating continuously since 1968. A special emphasis is placed on instruction for women, with women-only schools featuring female instructors. Personalized attention and

care is the rule, not the exception, here. A good starting place for beginners. Video analysis (including take-home tapes), and split-screen strobe effects are employed.

CRUMPIN-FOX CLUB
ADULT GOLF INSTITUTE

Location: Bernardston, Mass.
Head Instructor: Ron Beck.
Student/Teacher Ratios: 4/1.
Rates: From $500 for commuters.
Description: Video analysis, a digital printer, and a wide array of learning aids are employed at this school, which concentrates treats enjoyment of the game as seriously as teaching fundamentals of the swing. A complete learning center hosts the technical sessions, followed by nine-hole playing lessons each afternoon. The school teaches specialty, situational shots as well as the fundamentals of driving, iron play, putting and chipping. "The three most important bones in golf—the WISH bone, the Back bone, and the FUNNY bone, "goes the saying at the Institute. Junior programs offered weekly in the summer.

DAVE PELZ
SHORT GAME SCHOOL

Locations: Boca Raton, Fla.; La Quinta, Calif..
Head Instructor: Dave Pelz.
Student/Teacher Ratios: 4/1.
Rates: From $1700 for a three-day school.
Description: Dave Pelz is on most short lists of the top golf instructors, as his rates reflect, and this school is concentrated on the short game, where three strokes can be turned into two and where improvement has the most direct impact on scoring. Pelz combines theory and outdoor execution sessions for wedge play, pitching, chipping, sand play and putting. Pelz structures his teaching to players of all ability levels, and thus it has happened before that amateurs are learning side-by-side with PGA and LPGA tour pros! Pelz has a Putting Robot on-site, plus video analysis, laser alignment and practice aids, all grouped into a Short game Center designed to house the Short Game School.

DAVID LEADBETTER
GOLF ACADEMY

Locations: Orlando, Fla.
Head Instructor: David Leadbetter.
Student/Teacher Ratios: 2/1 on two-day retreats.
Rates: From $125 per hour; half-day sessions from $175, one-day schools from $550, and two-day retreats from $1200.
Description: A mixed bag—as highly-priced as instruction gets, but Leadbetter coaches Nick Price, David Frost, Ernie Els and Nick Faldo among dozens of pros

who have sought out his help, and thus Leadbetter has the results to justify the fees. His swing theories focus on movement of the big muscles of the torso and taking the hands out of the action; video swing analysis, the David Leadbetter Putting System, The Right Angle, Swing Mirror, Swing Links, and the Powerball are employed as devices to aid students. Leadbetter operates out of Lake Nona, one of the nation's ultimate golf-oriented communities, but his own operation is very low-key and understated. In short, not for everyone at these rates, but certainly at the top of the list for celebrity instruction and/or results.

DORAL GOLF LEARNING CENTER

Location: Miami, Fla. (800) 12-DORAL.
Head Instructor: Jim McLean.
Student/Teacher Ratios: N/A.
Rates: One-, two-, three- and five-day programs available.
Description: Doral was Jimmy Ballard's old hang-out, and now they have Jim McLean, also on everyone's short list of great American golf instructors. Students stay of course at the famed Doral Resort and can play the equally famed Blue Monster course in between sessions.

EXCELLER GOLF SCHOOLS

Location: Phoenix, Ariz.
Head Instructor: N/A.
Student/Teacher Ratios: N/A.
Rates: N/A.
Description: One of the more aggressive, new-style instruction schools, Exceller has several locations and features excellent programs for women golfers.

GALVANO INTERNATIONAL
GOLF ACADEMY

Locations: Wisconsin Dells, WI. (800) 234-6121.
Head Instructor: Phil Galvano.
Student/Teacher Ratios: N/A.
Rates: N/A.
Description: Bob Hope, Johnny Carson, Carol Burnett, Morey Amsterdam, Milton Berle, Willie Mosconi, and Dwight Eisenhower are a few of the many notable personalities who have attended the Academy, which was founded in 1941. Stop-action videoography is combined with a program of technical and mental preparedness training.

THE GOLF ACADEMY AT AVIARA

Location: Carlsbad, Calif. (800) 433-7468.
Head Instructor: Kip Puterbaugh.
Student/Teacher Ratios: 4/1.
Rates: From $150 for a half-day school.
Description: The practice facilities and classroom

areas offer students a state of the art learning situation, to aid in the understanding of the golf swing. Puterbaugh's goal is to have students hit more consistently good shots, and be able to self-analyze problems and develop improvements. Junior programs are available here, and unlimited play at Aviara is available after class on a space-available basis. Scott Simpson and Dennis Paulson are the PGA TOUR advisors at Aviara, which sometimes puts on a road show in Carmel, Calif. Corporate groups are a specialty here, too.

GOLF SCHOOLS OF SCOTTSDALE

Locations: Scottsdale, Ariz. Programs also available in Palm Springs. (800) 356-6678.
Head Instructor: Ned Mullen, Exec. Director.
Student/Teacher Ratios: 5/1.
Rates: From $495 for a full-day school; two-, three-, and five-day sessions available.
Description: This Scottsdale program is located at the Tatum Ranch G.C., in the foothills of the Sonoran Desert. The school's philosophy is to custom-fit instruction to the client's needs, and to concentrate on playing lessons. Video Analysis available, and a non-golfing spouse stays free at the Red Lion's La Posada Resort during the program. Not a bad idea at all for those on a budget.

THE GOLF UNIVERSITY AT SAN DIEGO

Locations: San Diego, Calif. (800) 426-0966.
Head Instructor: Dr. Ken Blanchard, Founder.
Student/Teacher Ratios: 5/1.
Rates: From $895 for a three-day commuter program; four-day programs available.
Description: Founded in 1988 by Ken Blanchard, co-author of The One Minute Manager and author of Playing the Great Game of Golf, to reach out to golfers and bring them an easy-to-learn, individualized golf curriculum. Blanchard's innovative management ideas are applied to golf in a way that enhances performance and enjoyment of the game. Includes video analysis with voice-over swing evaluation, playing lessons, and personal club fitting and evaluation.

GRAND CYPRESS ACADEMY OF GOLF

Locations: Orlando, Fla. ((800) 835-7377.
Head Instructor: Fred Griffin.
Student/Teacher Ratios: 3/1.
Rates: From $1,125 for a three-day mini-school; regular schools from $1,825.
Description: One of the most-highly regarded programs in the country, and situated at the elegant Grand Cypress Resort southwest of downtown Orlando. Only the best teach at Grand Cypress, including longtime director Fred Griffin, PGA Senior TOUR player Phil

Rodgers, and biomechanics expert Dr. Ralph Munn. Video analysis and comparison with the computer-enhanced "perfect swing" are two of the programs in this high-tech version of golf instruction. Personal teaching, club fitting, and the comprehensive analysis of all aspects of the student's playing style are the hallmarks of this very well designed program.

GRAND STRAND GOLF INSTRUCTIONS

Location: Myrtle Beach, S.C.
Head Instructor: Glen Davis.
Student/Teacher Ratios: 3/1.
Rates: From $180 for a three-day mini-school.
Description: Situated along "The Grand Strand," home to over 70 golf courses and an avalanche of avid golfers, the school concentrates on simplifying the golf swing. A focus is placed on achieving the correct tilt of the spine, the swing axis, and the position of the hands ahead of the ball at impact. They proudly state that they can take a chronic slicer and have them drawing the ball in less than ten minutes. Video analysis is employed, and results guaranteed.

GUARANTEED PERFORMANCE SCHOOL OF GOLF

Location: Bethel, Maine.
Head Instructor: Allen Conners.
Student/Teacher Ratios: 4/1.
Rates: From $420 for a three-day program.
Description: The school's philosophy is to guarantee to lower the student's score by focusing on the short game. Their method is based on the enhancement of the student's strength in dealing with fundamental problems in their golf swing. The comfort produced in this method allows for changes to happen in a positive and rewarding way. Video analysis is employed, and well as on-course instruction.

HIGH HAMPTON INN & COUNTRY CLUB

Location: Cashiers, N.C.
Head Instructor: Bonnie Rudolph.
Student/Teacher Ratios: 10/1.
Rates: From $545 for the five-day program.
Description: Bonnie Rudolph is one of the most female instructors in the country, and her program is a little out of the way (near Asheville, N.C.) but well worth a look. Starting with putting and chipping, the school graduates slowly into the full swing, enabling pupils to grow step-by-step. Video analysis is available, and an undercover range facility is also available in case of inclement weather.

HOWIE BARROW SCHOOL OF

GOLF AT GRENELEFE

Locations: Haines City, Fla.
Head Instructor: Howie Barrow..
Student/Teacher Ratios: 4/1.
Rates: From $125 per day for commuters; from $300 with room and meals.
Description: Rated as one of the best golf schools in Florida by Golfweek Magazine, Howie Barrow combines video analysis, the Perfect Swing Trainer, and individual training in this well-known and well-established program located at the Grenelefe Resort south of Orlando. Barrow places his major emphasis on the set-up and the basic swing fundamentals.

IMAGE GOLF, THE INSTRUCTIONAL SCHOOL

Location: Ocean Isle Beach, N.C.
Head Instructor: Ben Hunt.
Student/Teacher Ratios: 4/1.
Rates: From 125 for a one-day school; three- and five day programs available.
Description: Based at The Gauntlet in the Myrtle Beach area, Image Golf emphasizes the mental side of golf, underscoring a positive approach and the improvement of the grip and other fundamentals without drastic and unnecessary change. There is a heavy emphasis on the laws and principles of the golf swing and on teaching students how to implement same on the golf course.

INNISBROOK GOLF INSTITUTE

Location: Tarpon Springs, Fla.
Head Instructor: Jay Overton; Lew Smither III.
Student/Teacher Ratios: 4/1.
Rates: From $575 for a three-day school.
Description: Founded by legendary instructor and PGA TOUR veteran Jay Overton, this has been one of the top-ranked programs in the country for fifteen years. The unique teaching methods feature intensive on-line sessions and on-course instruction, providing golfers with both confidence and consistency in their games. The philosophy is summed up by Jay Overton as "P.G.A.—Posture, Grip, and Alignment." Awarded a "Best of the South" award by LINKS Magazine in 1992, and well-deserving the honor.This is the pinnacle.

JACK FLECK COLLEGE OF GOLF KNOWLEDGE

Locations: Magazine, AR. (501) 969-2203.
Head Instructor: Jack Fleck.
Student/Teacher Ratios: 1/1.
Rates: From $100 per hour; full-day program available.
Description: Any program taught by a man who beat Ben Hogan in a playoff for the U.S. Open is one that everyone should consider carefully. Jack teaches full-time out of Lil' Bit A Heaven G.C. in Arkansas but winters in the Palm Springs area, so West Coast residents can pick him up there. Jack emphasizes mental understanding of the golf swing and the golf game, and the promise of one-on-one sessions with the great man himself is hard to resist...especially at these rates.

JIMMY BALLARD GOLF WORKSHOPS

Location: Palm Beach, Fla.
Head Instructor: Jimmy Ballard.
Student/Teacher Ratios: 5/1.
Rates: From $795 for ten-hours.
Description: The one, the only, the inimitable Jimmy Ballard, one of the game's true characters and voted Teacher of the Decade by GOLF Magazine. Jimmy has worked with the majority of PGA TOUR players at some stage in his career: Curtis Strange, Seve Ballesteros, Sandy Lyle and Hal Sutton are Ballard alumni and have won ten majors between them. Jimmy emphasizes the fundamentals of the golf swing, based on analysis of the greatest ball strikers, and his theories such as the theory of connection throughout the swing have won general acceptance over the years. Ballard's school comes with a fair bit of machinery, including the Jimmy Ballard Swing Machine, the Swing Connector, and video analysis (in which he was also a pioneer). Ballard is dynamic and insistent—and students who take to his forthright style will reap significant rewards.

JOHN JACOBS' PRACTICAL GOLF SCHOOLS

Locations: 38 cities nationwide; national headquarters in Scottsdale, Ariz.
Head Instructor: John Jacobs; Shelby Futch.
Student/Teacher Ratios: 4/1.
Rates: From $195 for a half-day school; full-days sessions from $345.
Description: Founded by former British Ryder Cup captain and legendary instructor John Jacobs, the schools have grown into the nation's largest golf school concern by centering its activities around practical instruction, low teacher/student ratios, and attractive packages including accommodations at some of the nation's finer resorts. Shelby Futch, a renowned instructor in his own right, has been the day-to-day head of the schools for some time. John Jacobs' also has a course ownership and travel agency wing, which allows for complete control of the packaging process. A proven value.

KEN VENTURI GOLF TRAINING CENTERS

Locations: Hilton Head Island, S.C.; Rancho Mirage, Calif.

Head Instructor: Ken Venturi.
Student/Teacher Ratios: 4/1 maximum.
Rates: From $149 for a half-day school; full-days sessions from $299.
Description: Who could resist a lesson from the original "stroke Saver" himself, Ken Venturi, who has graced the CBS golf telecasts for years with his insights and instructional tips? Venturi appears at both schools on selected dates, but throughout the year his hand-picked staff of instructors teach the "Venturi System"— a proven program of basic fundamentals designed to meet the individual needs and goals of each student. Students are paired with others of similar abilities, and video swing analysis is employed. The Venturi School is well-grounded in the Venturi philosophy, and so one needn't wait for the maestro to make an appearance. But Kenny's worth the extra money if your calendar is flexible.

KINGSMILL GOLF SCHOOL

Location: Williamsburg, Va. (800) 832-5665.
Head Instructor: Tim Poland.
Student/Teacher Ratios: 3/1.
Rates: From $545 for a three-day school.
Description: Set in the historic Colonial Williamsburg area is the school based at the Kingsmill Resort (host of the Anheuser-Busch Classic), which concentrates on teaching connection, a unified motion relying on the big muscles of the body. The school covers set-up, alignment, backswing, downswing, finish, sand shots, pitch shots, chipping and putting, strategies, and the pre-shot routine. The school employs video analysis, the Sport Sense weight shift detector, and the Jimmy Ballard "Swing Connector."

LA COSTA SCHOOL OF GOLF

Location: La Jolla, Calif.
Head Instructor: John Jacobs; Shelby Futch.
Student/Teacher Ratios: 1/1.
Rates: $85 per hour for individual instruction; $100 per hour for two students.
Description: A "must-consider" golf school, under the direction of Carl Welty, who teaches Tom Kite, Curtis Strange, Davis Love III, and Sandy Lyle, among others. His specialty is videotape swing analysis, and La Costa is considered by ,most authorities to offer the best in this area. Welty is a featured instructor in the Tommy Armour PGA Teaching & Coaching Summit. Welty ignores most of the truisms of golf instruction for a simple "First we determine where the ball went. Second, we figure out where the club went. Then we can start to fix the problem." Fix it he will. At fairly low rates. And surrounded by the creature comforts of the La Costa Resort & Spa, which is only the favorite stop for the PGA TOUR players. Loofah scrubs and saunas abound. Think hard about this one.

MARLENE FLOYD'S "FOR WOMEN ONLY" GOLF SCHOOL

Location: Hilton Head, S.C. (800) 637-2694.
Head Instructor: Marlene Floyd.
Student/Teacher Ratios: 3/1.
Rates: $399 for a two-day program.
Description: Marlene is the younger sister of PGA TOUR star Raymond Floyd and an LPGA veteran in her own right, and offers a first-rate program twice a year at Palmetto Dunes Resort on Hilton Head. Marlene concentrates on natural club-swinging and brings with her a team of female PGA and LPGA instructors and helpers. Video analysis is offered, and of course Marlene's own charming and persuasive teaching style. If Marlene's schedule fits yours, this is definitely worth a look. Strong word-of-mouth and repeat traffic on this school.

MID PINES GOLF CLUB

Location: Southern Pines, N.C. (800) 323-2114.
Head Instructor: Chip King.
Student/Teacher Ratios: 2/1.
Rates: From $296 for a two-day instruction package.
Description: Another fine program in the Pinehurst area! Chip King heads this one based at the Mid Pines resort and its Donald Ross course (a course which was never remodeled from the original design, and thus is true to Ross' unique design principles and style). The school creates a simple, fun approach to the game and features a very low student/teacher ratio. One of the most rewarding aspects of the school is the chance to practice on the "crowned greens" that Donald Ross is so well-known for. No better place in the world to train on the short game and creative shot-making than a Ross course.

MOUNTAIN TOP GOLF SCHOOL

Location: Chittenden, Vermont. (800) 445-2100.
Head Instructor: Scott DeCandia.
Student/Teacher Ratios: 4/1.
Rates: Two-, three-, and five-day programs available.
Description: Headed by Scott DeCandia, former National Long Drive champion, this is obviously a place to go for instruction on hitting the long ball. But all aspects of the game. DeCandia emphasizes that the game is played at ground-level but analyzed at eye-level, and thus the ideal swing is much flatter than it is perceived to be—when students at Mountain Top practice the flatter swing, DeCandia states, they feel the swing motion better. Video analysis is employed.

MYRTLE BEACH GOLF SCHOOL

Locations: Myrtle Beach, S.C.
Head Instructor: Peter Anderson.
Student/Teacher Ratios: 4/1.
Rates: From $330 for a three-day school; five and seven-day sessions available.
Description: The School was voted the #1 golf school

value in 1989 by Northeast Golfer Magazine, and the program concentrates on tackling each student's individual weaknesses. After a video-taped swing analysis, an individual program is established. Radar guns, a swing analyzer, and multiple swing training aids (mirrors, hinged clubs, &c.) are employed. The school averages a reduction of 20% in handicap over the week-long programs.

NICKLAUS /FLICK GOLF SCHOOL

Locations: Palm Beach Gardens, Fla; Scottsdale, Ariz.; Pebble Beach, Calif.; Harbor Springs, Mich. (800) 642-5528.
Head Instructor: Jim Flick.
Student/Teacher Ratios: N/A.
Rates: N/A.
Description: Jim Flick has been one of the nation's top instructors for many years, and Jack Nicklaus needs little introduction either as a player or communicator within the game; but they teamed up late in their careers after Flick's advice had resulted in some noticeable improvements in the Nicklaus game. Their operation is part of the Golden Bear colossus in West Palm Beach, but they fan out to several sites throughout the country. Flick has trained probably more PGA TOUR pros that any contemporary instructor except perhaps Jimmy Ballard.

PALMETTO DUNES GOLF

Location: Hilton Head Island, S.C. (800) 785-1136.
Head Instructor: Chip Pellerin.
Student/Teacher Ratios: 6/1.
Rates: From $125 per student for a three-day school.
Description: Situated at the oceanside Palmetto Dunes Resort on Hilton Head Island, the school teaches the classic golf swing, emphasizing the use of the bigger muscles. Swinging the arms and letting the body follow is the key, here. Students will utilize the principles of the Bob Toski/Jim Flick book "How to become a Complete Golfer," which is also used by the PGA, and practice on the Robert Trent Jones course at the resort.

PHIL RITSON GOLF SCHOOL

Locations: 38 cities nationwide; national headquarters in Scottsdale, Ariz.
Head Instructor: John Jacobs; Shelby Futch.
Student/Teacher Ratios: 4/1.
Rates: From $195 for a half-=day school; full-days sessions from $345.
Description: Founded by former British Ryder Cup captain and legendary instructor John Jacobs, the schools have grown into the nation's largest golf school concern by centering its activities around practical instruction, low teacher/student ratios, and attractive packages including accommodations at some of the nation's finer resorts. Shelby Futch, a renowned instructor in his own right, has been the day-to-day head of the schools for some time. John Jacobs' also has a course ownership and travel agency wing, which allows for complete control of the packaging process. A proven value.

PINE NEEDLES

Locations: Pinehurst, N.C.
Head Instructor: Peggy Kirk Bell.
Student/Teacher Ratios: 4/1.
Rates: From $995 for the three-day Learning Center program, all meals and accommodations included.
Description: Pinehurst is loaded with top-flight instructors, but Peg Bell still shines head and shoulders above the rest—a legendary instructor for decades now, she still barks out her advice along with fellow instructors Dr. Jim Suttie and PGA TOUR professional Pat McGowan. Pine Needles, in addition, may be as close to golf heaven as one gets, with a Donald Ross course good enough to host the 1995 U.S. Women's Open, no crowds, and terrific instruction. Peggy Kirk Bell also offers highly-regarded youth camps and the famed Golfari, the women-only five-day program that did much to land Ms. Bell the Richardson Award for Lifetime Achievement from the Golf Writers' Association of America last year.

PINEHURST GOLF ADVANTAGE SCHOOL

Locations: Pinehurst, N.C. (800) 795-GOLF.
Head Instructor: Don Padgett.
Student/Teacher Ratios: 5/1.
Rates: From $495 for a two-day school; week long programs also available.
Description: The Pinehurst Resort never plays second fiddle to anyone in any arena connected with golf, and thus Don Padgett's school at the legendary Sandhills Resort offers one of the greatest shows on earth. Juniors and adults take weekends or week-long programs of instruction which include lodging at the Resort, daily green fees, video analysis, club fitting, and instruction both on-course and in the 4500 sq. ft. instruction facility. You'll be hard pressed to find a course better than Pinehurst No. 2, and hard-pressed to find a better preparation for the experience than in Don Padgett's school.

PROFESSIONAL GOLF SCHOOLS OF AMERICA

Locations: Maggie Valley, N.C.; Mt. Pocono, Penn.; Mesa, Ariz. (800) 447-2744.
Head Instructor: Robert Staples, Mike Lucas, Directors.
Student/Teacher Ratios: 4/1.
Rates: From $680 for a three-day school; five-day sessions available.

Description: PGA Professionals mold the students' motion through drills and a sound understanding of the golf swing. Their primary goal is to create an awareness of why things happen and why preswing fundamentals are essential to a better swing motion. video analysis and other swing aids are employed.

RILEY SCHOOL OF GOLF

Locations: Palm Springs, Calif.; San Diego, Calif.; Myrtle Beach, S.C. (800) 847-4539.
Head Instructor: Mike Schroeder.
Student/Teacher Ratios: 3/1.
Rates: From $559 for a three-day program; four- and five-day sessions available.
Description: Riley emphasizes personally fitted clubs and instruction in groups based on similar levels of ability. Technical instruction is balanced with physical training regimens, while leaving plenty of free time to apply lessons in unsupervised play or in enjoying the other resort amenities. A low student/instructor ratio is a decided bonus.

ROCKY MOUNTAIN FAMILY GOLF SCHOOL

Locations: Albuquerque, Tucson, and the school headquarters in Gunnison, Colo.
Head Instructor: Ollie Woods (teaches at Gunnison only).
Student/Teacher Ratios: 8/1.
Rates: From $185; 3-, 4-, and 5-day programs available.
Description: Teaches the "one swing" method, emphasizing that the game should be played simply and naturally. Ollie Woods has assembled an impressive staff in his remote location surrounded by the spectacular Gunnison National Forest: two of his four staff instructors have been inducted into the Golf Coaches of America Hall of Fame. A youth camp has recently been established. A relaxed atmosphere is provided, as well as video analysis and an electronic swing analyzer.

ROLAND STAFFORD GOLF SCHOOL

Locations: Windham, N.Y; Clymer, N.Y.; Francestwon, N.H.; Esterel, Quebec; Pembroke Pines, Fla.; Gulf Shores, Ala. (800) 447-8894.
Head Instructor: Roland Stafford.
Student/Teacher Ratios: 6/1.
Rates: From $379 for a two-day school; three- and five-day programs available.
Description: Roland Stafford is one of the most successful golf school operators in the country, and they attribute their success to their PGA-trained staff, the custom club-fitting program, the instructional tapes and books that are available of the Stafford method, the large student practice areas, small classes, and video analysis. The Stafford Method avoids over-analysis of the swing—he emphasizes grip, levels, connection, and tempo, which are demonstrated and explained in detail. All aspects of the short game are taught, including specialty shots designed to cut strokes off the student's game.

ROYAL GOLF ACADEMY

Location: Hilton Head Island, S.C.
Head Instructor: Keith Marks, Jr.
Student/Teacher Ratios: N/A.
Rates: N/A.
Description: Keith Marks is the second generation professional here at Hilton Head's Port Royal Resort (his father, Keith Marks, Sr., was also a noted instructor). Michael Jordan is among the celebrities who have graced the range at Port Royal and students at RGA will receive instruction in all aspects of the game while enjoying the oceanside resort and its three courses. Video analysis available.

SAMOSET GOLF SCHOOL

Location: Samoset Golf Resort, Rockport, ME. (800) 341-1650
Head Instructor: Bob O'Brian.
Student/Teacher Ratios: 4-5/1.
Rates: Three days/two nights; Single $484; Double $366.
Description: Quality instruction as opposed to quantity instruction. The three-day school features six hours of instruction concentrated on one or two areas of improvement each day, with a playing lesson on the final day. The Samoset course is very highly-ranked among resort courses and thus students will have an opportunity to try their new-found skills in a challenging and scenic environment.

SEA PINES ACADEMY OF GOLF

Location: Hilton Head Island, S.C.
Head Instructor: Don Trahan.
Student/Teacher Ratios: N/A.
Rates: N/A.
Description: This is the school that camps out in the shadow of the famed Harbour Town lighthouse at Harbour Town\ Golf Links. Don Trahan, "The Swing Surgeon," heads this school, which is based on the Trahan method as explained in his book "Golf Plain and Simple." Trahan offers video analysis and numerous teaching aids, and as an added benefit students can purchase Compu-Golf, a golf instruction system that gives individualized instruction via your personal computer! Trahan has been voted one of the top 50 instructors in America by Golf Magazine—his latest star pupil, who became the youngest person ever to qualify for the U.S. Junior Amateur, is his own son, D.J. Trahan.

SILVER SANDS GOLF

SCHOOL OF WISCONSIN

Locations: Wisconsin and Florida (Adults); Wisconsin only (juniors). (414) 275-6122.
Head Instructor: Wayne Rolfs.
Student/Teacher Ratios: 3-4/1.
Rates: 33-day program for adults; 6-day summer programs for juniors. 1995 Rates not available.
Description: Wayne Rolfs, author of "The 10-30 Power Swing," has held court at Silver Sands for 21 years, emphasizes clear, concise instruction and immediate improvement at his schools. The school address body, mind, technique, and proper equipment, as well as individual attention in five hours of instruction daily. Video analysis, playing analysis, club fitting, swing and training aids, and playing lessons are all part of the package.

SPORTS ENHANCEMENT ASSOCIATES, INC.

Location: Sedona, Ariz.
Head Instructor: Chuck Hogan.
Student/Teacher Ratios: N/A.
Rates: N/A.
Description: This is the school where Chuck Hogan hangs his hat, perhaps the best known of the coaches who focus on the mental side of instruction. Peter Jacobsen recalled a session with Hogan in which the coach pretended to toss five golf balls on the putting surface, telling Jacobsen, "Here, putt these first for me," and only accepted Jacobsen as a student after Jake reported making every one of the five imaginary putts. Hogan teaches all aspects of the game, but it's all given an unmistakable spin by the Master.

STANFORD GOLF SCHOOL FOR ADULTS

Locations: 38 cities nationwide; national headquarters in Scottsdale, Ariz.
Head Instructor: John Jacobs; Shelby Futch.
Student/Teacher Ratios: 4/1.
Rates: From $195 for a half-=day school; full-days sessions from $345.
Description: Founded by former British Ryder Cup captain and legendary instructor John Jacobs, the schools have grown into the nation's largest golf school concern by centering its activities around practical instruction, low teacher/student ratios, and attractive packages including accommodations at some of the nation's finer resorts. Shelby Futch, a renowned instructor in his own right, has been the day-to-day head of the schools for some time. John Jacobs' also has a course ownership and travel agency wing, which allows for complete control of the packaging process. A proven value.

STOW ACRES COUNTRY CLUB

Locations: Stow, Mass.
Head Instructor: Sal Ruggiero.
Student/Teacher Ratios: 5/1.
Rates: From $315 for a two-day school. Junior clinics from $100.
Description: Sal Ruggiero runs one of the most aggressive country-club instruction programs around, a real contrast to the resort locations of most other golf schools. They teach students to swing the club freely away from and to the target.In addition to teaching basic fundamentals, they outline several key phrases such as keeping muscles relaxed, swing levels, center rotation, connection and balance. Video analysis, mirrors, and a variety of other teaching aids are employed.

STRATTON GOLF SCHOOL

Location: Scottsdale, Ariz; Stratton Mountain, Vermont.
Head Instructor: Keith Lyford,
Student/Teacher Ratios: 5/1.
Rates: From $370 for a two-day school; three- and five-day programs available.
Description: Stratton emphasizes working on a few key areas of improvement rather than rebuilding the entire golf swing. Each student receives an instruction booklet with their instructor's written analysis and photos (sometimes before and after) of the specific positions they are working on. Extensive video analysis is a feature of the school, and teaching aids and drills are freely employed. "Different strokes for different folks" is the philosophy here, and instruction tailored to the needs of the individual student is the rule. Students even fill out a golfer profile before arriving at the school to give the staff a chance to learn the student's game.

SWING MASTERS

Location: Orange Tree Golf Resort, Scottsdale, Ariz. (800) 752-9162.
Head Instructor: Kieran Dunlavy, President.
Student/Teacher Ratios: 4/1.
Rates: Two-day programs from $355.
Description: They quote Ernest Jones" "Swing the Clubhead" theorems in earnest here, which is a very good sign; body position relative to the target line and blade position relative to the target are emphasized as the key to a free-flowing swing. Swing Masters offers full travel services, accommodations, ground transportation, advance tee time reservations, as well as videotaped swing analysis; Orange Tree is a fine, mid-priced Arizonan resort which is worth a look.

SWING'S THE THING GOLF SCHOOLS

Locations: Palm Springs, Calif.; Myrtle Beach, S.C.; Shawnee, Penn.; Orlando, Fla.; Ocean City, Maryland. (800) 221-6661.

Head Instructors: Rick McCord and Dick Farley.
Student/Teacher Ratios: N/A.
Rates: From $645 for a three-day school.
Description: Featuring a program headed by Dick Farley and Rick McCord (maker of training videos with Orville Moody, Miller Barber and Dale Douglas), this school has remained at the pinnacle for over a quarter-century now. Founder Harry Obitz established a simple system of moderate prices and a low-key instruction style; the school's success has reached now into the Japan, with the school creating a five-hour instruction series for NHK, the Japanese public television network. Both Farley and McCord were chosen by GOLF Magazine on their 50 Best Teachers in America list, and with small classes students see plenty of top-flight instruction. The school offers a one-day refresher course for alumni; beginner programs are available.

TEXAS TECH UNIVERSITY GRADUATE GOLF WORKSHOP

Location: Lubbock, Tex. (806) 742-3335.
Head Instructor: Danny Mason.
Student/Teacher Ratios: 10/1.
Rates: $500 for a three-week program.
Description: Junior students sneak sideways into this school, which actually is a three-week college credit training program for high school golf coaches. In the final week the coaches turn to practice teaching with juniors ages 13-17. For those in the golf teaching business, this represents an excellent refresher course in the fundamentals of the golf swing and in modern instruction technique. Very low rates, too—and college credit.

THE SCHOOL OF GOLF EXCLUSIVELY FOR WOMEN

Locations: El Cajon, Calif. (619) 270-6230.
Head Instructor: Shirley Spork.
Student/Teacher Ratios: 4-5/1.
Rates: From $1150 for the 3-day program; a five-day program is also available.
Description: This women-only school is headed by Shirley Spork, a founding member of the LPGA and twice its choice as Teacher of the Year. She's assembled a top-flight staff of moonlighters, including former LPGA Teaching Division president Barbra Crawford-O'Brien for the seven-times-a-year school. developing self-confidence and a positive mental attitude are keys to the instruction, as well as sound instruction in all areas of the game. Playing lessons are mixed with straight instruction, and the schools wrap up with a scramble tournament featuring coaches and students.

UNITED STATES SENIOR GOLF ACADEMY

Location: Melbourne, Fla.
Head Instructor: Roy Smith.

Student/Teacher Ratios: 3/1.
Rates: From $1685 for a five-day school.
Description: Roy Smith heads up one of the few programs that exclusively deals with the needs of the senior golfer. The school employs extensive video taping and analysis, equipment analysis and custom club fitting, a low student/teacher ratio, daily playing lessons with the professional staff, and a highly-trained staff of PGA and LPGA members. The schools allow for two rain days, so the package price includes a full week's lodging. One-on-one instruction available.

V.I.P. GOLF ACADEMY

Locations: Sebring, Fla. (800) 673-7686.
Head Instructor: Richard E. Cormier, Jr.
Student/Teacher Ratios: 1/1.
Rates: From $299 per day.
Description: One-on-one instruction is the calling-card of this unusual program, praised by 1987 LPGA Rookie of the Year Tammie Green who remarked "I have been very impressed with the knowledge and communication skills of Richard Cormier and his staff." Six hours of private instruction per day, on course playing lessons, video analysis, and sports psychology training are highlights of the school—and the students chooses which areas of the game to work on. Accommodations included in total package.

WINTERGREEN GOLF ACADEMY

Locations: Wintergreen, Va.
Head Instructor: Graeme Oliver.
Student/Teacher Ratios: 4/1.
Rates: From $250 for the one-day school. Two- and three-day programs also available.
Description: Small, extremely personalized instructional groups absorb the Wintergreen philosophy, "The Five Principles of Shot Structure," applied to the ability level of the individual. And all this at one of the East Coats's best-known golf resorts—Wintergreen—where students play the Stoney Creek C.C. course in between lessons. In addition to various instructional aids, video analysis is employed and students receive a personalized take-home tape.

WOODLAKE TOTAL PERFORMANCE GOLF SCHOOLS

Locations: Vass, N.C. (920) 245-4031
Head Instructor: Stuart Taylor.
Student/Teacher Ratios: 4/1.
Rates: From $90 for a one-day school.
Description: Pinehurst isn't well-noted for its golf bargains, but it does have one distinct bargain in instruction at The Woodlake school. Woodlake promises a new total golf concept for improving your game, which features golf-specific exercises, sports nutrition and a program to improve general health as well as golf ability. The program is based on the work of consultant John Davis. Video analysis is offered, as well as club fitting.

ECONOMICS AND DEVELOPMENT

OVERVIEW: *Key industry statistics from the National Golf Foundation and industry sources regarding course and facility construction, fees, spending trends, employment, TOUR finances, corporate sponsors, charitable donations, and a census of golfers since 1945.*

American Professional Tour Purses

Sources: PGA TOUR, LPGA, Senior PGA TOUR, and Nike TOUR. All figures in thousands.

Year	PGA	LPGA	Sr. PGA	Nike	TOTAL	%+(-)	PGA share
1938	158	—	—	—	158	—	100.0%
1939	121	—	—	—	121	(23.4)	100.0
1940	117	—	—	—	117	(3.3)	100.0
1941	169	—	—	—	169	44.4	100.0
1942	117	—	—	—	117	(30.8)	100.0
1943	17	—	—	—	17	(85.5)	100.0
1944	151	—	—	—	151	788.2	100.0
1945	435	—	—	—	435	188.1	100.0
1946	412	—	—	—	412	(5.3)	100.0
1947	353	—	—	—	353	(14.3)	100.0
1948	427	—	—	—	427	21.0	100.0
1949	338	—	—	—	338	(20.8)	100.0
1950	460	50	—	—	510	50.9	90.2
1951	460	70	—	—	530	3.9	86.8
1952	498	150	—	—	648	22.3	76.9
1953	563	120	—	—	683	5.4	82.4
1954	601	105	—	—	706	3.4	85.1
1955	782	135	—	—	917	29.9	85.3
1956	847	140	—	—	987	7.6	85.8
1957	820	148	—	—	968	(1.9)	84.7
1958	1,006	159	—	—	1,165	20.4	86.4
1959	1,225	203	—	—	1,428	22.6	85.8
1960	1,335	187	—	—	1,522	6.6	87.7
1961	1,462	289	—	—	1,751	15.0	83.5
1962	1,790	338	—	—	2,128	21.5	84.1
1963	2,045	345	—	—	2,390	12.3	85.6
1964	2,301	351	—	—	2,652	11.0	86.8
1965	2,849	356	—	—	3,205	20.9	88.9
1966	3,704	510	—	—	4,214	31.5	87.9
1967	3,979	435	—	—	4,414	4.7	90.1
1968	5,078	550	—	—	5,628	27.5	90.2
1969	5,466	597	—	—	6,063	7.7	90.2
1970	6,752	435	—	—	7,187	18.5	93.9
1971	7,116	559	—	—	7,675	6.8	92.7
1972	7,597	988	—	—	8,585	11.9	88.5
1973	8,657	1,471	—	—	10,128	18.0	85.5
1974	8,166	1,753	—	—	9,919	(2.1)	82.3
1975	7,895	1,742	—	—	9,637	(2.8)	81.9
1976	9,158	2,527	—	—	11,685	21.3	78.4
1977	9,689	3,058	—	—	12,747	9.1	76.0
1978	10,337	3,925	—	—	14,262	11.9	72.5
1979	12,801	4,400	—	—	17,201	20.6	74.4
1980	13,372	5,150	250	—	18,772	9.1	71.2
1981	14,175	5,800	750	—	20,725	10.4	68.4
1982	15,090	6,400	1,372	—	22,862	10.3	66.0

Year	PGA	LPGA	Sr. PGA	Nike	TOTAL	%+(-)	PGA share
1983	17,588	7,000	3,365	—	27,953	22.3	62.9
1984	21,251	8,000	5,156	—	34,407	23.1	61.8
1985	25,291	9,000	6,076	—	40,367	17.3	62.7
1986	25,442	10,000	6,300	—	41,742	3.4	61.0
1987	32,106	11,400	8,700	—	52,206	25.1	61.5
1988	36,959	12,510	10,500	—	59,969	14.9	61.6
1989	41,289	14,190	14,195	—	69,674	16.2	59.3
1990	46,252	17,100	18,323	3,050	84,725	21.6	54.6
1991	49,628	18,435	19,788	3,625	91,476	8.0	54.3
1992	49,387	21,325	21,025	4,200	95,937	4.9	51.5
1993	53,204	20,400	26,250	4,975	104,829	9.3	50.8
1994	54,750	21,975	28,850	5,675	111,250	6.1	49.2
TOTAL	624,038	214,781	170,900	21,525	1,031,244	—	60.5

Speed Of Play

Source: 1989 PGA Cost/Revenue Survey. 18 hole Regulation Length Courses.

Group or Facility type	4 hrs or less	4 to 4-1/2 hrs.	More than 4-1/2 hrs.	Average Round
All Facilities	44.2%	19.4%	36.4%	4 hrs 15 min
Municipal	27.8	19.1	53.1	4 hrs 27 min
Daily Fee	34.1	15.6	50.3	4 hrs 23 min
Private Non-Equity	46.5	25.5	27.9	4 hrs 11 min
Private Equity	58.2	19.5	22.3	4 hrs 06 min
Men	59.8	24.7	15.5	3 hrs 59 min
Women	58.9	14.5	26.6	4 hrs 04 min
0-9 handicap	67.7	14.6	17.7	3 hrs 49 min
10-19 handicap	62.2	27.6	10.2	3 hrs 52 min
20-29 handicap	55.3	27.1	17.6	4 hrs 05 min
30-49 handicap	54.5	19.8	25.7	4 hrs 14 min
50+ handicap	42.1	26.3	31.6	4 hrs 22 min

Course and Facility Development, 1981-92

Source: National Golf Foundation

Year	Courses Opened	Year	Courses Opened	Year	Courses Opened
1981	149	1985	109	1989	290
1982	140	1986	131	1990	351
1983	104	1987	145	1991	342
1984	136	1988	211	1992	351

PGA TOUR Charitable Contributions, 1977-1993

Source: PGA TOUR. Figures in thousands.

Year	Total Contributions	Year	Total Contributions
1977	$3,300	1985	$11,300
1978	$4,300	1986	$16,100
1979	$4,400	1987	$17,600
1980	$4,500	1988	$18,390
1981	$6,800	1989	$19,779
1982	$7,200	1990	$20,161
1983	$7,800	1991	$19,534
1984	$9,400	1992	$22,223
		1993	$22,752

Growth in the Golf Facility Supply, by Facility Type, 1931-1994

Source: National Golf Foundation

Year	Total	Private	Daily Fee	Muni.	Year	Total	Private	Daily Fee	Muni.
1931	5,691	4,448	700	543	1968	9,615	4,269	4,110	1,236
1934	5,727	4,155	1,006	566	1969	9,926	4,459	4,192	1,275
1937	5,196	3,489	1,070	637					
1939	5,303	3,405	1,199	699	1970	10,188	4,619	4,248	1,321
					1971	10,494	4,720	4,404	1,370
1941	5,209	3,288	1,210	711	1972	10,665	4,787	4,484	1,394
1946	4,817	3,018	1,076	723	1973	10,665	4,787	4,484	1,394
1947	4,870	3,073	1,061	736	1974	11,134	4,715	4,878	1,541
1948	4,901	3,090	1,076	735	1975	11,370	4,770	5,014	1,586
1949	4,926	3,068	1,108	750	1976	11,562	4,791	5,121	1,650
1950	4,931	3,049	1,141	741	1977	11,745	4,847	5,203	1,695
					1978	11,885	4,872	5,271	1,742
1951	4,970	2,996	1,214	760	1979	11,966	4,848	5,340	1,778
1952	5,026	3,029	1,246	751					
1953	5,056	2,970	1,321	765	1980	12,005	4,839	5,372	1,794
1954	5,076	2,878	1,392	806	1981	12,035	4,789	5,428	1,818
1955	5,358	2,801	1,692	865	1982	12,140	4,798	5,494	1,848
1956	5,358	2,801	1,692	865	1983	12,197	4,809	5,528	1,860
1957	5,553	2,887	1,832	834	1984	12,278	4,831	5,566	1,881
1958	5,745	2,986	1,904	855	1985	12,346	4,861	5,573	1,912
1959	5,991	3,097	2,023	871	1986	12,384	4,865	5,587	1,912
					1987	12,407	4,898	5,583	1,926
1960	6,385	3,236	2,254	895	1988	12,582	4,897	5,748	1,937
1961	6,623	3,248	2,363	912	1989	12,658	4,862	5,833	1,963
1962	7,070	3,503	2,636	931					
1963	7,477	3,615	2,868	994	1990	12,846	4,810	6,024	2,012
1964	7,893	3,764	3,114	1,015	1991	13,004	4,686	6,272	2,046
1965	8,323	3,887	3,368	1,068	1992	13,210	4,568	6,552	2,090
1966	8,672	4,016	3,483	1,173	1993	13,439	4,492	6,803	2,144
1967	9,336	4,166	3,960	1,210					

Census of U.S. Golfing Population and Rounds Played, 1960-1994

Source: National Golf Foundation. Figures in thousands.

Year	Golfers	Rounds	Rounds/Golfer	Year	Golfers	Rounds	Rounds/Golfer
1960	5,000	N/A	N/A	1984	17,000	403,000	23.7
				1985	17,500	415,000	23.7
1970	11,200	266,000	23.8	1986	19,900	419,000	21.1
				1987	21,200	431,000	20.3
1975	13,000	309,000	23.8	1988	23,000	484,000	21.0
				1989	24,200	469,000	19.4
1980	15,100	358,000	23.7				
1981	15,600	368,000	23.6	1990	27,800	502,000	18.1
1982	16,000	379,000	23.7	1991	24,800	479,000	19.3
1983	16,500	391,000	23.7	1992	24,800	505,000	20.4
				1993	24,500	499,000	20.4

U.S. Golfing Population, 1993

Source: National Golf Foundation. Figures in thousands.

	Nos. of Golfers		Nos. of Golfers		Nos. of Golfers
All Golfers	24,796	**Income cont'd**		**Education**	
Men	17,714	$20,000-$29,999	3,223	Non-H.S. Grad.	942
Women	5,247	$30,000-$39,999	3,943	H.S. Grad.	6,125
Juniors	1,835	$40,000-$49,999	3,645	Some College	6,868
		$50,000-$74,999	7,389	College Grad.	10,836
Age		$75,000 and over	4,265		
12-17	1,835			**Occupation**	
18-29	6,621	**Geographic Region**		Prof./Mgmt.	10,241
30-39	6,472	New England	1,364	Clerical/Sales	4,091
40-49	4,339	Middle Atlantic	3,447	Blue Collar	5,653
50-59	2,256	East North Central	6,174	Other	1,909
60-64	1,041	West North Central	2,504	Retired/Not Employ.	2,901
65 or over	2,232	South Atlantic	3,670		
		East South Central	843		
Income		West South Central	1,860		
Less than $10,000	422	Mountain	1,513		
$10,000-$19,999	1,934	Pacific	3,422		

U.S. Golfing Population, 1993— by Number of Rounds and Usual Facility Type

Source: National Golf Foundation. Figures in thousands.

Population	Numbers of Golfers	Population	Numbers of Golfers
All Adult Golfers	22,961	**Core (8-24 Rounds)**	11,481
Public course golfers	17,822	Public course golfers	4,906
Private course golfers	4,014	Private course golfers	905
Play both types equally	1,125	Play both types equally	333
Occasional (0-7 rounds)	11,480	**Avid Core (25+ rounds)**	5,348
Public course golfers	9,156	Public course golfers	3,760
Private course golfers	1,687	Private course golfers	1,433
Play both types equally	637	Play both types equally	155

Rounds of Golf Played in the United States, 1986-1993

Source: National Golf Foundation. Figures in millions.

Year	Total	Core	Occasional	Juniors	Year	Total	Core	Occasional	Juniors
1986	421.0	n/a	n/a	n/a	**1990**	501.6	437.2	42.7	21.7
1987	431.0	380.1	32.1	18.8	**1991**	478.6	418.4	36.7	23.5
1988	484.4	430.4	34.4	19.6	**1992**	505.4	449.9	36.7	18.8
1989	469.0	410.5	37.1	21.4	**1993**	499	n/a	n/a	n/a

U.S. Core Golfing Population, 1993

Source: National Golf Foundation. Figures in thousands.

Core golfers are defined as golfers over 18 years of age who play 8 or more rounds per year.

Population	Nos. of Golfers	Group	Nos. of Golfers	Group	Nos. of Golfers
All Core Golfers	24,796	$20,000-$29,999	3,223	Education	
		$30,000-$39,999	3,943	Non-H.S. Grad.	942
Men	17,714	$40,000-$49,999	3,645	H.S. Grad.	6,125
Women	5,247	$50,000-$74,999	7,389	Some College	6,868
		$75,000 and over	4,265	College Grad.	10,836
Age					
12-17	1,835	Geographic Region		Occupation	
18-29	6,621	New England	1,364	Prof./Mgmt.	10,241
30-39	6,472	Middle Atlantic	3,447	Clerical/Sales	4,091
40-49	4,339	East North Central	6,174	Blue Collar	5,653
50-59	2,256	West North Central	2,504	Other	1,909
60-64	1,041	South Atlantic	3,670	Retired/Not Empl.	2,901
65 or over	2,232	East South Central	843		
		West South Central	1,860		
Income:		Mountain	1,513		
Less than $10,000	422	Pacific	3,422		
$10,000-$19,999	1,934				

U.S. Avid Core Golfing Population, 1993

Source: National Golf Foundation. Figures in thousands.
Core golfers are defined as golfers over 18 years of age who play 25 or more rounds per year.

Population	Nos. of Golfers	Group	Nos. of Golfers	Group	Nos. of Golfers
All Core Golfers	24,796	$20,000-$29,999	3,223	Education	
		$30,000-$39,999	3,943	Non-H.S. Grad.	942
Men	17,714	$40,000-$49,999	3,645	H.S. Grad.	6,125
Women	5,247	$50,000-$74,999	7,389	Some College	6,868
		$75,000 and over	4,265	College Grad.	10,836
Age					
12-17	1,835	Geographic Region		Occupation	
18-29	6,621	New England	1,364	Prof./Mgmt.	10,241
30-39	6,472	Middle Atlantic	3,447	Clerical/Sales	4,091
40-49	4,339	East North Central	6,174	Blue Collar	5,653
50-59	2,256	West North Central	2,504	Other	1,909
60-64	1,041	South Atlantic	3,670	Retired/Not Empl.	2,901
65 or over	2,232	East South Central	843		
		West South Central	1,860		
Income:		Mountain	1,513		
Less than $10,000	422	Pacific	3,422		
$10,000-$19,999	1,934				

U.S. Golf Travel

Source: 1989 National Golf Foundation Consumer Survey.

Golf Travelers	8,100,000	Average number of		Golf Trips, Total	21,060,000
Median Income	$49,400	Golf Trips/Traveler	2.6	Golf rounds played	
Median Age	41.5	Average golf days	5.3	by travelers/year	42,930,000
Median Rounds/Year	31.1				

U.S. Golf Travel Destinations

Source: 1989 National Golf Foundation Consumer Survey.

State	% of Golf Trips	State	% of Golf Trips	State	% of Golf Trips
Florida	11.6%	South Carolina	5.0%	Texas	4.3%
California	10.1	Wisconsin	4.7	North Carolina	4.2
Arizona	5.1	Pennsylvania	4.3		

1993 U.S. Sales of Golf Equipment—Brand Leaders

Source: Golf Pro Census '94

WOODS

Brand	% of Shops	PI*
Callaway	36.2%	59
Taylor Made	10.6	18
Ping	8.0	12
Cobra	5.2	12

IRONS

Brand	% of Shops	PI*
Ping	44.2%	56
Tommy Armour	8.5	15
Cobra	5.1	14
Titleist	4.6	10

BALLS

Brand	% of Shops	PI*
Titleist	66.5%	69
Spalding	17.8	22
Slazenger	4.3	6
Wilson	3.8	5
Maxfli	3.1	4

WEDGES

Brand	% of Shops	PI*
Ping	20.7%	35
Cleveland	15.1	42
Wilson	12.1	33
Hogan	5.2	17

PUTTERS

Brand	% of Shops	PI*
Ping	64.7%	80
Ram	3.3	8
Titleist	2.6	5

SHAFTS—Brand

Brand	% of Shops Stocked
True Temper	87%
Aldila	82
Apollo	40
Brunswick	29
Ti-Shaft	23

SHAFTS (Woods)—Type

Type	%—1993	1992
Steel	31.8%	38.5
Light. Steel	16.4	20.3
Graphite	50.1	38.4
Titanium	1.6	2.7

SHAFTS (Irons)—Type

Type	%—1993	1992
Steel	48.9%	51.8
Light. Steel	25.5	27.9
Graphite	24.8	19.3
Titanium	0.6	1.0

MEN'S SHIRTS

Brand	% of Shops	PI*
Ashworth	22.6%	53
Aureus	6.6	17
Izod Club	6.4	17
PGA Tour	6.3	29

GLOVES

Brand	% of Shops	PI*
Foot-Joy	30.7%	51
Wilson	9.3	30
Kasco	9.0	23
Daiwa	7.8	36
Titleist	7.2	24

SHOES

Brand	% of Shops	PI*
Foot-Joy	54.2%	68
Etonic	16.8	34
Dexter	10.7	27

*PI— *Golf Pro's* exclusive **Performance Index** equals the number of shops where the brand is the top seller divided by the total number of shops carrying the brand, multiplied by 100.

Growth in U.S. Golf Driving Ranges 1987-1993

Source: Golf Data International

	# of New Ranges	% Growth		# of New Ranges	% Growth
1987	44	4.2%	1991	768	53.8%
1988	109	10.0%	1992	412	18.7%
1989	100	8.3%	1993	323	
1990	126	9.7%			

U.S. Golf Equipment Exports 1992-1993

Source: Sporting Goods Manufacturers Association

1992	$	1993	$
Balls	$82,672,000	Balls	$101,766,000
Clubs	$151,241,000	Clubs	$207,205,000
Club parts	$138,380,000	Club parts	$122,533,000
Other	$52,033,000	Other	$57,058,000
TOTAL	$424,326,000	TOTAL	$488,562,000

DIRECTORY OF ASSOCIATIONS AND GOVERNING ORGANIZATIONS OF GOLF

OVERVIEW: *Addresses, telephone numbers and fax numbers (if available) for the leading international, national, province, country and state golfing organizations.*

INTERNATIONAL GOLF ASSOCIATIONS

Asia-Pacific Golf Confederation
52,1st Floor, Jalan Hang,
Lekiu 50100
Kuala Lumpur.

European Golf Association
En Ballgue, Case Postale CH-1066,
Epalinges, Lausanne,
Switzerland
Tel: 010-4l-21-7843532 Telex 450804
Golf Fax: 41-21-7843536.

Royal & Ancient Golf Club,
St. Andrews, Fife, SCOTLAND
Tel: (0334) 72112 Fax: (0334) 77580

United States Golf Association
Golf House, Liberty Corner Rd., Far Hills,
NJ 07931
Tel: (201) 624-8400

International Golf Association
P.O. Box 176, Greenwich, CT 06831-0876
Tel: (203) 531-1113 Fax: (203) 531 4373

South American Golf Federation
Avda. Brasil 3025, Rib 50, Montevideo,
Uruguay

NATIONAL GOLF ASSOCIATIONS

ARGENTINA

Asociacion Argentina de Golf
Callè Corrientes 538 - piso 11
1043 Buenos Aires
Argentina
Tel: 54-1-325-7498

AUSTRALIA

Australian Golf Union
155 Cecil Street
South Melbourne
3205 Victoria
Australia
Tel: 61-03-699-7944

Australian Ladies' Golf Union
22 McKay Road,
Rowville 3178, Victoria.
Tel: (03) 7644019 Fax: (03)7645219

Australian Professional Golfers' Association - PGA Tour
4/140 George Street,
Hornsby 2077 New South Wales
Tel: (02) 47-6333 Fax: (02) 477-7625.

MEN'S STATE ASSOCIATIONS

Victorian Golf Association
15 Bardolph Street,
Burwood,Victoria.
Tel: (03) 296731 Fax: (03) 291077.

New South Wales Golf Association
17 Brisbane Street,
Darlinghurst, New South Wales.
Tel: (02) 1648433 Fax: (02) 2614750.

Tasmanian Golf Council
2 Queen Street
Bellerive, Tasmania 7018.
Tel: (002) 443600 Fax: (002) 443201.

Queensland Golf Union
Cur Wren Street & Walden Lane,
Bowen Hills, Queensland 4006.
Tel: (07) 8541105 Fax: (07)2571620.

Western Australian Golf Association
Suite 14, 49 Melville Parade
South Perth 6151 Western Australia.
Tel: (09) 3672490 Fax: (09) 3682255.

South Australian Golf Association
249 Henley Beach Road
Torrensville 5031 South Australia.
Tel: (08) 3526899 Fax: (08) 3523900.

WOMEN'S STATE ASSOCIATIONS

Victoria
598A Glenliuntly Road,
Elsternwick 3185, Victoria.
Tel: (03) 5238511 Fax: (03) 5281056.

New South Wales
17 Brisbane Street,
Darlinghurst 2010, New South Wales
Tel: (02) 2647327

Queensland
Unit 3, Cur Wren Street & Walden Lane
Bowen Hills, Queensland 4006.
Tel: (07) 2528155.

Western Australia
Unit 3, 66 Mill Point Road,
South Perth 6151, Western Australia
Tel: (09) 3682618.

South Australia
2 Marshall Street
Glengowne 5044 South Australia.
Tel: (08) 2947838

Tasmania
86 Roslyn Avenue
Kingston Beach 7050 Tasmania
Tel: (002) 296622.

AUSTRIA

Osterreichischer Golf-Verband
Prinz-Eugen Strasse 12
A-1040 Vienna
Austria
Tel: 43-222-505-3245

THE BAHAMAS

Bahamas Golf Federation
P.O. Box N 4568
Nassau
The Bahamas

BELGIUM

Federation Royale Belge de Golf
Chemin de Baudemont, 23
B-1400 Nivelles
Belgium
Tel: 32-67-220440

BERMUDA

Bermuda Golf Association
Box HM BX-433
Hamilton
Bermuda

BOLIVIA

Federacion Boliviana de Golf
Casilla de Corree 6130, La Paz
Bolivia

BOTSWANA

Botswana Golf Union
P.O. Box 1033, Galoorone.
Botswana

BRAZIL

Confederacao Braseleira de Golf
Rua 7de Abril
282- s/83
01044 Sao Paulo
Brazil

BURMA

Burma Golf Federation
c/o Aung San Stadium
Rangoon
Burma

CANADA

Canadian (Royal) Golf Association
Golf House, RR No. 2,
Oakville, Ontario L6J 4Z3.

Canadian Ladies' Golf Association
1600 James Naismith Drive, Gloucester,
Ontario KIB 5N4. Tel: (613) 7485642.

**Canadian Professional Golfers'
Association**
69 Berkeley Street, Toronto M5A 2W6.
Tel: (416) 368 6104.

PROVINCIAL GOLF ASSOCIATIONS

British Columbia
Room 22,1675 West 8th Ave,
Vancouver, BC V6J 1V2.

Alberta
200-H Haddon Road
Calgary, Alberta T2V 2Y6.

Saskatchewan
205 Victoria Avenue
Regina, Saskatchewan S4P 0S4.

Manitoba
1700 Etlice Ave.,
Winnipeg, Manitoba R3H 0B1.

Ontario
400 Esna Park Drive, Unit 11,
Markham, Ontario L3R 1H5.

Quebec
3300 Cavendish Blvd, Sinte 250,
Montreal, Quebec L4B 2M8.

New Brunswick
3 Sunset Lane
St. John, New Brunswick E2H 1GB.

Nova Scotia
4 Lanardo Drive
Dartmouth, Nova Scotia 3A3X4.

Newfoundland/Labrador
PG Box 5361
St. Johns, Newfoundland

Prince Edward Island
PG Box 51
Charlottetown, PEI C1A 7K2.

CHILE

Federacion Chilena de Golf
Vicuna Mackenna 40
Casilla 13307 Santiago
Chile

CHINA (TAIWAN)

**Professional Golfers' Association of
the Republic of China**
2nd Floor, No. 196 Pei Ling 5th Road,
Taipel, Taiwan,
Republic of China
Tel: (02)8220318 8229684

COLOMBIA

Federacion Colombiana de Golf
Carrera 7a N. 72-64, Of. Int. 26
Apartado Aereo 90985
Bogota, D.E. Columbia

COSTA RICA

Costa Rica Golf Association
c/o ANAGOLF
P.O. Box 2041-1000
San Jose
Costa Rica

CYPRUS

Cyprus Golf Union
c/o JSGC Dhekelia, BPPO 58
Cyprus

CZECH REPUBLIC

Czech Golf Federation
Na porici 12, CS-11530
Praha 1
Czech Republic
Tel: 42(2) 2350065-84

DENMARK

Danish Golf Union
Golfsvingt 2
2625 Vallensbaek
Denmark
Tel: 45-4-264-0666

DOMINICAN REPUBLIC

Dominican Golf Association
P.O. Box 641
Santa Domingo
Dominican Republic

ECUADOR

Federacion Ecuatoriana de Golf
Baquerizo Moreno 1120, P.O. Box 521
Guayaquil
Ecuador

EGYPT

The Egyptian Golf Federation
Gezira Sporting Club,
Gezira, Cairo, Egypt
Tel: (2) 80 6000

EL SALVADOR

Asociacion Salvadorena de Golf
Apartado Postal 631
San Salvador
El Salvador

ENGLAND

Amateur Golf Championship
Royal & Ancient Golf Club, St. Andrews.
Tel: (0334)72112 Fax: (0334) 77580.

Association of Public Golf Courses
35 Sinclarr Grove, Golders Green,
London NW11 9JH
Tel: 081-4585433.

British Association of Golf Course Architects
5 Oxford Street, Woodstock Oxford GX7 ITQ.
Tel: (0993) 811976.

British Association of Golf Course Constructors
Tellford Farm, Willingale, Ongar,
 Essex CM5 OQE
Tel: (0277) 896229 Fax: (0245) 491620.

British & International Golf Greenkeepers' Association
Aldwark Manor, Aldwark,
 Alne, York Y06 2NF.
Tel: (03473) 5812 Fax: (03473) 8864.

British Professional Golfers' Association, Apollo House, The Belfry,
Sutton Colfield, West Midlands, B76 9PT
Tel: (0676) 70333 Fax: (0675) 70674

Golf Foundation
57 London Road, Enfield,
Mliddlesex EN2 6DU.
Tel: 081-367 4404.

Golf Society of Great Britain
Southvlew, Warren Road, Thurlestone,
Devon TQ7 3NT
Tel: (0548) 560630.

Ladies' Golf Union
The Scores,
St. Andrews, Fife KYI6 9AT.
Tel: (0334)75811.

The Professional Golfers' Association
National Headquarters, Apollo House,
The Belfry Sutton ColdSeld, West
Midlands, B76 9PT.
Tel: (0675) 70333 Telex 338481
Fax: (0675) 70674.

PGA European Tour
European Tour, The Wentworth Club,
Wentworth Drive, Virginia Water, Surrey
GU25 4LS.
Tel: (0344)842881 Fax: (0344)842929.

**Women Professional Golfers'
European Tour**
The Tytherington Club, Macclesfield,
Cheshire SKIO 2JP
Tel: (0625) 611444.

Sports Turf Research Institute
Bingley West Yorkshire BDI6 IAU.
Tel: (0274) 566131 Fax: (0274) 561891.

COUNTY GOLF ASSOCIATIONS

Bedfordslure County Golf Union
8 Galusborough Avenue, St Albans,
Bedfordshire ALI 4NL.
Tel: (0727) 67834.

**Bedfordshire Ladies' County Golf
Association**
3 Sherbourne Avenue, Luton,
Bedfordshire LU2 7BB.
Tel: (0582) 675883.

**Berks, Bucks and Oxon
Union of Golf Clubs**
Leyscre, Lodersfield, Lechlade,
Gloucestershire GL7 3DJ.
Tel: (0637) 52926.

**Berkshire, Buckinghamshire and
Oxfordshire Golfers Alliance**
Wayside, Aylesbury Road, Monks
Risborough, Aylesbury, Bucks.

**Berkshire Ladies' County Golf
Association**
Hon Sec, Mrs BE Band, 11 Lynton
Green, College Road, Maldenhead,
Berkshire SL6 6AN.
Tel: (0628) 21462.

**Buckinghamshire Ladies' County Golf
Assoclation**
Springfield Bungalow, Butlers Cross,
Aylesbury, Buckinghamshire
Tel: (0296) 624376.

Cambridgeshire Area Golf Union
2a Dukes Meadow, Stapleford,
Cambridgeshire CB2 6BH.
Tel: (0223) 842062.

**Cambs and Hunts Ladies' County Golf
Association**
The Paddock, 14 Mingle Lane,
Stapletord Carobs. CB2 6BG.
Tel: (0223) 843267.

Channel Islands Ladies' GA
Oakertbilch, Park Estate, St Brelade,
Jersey
Tel: (0634) 42072.

**Cheshire County Ladies' Golf
Association**
12 Higher Downs, Knutsford, Cheshire
WAI 6 8AW

Cheshire Union of Golf Clubs
4 Curson Mews, Wimislow
Cheshire SK9 6A1.
Tel: (0626)632866.

Cornwall Golf Union
8 Lydcott Crescent, Widegates, Looe
Cornwall PLI3 IOG.
Tel: (06034) 492.

**Cornwall Ladies' County Golf
Association**
Hain Walk, St Ives, Cornwall.
Tel: (0736) 796392.

Cumbria Ladies'
County Golf Association
Cawdor, Garth Heads Road, Appleby
Cumbria CA6 6DD.
Tel: (07683) 61672.

Cumbria Union of Golf Clubs
Thorn Lea, Lazouby Penrith, Cumbria.
Tel: (0768) 83231.

Derbyshire Alliance
c/o Buxton & High Peak CC, Fanfield,
Buxton, Derbyshire.
Tel: (0298) 3112.

Derbyshire Ladies' County Golf
Association
11 Pine Close, Smalley,
Derbyshire DE7 6EH.
Tel: (0332) 880929.

Derbyshire PGA
Erewash Valley Golf Club
Stanton-by-Dale, Derbyshire
Tel: (0662) 324667.

Derbyshire Union of Golf Clubs
67 Portland Close, Mickleover,
Derbyshire DE3 6BR.
Tel: (0332) 612466

Devon County Golf Union
Appledowne, Keyberry Park,
Newton Abbot, Devonshire TQl2 lDF
Tel: (0626)62999.

Devon County Ladies' Golf
Association
The White House, Hansford, Sidmouth,
Devonshire

Devon Professional Golfers' Alliance
Surthaven, 2 Landscore Close,
Devonshire
Tel: (03632) 3146.

Dorset County Golf Union
38 Carlton Road, Bournemouth BHI 3TG.
Tel: (0202) 290821.

Dorset Ladies'
County Golf Association
4 Egdon Glen Crossways, Dorchester,
Dorsetshire DT2 8BQ.
Tel: (0306) 862647.

Durham County Golf Union
Iliginiam Lodge, Park Mews, Harilepeol,
Cleveland T526 ODX.
Tel: (0429) 273186.

Durham County
Ladies' Golf Association
107 Harlsey Road, Harthurn,
Stockton-on-Tees.

English Golf Union
1-3 Upper King Street,
Leicester LEt 6XF.
Tel: (0633) 663042 Fax: (0633) 471322.

Midland Group
Chantry Cottage, Friar Street, Droitwich,
Worns WR9 8EQ. Tel: (0906) 778660.

Northern Group
7 Northbrook Court, Harilepool,
Cleveland TS26 ODJ.
Tel: (0429) 274828.

South Eastern Group
22 Wye Court, Malvern Way Ealing,
London W13 BFA.
Tel: (081) 9977466.

South Western Group
Hariland, Potterne, Devizes,
Wills SNIII 6PA.
Tel: (0380) 3936.

English Ladies' Golf Association
Edgbaston Golf Club, Church Road,
Birmingham B16 3Th.
Tel: (02) 466 2088.

Northern Division
10 Cleehill Drive, North Shields, Tyne &
Weir NE29 9EW
Tel: (091) 267 6926.

Midlands Division
3 Leanolme Gardens, Pedmore,
Stourbridge, West Midlands DY9 OXX
Tel: (0662) 884682.

South-Eastern Division
71 Parkanaur Avenue, Thorpe Bay
Essex SSI 3JA.
Tel: (0702) 688336

South-Western Division
19 Ferndown Close,
Kingsweston, Bristol.
Tel: (0272) 683643.

Essex County Amateur Golf Union
9 Willow Walk, Hadleigh,
Benfleet, Essex SS7 2RW
Tel: (0702) 669871.

**Essex Ladies' County Golf
Association**
1 The Paddocks, Stock, Essex.
Tel: (0277) 810466.

**Gloucestershire and Somerset
Professional Golfers' Association**
Cotswold Hills CC
Tel: (0242) 616263.

Gloucestershire Golf Union
2 Hartley Close, Sandy Lane,
Chariton Kings, Cheltenham CL63 9DN.
Tel: (0242) 614024.

**Gloucester Ladies' County Golf
Association**
1 Avon Crescent, Cumberland Road,
Bristol BSI 6XQ.
Tel: (0272) 264606.

**Hampshire Ladies' County Golf
Association**
182 Bassett Green Road, Southampton,
Hampshire S02 3LW
Tel: (0703) 789273.

**Hampshire, Isle of Wight and Channel
Islands Golf Union**
Glyngarth,Tower Road, Hindhead,
Surrey CU26 6SL.
Tel: (042 873) 4090.

**Hampshire Professional Golfers'
Association**
3 Lily Close, Kempshott Down,
Basingstoke, Hants RC22 6NT
Tel: (0266) 466070.

**Hertfordshire County
Professional Golfers' Alliance**
1 Field Lane, Letchworth,
Hertfordshire SC6 3LF.
Tel: (0462) 682266.

**Hertfordshire County
Ladies' Golf Association**
22 The Avenue, Radlett,
Hertfordshire WD7 7DW
Tel: (0923) 867184.

Hertfordshire Golf Union
2 The Heath, Radlett,
Hertfordshire WD7 7DF.
Tel: (0923) 867184.

Isle of Man Golf Union
22 Mount View Road, Onchan,
Isle of Man.
Tel: (0624) 622991.

Isle of Wight Ladies' Golf Association
Rosloing, Solent View Road, Seaview,
Isle of Wight PO34 6HY.
Tel: (0988) 613266

Kent County Golf Union
62 Queens Road, Littlestone, New
Romney, Kent TN28 8LY.
Tel: (0679) 63613.

Kent County Ladies' Golf Association
Colleton House, North Road, Hythe,
Kent CT21 4AS.
Tel: (0303) 66286.

Kent Professional Golfers' Union
20 The Grove, Baritham, Kent.
Tel: (0227) 831666.

Lancashire Ladies' County Golf Association
26 Park Road, Colborne, Warringlon, Cheshire WA3 3PU

Lancashire PGA
32 Pembridge Road, Blackley
Manchester M9 2IE.
Tel: 061-7968647.

Lancashire Union of Golf Clubs
4 Cedarwood Close, Lytham Hall Park, Lytham, Lancashire FYB 4PD.
Tel: (0263) 733323.

Leicestershire and Rutland Ladies' County Golf Association
4 Bailey's Lane, Burton Overy
Leicestershire LE8 0DD.
Tel: (063) 769 2697.

Leicestershire and Rutland Golf Union
187 Leicester Road, Groby , Leicester.
Tel: (0633) 873676.

Leicestershire Professional Golfers' Association
218 Hamilton Lane, Scraptoft, Leicester.
Tel: (0633) 414736.

Lincolnshire Ladies' County Association
86 South Parade, Boston, Lincolnshire PE2l 7PN.
Tel: (0206) 69948.

Lincolnshire Professional Golfers' Association
Seacroft CC, Skegness, Lincolnshire.
Tel: (0764) 3020.

Lincolnshire Union of Golf Clubs
Allenby Ores, Fotherby Nr Louth
Lincolnshire, LNl 1 OLl.
Tel: (0607) 604298.

Middlesex County Golf Union
36 Grants Close, Mill Hill,
London NW7 lDD.
Tel: (081) 3490414.

Midland Golf Union
Chantry Cottage, Friar Street,
Droitwich, Worcestershire WR9 8EQ.
Tel: (0905) 778560.

Norfolk County Golf Union
2a Stanley Avenue, Norwich, Norfolk.
Tel: (0603) 31026.

Norfolk Ladies' County Association
17 Taylor Avenue, Cringleford,
Norfolk NR4 6XY.
Tel: (0603) 56049.

Northamptonshire Golf Union
10 12 Edge Hill Road, Duston,
Northampton lNS 6BY
Tel: (0604) 51031.

Northamptonshire Ladies' County Golf Association
534 Wellingborough Road,
Northampton NN3 3HZ.
Tel: (0604) 09298.

Northamptonshire PGA
Ivycroft, Back Lane, Chapel Trampton,
Northamptonshire.
Tel: (0605) 843305.

Northumberland Ladies' County Golf Association
23 Mast Lane, Ullercoats,
North Shields NE30 3DK
Tel: (091) 252 5382.

Northumberland Union of Golf Clubs
5 Calthursl Drive, Kenton Ark, Gosforth,
Newcastle-upon-Tyne NE3 4J5.

Nottinghamshire County Ladies' Golf Association
Cranmer Lodge, Maln
Steet, Kinoulton, Noos, NA12 3EL.
Tel (0949) 81201.

Nottinghamshire PGA
52 Barden Road, Mapperley,
Nottingham NG3 5QD.
Tel: (0602) 269635.

Nottinshire Union of Golf Clubs
48 Weaverthorpe Road, Aroodthorp,
Nottinghamshire NG5 4NB.
Tel: (0602) 266560.

Oxfordshire Ladies' County Golf Association
532 Banbury Road, Oxford 0X2 BEG.
Tel: (0865) 58300.

Sheffield PGA
Hillsborough CC, Worrall Road,
Sheffield S6 4BE.
Tel: (0742) 332666.

Sheffield Union of Golf Clubs
8 Newfield Court, 186 Fulwood Road,
Sheffield SIO 3QE.

Shropshire and Herefordshire Union of Golf Clubs
23 Poplar Crescent, Bayston il,
Shrewsbury SY3 0GB.
Tel: (0743) 722655.

Shropshire and Herefordshire PGA
Bridgorth Golf Club, Stanley Lane,
Bridgnorth, Shropshire.
Tel: (07462) 2045.

Shropshire Ladies' County Golf Association
122 Fieldhouse Drive, Muxton, Telford,
Shropshire TF8 8BB. Tel: (0952) 604522.

Somerset Golf Union
Longwood, Grange Road, Salford,
Bristol BS1B 3AC.
Tel: (0225) 872166.

Somerset Ladies' County Golf Association
Tresausen, Mill Lane, Corfe,
Taunton TA3 7AH.

South-Western Counties Golf Association
Hartland, Potterne, Devizes,
Wiltfordshire SNIO SPA.
Tel: (0380) 3935.

Staffordshire Ladies' County Golf Association
11 Westhill, Finchfield Hill,
Wolverhampton WV3 9HL.
Tel: (0902) 753279.

Staffordshire and Shropshire Union of Professional Golfers
22 Wyan Road, Penn, Wolverhamplon.

Staffordshire Union of Golf Clubs
19 Broadway Walsall,
West Midlands WSI 3EX.
Tel: (0922) 24988.

Suffolk County Golf Union
2 Barton Road, Felixstowe,
Suffolk WU 7JH.
Tel: (0394) 286429.

Suffolk Ladies' County Golf Association
20 Meadowside, Snowdon Hill,
Wickman Market, Woodbridge, Suffolk.
Tel: (0728) 747609.

Suffolk PGA
Bury St Edmunds CC,
Forubam All Saints, Bury St Edmunds,
Suffolk W28 2LG.
Tel: (0284) 755978.

Surrey County Golf Union
Rushmoor Cottage,
Rushrnoor Close,
Fleet, CUI3 9LD.
Tel: (0252) 614078.

Surrey Ladies' County Golf Association
Tel: (0883) 723163.

Surrey PGA
27 Lower Wood Road,
Claygate, Surrey
Tel: (0372) 63882.

Sussex County Golf Union
12 Redmell Avenue, Saltdean,
Brighton, E Sussex BN2 8LT
Tel: (0273) 304415.

**Sussex County Ladies' Golf
Association**
Flat 1, 22 Granville Road, Eastbourne,
East Sussex BN2O 7HA.
Tel: (0323) 28452.

Sussex Professional Golfers' Union
96 Cranston Avenue, Bexhill-on-Sea,
Sussex.
Tel: (0424) 221298.

**Warwickshire Ladies' County Golf
Association**
57 White House Green, Solihull, W.
Midlands 831 ISP
Tel: (021)705 8062.

Warwickshire PGA
S Church Lane, Stoneleigh,
Warwickshire.
Tel: (0203)418113.

Wiltshire County Golf Union
10 Priory Park, Bradford-on-Avon,
Wiltshire BAIS 1QU. Tel: (022 16) 6401.

**Wiltshire Ladies' County Golf
Association**
South Lodge, Northleigh,
Bradford-on-Avon, Wiltshire
Tel: (02216)3387.

Wiltshire PGA
Marlborough CC, The Coramon,
Marlborough, Wiltshire
Tel: (0672) 512493.

**Worcestershire Association of
Professional Golfers**
Droitwich CC, Ford Lane. Droitwich WR9
0BH, Worcestershire
Tel: (090S) 770207.

**Worcestershire County Ladies' Golf
Association**
12 Russeil Road,
Kidderminster, Worcestershire DYIO 3IIT.

Worcestershire Union of Golf Clubs
70 Cardinal Drive,
Kidderminster, Worcestershire DYIO 4RY.
Tel: (0562) 823109.

**Yorkshire Ladies' County Golf
Association**
Ingle Court, Lepton,
Huddersfield, Yorkshire
Tel: (0484) 602011.

**Yorkshire Professional Golfers'
Association**
1 Summerhill Gardens, Leeds,
Yorkshire LS8 2EL.
Tel: (0532) 664746.

Yorkshire Union of Golf Clubs
SO Bingley Road,
Bradford, West Yorkshire BD9 6HH.
Tel: (0274) 542661.

Fiji

Fiji Golf Association
P.O. Box 177
Suva
Fiji

Finland

Finnish Golf Union
Radiokatu 12, SF-00240
Helsinki
Finland
Tel: 358 (0) 158-2244

FRANCE

Federation Francaise de Golf
69 Victor Hugo
F-75783
Paris Cedex 16
France
Tel: 33 (1) 4-502-1355

French Professional Golfers'
Association
69 Avenue Victor Hugo
75116 Paris 16
France
Tel: Paris (1) 500-4372.

GERMANY

Deutscher Golf Verband
eV. Postfach 2106
Wiesbaden D-6200
Germany
Tel: 49 (6121) 526-041

Deutscher Golfiehier Verband (PGA)
Eberlestrasse 13
89 Augsburg
Germany
Tel: 010 49 (821) 628900

GHANA

Ghana Golf Association
PO Box 8, Achimola
Ghana

GUYANA

Guyana Golf Union
c/o Demerara Bauxite Co. Ltd.,
Mackenzie
Guyana

GREECE

Hellenic Golf Federation
P.O. Box 70003
GR 166 10 Athens
Greece
Tel: 30 (1) 894-1933

GUATEMALA

Federacion Guatemalteca de Golf
3a Avenida Finca
El Zapote Zona 2
Guatemala

HONDURAS

Asociacion Hondurena Golf
Apartado Postal No. 68-C
Tegucigalpa, D.C.
Honduras

HONG KONG

The Golf Association of Hong Kong
G.P.O. Box 9978. Room 110
Yu To Sang Building, 37 Queens Road,
Central Hong Kong

Hong Kong Professional Golfers'
Association
Hon Sec, AR Hamilton, PG Box 690,
Hong Kong.
Tel: (5) 222111. Telex IX73751.

HUNGARY

Hungarian Golf Federation
c/o Rodata RT
Budapest 1028
Hungary
Tel: 36 (1) 176-6722

ICELAND

Golfsamband Islands
P.O. Box 1076
Reykjavik IS-101
Iceland
Tel: 354-168-6686

INDIA

The Indian Golf Union
Tta Centre, 3rd. Floor
43 Chowringhee Road, Calcutta 700-071
India

INDONESIA

Indonesian Golf Association
J1. Rawamangun Muka Taya
Jakarta 13220
Indonesia

IRELAND

Irish Golf Union
Glencar House, 81
Eglinglon Road, Donnybrook, Dublin 4.
Tel: (0001) 694111.

COUNTY ASSOCIATIONS

Ulster Branch
High Street, Holywood,
Co Down, BTl8 9AE.
Tel: Holywood 3708

Leinster Branch
1 Clonskeagh Sguare,
Clonskeagh Road, Dublin 14.
Tel: (0001) 696977 / 696727.

Munster Branch
Sunvilte, Dromshgo, Mallow Co Cork.
Tel: (22)21117/ 221123 (office).

Coraacht Branch
Abbey Hotel, Roscummon.

Irish Ladies' Golf Union
1 Clonskeagh Square,
Clonskeagh Road, Dublin 14.
Tel: (0001) 696244.

Northern District
1 4D Adelalde Park, Belfast BT9 6FX.
Tel: (0232) 682152.

Southern District
11 Baritead Drive, Church Road,
Blackrock, Cork.
Tel: (21) 291698.

Eastern District
4 Castletown Court, Colbridge, Co.
Kildare.

Western District
Dooney Rock, Cleveragh Drive,
Sligo.
Tel: Sligo (71)62351.

Midland District
Glena Terrace, Spawell Road,
Wexford.
Tel: Wexford (53) 22866.

ISRAEL

Israel Golf Federation
P.O. Box 1010
Caesarea
Israel
(972) 6-361172

ITALY

Federazione Italiana Golf
Via Flaminia 388
Roma 1-00196
Italy
Tel: 39 (6) 394641

IVORY COAST

Federation Nationale du Golf
08 BP 1297
Abidjan 08
Cote D'Ivoire
Tel: 22-521-3874

JAMAICA

Jamaica Golf Association
P.O. Box 743
Kingston 8
Jamaica

JAPAN

National Golf Foundation Japan
3-3-4 Sebdagaya Shibuya-ku
Tokyo
Japan
Tel: 81 (03) 478-4355

Japan Golf Association
606-6th Floor, Palace Building,
Marunouchi, Chiyoda-ku,
Tokyo
Japan
Tel: (3) 2150003.

Japan Ladies' Professional Golfers' Association
Kuranae Kogyo Kalkan 7E
Slanbasi 2-19-10, Minato-ku,
Tokyo,
Japan
Tel: (3) 571 0928.

Japan Professional Golf Association
Thmin-Ueno Building, 4F, 1-7-15,
Higashi-Ueno,
Talto-Ku, Tokyo 110
Japan

KENYA

Kenya Golf Union
PG Box 49609
Nalrobi
Kenya
Tel: (2) 720074.

Kenya Ladies' Golf Union
PG Box 45615
Nalrobi
Kenya

KOREA

Korea Golf Association
Room 18 - 13 Floor Manhattan Building
36-2 Yeo Eui Do-Dong
Yeong Deung Po-Ku, Seoul
Korea
Tel: 82 (02) 783-4748

LIBYA

Libyan Golf Federation
P.O. Box 3674
Tripoli
Libya

LUXEMBOURG

Golf Club
Grand Ducal 1, Route de Treve
L-2633 Senningerberg
Luxembourg
Tel: (352) 34090

MALAWI

Malawi Golf Union
PG Box 1198
Blantyre
Malawi

Malawi Ladies' Golf Union
PG Box 5319
Inmbe
Malawi

MALAYSIA

Malaysian Golf Association
No. 12-A Persiaran Ampang
55000 Kuala Lumpur
Malaysia

MEXICO

Federacion Mexicana de Golf
Cincinati No 40-104
Col. Napoles, 03710
Mexico
Tel: (5) 563-9194

MOROCCO

Federation Royale Marociane de Golf Royal
Golf Rabat dar es Salam
Route des Zaers
Rabat
Morocco

NETHERLANDS

Nederlandse Golf Federatie
P.O. Box 221
3454 PV De Meern
Netherlands
Tel: (31) 34-06-21888

NEW ZEALAND

New Zealand Golf Association
Dominion Sports House, Mercer Street
P.O. Box 11842
Wellington
New Zealand

**New Zealand Professional Golfers'
Association**
PG Box 27337
Wellington
New Zealand
Tel: (04) 722687 Fax: (04) 712152.

New Zealand Ladies' Golf Union
PG Box 13-029,
Wellington 4.
New Zealand
Tel: (04) 793868.

NIGERIA

Nigeria Amateur Golf Association
National Sports Commission
P.O. Box 145, Lagos
Nigeria

NORWAY

Norwegian Golf Association
Hauger Skolevie 11351 Rud
Oslo
Norway
Tel: 47 (2) 518800

PAKISTAN

Pakistan Golf Federation
P.O. Box No. 1295
Rawalpindi
Pakistan

PANAMA

Panama Golf Association
P.O. Box 8613
Panama 5
Panama

PAPUA NEW GUINEA

**Papua New Guinea Amateur Golf
Association**
PG Box 382, Lao
Papua New Guinea

**Papua New Guinea Ladies' Golf
Association**
PG Box 1256,
Port Moresby
Papua New Guinea
Tel: 675214745,

PARAGUAY

Asociacion Paraguaya de Golf
Casilla de Correo 1795
Asuncion
Paraguay

PERU

Federation Peruana de Golf Estadio
Nacional Puerto 4, Piso 4
Casilla 5637 Lima
Peru

PHILLIPINES

**Republic of the Philippines Golf
Association**
Rm. 209 Administration Building
Rizal Memorial Sports Complex
Vito Cruz, Manila
The Philippines

PORTUGAL

Federacao Portuguesa de Golf
Rua Almeida Brandao, 39
P-1200 Lisboa
Portugal
Tel: 351 (1) 661121

PUERTO RICO

Puerto Rico Golf Association
GPO Box 3862
San Juan 00936
Puerto Rico
Tel: (809) 781-2070

SCOTLAND

Scottish Golf Union
The Cottage, I8la Whitehouse Road,
Barnton, Edinburgh EH4 68Y.
Tel: 031-339 7546.

Scottish Golfer's Alliance
5 Deveron Avenue, Gifinock,
Glasgow G48 6NH.

Scottish Ladies' Golfing Association
Chacewood, 49 Fullarton Drive, Troon
KAIO 6LF.
Tel: (0292) 313047.

Scottish Ladies' Golfing Association-County Golf
Straibdon, Nelson Street, Dumfries.
Tel: (0387) 54429.

Scottish Schools' Golf Association
Grangemouth High School,
Grangemouth, Central Region.

West of Scotland Girls' Golfing Association
7 Gardenside Avenue, Uddingston,
Glasgow G7 1 7BU.

COUNTY ASSOCIATIONS

Aberdeen Ladies' County Golf Association
9 Earlsweil Place, Cults,
Aberdeen AB1 9LG.
Tel: (0224) 861502.

Angus Ladies' County Golf Association
The Hawinorns, 1 Grange Avenue,

Mocifieth, Dundee.
Tel: (0382) 532799

Ayrshire Ladies' County Golf Association
8 Station Road, Prestwick KA9 IAG.
Tel: (0292) 77330.

Border Counties' Ladies Golf Association
Fultarton, Darnick, Metrose,
Roxburghshire.
Tel: (089682) 2962.

Dumfriesshire Ladies' County Golf Association
Strathdon, 10 Nelson Street, Dumfnes.
Tel: (0387) 54429.

East Lothian Ladies' County Association
Glenlair, Main Street, Gullane.
Tel: (0620) 842534.

Fife County Ladies' Golf Association
Greyfriars, Greyfriars Garden,
St Andrews.
Tel: (0334) 72639.

Galloway Ladies' County Golf Association
3 Seggies, Kirkcudbright.
Tel: (0557) 30542.

Lanarkshire Ladies' County Golf Association
76 Kenmure Gardens, Bishopbriggs,
Glasgow G64 2BZ.
Tel: (041) 772 1720.

Midlothian County Ladies' Golf Association
37 Thomson Drive, Currie,
Midlothian EH14 5EY.
Tel: 031-4493441.

Perth and Kinross Ladies' County Golf Association
Broom, Caleclonian Crescent,
Auchierarder, Perthshire.
Tel: (0764) 62254.

Renfrewshire Ladies' County Golf Association
21 Holmnead Road, Glasgow G443AS.
Tel: (041) 637 1307.

Stirling and Clackmannan Ladies' Golf Association
7 Craighorn Drive, FalkirkIKI 5NX.
Tel: (0324) 29672.

SIERRA LEONE

Sierra Leone Golf Federation
Freetown Golf Club,
PG Box 237,
Lumley Beach, Freetown
Sierra Leone

SINGAPORE

Singapore Golf Association
c/o C.L. Loong & Company
4 Battery Road #12000
Bank of China Building, Singapore 0104
Singapore

SLOVENIA

Golf Association of Slovenia
c/o Golf Club Bled
C. Svbode13
64260 Bled
Slovenia
38 (64) 78282

SOUTH AFRICA

South Africa Golf Union
P.O. Box 1537
Cape Town 8000
South Africa

South African Ladies' Golf Union
PG Box 135,
1930 Vereeniging, Transvaal
South Africa

South African PGA
PG Box 55253, Posbus Northlands
2116 Johannesburg

South Africa
Tel: (011) 884 3404 Fax: (011) 884 3436

PROVINCIAL ASSOCIATIONS

Border Golf Union
Box 1773
East Lendon 5200 CP
Tel: (0431) 403899.

Eastern Province Golf Union
PG Box 146,
Port Elizabeth 6000, OP
Tel: (041) 21919

Northern Cape Golf Union
PG Box 517,
Bloemfontein 9300, GFS
Tel: (051) 470511.

Natal Golf Union
PG Box 1939, Durban 4000,
Natal
Tel: (031) 223877

Transkei Golf Union
PC Box 210,
Umtata, Transkei

Transvaal Golf Union
PG Box 391661
Bramley 2018, Transvaal
Tel: (011) 6403714.

Western Province Golf Union
Box 153, Howard Place, 7450,
Orange Province
Tel: (021) 536728.

SPAIN

Real Federacion Espanola De Golf
Capitan Haya, 9-5
E-28020 Madrid
Tel: 34 (1) 555 2757

SRI LANKA

Ceylon Golf Union
P.O. Box 309, Model Farm Road
Colombo 8

SWAZILAND

Swaziland Golf Union
S Mabuza, PO Box 1739
Mbabane
Swaziland

SWEDEN

Svenska Golfforbundet
Box 84 (Kevingestrand)
A-182 11 Danderyd
Sweden
Tel: 46 (8) 753-0265

Swedish PGA
PO Box 35, S-181 21
Lidingo
Sweden
Tel: Stockholm (8) 767 83 23

SWITZERLAND

Association Suisse de Golf
EnBallque, Case Postale
1066 Epalinges
Switzerland
Tel: 41 (21) 784-3531

**Swiss Professional Golfers'
Association**
Perrelet 9, 2074
Marin
Tel: (038) 33 23 79

TANZANIA

Tanzania Golf Union
PG Box 4879,
Dar-es-Salaam

THAILAND

Thailand Golf Association
Railway Training Centre
Vibhavadee Rangsit Road
Bangkok

TRINIDAD & TOBAGO

Trinidad & Tobago Golf Association
7A Warner Street
NewTown
Port of Spain
Trinidad

UGANDA

Uganda Golf Union
Kitante Road
PG Box 2674
Kampala

UNITED STATES

**Professional Golfers' Association of
America**
100 Ave. of the Champions,
Palm Beach Gardens, FL 33418
Tel: (407) 624-8400

United States Golf Association
Golf House, Liberty Corner Rd.,
Far Hills, NJ 07931
Tel: (201) 624-8400

STATE AND CITY ASSOCIATIONS

Alabama Golf Association
1025 Montgomery Hwy., Ste. 210,
Birmingham, AL 35216
Tel: (205) 979-1234
Fax: (205) 979-1602

Anchorage Golf Association
P.O. Box 112210,
Anchorage AK 99511
Tel: (907) 349-4653

Arizona Golf Association
7226 North 16th Street, Suite 200,
Phoenix, AZ 85020
Tel: (602) 944-3035
Fax: (602) 944-3228

Cactus & Pine
Golf Course Superintendents
Association of Arizona
7418 Helm Dr., Suites 227/228,
Scottsdale, AZ 85260.
Tel: (602) 998-9059
Fax: (602) 951-9756

Junior Golf Association of Arizona
5040 E. Shea, #250, Scottsdale, AZ
85254
Tel: (602) 443-9009
Fax: (602) 443-9006

Arkansas Seniors Golf Association
7002 Lucerne Dr., Little Rock, AR 72205
Tel: (501) 666-0951

Arkansas State Golf Association
2311 Biscayne Dr., #308, Little Rock, AR
72207
Tel: (501) 227-8555
Fax: (501) 227-8234

L.A. Junior Chamber of Commerce
404 S. Bixel St., Los Angeles, CA 90017
Tel: (213) 482-1311

N. California Golf Association, P.O.
Box NCGA, 3200 Lopez Rd., Pebble
Beach, CA 93953
Tel: (408) 625-4653 Fax: (408) 625-
0150

San Diego Cty. Junior Golf
Association Jack Murphy Stadium
9449 Friars Rd.
San Diego, CA 92108-1771
Tel: (619) 280-8505
Fax: (619) 281-7947

San Diego Cty. Women's G. Assoc.
3102 Lavante St., Carlsbad, CA 92009
Tel: (619) 436-0266

S. California Pub. Links G. Assoc.
7035 Orangethorpe Ave., Ste. E, Buena
Park, CA 90621
Tel: (714) 994-4747

Women's S. California Golf Assoc
402 W. Arrow Hwy., Ste. 10
Tel: (714)592-1281
Fax: (714) 592-7542

Colorado Golf Association
5655 S. Yosemite, Ste. 101, Englewood,
CO 80111
Tel: (303) 779-4653
Fax: (303) 220-8397

Connecticut State Golf Assoc.
35 Cold Spring Rd., #212, Rocky Hill, CT
06067 Tel: (203) 257-4171
Fax: (203) 257-8355

Connecticut Women's Golf Assoc.,
183 Plagler Ave., Cheshire, CT 06410

Delaware State Golf Association,
7234 Lancaster Pike, #302B,
Hockessin, DE 19707-9273
Tel: (302) 234-3365
Fax: (302) 234-3359

Dade Amateur Golf Association
1802 N.W. 37th Ave., Miami, FL 33159
Tel: (305) 633-4563

Florida Golf Republic Association
P.O. Box 2280, Boca Raton, FL 33427
Tel: (407) 391-3292

Florida State Golf Association
P.O. Box 21177, Sarasota, FL 34276
Tel: Tel: (813) 921-5695
Fax: (813) 923-1254

Florida Turfgrass Association
302 S. Graham Ave.,
Orlando, FL 32803-6399
Tel: (407) 898-6721
Fax: (813) 923-1254

Pensacola Sports Association
201 E. Gregory St., Pensacola, FL
32501
Tel: (909) 939-4455

**Georgia Golf Course
Superintendents Association**
1141 Station Dr., Watkinsville, GA 30677
Tel: (706) 769-4076
Fax: (706) 769-4076

Georgia State Golf Association
121 Village Parkway, Bldg. 3,
Marietta, GA 30067
Tel: (404) 955-4272
Fax: (404) 955-1156

Hawaii Golf State Association
3599 Waielae Ave. #PH,
Honolulu, HI 96816-2759
Tel: (808) 732-9785

Idaho Golf Association, Inc.
P.O. Box 3025, Boise, ID 83703
Tel: (208) 342-4442
Fax: (208) 345-5959

**Central Illinois Golf Course
Superintendents Association**
5350 Old Jacksonville Rd.,
Springfield, IL 62707
Tel: (217) 787-7750

Chicago District Golf Association
619 Enterprise Dr., Oak Brook, IL 60521
Tel: (708) 954-2180
Fax: (708) 954-3650

Illinois Junior Golf Association
2100 Clearwater Dr., Suite 206,
Oak Brook, IL 60521
Tel: (708) 368-0000
Fax: (708) 990-7864

Western Golf Association
1 Briar Rd., Golf, IL 60029
Tel: (708) 724-4600
Fax: (708) 724-7133

Indiana Association of Nurserymen
2635 Yeager Rd, Ste. B, West Lafayette,
IN 47906
Tel: (317) 497-1100
Fax: (317) 463-0190

Indiana Golf Association
P.O. Box 516, Franklin, IN 46131
Tel: (317) 738-9696
Fax: (317) 738-9436

Indiana Junior Golf Association
P.O. Box 4454, Lafayette, IN 47903
Tel: (317) 447-1992
Fax: (317) 448-9969

Iowa Golf Association
1930 Saint Andrews Ct. N.E.,
Cedar Rapids, IA 52402
Tel: (319) 378-9142
Fax: (319) 378-9203

Kansas City Golf Association
9331 Ensley Lane, Leawood, KS 66206
Tel: (913) 649-8872
Fax: (913) 842-3831

Kansas Golf Association
3301 Clinton Parkway Ct. #4,
Lawrence, KS 66047
Tel: (913) 842-4833
Fax: (913) 842-3831

Kentucky Golf Association
4109 Bardstown Rd. #5A,
Louisville, KY, 40261
Tel: (502) 499-7255
Fax: (502) 499-7422

Louisiana Golf Association
1305 Emerson St., Monroe, LA 71201
Tel: (318) 342-1968
Fax: (318) 342-1989

Maine State Golf Association
11 Cook St., Auburn, ME 04210
Tel: (207) 582-6742
Fax: (207) 582-6743

Maryland State Golf Association
P.O. Box 16289, Baltimore, MD 21210
Tel: (410) 467-8899

Massachusetts Golf Association
190 Park Rd., Weston, MA 02193
Tel: (617) 891-4300
Fax: (617) 891-9471

Golf Association of Michigan
37935 12 Mile Rd., Ste 200,
Farmington Hills, MI 48331
Tel: (313) 553-4200
Fax: (313) 553-4438

Michigan Publinx Sr. Golf Assoc.
43525 W. 6 Mile Rd., Northville, MI 48167
Tel: (313) 349-2148

Minnesota Golf Association
6550 York Ave. S., Ste. 211,
Edina, MN 55435
Tel: (612) 927-4643

Trans-Mississippi Golf Association
240 Minnetonka Ave. S., #212,
Wayzata, MN 55391
Tel: (612) 473-3722
Fax: (612) 473-0576

Mississippi Golf Association
1019 N. 12th Ave. #3, Laurel, MS 39441
Tel: (601) 649-0570
Fax: (601) 649-1737

Missouri Golf Association
P.O. Box 104164,
Jefferson City, MO 65110
Tel: (314) 636-8994
Fax: (314) 636-4225

St Louis District Golf Association
537 N. Clay, Kirkwood, MO 63122
Tel: (314) 821-1511

Montana State Golf Association
P.O. Box 2289, Butte, MT
Tel: (406) 723-4312
Fax: (406) 782-9551

Nebraska Golf Association
5625 O Street, Ste. Fore,
Lincoln, NE 68510-2149
Tel: (402) 486-1440

Nevada State Golf Association
P.O. Box 5630, Sparks, NV 89432-5630
Tel: (702) 673-4653
Fax: (702) 673-1144

Southern Nevada Golf Association
1434 Cottonwood, Las Vegas, NV 89104
Tel: (702) 382-6616

New Hampshire Golf Association
45 Kearney St., Manchester, NH 03104
Tel: (603) 623-0396

New Jersey State Golf Association
1000 Broad St., Bloomfield, NJ 07003
Tel: (201) 338-8334
Fax: (201) 338-5525

Southern Jersey State Golf
277 Mayflower Dr., Buena, NJ 08310
Tel: (609) 697-9318

Trenton District Golf Association
7 High Acres Rd.,
West Trenton, NJ 08628
Tel: (609) 771-2191

**Sun Country
Amateur Golf Association**
10035 Country Club Ln. NW, #5,
Albuquerque, NM 87114
Tel: (505) 897-0864
Fax: (505) 897-3494

Buffalo District Golf Association
P.O. Box 19, Cheektowaga, NY 14225
Tel: (716) 632-1936

Metropolitan Golf Association
125 Spencer Pl.,
Mamaroneck, NY 10543
Tel: (914) 698-0390

Rochester District Golf Association
1106 Long Pond Rd. Ste 190,
Rochester, NY 14626
Tel: (716) 227-4053

Syracuse District Golf Association
2205 W. Genese St.,
Syracuse, NY 13219-1617
Tel: (315) 488-7391

Westchester Golf Association
106 N. Broadway, Irvington, NY 10533
Tel: (914) 591-4970

Carolinas Golf Association
P.O. Box 428, West End, NC 27376
Tel: (910) 673-1000
Fax: (910) 673-1001

Turfgrass Council of N. Carolina
231 W. Pennsylvania Ave., Southern
Pines, NC 28387
Tel: (910) 695-1333
Fax: (910) 695-1222

North Dakota State Golf Assoc.
P.O. Box 452, Bismark, ND 58502
Tel: (701) 223-2770
Fax: (701) 223-6719

Northern Ohio Golf Association
17800 Chillicothe Rd., Ste. 210,
Chagrin Falls, OH 44023
Tel: (216) 543-6320

Ohio Assoc. of Public Golf Courses
5874 Morray Ct., Dublin, OH 43017
Tel: (614) 761-1527

Ohio Golf Association
5300 McKitrick Blvd.,
Columbus, OH 43235
Tel: (614) 457-8169
Fax: (614) 457-8211

Toledo District Golf Association
Southwyck Blvd., Ste. 204,
Toledo, OH 43614-1505
Tel: (419) 866-4771
Fax: (419) 866-0388

Oklahoma Golf Association
P.O. Box 449, Edmond, OK 73083
Tel: (405) 340-6333
Fax: (405) 340-6333

Oregon Golf Association
8364 S.W. Nimbus Ave. #A1,
Beaverton, OR 97005
Tel: (503) 643-2610
Fax: (405) 340-6333

Erie District Golf Association
1223 Jonathan Dr., Erie, PA 16509
Tel: (814) 838-8524

Golf Association of Philadelphia
P.O. Drawer 808,
Southeastern, PA 19399
Tel: (215) 687-2340
Fax: (215) 687-2082

Keystone Public Golf Association
2186 Locust St., Export, PA 15632
Tel: (412) 468-8880
Fax: (412) 468-8897

Western Pennsylvania Golf Assoc.
1360 Old Freeport Rd. Ste 1BR,
Pittsburgh, PA 15238
Tel: (412) 963-9806
Fax: (412) 967-0612

Rhode Island Golf Association
10 Orms St., Ste. 326,
Providence, RI 02904
Tel: (401) 272-1350

South Carolina Golf Association
P.O. Box 286, Irmo, SC 29063
Tel: (803) 781-6992
Fax: (803) 781-6992

Women's S. Carolina Golf Assoc.
10638 Two Notch, Elgin, SC 29045
Tel: (803) 736-0081

South Dakota Golf Association
509 S. Holt, Sioux Falls, SD 57103
Tel: (605) 338-7499
Fax: (605) 334-3447

Dallas District Golf Association
4321 Live Oak, Dallas, TX 75204
Tel: (214) 823-6004

Houston Golf Association
1830 S. Millbend Dr.,
The Woodlands, TX 77380
Tel: (713) 367-7999
Fax: (713) 363-9888

San Antonio Golf Association
70 NE Loop 410, Ste. 370,
San Antonio, TX 78216
Tel: (512) 341-0823
Tel: (512) 340-1625

Utah Golf Association
1110 E. Englewood Dr.,
N. Salt Lake City, UT 84054
Tel: (801) 299-8421

Vermont Golf Association
P.O. Box 1612, Stn. A,
Rutland, VT 05701
Tel: (802) 773-7180
Fax: (802) 773-7061

Virginia State Golf Association
830 Southlake Blvd., Ste. A,
Richmond, VA 23236
Tel: (804) 378-2300
Fax: (804) 378-2369

Washington Metro. Golf Assoc.
8012 Colorado Springs Dr.,
Springfield, VA 22153
Tel: (703) 569-6311
Fax: (703) 569-6332

Pacific Northwest Golf Association
155 N.E. 100th St., #302
Seattle, WA 98125
Tel: (206) 526-1238
Fax: (206) 522-0281

Washington Junior Golf Assoc.
633 Mildred, Ste. C, Tacoma, WA 98406
Tel: (206) 564-0348
Fax: (206) 564-2602

West Virginia Golf Association
P.O. Box 8133,
Huntington, WV 25705-0133
Tel: (304) 525-0000

Golf Course Assoc. of Wisconsin
P.O. Box 65, Mauston, WI 53948
Tel: (608) 847-7968

Wisconsin State Golf Association
P.O. Box 35, Elm Grove, WI 53122
Tel: (414) 786-4301
Fax: (414) 786-4202

Wyoming Golf Association
501 First Ave. S., Greybull, WY 82426
Tel: (307) 568-3304

URUGUAY

Asociacion Uruguaya de Golf
Casilla de Correo 1484,
Montevideo

VENEZUELA

Federacion Venezolana de Golf
Unidad Comercial "La Florida," Local 5
Avenida Avila,
La Florida, Caracas 1050

WALES

Welsh Golfing Union
Powys House,
Cwmbran, Gwent NP44 1PB.

Welsh Ladies' Golf Union
Ysgoldy Gynt, Llanhennock, Newport,
Gwent NP6 1LT
Tel: (0633)420642

LOCAL ASSOCIATIONS

Anglesey Golf Union
20 Gwelfor Estate, Cemaes Bay
Anglesey
Tel: (0407) 710755

Brecon and Radnor Golf Union
Hon Sec CL Williams, 10 Penpentre,
Hanfees, Brecon.

Caernarvonshire and Anglesey Ladies' County Golf Association
Deunant, Llangefni,
Anglesey LL7 7YP.
Tel: (0248) 722338.

Caernarvonshire and District Golung Union
23 Bryn Rhos, Rhosbodrual,
Caernarfon, Gwynedd UL55 2BT
Tel: (0286) 3486.

Dyfed Golfing Union
55 Clover Par
Haverfordwest, Dyfed.

Flintshire Golfing Union
Cornist Lodge, Cornist Park,
Flint, Clwyd.
Tel: (03526) 2186.

**Glamorgan Ladies'
County Golf Association**
19 Trem-y-Don, Barry, South Glamorgan.
Tel: (0446) 734866.

Gwent Golf Union
3 Oak Court, Woodfield Park,
Blackwood, Gwent.
Tel: (0495) 223520.

**Mid Wales Ladies' County Golf
Association**
Ael-y-Byrn, Pontfaen Road, Lampeter,
Dyfed.
Tel: (0570) 422463.

**Monmouthshire Ladies' County Golf
Association**
Flat 2, 405 Chepstow Road, Newport,
Gwent.
Tel: (0633) 279638.

**South Wales Professional Golfers'
Association**
St Mellons Golf Club, MidGlamorgan
Tel: (0633) 680101.

ZAIRE

Zaire Golf Federation
Fres, Tshilombo Mwin
Tshitol, BP 1648 Lubumbashi.

ZAMBIA

Zambian Golf Union
PG Box 37446, Lusaka
Zambia
TelexZA 40098.

Zambia Ladies' Golf Union
PG Box 32150, Lusaka.
Tel: Lusaka (1) 251668, Telex ZA40098.

ZIMBABWE

Zimbabwe Golf Association
P.O. Box 3327
Harare

Zimbabwe Ladies' Golf Union
PG Box 3814
Harare

EASY GUIDE TO GOLFING TERMINOLOGY

OVERVIEW: *Simple definitions and explanations of golf's sometimes arcane and always unique vocabulary.*

Ace. Holing the ball on the first stroke. Also HOLE-IN-ONE.

Action. A strong backspin on a shot, usually a wedge or short iron to the green. Also JUICE.

Address. The position of the player immediately before commencing the backswing.

Albatross. (Rare) Three strokes under the PAR score for a hole; i.e. a hole-in-one on a par-four, or a two on a par-five. Also DOUBLE EAGLE.

Alternate Shot. A match format in which two players on one team play one ball, alternating shot for shot. Also FOURSOME, SCOTCH FOURSOME.

Approach. A stroke aimed to finish on the putting surface and close to the hole.

Apron. The area of close-cropped grass surrounding the putting surface. Also FRINGE or FROG HAIR.

Arnie. Making PAR after missing the fairway with the drive.

Baffie. An older golf club, now seldom in use, similar in design to the modern 3-iron. From the Scottish word "baff," to put a ball in the air.

Balata. A by-product of the rubber-tree used to make a golf-ball cover material which spins faster than other cover materials, although it tends to fly a shorter distance and cut easily.

Banana Ball. See CUT SHOT.

Barkie. Making PAR after hitting a tree on the approach shot.

Baseball Grip. See GRIP.

Best Ball. A team scoring format in which the team records only the lowest score among all the team members (sometimes the two lowest, as in "two best balls") .

Birdie. Holing the ball in one stroke under the PAR score.

Bisque. A handicap stroke that may be freely employed at any time during a match.

Blade. 1: The leading edge of an iron. 2: A narrow, forged iron favored by lower handicap players. 3: (Verb) To scull a ball, usually across and over the putting surface.

Blast. A lofted recovery from a greenside bunker, typically struck with the flanged-sole sand wedge and often accompanied by terrific backspin. Also EXPLOSION.

Bogey. Holing the ball in one stroke over the par score. Originally conceived as the average score by the mythical expert player, it has come to represent a mediocre effort in light of modern improvements in technique and equipment. A double-bogey is two over the par score, a triple-bogey is three over, &c.

Brassie. A golf club used prior to 1945, similar to the modern two-wood, so named because of a distinctive brass plate on the sole of the club.

Bump-and-run. A short (20-60 yard) shot in which the player employs a short, flattened backswing to produce a low, running ball which bounces rather than flies into the green. Used most effectively on windy or dry courses.

Bunker. A scrape or swale in the ground filled with sand, usually placed near the green to perplex the player. Also SAND TRAP.

Caddie. The associate who carries the player's clubs, cleans his equipment, and is the only person allowed under the rules to offer advice or information to the player during a round. Often an expert golfer, caddies have often formed life-long associations with top clubs or top professionals. The word comes from the French *cadet*, after the French pages brought to Scotland by Mary, Queen of Scots, who was a keen golfer.

Calcutta. An auction of players before a match—bettors bid for players and the resulting sum of wagers is put into a pool distributed to the winning players and bettors.

Callaway System. A scoring system used for players lacking formal HANDICAP ratings.

Captain's Choice. See SCRAMBLE.

Cast Irons. A technology for casting irons from a mold (rather than forging individually), which introduced the era of cavity-back irons. With weight re-distributed to the perimeter, cavity-back irons have enlarged Sweet Spots and provide more control and distance for off-center hits.

Casual Water. Collections of dew, rainfall, or ground moisture not considered a part of the course; a player is allowed a free drop away from casual water.

Cayman Ball. A ball developed for use on short golf courses which travels significantly less far than the modern golf ball while retaining its spin and control characteristics.

Chili Dip. The clubhead striking the ground well behind of the ball, resulting in a very weak and short shot, as well as an especially impressive DIVOT.

Chip. A shot around the green in which the player employs a putting stroke with a lofted iron; the result is a shot which flies a short distance before rolling toward the hole.

Cleek. (Rare) A golf club similar to the modern 4-wood.

Closed Face. Rotation of the golf clubface in a counter-clockwise direction to produce less loft, more overspin, and a more

pronounced DRAW.

Closed Stance. A stance in which a right-handed player's body is aligned right of the target.

Course Rating. The average score of a scratch handicap player on a course, as sanctioned by the United States Golf Association, the Royal & Ancient, or its designated representatives. See SLOPE RATING.

Cross-bunker. A typically narrow and wide bunker which stretches across the fairway, rather than parallel to it. A typical design feature in PENAL ARCHITECTURE.

Cut, The. The reduction of the field, typically after the second day's play, to the low 40-90 contestants. In pro events, only those players who make the cut earn prize money.

Cut Shot. A ball that spins for the right-hander from left to right. The cut shot typically travels a shorter distance than the DRAW, but is easier to control. Also FADE or, in severe and uncontrolled cases, SLICE or BANANA BALL.

Dance Floor. (Slang) The putting surface.

Dimple Pattern. The design of the small indentations in the golf ball that help lengthen its flight and control its spin.

Divot. The turf freed by a golf club when it strikes the ground. Making a DIVOT behind the ball produces a CHILI DIP; hitting after the ball produces BACKSPIN.

Dormie. A position in match play where one player is far enough ahead that he cannot be beaten, but has not yet achieved victory. E.g. five holes up with five to play.

Double Eagle. See ALBATROSS.

Drainpipe. A narrow, lightweight golf bag suitable for walking the course.

Draw. A ball that for the right-hander spins from right to left. The draw shot typically travels further than the FADE, but is less subject to precise control. Also known as a HOOK or, in severe and uncontrolled cases, as a DUCK HOOK. "You can't talk to a hook."—Lee Trevino.

Drive. An initial stroke on a hole, when played with a DRIVER. The stroke produces the longest shots in golf, at the risk of some loss in accuracy.

Driver. The longest, least-lofted club in the modern golf bag, almost exclusively used for tee shots, particularly where distance is a factor. Originally known as the PLAY-CLUB.

Duck Hook. See DRAW.

Eagle. Two strokes below the PAR score for a hole. E.g. a HOLE-IN-ONE on a par-three, two strokes on a par-four, and three strokes on a par-five.

Equitable Stroke Adjustment. An adjustment made in a player's score (for handicap purposes only), which limits the maximum score a player can record for an individual hole. The rule was established to prevent players inflating their handicaps with deliberately poor play. See SANDBAGGING.

Explosion. See BLAST.

Face. The front part of the clubhead.

Fade. See CUT SHOT.

Fairway. Short-cropped grass, usually in the 30-50 yards on either side of the center line of a hole, which is the preferred landing point of the player off the tee.

Fat. Hitting underneath the ball.

Feathery. One of the most ancient types of golf balls, it consisted of feathers tightly packed inside a leather cover. Costly and not particularly lively, the ball was superseded in the mid-19th century by the GUTTIE.

Flop Shot. A shot, typically employed in heavy rough, where the player opens the clubface so that it is almost parallel to the ground, to reduce resistance and allow the club to move through heavy grass without digging into the turf.

Forged Irons. See CAVITY-BACK IRONS.

Fourteen-club Rule. The rule instituted in the 1930s limiting a player to carrying a maximum of fourteen golf clubs in a round.

Forecaddie. A player's associate who does not carry the clubs, but in other ways fills the role of the CADDIE.

Four Ball. A match between two teams of two players each.

Foursome. In the United States, any grouping of four golfers. In the rest of the world, a foursome is a match format pitting four players in two-man teams in an ALTERNATE SHOT format. Also SCOTCH FOURSOME.

Fringe. See APRON.

Frog Hair. See APRON.

Frosty. See SNOWMAN.

Gimme. A putt conceded to a player by his opponent, typically a putt of less than two feet, or less than the length of a putter from the sole to the base of the grip.

Grain. The angle at which the grass is growing. Proper allowance for the "drag" caused when putting against the grain is an essential part of READING a green.

Green. Originally, the entire golf course, hence the design principle of "flow through the green," or the "greenkeeper." The modern definition is usually confined to the putting surface.

Greenie. A bonus bet won by the player who is closest to the pin on a par-three hole (and on the putting green).

Grip. The position of the hands on the shaft. The TEN-FINGER GRIP (also BASEBALL GRIP) is the oldest form, in which the hands work independently. The OVERLAPPING or VARDON GRIP has the little finger of the right hand (for a right-hander) overlapping the index finger on the left. The INTERLOCKING GRIP, popularized by Jack Nicklaus, has the little finger of the right hand interlocked between the index and middle fingers of the left hand, and is used primarily by players with small hands.

Gross Score. A player's actual score, before deductions for HANDICAP and EQUITABLE STROKE ADJUSTMENT.

Ground Under Repair. Ground usually defined as part of the golf course which, due to ground conditions, is ruled unplayable. Players who land here are allowed a drop without penalty.

Guttie. The gutta-percha ball, a solid rubber ball developed in the mid-19th century, superceded the FEATHERY and preceded the HASKELL ball. The Guttie had a tendency to fly quite low, and was difficult to control.

Halve. A tie between two players or two teams in a hole or match.

Handicap. An average of scores, expressed in strokes over par, for the individual player. E.g., a player who averages a score of eighteen strokes over par is said to have a handicap of 18. Handicaps were developed in the stroke play era to allow players of different abilities to compete in "NET SCORE" competitions.

Haskell Ball. The first modern rubber-cored golf ball, invented in 1902.

Hazard. A position within the course boundaries, such as a pond, where the ball is typically unplayable; the player may under penalty of one stroke drop the ball behind the point where the ball entered the hazard. See LATERAL HAZARD.

Heel. The edge of a clubhead nearest the shaft.

Heroic Architecture. A philosophy of course design, most closely associated with the designs of Robert Trent Jones, that presents golfers with difficult or "heroic" shots that, if risked and carried off, make eagle or birdie scores possible. The Heroic style flourished after the Second World War but has in recent decades been superseded by STRATEGIC ARCHITECTURE, which is closely related.

Hole-in-One. See ACE.

Honor. The player who recorded the lowest score on the preceding hole is said to have "the honor," and tees off first on the next hole.

Hook. See DRAW.

Horseshoe. A putted ball which spins around the entire rim of the cup without falling into the hole. Also PAINT-JOB.

Hosel. The point at which the shaft joins the clubhead.

Initial Velocity. The speed of a golf ball struck by the USGA's Iron Byron machine, when it first leaves the club-face. Golf balls which exceed the initial velocity specified by the United States Golf Association and the Royal and Ancient Golf Club are not recognized as legal for the purposes of competition.

Interlocking Grip. See GRIP.

Iron. The ancient Scottish word for "sword," it refers to the family of clubs, originally with iron club-heads, used for the short-to-medium length shots. Irons were first developed for use in unusual lies, but since Young Tom Morris demonstrated their ability to produce high, soft shots that stopped quickly (or, in modern times, backed up), they have been used anywhere from the tee to the green. Irons are numbered from 1 through 9; there are also several types of high-lofted or flanged irons known as Sand Wedge, Pitching Wedge, Lob Wedge, &c.

Juice. See ACTION.

Lag Putt. A long putt aimed to finish close to the hole for an easy tap-in.

Lateral Hazard. A water or other HAZARD area in which the player can take a penalty drop beside, rather than strictly behind, the hazard line.

Links. In the traditional sense, a course built atop land from which the ocean has receded, hence a course built on sandy soil. In practice, the term has expanded to include all seaside courses, and many Scottish-influenced designs. As a marketing term, it has been used to describe practically anything that resembles a golf course.

Marker. The score-keeper. Typically another competing player, although the Marker can either be a non-participant or a non-competing player.

Mashie. The old name for what is the modern 3-iron.

Match Play. A competition decided by the number of holes won. See MEDAL PLAY.

Medal Play. Competition decided by the total number of strokes taken, rather than holes won (as in MATCH PLAY).

Metal Wood. See WOOD.

Modified Stableford. See STABLEFORD.

Mulligan. Named for circa-1930s Winged Foot member David Mulligan, it is a replay of a shot without penalty. Forbidden under the Rules of Golf, the Mulligan is nonetheless universally, frequently, and cheerfully employed in amateur golf, particularly with novices. The original interpretation of a Mulligan was a replay of the first tee shot of the day, but the term has since grown to include any replay without penalty granted by a playing partner during the round.

Nassau. A match between two teams in which one-third of the bet is placed on the outcome of the first nine holes, the second third on the second nine, and the final third on the round as a whole. The most popular and enduring of golf wagers.

Net. A player's GROSS score less adjustments for HANDICAP.

Niblick. A golf club similar to the modern five-iron. This was the highest-lofted club manufactured until the 20th century.

Opened Face. Rotation of the clubface in a clockwise direction to produce more loft, more backspin, or a more pronounced FADE.

Opened Stance. A position at address in which a right-handed player is aligned left of the target.

Out of Bounds. Outside the boundary of the course. Any ball hit "O.B." must be replayed from the original position under a penalty of one stroke.

Overlapping Grip. See GRIP

Paint Job. See HORSESHOE.

Par. Of unknown origin, the term developed in the early 20th century to express the number of strokes the mythical expert player should take to complete a golf hole. Currently defined formally as: Under 225 yards, par 3; 225-474 yards, par 4; 475-575 yards, par 5; over 575 yards, par 6. Courses are not obliged to follow these USGA guidelines, and there are many exceptions. See BOGEY.

Penal Architecture. A philosophy of golf course instruction where errant shots are penalized with difficult lies and hazards. Pine Valley is one of the finer examples of the type. The penal architectural style flourished in the early 20th century but has fallen into disfavor.

Pitch Shot. A short (50-120 yards) shot typically played with a wedge in which the player lofts the ball high into the air to achieve a soft landing on the putting surface.

Play Club. See DRIVER.

Pneumatic Ball. An experimental ball from the early 20th century which, featuring a core of compressed air, had a reputation for flying great distances. When several competitors were injured by the ball exploding in warm temperatures, it was withdrawn from sale.

Pot Bunker. A small and typically deep bunker which is a common feature of Scottish and Scottish-influenced courses.

Pro-Am. A match format mixing professionals and amateurs in a team, often on the day before a professional tournament.

Punch Shot. A low-trajectory shot used in heavy wind or when the shot is crowded by trees. The classic stroke is played with a three-quarter swing and the ball aligned opposite the back foot.

Purse. The pool or prize-money in a professional tournament.

Putt. A stroke employed on the putting surface or close around the green in which the player rolls the ball along the ground instead of lofting it into the air.

Putter. The club employed typically for shots on the green, typically featuring a face with no loft.

Qualifying School. A qualifying tournament or series of tournaments in which professionals vie for a limited number of playing cards for professional tours.

Read. A player's estimate of the slope of the ground, an important factor in choosing the line for a putt.

Rough. Unmowed or heavy grass that is part of the golf-course but off the FAIRWAY.

Rub of the Green. An element of good or bad luck. E.g. a ball which strikes the flagstick and, in the one case, drops into the hole, but in another case rebounds into a water-hazard.

Rules of Golf. The official Rules of the Game as codified by the United States Golf Association and the Royal & Ancient Golf Club of St. Andrews.

Rut Iron. A de-lofted club used to hit a ball

from an embedded lie. In the modern game most embedded lies are allowed relief with a free drop, and the club has fallen out of use.

Sandbagging. (Slang) The practice of quoting a higher number than one's actual handicap in order to receive either more strokes in a tournament or match, or more favorable terms in a wager. Also refers to the practice of deliberately playing poorly to inflate one's handicap prior to a match or tournament.

Sandie. A ball holed in two shots ("up and down") from a sand-trap.

Scramble. A team format in which team members each hit a shot, choose the best result, and each drop a ball within a club-length and hit from that point. The routine is repeated until the ball is holed. The format, which often produces rashes of birdies and eagles and outrageously low scores, is usually employed with novice players or with groups of widely varying abilities; the format has become widely known through the annual Oldsmobile Scramble, a national amateur championship which employs the format. Also CAPTAIN'S CHOICE.

Scratch Handicap. A handicap of zero. Hence SCRATCH player.

Scull. To hit the ball with the lowest edge of an iron, causing a low-flying and often wildly-errant shot.

Shamble. Related to a SCRAMBLE, a team format in which team members each hit a shot, choose the best result, and thereafter play their own ball in.

Shank. A ball which is hit off the HOSEL, causing the ball to fly in a low and wildly off-line trajectory.

Skins. A match format in which points or prizes are awarded ("Skins") only when one player wins the hole outright. The format is often played with "carry-overs," in which prizes not awarded because of a halve on one hole are carried over to the next.

Slice. See CUT SHOT.

Slope Rating. The average score of BOGEY golfers over a course, divided by the average score of SCRATCH HANDICAP golfers (COURSE RATING). The purpose of slope is to enable the comparison of scores made by golfers of any ability on differing courses. Using COURSE RATINGS alone offers an effective comparison only for low handicap golfers.

Snowman. (Slang) A score of eight on a single hole. Also FROSTY.

Sole. The bottom edge of a golf club.

Spin-rate. The number of revolutions per second of a golf ball hit by the USGA's "Iron Byron" ball-striking machine.

Spoon. An older term for the fairway wood, now the three-, four- or five-wood.

Square. An alignment of the player at ADDRESS, or the clubface at impact, which is perpendicular to the target. Also, a position in a match where the players or teams are level.

Stableford. A scoring system which utilizes a points system, and which encourages bold play through heavy premiums placed on birdies and eagles. The Sprint International, a PGA TOUR event, uses a modified Stableford system.

Strategic Architecture. A philosophy of golf course design which emphasizes presenting options to the golfer, typically a safe route to PAR and a heroic route to BIRDIE or EAGLE. The Strategic style has become increasingly popular in the past twenty years, and is the dominant style in contemporary course design.

Stroke Play. See MEDAL PLAY.

Stymie. Until 1951, players could not mark and lift their balls on the putting surface, and a player whose path to the hole was blocked by another player's ball was "stymied." The stymie became increasingly unpopular with the introduction of greenkeeping and smooth putting surfaces in the 19th century. The subsequent development of the rolled putt (rather than the chipping style previously favored) creating loud demand for marking of balls on the green. Such an amendment was made to the RULES OF GOLF in 1951, and since then the stymie has been obsolete.

Surlyn. A patented formula for a hard

golf-ball cover which is resistant to scuffing and cutting, introduced by Spalding in 1972.

Sweet Spot. The center of gravity on a club FACE.

Target golf. The strategy of hitting highly lofted shots loaded with backspin that will hold on elevated, heavily watered greens. The strategy is most effective on American courses. In the rest of the world, drier and less elevated greens favor the BUMP-AND-RUN. Also referes to a style of architecture and play found in desert areas where, for water conservation purposes, there is a strict limitation on irrigated turf, and golfers play by hitting from target area to target area.

Tee. Originally a point one club-length or less from the hole where players would begin play on the next hole. The term still refers to the starting point for a hole, but in the modern game up to eight distinct teeing grounds may be designed for individual golf holes, to cut down on wear-and-tear as well as allowing for varying levels of ability or strength. The term also now commonly applies to the wooden pegs on which the ball is placed for the tee shot.

Ten-finger Grip. See GRIP.

Texas Wedge. A shot in which the player uses a putter to stroke the ball from a position off the putting surface.

Thin. Hitting slightly above the ball, producing a low-trajectory flight. A THIN shot in cold weather is one of golf's most memorable experiences.

Three-piece Ball. A ball with a cover, wound rubber strands and a rubber core.

Toe. The edge of a golf-club furthest from the shaft.

Topper. A swing which catches only the top of the ball, causing it to fly only a short distance with tremendous overspin.

Trap. See BUNKER.

Two-piece Ball. A ball with a cover and a solid core.

Unplayable Lie. A difficult lie in which the player, under penalty of one stroke, elects to take a drop within two club-lengths rather than attempting a stroke.

Vardon Grip. See GRIP.

Waggle. A part of the pre-shot routine, a to-and-fro motion utilized to set the tempo of the swing and build concentration for the shot.

Waste Area. A sandy area where the player is allowed to ground his club at address. Named after a bunker on the 16th hole at Harbour Town.

Whiff. A swing which misses the ball.

Winter Rules. Local rules imposed to protect turf during the off-season, allowing players to pick, clean, and place the ball on the fairway. Winter Rules are not endorsed in the Rules of Golf and, of course, by encouraging players to hit off the remaining undamaged turf can actually accelerate the deterioration of a golf course in the winter season. Winter Rules have nonetheless prospered because of their positive effect on scoring.

Wood. A club, originally with a large wooden clubhead, typically used for the longer distance shots in the modern game. Woods are numbered from 1 to 9, and since 1980 have been made with metal and ceramic heads in addition to the traditional persimmon wood.

Yips. A shaking of the hands experienced by older golfers trying to manipulate the small muscles in their hands, especially noticeable in the PUTTING stroke. Yips have destroyed many a fine golf round and even in some cases a career. The most famous example of yips is the WHIFF recorded by Harry Vardon while attempting to putt in the U.S. Open, which he went on to win anyway.

Zanesville Ceramics and other collectibles. A valuable series of ceramics depicting golf, created in the early 20th century. Golfers have been known to collect an astonishing range of useful and utterly useless items that have some remote connection with the grand old game. Collecting began in the late 18th century and encompasses books, clubs, balls, art, accessories, ceramics, toys and games, autographs, stamps, and the all-inclusive "ephemera."

GENERAL INDEX

AUSTRALIA

CANADA

LPGA PERSONALITIES

Acknowledgments

Any book of this size and scope requires some grateful acknowledgment to a large number of key people who have worked behind the scenes to bring this book to you. Thanks to:

Julie Merberg, Liz Perl, Donna Gould, Tim and Carisa Hays, David Shanks, Walt Spitzmiller, Russ Schaerer, Randy Guyton, Matt Sullivan, Alex Miceli, and most of all to Ann Rodewig Lane for all the help in putting this project together.

Thanks also to the following people for various tips, diskettes, jokes, and everything else that makes a book come together successfully:

To my crazy collection of friends from Byron Bay, The Archives, The Hub, *Harper's*, *LINKS*, WHHI-TV, KISS-FM, and all points in between—for the story assignments, the laughs, and all the good times.

To my family for their unwavering support of this project.

To Jack Purcell and Steve Nazaruk for giving me the green light to compile the Almanac when there was plenty else to do at *LINKS*. Thanks to Adam Kaplan for the backup work.

To the wonderful editorial, sales, and production staff at Perigee, in particular Bill Harris, Maureen Troy and the astonishing Paul Winkler.

To the following providers of raw data: Dave Lancer and staff at the PGA TOUR; Elaine Scott and the staff at the LPGA; Maxine at the USGA for many mad dashes for facts; the European PGA Tour; Augusta National Golf Club; Julius Mason and Sherry Major at the PGA of America; John Benda for some key assistance on South America; Mr. Sato at the Japanese PGA; Tom Place at the IGA; the staff at the Women's Pro Golf European Tour, the National Golf Foundation, and finally all the dedicated individuals who staff national golf associations around the world who took time to return surveys and provide background history.

Sammy Cahn was often asked "What comes first, the lyrics or the music?" "The phone call," he always replied. Thanks to Elvira Lopez and Brett Borton for mine.

Errata and amendments

In a book of this size, there is the possibility of a small error—no matter who the quoted source is for the material, the final responsibility rests entirely with me. Future editions of **The Complete Golfer's Almanac** will correct any and all errors which are detected.

James M. Lane
Hilton Head Island
December, 1994

This book is dedicated to
Annie and Isabel with love.

Sources

The primary source for contemporary information in this guide has been releases received at The Complete Golfer's Almanac or at LINKS Magazine. The Almanac also includes much original material supplied by state, regional, trade, and national golf associations throughout the world. 20th-century historical material has been compiled from records supplied by the organizations named below, through surveys conducted by The Complete Golfer's Almanac, and/or from a variety of secondary information sources. The organizations named below are staffed by tireless individuals who labor, usually in anonymity, to preserve golf history and collect and share golf data. Each of them merits your support through membership, subscription, or volunteer activity.

PRIMARY SOURCES
1994 Golfer's Almanac Survey of States
1994 Golfer's Almanac Survey of Nations
1994 Golfer's Almanac Survey of Courses
1994 Golfer's Almanac Survey of Schools
American Junior Golf Association
American Society of Golf Course Architects
Augusta National Golf Club
The Asian Tour
The European PGA
Golf Course Superintendents of America
Golf Data Online
The International Golf Association
The Japanese PGA
The LPGA
National Collegiate Athletic Association
National Golf Course Owner's Association
The National Golf Foundation
The PGA of America
The PGA TOUR
The South American Tour
Sporting Goods Manufacturers Association
The United States Golf Association
The Women's Professional Golf European Tour

SECONDARY SOURCES
1993 Merchandise Show Directory & Buyer's Guide
1994 Golf Almanac (Publications International/Signet: 1994)
1994 Yellow Pages of Golf
Allen, Sir Peter—The Sunley Book of Royal Golf (Stanley Paul: 1989)
Borton, Brett and Cherry, Ed, and the Editors of LINKS Magazine —The Endless Fairway

(Simon & Schuster: 1992-94)
Browning, Robert—A History of Golf (Dent: 1955)
Darwin, Bernard—The Golf Courses of the British Isles (Storey/Ailsa: 1988)
Golf Consumer Survey (National Golf Foundation: 1989)
Golf Digest
Golf Digest Almanac 1989
The Golfer's Handbook
Golf Magazine
Golf Magazine's Encyclopedia of Golf (HarperCollins: 1993)
Golf Participation in the United States (National Golf Foundation: 1988-1994)
Golf Pro—Census 1994
Golfweek Magazine
Golf World Magazine
Golf Writers Association of America 1994 directory
Hobbs, Michael—The Golfer's Companion (Macdonald/Queen Anne Press: 1988)
LINKS Magazine
LPGA Media Guide
PGA of America Media Guide
PGA of America Slow Play Survey (1989)
PGA TOUR Media Guide
Macdonald, Charles Blair—Scotland's Gift-Golf (Ailsa, Inc.: 1985)
The National Golf Course Directory (Sports Directories: 1994)
The United States Golf Association Media Guide
The World of Professional Golf (IMG: 1990-94)

We welcome all suggestions, corrections, and new material for inclusion in future editions. Please contact us at:

THE COMPLETE GOLFER'S ALMANAC
12 Evergreen Lane
Hilton Head Island, SC 29928
E-Mail: Gymbabwe@aol.com

Walt Spitzmiller
is one of the world's foremost sporting artists.

He has dedicated some of his finest work to portraying the many aspects of the game of golf— from its rich traditions to its heroes and most memorable competitions. Walt is one of only three individuals to be featured by The United States Golf Association Museum and Library with an exhibition showcasing his golf art.

Spitzmiller is perhaps best recognized for his many contributions to *Sports Illustrated, Golf* Magazine, *Senior Golfer,* *Golf Digest* and other popular magazines. His work is held in private collections throughout the world.

Corporate collections of Spitzmiller's portraits include CBS Sports, The PGA Tour, Titleist, Baseball Hall of Fame, and ABC Sports. Other collections are featured in the American Museum of Illustration, The National Art Museum of Sports, and The Professional Rodeo Hall of Champions Museum.

SPECIAL OFFER

The cover illustration for
THE COMPLETE GOLFER'S
ALMANAC 1995 was created by
Walt Spitzmiller for the 1994 PGA
Tour Poster Program. A limited
number of fine prints is being made
available to the readers of the
ALMANAC for the price of $95., plus
shipping and
handling. This
beautiful color
print celebrating
the great game of
golf, and the PGA
Tour, is already a
much sought-after
collector's item by
golf enthusiasts
around the world.
**The print is
21" by 30", on fine
art paper that is
acid-free neutral
PH stock.**